The logic of God

Introduction/The challenge of contemporary empiricism

by Malcolm L. Diamond

The logic of God/Theology

and verification

edited by **Malcolm L. Diamond**
and **Thomas V. Litzenburg, Jr.**

The Bobbs-Merrill Company, Inc.
Indianapolis

The Bobbs-Merrill Company, Inc.
4300 West 62nd Street
Indianapolis, Indiana 46268

First Edition
First Printing 1975
Designed by Betty Binns

Library of Congress Cataloging in Publication Data
Diamond, Malcolm Luria, comp.
The logic of God.

    1. Religion—Philosophy. I. Litzenburg, Thomas V.,
joint comp. II. Title.
BL51.D49   200'.1   74-32235
ISBN 0-672-60792-1

Contents

v

Preface

The editors have taught courses in the philosophy of religion for a number of years. We felt the need for an extensive book on theology and verification that would both introduce students to the central issues and provide them with a representative selection of the most important contributions.

The introductions do not presuppose knowledge of philosophy in general or of the variants of contemporary empiricism that appear in this book. They orient students to the issues so that they can follow the discussions in the essays and proceed to do further work in philosophy.

The essays included in this volume are representative, but by no means exhaustive. In many cases we have reprinted extended philosophical interchanges that should make students aware that philosophy proceeds by argument and that the views of even the most prestigious philosophers are debatable and subject to revision.

The original contributions to this volume (marked with asterisks in the table of contents) carry the issue of theology and verification to the frontiers of contemporary discussion.

A number of essays reprinted here, such as John Wisdom's

"Gods," the "University Discussion on Theology and Falsification," and Richard Braithwaite's "An Empiricist's View of the Nature of Religious Belief," have often been reprinted. We decided to reprint them again because they are indispensable to any responsible discussion of the issues and because the extensive introductory materials presented here make them far more accessible to the uninitiated reader and clarify their role in the continuing debate over the challenge of contemporary empiricism to theology.

In working on this project we have accumulated debts of gratitude far too numerous to list in full. We wish, however, to thank the following for valuable editorial advice and for reading early drafts of portions of the introductory sections: William H. Austin, associate professor of philosophy, Rice University; Van A. Harvey, professor of religion, University of Pennsylvania; Dallas M. High, associate professor of religion and philosophy, University of Kentucky; Edward Langerak, assistant professor of philosophy, St. Olaf College; Basil Mitchell, Nolloth Professor of the philosophy of the christian religion, Oxford University; Richard M. Rorty, professor of philosophy, Princeton University; Axel Steuer, instructor in religion, Princeton University; and Paul M. van Buren, professor of religious thought, Temple University. We also want to thank Miss Sandra Hurd for assisting in the preparation of the bibliography and Mrs. William Vaughan, Miss Susan Hotine, Mrs. Denise Landry, and Mrs. Mildred Jones for typing and retyping the introductory material and the bibliography. We also wish to acknowledge the generous financial assistance as well as the secretarial and library services provided us by Princeton University and Wells College. Finally, we gratefully note that as a 1970 recipient of the "E. Harris Harbison Award for Gifted Teaching" from the Danforth Foundation and a sabbatical leave from Princeton University, Professor Diamond was able to complete work on this and other related research projects.

The editors are grateful to the McGraw-Hill Book Company for permission to publish pages 3–54, 151–157, and 247–256 which appear as Part Two of the *Contemporary Empiricism and Religious Thought* by Malcolm L. Diamond.[1]

M. L. D.

T. V. L., JR.

Princeton, New Jersey
Aurora, New York
August, 1973

[1] Used by permission of McGraw-Hill, Inc., copyright 1974.

The logic of God

One/**Introduction**

Malcolm L. Diamond/The challenge of contemporary empiricism

VERIFICATION is one of the most important intellectual issues of the twentieth century. The term was set at the center of the philosophical stage by the work of the logical positivists who met in Vienna in the 1920s and consciously set out to revolutionize philosophy. Many of them were competent mathematicians and physicists who were at home with the sophisticated notations of twentieth-century logic and used them in the effort to generalize and unify the methods, and even the contents, of science. To this extent, their purpose was in harmony with the philosophical tradition. They were concerned to achieve the greatest possible clarity regarding our ability to know the world. They were at odds with the philosophical tradition insofar as they were not only hostile to traditional philosophical enterprises such as theology and metaphysics, but as we shall see, they tried to use the test of verification to eliminate these disciplines from serious philosophical consideration.

During the period of positivism's greatest influence (roughly from the thirties to the mid-fifties) it was widely assumed that verification could do the job assigned to it by the positivists. It could be used to demonstrate the fact that theology is not worthy of serious philosophical study. For well over a decade it has been evident that almost all the positivists' positions, especially their view of verification, had been oversold. Philosophical fashions have now moved in the opposite direction. Positivism and verification are dismissed as dated. As a result, in some theological circles it is assumed that religious thinkers can safely ignore the issue of verification. This is a mistake. The issue of theology and verification continues to be important because:

1. A mastery of verification and other issues arising from positivism is a precondition of philosophical literacy. Many contemporary philosophers look askance at the issue of verification on the grounds that "we have gone far beyond that." Yet they often use the basic terms of positivism in staking out their post-positivist claims. It is therefore imperative that students have a firm grasp of verification and other positivistic positions if they are to understand post-positivist philosophers who claim to have gone beyond them.

2. The positivists could not come up with an adequate statement of the test of verification; this was a major reason for the failure of their movement. Yet it is not certain that an adequate statement cannot be formulated. It is too early to judge the success of the most recent efforts but they are underway (see Section Ten).

3. The threat of verification to theology may well have been exaggerated, but it is still being debated, and the conclusion should not be taken for granted. In any case, religious thinkers who dismiss the challenge of verification on the grounds that it is passé will ignore important lessons, and repeat many of the mistakes of past theological eras.

4. The positivists used verification as an instrument to cut theology away from the living body of philosophy. However, many theologians who were sympathetic to the positivists' concern for clarity and rigor tried to show that verification could be used in a positive way to advance the cause of religious thought (see pp. 42).

5. Verification is the most impressive effort to date at adapting scientific thinking to philosophical purposes. It has been used to sharpen the attacks on religion that have been made in the name of science. The issue of theology and verification will, therefore,

continue to be important as long as religion and science continue to be regarded as intellectually significant.

The contributors to this volume either assume that the reader is familiar with technical terms like *verification,* or they introduce them in a sketchy way. Section one is designed to present a thorough introduction for readers who are unfamiliar with positivism. It covers the following major points:

1. the goals and terminology of the positivists;
2. the difficulties with verification as well as other factors that led to the demise of positivism;
3. a survey of the debate on theology and verification in the post-positivist era with emphasis on the relevance of the broader cultural issue of religion and science.

The goals and techniques of logical positivism

The story of contemporary empiricism is involved and difficult to follow. Its roots are in the nineteenth century and much of the important work was done early in the twentieth century by such thinkers as Bertrand Russell and G. E. Moore. This introduction will not attempt an over-all survey; that has already been done successfully.[1] I will focus on the logical positivists and their analytic successors because they used the test of verification to call the very existence of theology into question. One of the major points is that their effort traded heavily on the prestige of science.

It is generally understood that the rise of science challenged theology. It is less widely appreciated that it also constituted a serious challenge to philosophy. One of the most impressive features of science is its ability to progress. Newtonian science may have been overthrown by the developments of the twentieth century, but this has not led to a return to pre-Newtonian views like those of Ptolemaic astronomy. By contrast, philosophy seems static. The history of philosophy has often been written in terms

[1] J. O. Urmson, *Philosophical Analysis: Its Development between Two World Wars* (Oxford: Clarendon Press, 1956) is one of the best. John Passmore, *A Hundred Years of Philosophy* (London: Duckworth, 1957) sets contemporary empiricism in its broader philosophical context. Herbert Feigl, one of the Vienna Circle, writes on "The Origin and Spirit of Logical Positivism" in *The Legacy of Logical Positivism,* P. Achinstein and S. F. Barker, eds. (Baltimore: Johns Hopkins Press, 1969), pp. 3–24.

of the debates between metaphysicians who are oriented to realities that are supersensible and empiricists who are oriented to sense experience. In each generation the same issues came up and pretty much the same points were made, but in terms of different vocabularies. Immanual Kant (1724–1804) etched an invidious comparison between metaphysics and science:

> If it [metaphysics] be a science, how comes it that it cannot, like other science, obtain universal and permanent recognition? . . . Everybody, however ignorant in other matters, may deliver a final verdict, as in this domain there is as yet no standard weight and measure to distinguish sound knowledge from shallow talk.[2]

Kant's effort to establish weights and measures for metaphysics is one of the most impressive intellectual achievements in history. Yet his "critical" version of metaphysics failed to "obtain universal and permanent recognition." The logical positivists hoped to succeed where Kant had failed. They were impressed with the success of mathematics and science. They mined these rich veins of knowledge in an effort to find out what made them so rewarding. They concluded that Kant's mistake had been his effort to try to make metaphysics scientific.

The positivists adopted a number of Kant's important technical terms. The crucial ones were—'analytic,' 'synthetic,' 'a priori,' and 'a posteriori'—terms that will soon be clarified. Kant used them in an effort to reform metaphysics, but the positivists used them in an effort to eliminate it. They thought that philosophy could only achieve progress that was comparable to that of science if metaphysics, and theology as well, no longer received serious attention from philosophers.

It is hard for anyone who is not familiar with the history of philosophy to appreciate the startling character of this proposal. The cultural prestige of philosophy and even its subject matter seemed inescapably bound up with metaphysics and theology. As far as prestige is concerned, the issue hinges on the contrast between human beings and animals. Both use their senses to observe physical objects, but only humans can reason. Metaphysicians and theologians used reason to claim knowledge of realities of a higher order than the mere physical objects which animals can also observe. These realities transcend, that is, they are utterly beyond

[2] Kant, *Prolegomena to Any Future Metaphysics,* ed. Paul Carus (Chicago: Open Court Press, 1949), p. 2.

the reach of, the senses. Since God is an illustration of these transcendent realities, the high stakes involved should be obvious, but
it is worth noting that central concepts of leading philosophers,
such as Plato's Forms and Kant's thing-in-itself, are also transcendent realities.

The proposal to eliminate metaphysics and theology was not
only a threat to the philosophical mystique, it also threatened to
leave philosophy without a subject matter. Scientists work by
means of *observations* and they are very successful at it. The study
of *non-observable* realities like God and the Forms seemed to be
the special subject matter of philosophy. The proposal to eliminate
them from philosophy seemed like proposing to revise *Hamlet* by
eliminating the Prince of Denmark.

In his aggressively argued book, *Language, Truth and Logic*
(first edition, 1936), A. J. Ayer confronted English-speaking philosophers with the challenge of positivism.[3] His use of the term *metaphysics* was influential; it has been clearly stated by Kai Nielsen:

> Ayer defines 'metaphysics' as an inquiry into the nature of the
> reality "underlying or transcending the phenomena which the spe-
> cial sciences are content to study." . . . He [the metaphysician] is
> trying to attain nonexperiential knowledge of matters of fact; he
> wants to attain a deeper and more fundamental knowledge of real-
> ity than anything we could attain from even the most systematic
> and theoretical of the sciences. . . . And, typically at least, he tries
> to seek a knowledge of some reality that transcends empirical, sci-
> entifically knowable reality.[4]

The positivists were not the first philosophers to engage in
sharp criticisms of arguments to transcendent realities. Empiricism, that is, the view that all knowledge is rooted in sense experience, is a traditional philosophical position. It was directed against
rationalist metaphysicians who thought they could attain knowledge of transcendent realities by reason alone, "unsullied" by the
use of the senses. Yet the pre-positivist empiricists did not try to
eliminate metaphysics and theology; indeed, they had metaphysical and theological positions of their own. Furthermore, they ex-

---

[3] Alfred J. Ayer, *Language, Truth and Logic* (London: Victor Gollancz, 1936).

[4] Kai Nielsen, *Reason and Practice* (New York: Harper and Row, 1971), p. 416.
The chapters on "Empiricism and the Verification Principle," represent an
effort to defend the test of verification against many of the criticisms that
appear in this volume. The definition of metaphysics quoted by Nielsen appears on p. 33 of the second edition [1946] of *Language, Truth and Logic*.

pended a great deal of their energies in trying to show what was wrong with the arguments of rationalist metaphysicians and theologians. These were the ancient, "never get anywhere," disputes that Kant was complaining about in the paragraph quoted above.

In part, the positivists represented a continuation of the empiricist tradition, but they were also, as they claimed to be, revolutionary. Their effort to eliminate metaphysics differed radically from the traditional empiricist criticisms of individual metaphysical arguments. What was at issue will be clearer if we consider an analogy.

Imagine a great university that admits anyone who applies. The faculty then works over each and every candidate; some flunk out and others graduate. Now let us suppose that a number of young professors with new ideas reject these traditional procedures. They are convinced that the university will never progress in its task of advancing knowledge as long as time is wasted in flunking out candidates who shouldn't have been admitted in the first place. They propose a preliminary examination that will be taken by all candidates for admission. It is designed to be as simple as possible: an objective examination that can be graded by a computer. By means of it, they propose to eliminate candidates who are obviously unworthy. Those who pass and are admitted as qualified candidates for the degree are then examined just as carefully as under the old procedures. In the end, some graduate and others do not. The important gain of this new system is that the faculty confines its efforts to a select group of promising candidates, even though some of them will still fail to work out.

The traditional empiricists used techniques that were rather like the old admission procedures. They studied all metaphysical and theological works and tried to refute statements like "The Absolute is perfect" or "God is omnipotent." The revised admission procedure mirrors the goals of the logical positivists. They thought they had a preliminary check on philosophical works that would determine, with a minimum of time and effort, whether they were worth studying in detail. If a work failed to pass, it was set aside as worthless, and the positivists didn't even bother to argue with its author. If it passed, it would be studied very carefully. It might still be found wanting, but at least the positivists would have assured themselves beforehand that the study was worth the effort.

The preliminary examination applied to philosophical work

by the positivists was the test of verification. Before we can understand their use of it, we shall have to examine its construction
within the framework of the analytic/synthetic distinction.[5]

The analytic and the synthetic

"True," for a philosopher, is like the assayer's statement that "This
mineral is gold." It has been inspected and certified. It is the real
thing. The positivists, like all philosophers, are careful about
stamping *true* on any statements. In general, they focussed on language by means of questions like, "How can we know whether a
given statement has the capacity for being true?" and "How do we
decide whether a statement *is* true?"

It is obvious that there are many types of sentences which
could never, by virtue of their grammatical form, be used to make
true statements. These include questions: "What's for dinner?,"
exclamations: "O boy!," and imperatives: "Bring it now!" The
grammatical form of a sentence that can be labelled *true* is the
declarative, as in "Two plus three equals five" and "John F. Kennedy was elected President of the United States in 1960."[6] The distinctive feature of the positivists' challenge to metaphysics and
theology is to drive a wedge between proper grammatical form and
proper philosophical form. In saying that "The Absolute is perfect," the metaphysician makes a declarative statement which is
grammatically correct. He intends it as a cognitive claim, that is,
a claim to know that something is true. The positivists thought that
they could show that statements of this kind were incapable of
being true. Therefore, they cannot be genuine cognitive claims.

The positivists introduced a radical restriction on the kinds
of statements that had a capacity for being true. They insisted that
all such statements were members of one of two mutually exclusive classes, the analytic and the synthetic. Countless statements
from the philosophical tradition could not, by this standard, be
true, because statements like, "The Absolute is perfect," or "God

[5] This presentation will ignore an important element of the positivists' program, namely, the effort to construct an ideal language that would exclude
metaphysical, theological, and other types of statements that do not conform
to the positivists' standards. This effort is primarily associated with the work
of Rudolf Carnap. See especially, *The Logical Syntax of Language* (London:
Routledge and Kegan Paul, 1937).

[6] David Rynin correlates declarative and nondeclarative statements in "Cognitive Meaning and Cognitive Use," *Inquiry*, 9 (1966), pp. 121f.

is omnipotent," are, according to the positivists, neither analytic nor synthetic. Metaphysicians and theologians protested against the arbitrariness of this restriction. The positivists admitted that their procedures were radical, in fact they were proud of this. However, they denied that this restriction was arbitrary. It was rooted in their admiration for mathematics and science which are the two most successful modes of knowing that men have achieved.[7]

The analytic: the necessary truths of mathematics and logic

The positivists derived their use of the *analytic* by reflecting on the character of true statements made in mathematics and logic.

The main features of analytic statements, as the positivists understood them, are:

    1. Analytic statements are necessarily true; their denials are contradictions.

    2. They are known to be true a priori.

    3. They do not convey factual information.

Necessity. Philosophers have always been fascinated by mathematics. Statements like "two plus three equals five" have been their ideal illustrations of true statements. This is because of their peculiar property: they are not merely true, their truth is necessary. You cannot consider them false even for the sake of argument or fantasy. For the sake of argument we can imagine that the statement "John F. Kennedy was assassinated in 1963" is false. And for the sake of fantasy, we may, in reading the comic strip *Mandrake the Magician,* pretend that the statement "All men are visible to agents with normal vision," is false, because Mandrake is supposed to be able to make himself invisible. Mathematical statements, such as the one previously cited, cannot be treated this way. They force us to accept them as true. Provided that we keep our symbolism constant, even the most clever author of science fiction cannot change their truth value. They are true for everyone, at every time and every place.

    The analytic is not confined to mathematics. A limitless number of verbal statements have the same coercive power, for

---

[7] Hans Reichenbach, *The Rise of Scientific Philosophy* (Berkeley: University of California Press, 1951), p. 308 and Frederick C. Copleston, S. J., *Contemporary Philosophy* (Westminster, Md.: Newman Press, 1956), pp. 26–33.

example, "All bachelors are unmarried" and "It is snowing or it is not snowing." These statements, like those of mathematics, are analytic and necessarily true because their truth depends on their logical form. It is impossible to deny their truth because to do so involves one in contradictions and contradictions are necessarily false. The logical form of an analytic statement may not appear on the surface, but it is there. Consider the statement "All bachelors are unmarried." Remember that a crucial part of the definition of a *bachelor* is a person who is *"unmarried* and male." The statement can then be cast into logical form by letting "A" stand for "unmarried," and "B" for "male." It then reads, "All A-and-B are A." To deny the truth of this statement by talking of a married bachelor would involve a contradiction, because "A-and-B" can only be true if both A and B are true. Therefore, we cannot affirm the truth of "A-and-B" and simultaneously declare A to be false. To do so would be like saying that "A white horse is *not* white."

A priori.   An important feature of analytic statements is related to their logical character, they are known a priori, that is, they are known to be true independently of observations of the world. To check on the truth of the analytic statement "All bachelors are unmarried," we need only to reflect on the meaning of the terms and on the rules of the English language. We do not need to go out into the world and make observations like polling all bachelors in order to find out whether they are married.

The a priori character of analytic statements explains a peculiarity of our intellectual interaction. If someone challenges the truth of the statement "Alan Jones is unmarried" (a statement of fact which is not analytic), he calls the statement into question. If someone challenges the truth of "All bachelors are unmarried," he calls his understanding of the statement into question. If he persists in challenging the truth of this statement and of other statements like it, we would come to question his basic intellectual capacities.

Not factually informative.   The analytic is the domain of necessity. In it, statements are either necessarily true, such as, "A square has four sides" (because a square is, by definition, a four-sided figure), or contradictory, that is, necessarily false, as in the case of "This square has three sides." The contradiction can be made clear by observing the logical structure of this statement. A contradiction is the simultaneous affirmation of "*A* and not-*A*" where the sense of *A* does not change. The statement is contradictory because it amounts to saying that "This figure has four sides (four-sided being part of the meaning of square) and it does not have four sides".

Analytic statements are necessarily true, therefore, their truth is known with certainty, because it follows from an analysis of their logical structure. This certainty is, however, purchased at a price; analytic statements are not informative about states of affairs in the world. Analytic statements merely elaborate the rules governing our use of words and other symbols. Like all matters relating to the analytic, this point is obvious once you grasp it and baffling until you do. An illustration may help. It will deal with the analytic statement, "It is snowing or it is not snowing," which certainly seems to be about a state of affairs in the world, namely, about the weather.

I am at Aspen during the ski season, but there is no snow. I have no prospect of coming back and I am brooding about my bad luck in front of the fire in the basement lounge of a ski lodge. There are no windows so I can't see out. Suddenly a friend bursts into the lounge exuberantly shouting, "It is snowing!" I jump out of my chair and break for the stairs so that I can run to the picture window on the next floor and watch the beautiful stuff come down.

Now, let's try an instant replay on this scenario. I am in Aspen during the ski season and there is no snow. I am brooding in the windowless basement of the ski lodge when my friend bursts in and shouts, "It is snowing!" As I jump out of my chair and break for the stairs, he adds, "or it is not snowing." Collapse and fadeout!

The point is that the analytic statement "It is snowing or it is not snowing" only *appears* to be about the weather. Its truth is compatible with any weather whatever—with rain, sleet, or sunshine as well as with snow—because the statement is not about the weather at all. Actually, it illustrates the operation of "or" as a logical connective. We know that this statement is true a priori, that is, by inspecting the statement. We do not have to check the weather to know it, because any statement with the logical form "*A* or not-*A*" is necessarily true. In this case we substituted "It is snowing" for *A*, but the results would still be necessarily true if we changed the statement to "There are microbes or there are not microbes," "It is purple or it is not purple," and "It is a miracle or it is not a miracle." We can be sure that these statements are not informative about germs, colors, or religion. Like the statement about snow, they serve only to show how "or" functions logically. To deny their truth is impossible, but they are not capable of conveying information about states of affairs in the world. The truth of an analytic statement is compatible with any state of affairs whatever, because analytic statements are not informative with regard to any state of affairs.

This exposition may have given the impression that the analytic is trivial; it is not. After all, the analytic embraces two of the most important intellectual disciplines: mathematics and logic.

In addition, analytic statements may be said to be *informative* in some rather special, but important, senses of that term. A person who first comes to realize the truth of an analytic statement increases his personal store of information in the psychological sense. It is not, however, information about states of affairs in the world. Someone may, for example, know what a *cube* is without being aware of the fact that it has twelve edges. If this is pointed out, he receives additional information. It is, however, only information about the defining characteristic of cubes. Once you know some of them, the rest of the characteristics are logically tied in. It only requires reflection or proper stimulation to bring them to conscious awareness. To appreciate the point, contrast the statement, "A cube has twelve edges," with the statement, "The lobby of the Empire State Building is cubical." To check on the truth of the second statement, reflection on the defining characteristics of cubes is not enough; we must go out into the world and do some measuring.

The most important sense in which the analytic may be regarded as informative is that it provides information about the rules that control the use of symbolic systems. Without this information regarding mathematical and symbolic systems, we could hardly hope to do significant work in any field. Indeed without this information we cannot even speak a language, because we will not know how to hang words together. In this connection, we might consider the exchange between Alice and Humpty Dumpty in Lewis Carroll's *Through the Looking Glass*.

> *Humpty Dumpty* There are 364 days when you might get un-birthday presents . . . and only *one* for birthday presents, you know. There's glory for you.

> *Alice* I don't know what you mean by "glory."
>
> *Humpty Dumpty* Of course you don't—till I tell you. I meant "there's a nice knock-down argument" for you.
>
> *Alice* But "glory" doesn't mean "a nice knock-down argument!"
>
> *Humpty Dumpty* When I use a word, it means just what I choose it to mean—neither more nor less.
>
> *Alice* The question is whether you *can* make words mean different things.
>
> *Humpty Dumpty* The question is, which is to be master—that's all.

It is important to note that if Humpty Dumpty's linguistic policies were actually in force, this delightful interchange could not take place. There could be no linguistic communication, because words would not have fixed meanings. They could not even be used for the purpose of saying that *glory* means "there's a nice knock-down argument."

The analytic, then, is important, and it is even, in some special senses, "informative." Analytic statements deal with the internal (syntactical) relations of words and numbers. They deal with the way that words and numbers must necessarily relate to one another if they are to be used meaningfully. They do not deal with the way that words and numbers are used (semantically) to refer to states of affairs in the world. They do not deal with matters of fact.

The synthetic: the possible truths of fact

According to the positivists, there is only one other class of statements that are capable of being true, the synthetic. The defining characteristics of the synthetic can be contrasted with those of the analytic:

1. It is possible for synthetic statements to be either true or false.
2. Their truth or falsity is determined a posteriori.
3. They convey factual information.

Synthetic statements may be either true or false. In contrast to analytic statements, which are necessarily true or contradictory (necessarily false), it is possible for synthetic statements to be either true or false. To appreciate the difference, we need only add the word *not* to an example of each class. Vary one of the standard examples of an analytic statement in this way, and it yields, "All bachelors are not unmarried," which cannot possibly be true; it is a contradiction. On the other hand, we have already considered a good example of a synthetic statement, "Alan Jones is unmarried." Add the word *not,* and the result, "Alan Jones is *not* unmarried," makes just as much sense as the original statement that he *is* unmarried. Both statements may be either true or false. To find out whether either of them is actually true or actually false, we must check them out by means of observation.

A posteriori.   In checking on the truth of synthetic state-ments by observations we use our senses—primarily, sight, hear-ing, and touch. In checking on "Alan Jones is unmarried," we would observe his habits, his residence, and we would check the records in Town Hall to see if we could find a marriage license with his name on it. We would also resort to other checks, such as asking his friends about him. Philosophers call this method of checking the truth of statements 'a posteriori.' It means roughly, *after,* that is, the truth of the statement is determined after obser-vation, which contrasts sharply with the *a priori* which is used in determining the truth of analytic statements.

Factually informative.   We have already considered exam-ples of the factually informative character of synthetic statements. "It is snowing," is used to provide information about a state of affairs "out there." "Alan Jones is a bachelor" is intended to tell us something specific about a particular person. These synthetic state-ments convey information that cannot be derived from mere re-flection on the meaning of the words used in them.

Analytic statements are functions of definitions that enable symbolic games to be played; synthetic statements tell us what is the case out there in the world. In a rough sense it is comparable to chess. "Bishops are those pieces which move diagonally" is, within the game of chess, an analytic statement. It tells us about the patterns in which bishops necessarily move, but it doesn't in-form us about specific moves in any particular game of chess. By contrast, a newspaper account of a championship match will con-tain statements like, "Fischer, playing white, moved his queen's bishop to K5." This move was not necessary. Within the rules of chess, he might have moved differently. The specific move is a matter of fact; the statement of it is synthetic.

Pseudo-synthetic

The positivists claimed to have uncovered a type of statement that appeared to be synthetic or factual but which was not the genuine article. They used the prefix *pseudo,* that is, pretended or unreal, to mark them off from the genuine article. Pseudo-synthetic statements are grammatically similar to genuine ones, and like them, they appear to convey information about a state of affairs in the world. Positivists charged that pseudo-synthetic statements were incapable of doing any such thing because they lack all capacity for being true. The instrument by which the positivists tried to demonstrate this was the test of verification. Before discussing this test in detail it will be useful to develop a sense for the kinds of analyses that led positivists to categorize statements as pseudo-synthetic.

The status of a statement is a matter of language. It might, therefore, seem that a mere inspection of the words of a statement would enable us to classify it. The issue is, however, more complex. The determination of the status of a statement is affected by such factors as the philosopher's use of his words, his consistency with regard to usage, and his openness to evidence that challenges the truth of his statements.

Intention and practice. The status of a statement cannot be determined independently of the intention of the person making it. A metaphysician may write that "All substances are invisible." If he intends to use the word *substance* in the ordinary way to mean some physical stuff, it is patently false. We see substances, in this sense, all around us. That is why we should avoid reading traditionally minded metaphysicians and theologians in an insensitive way. Generally speaking, a metaphysician would not intend a statement of this kind as synthetic. He would be introducing *substance* as a technical term whose meaning, at least in part, is "invisible." In that case, *within his system,* the statement "All substances are invisible" would be analytic. It would be parallel to the status, in ordinary English, of the statement "All bachelors are unmarried." So far, so good. The status is analytic and the label "pseudo-synthetic" does not come into play.

We have, however, noted that while analytic statements are necessarily true, they are not informative about states of affairs in the world. Yet, according to the positivists, a metaphysician, having defined his peculiar use of *substance,* often fails to stick to it. Sooner or later he trades on the ordinary meaning of the word and suggests that what he is saying about substances is factually informative. If he then makes a statement like "All substances are invisible" with overtones that convey the impression that it is factually informative, the positivist claims that the statement is masquerading as a synthetic statement and brands it as "pseudo-synthetic."

The refusal to accept counter-evidence. A more common application of the label *pseudo-synthetic* results from circumstances in which a metaphysician or theologian makes a statement that seems to be straightforwardly synthetic. The positivist asks for a specification of the kinds of evidence that would determine its truth or falsity. The thinker who made the statement refuses but insists, all the same, that the statement tells us something about states of affairs in the world. The positivist then charges that the statement in question is pseudo-synthetic. The application of this line of analysis to the theological statement "God loves us as a father loves his children" is one of the major issues in this volume. It is considered at length in Section Seven and need not be discussed here. At this point it will be more helpful to consider examples that are neither theological nor philosophical.

We all know people who are addicted to making large scale generalizations about minorities. These are often derogatory, but in an effort to keep psychological sensitivities low and logical awareness high, let me present a few flattering ones: "All Irishmen are charming," "All Jews are intelligent," and "All Blacks are graceful." The statements are intended to be synthetic because the person making them assures his hearers that these are characteristics they can expect to find in each and every member of certain identifiable groups. In that case, one instance of a surly Irishman, a stupid Jew, or an awkward Black should be enough to show that each of the statements is false. If the person making the statement accepts the counter-evidence and admits that his statement is false, well and good. His statement was both intended to be synthetic (factual) and it proved to be genuinely synthetic, because he was receptive to observations that showed the statement to be untrue.

Yet people who make generalizations of this kind are notoriously reluctant to accept counter-evidence. Tell a person who claims that "All Irishmen are charming" that you have an Irish friend who is not charming and you are apt to get answers of this kind: "When you get to know him better you'll see that he *really* is charming," or "If he isn't charming then he can't *really* be Irish." Under cross-examination it becomes clear that the person intends to make a synthetic statement and that he will not let any observations count against its truth. In that case, the positivists insist that the statement is pseudo-synthetic.

Pseudo-synthetic statements cannot be either true or false. We are now in a position to understand the positivists' claim that pseudo-synthetic statements lack *truth-capacity* as well as truth. The positivists insist that there are two and only two procedures appropriate to determining the truth of a statement: either the a priori procedures used for analytic statements or the a posteriori ones that are applied to synthetic statements. In the case of a pseudo-synthetic statement both are ruled out by the person making it. The a priori is ruled out by his intention to use the statement to convey factual information or by his lapsing into that use. In that case, positivists insist that he should be willing to accept the a posteriori method of checking on synthetic statements. This involves checking by means of observations. Yet the person making the statement resolutely refuses to specify any observations that would be relevant to determining its truth or falsity. In that case, he has ruled out *all* procedures by which the truth of his statement might be determined and it is shown to be without any capacity for truth.

Since pseudo-synthetic statements have no capacity for truth, it is obvious that they are not actually true. What is less obvious is the further point urged by the positivists, namely, that pseudo-synthetic statements cannot be false either. They fall outside the range of statements that can be either true or false. It follows that in the positivists' scheme of things, *false* is something of a compliment. Of course, it is not nearly as much of a compliment as *true,* but at least a false statement like "Adlai Stevenson was elected President of the United States in 1952" is genuinely synthetic. It might have been true; it merely happens to be false. By contrast, a pseudo-synthetic statement, cannot possibly be false any more than it can be true. Therefore, the positivists declared that pseudo-synthetic statements were "factually meaningless."

When positivists refer to a statement as factually meaningless they are using the word *meaningless* (and its contrast term *meaningful*) in a special sense. It can only be understood in the context of their philosophical program.

If supposedly synthetic statements are found to be capable of being either true or false they make a genuine cognitive claim. Positivists certify them as genuinely synthetic and regard them as "cognitively meaningful" or "factually meaningful" (*empirical* may be substituted for *factual*). The terms are often used interchangeably, but as I use them cognitively meaningful is broader than factually meaningful (see p. 497). A statement is *cognitively meaningful* if and only if it is *analytic* or *genuinely synthetic*. A statement is *factually (or empirically) meaningful* if and only if it is *genuinely synthetic*. Since pseudo-synthetic statements are incapable of being either true or false, it is clear that they are both cognitively and factually meaningless. There is no point in making an effort to determine their truth value, because they simply do not, and cannot, have a truth value.

As used in this context, the word *meaningless* is misleading. It suggests that a statement like "God loves us as a father loves his children," which is labelled "pseudo-synthetic" cannot be understood. This is not the case. Soon after the positivists introduced the notion of cognitive meaninglessness philosophers began to criticize it. They noted that the positivists obviously understood a great number of the pseudo-synthetic statements that they nevertheless claimed were cognitively meaningless. After all, unless the positivists understood them, they would not have been able to demonstrate (at least to their own satisfaction) that they could not possibly be true (see pp. 227 f.). Actually, by claiming that metaphysical and theological statements are factually (or cognitively) meaningless, the positivists were not (in general) trying to say that these statements were utterly unintelligible gibberish. The positivists were, rather, trying to expose the pretentiousness of these statements. It is precisely because they are not gibberish that these statements seem to convey information about the world. Yet the positivists were convinced that they were incapable of doing so. "Factually meaningless" can therefore be paired with "pseudo-synthetic" as labels that expressed the positivists' confidence; they had seen through the deceptive appearances of metaphysical and theological statements.

Far from claiming that metaphysical and theological statements were meaningless gibberish, the positivists actually assigned a special type of meaning to them, namely, "emotive meaning." According to the positivists, a statement like "God loves us as a father loves his children" cannot, when understood literally, be capable of being shown to be either true or false. Therefore it cannot have factual meaning. It can, however, have emotive meaning which involves the fairly consistent set of emotional responses it elicits from people who have been conditioned to expressions of this kind (see pp. 74 ff.).

Furthermore, the positivists conceded the sincerity of the metaphysicians and theologians who made pseudo-synthetic statements. They were not accusing these thinkers of deliberately trying to mislead their readers.[8] After all, the positivists' claim to revolutionary significance was bound up with the fact that the cognitive meaninglessness of metaphysical and theological statements was not easily uncovered. These statements had been regarded as cognitively meaningful by generations of philosophers, even by pre-positivistic empiricists who often challenged their truth.

The question of why previous generations of philosophers had been deceived is an interesting one.[9] One possible explanation involves the appeal to a cultural gap. Scientists achieved unprecedented knowledge of the world, but it took a long while for the implications of scientific method to register. The positivists could claim that they were the first philosophers who fully understood these implications. They claimed that scientific statements are genuinely synthetic and that metaphysical and theological statements are parasitic on them (as well as on commonsense statements of fact). A theological statement like "God loves us" seems to be just as synthetic as the statement "Hydrogen atoms have one electron." Theologians who make statements of this kind seem to be providing important information about the world. Yet, unlike scientists, they do not specify observations that would verify the truth of their claims. The possibility of checking on the truth or falsity of supposedly synthetic statements by means of observations is what the issue of verification is all about.

Verification: the test for factual meaningfulness

An obvious question arises at this point: "How do we determine whether a supposedly synthetic statement is capable of being true

[8] Hans Reichenbach, *The Rise of Scientific Philosophy*, p. 34.
[9] Kai Nielsen presents a psychological explanation; see, *Reason and Practice*, p. 417.

or false?" In answering this question the positivists proposed the test of verification which has also been called the empiricist criterion of meaning.[10] It was intended to be as quick and simple as the litmus paper test that determines whether a solution is acidic or alkaline. In using this test as a preliminary examination for all philosophical statements, the positivists were not attempting to defeat metaphysicians in the philosophical arena. They were attempting to deny them the status of legitimate combatants.

The positivists probed the scientific method in an effort to find the element that made scientific work so successful. They were certain that it could not be common sense; after all sophisticated scientific work like theoretical physics is written in a notation that is almost purely logical and mathematical. A literate person who has not studied the field cannot even read a page of it. It is so abstract that scientists themselves may forget that their theories relate to states of affairs in the world. Yet the truth and falsity of even the most rarified theories are ultimately determined by means of experiments that involve observations. The theories generate expectations. If the observations made conform with the results that the theory leads the scientists to anticipate, then, to that extent, the statement of the theory is verified; it is true. If the observations fail to conform to the expectations, then (provided that the accuracy of the experiments and similar factors have been checked out), the theory is falsified. Once falsified it can be discarded, and scientists are free to pursue more fruitful lines of inquiry. In this way science can progress.

Verification is the positivists' adaptation of the role of experimental work in science to philosophical purposes. If a grammatical and philosophical analysis shows that a statement is supposed to be synthetic, positivists ask: "How can it be verified?" If it is *not* possible to specify observations that would verify it, then it is pseudo-synthetic. It has failed the preliminary examination and is not worthy of serious philosophical consideration. It can be stored in a "dead file" labelled "factually meaningless."

If it is possible to specify observations that would check out a putatively synthetic statement, well and good, one can proceed to do so. If the observations correspond to the state of affairs communicated by the statement, it is true; if they do not match, it is false. In verifying "This book has white pages and black print" one has only to look at the book in your hands to see that it is true.

---

[10] Verification has also been used as a theory of meaning; see pp. 124f. for a discussion of its relevance to theology.

The statement "This book has yellow pages and red print," is checked out in the same way. It is false, but it is a perfectly meaningful synthetic or factual statement that might have been true.

The verification of a commonsense statement like "This book has white pages and black print" is the easiest case to understand. It is also the kind of statement that is least relevant to a discussion of verification and theology. On the one hand, it is not particularly relevant to the verification of scientific hypotheses. They are verified by observations, but the relation is not as simple as it is in the case of checking on the colors of a book (see pp. 395 ff.). On the other hand, it should be obvious that theological statements about God, are not *intended* to be verified by direct observations. God is not like a unicorn or a flying saucer, that is, an object that is supposed to be observable, but whose existence is called into question because no reliable observations ever turn up. Only idols are directly observable.

The issue of verification and theology pivots around the positivists' claim that verification plays a crucial and a successful role in scientific work, and that it is not operative at all, or not successfully, in the work of theologians.

The difficulties of verification and its reformulations

In the early years of the movement, the positivists were confident that verification would serve as a preliminary examination that would effectively eliminate metaphysics and theology from the philosophical scene. There seemed to be good grounds for their confidence. Verification is a crucial factor in scientific work and they hoped for success in applying it to philosophy. Yet they soon found themselves involved in a complicated network of problems.

Michael Tooley notes that a crucial consideration in appraising the adequacy of a criterion of factual meaning is that it should yield acceptable results in noncontroversial cases (see p. 493). Examples of statements that philosophers today find noncontroversial are: "There is molten metal at the earth's core," "All crows are black," and "Unicorns exist." They are commonsense statements whose factual meaningfulness seems obvious. Similarly, the factual meaningfulness of statements of well-established scientific laws, like the law of gravity, seem noncontroversial. Yet, as we shall soon see, positivist versions of verification that denied factual meaningfulness to metaphysical and theological statements also denied them to these seemingly noncontroversial commonsense and scientific statements.

A large number of criticisms have been directed against the positivists' versions of verification. Michael Tooley presents a number of them in his contribution to this volume (see pp. 494 f.); I shall deal briefly with others.[11] The positivists quickly overcame the first difficulty I shall present. They were never able to solve the problems connected with the other three.

1. Many statements that the positivists regarded as factually meaningful could not be verified because of practical difficulties.

2. The test of verification was too restrictive. It excluded metaphysics and theology, but it also excluded as factually meaningless many scientific and commonsense statements that the positivists regarded as meaningful.

3. An effort to recast the test of verification in terms of falsification proved to be too restrictive in this same sense.

4. The test of verification was modified to confirmation in order to include as factually meaningful some standard scientific and commonsense statements. This proved too permissive, it also "passed" metaphysical and theological statements.

Verifiability: statements that can be verified in principle

Early in the game, positivists introduced a major modification of their test. Initially they insisted that the only statements which were factually meaningful were those which could actually be verified like "This book has white pages and black print." The positivists were soon to acknowledge the excessive restrictiveness of this criterion. "There is molten metal at the earth's core" is probably true, but it is a statement whose truth we cannot actually verify. Even at our present state of advanced technology, there is no way of burrowing to the center of the earth. Yet we know what molten metal looks like; if we could reach the center of the earth, we would know what to look for in the effort to verify this statement.

11 My presentation is heavily indebted to Carl G. Hempel, "The Empiricist Criterion of Meaning" in *Logical Positivism*, ed. A. J. Ayer (Glencoe, Illinois: Free Press, 1959), pp. 108–129. As a positivist, he earnestly hoped that these difficulties could be overcome, but he exposed them with rigor and clarity.

The statement, "There is a gold sphere, twenty feet in diameter, at the earth's core," is almost certainly false. Yet, if we could get to the earth's core, it would be easy to check on it, because in this case as well, we would know what to look for. The crucial point is not whether the statement would turn out to be true or false; it is whether there are *conceivable* observations that would, in principle, verify or falsify it. Both statements we have just considered seem to be factually meaningful, yet the highly restrictive version of verification first used by the positivists denied them this status.

The positivists successfully overcame this difficulty. They modified their earlier position and conceded factually meaningful status to statements that could be verified *in principle* ("We'd know what to look for, if we could get there"), even though, for *practical* reasons, they cannot be verified in fact (see pp. 66 f.).

To illustrate, like the statements about molten metal and the gold sphere, the statement "There are twenty daemons at the center of the earth" is supposedly synthetic. There is, however, a crucial difference; daemons are defined as being inaccessible to the senses. Therefore even if we could burrow to the center of the earth, we wouldn't know what to look for when we got there. For this reason, the statement "There are twenty daemons at the center of the earth" is unverifiable *in principle*. Positivists would, with maximal confidence, classify it as pseudo-synthetic, and declare it to be factually meaningless.

Verification eliminates common sense and science

The test of verifiability, that is, verification in principle, may be phrased: "A statement is factually meaningful if and only if there are observations that could, in principle, verify it." The difficulties of verifiability involve the use of such apparently simple words as *all*, *some*, and *exists*. This discussion will focus on *all*, a word that is unproblematic in ordinary English, but which proves treacherous in the context of verification.

"All crows are black" seems to be a straightforward synthetic statement. It is intended to convey information about a state of affairs in the world, and it can be checked by observations. It is almost certainly true, as well as factually meaningful. Yet philosophical reflection uncovers a peculiarity of this statement arising from the word *all*. In order to appreciate it, compare the statement "All crows are black" with "This crow is black." The statement about "this crow" is conclusively verifiable. To establish its truth, we have only to look at the crow which is being pointed out. The statement about "all crows" seems to allow for the same verification procedure, we merely look at crows. Yet this is not the case. No matter how many crows are checked out in the course of history, there is always the possibility that an exception will turn up: A yellow bird, born of two black crows, and incontestably crow-like in all other respects, in other words, a yellow crow! Therefore, *as long as it is not qualified by a limitation of time,* (as in "All crows *now living* are black") the statement "All crows are black" is not verifiable, not even in principle.

At first it might seem as though the difficulty with "All crows are black" is like the problem associated with one of our earlier statements: "There is molten metal at the earth's core." Both statements cannot be verified, yet both seem factually meaningful and probably true. Actually, the two statements are quite different. There is a technological problem associated with the statement about the core of the earth. Anytime we could manage to get there, we would have no difficulty in verifying this statement. Therefore, it is factually meaningful. There is also a merely practical difficulty involved in verifying the statement "All crows now living are black"; it would be hard to assemble them. By contrast, the difficulty with the statement "All crows are black" is *logical*. The statement is not verifiable, even in principle, because we cannot, logically cannot, exclude the possibility of contrary evidence emerging at some future date. "All crows are black" is, then, by the test of verifiability, factually meaningless. Yet it is a kind of noncontroversial statement whose meaningfulness the positivists had no desire to challenge.

From the positivists' standpoint, an even more regrettable consequence of this excessive restrictiveness of the principle of verifiability is the fact that scientific laws are caught in this same net. The law of gravity, for example, has the same logical form as the statement about crows: "All bodies falling freely from rest will accelerate at a rate of 32 feet per second per second." The statement is universal ("All bodies") and it is unrestricted with regard to time. According to the test of verifiability, it too is factually meaningless. This was especially embarrassing for the positivists. The application of their most distinctive principle resulted in the denial of meaning to well-established scientific laws. This meant that, if valid, their work would undercut the prestige of science. Yet this was a case of the positivists sawing off the limb they were sitting on, because the appeal of their program was heavily dependent on this prestige.

Falsification is too restrictive

A leading philosopher of science, Karl Popper, was sympathetic to the positivists' effort to discriminate the factually meaningful statements of science from the nonempirical statements of the metaphysicians.[12] He thought that the positivists had got off on the wrong foot by working with verifiability. No matter how many observations verify a scientific generalization, it is always possible that an exception to it will be observed in the future. For this reason Popper thought that verifiability was not the distinctive feature of science; its distinctive feature is *falsification*. "All bodies falling freely from rest will accelerate at a rate of 32 feet per second per second" is a scientific law now regarded as true. Countless observations have verified it, but none are conclusive because one properly certified exception to it will falsify it, that is, it will force us to label it *false*. To label a statement *false,* is, as we have seen, to concede that it is factually meaningful. It might have been true, but it happens, as things go in the world, to be false. Popper concluded that falsifiability rather than verifiability is the litmus paper type of test that the positivists had been seeking in their effort to discriminate between scientific and metaphysical statements. It can be phrased: "A statement is factually meaningful if and only if there are observations that could, in principle, falsify it."

The test of verifiability founders on statements that deal with every member of a class. Falsification, as Popper himself noted, ran into trouble in coping with statements that deal with at least one member of a class. Consider the statement, "Unicorns exist." It can be rephrased as "There is at least one unicorn." This is a noncontroversial statement whose truth would be denied by everyone; yet no one, including the positivists, would want to deny

[12] Karl Popper, *The Logic of Scientific Discovery* (London: Hutchinson, 1959), see especially, pp. 32–42, 64–72, 78–92. The English version of the book is a revision of the German, *Logic der Forschuung*, (Vienna, 1935).

that it is factually meaningful. Furthermore, it seems as though it would be easy to falsify it. We begin by considering the description: a white animal, with the body of a horse, and a long thin horn protruding from its forehead. We then try to find a beast that actually conforms to this description. If no relevant observations are made, we would say that the statement, "There is at least one unicorn," is falsified. Here we seem to have a clear-cut case of a supposedly synthetic statement passing the test; it is found to be factually meaningful, although false. Yet reflection on the logic of this statement shows that it cannot, in principle, be falsified, even though it is almost certainly false. The statement, like the one about "all crows," is not restricted with regard to time. Therefore, no matter how long the quest for a unicorn might prove fruitless, there is always the possibility that one will turn up. This analysis can be extended to any claim that some kind of thing exists, for example, a scientific claim about genes: "There is a gene that produces sexless human beings." It is clear that the test of falsification, like verification, denies meaningfulness to statements of common sense and science, whose meaning the positivists had no desire to challenge.

It is not surprising that falsification is no more effective than verification, because there is a logical relation between universal and particular statements that links verification and falsification. The denial of a universal statement is expressed in terms of a particular statement, and the denial of a particular statement is expressed in terms of a universal statment. Thus the denial of "All crows are black" (a universal statement which, as we have seen, is nonverifiable) may be formulated in terms of the particular statement "There is at least one non-black crow," (which, we have seen, is nonfalsifiable). By the same token, the denial of the particular statement "There is at least one unicorn," which served as the key example of a nonfalsifiable statement, is the universal (and therefore nonverifiable) statement "All animals are non-unicorns."

Once you come to appreciate the motivation and operation of verification, it comes to have an almost intuitive appeal. After all, there does not seem to be anything conclusively verifiable or falsifiable about theological statements like "God loves us as a father loves his children" or metaphysical statements like "The Absolute enters into, but is itself incapable of, evolution and progress." By contrast, even though "All crows are black" is not conclusively verifiable, it is conclusively falsifiable. One validated instance of a yellow crow would falsify it, in the way that the actual existence of black swans conclusively falsifies "All swans are white." In like fashion, even though the statement "There is at least one unicorn" (or "Unicorns exist") cannot be conclusively falsified, one valid unicorn find would conclusively verify it. We would only need to find an actual white animal with the body of a horse and a horn like an ibex. One might, therefore, suggest that the statement of the test be modified as follows: "A statement is factually meaningful if and only if it is either conclusively verifiable or conclusively falsifiable." In that case universal statements like "All crows are black" would be factually meaningful because they are conclusively falsifiable. The negation of this statement, namely, the particular statement that "There is at least one non-black crow" would also be factually meaningful because it is conclusively verifiable. This would seem to answer all the difficulties encountered so far.

Unfortunately, there are a limitless number of statements which turn out to be factually meaningless by this criterion, but which are instances of the kind of statement whose factual meaningfulness seemed noncontroversial to the positivists. Examples are: "Beyond every star there is another one" and "For any substance there exists some solvent."[13] The terms *every* and *any,* like *all,* are of unrestricted generality, that is, they are used to make a universal statement. We have seen that, when unrestricted as to time, they are not verifiable. *Some* and *another* mean "at least one" which are the marks of particular statements; we have seen that, when unrestricted as to time, they are not falsifiable. The revised statement of the test asks only that a factually meaningful statement be *either* verifiable *or* falsifiable. However, statements of this kind—which logicians refer to as involving mixed quantification (universal and particular)—are *neither* verifiable *nor* falsifiable because the universal part is not verifiable and the particular part is not falsifiable. Furthermore, the universal and particular components cannot be detached from one another without changing the meaning of the statement. Therefore, this revised criterion, like the others, is too restrictive. Its use forces the positivist to brand statements whose factual meaningfulness he has no desire to challenge with the label pseudo-synthetic.

[13] Carl G. Hempel, *Aspects of Scientific Explanation* (New York: Free Press, 1965), p. 105.

With the greatest reluctance, the positivists concluded that both verification and falsification were too restrictive. A rigorous application of either test eliminated scientific babies with the metaphysical bathwater.

Confirmation is too permissive

The positivists' reaction to the excessive restrictiveness of verification and falsification was predictable. They modified their criterion of meaning in the effort to make it restrictive enough to exclude metaphysics and theology but permissive enough to include science.

Reams of literature have been written on this subject. Almost all of it is highly technical, as might be expected, since the issue concerns the theoretical frontiers of logic in its relation to the philosophy of science.[14] In dealing with it here, I shall include only enough material to enable us to understand its relevance to theology.

The problem that emerged in connection with the positivists' test for eliminating metaphysics is that many common-sense and scientific statements also fail to be verifiable or falsifiable. Positivists located the difficulty in the demand for conclusiveness. This is especially clear in the case of falsification because this test is modelled on crucial scientific experiments. If one valid exception to a scientific generalization turns up, we then label the statement of the generalization as *false*. Yet verification was initially thought of in pretty much the same terms, namely, in terms of a single conclusive case. "This book has white pages and black print" is conclusively verified if you look at it.

The answer to the difficulty seemed obvious: eliminate the need for conclusive verification or falsification. The positivists substituted the test of confirmation, roughly, "A statement is factually meaningful if and only if there are, in principle, observations that would count as evidence for its truth and observations that would count against it." These observations would not count conclusively for its truth, they are partial *confirmations* of the truth, hence the term *confirmation*.

Positivists thought this modified test would work because,

[14] *Ibid.,* Section I, 1. See also Israel Scheffler, *The Anatomy of Inquiry* (New York: Alfred A. Knopf, 1963), Part III.

as we have noted, they were certain of one basic distinction between scientific statements on the one hand, and metaphysical and theological statements on the other. Observations are relevant to establishing the truth of science; they are not relevant to establishing the truth of metaphysics and theology. The positivists were right, up to a point. God and metaphysical realities like the Absolute, universals, and substances are not directly observable, even in principle. Therefore, statements about them cannot be conclusively verified by observation. You cannot observe a metaphysical reality to verify a statement like, "The Absolute is perfect." You cannot observe a metaphysical relation in order to verify, for example, the truth of the statement "All shades of grey participate in the universal 'greyness.'" Yet metaphysicians and theologians are by no means prepared to concede the point that there are no observations that could *confirm* the truth of their statements. If the demand for conclusive verification and falsification is abandoned, then some metaphysicians and theologians are willing to specify observations that count for the truth of their statements. To appreciate this willingness we must refine the notion of confirmation to take account of *indirect* as well as *direct* checks.

Many statements can be verified conclusively by direct inspection. "This book has white pages and black print" is an example that has come up a number of times. Since you have the book in your hands, you can look at and verify it.

Statements which cannot be verified directly can often be confirmed indirectly. They are confirmable by evidence that counts for or against their truth. In some cases, the evidence is the observation of one part of a process that we have, on other occasions, observed fully. Thus, "Johnny has been eating chocolate ice cream," where the evidence is a brown smudge on his chin. In this case we say that the smudge counts as confirmation of the statement. We could not verify it directly, because we did not actually see him eat it. Yet it is a solid indirect check, because we have often directly observed him eating ice cream and watched him produce just this kind of smudge.

In other cases, we have evidence that confirms a statement about a nonobservable reality. Statements about subatomic particles are a case in point. Electrons cannot be observed directly, but we regard statements about the behavior of drops of oil between charged plates as evidence that confirms the existence of electrons (see pp. 124 f., 494 f.).

The existence of metaphysical entities like universals and the Absolute cannot be verified by direct inspection, because they are nonobservable. Yet metaphysicians can argue that once the demand for conclusive verification is dropped, they can specify observations which confirm the existence of metaphysical entities. Every observation of a grey-colored object may be taken as, in some sense, confirming the statement "All shades of grey participate in the universal greyness." Of course, the connection between the statement and the observations that are relevant to its confirmation is none too obvious. It must be considered in the context of a metaphysical system. Yet the same point applies to the connection between statements about electrons and the evidence that confirms them. Considerable mastery of physics is required for its appreciation.

Metaphysicans may, therefore, argue that if *confirmation* is the test, metaphysical statements, by the positivists' own standards, are factually meaningful. Basil Mitchell shows that the same point can be made with regard to theological statements (see pp. 250 ff., 263 ff.).

Confirmation, then, was too permissive. When the positivists weakened the test to make sure that it did not exclude science and common sense, it failed to exclude metaphysics and theology.

From positivism to analysis

Since the mid-fifties, there have been few philosophers who accept the label, *logical positivist.* The central concerns of the positivists and their terminology are still part of the philosophical scene, but their positions have been either rejected or refined. Their successors are a large company of empiricist philosophers. All of them practice philosophy by exploring the nature of language and its spectrum of legitimate meanings (in the philosophical, not the dictionary sense). They agree that the gleaning of factual information about things and minds is best left to scientists. They remain hostile to speculative systems of philosophy in the grand style of G. W. Hegel and F. H. Bradley. Their work, however, is much more varied than that of the positivists, and some of it is even reminiscent of what metaphysicians have done in the past. These contemporary empiricists are called by many names. The most general one is *philosophical analysts,* or simply, *analysts.*

There is no sharp line dividing the analysts from their positivist predecessors. The work of refining positivism was largely a self-critical enterprise. The positivists' ability to nail down the reasons for the inadequacy of the various formulations of the test for factual meaning is evidence of a rigor that contrasts favorably with much of the traditional metaphysical and theological writing that they rejected. Some of the positivists of the Vienna Circle, such as Rudolph Carnap and Herbert Feigl became leading figures on the analytic scene. So too did A. J. Ayer whose *Language, Truth and Logic* (1936) did so much to bring positivism to the attention of philosophers in the English-speaking world. These thinkers abandoned or modified positivistic conclusions while retaining the respect for science and the bias against metaphysics and theology that characterized their earlier work.

On the English scene, analysis has been less oriented to science and mathematics and more concerned with articulating and emphasizing the importance of ordinary language to philosophy. Gilbert Ryle and J. L. Austin have been significant representatives of this tendency, but the greatest influence was that of the work of the late Ludwig Wittgenstein. He provided an impetus to the abandonment of positivistic rigidity in favor of more supple approaches to meaning and also to the wider range of concerns that contemporary analysts manifest. By lecturing on these matters at Cambridge during the thirties and forties he influenced a generation of philosophers, among them Elizabeth Anscombe, Peter Geach, Norman Malcolm, and John Wisdom. His influence became much greater when a number of his books were posthumously published in the sixties.

There are many reasons for the demise of positivism as a self-confident and integrated movement. In this connection, Michael Tooley's contribution to this volume is very important, especially his discussion of the problems of observation statements (see pp. 509 ff.). I will deal with a number of the problems of positivism here.

Verification did not eliminate metaphysics and theology

The test of verification was the key element in the positivists' program. There seemed to be good reasons for their confidence that it could be used to eliminate disciplines like metaphysics and theology from the philosophical scene. Once the test is understood, it seems almost intuitive. Furthermore, as has already been noted (pp. 21 f.), it carried with it the prestige of being a crucial element in scientific methodology.

Inadequacies of the test of verification

The confidence of the positivists was eroded by the fact that the test of verification, which was supposed to enable philosophy to progress in a manner comparable to scientific progress, itself became mired in difficulties of a peculiarly philosophical kind.

Difficulties of practical application. Some of the difficulties of applying the test of verification (and the various reformulations of it) to specific statements have already been considered (see pp. 24 ff.). Further instances are presented in Michael Tooley's contribution to this volume (see pp. 494 ff.). The positivists never seemed able to come up with the right combination of restrictiveness (metaphysics and theology "out") and permissiveness (common sense and science "in"). There was another important difficulty which should now be considered.

Is the statement of the test of verification itself cognitively meaningful? The positivists claimed that only two classes of statements were capable of being true and therefore cognitively meaningful: the analytic and the synthetic. They soon suffered the embarrassment of having their philosophical opponents note that standard statements of the test of verification (and falsification and confirmation as well) were not members of either class. It follows that by the positivists' own standards, they were cognitively meaningless, or incapable of being true and, therefore, no threat to metaphysics and theology. (Father Copleston urges this point against Professor Ayer on p. 118).

Opponents of the positivists used many arguments in the effort to make good their charge of cognitive meaninglessness regarding standard statements of the test of verification like "A statement is factually meaningful if and only if there are observations that could, in principle, verify it."[15] I will present a very small sampling of them.

[15] For an extended treatment of this issue, see A. C. Ewing, "Meaninglessness," in *A Modern Introduction to Philosophy*, ed. P. Edwards and A. Pap, 2nd edition (New York: Free Press, 1965), pp. 705ff.

Analytic. As we have seen, the positivists claimed that analytic statements are necessarily true because their denials involve us in contradictions. The truth of statements like "All bachelors are unmarried" is, therefore, universally acknowledged. When we consider the statement of the test of verification things are quite different. (1) No contradiction is involved in denying that "A statement is factually meaningful if and only if there are observations that would, in principle, verify it." (2) When the positivists first formulated their statement of the test, they were a radical minority. Most philosophers at the time not only thought that the statement of the test could be denied without contradiction, but they thought that the *denial* of the *statement* of the test was *true.* Therefore, the positivists could not claim that the statement of the test was cognitively meaningful on the grounds that it is analytic, because it lacks the necessity and universality required for analytic status.

Synthetic. The other option was to claim that the statement of the test was a true synthetic statement. In other words, that as a matter of fact it is true that "A statement is factually meaningful if and only if there are observations that would, in principle, verify it." There are many difficulties with this claim, one of them being that it involves circular argument in the vicious sense of that term. The positivists' job was to show that the statement of the test is synthetic, that is, a genuine statement of fact, and also that it is true. By the positivists' standards, the only way to achieve this would be to specify observations that would verify it. However, to proceed in this way involves the assumption that the statement of the test is both factually meaningful and true. If this were not the case, the procedure would make no sense. Yet, by making this assumption the positivists invalidate their procedure because they proceed by assuming that the statement of the test of verification is a true synthetic statement—which is the very point at issue.[16]

It follows that the statement of the test of verification cannot be shown to be either analytic or synthetic and that, by the positivists' own standards, it is cognitively meaningless.

[16] Axel Steuer helped me to formulate the issue of circularity which is developed by A. J. Ayer, "Demonstration of the Impossibility of Metaphysics" in *A Modern Introduction to Philosophy,* ed. P. Edwards and A. Pap, pp. 692f. Hare's discussion of "bliks," in this volume, is a colorful formulation of one aspect of this issue, namely, the difference in the empirical status of the statement of a criterion itself, and the statements to which we apply it (see pp. 260ff.).

Proposal: Faced with this unhappy state of affairs regarding the status of the statement of the test of verification, the positivists denied that it was a statement (or an *assertion* or a *proposition,* which are terms that the positivists interchanged with *statement*). C. G. Hempel put it in the following terms: "One might think of construing the criterion as a definition which indicates what empiricists propose to understand by a cognitively significant sentence; thus understood, it would not have the character of an assertion and would be neither true nor false. But this conception would attribute to the criterion a measure of arbitrariness which cannot be reconciled with the heated controversies it has engendered. . . ."[17] To elaborate, as a proposal the statement of the test of verification (which Hempel refers to as "the empiricist criterion of meaning") would have the *grammatical form* of an *imperative sentence* in the first person plural, that is the form of sentence that begins with the phrase "Let us." In this case, the proposal might be put as follows: "Let us restrict factual meaningfulness to statements that are verifiable in principle." This would, on *grammatical* grounds alone—without further philosophical analysis—preclude the possibility that the proposal could be cognitively meaningful because, as we have seen, only *declarative sentences* can be either analytic or synthetic (see p. 9). As Hempel notes, in the case of the proposal, which is an imperative, the question of its truth or falsity does not even come up. Furthermore, as Hempel also notes, there is an element of arbitrariness involved in proposing to restrict factual meaningfulness to statements that are verifiable in principle. The positivists may choose to do so, but their opponents are free to propose different definitions of factually meaningful.

  Although the positivists conceded the point that the statement of the test of verification was itself neither analytic nor synthetic, they were confident that the test's effectiveness in practice would compensate for the theoretical flaw pertaining to its status as a statement. Yet success in practice is a standard that varies according to one's purposes. At first, the positivists were happy with the way the test worked in practice, because it seemed to do the job of excluding metaphysics and theology without damaging the status of scientific or commonsense statements. Obviously, metaphysicians and theologians would not be at all happy with this sort of "practice." They were, therefore, by no means pre-

[17] Carl G. Hempel, "The Empiricist Criterion of Meaning," *Logical Positivism,* p. 124.

pared to ignore the theoretical flaw pertaining to its status and to accept the test of varifiability as a useful proposal.

In any case, as we have seen, the positivists themselves discovered flaws in the way the test operated in practice and this made it far less useful for the positivists' anti-metaphysical and anti-theological purposes.

Positivistic pessimism about the test of verification

In 1951, C. G. Hempel published an important survey of the formulations and reformulations of the test of verification. He concluded it on the following note: "It is to be hoped that before long . . . our last version of the empiricist meaning criterion [the test of verification] will be replaced by another more adequate one."[18] Some fifteen years later he indicated that this hope had still not been realized.[19] This shift from revolutionary confidence to long-range hope took place in a period of only two decades. Yet in terms of the application of verification to metaphysics and theology, Ayer's shift is even more significant. In the first edition of *Language, Truth and Logic* (1936) he was confident to the point of being cocky. Ten years later, when he wrote the introduction to the second edition, he stated that:

> . . . although I should still defend the use of the criterion of verifiability as a methodological principle, I realize that for the effective elimination of metaphysics it needs to be supported by detailed analyses of particular metaphysical arguments.[20]

This statement is, to put it mildly, ironical, because the test of verification was designed as an instant metaphysical purgative which would eliminate the need for "the detailed analyses of particular metaphysical arguments." After all, "detailed analysis" is what the pre-positivistic empiricists applied to metaphysics; there was nothing revolutionary in that.

Post-positivistic optimism with regard to verification

The failure to achieve an adequate statement of the test of verification was a major factor in eroding the prestige of positivism even

---

[18] *Ibid.,* p. 126.
[19] Carl G. Hempel, *Aspects of Scientific Explanation,* pp. 120ff.
[20] Alfred J. Ayer, *Language, Truth and Logic,* 2nd edition, p. 16.

among empiricist philosophers. David Rynin attempted to stem the tide by answering C. G. Hempel's criticisms of the various versions of verification and falsification.[21] Yet Rynin not only concedes the point that his reformulation of verification will not serve as a litmus test that would eliminate theology and transcendental metaphysics, he sharply dissociates himself from this kind of positivistic dogmatism.[22] Therefore, from the standpoint of the original revolutionary purposes of the positivists, Rynin's optimism about verifiability amounts to the same thing as the pessimism that the work of Hempel and others inspired: verifiability could not do the job of eliminating theology from the realm of cognitive discourse.

A major point of Michael Tooley's contribution to this volume is to insist that this widespread pessimism on the part of empiricists was premature. He claims that Wesley Salmon's essay on "Verifiability and Logic" (1966) constitutes a fresh and viable approach to this issue.[23]

Tooley is right in claiming that Salmon's statement of verifiability represents a fresh departure. The question of its effectiveness is more problematic. In any case, as Salmon noted in his introductory remarks, pessimism about verification was so widespread that we were in the post-positivistic period by the time his essay appeared. There were other problems that led to the abandonment of positivism; I will consider a few of them.

Quine's rejection of the analytic

An important milestone on the road to the post-positivistic scene in philosophy was the appearance in 1953 of W. V. Quine's essay "Two Dogmas of Empiricism."[24] He did not elaborate on the difficulties of the test of verification; he assumed them. He trained his fire on the positivists' distinction between the analytic and the syn-

[21] David Rynin, "The Vindication of L*g*c*l P*s*t*v*sm," *Proceedings and Addresses of the American Philosophical Association,* XXX (1957), pp. 45–67 and "Cognitive Meaning and Cognitive Use," *op. cit.,* pp. 109–131.

[22] David Rynin, "The Vindication of L*g*c*l P*s*t*v*sm," *op. cit.,* pp. 56f., 65ff. Rynin's use of this strange spelling in the title of his essay is, in part, to symbolize his abandonment of positivistic dogma regarding metaphysics and theology.

[23] Wesley Salmon, "Verifiability and Logic," in *Mind, Matter and Method,* ed. P. K. Feyerabend and G. Maxwell (St. Paul: University of Minnesota Press, 1966), pp. 354–376. [Reprinted in this volume, pp. 456–480.—Editors]

[24] Reprinted in Willard V. Quine, *From a Logical Point of View* (New York: Harper and Row, 1963), see especially pp. 20–37, 44–46.

thetic. This was a rude jolt to the positivists. By 1953 they knew very well that they were in trouble on verification, but the analytic was regarded as a bulwark of their program. It rested on the self-evident and necessary character of logic. Yet Quine denied that any statements are necessary in the sense that the positivists claimed necessity for analytic statements.

Quine has tried to demonstrate that the analytic is a philosophical chimera. The technical details of his treatment of the analytic, and the question of whether his position will ultimately be validated, are not relevant to this discussion of theology and verification. What is important is that his assault on the analytic contributed to the passing of positivism from the center of the philosophical stage. A brilliant logician and philosopher who was sympathetic to the empiricism of the positivists attacked its strongest point. It was bound to shake up the philosophical scene.

The break with dogmatism

At first, philosophers were inclined to take the positivists at face value and to regard their enterprise as a vigorous manifestation of the scientific spirit within the philosophical camp; as time went on, they began to wonder whether the positivists were not merely partisan. There was, after all, something prejudicial and dogmatic about the tortuous efforts of the positivists to achieve a version of the verifiability principle with the right combination of permissiveness ("science-in") and restrictiveness ("metaphysics-out"). A scientific inquiry into meaningfulness should have been more open-ended. It might have begun with a sense of the meaningfulness of certain types of statements and of the meaninglessness of other types, but the investigators would have been open to the possibility that things might not turn out that way. The positivists, by contrast, clung to their favorite metaphysical whipping boys: Platonic, Hegelian, Heideggerian, and theological statements. These were to be shown to be factually meaningless come what may! Then the job was to find the philosophical broadsword that would hack them from the scene without injuring any innocent "scientific" or "commonsense" bystanders.

Did the positivists use "umbrella-words"?

Philosophers have often divided subjects by grand distinctions which yield two vast classes, like the subjective and the objective, the material and the mental, and the I-It and the I-Thou. Among the post-positivistic analysts comprehensive terms like *subjective* and *objective* are suspect. These terms embrace and obscure so many important distinctions that Gilbert Ryle calls them "umbrella-words."[25] He clearly refers to a very large covering that has a considerable variety of objects sheltered under it. Some of the positivists' distinctions came to seem embarrassingly like these great and overblown classifications of the philosophical tradition. The positivist divisions of statements into the "analytic/synthetic" and the "genuinely synthetic/pseudo-synthetic" were regarded as too crudely drawn. Too many important distinctions were covered by single terms like *analytic* and *pseudo-synthetic*. Morton White, himself a contemporary analytic empiricist, paid tribute to the creative impetus of the early positivists, but was sharply critical of the dogmatic spirit which quickly set in and led to an emphasis on umbrella words:

> . . . ancient metaphysical generalizations about everything being
> fire or water were erased and replaced by equally indefensible
> universal theses, according to which all logical statements are like
> this, and all physical statements are like that, and all ethical state-
> ments are very different from both.[26]

Wittgenstein: meaning as use

The impetus to break with the dogmatism represented by the umbrella words of positivism received its strongest support from Wittgenstein's later work. Wittgenstein was by no means the first philosopher to make the point in print; his influence was a function of his enormous prestige. He was a philosophical "loner" who had never been a member of the Vienna Circle, but his *Tractatus Logico-Philosophicus* (1921) was a major influence on the development of logical positivism. Everyone knew that he had been rethinking his position during the thirties and forties and the posthumous appearance of his *Philosophical Investigations* (1953) was one of the major events of the century.[27] In this later work he repudiated the

25 Gilbert Ryle, "Heterologicality" in *Philosophy and Analysis*, ed. M. Mac-Donald (Oxford: Basil Blackwell, 1954), p. 51.
26 Morton White, *Toward Reunion in Philosophy* (New York: Atheneum, 1963), p. 290.
27 Ludwig Wittgenstein, *Tractatus Logico-Philosophicus*, 2d ed. rev., tr. D. F. Pears and B. F. McGuiness (London: Routledge and Kegan Paul, 1961), *Philosophical Investigations*, 3d ed., tr. G. E. M. Anscombe (New York: Macmillan, 1969). David Rynin, in "Cognitive Meaning and Cognitive Use," *op. cit.*, pp.

rigidities of the *Tractatus*, with its picture theory of meaning, along with the rigidities of the positivism that it helped to inspire. He no longer believed that the incredible variety of cognitively meaningful language could be forced into prefabricated molds. Conclusions that may be drawn from his later work are:

1. Cognitive meaning should not be restricted to the cases that conform to the standards of mathematics and physics;

2. In any case, even within these disciplines meanings are far more complicated than can be indicated by the sweeping terms *analytic* and *synthetic;*

3. It is a mistake to consider the meaning of individual words and statements without paying close attention to the nuances of their larger linguistic context. *White* and *black* must be understood in the context of the function of color terms in ordinary English. One of Wittgenstein's major contributions was to show that this is far more complicated than we usually take it to be. A child may be able to say "black" when you point to a black chair, and "white" when you point to a white one, without really grasping the meaning of *black* and *white.* He might associate the colors with the shape of the chairs or with the texture of the materials used to cover them. Checking on whether someone has mastered color words cannot be done by simplistic tests that are confined to the verification of isolated statements like "This book has white pages and black print." Wittgenstein's analysis is obviously even more relevant to disciplines with complex fabrics of meaning like law, physics, architecture, and, of course, theology. As he put it, "For a *large* class of cases—though not for all—in which we employ the word 'meaning' it can be defined thus: the meaning of a word is its use in the language."[28]

119f., claims that the *Investigations* does not represent a radical departure from the *Tractatus* and that the relation between meaning and use had been explored long before the *Investigations* appeared. The point, to be sure, has been made by a number of other interpreters of Wittgenstein and now is supported by the translation and publication of two of Wittgenstein's works that bridge the span between the *Tractatus* and the *Investigations;* see *Philosophical Remarks*, ed. Rush Rhees, trs. Raymond Hargreaves and Roger White (Oxford: Basil Blackwell, 1974) and *Philosophical Grammar*, ed. Rush Rhees, tr. Anthony Kenny (Oxford: Basil Blackwell, 1974). Even if this is so, Rynin, in making the point, acknowledged that the *impact* of the *Investigations* was that of a radical departure that initiated a fresh emphasis on meaning as use.

[28] Ludwig Wittgenstein, *Philosophical Investigations*, p. 20. The general discussion of "meaning as use" runs from pp. 10–31.

In philosophy an important insight is rarely a wrap-up, it is generally a point of departure for a fresh discussion. This was the case with Wittgenstein's theory of "meaning as use." It helped to get contemporary empiricists out of the analytic and the synthetic ruts, but it did not resolve all the important questions of cognitive meaning. Initially, some thinkers misunderstood it; they thought it involved the consequence that "anything goes." Some religious thinkers, for example, hailed this departure as a conclusive answer to the challenge of the positivists, because the word *God* certainly has a meaning in English and it is well established.[29] Part of this meaning involves the idea that God is an existing reality. It would, therefore, seem that according to Wittgenstein's standard of "meaning as use," God must exist. Obviously, this line of reasoning is too simplistic. Even if we accept Wittgenstein's statement that the meaning of a word is its use in the language, there are complications that should be noted: one is that Wittgenstein did not claim that his standard of meaning applies to all cases; another is that God is obviously a controversial case. In addition, we realize that we are not stuck with the common use of words, but that we often react critically to them. Take for example the use of *daemon* in a culture where daemons are believed to exist. Existence is, for them, part of the meaning of daemon. Yet people of *our* culture will not accept the existence of daemons on this basis. Indeed, as noted earlier, the rise of science has called the meaning of God in our western culture into question. Although believers still regard existence as part of its meaning, vast numbers of sceptics challenge this use. This point applies to facile efforts to invoke Wittgenstein's prestige on behalf of the claim that God exists merely by noting that generations of believers have used the term *God* to refer to an actual agent.

On the other hand, *critics* of theology can also be too facile. Wittgenstein's theory of meaning as use is an antidote to the all too common practice of demanding that theologians produce evidence for "God exists" that would be comparable to evidence for "The Abominable Snowman exists." This is misguided because the

[29] For a discussion of this point see Jerry H. Gill, *Possibility of Religious Knowledge* (Grand Rapids: Eerdmans Publishing House, 1971), p. 232, n. 31; Dallas M. High, *Language, Persons and Belief* (New York: Oxford University Press, 1967), pp. 134f; Ronald Hepburn, "From World to God," in *Philosophy of Religion,* ed. B. Mitchell (London: Oxford University Press, 1971), pp. 168f, and, for an effort to answer this charge, see D. Z. Phillips, "Religious Beliefs and Language Games," in *Philosophy of Religion,* ed. B. Mitchell, pp. 121–142.

term *God* is not used to refer to a reality that is supposed to be observable. Wittgenstein alerts us to the need to consider terms like *God* and statements like "God loves us" in their theological contexts.

Wittgenstein has influenced a considerable number of contemporary religious thinkers.[30] Some of them invoke his name merely for the purpose of making the point that positivism didn't eliminate theology. Others, who regard themselves as philosophical empiricists, apply his thought more directly and positively to their own work, as in the following statements by Basil Mitchell:

> How will philosophers of this persuasion [that is, post-positivistic analysts who have been influenced by Wittgenstein] tend to approach theology? Three things are, I think, clear.
>
> (1) They will not, as did the Idealists, put forward . . . a worldview or philosophy of life, which might conflict with Christianity; because they regard the development of such world-views as no part of a philosopher's business.
>
> (2) They will not . . . rule out theological statements from the start on the ground that they are meaningless, as the logical positivists did.

[30] Ludwig Wittgenstein, *Lectures and Conversations on Aesthetics, Psychology and Religious Belief,* ed. Cyril Barrett (Oxford: Basil Blackwell, 1966), published posthumously, deals with religious belief, pp. 53–72. Among thinkers on religion who have been influenced by Ludwig Wittgenstein are: John Wisdom, "Gods," *Philosophy and Psychoanalysis* (Oxford: Basil Blackwell, 1953), pp. 149–168; see also his *Paradox and Discovery* (Oxford: Basil Blackwell, 1965), especially, "The Logic of 'God,' " pp. 1–22; Dallas M. High, *Language, Persons and Belief;* Paul L. Holmer, "Wittgenstein and Theology," in *New Essays on Religious Language,* ed. Dallas M. High (New York: Oxford University Press, 1969), pp. 25–35, and Paul L. Holmer, "The Nature of Religious Propositions," in *Religious Language and the Problem of Religious Knowledge,* ed. Ronald E. Santoni (Bloomington: Indiana University Press, 1968) pp. 233–247; W. D. Hudson, *Ludwig Wittgenstein: The Bearing of His Philosophy on Religious Belief* (Richmond: John Knox Press, 1968); Norman Malcolm, "Is it a Religious Belief that God Exists?," in *Faith and the Philosophers,* ed. John Hick (New York: St. Martin's Press, 1964), pp. 103–110; D. Z. Phillips, *Faith and Philosophical Inquiry* (London: Routledge and Kegan Paul, 1970); James Richmond, *Theology and Metaphysics* (London: SCM Press, 1970); Paul M. van Buren, *The Edges of Language* (New York: Macmillan, 1972); Peter Winch, *The Idea of a Social Science* (London: Routledge and Kegan Paul, 1958). In the following note there is a reference to a collection of essays by the "Metaphysicals," an Oxford-based group of religious thinkers who were influenced by Wittgenstein. Kai Nielsen, in "Wittgensteinian Fideism," *Philosophy,* 42 (1967), 191–209, subjects the religiously oriented Wittgensteinians to a searching criticism. W. D. Hudson replies in "On Two Points Against Wittgensteinian Fideism," *Philosophy,* 43 (1968), 269–273, to whom Nielsen replies in "Wittgensteinian Fideism: A Reply to Hudson," *Philosophy,* 44 (1969), 63–65.

(3) They will ask the same sort of questions about theological statements as they do about statements of other kinds, viz. "How are they verified? What sorts of arguments or observations tend to confirm or refute them?" In short, "What is their logic?"[31]

Theology and analysis

By the time that Wittgenstein's *Philosophical Investigations* began to take hold, it was clear that the deployment of verification would not eliminate metaphysics or theology by means of a preliminary examination. This is the crowning irony of the story of positivism. One of the main objectives of the positivists was the elimination of metaphysics and theology, yet they continue to flourish after positivism has passed from the scene.

The varied responses of religious thinkers to the challenge of verification will be treated in the remaining sections of this text. The rest of this discussion will be devoted to a summary of the state of the debate today. It begins with the effort to eliminate a source of confusion. The positivists' challenge was not directed against fundamentalism (which is what many people still have in mind when they think of Christianity), but against more sophisticated theological positions.

The theological targets of verification

Fundamentalism is an approach to religion that cuts across many of the denominational and sectarian distinctions of Protestantism. It must be understood as a reaction against theological accommodation to the scientific outlook. Fundamentalists try to overwhelm modern culture by appealing to the authority of the Bible. Their sense of its authority is rooted in their conviction that every word of it, as literally understood, is divinely inspired and, therefore, guaranteed against error. Their policy is that if science conflicts with the Bible, then so much the worse for science.

Sophisticated theologians are embarrassed by the miraculous elements of the Bible. They cope with them in various ways. They often interpret them rationalistically as when the instantaneous healings of Jesus are regarded as examples of psychosomatic

[31] Basil Mitchell, ed., *Faith and Logic* (London: George Allen and Unwin, 1957); see the editor's Introduction, p. 5.

medicine. Some sophisticated theologians try to eliminate miracles altogether by claiming that they are outmoded myths that are part of the Bible, but not part of its essential message. By contrast, the fundamentalists vehemently reject efforts to downgrade biblical miracles.

Now we can see why fundamentalists are not vulnerable to the challenge of verification. Suppose a fundamentalist makes the statement, "God freed the Israelites from slavery in Egypt." If he is then challenged to verify it, he can not only appeal to observations, but to observations that are, to say the least, startling. He can appeal to the parting of the raging waters of the Red Sea and to their standing in "walls." Furthermore, the fundamentalist claims that these events are so utterly extraordinary that they could not have happened without God's supernatural intervention. Naturally, he can then be challenged to show that these events really happened. Here too, the fundamentalist is, within his own frame of reference, on sound ground. He claims that the accuracy of the observations recorded in the Bible is guaranteed by God's inspiration.

Another important aspect of fundamentalism's invulnerability to the challenge of verification is the special character of some of the observations recorded, the most important being the resurrection of Jesus Christ. This miracle verifies the truth of Christian statements, and only of Christian statements. It would not serve equally well to verify theological statements of other religions like Judaism and Islam. Therefore, fundamentalists can claim that the miracles are distinctive observations which verify, or at least confirm, the theological statements of Christendom, and which do not and cannot verify any other statements whatever.

This is not the place to go into the thinking that has led to the rejection of fundamentalism within Christendom as well as in sceptical circles.[32] Basically, it amounts to the inability of fundamentalists to make a case for their view of biblical authority. They now exist in cultural isolation since nonfundamentalists no longer bother to argue with them.

Contemporary empiricists concede the factual meaningfulness of fundamentalist theology.[33] However, they regard funda-

---

[32] There is an extended discussion of this point in Malcolm L. Diamond, *Contemporary Empiricism and Religious Thought: An Introduction to the Philosophy of Religion* (New York: McGraw-Hill, 1974), pp. 57–71.

[33] Rudolf Carnap, "The Elimination of Metaphysics" in *Logical Positivism*, ed. A. J. Ayer, pp. 66f.

mentalism as so hopelessly outmoded by the development of scientific standards of believability, that they do not even bother to challenge the thrust of its factually meaningful statements. The failure to appreciate the attitude of contemporary empiricists toward fundamentalism can lead to unfortunate results. For example, R. S. Heimbeck, in a recent defense of the factual meaningfulness of theological statements, displays considerable sophistication in tracing the changes in the theory of meaning that have taken place in contemporary empiricist philosophy. Yet his approach to theology is utterly naïve. He defends the factual meaningfulness of theological statements by appealing to literal approaches to the miracles of the Red Sea and the Resurrection.[34] This literalism would not be accepted by sophisticated theologians of our time. Indeed, John Wisdom's influential essay, "Gods," takes its point of departure from the fact that religious thinkers no longer appeal to literalistic accounts of miracles—like the fire from heaven that consumed Elijah's altar—to verify religious or theological statements (see p. 159).

In Protestant circles, important theologians from Friedrich Schleiermacher (1768–1834), to Rudolph Bultmann (1844–   ) have rejected fundamentalism and accepted the implications of a scientifically oriented culture. This does not merely involve the acceptance of specific scientific theories like evolution; it involves the acceptance of scientific assumptions about the natural world. They accept the uniformity of nature, and along with it, the view that any occurrence that can be observed can, in principle, be explained naturally. The positivists directed their fire at the sophisticated theologies that were influential during their heyday. Thomism dominated the Catholic scene, and the Protestant scene was dominated by liberalism and neo-Orthodoxy.

Thomism is an Aristotelian form of theology which antedated the rise of science but was sophisticated enough to avoid being forced into the reactive posture of fundamentalism. It is a speculative metaphysical system. As such, it was, naturally, one of the primary targets of the positivists (see Section Three).

Many of the liberal theologians and the representatives of the new orthodoxy reject fundamentalism and with it the traditional view of miracle. They retain the belief in a personal God

[34] Raeburne S. Heimbeck, *Theology and Meaning* (Stanford, California: Stanford University Press, 1969), pp. 154f., 172f., 196–200, 221f. Flew discusses Heimbeck's position on pp. 275f. Heimbeck's discussions of theories of meaning are replete with helpful bibliographical references.

who transcends, that is, who is utterly beyond the world, yet nevertheless interacts with it. They do not, however, think of God's actions in terms that suggest supernatural causes, for example, dead men being restored to life, raging seas dividing and standing in "walls," and bushes burning without being charred or damaged in any other way. They are sceptical of biblical accounts of these sorts of occurrences, because the rise of scientific standards of understanding nature and of historical research have affected their standards of believability. They think of God as acting within the natural regularities that scientists formulate in their theories and laws; God does not act by suspending or violating them. Liberal theologians tend to find God in distinctively religious and moral experiences. Neo-orthodox theologians tend to be more oriented to the dramatic tensions of historical crises. Insofar as they are precluded, by their own choice, from appealing to miracles as evidence for God's supernatural activity, both liberal and neo-orthodox theologians are peculiarly vulnerable to the challenge of verification. Yet the confrontations which appear in the balance of this volume show that even these "vulnerable" theologies are not as vulnerable as the positivists thought they were.

In this post-positivistic era theology is as varied as it has ever been. Theologians, as always, argue even more with one another than they do with sceptics. In response to fresh insights and to contemporary cultural crises they develop new directions like the "death of God theology" and the "theology of hope." More established approaches such as liberalism, neo-orthodoxy, religious existentialism, and even fundamentalism, all have their adherents, as do metaphysical types of theology such as Thomistic and Whiteheadian thought. Finally, there are a considerable number of religious thinkers who work with analytic categories. They display the variety of approaches that are found in post-positivistic empiricism. Some are oriented to the logical concerns of contemporary empiricism; others take a Wittgensteinian tack and work with ordinary language. They share the conviction that the positivists grossly oversimplified the questions involved in dealing with the cognitive significance of religious and theological language.[35]

In light of the failure of verification to do the jobs for which

[35] A sketch of representative thinkers and the major tendencies they exemplify should be helpful; for full references see the bibliography (pp. 531–554). These categorizations are not intended to be hard and fast; there is some overlapping:

it was designed, many theologians may feel justified in treating the positivist episode as a philosophical nightmare. Now that it is over, they feel they can return to business as usual (see p. 229). This reaction would be misguided, because the challenge of contemporary empiricism remains a formidable one and there are important lessons to be learned from it.

The struggle for clarity

Contemporary empiricists have raised the standards of philosophical argument, partly as a result of their passion for clarity. This is not to say that they are the first philosophers who have sought clarity (think of Spinoza's efforts to do ethics in the manner of geometry) or that they are necessarily clearer than other philosophers (the contemporary idealist Brand Blanshard writes more clearly than most analysts). The virtue of the contemporary empiricists is to have made clarity a central issue in philosophy. They insist on a clear formulation of questions and on clarity in answering them. One positive outcome of the emphasis on verification has been the demand for precision in saying what counts for a thesis, what counts against it, and why.

Another beneficial result of the empiricist emphasis on clarity has been the debunking of technical jargon that masquerades as profundity. Too much theological writing is still vulnerable to the jibe of W. S. Gilbert "And every one will say, / as you

---

a. *Thinkers oriented to formal logic*
    Joseph Bochenski, O.P., Robert Coburn, George I. Mavrodes, Alvin Plantinga, James F. Ross, and Michael Tooley.
b. *Thinkers oriented to ordinary language*
    Donald D. Evans, Frederick Ferré, Van A. Harvey, D. Z. Phillips, Ian Ramsey, Ninian Smart, and an Oxford group called "The Metaphysicals," who produced *Faith and Logic,* edited by Basil Mitchell.
c. *Analytic thinkers who deal with Thomism*
    Peter Geach, Anthony Kenny, Victor Preller, and James F. Ross.
d. *Positivistic thinkers*
    John Hick and William Zurdeeg have produced full length studies of religious thought that are positivistic in orientation. Paul van Buren has a positivistic approach in his *The Secular Meaning of the Gospel* (1963), but in his *Theological Explorations* (1968) and *The Edges of Language* (1972) he shifts to a post-positivist orientation to religious thought that stresses ordinary language and is much indebted to Wittgenstein. Finally, it should be noted that Michael Tooley, in his contribution to this volume (see Section Ten) tries to revive some important positivist positions.

walk your mystic way, / if this young man expresses himself in terms too deep for me, / why what a very singularly deep young man this deep young man must be" (*Patience*). Analysts challenge theologians to get as clear as they possibly can in presenting their views. The writing of theologians who avoid the discipline provided by the study of contemporary empiricism is frequently so turgid that it is all but impossible to understand. The title essay of a recent collection of philosophical essays was called, "Clarity is not Enough."[36] This is true, but clarity is a great help.

The burden of proof

One of the major issues between analysts and theologians is the question of who bears the burden of proof. Theologians attempt to shift it to the analysts by saying that until the analysts prove the adequacy of some version of the test of verification, theologians need not worry about the empiricist challenge. Analysts attempt to shift it to the theologians by saying that until theologians prove that at least some of their important statements are capable of being factually meaningful—if not in terms of verifiability, then in terms of some other publicly acceptable standard—they need not take theology seriously.

I shall not elaborate the issue here, because it comes up so frequently in the rest of this volume. In the debate between A. J. Ayer and Father Copleston in Section Three, each of them tries to shift the burden to the other. In Section Six G. I. Mavrodes provides an excellent illustration of the way religious thinkers try to shift the burden to sceptics. Antony Flew in Section Eight tries to thrust the burden on theologians in general, and T. V. Litzenburg tries to shift it right back to Flew. In Section Nine the question emerges in the form of comparison between science and religion.

The tu quoque

The positivists' revolution was born of disgust and launched in hope. They were disgusted at the fact that philosophy, after hundreds of years of effort by some of history's most brilliant men, seemed incapable of getting anywhere. Their hope was that by

[36] H. H. Price, "Clarity is not Enough" in *Clarity is not Enough*, ed. H. D. Lewis (London: Allen and Unwin, 1963), pp. 15–41.

eliminating incurably futile enterprises, especially metaphysics and theology, they could get philosophy to progress like science.

Theologians can hardly be expected to concede the point that contemporary empiricists have achieved philosophical progress. The test of verification was their main instrument for achieving it, but, as we have seen, it is itself bogged down in a quagmire of difficulties of a peculiarly philosophical kind. The post-positivist scene is even less encouraging from the standpoint of the revolutionary progress that empiricists hoped to achieve.[37]

Theologians, therefore, direct a standard form of argument, the *tu quoque* ("you're another") against contemporary empiricists.[38] It is used to accuse the critic of suffering from the very defect with which he charges his opponent. In this case, the theologians claim that if the failure to achieve progress comparable to that of science is a defect in theology, it is also a defect in contemporary empiricism (see pp. 292 f. for Schubert Ogden's use of the *tu quoque* against Anthony Flew).

The *tu quoque* is one of the most effective replies that theologians can make to analytic philosophers. Its effectiveness is eroded, though not completely eliminated, by noting their different points of departure. Analytic sceptics confine their theorizing to mathematics, science, and common sense; theologians necessarily theorize about religion. The work of G. E. Moore (1873–1958) points up the importance of this difference.

Moore protested against the philosophical tendency to deny the obvious in the name of the obscure. People manage quite well with commonsense statements of fact like "This page is white," even though generations of philosophers have been unable to come up with a satisfactory theoretical account of how we know it. Moore insisted that our inability to provide an adequate theoretical account of our knowledge of this statement should not lead us to deny its truth. Indeed, he claimed that if a theory of knowledge involves the denial of the truth of this kind of statement, that is a sign that the theory rather than the statement is questionable.[39]

[37] For a penetrating discussion of this issue see Richard Rorty, "Metaphilosophical Difficulties of Linguistic Philosophy" in *The Linguistic Turn*, ed. R. Rorty (Chicago: University of Chicago Press, 1967), pp. 1–39.

[38] For an extended statement of the theological use of this argument and a contemporary empiricist's effort to answer it, see William W. Bartley III, *The Retreat to Commitment* (New York: Alfred A. Knopf, 1962), pp. 86–95, 146–156.

[39] George E. Moore, *Philosophical Papers* (London: Allen and Unwin, 1959), pp. 23ff.

This approach can be extrapolated from commonsense contexts to the more rarified domains of mathematics and science. Mathematicians and scientists seem to operate quite well at practicing their disciplines even though the philosophy of mathematics and the philosophy of science continue to be highly controversial subjects.

Analytic sceptics can, therefore, acknowledge the force of the theologians' appeal to the *tu quoque* at the theoretical level. They can admit that epistemology (the theory of knowledge), the philosophy of mathematics, and the philosophy of science are shot through with intractable problems; in this sense they are comparable to theology. Yet analysts can then deny the effectiveness of the *tu quoque* at the level of ordinary practice, because there do not seem to be statements of religious belief that are obviously true in Moore's sense. Furthermore, neither the statements of ordinary believers nor those of theologians seem to achieve the kind of operative consensus found among mathematicians and scientists. That is why analysts can refuse to concede the point that theology is no more problematical than such theoretical enterprises as epistemology and the philosophy of science (see pp. 185 f.). They are convinced that the problems of the philosophy of science are worth studying and resolvable because science is a successful mode of knowing. They charge that theology is intrinsically futile and its problems are not worth studying because, to the extent that religion involves claims to knowledge, it is incapable of making any of them good.

Theologians can reply that even if Moore's position on commonsense statements is valid, it is treacherous to apply his position to scientific statements. Statements about theoretical particles in physics or about genes in biochemistry are not on the same level as statements like "This page is white." It is, therefore, open to the theologians to insist that the statements of science are no more like those of common sense than are religious statements. In other words, the theologian can take the position that science and religion are not that dissimilar in their logical structure (see Section Nine). Indeed, theologians could even admit that religion is more problematic than science without conceding the point that this difference undercuts the effectiveness of the *tu quoque*. Theologians can point to the fact that religion deals with the ultimate mysteries of God and the universe. These are obviously more difficult subjects than the limited aspects of the universe that scientists study. Given the difference in subject matter, theologians can claim that in a comparison with science, religion doesn't do that badly.[40]

Theologians can also try to blunt the force of invidious comparisons between religion and science (as cognitive enterprises) by appealing to the "limitations of science." There is a considerable body of literature devoted to this topic, a good deal of it being marred by misunderstandings of science and by sloppy thinking. At its best, it succeeds in raising the possibility that in dealing with such matters as freedom, trust, and love, the scientific approach is not only unsuccessful, but is misguided. The same could be said of other instances of what Donald Evans calls "depth experiences" (see pp. 282 ff.). If this point could be sustained, theologians could claim that religious thought achieves knowledge of areas that are beyond the reach of science.

Analytic sceptics do not find this appeal convincing; they raise the following kinds of questions: (1) Do religious sources actually provide insights into freedom, love, and other important concerns that cannot equally be obtained independently of religion? (2) Even if the answer to the first question is "yes," are these insights the sorts of things that can be labelled "true," and, therefore, regarded as cognitive? There does not seem to be a reliable method, comparable to that of science, for transmitting these religious insights. The sceptics insist that if we are ever to attain *knowledge* of these areas, it will be by applying the scientific method.

This sketch of the debate is designed to show that the appeal to science represents a formidable challenge to religious thought. However, the debate to date does not provide a clinching demonstration of the sceptic's case. One way of making this point is to ask the question: "Is there an adequate test of factual meaningfulness (adequate by the standards of contemporary empiricists) that is positive on electrons and negative on God?" We find that, to date, the answer is: "No!"

Finally, as a needed counter-emphasis to my focus on religion and science, readers should note Ogden's metaphysical response to Flew's latest version of the falsification challenge (see pp. 290 ff.).

[40] Richard Brandt in *Faith and the Philosophers*, ed. J. Hick (New York: St. Martin's Press, 1964), pp. 152ff.

Cultural shift: fundamentalism
and theology

A considerable number of brilliant philosophers have tried to discredit theology as a cognitive enterprise. They have not succeeded. The only thing they have demonstrated is that it is very different from mathematics and science.[41] It is doubtful that philosophers will ever come up with a convincing demonstration of the cognitive meaninglessness of theology or even of the falsity of the theological statement "God exists." If theology is ever discredited it will probably be the result of a cultural shift that leads people to lose interest in it. This is what happened with fundamentalism.

Two contributors to this volume deal explicitly with the issue of cultural shift. John Wisdom tries to show how the arguments between theists and atheists have changed after the abandonment of fundamentalism by religious believers (see pp. 158 ff.). D. Z. Phillips uses Wittgensteinian categories to show the importance of the cultural setting to loss of belief and then to relate it to the issue of theology and verification (see pp. 341 ff.). I shall deal with it here in my own terms.

The parallel I am about to draw between the present state of fundamentalism and a possible future state of theology was suggested by a conversation with a theologically sophisticated graduate student. He was outraged at the narrowness of analytically oriented philosophy students. In response to the suggestion that they read Heidegger, one of them said, "Why waste time reading that stuff?" In reporting this incident, my friend clearly expected me to share his outrage. Instead, I asked him, "How many volumes of fundamentalist theology have you read in the past year?" The answer was that he had not read a single volume of it at any time.

I asked this question in order to suggest that we all have cut off points where we decide that a given option is no longer a live one. Decisions of this kind involve a variety of factors; many of them are not logical. Most theologians no longer regard fundamentalism as a live option; it has never been refuted by a logically conclusive argument. It is rejected because its basic assumptions conflict with the scientifically oriented world view of many theologians, and because they think that fundamentalists understand

---

[41] Alfred J. Ayer, "Editor's Introduction" in *Logical Positivism*, pp. 15f.

religious belief in magical terms rather than in terms of existential faith.

Fundamentalists, of course, insist that their option is a live one. They rightly claim that there has been no conclusive disproof of their view that God dictated the words of the Bible to the prophets and apostles (or inspired them to verbal infallibility by some other device). The same holds true of their belief that God suspends or violates the laws of nature in order to perform miracles. They claim that the major arguments against these views have been advanced by thinkers who assume the very points at issue. That is, thinkers who reject fundamentalism assume that it is impossible to conceive of the God who utterly transcends the senses dictating anything to anyone. They also assume that the rise of science has decisively influenced our standards of believability both with regard to natural occurrences and to the reliability of historical reports of the utterly extraordinary. They assume, for example, that it is utterly implausible to think of obtaining valid evidence for the occurrence of miracles like the waters standing in "walls" at the Red Sea.

Fundamentalists press their case even further by insisting that they are oriented to the unchanging words of the eternal God that are found in the Bible. Their opponents accept higher criticism which involves the study of the Bible by modern methods of literary and historical research. The conclusions of the higher critics have varied a great deal over the years, and no responsible critic can claim that a consensus now prevails on important issues such as the quest for the historical Jesus. As far as the fundamentalists are concerned, the controversies prevailing among higher critics is just what one would expect when God's infallible words are polluted with the fallibilities of human research.

In light of their opponents' failure to present a logically conclusive refutation of fundamentalism, and in light of the confusions that plague the higher critics, fundamentalists vehemently protest the fact that in so many great centers of theological learning the validity of the critical approach to the Bible is simply assumed and not argued for.

Higher critics used to spend a great deal of their time and energy arguing with fundamentalists. Now they ignore them and get on with their work, for example, by devising better tools like carbon tests for dating manuscripts.

I am suggesting that it is possible for theology, in the future, to find itself in the cultural situation that fundamentalism is in today. Philosophers might find themselves unable to prove that theology is cognitively meaningless but, instead of becoming more interested in doing so, they might lose all interest in this effort and in theology in general. They would then ignore it in the way that sophisticated theologians and biblical critics ignore fundamentalism. Clearly, the situation has not reached this point, and the failure of the positivists' program makes it less likely that it will. Yet Gilbert Ryle provides an interesting illustration of an analytic sceptic whose view of theology is that it is going, going . . . , even though not quite gone.

> The theological fire has died down, but it has not quite gone out and the kettle of theological philosophy, though far from even simmering, is not quite stone cold. Some philosophers, some of the time, do take some interest in tensions between theological, scientific and moral ideas. Others are at least polemically interested enough to deny that theological dictions convey any ideas at all. But most of us, most of the time, do just forget about the subject.[42]

Ryle made these observations in the mid-fifties. Since then it is clear that the failure of the positivists' program has, in the technical sense, given theology a new lease on life. Many religious thinkers are now working at the job of developing theologies that will take account of the challenge of contemporary empiricism. This is a necessary but not sufficient condition of theological vitality. It is just as important to show the relevance of theology to broader cultural concerns such as art, politics, and economics; but this issue goes beyond the scope of this book.

[42] Gilbert Ryle, "Final Discussion," in *The Nature of Metaphysics*, ed. D. F. Pears (London: Macmillan, 1957), p. 160. See also pp. 144f.

Two/The elimination of metaphysics and theology

Introduction/**Problems of confirmation**

T HERE are many statements of the challenge of verification to metaphysics and theology. Ayer's are reprinted here because his statement (from Language, Truth and Logic, 1936) has attained the status of a
classic. It communicates the confidence and revolutionary fervor that
characterized positivism in its prime.

The elimination of metaphysics

The best way to appreciate Ayer's effort to eliminate metaphysics is to
focus on his treatment of F. H. Bradley (see pp. 66 f.). Ayer quotes "at random" the remark that "The absolute enters into, but is itself incapable of,
evolution and progress."[1] Clearly Bradley thinks that this statement tells

From Language, Truth and Logic by Alfred J. Ayer (London: Victor Gollancz,
1936; 2d ed. London: Victor Gollancz, New York: Dover Publications, 1946),
pp. 5–16, 33–45, 114–120. Reprinted by permission of Victor Gollancz, Ltd.,
Dover Publications, Inc., and the author.

[1] F. H. Bradley, Appearance and Reality (Oxford: Oxford University Press,
1893), p. 499.

us something important about reality. Ayer is convinced that Bradley does not intend it to be analytic, but rather that it is intended as synthetic. Yet Bradley would not have wished to, nor would he have been able to, specify observations that would verify it. This procedure would be contrary to Bradley's view of metaphysics. Ayer concludes that the statement is pseudo-synthetic, and, when understood literally, cognitively meaningless. Furthermore, it is obvious that this statement is typical of the book, because "The Absolute" is central to Bradley's philosophy.

Appearance and Reality clearly fails the preliminary examination. Ayer is confident that he has no need of considering the intricacies of Bradley's extended arguments in an effort to refute them. Indeed, in quoting the passage about the Absolute entering into progress, Ayer does not even cite the page upon which it appears. Obviously, he thinks that anyone who makes statements of this kind can be dismissed out of hand. By failing to cite the page from which he quotes, Ayer is urging his readers to follow his example; they need not argue with Bradley, but should spend their time on philosophical works that are worthy of serious attention. This is what I mean by the "revolutionary fervor" of positivism.

Ayer on confirmation

By the time that Ayer wrote Language, Truth and Logic (1936), both conclusive verification and conclusive falsification had been found wanting. They eliminated metaphysics, but they also eliminated statements of common sense and science (see pp. 25 ff.). Ayer proposes a weakened test, the test of confirmation in principle. It is designed to guarantee the factual meaningfulness of the highly theoretical statements of science.

Atoms are not directly observable. Therefore, one cannot formulate observation statements that verify them directly, as would be the case with the statement, "This is a picture of a hydrogen atom." The statement cannot be made, because the picture cannot be taken. Yet when statements about hydrogen atoms are set in the context of theoretical physics, observation statements can be deduced from them. According to Ayer, these observation statements would not be deducible from the body of physical theory without the addition of the statements about hydrogen atoms. They would also not be deducible from isolated statements about hydrogen atoms that were not set into the body of theoretical physics. They are, however, deducible from statements about hydrogen atoms, when they are set in the context of physics. Some of these observation statements deal with obscure marks on photographic

plates and other rarified details that only a physicist could observe.
Other observation statements that can be deduced from statements about
hydrogen atoms in the context of scientific theory may be as spectacular
as statements about thermonuclear explosions. These explosions can
then be taken as confirmations of the theory. This is the background of
Ayer's statement of confirmation: "It is the mark of a genuine factual
proposition [or statement] . . . that some experiential propositions [that
is statements of observations] can be deduced from it in conjunction
with certain other premises without being deducible from these other
premises alone." (see p. 69).

This test succeeded in allowing for the factual meaningfulness of
the highly general and theoretical statements of science. However, it
proved to be too permissive. It also bestowed factual meaningfulness on
metaphysical statements, theological statements, and even on statements
that were patently nonsensical. In the second edition of Language, Truth
and Logic (1946), Ayer himself, drawing on a critical essay of Isaiah Berlin, shows why this version of the test is too permissive (see p. 88).
Unfortunately, readers who are not familiar with logic, will not be able
to follow either Ayer's demonstration or this introduction to it. Ayer
uses a basic rule of inference called modus ponens:

> If p then q
> p
> therefore q

An important metaphysical statement, "The Absolute is perfect," can be
substituted for p. An observation statement, "This page is white," can
be substituted for q. Readers who are familiar with logic will realize
that it is logically legitimate to combine any two statements into one
hypothetical statement of the "If p then q" form. This procedure yields
the statement "If the Absolute is perfect, then this page is white." This
statement can then be made the first premise of a modus ponens argument which runs as follows:

> If the Absolute is perfect, then this page is white.
> The Absolute is perfect.
> Therefore, this page is white.

According to Ayer's first edition version of confirmation, the factual meaningfulness of the metaphysical statement "The Absolute is
perfect" has been demonstrated. Why? Because the observation statement "This page is white" could not have been deduced from the isolated

statement "If the Absolute is perfect, then this page is white." It could also not have been deduced from the isolated statement "The Absolute is perfect." Yet it has been deduced from the statements taken together. This is all that Ayer's first edition test demands.

Of course, it may be objected that there is something wrong with the argument; the second premise, "The Absolute is perfect," has not been shown to be true. This would be a telling objection to the argument if it were being used to demonstrate the truth of the metaphysical statement "The Absolute is perfect." However, we are not concerned with its truth but with its truth-capacity, that is, with its cognitive meaningfulness. By showing that, in combination with the statement "If the Absolute is perfect, then this page is white," observation statements can be deduced from it, we have shown that it passes Ayer's first edition version of the test of confirmation. Therefore, it is cognitively meaningful. Indeed it must be considered a genuine synthetic statement with factual content.

Ayer continues the Introduction to the second edition of Language, Truth and Logic by trying to take account of these criticisms. He formulates a new version of confirmation. It too was subjected to criticisms that have generally been accepted as decisive (see pp. 452 ff.). Alvin Plantinga continues this story and concludes that the effort to achieve a satisfactory statement of verification has been such a total failure that it is hard to see why theologians have been so troubled by the issue (see, p. 455).

The elimination of theology

Ayer's effort to eliminate theology as a domain of serious philosophical study is tersely expressed. He fails to specify the theological position that he is attacking. It should be obvious that his challenge is not directed to fundamentalist theologians who would try to verify theological statements by means of an appeal to miracles. Ayer is criticizing thinkers, like the representatives of liberal Protestant theology, who continue to talk of God in personal terms, while rejecting fundamentalism. These thinkers claim that God does not disrupt the regularities of nature, He communicates His will to men through the very regularities that scientists uncover.

The best way of getting at Ayer's criticism is to consider a theological statement that expresses the conviction that God controls the regularities of nature. A typical example is, "God is the sustainer of the

world." The point at issue may be clarified by considering the following
passage from a study of St. Thomas Aquinas:

> Though the word 'God' is introduced to refer to the Maker and
> Sustainer of the world, that is not its definition. The term 'helium'
> was first introduced to refer to an element that produced a certain
> line in the solar spectrum; but 'source of such-and-such a line in
> the solar spectrum' was not the definition of the term 'helium';
> 'helium' was introduced as a new term in the category of 'nouns
> of material,' like 'hydrogen' and 'gold,' to refer to a material
> known only by inference, not by an examination of samples. Simi-
> larly, 'God' refers to the type of life that would belong to the
> Maker and Sustainer of the world, rather than to the acts of mak-
> ing and sustaining the world. . . .[2]

Ayer challenges the factual meaningfulness of the theological statements
like that "God is the Sustainer of the world." The comparison with the
statement about helium should help us to appreciate the reason. The evi-
dence for helium is such that it could not be explained except by positing
this "noun of material." If the data could be explained without positing
the reality of this material, then scientists would not accept the notion
that helium exists. Fundamentalists claim that miraculous occurrences
like the behavior of the waters of the Red Sea cannot be explained ex-
cept by reference to the activity of God, the sustainer of the world. He
imposes the regularities of nature by His act of will and He can, by an-
other act of will, violate them.

Theologians who are not fundamentalists, like the representatives
of liberal Protestant theology, continue to claim that "God is the sus-
tainer of the world." When a positivist asks, "How would you verify
that statement?" they cannot appeal to miracles in the traditional super-
natural sense of the term. This mode of verification is closed off to them
by their rejection of fundamentalism. Yet they are not without an an-
swer to this challenge. They can appeal to a limitless number of observa-
tions that verify the statement that "God is the sustainer of the world."
They can appeal to each and every instance of natural processes from
the course of the stars in the heavens to the reproduction of one-celled
organisms. They can claim that it is because of God's sustaining activity
that the sun shines and the rains fall. In that case, every observation of
the sun shining and rains falling will verify the statement, "God is the
sustainer of the world." If this verifying procedure were to be accepted

[2] G. E. M. Anscombe and Peter Geach, *Three Philosophers* (Oxford: Blackwell, 1961), pp. 109ff.

at face value, the statement would be genuinely synthetic and factually meaningful; indeed theologians would claim that it is true.

Ayer is concerned to reject this mode of verification. He rejects it on the grounds that it is too all-embracing. To appreciate the point, we may compare this mode of verification with Elijah's challenge to the priests of Baal (see p. 159). Elijah proposed a test that was discriminatory. If Baal was the true God, one altar would be consumed, if Yahweh was the true God, a different altar would be consumed. By contrast, the appeal to all natural regularities, does not show the specific difference that God's purported sustaining activity makes to the way things happen in the world.

In the absence of an appeal to God's special and miraculous interventions into the natural order, God's existence is compatible with any course of natural events. Compatibility with all states of affairs is, as we have seen (see pp. 12 f.), characteristic of analytic statements. Yet the statement "God is the sustainer of the world" is clearly intended to be informative regarding the cause of events in the world. Therefore, it is not analytic. It is supposedly synthetic. Yet because it is compatible with all states of affairs in the world it is not genuinely synthetic. It is pseudo-synthetic, and, therefore, factually meaningless.

Ayer insists that his position must be distinguished from atheism and agnosticism. An atheist thinks that belief in God is factually meaningful, but false. An agnostic thinks that this belief in factually meaningful, but that we cannot know whether it is true or false. Ayer thinks that it cannot be either true or false; it is literally nonsensical and not worth discussing.

Ayer's position has proved vulnerable to criticisms; some of them have been made by Father Copleston in the course of their debate, which is reprinted in the next section. Michael Tooley's extensive discussion of Ayer's "translatability challenge" appears in Section Ten.[3]

---

[3] See also, C. G. Hempel, "The Empiricist Criterion of Meaning," in *Logical Positivism*, ed. A. J. Ayer, pp. 116–122.

Alfred J. Ayer/The elimination of metaphysics

The traditional disputes of philosophers are, for the most part, as unwarranted as they are unfruitful. The surest way to end them is to establish beyond question what should be the purpose and method of a philosophical enquiry. And this is by no means so difficult a task as the history of philosophy would lead one to suppose. For if there are any questions which science leaves it to philosophy to answer, a straightforward process of elimination must lead to their discovery.

We may begin by criticising the metaphysical thesis that philosophy affords us knowledge of a reality transcending the world of science and common sense. Later on, when we come to define metaphysics and account for its existence, we shall find that it is possible to be a metaphysician without believing in a transcendent reality; for we shall see that many metaphysical utterances are due to the commission of logical errors, rather than to a conscious desire on the part of their authors to go beyond the limits of experience. But it is convenient for us to take the case of those who believe that it is possible to have knowledge of a transcendent reality as a starting-point for our discussion. The arguments which we use to refute them will subsequently be found to apply to the whole of metaphysics.

One way of attacking a metaphysician who claimed to have knowledge of a reality which transcended the phenomenal world would be to enquire from what premises his propositions were deduced. Must he not begin, as other men do, with the evidence of his senses? And if so, what valid process of reasoning can possibly lead him to the conception of a transcendent reality? Surely from empirical premises nothing whatsoever concerning the properties, or even the existence, of anything super-empirical can legitimately be inferred. But this objection would be met by a denial on the part of the metaphysician that his assertions were ultimately based on the evidence of his senses. He would say that he was endowed with a faculty of intellectual intuition which enabled him to know facts that could not be known through sense-experience. And even if it could be shown that he was relying on empirical premises, and that his venture into a non-empirical world was therefore logically unjustified, it would not follow that the assertions which he made concerning this non-empirical world could not be true. For the fact that a conclusion does not follow from its putative premise is not sufficient to show that it is false. Consequently one cannot overthrow a system of transcendent metaphysics merely by criticising the way in which it comes into being. What is required is rather a criticism of the nature of the actual statements which comprise it. And this is the line of argument which we shall, in fact, pursue. For we shall maintain that no statement which refers to a "reality" transcending the limits of all possible sense-experience can possibly have any literal significance; from which it must follow that the labours of those who have striven to describe such a reality have all been devoted to the production of nonsense.

It may be suggested that this is a proposition which has already been proved by Kant. But although Kant also condemned transcendent metaphysics, he did so on different grounds. For he said that the human understanding was so constituted that it lost itself in contradictions when it ventured out beyond the limits of possible experience and attempted to deal with things in themselves. And thus he made the impossibility of a transcendent metaphysic not, as we do, a matter of logic, but a matter of fact.

He asserted, not that our minds could not conceivably have had the power of penetrating beyond the phenomenal world, but merely that they were in fact devoid of it. And this leads the critic to ask how, if it is possible to know only what lies within the bounds of sense-experience, the author can be justified in asserting that real things do exist beyond, and how he can tell what are the boundaries beyond which the human understanding may not venture, unless he succeeds in passing them himself. As Wittgenstein says, "in order to draw a limit to thinking, we should have to think both sides of this limit,"[1] a truth to which Bradley gives a special twist in maintaining that the man who is ready to prove that metaphysics is impossible is a brother metaphysician with a rival theory of his own.[2]

Whatever force these objections may have against the Kantian doctrine, they have none whatsoever against the thesis that I am about to set forth. It cannot here be said that the author is himself overstepping the barrier he maintains to be impassable. For the fruitlessness of attempting to transcend the limits of possible sense-experience will be deduced, not from a psychological hypothesis concerning the actual constitution of the human mind, but from the rule which determines the literal significance of language. Our charge against the metaphysician is not that he attempts to employ the understanding in a field where it cannot profitably venture, but that he produces sentences which fail to conform to the conditions under which alone a sentence can be literally significant. Nor are we ourselves obliged to talk nonsense in order to show that all sentences of a certain type are necessarily devoid of literal significance. We need only formulate the criterion which enables us to test whether a sentence expresses a genuine proposition about a matter of fact, and then point out that the sentences under consideration fail to satisfy it. And this we shall now proceed to do. We shall first of all formulate the criterion in somewhat vague terms, and then give the explanations which are necessary to render it precise.

The criterion which we use to test the genuineness of apparent statements of fact is the criterion of verifiability. We say that a sentence is factually significant to any given person, if, and only if, he knows how to verify the proposition which it purports to express—that is, if he knows what observations would lead him,

[1] *Tractatus Logico-Philosophicus*, Preface.
[2] Bradley, *Appearance and Reality*, 2nd ed., p. 1.

under certain conditions, to accept the proposition as being true, or reject it as being false. If, on the other hand, the putative proposition is of such a character that the assumption of its truth, or falsehood, is consistent with any assumption whatsoever concerning the nature of his future experience, then, as far as he is concerned, it is, if not a tautology, a mere pseudo-proposition. The sentence expressing it may be emotionally significant to him; but it is not literally significant. And with regard to questions the procedure is the same. We enquire in every case what observations would lead us to answer the question, one way or the other; and, if none can be discovered, we must conclude that the sentence under consideration does not, as far as we are concerned, express a genuine question, however strongly its grammatical appearance may suggest that it does.

As the adoption of this procedure is an essential factor in the argument of this book, it needs to be examined in detail.

In the first place, it is necessary to draw a distinction between practical verifiability, and verifiability in principle. Plainly we all understand, in many cases believe, propositions which we have not in fact taken steps to verify. Many of these are propositions which we could verify if we took enough trouble. But there remain a number of significant propositions, concerning matters of fact, which we could not verify even if we chose; simply because we lack the practical means of placing ourselves in the situation where the relevant observations could be made. A simple and familiar example of such a proposition is the proposition that there are mountains on the farther side of the moon.[3] No rocket has yet been invented which would enable me to go and look at the farther side of the moon, so that I am unable to decide the matter by actual observation. But I do know what observations would decide it for me, if, as is theoretically conceivable, I were once in a position to make them. And therefore I say that the proposition is verifiable in principle, if not in practice, and is accordingly significant. On the other hand, such a metaphysical pseudo-proposition as "the Absolute enters into, but is itself incapable of, evolution and progress,"[4] is not even in principle verifiable. For one cannot conceive of an observation which would enable one to determine whether the Absolute did, or did

[3] This example has been used by Professor Schlick to illustrate the same point.
[4] A remark taken at random from *Appearance and Reality*, by F. H. Bradley.

not, enter into evolution and progress. Of course it is possible that the author of such a remark is using English words in a way in which they are not commonly used by English-speaking people, and that he does, in fact, intend to assert something which could be empirically verified. But until he makes us understand how the proposition that he wishes to express would be verified, he fails to communicate anything to us. And if he admits, as I think the author of the remark in question would have admitted, that his words were not intended to express either a tautology or a proposition which was capable, at least in principle, of being verified, then it follows that he has made an utterance which has no literal significance even for himself.

A further distinction which we must make is the distinction between the "strong" and the "weak" sense of the term "verifiable." A proposition is said to be verifiable, in the strong sense of the term, if, and only if, its truth could be conclusively established in experience. But it is verifiable, in the weak sense, if it is possible for experience to render it probable. In which sense are we using the term when we say that a putative proposition is genuine only if it is verifiable?

It seems to me that if we adopt conclusive verifiability as our criterion of significance, as some positivists have proposed,[5] our argument will prove too much. Consider, for example, the case of general propositions of law—such propositions, namely, as "arsenic is poisonous"; "all men are mortal"; "a body tends to expand when it is heated." It is of the very nature of these propositions that their truth cannot be established with certainty by any finite series of observations. But if it is recognised that such general propositions of law are designed to cover an infinite number of cases, then it must be admitted that they cannot, even in principle, be verified conclusively. And then, if we adopt conclusive verifiability as our criterion of significance, we are logically obliged to treat these general propositions of law in the same fashion as we treat the statements of the metaphysician.

In face of this difficulty, some positivists[6] have adopted the heroic course of saying that these general propositions are indeed

[5] e.g. M. Schlick, "Positivismus and Realismus," Erkenntnis, Vol. I, 1930; F. Waismann, "Logische Analyse des Warscheinlichkeitsbegriffs," Erkenntnis, Vol. I, 1930.
[6] e.g. M. Schlick, "Die Kausalität in der gegenwartigen Physik," Naturwissenschaft, Vol. 19, 1931.

pieces of nonsense, albeit an essentially important type of non-sense. But here the introduction of the term "important" is simply an attempt to hedge. It serves only to mark the authors' recognition that their view is somewhat too paradoxical, without in any way removing the paradox. Besides, the difficulty is not confined to the case of general propositions of law, though it is there revealed most plainly. It is hardly less obvious in the case of propositions about the remote past. For it must surely be admitted that, however strong the evidence in favour of historical statements may be, their truth can never become more than highly probable. And to maintain that they also constituted an important, or unimportant, type of nonsense would be unplausible, to say the very least. Indeed, it will be our contention that no proposition, other than a tautology, can possibly be anything more than a probable hypothesis. And if this is correct, the principle that a sentence can be factually significant only if it expresses what is conclusively verifiable is self-stultifying as a criterion of significance. For it leads to the conclusion that it is impossible to make a significant statement of fact at all.

Nor can we accept the suggestion that a sentence should be allowed to be factually significant if, and only if, it expresses something which is definitely confutable by experience.[7] Those who adopt this course assume that, although no finite series of observations is ever sufficient to establish the truth of a hypothesis beyond all possibility of doubt, there are crucial cases in which a single observation, or series of observations, can definitely confute it. But, as we shall show later on, this assumption is false. A hypothesis cannot be conclusively confuted any more than it can be conclusively verified. For when we take the occurrence of certain observations as proof that a given hypothesis is false, we presuppose the existence of certain conditions. And though, in any given case, it may be extremely improbable that this assumption is false, it is not logically impossible. We shall see that there need be no self-contradiction in holding that some of the relevant circumstances are other than we have taken them to be, and consequently that the hypothesis has not really broken down. And if it is not the case that any hypothesis can be definitely confuted, we cannot hold that the genuineness of a proposition depends on the possibility of its definite confutation.

Accordingly, we fall back on the weaker sense of verifica-

---

[7] This has been proposed by Karl Popper in his *Logik der Forschung*.

tion. We say that the question that must be asked about any putative statement of fact is not, Would any observations make its
truth or falsehood logically certain? but simply, Would any observations be relevant to the determination of its truth or falsehood?
And it is only if a negative answer is given to this second question
that we conclude that the statement under consideration is
nonsensical.

To make our position clearer, we may formulate it in another way. Let us call a proposition which records an actual or
possible observation an experiential proposition. Then we may
say that it is the mark of a genuine factual proposition, not that it
should be equivalent to an experiental propositon, or any finite
number of experiential propositions, but simply that some experiential propositions can be deduced from it in conjunction with
certain other premises without being deducible from those other
premises alone.[8]

This criterion seems liberal enough. In contrast to the principle of conclusive verifiability, it clearly does not deny significance to general propositions or to propositions about the past.
Let us see what kinds of assertions it rules out.

A good example of the kind of utterance that is condemned
by our criterion as being not even false but nonsensical would be
the assertion that the world of sense-experience was altogether
unreal. It must, of course, be admitted that our senses do sometimes deceive us. We may, as the result of having certain sensations, expect certain other sensations to be obtainable which
are, in fact, not obtainable. But, in all such cases, it is further
sense-experience that informs us of the mistakes that arise out of
sense-experience. We say that the senses sometimes deceive us,
just because the expectations to which our sense-experiences give
rise do not always accord with what we subsequently experience.
That is, we rely on our senses to substantiate or confute the judgements which are based on our sensations. And therefore the fact
that our perceptual judgements are sometimes found to be
erroneous has not the slightest tendency to show that the world
of sense-experience is unreal. And, indeed, it is plain that no
conceivable observation, or series of observations, could have
any tendency to show that the world revealed to us by sense-
experience was unreal. Consequently, anyone who condemns the

[8] This is an over-simplified statement which is not literally correct. I give what
I believe to be the correct formulation in the Introduction, p. 13. [Reprinted
here, p. 89.—Editors]

sensible world as a world of mere appearance, as opposed to reality, is saying something which, according to our criterion of significance, is literally nonsensical.

   An example of a controversy which the application of our criterion obliges us to condemn as fictitious is provided by those who dispute concerning the number of substances that there are in the world. For it is admitted both by monists, who maintain that reality is one substance, and by pluralists, who maintain that reality is many, that it is impossible to imagine any empirical situation which would be relevant to the solution of their dispute. But if we are told that no possible observation could give any probability either to the assertion that reality was one substance or to the assertion that it was many, then we must conclude that neither assertion is significant. We shall see later on[9] that there are genuine logical and empirical questions involved in the dispute between monists and pluralists. But the metaphysical question concerning "substance" is ruled out by our criterion as spurious.

   A similar treatment must be accorded to the controversy between realists and idealists, in its metaphysical aspect. A simple illustration, which I have made use of in a similar argument elsewhere,[10] will help to demonstrate this. Let us suppose that a picture is discovered and the suggestion made that it was painted by Goya. There is a definite procedure for dealing with such a question. The experts examine the picture to see in what way it resembles the accredited works of Goya, and to see if it bears any marks which are characteristic of a forgery; they look up contemporary records for evidence of the existence of such a picture, and so on. In the end, they may still disagree, but each one knows what empirical evidence would go to confirm or discredit his opinion. Suppose, now, that these men have studied philosophy, and some of them proceed to maintain that this picture is a set of ideas in the perceiver's mind, or in God's mind, others that it is objectively real. What possible experience could any of them have which would be relevant to the solution of this dispute one way or the other? In the ordinary sense of the term "real," in which it is opposed to "illusory," the reality of the picture is not in doubt. The disputants have satisfied themselves that the picture is real, in this sense, by obtaining a correlated series of sensations

---

[9] In Chapter VIII.
[10] Vide "Demonstration of the Impossibility of Metaphysics," Mind, 1934, p. 339.

of sight and sensations of touch. Is there any similar process by which they could discover whether the picture was real, in the sense in which the term "real" is opposed to "ideal"? Clearly there is none. But, if that is so, the problem is fictitious according to our criterion. This does not mean that the realist-idealist controversy may be dismissed without further ado. For it can legitimately be regarded as a dispute concerning the analysis of existential propositons, and so as involving a logical problem which, as we shall see, can be definitively solved.[11] What we have just shown is that the question at issue between idealists and realists becomes fictitious when, as is often the case, it is given a metaphysical interpretation.

There is no need for us to give further examples of the operation of our criterion of significance. For our object is merely to show that philosophy, as a genuine branch of knowledge, must be distinguished from metaphysics. We are not now concerned with the historical question how much of what has traditionally passed for philosophy is actually metaphysical. We shall, however, point out later on that the majority of the "great philosophers" of the past were not essentially metaphysicians, and thus reassure those who would otherwise be prevented from adopting our criterion by considerations of piety.

As to the validity of the verification principle, in the form in which we have stated it, a demonstration will be given in the course of this book. For it will be shown that all propositions which have factual content are empirical hypotheses; and that the function of an empirical hypothesis is to provide a rule for the anticipation of experience.[12] And this means that every empirical hypothesis must be relevant to some actual, or possible, experience, so that a statement which is not relevant to any experience is not an empirical hypothesis, and accordingly has no factual content. But this is precisely what the principle of verifiability asserts.

It should be mentioned here that the fact that the utterances of the metaphysican are nonsensical does not follow simply from the fact that they are devoid of factual content. It follows from that fact, together with the fact that they are not a priori propositions. And in assuming that they are not a priori propositions, we are once again anticipating the conclusions of a later chapter

[11] Vide Chapter VIII.
[12] Vide Chapter V.

in this book.[13] For it will be shown there that *a priori* propositions, which have always been attractive to philosophers on account of their certainty, owe this certainty to the fact that they are tautologies. We may accordingly define a metaphysical sentence as a sentence which purports to express a genuine proposition, but does, in fact, express neither a tautology nor an empirical hypothesis. And as tautologies and empirical hypotheses form the entire class of significant propositions, we are justified in concluding that all metaphysical assertions are nonsensical. Our next task is to show how they come to be made.

The use of the term "substance," to which we have already referred, provides us with a good example of the way in which metaphysics mostly comes to be written. It happens to be the case that we cannot, in our language, refer to the sensible properties of a thing without introducing a word or phrase which appears to stand for the thing itself as opposed to anything which may be said about it. And, as a result of this, those who are infected by the primitive superstition that to every name a single real entity must correspond assume that it is necessary to distinguish logically between the thing itself and any, or all, of its sensible properties. And so they employ the term "substance" to refer to the thing itself. But from the fact that we happen to employ a single word to refer to a thing, and make that word the grammatical subject of the sentences in which we refer to the sensible appearances of the thing, it does not by any means follow that the thing itself is a "simple entity," or that it cannot be defined in terms of the totality of its appearances. It is true that in talking of "its" appearances we appear to distinguish the thing from the appearances, but that is simply an accident of linguistic usage. Logical analysis shows that what makes these "appearances" the "appearances of" the same thing is not their relationship to an entity other than themselves, but their relationship to one another. The metaphysician fails to see this because he is misled by a superficial grammatical feature of his language.

A simpler and clearer instance of the way in which a consideration of grammar leads to metaphysics is the case of the metaphysical concept of Being. The origin of our temptation to raise questions about Being, which no conceivable experience would enable us to answer, lies in the fact that, in our language, sen-

[13] Chapter IV.

tences which express existential propositons and sentences which express attributive propositions may be of the same grammatical form. For instance, the sentences "Martyrs exist" and "Martyrs suffer" both consist of a noun followed by an intransitive verb, and the fact that they have grammatically the same appearance leads one to assume that they are of the same logical type. It is seen that in the proposition "Martyrs suffer," the members of a certain species are credited with a certain attribute, and it is sometimes assumed that the same thing is true of such a proposition as "Martyrs exist." If this were actually the case, it would, indeed, be as legitimate to speculate about the Being of martyrs as it is to speculate about their suffering. But, as Kant pointed out,[14] existence is not an attribute. For, when we ascribe an attribute to a thing, we covertly assert that it exists: so that if existence were itself an attribute, it would follow that all positive existential propositions were tautologies, and all negative existential propositions self-contradictory; and this is not the case.[15] So that those who raise questions about Being which are based on the assumption that existence is an attribute are guilty of following grammar beyond the boundaries of sense.

A similar mistake has been made in connection with such propositions as "Unicorns are fictitious." Here again the fact that there is a superficial grammatical resemblance between the English sentences "Dogs are faithful" and "Unicorns are fictitious," and between the corresponding sentences in other languages, creates the assumption that they are of the same logical type. Dogs must exist in order to have the property of being faithful, and so it is held that unless unicorns in some way existed they could not have the property of being fictitious. But, as it is plainly self-contradictory to say that fictitious objects exist, the device is adopted of saying that they are real in some non-empirical sense—that they have a mode of real being which is different from the mode of being existent things. But since there is no way of testing whether an object is real in this sense, as there is for testing whether it is real in the ordinary sense, the assertion that fictitious objects have a special non-empirical mode of real being is devoid of all literal significance. It comes to be

[14] Vide *The Critique of Pure Reason*, "Transcendental Dialectic," Book II, Chapter iii, section 4.
[15] This argument is well stated by John Wisdom, *Interpretation and Analysis*, pp. 62, 63.

made as a result of the assumption that being fictitious is an attribute. And this is a fallacy of the same order as the fallacy of supposing that existence is an attribute, and it can be exposed in the same way.

In general, the postulation of real non-existent entities results from the superstition, just now referred to, that, to every word or phrase that can be the grammatical subject of a sentence, there must somewhere be a real entity corresponding. For as there is no place in the empirical world for many of these "entities," a special non-empirical world is invoked to house them. To this error must be attributed, not only the utterances of a Heidegger, who bases his metaphysics on the assumption that "Nothing" is a name which is used to denote something peculiarly mysterious,[16] but also the prevalence of such problems as those concerning the reality of propositions and universals whose senselessness, though less obvious, is no less complete.

These few examples afford a sufficient indication of the way in which most metaphysical assertions come to be formulated. They show how easy it is to write sentences which are literally nonsensical without seeing that they are nonsensical. And thus we see that the view that a number of the traditional "problems of philosophy" are metaphysical, and consequently fictitious, does not involve any incredible assumptions about the psychology of philosophers.

Among those who recognise that if philosophy is to be accounted a genuine branch of knowledge it must be defined in such a way as to distinguish it from metaphysics, it is fashionable to speak of the metaphysician as a kind of misplaced poet. As his statements have no literal meaning, they are not subject to any criteria of truth or falsehood: but they may still serve to express, or arouse, emotion, and thus be subject to ethical or aesthetic standards. And it is suggested that they may have considerable value, as means of moral inspiration, or even as works of art. In this way, an attempt is made to compensate the metaphysician for his extrusion from philosophy.[17]

16 Vide *Was ist Metaphysik*, by Heidegger: criticised by Rudolf Carnap in his "Überwindung der Metaphysik durch logische Analyse der Sprache," *Erkenntnis*, Vol. II, 1932.
17 For a discussion of this point, see also C. A. Mace, "Representation and Expression," *Analysis*, Vol. I, No. 3; and "Metaphysics and Emotive Language," *Analysis*, Vol. II, Nos. 1 and 2.

I am afraid that this compensation is hardly in accordance with his deserts. The view that the metaphysician is to be reckoned among the poets appears to rest on the assumption that both talk nonsense. But this assumption is false. In the vast majority of cases the sentences which are produced by poets do have literal meaning. The difference between the man who uses language scientifically and the man who uses it emotively is not that the one produces sentences which are incapable of arousing emotion, and the other sentences which have no sense, but that the one is primarily concerned with the expression of true propositions, the other with the creation of a work of art. Thus, if a work of science contains true and important propositions, its value as a work of science will hardly be diminished by the fact that they are inelegantly expressed. And similarly, a work of art is not necessarily the worse for the fact that all the propositions comprising it are literally false. But to say that many literary works are largely composed of falsehoods, is not to say that they are composed of pseudo-propositions. It is, in fact, very rare for a literary artist to produce sentences which have no literal meaning. And where this does occur, the sentences are carefully chosen for their rhythm and balance. If the author writes nonsense, it is because he considers it most suitable for bringing about the effects for which his writing is designed.

The metaphysician, on the other hand, does not intend to write nonsense. He lapses into it through being deceived by grammar, or through committing errors of reasoning, such as that which leads to the view that the sensible world is unreal. But it is not the mark of a poet simply to make mistakes of this sort. There are some, indeed, who would see in the fact that the metaphysician's utterances are senseless a reason against the view that they have aesthetic value. And, without going so far as this, we may safely say that it does not constitute a reason for it.

It is true, however, that although the greater part of metaphysics is merely the embodiment of humdrum errors, there remain a number of metaphysical passages which are the work of genuine mystical feeling; and they may more plausibly be held to have moral or aesthetic value. But, as far as we are concerned, the distinction between the kind of metaphysics that is produced by a philosopher who has been duped by grammar, and the kind that is produced by a mystic who is trying to express the inexpressible, is of no great importance: what is important to us is to realise that even the utterances of the metaphysician who is attempting to expound a vision are literally senseless; so that henceforth we may pursue our philosophical researches with as little regard for them as for the more inglorious kind of metaphysics which comes from a failure to understand the workings of our language.

It is now generally admitted, at any rate by philosophers, that the existence of a being having the attributes which define the god of any non-animistic religion cannot be demonstratively proved. To see that this is so, we have only to ask ourselves what are the premises from which the existence of such a god could be deduced. If the conclusion that a god exists is to be demonstratively certain, then these premises must be certain; for, as the conclusion of a deductive argument is already contained in the premises, any uncertainty there may be about the truth of the premises is necessarily shared by it. But we know that no empirical proposition can ever be anything more than probable. It is only *a priori* propositions that are logically certain. But we cannot deduce the existence of a god from an *a priori* proposition. For we know that the reason why *a priori* propositions are certain is that they are tautologies. And from a set of tautologies nothing but a further tautology can be validly deduced. It follows that there is no possibility of demonstrating the existence of a god.

What is not so generally recognised is that there can be no way of proving that the existence of a god, such as the God of Christianity, is even probable. Yet this also is easily shown. For if the existence of such a god were probable, then the proposition that he existed would be an empirical hypothesis. And in that case it would be possible to deduce from it, and other empirical hypotheses, certain experiential propositions which were not deducible from those other hypotheses alone. But in fact this is not possible. It is sometimes claimed, indeed, that the existence of a certain sort of regularity in nature constitutes sufficient evidence for the existence of a god. But if the sentence "God exists" entails no more than that certain types of phenomena occur in certain sequences, then to assert the existence of a god will be simply equivalent to asserting that there is the requisite regularity in nature; and no religious man would admit that this was all he intended to assert in asserting the existence of a god. He would say that in talking about God, he was talking about a transcendent being who might be known through certain empirical manifestations, but certainly could not be defined in terms of those manifestations. But in that case the term "god" is a metaphysical term. And if "god" is a metaphysical term, then it cannot be even probable that a god exists. For to say that "God exists" is to make a metaphysical utterance which cannot be either true or false. And by the same criterion, no sentence which purports to describe the nature of a transcendent god can possess any literal significance.

It is important not to confuse this view of religious assertions with the view that is adopted by atheists, or agnostics.[18] For it is characteristic of an agnostic to hold that the existence of a god is a possibility in which there is no good reason either to believe or disbelieve; and it is characteristic of an atheist to hold that it is at least probable that no god exists. And our view that all utterances about the nature of God are nonsensical, so far from being identical with, or even lending any support to, either of these familiar contentions, is actually incompatible with them. For if the assertion that there is a god is nonsensical, then the atheist's assertion that there is no god is equally nonsensical, since it is only a significant proposition that can be significantly contradicted. As for the agnostic, although he refrains from saying either that there is or that there is not a god, he does not deny that the question whether a transcendent god exists is a genuine question. He does not deny that the two sentences "There is a transcendent god" and "There is no transcendent god" express propositions one of which is actually true and the other false. All he says is that we have no means of telling which of them is true, and therefore ought not to commit ourselves to either. But we have seen that the sentences in question do not express propositions at all. And this means that agnosticism also is ruled out.

Thus we offer the theist the same comfort as we gave to the moralist. His assertions cannot possibly be valid, but they cannot be invalid either. As he says nothing at all about the world, he cannot justly be accused of saying anything false, or anything for which he has insufficient grounds. It is only when the theist claims that in asserting the existence of a transcendent god he is expressing a genuine proposition that we are entitled to disagree with him.

It is to be remarked that in cases where deities are identified with natural objects, assertions concerning them may be allowed

18 This point was suggested to me by Professor H. H. Price.

to be significant. If, for example, a man tells me that the occurrence of thunder is alone both necessary and sufficient to establish the truth of the proposition that Jehovah is angry, I may conclude that, in his usage of words, the sentence "Jehovah is angry" is equivalent to "It is thundering." But in sophisticated religions, though they may be to some extent based on men's awe of natural process which they cannot sufficiently understand, the "person" who is supposed to control the empirical world is not himself located in it; he is held to be superior to the empirical world, and so outside it; and he is endowed with super-empirical attributes. But the notion of a person whose essential attributes are non-empirical is not an intelligible notion at all. We may have a word which is used as if it named this "person," but, unless the sentences in which it occurs express propositions which are empirically verifiable, it cannot be said to symbolize anything. And this is the case with regard to the word "god," in the usage in which it is intended to refer to a transcendent object. The mere existence of the noun is enough to foster the illusion that there is a real, or at any rate a possible entity corresponding to it. It is only when we enquire what God's attributes are that we discover that "God," in this usage, is not a genuine name.

It is common to find belief in a transcendent god conjoined with belief in an after-life. But, in the form which it usually takes, the content of this belief is not a genuine hypothesis. To say that men do not ever die, or that the state of death is merely a state of prolonged insensibility, is indeed to express a significant proposition, though all the available evidence goes to show that it is false. But to say that there is something imperceptible inside a man, which is his soul or his real self, and that it goes on living after he is dead, is to make a metaphysical assertion which has no more factual content than the assertion that there is a transcendent god.

It is worth mentioning that, according to the account which we have given of religious assertions, there is no logical ground for antagonism between religion and natural science. As far as the question of truth or falsehood is concerned, there is no opposition between the natural scientist and the theist who believes in a transcendent god. For since the religious utterances of the theist are not genuine propositions at all, they cannot stand in any logical relation to the propositions of science. Such antagonism as there is between religion and science appears to consist in the fact that science takes away one of the motives which make men religious. For it is acknowledged that one of the ultimate sources of religious feeling lies in the inability of men to determine their own destiny; and science tends to destroy the feeling of awe with which men regard an alien world, by making them believe that they can understand and anticipate the course of natural phenomena, and even to some extent control it. The fact that it has recently become fashionable for physicists themselves to be sympathetic towards religion is a point in favour of this hypothesis. For this sympathy towards religion marks the physicists' own lack of confidence in the validity of their hypotheses, which is a reaction on their part from the anti-religious dogmatism of nineteenth-century scientists, and a natural outcome of the crisis through which physics has just passed.

It is not within the scope of this enquiry to enter more deeply into the causes of religious feeling, or to discuss the probability of the continuance of religious belief. We are concerned only to answer those questions which arise out of our discussion of the possibility of religious knowledge. The point which we wish to establish is that there cannot be any transcendent truths of religion. For the sentences which the theist uses to express such "truths" are not literally significant.

An interesting feature of this conclusion is that it accords with what many theists are accustomed to say themselves. For we are often told that the nature of God is a mystery which transcends the human understanding. But to say that something transcends the human understanding is to say that it is unintelligible. And what is unintelligible cannot significantly be described. Again, we are told that God is not an object of reason but an object of faith. This may be nothing more than an admission that the existence of God must be taken on trust, since it cannot be proved. But it may also be an assertion that God is the object of a purely mystical intuition, and cannot therefore be defined in terms which are intelligible to the reason. And I think there are many theists who would assert this. But if one allows that it is impossible to define God in intelligible terms, then one is allowing that it is impossible for a sentence both to be significant and to be about God. If a mystic admits that the object of his vision is something which cannot be described, then he must also admit that he is bound to talk nonsense when he describes it.

For his part, the mystic may protest that his intuition does reveal truths to him, even though he cannot explain to others what these truths are; and that we who do not possess this faculty of intuition can have no ground for denying that it is a cognitive faculty. For we can hardly maintain *a priori* that there are no ways of discovering true propositions except those which we ourselves employ. The answer is that we set no limit to the number of ways in which one may come to formulate a true proposition. We do not in any way deny that a synthetic truth may be discovered by purely intuitive methods as well as by the rational method of induction. But we do say that every synthetic proposition, however it may have been arrived at, must be subject to the test of actual experience. We do not deny *a priori* that the mystic is able to discover truths by his own special methods. We wait to hear what are the propositions which embody his discoveries, in order to see whether they are verified or confuted by our empirical observations. But the mystic, so far from producing propositions which are empirically verified, is unable to produce any intelligible propositions at all. And therefore we say that his intuition has not revealed to him any facts. It is no use his saying that he has apprehended facts but is unable to express them. For we know that if he really had acquired any information, he would be able to express it. He would be able to indicate in some way or other how the genuineness of his discovery might be empirically determined. The fact that he cannot reveal what he "knows," or even himself devise an empirical test to validate his "knowledge," shows that his state of mystical intuition is not a genuinely cognitive state. So that in describing his vision the mystic does not give us any information about the external world; he merely gives us indirect information about the condition of his own mind.

These considerations dispose of the argument from religious experience, which many philosophers still regard as a valid argument in favour of the existence of a god. They say that it is logically possible for men to be immediately acquainted with God, as they are immediately acquainted with a sense-content, and that there is no reason why one should be prepared to believe a man when he says that he is seeing a yellow patch, and refuse to believe him when he says that he is seeing God. The answer to this is that if the man who asserts that he is seeing God is merely asserting that he is experiencing a peculiar kind of sense-content, then we do not for a moment deny that his assertion may be true. But, ordinarily, the man who says that he is seeing God is saying not merely that he is experiencing a religious emotion, but also that there exists a transcendent being who is the object of this emotion; just as the man who says that he sees a yellow patch is ordinarily saying not merely that his visual sense-field contains a yellow sense-content, but also that there exists a yellow object to which the sense-content belongs. And it is not irrational to be prepared to believe a man when he asserts the existence of a yellow object, and to refuse to believe him when he asserts the existence of a transcendent god. For whereas the sentence "There exists here a yellow-coloured material thing" expresses a genuine synthetic proposition which could be empirically verified, the sentence "There exists a transcendent god" has, as we have seen, no literal significance.

We conclude, therefore, that the argument from religious experience is altogether fallacious. The fact that people have religious experiences is interesting from the psychological point of view, but it does not in any way imply that there is such a thing as religious knowledge, any more than our having moral experiences implies that there is such a thing as moral knowledge. The theist, like the moralist, may believe that his experiences are cognitive experiences, but, unless he can formulate his "knowledge" in propositions that are empirically verifiable, we may be sure that he is deceiving himself. It follows that those philosophers who fill their books with assertions that they intuitively "know" this or that moral or religious "truth" are merely providing material for the psycho-analyst. For no act of intuition can be said to reveal a truth about any matter of fact unless it issues in verifiable propositions. And all such propositions are to be incorporated in the system of empirical propositions which constitutes science.

Introduction

In the ten years that have passed since *Language, Truth and Logic* was first published, I have come to see that the questions with which it deals are not in all respects so simple as it makes them appear; but I still believe that the point of view which it expresses is substantially correct.[1] Being in every sense a young man's book, it was written with more passion than most philosophers allow themselves to show, at any rate in their published work, and while this probably helped to secure it a larger audience than it might have had otherwise, I think now that much of its argument would have been more persuasive if it had not been presented in so harsh a form. It would, however, be very difficult for me to alter the tone of the book without extensively re-writing it, and the fact that, for reasons not wholly dependent upon its merits, it has achieved something of the status of a text-book is, I hope, a sufficient justification for reprinting it as it stands. At the same time, there are a number of points that seem to me to call for some further explanation, and I shall accordingly devote the remainder of this new introduction to commenting briefly upon them.

The principle of verification

The principle of verification is supposed to furnish a criterion by which it can be determined whether or not a sentence is literally meaningful. A simple way to formulate it would be to say that a sentence had literal meaning if and only if the proposition it expressed was either analytic or empirically verifiable. To this, however, it might be objected that unless a sentence was literally meaningful it would not express a proposition;[2] for it is commonly assumed that every proposition is either true or false, and to say that a sentence expressed what was either true or false would entail saying that it was literally meaningful. Accordingly, if the principle of verification were formulated in this way, it might be argued not only that it was incomplete as a criterion of meaning, since it would not cover the case of sentences which did not express any propositions at all, but also that it was otiose, on the ground that the question which it was designed to answer must already have been answered before the principle could be applied. It will be seen that when I introduce the principle in this book I try to avoid this difficulty by speaking of "putative propositions" and of the proposition which a sentence "purports to express";

[1] In the Introduction to the Second Edition (1946) of *Language, Truth and Logic,* Ayer attempts to take criticisms of the test of confirmation into account by formulating a new version.—[Editors' note]
[2] Vide M. Lazerowitz, "The Principle of Verifiability," *Mind,* 1937, pp. 372–8.

but this device is not satisfactory. For, in the first place, the use of words like "putative" and "purports" seems to bring in psychological considerations into which I do not wish to enter, and secondly, in the case where the "putative proposition" is neither analytic nor empirically verifiable, there would, according to this way of speaking, appear to be nothing that the sentence in question could properly be said to express. But if a sentence expresses nothing there seems to be a contradiction in saying that what it expresses is empirically unverifiable; for even if the sentence is adjudged on this ground to be meaningless, the reference to "what it expresses" appears still to imply that something is expressed.

This is, however, no more than a terminological difficulty, and there are various ways in which it might be met. One of them would be to make the criterion of verifiability apply directly to sentences, and so eliminate the reference to propositions altogether. This would, indeed, run counter to ordinary usage, since one would not normally say of a sentence, as opposed to a proposition, that it was capable of being verified, or, for that matter, that it was either true or false; but it might be argued that such a departure from ordinary usage was justified, if it could be shown to have some practical advantage. The fact is, however, that the practical advantage seems to lie on the other side. For while it is true that the use of the word "proposition" does not enable us to say anything that we could not, in principle, say without it, it does fulfil an important function; for it makes it possible to express what is valid not merely for a particular sentence s but for any sentence to which s is logically equivalent. Thus, if I assert, for example, that the proposition p is entailed by the proposition q I am indeed claiming implicitly that the English sentence s which expresses p can be validly derived from the English sentence r which expresses q, but this is not the whole of my claim. For, if I am right, it will also follow that any sentence, whether of the English or any other language, that is equivalent to s can be validly derived, in the language in question, from any sentence that is equivalent to r; and it is this that my use of the word "proposition" indicates. Admittedly, we could decide to use the word "sentence" in the way in which we now use the word "proposition," but this would not be conducive to clarity, particularly as the word "sentence" is already ambiguous. Thus, in a case of repetition, it can be said either that there are two different sentences or that the same sentence has been formulated twice. It is in the latter sense that I have so far been using the word, but the other usage is equally legitimate. In either usage, a sentence which was expressed in English would be accounted a different sentence from its French equivalent, but this would not hold good for the new usage of the word "sentence" that we should be introducing if we substituted "sentence" for "proposition." For in that case we should have to say that the English expression and its French equivalent were different formulations of the same sentence. We might indeed be justified in increasing the ambiguity of the word "sentence" in this way if we thereby avoided any of the difficulties that have been thought to be attached to the use of the word "proposition"; but I do not think that this is to be achieved by the mere substitution of one verbal token for another. Accordingly, I conclude that this technical use of the word "sentence," though legitimate in itself, would be likely to promote confusion, without securing us any compensatory advantage.

A second way of meeting our original difficulty would be to extend the use of the word "proposition," so that anything that could properly be called a sentence would be said to express a proposition, whether or not the sentence was literally meaningful. This course would have the advantage of simplicity, but it is open to two objections. The first is that it would involve a departure from current philosophical usage; and the second is that it would oblige us to give up the rule that every proposition is to be accounted either true or false. For while, if we adopted this new usage, we should still be able to say that anything that was either true or false was a proposition, the converse would no longer hold good; for a proposition would be neither true nor false if it was expressed by a sentence which was literally meaningless. I do not myself think that these objections are very serious, but they are perhaps sufficiently so to make it advisable to solve our terminological problem in some other way.

The solution that I prefer is to introduce a new technical term; and for this purpose I shall make use of the familiar word "statement," though I shall perhaps be using it in a slightly unfamiliar sense. Thus I propose that any form of words that is grammatically significant shall be held to constitute a sentence, and that every indicative sentence, whether it is literally meaningful or not, shall be regarded as expressing a statement. Furthermore, any two sentences which are mutually translatable will be said to express the same statement. The word "proposition," on the other hand, will be reserved for what is expressed by sentences which are literally meaningful. Thus, the class of propositions becomes, in this usage, a sub-class of the class of statements, and one way of describing the use of the principle of verification would be to say that it provided a means of determining when an indicative sentence expressed a proposition, or, in other words, of distinguishing the statements that belonged to the class of propositions from those that did not.

It should be remarked that this decision to say that sentences express statements involves nothing more than the adoption of a verbal convention; and the proof of this is that the question, "What do sentences express?" to which it provides an answer is not a factual question. To ask of any particular sentence what it is that it expresses may, indeed, be to put a factual question; and one way of answering it would be to produce another sentence which was a translation of the first. But if the general question, "What do sentences express?" is to be interpreted factually, all that can be said in answer is that, since it is not the case that all sentences are equivalent, there is not any one thing that they all express. At the same time, it is useful to have a means of referring indefinitely to "what sentences express" in cases where the sentences themselves are not particularly specified; and this purpose is served by the introduction of the word "statement" as a technical term. Accordingly, in saying that sentences express statements, we are indicating how this technical term is to be understood, but we are not thereby conveying any factual information in the sense in which we should be conveying factual information if the question we were answering was empirical. This may, indeed, seem a point too obvious to be worth making; but the question, "What do sentences express?" is closely analogous to the question, "What do sentences mean?" and, as I have tried to show elsewhere,[3] the question, "What do sentences mean?" has been a source of confusion to philosophers because they have mistakenly thought it to be factual. To say that indicative sentences mean propositions is indeed legitimate, just as it is legitimate to say that they express statements. But what we are doing, in giving answers of this kind, is to lay down conventional definitions; and it is important that these conventional definitions should not be confused with statements of empirical fact.

[3] In The Foundations of Empirical Knowledge, pp. 92–104.

Returning now to the principle of verification, we may, for the sake of brevity, apply it directly to statements rather than to the sentences which express them, and we can then reformulate it by saying that a statement is held to be literally meaningful if and only if it is either analytic or empirically verifiable. But what is to be understood in this context by the term "verifiable"? I do indeed attempt to answer this question in the first chapter of this book; but I have to acknowledge that my answer is not very satisfactory.

To begin with, it will be seen that I distinguish between a "strong" and a "weak" sense of the term "verifiable," and that I explain this distinction by saying that "a proposition is said to be verifiable in the strong sense of the term, if and only if its truth could be conclusively established in experience," but that "it is verifiable, in the weak sense, if it is possible for experience to render it probable." And I then give reasons for deciding that it is only the weak sense of the term that is required by my principle of verification. What I seem, however, to have overlooked is that, as I represent them, these are not two genuine alternatives.[4] For I subsequently go on to argue that all empirical propositions are hypotheses which are continually subject to the test of further experience; and from this it would follow not merely that the truth of any such proposition never was conclusively established but that it never could be; for however strong the evidence in its favour, there would never be a point at which it was impossible for further experience to go against it. But this would mean that my "strong" sense of the term "verifiable" had no possible application, and in that case there was no need for me to qualify the other sense of "verifiable" as weak; for on my own showing it was the only sense in which any proposition could conceivably be verified.

If I do not now draw this conclusion, it is because I have come to think that there is a class of empirical propositions of which it is permissible to say that they can be verified conclusively. It is characteristic of these propositions, which I have elsewhere[5] called "basic propositions," that they refer solely to the content of a single experience, and what may be said to verify them conclusively is the occurrence of the experience to which they uniquely refer. Furthermore, I should now agree with those

[4] Vide M. Lazerowitz, "Strong and Weak Verification," *Mind*, 1939, pp. 202–13.

[5] "Verification and Experience," *Proceedings of the Aristotelian Society*, Vol. XXXVII; cf. also *The Foundations of Empirical Knowledge*, pp. 80–4.

who say that propositions of this kind are "incorrigible," assuming
that what is meant by their being incorrigible is that it is impossible to be mistaken about them except in a verbal sense. In a verbal
sense, indeed, it is always possible to misdescribe one's experience; but if one intends to do no more than record what is experienced without relating it to anything else, it is not possible to be
factually mistaken; and the reason for this is that one is making
no claim that any further fact could confute. It is, in short, a case
of "nothing venture, nothing lose." It is, however, equally a case
of "nothing venture, nothing win," since the mere recording of
one's present experience does not serve to convey any information
either to any other person or indeed to oneself; for in knowing a
basic proposition to be true one obtains no further knowledge than
what is already afforded by the occurrence of the relevant experience. Admittedly, the form of words that is used to express a
basic proposition may be understood to express something that is
informative both to another person and to oneself, but when it is
so understood it no longer expresses a basic proposition. It was for
this reason, indeed, that I maintained, in the fifth chapter of this
book, that there could not be such things as basic propositions,
in the sense in which I am now using the term; for the burden of
my argument was that no synthetic proposition could be purely
ostensive. My reasoning on this point was not in itself incorrect,
but I think that I mistook its purport. For I seem not to have per-
ceived that what I was really doing was to suggest a motive for
refusing to apply the term "proposition" to statements that "directly recorded an immediate experience"; and this is a terminological point which is not of any great importance.

    Whether or not one chooses to include basic statements in
the class of empirical propositions, and so to admit that some
empirical propositions can be conclusively verified, it will remain
true that the vast majority of the propositions that people actually
express are neither themselves basic statements, nor deducible
from any finite set of basic statements. Consequently, if the principle of verification is to be seriously considered as a criterion of
meaning, it must be interpreted in such a way as to admit statements that are not so strongly verifiable as basic statements are
supposed to be. But how then is the word "verifiable" to be understood?

    It will be seen that, in this book, I begin by suggesting that
a statement is "weakly" verifiable, and therefore meaningful, ac-

cording to my criterion, if "some possible sense-experience would be relevant to the determination of its truth or falsehood." But, as I recognize, this itself requires interpretation; for the word "relevant" is uncomfortably vague. Accordingly, I put forward a second version of my principle, which I shall restate here in slightly different terms, using the phrase "observation-statement," in place of "experiential proposition," to designate a statement "which records an actual or possible observation." In this version, then, the principle is that a statement is verifiable, and consequently meaningful, if some observation-statement can be deduced from it in conjunction with certain other premises, without being deducible from those other premises alone.

I say of this criterion that it "seems liberal enough," but in fact it is far too liberal, since it allows meaning to any statement whatsoever. For, given any statement "S" and an observation-statement "O", "O" follows from "S" and "if S then O" without following from "if S then O" alone. Thus, the statements "the Absolute is lazy" and "if the Absolute is lazy, this is white" jointly entail the observation-statement "this is white," and since "this is white" does not follow from either of these premises, taken by itself, both of them satisfy my criterion of meaning. Furthermore, this would hold good for any other piece of nonsense that one cared to put, as an example, in place of "the Absolute is lazy," provided only that it had the grammatical form of an indicative sentence. But a criterion of meaning that allows such latitude as this is evidently unacceptable.[6]

It may be remarked that the same objection applies to the proposal that we should take the possibility of falsification as our criterion. For, given any statement "S" and any observation-statement "O", "O" will be incompatible with the conjunction of "S" and "if S then not O." We could indeed avoid the difficulty, in either case, by leaving out the stipulation about the other premises. But as this would involve the exclusion of all hypotheticals from the class of empirical propositions, we should escape from making our criteria too liberal only at the cost of making them too stringent.

Another difficulty which I overlooked in my original attempt to formulate the principle of verification is that most empirical

[6] Vide I. Berlin, "Verifiability in Principle," *Proceedings of the Aristotelian Society,* Vol. XXXIX.

propositions are in some degree vague. Thus, as I have remarked elsewhere,[7] what is required to verify a statement about a material thing is never the occurrence of precisely this or precisely that sense-content, but only the occurrence of one or other of the sense-contents that fall within a fairly indefinite range. We do indeed test any such statement by making observations which consist in the occurrence of particular sense-contents; but, for any test that we actually carry out, there is always an indefinite number of other tests, differing to some extent in respect either of their conditions or their results, that would have served the same purpose. And this means that there is never any set of observation-statements of which it can truly be said that precisely they are entailed by any given statement about a material thing.

Nevertheless, it is only by the occurrence of some sense-content, and consequently by the truth of some observation-statement, that any statement about a material thing is actually verified; and from this it follows that every significant statement about a material thing can be represented as entailing a disjunction of observation-statements, although the terms of this disjunction, being infinite, cannot be enumerated in detail. Consequently, I do not think that we need be troubled by the difficulty about vagueness, so long as it is understood that when we speak of the "entailment" of observation-statements, what we are considering to be deducible from the premises in question is not any particular observation-statement, but only one or other of a set of such statements, where the defining characteristic of the set is that all its members refer to sense-contents that fall within a certain specifiable range.

There remains the more serious objection that my criterion, as it stands, allows meaning to any indicative statement whatsoever. To meet this, I shall emend it as follows. I propose to say that a statement is directly verifiable if it is either itself an observation-statement, or is such that in conjunction with one or more observation-statements it entails at least one observation-statement which is not deducible from these other premises alone; and I propose to say that a statement is indirectly verifiable if it satisfies the following conditions: first, that in conjunction with certain other premises it entails one or more directly verifiable statements which are not deducible from these other premises alone; and

<hr>

[7] The Foundations of Empirical Knowledge, pp. 240–1.

secondly, that these other premises do not include any statement that is not either analytic, or directly verifiable, or capable of being independently established as indirectly verifiable. And I can now reformulate the principle of verification as requiring of a literally meaningful statement, which is not analytic, that it should be either directly or indirectly verifiable, in the foregoing sense.

It may be remarked that in giving my account of the conditions in which a statement is to be considered indirectly verifiable, I have explicitly put in the proviso that the "other premises" may include analytic statements; and my reason for doing this is that I intend in this way to allow for the case of scientific theories which are expressed in terms that do not themselves designate anything observable. For while the statements that contain these terms may not appear to describe anything that anyone could ever observe, a "dictionary" may be provided by means of which they can be transformed into statements that are verifiable; and the statements which constitute the dictionary can be regarded as analytic. Were this not so, there would be nothing to choose between such scientific theories and those that I should dismiss as metaphysical; but I take it to be characteristic of the metaphysician, in my somewhat pejorative sense of the term, not only that his statements do not describe anything that is capable, even in principle, of being observed, but also that no dictionary is provided by means of which they can be transformed into statements that are directly or indirectly verifiable.

Metaphysical statements, in my sense of the term, are excluded also by the older empiricist principle that no statement is literally meaningful unless it describes what could be experienced, where the criterion of what could be experienced is that it should be something of the same kind as actually has been experienced.[8] But, apart from its lack of precision, this empiricist principle has, to my mind, the defect of imposing too harsh a condition upon the form of scientific theories; for it would seem to imply that it was

---

[8] cf. Bertrand Russell, *The Problems of Philosophy*, p. 91: "Every proposition which we can understand must be composed wholly of constituents with which we are acquainted." And, if I understand him correctly, this is what Professor W. T. Stace has in mind when he speaks of a "Principle of Observable Kinds." Vide his "Positivism," *Mind*, 1944. Stace argues that the principle of verification "rests upon" the principle of observable kinds, but this is a mistake. It is true that every statement that is allowed to be meaningful by the principle of observable kinds is also allowed to be meaningful by the principle of verification: but the converse does not hold.

illegitimate to introduce any term that did not itself designate
something observable. The principle of verification, on the other
hand, is, as I have tried to show, more liberal in this respect, and in
view of the use that is actually made of scientific theories which
the other would rule out, I think that the more liberal criterion
is to be preferred.

It has sometimes been assumed by my critics that I take the
principle of verification to imply that no statement can be evidence
for another unless it is a part of its meaning; but this is not the
case. Thus, to make use of a simple illustration, the statement
that I have blood on my coat may, in certain circumstances, confirm the hypothesis that I have committed a murder, but it is not
part of the meaning of the statement that I have committed a murder that I should have blood upon my coat, nor, as I understand it,
does the principle of verification imply that it is. For one statement
may be evidence for another, and still neither itself express a necessary condition of the truth of this other statement, nor belong to
any set of statements which determines a range within which such
a necessary condition falls; and it is only in these cases that the
principle of verification yields the conclusion that the one statement is part of the meaning of the other. Thus, from the fact that it
is only by the making of some observation that any statement
about a material thing can be directly verified it follows, according
to the principle of verification, that every such statement contains
some observation-statement or other as part of its meaning, and it
follows also that, although its generality may prevent any finite
set of observation-statements from exhausting its meaning, it does
not contain anything as part of its meaning that cannot be represented as an observation-statement; but there may still be many
observation-statements that are relevant to its truth or falsehood
without being part of its meaning at all. Again, a person who affirms the existence of a deity may try to support his contention by
appealing to the facts of religious experience; but it does not follow from this that the factual meaning of his statement is wholly
contained in the propositions by which these religious experiences
are described. For there may be other empirical facts that he would
also consider to be relevant; and it is possible that the descriptions
of these other empirical facts can more properly be regarded as
containing the factual meaning of his statement than the descriptions of the religious experiences. At the same time, if one accepts
the principle of verification, one must hold that his statement does

not have any other factual meaning than what is contained in at least some of the relevant empirical propositions; and that if it is so interpreted that no possible experience could go to verify it, it does not have any factual meaning at all.

In putting forward the principle of verification as a criterion of meaning, I do not overlook the fact that the word "meaning" is commonly used in a variety of senses, and I do not wish to deny that in some of these senses a statement may properly be said to be meaningful even though it is neither analytic nor empirically verifiable. I should, however, claim that there was at least one proper use of the word "meaning" in which it would be incorrect to say that a statement was meaningful unless it satisfied the principle of verification; and I have, perhaps tendentiously, used the expression "literal meaning" to distinguish this use from the others, while applying the expression "factual meaning" to the case of statements which satisfy my criterion without being analytic. Furthermore, I suggest that it is only if it is literally meaningful, in this sense, that a statement can properly be said to be either true or false. Thus, while I wish the principle of verification itself to be regarded, not as an empirical hypothesis,[9] but as a definition, it is not supposed to be entirely arbitrary. It is indeed open to anyone to adopt a different criterion of meaning and so to produce an alternative definition which may very well correspond to one of the ways in which the word "meaning" is commonly used. And if a statement satisfied such a criterion, there is, no doubt, some proper use of the word "understanding" in which it would be capable of being understood. Nevertheless, I think that, unless it satisfied the principle of verification, it would not be capable of being understood in the sense in which either scientific hypotheses or common-sense statements are habitually understood. I confess, however, that it now seems to me unlikely that any metaphysician would yield to a claim of this kind; and although I should still defend the use of the criterion of verifiability as a methodological principle, I realize that for the effective elimination of metaphysics it needs to be supported by detailed analyses of particular metaphysical arguments.

[9] Both Dr. A. C. Ewing, "Meaninglessness," Mind, 1937, pp. 347–64, and Stace, op. cit., take it to be an empirical hypothesis.

Three/**The thomistic response**

Introduction/Is theology a legitimate language game?

THOMISM is the school of philosophical theology practiced by followers of St. Thomas Aquinas who are largely, but by no means exclusively, Roman Catholic. Thomists do metaphysics in the grand manner and, what is more, they put it in the service of rationally proving the existence of God. The mainspring of Thomism is the cosmological argument which is used to demonstrate that "the existence of what we call the world not only is compatible with God's existence, but demands the conclusion that God exists" (see p. 115). For this reason it has been characterized as "metaphysical in that strongest (and most abhorred [by the positivists]) sense: it tries to infer an unobserved and unobservable entity from some highly general fact about the world."[1]

In the debate between A. J. Ayer and Father F. C. Copleston, S. J., we find Ayer's positivism challenged by a Thomist who is one of the leading historians of philosophy in our time.

Ayer claims that verifiability shows that metaphysical statements

[1] Ronald Hepburn, *Christianity and Paradox* (London: C. A. Watts, 1958), p. 156.

are pseudo-synthetic and factually meaningless. Copleston replies that verifiability cannot be used to show this, because it is not a neutral instrument that can be used to check for factual meaningfulness in the way that a Geiger counter is used to check for radioactivity. The use of verifiability is arbitrary and illegitimate unless the positivists can show that their empiricism is valid independently of the appeal to verifiability. Yet, what the positivists actually do is to appeal to verifiability in order to show that positivism is valid. This is a circular argument in the vicious sense of the term, because there is no reason to think that verifiability is a legitimate test of factual meaningfulness unless positivism is valid.

Ayer replies to the charge of circularity by insisting that positivism gets important jobs done by using verification. Therefore, its circularity is not vicious, and its standards are not arbitrary. He also insists that positivism is not unduly restrictive. He does not claim that all explanation must be scientific or that sense experience is the only type of experience that can verify factual assertions. He merely demands evidence of the effectiveness of metaphysical explanations and of the way that religious experience operates to confirm theological statements. He claims that no metaphysician or theologian has ever provided it.

Copleston is sceptical of Ayer's claim that he is not unduly restrictive. He insists that as soon as one departs from patterns appropriate to mathematics, commonsense statements of fact, or scientific hypotheses, Ayer cries "Foul!" The only conditions under which Ayer will concede the cognitive legitimacy of metaphysical and theological statements is a condition that metaphysicians and theologians cannot accept, namely, that they be transformed into statements of science or into analytic statements.

This debate took place in 1949. At that time most philosophers in the English-speaking world would have felt that Father Copleston was stubbornly refusing to concede that "the jig was up" with his kind of metaphysical theology. Yet it was positivism's days that were numbered. After the appearance of Wittgenstein's Philosophical Investigations in 1953, theologians who made the kinds of points that Copleston makes here could draw support from the work of one of the founding fathers of contemporary empiricism. Theologians could insist that the meaning of the word God can only be determined by its use in religious and theological language. It is arbitrary and dogmatic to say that it cannot have cognitive meaning unless it conforms to the pattern of mathematical symbols on the one hand or of electrons on the other. Against Ayer, and other empiricists who demonstrated the pseudo-synthetic character of theological statements, theologians could protest that these statements are not "pseudo" anything. They are genuinely theological. In Wittgensteinian terms, theology and metaphysics are legitimate "language games" with their own distinctive assumptions and rules. Indeed, Ayer himself was soon to acknowledge this point.[2]

2 Alfred J. Ayer, "Editor's Introduction," in Logical Positivism, pp. 15f.

Alfred J. Ayer and Frederick C. Copleston/**Logical positivism — a debate**

Ayer: Well, Father Copleston, you've asked me to summarize Logical Positivism for you and it's not very easy. For one thing, as I understand it, Logical Positivism is not a system of philosophy. It consists rather in a certain technique—a certain kind of attitude towards philosophic problems. Thus, one thing which those of us who are called logical positivists tend to have in common is that we deny the possibility of philosophy as a speculative discipline. We should say that if philosophy was to be a branch of knowledge, as distinct from the sciences, it would have to consist in logic or in some form of analysis, and our reason for this would be somewhat as follows. We maintain that you can divide propositions into two classes, formal and empirical. Formal propositions, like those of

From "Logical Positivism—A Debate," Third Program, British Broadcasting Corporation (June 13, 1949), by Alfred J. Ayer and Frederick C. Copleston, S. J. Reprinted by permission of Alfred J. Ayer and Frederick C. Copleston. [An unedited version of this material has been reprinted in *A Modern Introduction to Philosophy*, ed. P. Edwards and A. Pap, 2d ed. rev. [New York: The Free Press, 1965], 726–756.]

logic and mathematics, depend for their validity on the conventions of a symbol system. Empirical propositions, on the other hand, are statements of actual or possible observation, or hypotheses, from which such statements can be logically derived; and it is they that constitute science in so far as science isn't purely mathematical. Now our contention is that this exhausts the field of what may be called speculative knowledge. Consequently we reject metaphysics, if this be understood, as I think it commonly has been, as an attempt to gain knowledge about the world by non-scientific means. In as much as metaphysical statements are not testable by observation, we hold they are not descriptive of anything. And from this we should conclude that if philosophy is to be a cognitive activity it must be purely critical. It would take the form of trying to elucidate the concepts that were used in science or mathematics or in everyday language.

Copleston: Well, Professor Ayer, I can quite understand, of course, philosophers confining themselves to logical analysis if they wish to do so, and I shouldn't dream of denying or of belittling in any way its utility: I think it's obviously an extremely useful thing to do to analyse and clarify the concepts used in science. In everyday life, too, there are many terms used that practically have taken on an emotional connotation—"progressive" or "reactionary" or "freedom" or "the modern mind":—to make clear to people what's meant or what they mean by those terms, or the various possible meanings, is a very useful thing. But if the Logical Positivist means that logical analysis is the *only* function of philosophy—that's the point at which I should disagree with him. And so would many other philosophers disagree—especially on the Continent. Don't you think that by saying what philosophy is, one presupposes a philosophy, or takes up a position as a philosopher? For example, if one divides significant propositions into two classes, namely, purely formal propositions and statements of observation, one is adopting a philosophical position: one is claiming that there are no necessary propositions which are not purely formal. Moreover, to claim that metaphysical propositions, to be significant, should be verifiable as scientific hypotheses are verifiable is to claim that metaphysics, to be significant, should not be metaphysics.

Ayer: Yes, I agree that my position is philosophical, but not that it is metaphysical, as I hope to show later. To say what philosophy is, is certainly a philosophical act, but by this I mean that it is itself a question of philosophical analysis. We have to decide, among other things, what it is that we are going to call "philosophy" and I have given you my answer. It is not, perhaps, an obvious answer but it at least has the merit that it rescues philosophical statements from becoming either meaningless or trivial. But I don't suppose that we want to quarrel about how we're going to use a word, so much as to discuss the points underlying what you've just said. You would hold, I gather, that in the account I gave of the possible fields of knowledge something was left out.

Copleston: Yes.

Ayer: And that which is left out is what people called philosophers might well be expected to study?

Copleston: Yes, I should hold that philosophy, at any rate metaphysical philosophy, begins, in a sense, where science leaves off. In my personal opinion, one of the chief functions of metaphysics is to open the mind to the Transcendent—to remove the ceiling of the room, as it were, the room being the world as amenable to scientific handling and investigation. But this is not to say that the metaphysician is simply concerned with the Transcendent. Phenomena themselves (objects of what you would probably call "experience") can be considered from the metaphysical angle. The problem of universals, for instance, is a metaphysical problem. I say that metaphysical philosophy begins, *in a sense,* where science leaves off, because I do not mean to imply that the metaphysician cannot begin until science has finished its work. If this were so, the metaphysician would be quite unable to start. I mean that he asks other questions than those asked by the scientist and pursues a different method.

Ayer: To say that philosophy begins where science leaves off is perfectly all right if you mean that the philosopher takes the results of the scientist, analyses them, shows the logical connection of one proposition with another, and so on. But if you say that it leaps into a quite different realm—the realm which you describe as the "transcendent"—then I think I cease to follow you. And I think I can explain why I cease to follow you. I hold a principle, known as the principle of verification, according to which a statement intended to be a statement of fact is meaningful only if it's either formally valid, or some kind of observation is relevant to its truth or falsehood. My difficulty with your so-called transcendent statements is that their truth or falsehood doesn't, it seems to me, make the slightest difference to anything that any one experiences.

Copleston: I don't care for the phrase "transcendent statement." I think myself that some positive descriptive statements about the Transcendent are possible; but, leaving that out of account, I think that one of the possible functions of the philosopher (a function which you presumably exclude) is to reveal the limits of science as a complete and exhaustive description and analysis of reality.

Ayer: Limits of science? You see I can quite well understand your saying that science is limited if you mean only that many more things may be discovered. You may say, for example, that the physics of the seventeenth century was limited in so far as physicists of the eighteenth, nineteenth and twentieth centuries have gone very much further.

Copleston: No, I didn't mean that at all. Perhaps I can illustrate what I mean in reference to anthropology. The biochemist can describe Man within his own terms of reference and up to a certain extent. But, although biochemistry may doubtless continue to advance, I see no reason to suppose that the biochemist will be able to give an exhaustive analysis of Man. The psychologist certainly would not think so. Now, one of the possible functions of a philosopher is to show how all these scientific analyses of man—the analyses of the biochemist, the empirical psychologist and so on—are unable to achieve the exhaustive analysis of the individual human being. Karl Jaspers, for example, would maintain that Man as free, i.e. precisely as free, cannot be adequately handled by any scientist who presupposes the applicability of the principle of deterministic causality and conducts his investigations with that presupposition in mind. I am not a follower of Karl Jaspers; but I think that to call attention to what he calls *Existenz* is a legitimate philosophical procedure.

Copleston: Well, perhaps we'd better attend to your principle of verifiability. You mentioned the principle of verification earlier. I thought possibly you'd state it, Professor, would you?

Ayer: Yes. I'll state it in a fairly loose form, namely that to be significant a statement must be either, on the one hand, a formal statement, one that I should call analytic, or on the other hand empirically testable, and I should try to derive this principle from an analysis of understanding. I should say that understanding a statement meant knowing what would be the case if it were true. Knowing what would be the case if it were true means knowing what observations would verify it, and that in turn means being disposed to accept certain situations as warranting the acceptance or rejection of the statement in question. From which there are two corollaries: one, which we've been talking about to some extent, that statements to which no situations are relevant one way or the other are ruled out as non-factual; and, secondly, that the content of the statement, the cash value, to use James's term, consists of a range of situations, experiences, that would substantiate or refute it.

Copleston: Thank you. Now I don't want to misinterpret your position, but it does seem to me that you are presupposing a certain philosophical position. What I mean is this. If you say that any factual statement, in order to be meaningful, must be verifiable, and if you mean by "verifiable" verifiable by sense-experience, then surely you are presupposing that all reality is given in sense-experience. If you are presupposing this, you are presupposing that there can be no such thing as a metaphysical reality. And if you presuppose this, you are presupposing a philosophical position which cannot be demonstrated by the principle of verification. It seems to me that logical positivism claims to be what I might call a "neutral" technique, whereas in reality it presupposes the truth of positivism. Please pardon my saying so, but it looks to me as though the principle of verifiability were excogitated partly *in order to* exclude metaphysical propositions from the range of meaningful propositions.

Ayer: Even if that were so, it doesn't prove it invalid. But, to go back, I certainly should not make any statement about *all* reality. That is precisely the kind of statement that I use my principle in order not to make. Nor do I wish to restrict experience to sense-experience: I should not at all mind counting what might be called introspectible experiences, or feelings, mystical experiences if you like. It would be true, then, that people who haven't had certain experiences won't understand propositions which refer to them; but that I don't mind either. I can quite well believe that you have experiences different from mine. Let us assume (which after all is an empirical assumption) that you have even a sense different from mine. I should be in the position of the blind man, and then I should admit that statements which are unintelligible to me might be meaningful for you. But I should then go on to say that the factual content of your statements *was* determined by the experiences which counted as their verifiers or falsifiers.

Copleston: Yes, you include introspection, just as Hume did. But my point is that you assume that a factually informative statement is significant only if it is verifiable, at least in principle, by direct observation. Now obviously the existence of a metaphysical reality is not verifiable by direct observation, unless you are willing to recognize a purely intellectual intuition as observation. I am not keen on appealing to intuition, though I see no compelling reason to rule it out from the beginning. However, if you mean by "verifiable" verifiable by direct sense-observation and/or introspection, you seem to me to be ruling out metaphysics from the start. In other words, I suggest that acceptance of the principle of verifiability, as you appear to understand it, implies the acceptance of philosophical positivism. I should probably be prepared to accept the principle if it were understood in a very wide sense, that is, if "verifiable by experience" is understood as including intellectual intuition and also as meaning simply that some experience, actual or conceivable, is relevant to the truth or falsity of the proposition concerned. What I object to is any statement of the principle of verifiability which tacitly assumes the validity of a definite philosophical position.

   Now, you'd make a distinction, I think, between analytic statements on the one hand, and empirical statements, and metaphysical and ethical statements on the other. Or at any rate metaphysical statements; leave ethical out of it. You'd call the first group cognitive, and the second emotive. Is that so?

Ayer: I think the use of the word emotive is not very happy, although I have used it in the past, because it suggests that they're made with emotion, which isn't necessarily the case; but I accept what you say, if you mean by "emotive" simply "non-cognitive."

Copleston: Very well. I accept, of course, your substitution of "non-cognitive" for "emotive." But my objection still remains. By cognitive statements I presume that you mean statements which satisfy the criterion of meaning, that is to say, the principle of verifiability: and by non-cognitive statements I presume you mean statements which do not satisfy that criterion. If this is so, it seems to me that when you say that metaphysical statements are non-cognitive you are not saying much more than that statements which do not satisfy the principle of verifiability do not satisfy the principle of verifiability. In this case, however, no conclusion follows as to the significance or non-significance of metaphysical propositions. Unless, indeed, one has previously accepted your philosophical position; that is to say, unless one has first assumed that they are non-significant.

Ayer: No, it's not as simple as that. My procedure is this: I should claim that the account I've given you of what understanding a statement is, is the account that does apply to ordinary common-sense statements, and to scientific statements, and then I would give a different account of how mathematical statements functioned, and a different account again of value-judgments.

Copleston: Yes.

Ayer: I then say that statements which don't satisfy these conditions are not significant, not to be understood; and I think you can quite correctly object that by putting my definitions together, all I come down to saying is that statements that are not scientific or common-sense statements are not scientific or common-sense statements. But then I want to go further and say that I totally fail to understand—again, I'm afraid, using my own use of understanding: what else can I do?—I fail to understand what these other non-scientific statements and non-common-sense statements, which don't satisfy these criteria, are supposed to be. Someone may say he understands them, in some sense of understanding other than the one I've defined. I reply, It's not clear to me what this sense of understanding is, nor, *a fortiori* of course, what it is he understands, nor how these statements function. But of course you may say that in making it a question of how these statements function, I'm presupposing my own criterion.

Copleston: Well, then, in your treatment of metaphysical propositions you are either applying the criterion of verifiability or you are not. If you are, then the significance of metaphysical propositions is ruled out of court *a priori,* since the truth of the principle of verifiability, as it seems to be understood by you, inevitably involves the non-significance of such propositions. In this case the application of the criterion to concrete metaphysical propositions constitutes a proof neither of the non-significance of these propositions nor of the truth of the principle. All that is shown, it seems to me, is that metaphysical propositions do not satisfy a definite assumed criterion of meaning. But it does not follow that one must accept that criterion of meaning. You may legitimately say, if you like, "I will accept as significant factual statements only those statements which satisfy these particular demands"; but it does not follow that I, or anyone else, has to make those particular demands before we are prepared to accept a statement as meaningful.

Ayer: What I do is to give a definition of certain related terms: understanding, meaningful, and so on. I can't force you to accept them, but I can perhaps make you unhappy about the consequences of not accepting them. What I should do is this. I should take any given proposition, and show how it functioned. In the case of a scientific hypothesis, I would show that it had a certain function, namely that, with other premises, you could deduce certain observational consequences from it. I should then say, This is how this proposition works, this is what it does, this is what it amounts to. I then take a mathematical proposition and play a slightly different game with that, and show that it functions in a certain way, in a calculus, in a symbolic system. You then present me with these other statements, and I then say: On the one hand, they have no observational consequences; on the other hand, they aren't statements of logic. All right. So you understand them. I have given a definition of understanding according to which they're not, in my usage of the term, capable of being understood. Nevertheless you reject my definition. You're perfectly entitled to, because you can give understanding a different meaning if you like. I can't stop you. But now I say, Tell me more about them. In what sense are they understood? They're not understood in my sense. They aren't parts of a symbolic system. You can't do anything with them, in the sense of deriving any observational consequences from them. What *do* you want to say about them? Well, you may just want to say, "They're facts," or something of that sort. Then again I press you on your use of the word "facts."

Copleston: You seem to me to be demanding that in order for a factual statement to be significant one must be able to deduce observational consequences from it. But I do not see why this should be so. If you mean directly observable consequences, you appear to me to be demanding too much. In any case are there not some propositions which are not verifiable, even in principle, but which would yet be considered by most people to have meaning and to be either true or false? Let me give an example. I don't want to assume the mantle of a prophet, and I hope that the statement is false; but it is this: "Atomic warfare will take place, and it will blot out the entire human race." Now, most people would think that this statement has meaning; it means what it says. But how could it possibly be verified empirically? Supposing it were fulfilled, the last man could not say with his last breath, "Copleston's prediction has been verified," because he would not be entitled to say this until he was dead, that is, until he was no longer in a position to verify the statement.

Ayer: It's certainly practically unverifiable. You can't be man, surviving all men. On the other hand, there's no doubt it describes a possible situation. Putting the observer outside the story, one knows quite well what it would be like to observe devastation, and fail to observe any men. Now it wouldn't necessarily be the case that, in order to do that, one had to observe oneself. Just as, to take the case of the past, there were dinosaurs before there were men. Clearly, no man saw that, and clearly I, if I am the speaker, can't myself verify it: but one knows what it would be like to have observed animals and not to have observed men.

Copleston: The two cases are different. In regard to the past we have empirical evidence. For example, we have fossils of dinosaurs. But in the case of the prediction I mentioned there would be nobody to observe the evidence and so to verify the proposition.

Ayer: In terms of the evidence, of course, it becomes very much easier for me. That would be too easy a way of getting out of our difficulty, because there is also evidence for the atomic thing.

Copleston: Yes, but there would be no evidence for the prediction that it will blot out the human race, even if one can imagine the state of affairs that would verify it. Thus by imagining it, one's imagining oneself into the picture.

Ayer: No, no.

Copleston: Yes, yes. One can imagine the evidence and one can imagine oneself verifying it; but, in point of fact, if the prediction were fulfilled there would be no one there to verify. By importing yourself imaginatively into the picture, you are cancelling out the condition of the fulfillment of the prediction. But let us drop the prediction. You have mentioned imagination. Now, what I should prefer to regard as the criterion of the truth or falsity of an existential proposition is simply the presence or absence of the asserted fact or facts, quite irrespective of whether I can know whether there are corresponding facts or not. If I can at last imagine or conceive the facts, the existence of which would verify the proposition, the proposition has significance for me. Whether I can or cannot know that the facts correspond is another matter.

Ayer: I don't at all object to your use of the word "facts" so long as you allow them to be observable facts. But take the contrary case. Suppose I say, "There's a 'drogulus' over there," and you say "What?" and I say "Drogulus," and you say "What's a drogulus?" Well, I say "I can't describe what a drogulus is, because it's not the sort of thing you can see or touch, it has no physical effects of any kind, but it's a disembodied being." And you say, "Well how am I to tell if it's there or not?" and I say "There's no way of telling. Everything's just the same if it's there or it's not there. But the fact is it's there. There's a drogulus there standing just behind you, spiritually behind you." Does that make sense?

Copleston: It seems to me to do so. I should say that to state that there is a drogulus in the room or not is true or false, provided that you can—that you, at any rate, have some idea of what is meant by a drogulus; and if you can say to me it's a disembodied spirit, then I should say that the proposition is either true or false whether one can verify it or not. If you said to me "By drogulus I merely mean the word 'drogulus,' and I attach no other significance to it whatsoever," then I should say that it isn't a proposition any more than if I said "piffle" was in the room.

Ayer: That's right. But what is "having some idea" of something? I want to say that having an idea of something is a matter of knowing how to recognize it. And you want to say that you can have ideas of things even though there's no possible situation in which you could recognize them, because nothing would count as finding them. I would say that I understand the words "angel," "table," "cloth," "drogulus," if I'm disposed to accept certain situations as verifying the presence or absence of what the word is supposed to stand for. But you want to admit these words with-out any reference to experience. Whether the thing they are sup-posed to stand for exists or not, everything is to go on just the same.

Copleston: No. I should say that you can have an idea of some-thing if there's some experience that's relevant to the formation of the idea, not so much to its verification. I should say that I can form the idea of a drogulus or a disembodied-spirit from the idea of body and the idea of mind. You may say that there's no mind and there's no spirit, but at any rate there are, as you'll admit, cer-tain internal experiences of thinking and so on which at any rate account for the formation of the idea. Therefore I can say I have an idea of a drogulus or whatever it is, even though I'm quite unable to know whether such a thing actually exists or not.

Ayer: You would certainly not have to know that it exists, but you would have to know what would count as its existing.

Copleston: Yes. Well, if you mean by "count as its existing" that there must be some experience relevant to the formation of the idea, then I should agree.

Ayer: Not to the formation of the idea, but to the truth or falsity of the propositions in which it is contained.

Copleston: The word "metaphysics" and the phrase "metaphys-ical reality" can have more than one meaning: but when I refer to a metaphysical reality in our present discussion, I mean a being which in principle, and not merely in fact, transcends the sphere of what can be sensibly experienced. Thus God is a metaphysical reality. Since God is *ex hypothesi* immaterial, He cannot *in prin-ciple* be apprehended by the senses. May I add two remarks? My first remark is that I do not mean to imply that no sense-experience is in any way relevant to establishing or discovering the existence of a metaphysical reality. I certainly do believe that metaphysics must be based on experiences of some sort. But metaphysics in-volves intellectual reflection on experience: no amount of immedi-ate sense-experience will disclose the existence of a metaphysical reality. In other words, there is a half-way house between admit-ting only the immediate data of experience and on the other hand leaping to the affirmation of a metaphysical reality without any reference to experience at all. You yourself reflect on the data of

experience. The metaphysician carries that reflection a stage further. My second remark is this: Because one cannot have a sense-
experience of a metaphysical reality, it does not follow that one
could not have another type of experience of it. And if anyone
has such an experience, it does not mean that the metaphysical
reality is deprived, as it were, of its metaphysical character and
becomes non-metaphysical. I think that this is an important point.

Ayer: Yes, but asking are these metaphysical realities isn't like
asking are there still wolves in Asia, is it? It looks as if you've got
a clear usage for metaphysical reality, and are then asking "Does
it occur or not? Does it exist or not?" and as if I'm arbitrarily
denying that it exists. My difficulty is not in answering the question "Are there, or are there not, metaphysical realities?" but in
understanding what usage is being given to the expression "metaphysical reality." When am I to count a reality as metaphysical?
What would it be like to come upon a metaphysical reality? That's
my problem. It isn't that I arbitrarily say there can't be such things,
already admitting the use of the term, but that I'm puzzled about
the use of the term. I don't know what people who say there are
metaphysical realities *mean* by it.

Copleston: Well, that brings us back to the beginning, to the function of philosophy. I should say that one can't simply raise in the
abstract the question "Are there metaphysical realities?" Rather
one asks, "Is the character of observable reality of such a kind
that it leads one to postulate a metaphysical reality, a reality beyond the physical sphere?" If one grants that it is, even then one
can only speak about that metaphysical reality within the framework of human language. And language is after all primarily
developed to express our immediate experience of surrounding
things, and therefore there's bound to be a radical inadequacy in
any statements about a metaphysical reality.

Ayer: But you're trying to have it both ways, you see. If it's something that you say doesn't have a meaning in my language, then I
don't understand it. It's no good saying "Oh well, of course it
really has a meaning," because what meaning could it have except
in the language in which it's used?

Copleston: Let's take a concrete example. If I say, for example,
"God is intelligent," well, you may very well say to me "What
meaning can you give to the word 'intelligent,' because the only

intelligence you have experienced is the human intelligence, and are you attributing that to God?" And I should have to say no, because I'm not. Therefore, if we agreed to use the word intelligent simply to mean human intelligence, I should have to say "God is not intelligent"; but when I said that a stone is not intelligent, I should mean that a stone was, speaking qualitatively, less than intelligent. And when I said that God was intelligent, I should mean that God was more than intelligent, even though I could give no adequate account of what that intelligence was in itself.

Ayer: Do you mean simply that he knows more than any given man knows? But to what are you ascribing this property? You haven't begun to make that clear.

Copleston: I quite see your point, of course. But what you are inviting me to do is to describe God in terms which will be as clear to you as the terms in which one might describe a familiar object of experience, or an unfamiliar object which is yet so like to familiar objects that it can be adequately described in terms of things which are already familiar to you. But God is ex hypothesi unique; and it is quite impossible to describe Him adequately by using concepts which normally apply to ordinary objects of experience. If it were possible, He would not be God. So you are really asking me to describe God in a manner which would be possible only if He were not God. I not only freely admit that human ideas of God are inadequate, but also affirm that this must be so, owing to the finitude of the human intellect and to the fact that we can come to a philosophical knowledge of God only through reflection on the things we experience. But it does not follow that we can have no knowledge of God, though it does follow that our philosophical knowledge of God cannot be more than analogical.

Ayer: Yes, but in the case of an ordinary analogy, when you say that something is like something else you understand what both things are. But in this case if you say something is analogical, I say "analogical of what?" And then you don't tell me of what. You merely repeat the first term of analogy. Well, I got no analogy. It's like saying that something is "taller than," and I say "taller than?" and you repeat the first thing you say. Then I understand it's taller than itself, which is nonsense.

Copleston: I think that one must distinguish physical analogy and metaphysical analogy. If I say that God is intelligent, I do not say so simply because I want to call God intelligent, but either because I think that the world is such that it must be ascribed in certain aspects at least to a Being which can be described in human terms only as intelligent, or because I am satisfied by some argument that there exists an Absolute Being and then deduce that that Being must be described as intelligent. I am perfectly aware that I have no adequate idea of what that intelligence is in itself. I am ascribing to God an attribute which, translated into human terms, must be called intelligence. After all, if you speak of your dog as intelligent, you are using the word in an analogous sense, and it has some meaning for you, even though you do not observe the dog's physical operations. Mathematicians who speak of multi-dimensional space have never observed such a space, but presumably they attach some meaning to the term. When we speak of "extra-sensory perception" we are using the word "perception" analogously.

Ayer: Yes, but mathematical physicists do test their statements by observation, and I know what counts as a case of extra-sensory perception. But in the case of your statements I don't know what counts. Of course you *might* give them an empirical meaning, you might say that by "God is intelligent" you meant that the world had certain features. Then we'd inspect it to see if it had these features or not.

Copleston: Well of course I should prefer to start from the features of the world before going to God. I shouldn't wish to argue from God to the features of the world. But to keep within your terms of reference of empiricism, well then I'd say that if God is personal, then He's capable, for example, of entering into relationship with human beings. And it's possible to find human beings who claim to have a personal intercourse with God.

Ayer: Then you've given your statement a perfectly good empirical meaning. But it would then be like a scientific theory, and you would be using this in exactly the same way as you might use a concept like electron to account for, explain, predict, a certain range of human experience, namely, that certain people did have these experiences which they described as "entering into communion with God." Then one would try to analyse it scientifically, find out in what conditions these things happened, and then you might put it up as a theory. What you'd have done would be psychology.

Copleston: Well, as I said, I was entering into your terms of reference. I wouldn't admit that when I say God is personal I merely mean that God can enter into intercourse with human beings. I should be prepared to say that He was personal even if I had no reason for supposing that He entered into intercourse with human beings.

Ayer: No, but it's only in that case that one has anything one can control. The facts are that these human beings have these experiences. They describe these experiences in a way which implies more than that they're having these experiences. But if one asks what more, then what answer does one get? Only, I'm afraid, a repetition of the statement that was questioned in the first place.

Copleston: Let's come back to this religious experience. However you subsequently interpret the religious experience, you'd admit that it was relevant to the truth or falsity of the proposition that, say, God existed.

Ayer: Relevant in so far as the proposition that God existed is taken as a description or prediction of the occurrence of these experiences. But not, of course, relevant to any inference you might want to draw, such as that the world was created, or anything of that kind.

Copleston: No, we'll leave that out. All I'm trying to get at is that you'd admit that the proposition "God exists" could be a meaningful form of metaphysical proposition.

Ayer: No, it wouldn't then be a metaphysical proposition. It'd be a perfectly good empirical proposition like the proposition that the unconscious mind exists.

Copleston: The proposition that people have religious experiences would be an empirical proposition; and the proposition that God exists would also be an empirical proposition, provided that all I meant by saying that God exists was that some people have a certain type of experience. But it is *not* all I mean by it. All I originally said was that if God is personal, then one of the consequences would be that He could enter into communication with human beings. If He does so, that does not make God an empirical reality, in the sense of not being a metaphysical reality. God can perfectly well be a metaphysical reality, that is, independent of *physis* or nature, even if intelligent creatures have a non-sensible experience of Him. However, if you wish to call metaphysical propositions empirical propositions, by all means do so. It then becomes a question of terminology.

Ayer: No. I suggest that you're trying to have it both ways. You see, you allow me to give these words, these shapes or noises, an empirical meaning. You allow me to say that the test whereby what you call God exists or not is to be that certain people have experiences, just as the test for whether the table exists or not is that certain people have experiences, only the experiences are of a different sort. Having got that admission you then shift the meaning of the words "God exists." You no longer make them refer simply to the possibility of having these experiences, and so argue that I have admitted a metaphysical proposition, but of course I haven't. All I've admitted is an empirical proposition, which you've chosen to express in the same words as you also want to use to express your metaphysical proposition.

Copleston: Pardon me, but I did not say that the test whereby what I call God exists or not is that certain people have certain experiences. I said that if God exists, one consequence would be that people could have certain experiences. However, even if I accept your requirements, it follows that in one case at least you are prepared to recognize the word "God" as meaningful.

Ayer: Of course I recognize it as meaningful if you give it an empirical meaning, but it doesn't follow there's any empirical evidence for the truth of your metaphysical proposition.

Copleston: But then I don't claim that metaphysical propositions are not in some way founded on reflection on experience. In a certain sense I should call myself an empiricist, but I think that your empiricism is too narrow. Another point. You will not allow a factual statement to be significant unless it is verifiable. Now, suppose I say that we both have immortal souls. If we have, then the proposition will be empirically verified in due course. Are you then prepared to admit that my statement that we both have immortal souls is a significant statement? If you are not prepared, is this because you demand a particular kind of verification and reject any other type? Such an attitude would not seem to me to be warranted. And I don't see that thereby any statement about reality to which one concludes via the experience is derived of its metaphysical character, and introduced into the empirical sphere.

Ayer: Oh, surely. Let us take a case of a common-sense proposition, such as that there is a glass of water in front of us. The evidence of that is my seeing it, touching it. But of course the meaning of that proposition, the factual content of that proposition, isn't exhausted by any one particular piece of evidence of that sort. I may be having a hallucination. What my proposition predicts is more evidence of the same kind. It isn't that my seeing what I do is evidence for the existence of something totally unobservable. I go beyond the immediate evidence only in so far as I take this experience to be one of an indefinite series of experiences of seeing, touching it, etc., which my statement covers. Equally, in the case of your statement I should want to say that if you want to treat it empirically, you must then treat it as predicting, in exactly the same way, in certain conditions, religious experiences. What it will mean will be the possibility of further religious experiences.

Copleston: It's this predicting that I don't like, because it doesn't seem to me that even a scientific proposition necessarily consists in a prediction. Surely it's explicative, and also can be simply explicative, not necessarily a prediction.

Ayer: But isn't it explicative in the sense that it links up with a particular phenomenon, or with lots and lots of other ones that either will occur, have occurred, or would occur in certain circumstances? Take the case of physics. Do you want a world of electrons somehow behind the perceptual world? Is that what you're after?

Copleston: No. We'll take the electronic theory. I should have thought that its function was to explain certain phenomena; that it originated in an endeavour to explain certain phenomena or, more generally, that it is part of the attempt to discover the constitution of matter. I should not describe it as an attempt to predict events, except secondarily perhaps.

Ayer: Oh, I don't want to make the prediction a practical question, but I do want to say that understanding phenomena is a matter of lining them, of grouping them, and that the test of an explanation is that it applies to the hitherto unobserved cases. Suppose I am describing the path of a body and I draw a graph. Then the test of my having explained the observations is that hitherto unobserved points fall on the line I draw.

Copleston: Then my idea of metaphysics would be that of ex-plaining, as I said at the beginning, the series of phenomena, so that the reasoning would rise out of the phenomena themselves, or out of things themselves. In that sense it would be based on experience, even though the term of the reasoning might not itself be an object of experience. I can understand your ruling out all that reflective enquiry and reasoning that constitutes metaphysics, but if you rule it out it would seem to me to be in virtue of a presupposed philosophy.

Ayer: No, I want to say that I rule out nothing as an explanation so long as it explains. I make no statements about what is real and what is not real. That seems to me again an empirical question. My objection to the kind of statements that we've agreed to call metaphysical is that they don't explain.

Copleston: That's a matter for detailed argument and detailed dis-cussion of some particular argument. It's distinct, it seems to me, from the question of meaning. I can quite imagine somebody say-ing, "Your argument for, say, the existence of God is false. Your principles on which you're arguing are quite false." And if so, there's a conclusion.

Ayer: No, I don't want to say it isn't an accurate explanation. What I want to say is that it isn't an explanation at all. That's to say it doesn't even purport to do the work that an explanation does, simply because any given observation or situation is com-patible with it. Now if you want to say that you are using the word in some peculiar sense, of course I can't stop you, but equally I should say that (a) it isn't the ordinary sense, and (b) that this peculiar sense hasn't been made clear to me.

Copleston: But you see I consider that the existence of what we call the world not only is compatible with God's existence, but demands the conclusion that God exists. I may have misunder-stood you: but you seem to me to be saying that if the proposition that God exists means anything, one should be able to deduce some observation-statement from it. If you mean by deducing an observation-statement deducing a thing, I certainly do not think that one can do this. I believe that the existence of God can be inferred from the existence of the world, but I do not think that the world can be deduced from God. Spinoza might think other-wise, of course. If you are demanding that I should deduce the world from God, if I am to make the proposition "God exists" significant, you are demanding that I should adopt a particular idea of God and of creation. For, if one could deduce the world from God, creation would be necessary, and God would create necessarily. If I say that I cannot deduce observation-statements from the existence of God, it is not because I have no idea of God, but because my idea of God will not permit me to say this.

Ayer: You said that the existence of the world demands the conclusion that God exists. Do you mean that this conclusion follows logically, or follows causally?

Copleston: I should say causally. I'm certainly not going to say that God exists means that a world exists, if by that you mean that the world follows necessarily from God, but given the world then I should say that there is a necessary relationship.

Ayer: Logical or causal?

Copleston: Causal.

Ayer: Well, then we're back on the point we've already been over, aren't we?—this difficulty of a notion of causation that isn't the ordinary notion of causation, a notion that's still totally unexplained.

Copleston: On the contrary. I mentioned earlier on that what I mean by the principle of causality is that anything which comes into existence owes that existence to an extrinsic reality, which I term "cause." Incidentally, this notion of causality is much more like the ordinary notion of causation than the phenomenalistic notion which you would regard as the scientific notion. However, I agree that we are back where we were, namely at the question whether there are any principles which can be called certain metaphysical principles. That seems to me one of the chief issues between [the] logical positivist and the metaphysician.

Ayer: It seems to me, indeed, that this has been my quarrel with you all along, that you fail to supply any rules for the use of your expressions. I am not asking for explicit definitions. All that I require is that some indication be given of the way in which the expression relates to some possible experience. It is only when a statement fails to refer, even indirectly, to anything observable that I wish to dismiss it as metaphysical. It is not necessary that the observations should actually be made. There are cases, as you have pointed out, where for practical, or even for theoretical, reasons, the observations could not in fact be made. But one knows what it would be like to make them. The statements which refer to them may be said to be verifiable in principle, if not in fact. To put the point more simply, I understand a statement of fact if I know what to look for on the supposition that it is true. And my knowing what to look for is itself a matter of my being able to interpret the statement as referring at least to some possible experience.

Now, you may say, indeed you have said, that this is all entirely arbitrary. The principle of verifiability is not itself a descriptive statement. Its status is that of a persuasive definition. I am persuaded by it, but why should you be? Can I prove it? Yes, on the basis of other definitions. I have, in fact, tried to show you how it can be derived from an analysis of understanding. But if you are really obstinate, you will reject these other definitions too. So it looks as if we reach a deadlock. But let us then see in what positions we are left. I claim for my method that it does yield valuable results in the way of analysis, and with this you seem disposed to agree. You do not deny the importance of the analytic method in philosophy, nor do you reject all the uses to which I put it. Thus you accept in the main the account that I give of empirical propositions. You have indeed objected to my treatment of the propositions of logic, but there I think that I am in the right. At least I am able to account for their validity: whereas on your view it is utterly mysterious. The main difference between us is that you want to leave room for metaphysics. But now look at the results you get. You put forward your metaphysical statements as ultimate explanations of fact, but you admit that they are not explanations, in any accepted sense of the term, and you cannot say in what sense they are explanations. You cannot show me how they are to be tested, and you seem to have no criterion for deciding whether they are true or false. This being so, I say they are unintelligible. You say, No, you understand them; but for all the good they do you (I mean cognitively, not emotionally) you might just as well abandon them. This is my case against your metaphysical statements. You may decline to be persuaded by it, but what sort of a case can you make for them? I leave the last word to you.

Copleston: I have enjoyed our discussion very much. I have contended that a metaphysical idea has meaning if some experience is relevant to the formation of that idea, and that a rational metaphysic is possible if there are, as I think there are, principles which express an intellectual apprehension of the nature of being. I think that one *can* have an intellectual experience—or intuition if you like—of being. A metaphysical proposition is testable by rational discussion, but not by purely empirical means. When you say that metaphysical propositions are meaningless because they are unverifiable in your sense, I do not think that this amounts to more than saying that metaphysics are not the same thing as empirical science. In short, I consider that logical positivism, apart from its theory of analytic propositions, simply embodies the notion of nineteenth-century positivism that the terms "rational" and "scientific" have the same extension. This notion may correspond to a popular prejudice, but I see no adequate reason for accepting it.

I still find it difficult to understand the status of the principle of verification. It is either a proposition or no proposition. If it is, it must be, on your premises, either a tautology or an empirical hypothesis. If the former, no conclusion follows as to metaphysics. If the latter, the principle itself would require verification. But the principle of verification cannot itself be verified. If, however, the principle is not a proposition, it must, on your premises, be meaningless. In any case, if the meaning of an existential proposition consists, according to the principle, in its verifiability, it is impossible, I think, to escape an infinite regress, since the verification will itself need verification, and so on indefinitely. If this is so, then all propositions, including scientific ones, are meaningless.

Four/The noncognitivist response

Introduction/**Verification as a theory of meaning**

THE most radical response to the challenge of verification to theology is to admit that the positivists are right: Theological and religious languages are noncognitive. From the standpoint of most theologians this is an outright surrender. From the standpoint of thinkers who advocate this radical response it involves nothing more than a clarification of what religious language has always been about.

The meaning of "noncognitive"

Cognitively meaningful statements are those that (when understood literally) have a capacity of being true. A small child may understand the statement "Santa Claus brought your Christmas present" as making a cognitive claim. Later he learns that there is no Santa Claus and he accepts statements about Santa as expressions of the Christmas spirit. This involves a shift in the role that these statements play in his life, a shift from a factual function which is cognitive to an emotional function which is noncognitive.

In dealing with religious statements like "God loves us," theologians have manifested a wide range of views. They differ in the understanding of the terms God and love. They also disagree about the kind of evidence that can be used to support this claim and about the strength of the support provided. Yet traditionally, and even today, theologians generally agree that their statements are cognitive.

Positivists used the test of verification in the effort to show that large classes of statements that were regarded as cognitively meaningful are incapable of having cognitive meaning. Theological statements were one of their major targets. In his essay "An Empiricist's View of the Nature of Religious Belief," R. B. Braithwaite defends the positivist position and presents a noncognitivist interpretation of the meaning of religious language.

Braithwaite's essay is important; it cover the ground clearly and briefly. One important limitation is that he writes as an empiricist who is trying to make sense of religious language. Readers who are interested in noncognitivist approaches to theological language should, therefore, also read Paul van Buren's The Secular Meaning of the Gospel.[1] van Buren provides an example of a fairly conservative theologian who responded to the challenge of verification by shifting from a cognitivist to a noncognitivist position. Furthermore, in doing so, he reinterprets some of the main creedal and theological statements of Christendom. He tries to show that his noncognitivism frees these statements from outmoded mythological forms and enables the Christian message to speak effectively to this secular age.

The term noncognitive, as used in statements like "Theological statements are noncognitive," is rather like the term noninformative, as used in "Analytic statements are noninformative." In both cases the point is more limited than the language suggests. We have already considered the case of analytic statements (see pp. 11 ff.). They are noninformative in the limited sense of not providing factual information about states of affairs. In the case of the noncognitive understanding of religious language, it is clear that Braithwaite thinks that some cognition or knowledge is involved. The believer can, for example, claim to know a great deal about the way people interact and about Christian requirements for moral action. What Braithwaite's noncognitivist understanding of religious language denies is that Christianity (or any other religion) enables us to make true statements about a transcendent agent of infinite goodness, knowledge, and power. Braithwaite agrees with Ayer on this

[1] Paul van Buren, The Secular Meaning of the Gospel (London: SCM Press, 1963).

point. *These statements (when literally understood) are not true, but they are not false either. They are incapable of being either true or false, because they are not cognitively meaningful. As Braithwaite expresses it, they are not members of the three classes of cognitively meaningful statements: "(1) statements about particular matters of empirical fact; (2) scientific hypotheses and other general empirical statements; and (3) the logically necessary statements of logic and mathematics" (see p. 129).*

Verification as a theory of meaning

Throughout this book verification has been used as a criterion or standard of factual meaningfulness. It may be stated as follows: "A statement is factually meaningful if and only if there are, in principle, observations that would verify (or confirm) it." This criterion is used to expose the pretensions of pseudo-synthetic statements, and to brand them as factually meaningless. Braithwaite begins with an appeal to an earlier view of verification, namely as a theory of meaning. "I will start with the verification principle in the form in which it was originally propounded by logical positivists—that the meaning of a statement is given by its method of verification"—as a criterion of meaning.

As a criterion of factual meaningfulness, verification is intended to be a quick check for the truth capacity of statements. It is used to check out putatively synthetic statements, that is, statements that are intended to tell us something about a state of affairs in the world. If a statement passes the test it is then certified as factually meaningful, that is, as genuinely synthetic. In the context of the use of verification as a criterion of factual meaningfulness, this is the end of the matter. Verification need not be put to the further use of spelling out the meaning of the genuinely synthetic statement.

The use of verification as a theory of meaning is more complex than its use as a criterion of factual meaningfulness. The theory incorporates the criterion but goes further. As we have seen, the criterion may be stated as follows: "A statement is factually meaningful if and only if there are, in principle, observations that would verify it." When verification is used as a theory of factual meaning, the following claim is added: "The factual meaning of a statement is its method of verification."

In order to understand this theory consider the statement "There is an electric current in the wire." It seems quite similar to the straightforward factual statement "There is a fast current of water in the river." One difference between the two statements immediately comes to mind.

*Water currents are visible—we can watch them flow—but electric cur-
rents cannot be seen. The statement "There is an electric current in the
wire" is verified by observations like seeing a voltmeter reading change
on contact with the wire, seeing it used to light an electric lamp, and
being shocked when you touch it. It is arguable that over and above
these sorts of observations there is no meaning to the statement "There
is an electric current in the wire." In which case, the meaning of this
statement might properly be regarded as its method of verification, that
is, as the variety of observations we make in testing it. This view has
been generalized by philosophers of science who adopt the operationalist position. They claim that the meanings of statements in a theoretical science like physics are also determined by the procedures involved
in verifying them. This would apply to statements about subatomic particles, for example, "The hydrogen atom has one electron."*

*The status of theoretical entities like electrons is a controversial
issue in the philosophy of science. The operationalists deny that entities
of this kind really exist. They regard them as useful conceptual constructs, that is, as terms that are invented as a shorthand or symbol for
the evidence that has been accumulated in the laboratory (see pp. 219 f.).
Other philosophers of science maintain that they are real entities, but
that they are unobservable in principle. Still others consider them as real
and observable in principle, but not in fact, because we do not yet have
instruments that will enable us to observe them.[2]*

*It is tempting to apply verification as a theory of meaning to both
theological and religious statements, because statements about God, like
those about electrons, deal with an unobservable reality. Braithwaite, for
one, cannot resist this temptation. Yet, apart from all the complications
involved in comparisons of religion and science (see Section Nine), there
is another problem involved. Verification as a theory of meaning had a
very short life. There were too many classes of statements that it could
not handle. It was especially deficient in dealing with statements about
the past. A historian verifies statements about Lincoln's activities on
November 19, 1863, by going to the library and reading books, news-
papers, journals, and manuscripts. Yet the meaning of the statement "On
November 19, 1863, Lincoln delivered the Gettysburg Address" is not to*

[2] For a useful review of this controversy, see Grover Maxwell, "The Ontological Status of Theoretical Entities" in Minnesota Studies in the Philosophy
of Science, vol. III, ed. H. Feigl and G. Maxwell (Minneapolis: University of
Minnesota Press, 1962), pp. 3–27 and Sidney Morgenbesser, "The Realist-
Instrumentalist Controversy" in Philosophy, Science and Method, ed. S.
Morgenbesser, P. Suppes and M. White (New York: St. Martin's Press, 1969),
pp. 200–218.

be found in statements about what historians do in a library by way of checking it out.

Braithwaite interprets religious language as language which is concerned with human intentions and actions. Applying his view to the statement "God loves us," involves the view that it means, "I hereby resolve to treat my fellowmen as though they were loved by God." Now this may be a good conclusion to draw from the statement "God loves us." We might even consider it a good test of whether a man genuinely believes the statement "God loves us." But one thing is clear, whether the statement "God loves us" is cognitively meaningful or not, it does not mean "I hereby resolve to treat my fellowmen as though they were loved by God."

Braithwaite's appeal to meaning as use

Braithwaite's essay begins with an appeal to a positivistic version of the verification principle. He appeals to it in order to affirm the positivistic view that religious language cannot have the cognitive meaningfulness that theologians and believers attribute to it. He then shifts to Wittgenstein's view that "the meaning of any statement is given by the way it is used" (see p. 133). He invokes this principle to show the meaning that can properly be ascribed to religious language. Basically, his view is that religious language is a way of intensifying morality by means of the appeal to stories like that of the Good Samaritan.[3]

His appeal to meaning as use seems to carry Braithwaite's discussion into the post-positivistic era, but in this case, the appearance is deceiving. Wittgenstein developed his view in reaction against positivistic restrictiveness. He warned philosophers against dismissing terms and statements as meaningless simply because they do not conform to the patterns of common sense, science, or mathematics. He urged them to study the role that terms and statements play in the broader context of ordinary language so that they can discover the meanings they actually have.

Braithwaite's appeal to Wittgenstein is, therefore, very odd. By

[3] Braithwaite's view of moral language is subjected to searching criticisms by John Passmore in "Christianity and Positivism," *Australasian Journal of Philosophy*, vol. 36 (1958), pp. 131ff. See also the discussion by J. N. Schofield, D. MacKinnon, and I. Ramsey with a reply by Braithwaite, reprinted from the *Cambridge Review*, in *Christian Ethics and Contemporary Philosophy*, ed. I. Ramsey (New York: Macmillan, 1966), pp. 76–94.

insisting that religious language cannot be cognitive because it does not conform to the patterns of common sense, science, or mathematics, Braithwaite displays the kind of positivistic rigidity that Wittgenstein rejected. Then, ironically, he invokes Wittgenstein's theory of meaning as use to defend his positivistic interpretation of the noncognitive significance of religious language.

Braithwaite's position is far out, but it is not entirely beyond the pale of contemporary theological discussions, because the question of the meaning of religious language is still a subject of controversy among theologians. Therefore, Braithwaite's noncognitivist interpretation of religious language should not be cavalierly dismissed. Nevertheless, his own presentation of this point of view is marred by its hard core positivism.

Richard B. Braithwaite/An empiricist's view of the nature of religious belief

'The meaning of a scientific statement is to be ascertained by reference to the steps which would be taken to verify it.' Eddington wrote this in 1939. Unlike his heterodox views of the *a priori* and epistemological character of the ultimate laws of physics, this principle is in complete accord with contemporary philosophy of science; indeed it was Eddington's use of it in his expositions of relativity theory in the early 1920's that largely contributed to its becoming the orthodoxy. Eddington continued his passage by saying: 'This [principle] will be recognised as a tenet of logical positivism—only if it is there extended to all statements.'[1] Just as the tone was set to the empiricist tradition in British philosophy—the tradition running from Locke through Berkeley, Hume, Mill to Russell in our own time—by Locke's close association with the

From *An Empiricist's View of the Nature of Religious Belief* by Richard B. Braithwaite (Cambridge and New York: Cambridge University Press, 1955). Reprinted by permission of Cambridge University Press and the author.
[1] A. S. Eddington, *The Philosophy of Physical Science* (1939), p. 189.

scientific work of Boyle and the early Royal Society, so the contemporary development of empiricism popularly known as logical positivism has been greatly influenced by the revolutionary changes this century in physical theory and by the philosophy of science which physicists concerned with these changes—Einstein and Heisenberg as well as Eddington—have thought most consonant with relativity and quantum physics. It is therefore, I think, proper for me to take the verificational principle of meaning, and a natural adaptation of it, as that aspect of contemporary scientific thought whose bearing upon the philosophy of religion I shall discuss this afternoon. Eddington, in the passage from which I have quoted, applied the verificational principle to the meaning of scientific statements only. But we shall see that it will be necessary, and concordant with an empiricist way of thinking, to modify the principle by allowing *use* as well as *verifiability* to be a criterion for meaning; so I believe that all I shall say will be in the spirit of a remark with which Eddington concluded an article published in 1925: 'The scientist and the religious teacher may well be content to agree that the *value* of any hypothesis extends just so far as it is verified by actual experience.'[2]

I will start with the verificational principle in the form in which it was originally propounded by logical positivists—that the meaning of any statement is given by its method of verification.[3]

The implication of this general principle for the problem of religious belief is that the primary question becomes, not whether a religious statement such as that a personal God created the world is true or is false, but how it could be known either to be true or to be false. Unless this latter question can be answered, the religious statement has no ascertainable meaning and there is nothing expressed by it to be either true or false. Moreover a religious statement cannot be believed without being understood, and it can only be understood by an understanding of the circumstances which would verify or falsify it. Meaning is not logically prior to the possibility of verification: we do not first learn the meaning of a statement, and afterwards consider what would make us call it true or false; the two understandings are one and indivisible.

It would not be correct to say that discussions of religious belief before this present century have always ignored the problem of

2 *Science, Religion and Reality*, ed. by J. Needham (1925), p. 218 (my italics).
3 The principle was first explicitly stated by F. Waismann, in *Erkenntnis*, vol. 1 (1930), p. 229.

meaning, but until recently the emphasis has been upon the question of the truth or the reasonableness of religious beliefs rather than upon the logically prior question as to the meaning of the statements expressing the beliefs. The argument usually proceeded as if we all knew what was meant by the statement that a personal God created the world; the point at issue was whether or not this statement was true, or whether there were good reasons for believing it. But if the meaning of a religion has to be found by discovering the steps which must be taken to ascertain its truth-value, an examination of the methods for testing the statement for truth-value is an essential preliminary to any discussion as to which of the truth-values—truth or falsity—holds of the statement.

There are three classes of statement whose method of truth-value testing is in general outline clear: statements about particular matters of empirical fact, scientific hypotheses and other general empirical statements, and the logically necessary statements of logic and mathematics (and their contradictories). Do religious statements fall into any of these three classes? If they do, the problem of their meaningfulness will be solved: their truth-values will be testable by the methods appropriate to empirical statements, particular or general, or to mathematical statements. It seems to me clear that religious statements, as they are normally used, have no place in this trichotomy. I shall give my reasons very briefly, since I have little to add here to what other empiricist philosophers have said.

1. Statements about particular empirical facts are testable by direct observation. The only facts that can be directly known by observation are that the things observed have certain observable properties or stand in certain observable relations to one another. If it is maintained that the *existence* of God is known by observation, for example, in the 'self-authenticating' experience of 'meeting God', the term 'God' is being used merely as part of the description of that particular experience. Any interesting theological proposition, e.g. that God is personal, will attribute a property to God which is not an observable one and so cannot be known by direct observation. Comparison with our knowledge of other people is an unreal comparison. I can get to know things about an intimate friend at a glance, but this knowledge is not self-authenticating; it is based upon a great deal of previous knowledge about the connection between facial and bodily expressions and states of mind.

2. The view that would class religious statements with scientific hypotheses must be taken much more seriously. It would be very unplausible if a Baconian methodology of science had to be employed, and scientific hypotheses taken as simple generalizations from particular instances, for then there could be no understanding of a general theological proposition unless particular instances of it could be directly observed. But an advanced science has progressed far beyond its natural history stage; it makes use in its explanatory hypotheses of concepts of a high degree of abstractness and at a far remove from experience. These theoretical concepts are given a meaning by the place they occupy in a deductive system consisting of hypotheses of different degrees of generality in which the least general hypotheses, deducible from the more general ones, are generalizations of observable facts. So it is no valid criticism of the view that would treat God as an empirical concept entering into an explanatory hypothesis to say that God is not directly observable. No more is an electric field of force or a Schrodinger wave-function. There is no *prima facie* objection to regarding such a proposition as that there is a God who created and sustains the world as an explanatory scientific hypothesis.

But if a set of theological propositions are to be regarded as scientific explanations of facts in the empirical world, they must be refutable by experience. We must be willing to abandon them if the facts prove different from what we think they are. A hypothesis which is consistent with every possible empirical fact is not an empirical one. And though the theoretical concepts in a hypothesis need not be explicitly definable in terms of direct observation— indeed they must not be if the system is to be applicable to novel situations—yet they must be related to some and not to all of the possible facts in the world in order to have a non-vacuous significance. If there is a personal God, how would the world be different if there were not? Unless this question can be answered God's existence cannot be given an empirical meaning.

At earlier times in the history of religion God's personal existence has been treated as a scientific hypothesis subjectable to empirical test. Elijah's contest with the prophets of Baal was an experiment to test the hypothesis that Jehovah and not Baal controlled the physical world. But most educated believers at the present time do not think of God as being detectable in this sort of way, and hence do not think of theological propositions as explanations of facts in the world of nature in the way in which established scientific hypotheses are.

It may be maintained, however, that theological propositions explain facts about the world in another way. Not perhaps the physical world, for physical science has been so successful with its own explanations; but the facts of biological and psychological development. Now it is certainly the case that a great deal of traditional Christian language—phrases such as 'original sin', 'the old Adam', 'the new man', 'growth in holiness'—can be given meanings within statements expressing general hypotheses about human personality. Indeed it is hardly too much to say that almost all statements about God as immanent, as an indwelling spirit, can be interpreted as asserting psychological facts in metaphorical language. But would those interpreting religious statements in this way be prepared to abandon them if the empirical facts were found to be different? Or would they rather re-interpret them to fit the new facts? In the latter case the possibility of interpreting them to fit experience is not enough to give an empirical meaning to the statements. Mere consistency with experience without the possibility of inconsistency does not determine meaning. And a metaphorical description is not in itself an explanation. This criticism also holds against attempts to interpret theism as an explanation of the course of history, unless it is admitted (which few theists would be willing to admit) that, had the course of history been different in some specific way, God would not have existed.

Philosophers of religion who wish to make empirical facts relevant to the meaning of religious statements but at the same time desire to hold on to these statements whatever the empirical facts may be are indulging, I believe, in a sort of 'double-think' attitude: they want to hold that religious statements both are about the actual world (i.e. are empirical statements) and also are not refutable in any possible world, the characteristic of statements which are logically necessary.

3. The view that statements of natural theology resemble the propositions of logic and mathematics in being logically necessary would have as a consequence that they make no assertion of existence. Whatever exactly be the status of logically necessary propositions, Hume and Kant have conclusively shown that they are essentially hypothetical. $2 + 3 = 5$ makes no assertion about there being any things in the world; what it says is that, if there is a class of five things in the world, then this class is the union of two mutually exclusive sub-classes one comprising two and the other comprising three things. The logical-positivist thesis, due to Wittgenstein, that the truth of this hypothetical proposition is veri-

fied not by any logical fact about the world but by the way in which we use numerical symbols in our thinking goes further than Kant did in displacing logic and mathematics from the world of reality. But it is not necessary to accept this more radical thesis in order to agree with Kant that no logically necessary proposition can assert existence; and this excludes the possibility of regarding theological propositions as logically necessary in the way in which the hypothetical propositions of mathematics and logic are necessary.

The traditional arguments for a Necessary God—the onto-logical and the cosmological—were elaborated by Anselm and the scholastic philosophers before the concurrent and inter-related development of natural science and of mathematics had enabled necessity and contingency to be clearly distinguished. The necessity attributed by these arguments to the being of God may perhaps be different from the logical necessity of mathematical truths; but, if so, no method has been provided for testing the truth-value of the statement that God is necessary being, and consequently no way given for assigning meaning to the terms 'necessary being' and 'God'.

If religious statements cannot be held to fall into any of these three classes, their method of verification cannot be any of the standard methods applicable to statements falling in these classes. Does this imply that religious statements are not verifiable, with the corollary, according to the verificational principle, that they have no meaning and, though they purport to say something, are in fact nonsensical sentences? The earlier logical positivists thought so: they would have echoed the demand of their precursor Hume that a volume ('of divinity or school methaphysics') which contains neither 'any abstract reasoning concerning quantity or number' nor 'any experimental reasoning concerning matter of fact and existence' should be committed to the flames; though their justification for the holocaust would be even more cogent than Hume's. The volume would not contain even 'sophistry and illusion': it would contain nothing but meaningless marks of printer's ink.

Religious statements, however, are not the only statements which are unverifiable by standard methods; moral statements have the same peculiarity. A moral principle, like the utilitarian principle that a man ought to act so as to maximize happiness, does not seem to be either a logically necessary or a logically impossible proposition. But neither does it seem to be an empirical proposition, all the attempts of ethical empiricists to give naturalistic analyses having failed. Though a tough-minded logical positivist might be prepared to say that all religious statements are sound and fury, signifying nothing, he can hardly say that of all moral statements. For moral statements have a use in guiding conduct; and if they have a use they surely have a meaning—in some sense of meaning. So the verificational principle of meaning in the hands of empiricist philosophers in the 1930's became modified either by a glossing of the term 'verification' or by a change of the verification principle into the use principle: the meaning of any statement is given by the way in which it is used.[4]

Since I wish to continue to employ verification in the restricted sense of ascertaining truth-value, I shall take the principle of meaning in this new form in which the word 'verification' has disappeared. But in removing this term from the statement of the principle, there is no desertion from the spirit of empiricism. The older verificational principle is subsumed under the new use principle: the use of an empirical statement derives from the fact that the statement is empirically verifiable, and the logical-positivist thesis of the 'linguistic' character of logical and mathematical statements can be equally well, if not better, expressed in terms of their use than of their method of verification. Moreover the only way of discovering how a statement is used is by an empirical enquiry; a statement need not itself be empirically verifiable, but that it is used in a particular way is always a straightforwardly empirical proposition.

The meaning of any statement, then, will be taken as being given by the way it is used. The kernel for an empiricist of the problem of the nature of religious belief is to explain, in empirical terms, how a religious statement is used by a man who asserts it in order to express his religious conviction.

Since I shall argue that the primary element in this use is that the religious assertion is used as a moral assertion, I must first consider how moral assertions are used. According to the view developed by various moral philosophers since the impossibility of regarding moral statements as verifiable propositions was recognized, a moral assertion is used to express an *attitude* of the man making the assertion. It is not used to assert the proposition that

[4] See L. Wittgenstein, *Philosophical Investigations* (1953), especially §§ 340, 353, 559, 560.

he has the attitude—a verifiable psychological proposition; it is used to show forth or evince his attitude. The attitude is concerned with the action which he asserts to be right or to be his duty, or the state of affairs which he asserts to be good; it is a highly complex state, and contains elements to which various degrees of importance have been attached by moral philosophers who have tried to work out an 'ethics without propositions'. One element in the attitude is a feeling of approval towards the action; this element was taken as the fundamental one in the first attempts, and views of ethics without propositions are frequently lumped together as 'emotive' theories of ethics. But discussion of the subject during the last twenty years has made it clear, I think, that no emotion or feeling of approval is fundamental to the use of moral assertions; it may be the case that the moral asserter has some specific feeling directed on to the course of action said to be right, but this is not the most important element in his 'pro-attitude' towards the course of action: what is primary is his intention to perform the action when the occasion for it arises.

The form of ethics without propositions which I shall adopt is therefore a conative rather than an emotive theory: it makes the primary use of a moral assertion that of expressing the intention of the asserter to act in a particular sort of way specified in the assertion. A utilitarian, for example, in asserting that he ought to act so as to maximize happiness, is thereby declaring his intention to act, to the best of his ability, in accordance with the policy of utilitarianism: he is not asserting any proposition, or necessarily evincing any feeling of approval; he is subscribing to a policy of action. There will doubtless be empirical propositions which he may give as reasons for his adherence to the policy (e.g. that happiness is what all, or what most people, desire), and his having the intention will include his understanding what is meant by pursuing the policy, another empirically verifiable proposition. But there will be no specifically moral proposition which he will be asserting when he declares his intention to pursue the policy. This account is fully in accord with the spirit of empiricism, for whether or not a man has the intention of pursuing a particular behaviour policy can be empirically tested, both by observing what he does and by hearing what he replies when he is questioned about his intentions.

Not all expressions of intentions will be moral assertions: for the notion of morality to be applicable it is necessary either that the policy of action intended by the asserter should be a general policy (e.g. the policy of utilitarianism) or that it should be subsumable under a general policy which the asserter intends to follow and which he would give as the reason for his more specific intention. There are difficulties and vaguenesses in the notion of a general policy of action, but these need not concern us here. All that we require is that, when a man asserts that he ought to do so-and-so, he is using the assertion to declare that he resolves, to the best of his ability, to do so-and-so. And he will not necessarily be insincere in his assertion if he suspects, at the time of making it, that he will not have the strength of character to carry out his resolution.

The advantage this account of moral assertions has over all others, emotive non-propositional ones as well as cognitive propositional ones, is that it alone enables a satisfactory answer to be given to the question: What is the reason for my doing what I think I ought to do? The answer it gives is that, since my thinking that I ought to do the action is my intention to do it if possible, the reason why I do the action is simply that I intend to do it, if possible. On every other ethical view there will be a mysterious gap to be filled somehow between the moral judgment and the intention to act in accordance with it: there is no such gap if the primary use of a moral assertion is to declare such an intention.

Let us now consider what light this way of regarding moral assertions throws upon assertions of religious conviction. The idealist philosopher McTaggart described religion as 'an emotion resting on a conviction of a harmony between ourselves and the universe at large',[5] and many educated people at the present time would agree with him. If religion is essentially concerned with emotion, it is natural to explain the use of religious assertions on the lines of the original emotive theory of ethics and to regard them as primarily evincing religious feelings or emotions. The assertion, for example, that God is our Heavenly Father will be taken to express the asserter's feeling secure in the same way as he would feel secure in his father's presence. But explanations of religion in terms of feeling, and of religious assertions as expressions of such feelings, are usually propounded by people who stand outside any religious system; they rarely satisfy those who speak from inside. Few religious men would be prepared to admit that their religion was a matter merely of feeling: feelings—of joy,

[5] J. M. E. McTaggart, *Some Dogmas of Religion* (1906), p. 3.

of consolation, of being at one with the universe—may enter into
their religion, but to evince such feelings is certainly not the primary use of their religious assertions.

This objection, however, does not seem to me to apply to
treating religious assertions in the conative way in which recent
moral philosophers have treated moral statements—as being primarily declarations of adherence to a policy of action, declarations of commitment to a way of life. That the way of life led by
the believer is highly relevant to the sincerity of his religious conviction has been insisted upon by all the moral religions, above all,
perhaps, by Christianity. 'By their fruits ye shall know them.' The
view which I put forward for your consideration is that the intention of a Christian to follow a Christian way of life is not only the
criterion for the sincerity of his belief in the assertions of Christianity; it is the criterion for the meaningfulness of his assertions.
Just as the meaning of a moral assertion is given by its use in expressing the asserter's intention to act, so far as in him lies, in
accordance with the moral principle involved, so the meaning of
a religious assertion is given by its use in expressing the asserter's
intention to follow a specified policy of behaviour. To say that it
is belief in the dogmas of religion which is the cause of the believer's intending to behave as he does is to put the cart before
the horse: it is the intention to behave which constitutes what is
known as religious conviction.

But this assimilation of religious to moral assertions lays
itself open to an immediate objection. When a moral assertion is
taken as declaring the intention of following a policy, the form of
the assertion itself makes it clear what the policy is with which the
assertion is concerned. For a man to assert that a certain policy
ought to be pursued, which on this view is for him to declare his
intention of pursuing the policy, presupposes his understanding
what it would be like for him to pursue the policy in question. I
cannot resolve not to tell a lie without knowing what a lie is. But if
a religious assertion is the declaration of an intention to carry out
a certain policy, what policy does it specify? The religious statement itself will not explicitly refer to a policy, as does a moral
statement; how then can the asserter of the statement know what
is the policy concerned, and how can he intend to carry out a
policy if he does not know what the policy is? I cannot intend to do
something I know not what.

The reply to this criticism is that, if a religious assertion is regarded as representative of a large number of assertions of the same religious system, the body of assertions of which the particular one is a representative specimen is taken by the asserter as implicitly specifying a particular way of life. It is no more necessary for an empiricist philosopher to explain the use of a religious statement taken in isolation from other religious statements than it is for him to give a meaning to a scientific hypothesis in isolation from other scientific hypotheses. We understand scientific hypotheses, and the terms that occur in them, by virtue of the relation of the whole system of hypotheses to empirically observable facts; and it is the whole system of hypotheses, not one hypothesis in isolation, that is tested for its truth-value against experience. So there are good precedents, in the empiricist way of thinking, for considering a system of religious assertions as a whole, and for examining the way in which the whole system is used.

If we do this the fact that a system of religious assertions has a moral function can hardly be denied. For to deny it would require any passage from the assertion of a religious system to a policy of action to be mediated by a moral assertion. I cannot pass from asserting a fact, of whatever sort, to intending to perform an action, without having the hypothetical intention to intend to do the action if I assert the fact. This holds however widely fact is understood—whether as an empirical fact or as a non-empirical fact about goodness or reality. Just as the intention-to-act view of moral assertions is the only view that requires no reason for my doing what I assert to be my duty, so the similar view of religious assertions is the only one which connects them to ways of life without requiring an additional premise. Unless a Christian's assertion that God is love (agape)—which I take to epitomize the assertions of the Christian religion—be taken to declare his intention to follow an agapeistic way of life, he could be asked what is the connection between the assertion and the intention, between Christian belief and Christian practice. And this question can always be asked if religious assertions are separated from conduct. Unless religious principles are moral principles, it makes no sense to speak of putting them into practice.

The way to find out what are the intentions embodied in a set of religious assertions, and hence what is the meaning of the assertions, is by discovering what principles of conduct the asserter takes the assertions to involve. These may be ascertained both by asking him questions and by seeing how he behaves, each test being supplemental to the other. If what is wanted is not the meaning of the religious assertions made by a particular man but what the set of assertions would mean were they to be made by anyone of the same religion (which I will call their *typical* meaning), all that can be done is to specify the form of behaviour which is in accordance with what one takes to be the fundamental moral principles of the religion in question. Since different people will take different views as to what these fundamental moral principles are, the typical meaning of religious assertions will be different for different people. I myself take the typical meaning of the body of Christian assertions as being given by their proclaiming intentions to follow an agapeistic way of life, and for a description of this way of life—a description in general and metaphorical terms, but an empirical description nevertheless—I should quote most of the Thirteenth Chapter of I Corinthians. Others may think that the Christian way of life should be described somewhat differently, and will therefore take the typical meaning of the assertions of Christianity to correspond to their different view of its fundamental moral teaching.

My contention then is that the primary use of religious assertions is to announce allegiance to a set of moral principles: without such allegiance there is no 'true religion'. This is borne out by all the accounts of what happens when an unbeliever becomes converted to a religion. The conversion is not only a change in the propositions believed—indeed there may be no specifically intellectual change at all; it is a change in the state of will. An excellent instance is C. S. Lewis's recently published account of his conversion from an idealist metaphysic—'a religion [as he says] that cost nothing'—to a theism where he faced (and he quotes George Mac-Donald's phrase) 'something to be neither more nor less nor other than *done*'. There was no intellectual change, for (as he says) 'there had long been an ethic (theoretically) attached to my Idealism'; it was the recognition that he had to do something about it, that 'an attempt at complete virtue must be made'.[6] His conversion was a re-orientation of the will.

In assimilating religious assertions to moral assertions I do not wish to deny that there are any important differences. One is the fact already noticed that usually the behaviour policy intended

[6] C. S. Lewis, *Surprised by Joy* (1955), pp. 198, 212–13.

is not specified by one religious assertion in isolation. Another difference is that the fundamental moral teaching of the religion is frequently given, not in abstract terms, but by means of concrete examples—of how to behave, for instance, if one meets a man set upon by thieves on the road to Jericho. A resolution to behave like the good Samaritan does not, in itself, specify the behaviour to be resolved upon in quite different circumstances. However, absence of explicitly recognized general principles does not prevent a man from acting in accordance with such principles; it only makes it more difficult for a questioner to discover upon what principles he is acting. And the difficulty is not only one way round. If moral principles are stated in the most general form, as most moral philosophers have wished to state them, they tend to become so far removed from particular courses of conduct that it is difficult, if not impossible, to give them any precise content. It may be hard to find out what exactly is involved in the imitation of Christ; but it is not very easy to discover what exactly is meant by the pursuit of Aristotle's *eudaemonia* or of Mill's *happiness*. The tests for what it is to live agapeistically are as empirical as are those for living in quest of happiness; but in each case the tests can best be expounded in terms of examples of particular situations.

A more important difference between religious and purely moral principles is that, in the higher religions at least, the conduct preached by the religion concerns not only external but also internal behaviour. The conversion involved in accepting a religion is a conversion, not only of the will, but of the heart. Christianity requires not only that you should behave towards your neighbour as if you loved him as yourself: it requires that you should love him as yourself. And though I have no doubt that the Christian concept of *agape* refers partly to external behaviour—the agapeistic behaviour for which there are external criteria—yet being filled with *agape* includes more than behaving agapeistically externally: it also includes an agapeistic frame of mind. I have said that I cannot regard the expression of a feeling of any sort as the primary element in religious assertion; but this does not imply that intention to feel in a certain way is not a primary element, nor that it cannot be used to discriminate religious declarations of policy from declarations which are merely moral. Those who say that Confucianism is a code of morals and not, properly speaking, a religion are, I think, making this discrimination.

The resolution proclaimed by a religious assertion may then

be taken as referring to inner life as well as to outward conduct. And the superiority of religious conviction over the mere adoption of a moral code in securing conformity to the code arises from a religious conviction changing what the religious man wants. It may be hard enough to love your enemy, but once you have succeeded in doing so it is easy to behave lovingly towards him. But if you continue to hate him, it requires a heroic perseverance continually to behave as if you loved him. Resolutions to feel, even if they are only partly fulfilled, are powerful reinforcements of resolutions to act.

But though these qualifications may be adequate for distinguishing religious assertions from purely moral ones, they are not sufficient to discriminate between assertions belonging to one religious system and those belonging to another system in the case in which the behaviour policies, both of inner life and of outward conduct, inculcated by the two systems are identical. For instance, I have said that I take the fundamental moral teaching of Christianity to be the preaching of an agapeistic way of life. But a Jew or a Buddhist may, with considerable plausibility, maintain that the fundamental moral teaching of his religion is to recommend exactly the same way of life. How then can religious assertions be distinguished into those which are Christian, those which are Jewish, those which are Buddhist, by the policies of life which they respectively recommend if, on examination, these policies turn out to be the same?

Many Christians will, no doubt, behave in a specifically Christian manner in that they will follow ritual practices which are Christian and neither Jewish nor Buddhist. But though following certain practices may well be the proper test for membership of a particular religious society, a church, not even the most ecclesiastically-minded Christian will regard participation in a ritual as the fundamental characteristic of a Christian way of life. There must be some more important difference between an agapeistically policied Christian and an agapeistically policied Jew than that the former attends a church and the latter a synagogue.

The really important difference, I think, is to be found in the fact that the intentions to pursue the behaviour policies, which may be the same for different religions, are associated with thinking of different stories (or sets of stories). By a story I shall here mean a proposition or set of propositions which are straightforwardly empirical propositions capable of empirical test and which

are thought of by the religious man in connection with his resolution to follow the way of life advocated by his religion. On the
assumption that the ways of life advocated by Christianity and by
Buddhism are essentially the same, it will be the fact that the intention to follow this way of life is associated in the mind of a
Christian with thinking of one set of stories (the Christian stories)
while it is associated in the mind of a Buddhist with thinking of
another set of stories (the Buddhist stories) which enables a Christian assertion to be distinguished from a Buddhist one.

A religious assertion will, therefore, have a propositional
element which is lacking in a purely moral assertion, in that it will
refer to a story as well as to an intention. The reference to the
story is not an assertion of the story taken as a matter of empirical fact: it is a telling of the story, or an alluding to the story, in
the way in which one can tell, or allude to, the story of a novel
with which one is acquainted. To assert the whole set of assertions
of the Christian religion is both to tell the Christian doctrinal story
and to confess allegiance to the Christian way of life.

The story, I have said, is a set of empirical propositions, and
the language expressing the story is given a meaning by the standard method of understanding how the story-statements can be
verified. The empirical story-statements will vary from Christian
to Christian; the doctrines of Christianity are capable of different
empirical interpretations, and Christians will differ in the interpretations they put upon the doctrines. But the interpretations will
all be in terms of empirical propositions. Take, for example, the
doctrine of Justification by means of the Atonement. Matthew
Arnold imagined it in terms of

> . . . a sort of infinitely magnified and improved Lord Shaftesbury,
> with a race of vile offenders to deal with, whom his natural good-
> ness would incline him to let off, only his sense of justice will not
> allow it; then a younger Lord Shaftesbury, on the scale of his
> father and very dear to him, who might live in grandeur and
> splendour if he liked, but who prefers to leave his home, to go
> and live among the race of offenders, and to be put to an igno-
> minious death, on condition that his merits shall be counted
> against their demerits, and that his father's goodness shall be re-
> strained no longer from taking effect, but any offender shall be
> admitted to the benefit of it on simply pleading the satisfaction
> made by the son;—and then, finally, a third Lord Shaftesbury,
> still on the same high scale, who keeps very much in the back-

ground, and works in a very occult manner, but very effica-
ciously nevertheless, and who is busy in applying everywhere the
benefits of the son's satisfaction and the father's goodness.[7]

Arnold's 'parable of the three Lord Shaftesburys' got him into a lot
of trouble: he was 'indignantly censured' (as he says) for wounding
'the feelings of the religious community by turning into ridicule an
august doctrine, the object of their solemn faith'.[8] But there is no
other account of the Anselmian doctrine of the Atonement that I
have read which puts it in so morally favourable a light. Be that as
it may, the only way in which the doctrine can be understood veri-
ficationally is in terms of human beings—mythological beings, it
may be, who never existed, but who nevertheless would have been
empirically observable had they existed.

For it is not necessary, on my view, for the asserter of a religious assertion to believe in the truth of the story involved in
the assertions: what is necessary is that the story should be entertained in thought, i.e. that the statement of the story should be
understood as having a meaning. I have secured this by requiring
that the story should consist of empirical propositions. Educated
Christians of the present day who attach importance to the doctrine of the Atonement certainly do not believe an empirically
testable story in Matthew Arnold's or any other form. But it is the
fact that entertainment in thought of this and other Christian
stories forms the context in which Christian resolutions are made
which serves to distinguish Christian assertions from those made
by adherents of another religion, or of no religion.

What I am calling a *story* Matthew Arnold called a *parable*
and a *fairy-tale*. Other terms which might be used are *allegory,
fable, tale, myth*. I have chosen the word 'story' as being the most
neutral term, implying neither that the story is believed nor that
it is disbelieved. The Christian stories include straightforward historical statements about the life and death of Jesus of Nazareth; a
Christian (unless he accepts the unplausible Christ-myth theory)
will naturally believe some or all of these. Stories about the beginning of the world and of the Last Judgment as facts of past or
of future history are believed by many unsophisticated Christians.
But my contention is that belief in the truth of the Christian stories
is not the proper criterion for deciding whether or not an assertion

[7] Matthew Arnold, *Literature and Dogma* (1873), pp. 306–7.
[8] Matthew Arnold, *God and the Bible* (1875), pp. 18–19.

is a Christian one. A man is not, I think, a professing Christian unless he both proposes to live according to Christian moral principles and associates his intention with thinking of Christian stories; but he need not believe that the empirical propositions presented by the stories correspond to empirical fact.

But if the religious stories need not be believed, what function do they fulfil in the complex state of mind and behaviour known as having a religious belief? How is entertaining the story related to resolving to pursue a certain way of life? My answer is that the relation is a psychological and causal one. It is an empirical psychological fact that many people find it easier to resolve upon and to carry through a course of action which is contrary to their natural inclinations if this policy is associated in their minds with certain stories. And in many people the psychological link is not appreciably weakened by the fact that the story associated with the behaviour policy is not believed. Next to the Bible and the Prayer Book the most influential work in English Christian religious life has been a book whose stories are frankly recognized as fictitious—Bunyan's *Pilgrim's Progress*; and some of the most influential works in setting the moral tone of my generation were the novels of Dostoevsky. It is completely untrue, as a matter of psychological fact, to think that the only intellectual considerations which affect action are beliefs: it is *all* the thoughts of a man that determine his behaviour; and these include his phantasies, imaginations, ideas of what he would wish to be and do, as well as the propositions which he believes to be true.

This important psychological fact, a commonplace to all students of the influence of literature upon life, has not been given sufficient weight by theologians and philosophers of religion. It has not been altogether ignored; for instance, the report of the official Commission on Doctrine in the Church of England, published in 1938, in a section entitled 'On the application to the Creeds of the conception of symbolic truth' says: 'Statements affirming particular facts may be found to have value as pictorial expressions of spiritual truths, even though the supposed facts themselves did not actually happen. . . . It is not therefore of necessity illegitimate to accept and affirm particular clauses of the Creeds while understanding them in this symbolic sense.[9] But the patron saint whom I claim for my way of thinking is that great

[9] *Doctrine in the Church of England* (1938), pp. 37–8.

but neglected Christian thinker Matthew Arnold, whose parable of the three Lord Shaftesburys is a perfect example of what I take a religious story to be. Arnold's philosophy of religion has suffered from his striking remarks being lifted from their context: his description of religion as *morality touched by emotion* does not adequately express his view of the part played by imagination in religion. Arnold's main purpose in his religious writings was that of 'cementing the alliance between the imagination and conduct'[10] by regarding the propositional element in Christianity as 'literature' rather than as 'dogma.' Arnold was not prepared to carry through his programme completely; he regarded *the Eternal not ourselves that makes for righteousness* more dogmatically than fictionally. But his keen insight into the imaginative and poetic element in religious belief as well as his insistence that religion is primarily concerned with guiding conduct make him a profound philosopher of religion as well as a Christian teacher full of the 'sweet reasonableness' he attributed to Christ.

> *God's wisdom and God's goodness!*—Ay, but fools
> Mis-define these till God knows them no more.
> *Wisdom and goodness, they are God!*—what schools
> Have yet so much as heard this simpler lore?[11]

To return to our philosophizing. My contention that the propositional element in religious assertions consists of stories interpreted as straightforwardly empirical propositions which are not, generally speaking, believed to be true has the great advantage of imposing no restriction whatever upon the empirical interpretation which can be put upon the stories. The religious man may interpret the stories in the way which assists him best in carrying out the behaviour policies of his religion. He can, for example, think of the three persons of the Trinity in visual terms, as did the great Christian painters, or as talking to one another, as in the poems of St John of the Cross. And since he need not believe the stories he can interpret them in ways which are not consistent with one another. It is disastrous for anyone to try to believe empirical propositions which are mutually inconsistent, for the courses of action appropriate to inconsistent beliefs are not compatible. The needs of practical life require that the body of believed propositions should be purged of inconsistency. But there is no action which is

[10] Matthew Arnold, *God and the Bible* (1875), p. xiii.
[11] From Matthew Arnold's sonnet 'The Divinity' (1867).

appropriate to thinking of a proposition without believing it; thinking of it may, as I have said, produce a state of mind in which it is easier to carry out a particular course of action, but the connection is causal: there is no intrinsic connection between the thought and the action. Indeed a story may provide better support for a long-range policy of action if it contains inconsistencies. The Christian set of stories, for example, contains both a pantheistic sub-set of stories in which everything is a part of God and a dualistic Manichaean sub-set of stories well represented by St Ignatius Loyola's allegory of a conflict between the forces of righteousness under the banner of Christ and the forces of darkness under Lucifer's banner. And the Marxist religion's set of stories contains both stories about an inevitable perfect society and stories about a class war. In the case of both religions the first sub-set of stories provides confidence, the second spurs to action.

There is one story common to all the moral theistic religions which has proved of great psychological value in enabling religious men to persevere in carrying out their religious behaviour policies —the story that in so doing they are doing the will of God. And here it may look as if there is an intrinsic connection between the story and the policy of conduct. But even when the story is literally believed, when it is believed that there is a magnified Lord Shaftesbury who commands or desires the carrying out of the behaviour policy, that in itself is no reason for carrying out the policy: it is necessary also to have the intention of doing what the magnified Lord Shaftesbury commands or desires. But the intention to do what a person commands or desires, irrespective of what this command or desire may be, is no part of a higher religion; it is when the religious man finds that what the magnified Lord Shaftesbury commands or desires accords with his own moral judgment that he decides to obey or to accede to it. But this is no new decision, for his own moral judgment is a decision to carry out a behaviour policy; all that is happening is that he is describing his old decision in a new way. In religious conviction the resolution to follow a way of life is primary; it is not derived from believing, still less from thinking of, any empirical story. The story may psychologically support the resolution, but it does not logically justify it.

In this lecture I have been sparing in my use of the term 'religious belief' (although it occurs in the title), preferring instead to speak of religious assertions and of religious conviction. This was because for me the fundamental problem is that of the meaning of statements used to make religious assertions, and I have accordingly taken my task to be that of explaining the use of such assertions, in accordance with the principle that meaning is to be found by ascertaining use. In disentangling the elements of this use I have discovered nothing which can be called 'belief' in the senses of this word applicable either to an empirical or to a logically necessary proposition. A religious assertion, for me, is the assertion of an intention to carry out a certain behaviour policy, subsumable under a sufficiently general principle to be a moral one, together with the implicit or explicit statement, but not the assertion, of certain stories. Neither the assertion of the intention nor the reference to the stories includes belief in its ordinary senses. But in avoiding the term 'belief' I have had to widen the term 'assertion', since I do not pretend that either the behaviour policy intended or the stories entertained are adequately specified by the sentences used in making isolated religious assertions. So assertion has been extended to include elements not explicitly expressed in the verbal form of the assertion. If we drop the linguistic expression of the assertion altogether the remainder is what may be called religious belief. Like moral belief, it is not a species of ordinary belief, of belief in a proposition. A moral belief is an intention to behave in a certain way: a religious belief is an intention to behave in a certain way (a moral belief) together with the entertainment of certain stories associated with the intention in the mind of the believer. This solution of the problem of religious belief seems to me to do justice both to the empiricist's demand that meaning must be tied to empirical use and to the religious man's claim for his religious beliefs to be taken seriously.

Seriously, it will be retorted, but not objectively. If a man's religion is all a matter of following the way of life he sets before himself and of strengthening his determination to follow it by imagining exemplary fairy-tales, it is purely subjective: his religion is all in terms of his own private ideals and of his own private imaginations. How can he even try to convert others to his religion if there is nothing objective to convert them to? How can he argue in its defence if there is no religious proposition which he believes, nothing which he takes to be the fundamental truth about the universe? And is it of any public interest what mental techniques he uses to bolster up his will? Discussion about religion must be more than the exchange of autobiographies.

But we are all social animals; we are all members one of another. What is profitable to one man in helping him to persevere in the way of life he has decided upon may well be profitable to another man who is trying to follow a similar way of life; and to pass on information that might prove useful would be approved by almost every morality. The autobiography of one man may well have an influence upon the life of another, if their basic wants are similar.

But suppose that these are dissimilar, and that the two men propose to conduct their lives on quite different fundamental principles. Can there be any reasonable discussion between them? This is the problem that has faced the many moral philosophers recently who have been forced, by their examination of the nature of thinking, into holding non-propositional theories of ethics. All I will here say is that to hold that the adoption of a set of moral principles is a matter of the personal decision to live according to these principles does not imply that beliefs as to what are the practical consequences of following such principles are not relevant to the decision. An intention, it is true, cannot be logically based upon anything except another intention. But in considering what conduct to intend to practise, it is highly relevant whether or not the consequences of practising that conduct are such as one would intend to secure. As R. M. Hare has well said, an ultimate decision to accept a way of life, 'far from being arbitrary . . . would be the most well-founded of decisions, because it would be based upon a consideration of everything upon which it could possibly be founded.'[12] And in this consideration there is a place for every kind of rational argument.

Whatever may be the case with other religions Christianity has always been a personal religion demanding personal commitment to a personal way of life. In the words of another Oxford philosopher, 'the questions "What shall I do?" and "What moral principles should I adopt?" must be answered by each man for himself.'[13] Nowell-Smith takes this as part of the meaning of morality: whether or not this is so, I am certain that it is of the very essence of the Christian religion.

[12] R. M. Hare, The Language of Morals (1952), p. 69.
[13] P. H. Nowell-Smith, Ethics (1954), p. 320.

Five/The complexities of arguments between believers and atheists

Introduction/**The facts are not enough**

JOHN Wisdom's "Gods," which appeared in 1946, is one of the most influential essays on religious thought to appear in this century. Part of this influence may be attributed to the elusiveness of Wisdom's style. He does not state positions, but rather suggests them by means of imaginative illustrations like his parable of The Invisible Gardener. As a result, the essay can be interpreted in different ways. The contributions which appear in the next three sections take off from "Gods" in one way or another, but the authors do not agree about its meaning.

John Hick, like Wisdom, emphasizes the role of theological statements in providing us with a distinctive perspective on reality in Section Six, pp. 194 f. Yet Hick regards Wisdom as a noncognitivist. Therefore, Hick tries to show that theological statements are factually meaningful because they can be verified by experiences in the afterlife.

Antony Flew interprets Wisdom, in Section Seven, p. 257, as using the parable of the Invisible Gardener to make cognitive claims for religious statements. He then appeals to falsification to show that these claims cannot be made good, because Wisdom's invisible gardener amounts to no gardener at all.

Ian Crombie's essay in Section Eight comes closest to Wisdom's treatment of the complexities of theological arguments, even though

151

Crombie does not mention Wisdom. He follows Wisdom's lead in rejecting the positivists' options for theological statements. He rejects the
view that if theological statements are to be regarded as factually meaningful, they must conform to the patterns of scientific or commonsense
statements. Furthermore, the interchange between Crombie and Nielsen
(see pp. 312–340) provides a beautiful example of the kinds of arguments
between believers and sceptics that Wisdom describes in "Gods." In his
discussion with J. R. Jones, which appears at the end of Section Eight,
D. Z. Phillips reflects the influence of Wisdom as well as Wittgenstein.

By the time he wrote "Gods," Wisdom had been greatly influenced by Wittgenstein, and this essay shows it. Wisdom does not consider isolated theological statements like "God is the sustainer of the
universe," or "God loves us," and then test them by the criterion of verification. He considers the notion of theological arguments and explores
their complexities and their changing patterns. His parable of the Invisible Gardener may be understood as emphasizing a distinction drawn by
Wittgenstein between "seeing" and "seeing as."[1]

I. Idle disputes

In reading Wisdom's discussion of arguments between atheists and believers it is important to realize that he had previously formulated a
standard of utterly futile arguments or, as he calls them, "idle disputes."[2]
He illustrated it by means of two apparently conflicting explanations of
why a watch is not working. One expert claims that the source of the
trouble is a leprechaun that's messing up the works, the other one claims
that it's a brownie. It seems like a genuine difference as to the facts, the
sort of thing that could be settled by opening the watch and looking inside to see which expert is right. Yet when the experts are pressed, this
apparent difference vanishes. Neither leprechauns nor brownies turn out
to be the sort of things that can be seen, heard, touched, tasted, or
smelled. Furthermore, neither expert is willing to propose a test that will

[1] I shall not expound Wittgenstein's distinction. Readers who are not familiar
with it should be able to get the gist of it from the discussion of the parable
of the Invisible Gardener (see pp. 164f.). Wittgenstein discusses it in
Philosophical Investigations, pp. 193–216. It is applied to religious thought
in James Richmond, *Theology and Metaphysics* (London: SCM Press, 1970),
pp. 49–62 and John Hick, "Religious Faith as Experiencing-As," in *Talk of
God*, Royal Institute of Philosophy Lectures, vol. 2 (London: Macmillan, 1969),
pp. 20–35.

[2] John Wisdom, *Other Minds* (Oxford: Basil Blackwell, 1952), p. 11.

settle the issue; there are no observable consequences of either hypothesis. We cannot, for example, leave milk near the watch on the grounds that leprechauns will drink it whereas brownies will not. Therefore, the difference between the experts is merely verbal, and the dispute is an idle one. It is clear that "idle" is to disputes as "pseudo-synthetic" is to statements.

When he explores the nature of the disputes between theists and atheists, Wisdom deals with two different questions; it is important to keep them distinct even if he himself failed to do so:

1. Can an empirical dispute change its character in such a way that it is no longer a dispute about the facts, and yet is not an idle dispute?

2. Assuming that this has happened in the case of the dispute between theists and atheists, what kind of dispute are they now engaged in?

It is obvious that if he is to answer the first question affirmatively, Wisdom must provide a convincing answer to the second question. Unfortunately, his use of the Parable of the Invisible Gardener to provide a vivid answer to the first question has led to misunderstandings of his answers to the second one.

How the argument between theists and atheists has changed

In answering the first question, Wisdom begins by showing us how things were in the days before science discredited the idea of God's miraculous intervention in the world. He refers to the story of Elijah's challenge to the priests of the pagan deity, Baal. Altars to Baal and to Yahweh (The Lord of Israel) are erected. The true God is to prove himself by consuming his altar with fire. Here the dispute involves observable consequences, namely, which altar will be consumed. When the fire from heaven consumes the altar to Yahweh, the Israelites shout, "Yahweh is God."

Wisdom then shows how the dispute between atheists and theists has changed. Theologians are now too much oriented to science to propose a test by miracle. It is in this context that he tells his parable of The Invisible Gardener. Two men come upon their long neglected garden and find it overgrown with weeds. Yet they also find some of the flowers still flourishing and even arranged in beautiful patterns. They respond in contrasting ways. One of them insists that the flowers are evidence that a gardener tends it, the other focuses on the weeds and insists that a gardener would not allow them to proliferate. Initially, the dispute is over the facts. A thorough investigation of all relevant facts finally satisfies both parties: no gardener has been seen working on this garden. Yet the man who thinks it is tended persists in his view. The evidence of care and purpose that he finds in the garden is more impressive to him than the failure to produce evidence of the presence of a gardener. He claims that an invisible gardner must tend it. The dispute has changed from one about the facts to a dispute about their responses to the garden as a whole. In other words, they have both looked at and investigated the same area; the atheist sees it as untended, the believer sees it as tended.

Wisdom uses this parable to show how an argument can shift in character. Fundamentalists (and pre-scientific generations of Christians) might have differed with atheists about the facts. Sophisticated contemporary theologians differ with them in more complicated ways. Wisdom did not intend the parable of The Invisible Gardner to serve as a model for sophisticated theological arguments. The invisible gardner cannot serve as a model for God, because gardners are the kinds of things that are supposed to be visible. By contrast the word "God" is not intended to refer to a visible being. It is unfortunate that Flew's passionate and important challenge to the meaningfulness of theological language is marred by a misunderstanding of this point. He suggests both that the invisible gardner is a model for God and that Wisdom's account of the dispute over the garden is intended to serve as a model for disputes between sophisticated theologians and atheists.[3]

Flew's interpretation is plausible, because the garden can readily be taken for the world as a whole and it seems as though the invisible gardner must stand for God. Indeed, if that were not Wisdom's intention, then actual gardens are under discussion. In that case, the man who continues, against the evidence, to believe in the presence of an invisible gardener must be operating under a delusion.

Wisdom left himself wide open to Flew's unsympathetic interpretation. A more sympathetic one cannot be attempted within the framework of the parable of The Invisible Gardener. It must come, rather, from an examination of his subsequent efforts in this essay to elaborate the nature of the dispute between sophisticated theists and atheists.

[3] An interpretation of the parable and its relation to the rest of Wisdom's thought on religion is found in James Richmond, *Theology and Metaphysics*, pp. 63ff.

The argument between sophisticated theists and atheists

Having shown to his satisfaction that an empirical argument can cease to be an argument about facts and yet not become an idle dispute, Wisdom examines the nature of the dispute between sophisticated theists and atheists. After warning us not to treat theological arguments as disputes over the facts, he then warns us against regarding them as deductions of the kind we use in mathematics. Wisdom, like the existentialists, shifts our focus from mathematics and science to the subtleties and complexities of human interaction: to the sorts of things handled by judges, historians, and novelists.

The legal model. *Against the use of mathematical or scientific models of argument, Wisdom appeals to the legal model.[4] In legal arguments there are special cases where both sides agree on the facts; the conflict then centers on their arrangement and presentation. "For sometimes when there is agreement as to the facts there is still argument as to whether defendent did or did not 'exercise reasonable care,' or was or was not 'negligent' " (see pp. 166 f.).*

Wisdom presents these examples in order to suggest that the positivists' obsession with the appeal to "the facts" was misguided. There is more to empirical judgment than that. "It is possible," he notes, "to have before one's eyes all the items of a pattern and still to miss the pattern" (see p. 162). It is clear that Wisdom believes that the patterns in which facts are arranged and the connections that are drawn between one set of facts and another, has as much to do with factual meaningfulness as does the narrower question of establishing the facts. "What is so," he insists, "isn't merely a matter of 'the facts' " (see p. 163). Wisdom regards legal arguments of this kind as illuminating models for theology. A statement like "God loves us" should not be regarded as if it were intended as a commonsense statement of fact. A great many facts are relevant to establishing it, but it is part of a religious outlook. It ought, therefore, to be evaluated within the context of the patterns of the experiences and beliefs that are part of the fabric of Christianity. Wisdom

---

[4] For a study that uses legal arguments rather than mathematical demonstrations as the model for logic, see, Stephen Toulmin, *The Uses of Argument* (Cambridge: Cambridge University Press, 1958) and J. L. Austin, "A Plea for Excuses," in his *Philosophical Papers*, ed. J. O. Urmson and G. J. Warnock, 2d ed. rev. (New York: Oxford University Press, 1970), pp. 175–204.

suggests this approach. In his contribution to this volume, Ian Crombie carries it out.

Beauty and love.   *"The difference as to whether a God exists involves our feelings more than most scientific disputes and in this respect is more like a difference as to whether there is beauty in a thing"* (see p. 168). With this remark Wisdom broadens the scope of his treatment. The legal analogy is designed to show that narrow views of induction and deduction won't do for dealing with theological arguments. He then turns to beauty and love to show that our feelings can be strongly engaged in arguments and yet the arguments need be neither idle nor irrational.

If two people stand in front of a painting, they cannot disagree about "the facts" of it, because the facts are right there, on the canvas. Nevertheless, people in this situation disagree, even violently, about the meaning and the worth of paintings. The positivists regarded these disagreements as emotive; they merely reflect the feelings and associations of the participants. The disputes have no cognitive content. Wisdom rejects this view. He insists that these disputes are factually meaningful even though they are not arguments about the facts. One reason for Wisdom's position is that there are rational procedures for conducting these arguments. The individuals involved can go over the painting connecting some parts with other aspects of experience, say of other paintings. The hope is that the connections will trigger similar responses in the other individual and persuade him to share a similar perspective on the painting.

Later in his essay, Wisdom deals with the case of a lover. Here the involvement with the other is maximally intense and people are inclined to think that rational judgment of the beloved is impossible. Yet Wisdom applies his technique to lovers as well. A close friend, who doesn't think she is right for him, may exert a negative influence on the lover. First, he might describe her behavior in patterns that the lover acknowledges. If he can then connect these patterns to behavior that the lover admittedly finds repugnant in any one but his beloved, the lover may be shaken. If the lover (of paintings as well as women) is aware of the flaws that the critic emphasizes and nevertheless persists in his love, the influence may run the other way. The lover can say: "I know she can be cutting. I've been aware of it from the time we met, but when she's relaxed she's sensitive and tender." If the counter-patterns are impressive enough, the critic may come round to the lover's point of view.

These disputes, as far as Wisdom is concerned, are not idle, because both parties are subject to being persuaded, on rational grounds, to change their minds.

In the concluding section of the essay, where he discusses the reasonableness of belief in gods, Wisdom is more elusive and allusive than ever. He suggests that there may be more reasonableness to this belief than meets the eye, but he confines himself to a series of darting hints about art and psychoanalysis.[5]

In the context of the discussion of theology and verification the moral of Wisdom's essay is clear: "What is so isn't merely a matter of 'the facts' ". Therefore, theological statements can have empirical meaning in the broad sense, without being verifiable in a clearcut way.

[5] For an excellent discussion of the concluding sections (as well as the rest of the essay) see, D. Z. Phillips, *Faith and Philosophical Enquiry* (London: Routledge and Kegan Paul, 1970), pp. 170–203, especially, pp. 183–187.

John Wisdom/**Gods**

1. *The existence of God is not an experimental issue in the way it was.* An atheist or agnostic might say to a theist "You still think there are spirits in the trees, nymphs in the streams, a God of the world." He might say this because he noticed the theist in time of drought pray for rain and make a sacrifice and in the morning look for rain. But disagreement about whether there are gods is now less of this experimental or betting sort than it used to be. This is due in part, if not wholly, to our better knowledge of why things happen as they do.

It is true that even in these days it is seldom that one who believes in God has no hopes or fears which an atheist has not. Few believers now expect prayer to still the waves, but some think it makes a difference to people and not merely in ways the atheist would admit. Of course with people, as opposed to waves

From "Gods," *Proceedings of the Aristotelian Society*, 45 (1944–45), 185–206, by John Wisdom. Copyright 1944–45, The Aristotelian Society. Reprinted by permission of the editor of The Aristotelian Society and the author.

and machines, one never knows what they won't do next, so that expecting prayer to make a difference to them is not so definite a thing as believing in its mechanical efficacy. Still, just as primitive people pray in a business-like way for rain so some people still pray for others with a real feeling of doing something to help. However, in spite of this persistence of an experimental element in some theistic belief, it remains true that Elijah's method on Mount Carmel of settling the matter of what god or gods exist would be far less appropriate to-day than it was then.

2. *Belief in gods is not merely a matter of expectation of a world to come.* Someone may say "The fact that a theist no more than an atheist expects prayer to bring down fire from heaven or cure the sick does not mean that there is no difference between them as to the facts, it does not mean that the theist has no expectations different from the atheist's. For very often those who believe in God believe in another world and believe that God is there and that we shall go to that world when we die."

This is true, but I do not want to consider here expectations as to what one will see and feel after death nor what sort of reasons these logically unique expectations could have. So I want to consider those theists who do not believe in a future life, or rather, I want to consider the differences between atheists and theists in so far as these differences are not a matter of belief in a future life.

3. *What are these differences? And is it that theists are superstitious or that atheists are blind?* A child may wish to sit a while with his father and he may, when he has done what his father dislikes, fear punishment and feel distress at causing vexation, and while his father is alive he may feel sure of help when danger threatens and feel that there is sympathy for him when disaster has come. When his father is dead he will no longer expect punishment or help. Maybe for a moment an old fear will come or a cry for help escape him but he will at once remember that this is no good now. He may feel that his father is no more until perhaps someone says to him that his father is still alive though he lives now in another world and one so far away that there is no hope of seeing him or hearing his voice again. The child may be told that nevertheless his father can see him and hear all he says. When he has been told this the child will still fear no punishment nor expect any sign of his father, but now, even more than he did when his father was alive, he will feel that his father sees him all

the time and will dread distressing him and when he has done something wrong he will feel separated from his father until he has felt sorry for what he has done. Maybe when he himself comes to die he will be like a man who expects to find a friend in the strange country where he is going. But even when this is so, it is by no means all of what makes the difference between a child who believes that his father lives still in another world and one who does not.

Likewise one who believes in God may face death differently from one who does not, but there is other difference between them beside this. This other difference may still be described as belief in another world, only this belief is not a matter of expecting one thing rather than another here or hereafter, it is not a matter of a world to come but of a world that now is, though beyond our senses.

We are at once reminded of those other unseen worlds which some philosophers "believe in" and others "deny," while non-philosophers unconsciously "accept" them by using them as models with which to "get the hang of" the patterns in the flux of experience. We recall the timeless entities whose changeless connexions we seek to represent in symbols, and the values which stand firm[1] amidst our flickering satisfaction and remorse, and the physical things which, though not beyond the corruption of moth and rust, are yet more permanent than the shadows they throw upon the screen before our minds. We recall, too, our talk of souls and of what lies in their depths and is manifested to us partially and intermittently in our own feelings and the behaviour of others. The hypothesis of mind, of other human minds and of animal minds, is reasonable because it explains for each of us why certain things behave so cunningly all by themselves unlike even the most ingenious machines. Is the hypothesis of minds in flowers and trees reasonable for like reasons? Is the hypothesis of a world mind reasonable for like reasons—someone who adjusts the blossom to the bees, someone whose presence may at times be felt— in a garden in high summer, in the hills when clouds are gathering, but not, perhaps, in a cholera epidemic?

4. *The question "Is belief in gods reasonable?" has more than one source.* It is clear now that in order to grasp fully the logic of belief in divine minds we need to examine the logic of

---

[1] In another world, Dr. Joad says in the *New Statesman* recently.

belief in animal and human minds. But we cannot do that here and so for the purposes of this discussion about divine minds let us acknowledge the reasonableness of our belief in human minds without troubling ourselves about its logic. The question of the reasonableness of belief in divine minds then becomes a matter of whether there are facts in nature which support claims about divine minds in the way facts in nature support our claims about human minds.

In this way we resolve the force behind the problem of the existence of gods into two components, one metaphysical and the same which prompts the question "Is there *ever any* behaviour which gives reason to believe in *any* sort of mind?" and one which finds expression in "Are there other mind-patterns in nature beside the human and animal patterns which we can all easily detect, and are these other mind-patterns super-human?"

Such over-determination of a question syndrome is common. Thus, the puzzling questions "Do dogs think?", "Do animals feel?" are partly metaphysical puzzles and partly scientific questions. They are not purely metaphysical; for the reports of scientists about the poor performances of cats in cages and old ladies' stories about the remarkable performances of their pets are not irrelevant. But nor are these questions purely scientific; for the stories never settle them and therefore they have other sources. One other source is the metaphysical source we have already noticed, namely, the difficulty about getting behind an animal's behaviour to its mind, whether it is a non-human animal or a human one.

But there's a third component in the force behind these questions, these disputes have a third source, and it is one which is important in the dispute which finds expression in the words "I believe in God," "I do not." This source comes out well if we consider the question "Do flowers feel?" Like the questions about dogs and animals this question about flowers comes partly from the difficulty we sometimes feel over inference from *any* behaviour to thought or feeling and partly from ignorance as to what behaviour is to be found. But these questions, as opposed to a like question about human beings, come also from hesitation as to whether the behaviour in question is *enough* mind-like, that is, is it enough similar to or superior to human behaviour to be called "mind-proving?" Likewise, even when we are satisfied that human behaviour shows mind and even when we have learned whatever mind-suggesting things there are in nature which are not explained by human and animal minds, we may still ask "But are these things sufficiently striking to be called a mind-pattern? Can we fairly call them manifestations of a divine being?"

"The question," someone may say, "has then become merely a matter of the application of a name. And 'What's in a name?' "

5. *But the line between a question of fact and a question or decision as to the application of a name is not so simple as this way of putting things suggests.* The question "What's in a name?" is engaging because we are inclined to answer both "Nothing" and "Very much." And this "Very much" has more than one source. We might have tried to comfort Heloise by saying "It isn't that Abelard no longer loves you, for this man isn't Abelard"; we might have said to poor Mr. Tebrick in Mr. Garnet's *Lady into Fox* "But this is no longer Silvia." But if Mr. Tebrick replied "Ah, but it is!" this might come not at all from observing facts about the fox which we had not observed, but from noticing facts about the fox which we had missed, although we had in a sense observed all that Mr. Tebrick had observed. It is possible to have before one's eyes all the items of a pattern and still to miss the pattern. Consider the following conversation:

'And I think Kay and I are pretty happy. We've always been happy.'

Bill lifted up his glass and put it down without drinking.

'Would you mind saying that again?' he asked.

'I don't see what's so queer about it. Taken all in all, Kay and I have really been happy.'

'All right,' Bill said gently, 'Just tell me how you and Kay have been happy.'

Bill had a way of being amused by things which I could not understand.

'It's a little hard to explain,' I said. 'It's like taking a lot of numbers that don't look alike and that don't mean anything until you add them all together.'

I stopped, because I hadn't meant to talk to him about Kay and me.

'Go ahead,' Bill said. 'What about the numbers.' And he began to smile.

'I don't know why you think it's so funny,' I said. 'All the things that two people do together, two people like Kay and me, add up to something. There are the kids and the house and the dog and all the people we have known and all the times we've been out to dinner. Of course, Kay and I do quarrel sometimes but when you add it all together, all of it isn't as bad as the parts of it seem. I mean, maybe that's all there is to anybody's life.'

Bill poured himself another drink. He seemed about to say something and checked himself. He kept looking at me.[2]

Or again, suppose two people are speaking of two characters in a story which both have read[3] or of two friends which both have known, and one says "Really she hated him," and the other says "She didn't, she loved him." Then the first may have noticed what the other has not although he knows no incident in the lives of the people they are talking about which the other doesn't know too and the second speaker may say "She didn't, she loved him" because he hasn't noticed what the first noticed, although he can remember every incident the first can remember. But then again he may say "She didn't, she loved him" not because he hasn't noticed the patterns in time which the first has noticed but because though he has noticed them he doesn't feel he still needs to emphasize them with "Really she hated him." The line between using a name because of how we feel and because of what we have noticed isn't sharp. "A difference as to the facts," "a discovery," "a revelation," these phrases cover many things. Discoveries have been made not only by Christopher Columbus and Pasteur, but also by Tolstoy and Dostoiefsky and Freud. Things are revealed to us not only by the scientists with microscopes but also by the poets, the prophets and the painters. What is so isn't merely a matter of "the facts." For sometimes when there is agreement as to the facts there is still argument as to whether defendant did or did not "exercise reasonable care," was or was not "negligent."

And though we shall need to emphasize how much "There is a God" evinces an attitude to the familiar[4] we shall find in the end that it also evinces some recognition of patterns in time easily missed and that, therefore, difference as to there being any gods is in part a difference as to what is so and therefore as to the facts, though not in the simple ways which first occurred to us.

6. *Let us now approach these same points by a different road.*

[2] *H. M. Pulham, Esq.,* p. 320, by John P. Marquand.

[3] *e.g.,* Havelock Ellis's autobiography.

[4] *Persuasive Definitions, Mind,* July, 1938, by Charles Leslie Stevenson, should be read here. It is very good.

6.1 *How it is that an explanatory hypothesis, such as the existence of God, may start by being experimental and gradually become something quite different can be seen from the following story:*

Two people return to their long neglected garden and find among the weeds a few of the old plants surprisingly vigorous. One says to the other "It must be that a gardener has been coming and doing something about these plants." Upon enquiry they find that no neighbour has ever seen anyone at work in their garden. The first man says to the other "He must have worked while people slept." The other says "No, someone would have heard him and besides, anybody who cared about the plants would have kept down these weeds." The first man says "Look at the way these are arranged. There is purpose and a feeling for beauty here. I believe that someone comes, someone invisible to mortal eyes. I believe that the more carefully we look the more we shall find confirmation of this." They examine the garden ever so carefully and sometimes they come on new things suggesting that a gardener comes and sometimes they come on new things suggesting the contrary and even that a malicious person has been at work. Besides examining the garden carefully they also study what happens to gardens left without attention. Each learns all the other learns about this and about the garden. Consequently, when after all this, one says "I still believe a gardener comes" while the other says "I don't" their different words now reflect no difference as to what they have found in the garden, no difference as to what they would find in the garden if they looked further and no difference about how fast untended gardens fall into disorder. At this stage, in this context, the gardener hypothesis has ceased to be experimental, the difference between one who accepts and one who rejects it is now not a matter of the one expecting something the other does not expect. What is the difference between them? The one says "A gardener comes unseen and unheard. He is manifested only in his works with which we are all familiar," the other says "There is no gardener" and with this difference in what they say about the gardener goes a difference in how they feel towards the garden, in spite of the fact that neither expects anything of it which the other does not expect.

But is this the whole difference between them—that the one calls the garden by one name and feels one way towards it, while the other calls it by another name and feels in another way towards it? And if this [is] what the difference has become then is it any longer appropriate to ask "Which is right?" or "Which is reasonable?"

And yet surely such questions *are* appropriate when one person says to another "You still think the world's a garden and not a wilderness, and that the gardener has not forsaken it" or "You still think there are nymphs of the streams, a presence in the hills, a spirit of the world." Perhaps when a man sings "God's in his heaven" we need not take this as more than an expression of how he feels. But when Bishop Gore or Dr. Joad write about belief in God and young men read them in order to settle their religious doubts the impression is not simply that of persons choosing exclamations with which to face nature and the "changes and chances of this mortal life." The disputants speak as if they are concerned with a matter of scientific fact, or of trans-sensual, trans-scientific and metaphysical fact, but still of fact and still a matter about which reasons for and against may be offered, although no scientific reasons in the sense of field surveys for fossils or experiments on delinquents are to the point.

6.2. *Now can an interjection have a logic?* Can the manifestation of an attitude in the utterance of a word, in the application of a name, have a logic? When all the facts are known how can there still be a question of fact? How can there still be a question? Surely as Hume says ". . . after every circumstance, every relation is known, the understanding has no further room to operate?"[5]

6.3. When the madness of these questions leaves us for a moment *we can all easily recollect disputes which though they cannot be settled by experiment are yet disputes in which one party may be right and the other wrong and in which both parties may offer reasons and the one better reasons than the other. This may happen in pure and applied mathematics and logic.* Two accountants or two engineers provided with the same data may reach different results and this difference is resolved not by collecting further data but by going over the calculations again. Such differences indeed share with differences as to what will win a race, the honour of being among the most "settlable" disputes in the language.

6.4. *But it won't do to describe the theistic issue as one*

---

[5] Hume. *An Enquiry concerning the Principles of Morals*. Appendix I.

settlable by such calculation, or as one about what can be deduced in this *vertical* fashion from the facts we know. No doubt dispute about God has sometimes, perhaps especially in mediaeval times, been carried on in this fashion. But nowadays it is not and we must look for some other analogy, some other case in which a dispute is settled but not by experiment.

6.5. *In courts of law* it sometimes happens that opposing counsel are agreed as to the facts and are not trying to settle a question of further fact, are not trying to settle whether the man who admittedly had quarrelled with the deceased did or did not murder him, but are concerned with whether Mr. A who admittedly handed his long-trusted clerk signed blank cheques did or did not exercise reasonable care, whether a ledger is or is not a document,[6] whether a certain body was or was not a public authority.

In such cases we notice that the process of argument is not a *chain* of demonstrative reasoning. It is a presenting and re-presenting of those features of the case which *severally co-operate* in favour of the conclusion, in favour of saying what the reasoner wishes said, in favour of calling the situation by the name by which he wishes to call it. The reasons are like the legs of a chair, not the links of a chain. Consequently although the discussion is *a priori* and the steps are not a matter of experience, the procedure resembles scientific argument in that the reasoning is not *vertically* extensive but *horizontally* extensive—it is a matter of the cumulative effect of several independent premises, not of the repeated transformation of one or two. And because the premises are severally inconclusive the process of deciding the issue becomes a matter of weighing the cumulative effect of one group of severally inconclusive items against the cumulative effect of another group of severally inconclusive items, and thus lends itself to description in terms of conflicting "probabilities." This encourages the feeling that the issue is one of fact

---

6 *The Times,* March 2, 1945. Also in *The Times* of June 13, 1945, contrast the case of Hannah v. Peel with that of the cruiser cut in two by a liner. In the latter case there is not agreement as to the facts. See also the excellent articles by Dr. Glanville L. Williams in the *Law Quarterly Review, Language and the Law,* April and January, 1945, and *The Doctrine of Repugnancy,* October, 1943, January, 1944 and April, 1944. The author, having set out how arbitrary are many legal decisions, needs now to set out how far from arbitrary they are—if his readers are ready for the next phase in the dialectic process.

—that it is a matter of guessing from the premises at a further fact, at what is to come. But this is a muddle. *The dispute does not cease to be a priori because it is a matter of the cumulative effect of severally inconclusive premises.* The logic of the dispute is not that of a chain of deductive reasoning as in a mathematic calculation. But nor is it a matter of collecting from several inconclusive items of information an expectation as to something further, as when a doctor from a patient's symptoms guesses at what is wrong, or a detective from many clues guesses the criminal. It has its own sort of logic and its own sort of end—the solution of the question at issue is a decision, a ruling by the judge. But it is not an arbitrary decision though the rational connexions are neither quite like those in vertical deductions nor like those in inductions in which from many signs we guess at what is to come; and though the decision manifests itself in the application of a name it is no more merely the application of a name than is the pinning on of a medal merely the pinning on of a bit of metal. Whether a lion with stripes is a tiger or a lion is, if you like, merely a matter of the application of a name. Whether Mr. So and So of whose conduct we have so complete a record did or did not exercise reasonable care is not merely a matter of the application of a name or, if we choose to say it is, then we must remember that with this name a game is lost and won and a game with very heavy stakes. With the judges choice of a name for the facts goes an attitude, and the declaration, the ruling, is an exclamation evincing that attitude. But *it is an exclamation which not only has a purpose but also has a logic,* a logic surprisingly like that of "futile," "deplorable," "graceful," "grand," "divine."

6.6. *Suppose two people are looking at a picture or natural scene.* One says "Excellent" or "Beautiful" or "Divine"; the other says "I don't see it." He means he doesn't see the beauty. And this reminds us of how we felt the theist accuse the atheist of blindness and the atheist accuse the theist of seeing what isn't there. And yet surely each sees what the other sees. It isn't that one can see part of the picture which the other can't see. So the difference is in a sense not one as to the facts. And so it cannot be removed by the one disputant discovering to the other what so far he hasn't seen. It isn't that the one sees the picture in a different light and so, as we might say, sees a different picture. Consequently the difference between them cannot be resolved by putting the picture in a different light. And yet surely this is just what can be done in such a case—not by moving the picture but by talk perhaps. To settle a dispute as to whether a piece of music is good or better than another we listen again, with a picture we look again. Someone perhaps points to emphasize certain features and we see it in a different light. Shall we call this "field work" and "the last of observation" or shall we call it "reviewing the premises" and "the beginning of deduction (horizontal)"?

If in spite of all this if we choose to say that a difference as to whether a thing is beautiful is not a factual difference we must be careful to remember that there is a procedure for settling these differences and that this consists not only in reasoning and re-description as in the legal case, but also in a more literal re-setting-before with re-looking or re-listening.

6.7. *And if we say as we did at the beginning that when a difference as to the existence of a God is not one as to future happenings then it is not experimental and therefore not as to the facts, we must not forthwith assume that there is no right and wrong about it,* no rationality or irrationality, no appropriateness or inappropriateness, no procedure which tends to settle it, *nor even that this procedure is in no sense a discovery of new facts.* After all even in science this is not so. Our two gardeners even when they had reached the stage when neither expected any experimental result which the other did not, might yet have continued the dispute, each presenting and re-presenting the features of the garden favouring his hypothesis, that is, fitting his model for describing the accepted fact; each emphasizing the pattern he wishes to emphasize. True, in science, there is seldom or never a pure instance of this sort of dispute, for nearly always with difference of hypothesis goes some difference of expectation as to the facts. But scientists argue about rival hypotheses with a vigour which is not exactly proportioned to difference in expectations of experimental results.

The difference as to whether a God exists involves our feelings more than most scientific disputes and in this respect is more like a difference as to whether there is beauty in a thing.

7. *The Connecting Technique.* Let us consider again the technique used in revealing or proving beauty, in removing a blindness, in inducing an attitude which is lacking, in reducing a reaction that is inappropriate. Besides running over in a special way the features of the picture, tracing the rhythms, making sure that this and that are not only seen but noticed, and their relation

to each other—besides all this—there are other things we can do to justify our attitude and alter that of the man who cannot see. For features of the picture may be brought out by setting beside it other pictures; just as the merits of an argument may be brought out, proved, by setting beside it other arguments, in which striking but irrelevant features of the original are changed and relevant features emphasized; just as the merits and demerits of a line of action may be brought out by setting beside it other actions. To use Susan Stebbing's example: Nathan brought out for David certain features of what David had done in the matter of Uriah the Hittite by telling him a story about two sheep owners. This is the kind of thing we very often do when someone is "inconsistent" or unreasonable. This is what we do in referring to other cases in law. The paths we need to trace from other cases to the case in question are often numerous and difficult to detect and the person with whom we are discussing the matter may well draw attention to connexions which, while not incompatible with those we have tried to emphasize, are of an opposite inclination. A may have noticed in B subtle and hidden likenesses to an angel and reveal these to C, while C has noticed in B subtle and hidden likenesses to a devil which he reveals to A.

Imagine that a man picks up some flowers that lie half withered on a table and gently puts them in water. Another man says to him "You believe flowers feel." He says this although he knows that the man who helps the flowers doesn't expect anything of them which he himself doesn't expect; for he himself expects the flowers to be "refreshed" and to be easily hurt, injured, I mean, by rough handling, while the man who puts them in water does not expect them to whisper "Thank you." The Sceptic says "You believe flowers feel" because something about the way the other man lifts the flowers and puts them in water suggests an attitude to the flowers which he feels inappropriate although perhaps he would not feel it inappropriate to butterflies. He feels that this attitude to flowers is somewhat crazy *just as it is sometimes felt that a lover's attitude is somewhat crazy even when this is not a matter of his having false hopes about how the person he is in love with will act.* It is often said in such cases that reasoning is useless. But the very person who says this feels that the lover's attitude is crazy, is inappropriate like some dreads and hatreds, such as some horrors of enclosed places. And often one who says "It is useless to reason" proceeds at once to reason with the lover, nor is this reasoning always quite without effect. We may draw the lover's attention to certain things done by her he is in love with and trace for him a path to these from things done by others at other times[7] which have disgusted and infuriated him. And by this means we may weaken his admiration and confidence, make him feel it unjustified and arouse his suspicion and contempt and make him feel our suspicion and contempt reasonable. It is possible, of course, that he has already noticed the analogies, the connexions, we point out and that he has accepted them—that is, he has not denied them nor passed them off. He has recognised them and they have altered his attitude, altered his love but he still loves. We then feel that perhaps it is we who are blind and cannot see what he can see.

8. *Connecting and Disconnecting.* But before we confess ourselves thus inadequate there are other fires his admiration must pass through. For when a man has an attitude which it seems to us he should not have or lacks one which it seems to us he should have then, not only do we suspect that he is not influenced by connexions which we feel should influence him and draw his attention to these, but also we suspect he is influenced by connexions which should not influence him and draw his attention to these. It may, for a moment, seem strange that we should draw his attention to connexions which we feel should not influence him, and which, since they do influence him, he has in a sense already noticed. But we do—such is our confidence in "the light of reason."

Sometimes the power of these connexions comes mainly from a man's mismanagement of the language he is using. This is what happens in the Monte Carlo fallacy, where by mismanaging the laws of chance a man passes from noticing that a certain colour or number has not turned up for a long while to an improper confidence that now it soon will turn up. In such cases our showing up of the false connexions is a process we call "explaining a fallacy in reasoning." To remove fallacies in reasoning we urge a man to call a spade a spade, ask him what he means by "the State" and having pointed out ambiguities and vaguenesses ask him to reconsider the steps in his argument.

10. *Unspoken Connexions. Usually, however, wrongheadedness or wrongheartedness in a situation, blindness to what is*

[7] Thus, like the scientist, the critic is concerned to show up the irrelevance of time and space.

there or seeing what is not, does not arise merely from mismanagement of language but is more due to connexions which are not
mishandled in language, for the reason that they are not put into
language at all. And often these misconnexions too, weaken in the
light of reason, if only we can guess where they lie and turn it on
them. In so far as these connexions are not presented in language
the process of removing their power is not a process of correcting
the mismanagement of language. But it is still akin to such a
process; for though it is not a process of setting out fairly what
has been set out unfairly, it is a process of setting out fairly what
has not been set out at all. And we must remember that the line
between connexions ill-presented or half-presented in language
and connexions operative but not presented in language, or only
hinted at, is not a sharp one.

Whether or not we call the process of showing up these
connexions "reasoning to remove bad unconscious reasoning" or
not, it is certain that in order to settle in ourselves what weight
we shall attach to someone's confidence or attitude we not only
ask him for his reasons but also look for unconscious reasons both
good and bad; that is, for reasons which he can't put into words,
isn't explicitly aware of, is hardly aware of, isn't aware of at all—
perhaps it's long experience which he doesn't recall which lets him
know a squall is coming, perhaps it's old experience which he
can't recall which makes the cake in the tea mean so much and
makes Odette so fascinating.[8]

I am well aware of the distinction between the question
"What reasons are there for the belief that S is P?" and the question "What are the sources of beliefs that S is P?" There are cases
where investigation of the rationality of a claim which certain
persons make is done with very little enquiry into why they say
what they do, into the causes of their beliefs. This is so when we
have very definite ideas about what is really logically relevant to
their claim and what is not. Offered a mathematical theorem we
ask for the proof; offered the generalization that parental discord
causes crime we ask for the correlation co-efficients. But even in
this last case, if we fancy that only the figures are reasons we
underestimate the complexity of the logic of our conclusion; and
yet it is difficult to describe the other features of the evidence
which have weight and there is apt to be disagreement about the

[8] Proust. Swan's Way, Vol. 1, p. 58, Vol. 2. Phœnix Edition.

weight they should have. In criticizing other conclusions and especially conclusions which are largely the expression of an attitude,
we have not only to ascertain what reasons there are for them
but also to decide what things are reasons and how much. This
latter process of sifting reasons from causes is part of the critical
process for every belief, but in some spheres it has been done
pretty fully already. In these spheres we don't need to examine
the actual processes to belief and distil from them a logic. But in
other spheres this remains to be done. Even in science or on the
stock exchange or in ordinary life we sometimes hesitate to condemn a belief or a hunch[9] merely because those who believe it
cannot offer the sort of reasons we had hoped for. And now suppose Miss Gertrude Stein finds excellent the work of a new artist
while we see nothing in it. We nervously recall, perhaps, how
pictures by Picasso which Miss Stein admired and others rejected,
later came to be admired by many who gave attention to them,
and we wonder whether the case is not a new instance of her
perspicacity and our blindness. But if, upon giving all our attention to the work in question, we still do not respond to it, and we
notice that the subject matter of the new pictures is perhaps birds
in wild places and learn that Miss Stein is a bird-watcher, then
we begin to trouble ourselves less about her admiration.

It must not be forgotten that our attempt to show up misconnexions in Miss Stein may have an opposite result and reveal
to us connexions we had missed. Thinking to remove the spell
exercised upon his patient by the old stories of the Greeks the
psychoanalyst may himself fall under that spell and find in them
what his patient has found and, incidentally, what made the
Greeks tell those tales.

11. *Now what happens, what should happen, when we enquire in this way into the reasonableness, the propriety of belief
in gods?* The answer is: A double and opposite-phased change.
Wordsworth writes:

"......And I have felt
A presence that disturbs me with the joy
Of elevated thoughts, a sense sublime
Of something far more deeply interfused,
Whose dwelling is the light of setting suns,
And the round ocean and the living air,

[9] Here I think of Mr. Staces' interesting reflexions in *Mind*, January, 1945,
The Problems of Unreasoned Beliefs.

And the blue sky, and in the mind of man
A motion and a spirit, that impels
All thinking things, all objects of all thoughts,
And rolls through all things . . . ."[10]

We most of us know this feeling. But is it well placed like the feeling that here is first-rate work, which we sometimes rightly have even before we have full grasped the picture we are looking at or the book we are reading? Or is it misplaced like the feeling in a house that has long been empty that someone secretly lives there still. Wordsworth's feeling is the feeling that the world is haunted, that something watches in the hills and manages the stars. The child feels that the stone tripped him when he stumbled, that the bough struck him when it flew back in his face. He has to learn that the wind isn't buffeting him, that there is not a devil in it, that he was wrong, that his attitude was inappropriate. And as he learns that the wind wasn't hindering him so he also learns it wasn't helping him. But we know how, though he learns, his attitude lingers. It is plain that Wordsworth's feeling is of this family.

Belief in gods, it is true, is often very different from belief that stones are spiteful, the sun kindly. For the gods appear in human form and from the waves and control these things and by so doing reward and punish us. But varied as are the stories of the gods they have a family likeness and we have only to recall them to feel sure of the other main sources which co-operate with animism to produce them.

What are the stories of the gods? What are our feelings when we believe in God? They are feelings of awe before power, dread of the thunderbolts of Zeus, confidence in the everlasting arms, unease beneath the all-seeing eye. They are feelings of guilt and inescapable vengeance, of smothered hate and of a security we can hardly do without. We have only to remind ourselves of these feelings and the stories of the gods and goddesses and heroes in which these feelings find expression, to be reminded of how we felt as children to our parents and the big people of our childhood. Writing of a first telephone call from his grandmother Proust says:

" . . . . . . it was rather that this isolation of the voice was like a symbol, a presentation, a direct consequence of another isolation,

[10] Tintern Abbey.

that of my grandmother, separated for the first time in my life, from myself. The orders or prohibitions which she addressed to me at every moment in the ordinary cause of my life, the tedium of obedience or the fire of rebellion which neutralized the affection that I felt for her were at this moment eliminated. . . . . . . 'Granny!' I cried to her . . . . . . but I had beside me only that voice, a phantom, as unpalpable as that which would come to revisit me when my grandmother was dead. 'Speak to me!' but then it happened that, left more solitary still, I ceased to catch the sound of her voice. My grandmother could no longer hear me . . . . . . I continued to call her, sounding the empty night, in which I felt that her appeals also must be straying. I was shaken by the same anguish which, in the distant past, I had felt once before, one day when, a little child, in a crowd, I had lost her."

Giorgio de Chirico, writing of Courbet, says: "The word yesterday envelopes us with its yearning echo, just as, on waking, when the sense of time and the logic of things remain a while confused, the memory of a happy hour we spent the day before may sometimes linger reverberating within us. At times we think of Courbet and his work as we do of our own father's youth."

When a man's father fails him by death or by weakness how much he needs another father, one in the heavens with whom is "no variableness nor shadow of turning."

We understood Mr. Kenneth Graham when he wrote of the Golden Age we feel we have lived in under the Olympians. Freud says: "The ordinary man cannot imagine this Providence in any other form but that of a greatly exalted father, for only such a one could understand the needs of the sons of men, or be softened by their prayers and be placated by the signs of their remorse. The whole thing is so patently infantile, so incongruous with reality. . . . . ." "So incongruous with reality"! It cannot be denied.

But here a new aspect of the matter may strike us.[11] For the very facts which make us feel that now we can recognize systems of superhuman, sub-human, elusive, beings for what they are—the persistent projections of infantile phantasies—include facts which make these systems less fantastic. What are these

[11] This different aspect of the matter and the connexion between God, the heavenly Father and "the good father" of the psycho-analysts was put into my head by some remarks by Dr. Susan Isaacs.

facts? They are patterns in human reactions which are well described by saying that we are as if there were hidden within us
powers, persons, not ourselves and stronger than ourselves. That
this is so may perhaps be said to have been common knowledge
yielded by ordinary observation of people,[12] but we did not know
the degree in which this is so until recent study of extraordinary
cases in extraordinary conditions had revealed it. I refer, of
course, to the study of multiple personalities and the wider studies
of psycho-analysts. Even when the results of this work are reported to us that is not the same as tracing the patterns in the
details of the cases on which the results are based; and even that
is not the same as taking part in the studies oneself. One thing not
sufficiently realized is that some of the things shut within us are
not bad but good.

   Now the gods, good and evil and mixed, have always been
mysterious powers outside us rather than within. But they have
also been within. It is not a modern theory but an old saying
that in each of us a devil sleeps. Eve said: "The serpent beguiled
me." Helen says to Menelaus:

> " . . . . . . And yet how strange it is!
> I ask not thee; I ask my own sad thought,
> What was there in my heart, that I forgot
> My home and land and all I loved, to fly
> With a strange man? Surely it was not I,
> But Cypris there!"[13]

Elijah found that God was not in the wind, nor in the thunder,
but in a still small voice. The kingdom of Heaven is within us,

[12] Consider Tolstoy and Dostoievsky—I do not mean, of course, that their
observation was ordinary.

[13] Euripides. *The Trojan Women*, Gilbert Murray's Translation. Roger Hinks
in *Myth and Allegory in Ancient Art* writes (p. 108): "Personifications made
their appearance very early in Greek poetry . . . . . . It is out of the question
to call these terrible things 'abstractions' . . . . . . They are real daemons to
be worshipped and propitiated . . . . . . These beings we observe correspond
to states of mind. The experience of man teaches him that from time to time
his composure is invaded and overturned by some power from outside: panic,
intoxication, sexual desire."

> "What use to shoot off guns at unicorns?
> Where one horn's hit another fierce horn grows.
> These beasts are fabulous, and none were born
> Of woman who could lay a fable low."—*The Glass Tower*.
>
> Nicholas Moore, p. 100.

Christ insisted, though usually about the size of a grain of mustard seed, and he prayed that we should become one with the Father in Heaven.

New knowledge made it necessary either to give up saying "The sun is sinking" or to give the words a new meaning. In many contexts we preferred to stick to the old words and give them a new meaning which was not entirely new but, on the contrary, *practically* the same as the old. The Greeks did not speak of the dangers of repressing instincts but they did speak of the dangers of thwarting Dionysos, of neglecting Cypris for Diana, of forgetting Poseidon for Athena. We have eaten of the fruit of a garden we can't forget though we were never there, a garden we still look for though we can never find it. Maybe we look for too simple a likeness to what we dreamed. Maybe we are not as free as we fancy from the old idea that Heaven is a happy hunting ground, or a city with streets of gold. Lately Mr. Aldous Huxley has recommended our seeking not somewhere beyond the sky or late in time but a timeless state not made of the stuff of this world, which he rejects, picking it into worthless pieces. But this sounds to me still too much a looking for another place, not indeed one filled with sweets but instead so empty that some of us would rather remain in the Lamb or the Elephant, where, as we know, they stop whimpering with another bitter and so far from sneering at all things, hang pictures of winners at Kempton and stars of the 'nineties. Something good we have for each other is freed there, and in some degree and for a while the miasma of time is rolled back without obliging us to deny the present.

The artists who do most for us don't tell us only of fairylands. Proust, Manet, Breughel, even Botticelli and Vermeer show us reality. And yet they give us for a moment exhilaration without anxiety, peace without boredom. And those who, like Freud, work in a different way against that which too often comes over us and forces us into deadness or despair,[14] also deserve critical, patient and courageous attention. For they, too, work to release us from human bondage into human freedom.

Many have tried to find ways of salvation. The reports they bring back are always incomplete and apt to mislead even when they are not in words but in music or paint. But they are by no means useless; and not the worst of them are those which speak of

[14] Matthew Arnold. *Summer Night.*

oneness with God. But in so far as we become one with him he becomes one with us. St. John says, he is in us as we love one another.

This love, I suppose, is not benevolence but something that comes of the oneness with one another of which Christ spoke.[15] Sometimes it momentarily gains strength.[16] Hate and the Devil do too. And what is oneness without otherness?

[15] St. John xvi, 21.
[16] *The Harvesters* in *The Golden Age*, Kenneth Graham.

Six/Eschatological verification

Introduction/**Verification: theoretical and practical**

JOHN Hick is an important figure in the study of theology and verification because he is a religious thinker who has attempted to answer the challenge of verification in positivistic terms. Hick thinks that Wisdom's parable of The Invisible Gardener is useful in illuminating one side of Christian Faith, namely, that it is a way of seeing the world. Yet Hick insists that Christian Faith is also factually meaningful because it can be verified eschatologically, that is, in the afterlife. In order to show the limitations of what he takes to be Wisdom's perspectival understanding of Christianity, Hick counters with his parable of The Two Travellers.

Verification in the celestial city

Hick's two travellers are the Christian and the nonbeliever. Throughout life's journey they make the same kinds of observations. The Christian does not see men walking on water, converting water into wine, or any other extraordinary occurrences that cannot be explained in natural

181

terms. The believer sees the same types of things that the unbeliever sees. This means that, insofar as observations in this life are concerned, Hick is in the same boat as other sophisticated theologians. He cannot answer Ayer's challenge by appealing to distinctive types of observations, that is, miracles, that would verify, or at least confirm, theological statements like "God is the sustainer of the world."

Hick's point of departure for his answer to Ayer is that Christians, in this life, differ from nonbelievers in holding an important and distinctive hope. The Christian traveller believes that this earthly voyage has a supernatural destination, the Celestial City. This eschatological belief is, according to Hick, verifiable. Basically, Hick's eschatological verification amounts to the following:

1. In his afterlife in the Celestial City the individual can identify himself both because he continues to remember his earthly life and because he has a "resurrection body" which is not material, but is identifiable.

2. He meets members of his family and historical figures that he knows are dead. He is able to identify them because they too have resurrection bodies.

3. The Celestial City is a community ruled by Jesus Christ and in it, the individual constantly experiences the sense of communion with God.

Hick does not think that eschatological experiences of this kind would conclusively verify the existence of the transcendent God. This God cannot be observed. Yet Hick claims that experiences of this kind would constitute a powerful confirmation of his existence.

Hick further recommends this strategy by pursuing a point made by A. C. Ewing, namely that eschatological verification confronts the sceptic with a "heads I win, tails you lose" situation.[1] Christian eschatological beliefs can be verified but not falsified. If the Christian is right, his beliefs will be verified in the manner stated above. If the sceptic is right, he cannot falsify the Christian's beliefs, because death means the extinction of all experience.

Hick has not tried to demonstrate the existence of God, the truth of Christian beliefs, or the plausibility of its eschatology. He has only tried to show that theological language is factually meaningful. He claims that the Christian beliefs about the afterlife involve observable consequences. Therefore, they serve to confirm the truth of theological statements. This is the major point of his reply to Nielsen (see p. 243).

[1] A. C. Ewing, "Meaninglessness," in *A Modern Introduction to Philosophy*, 2nd ed., ed. P. Edwards and A. Pap (New York: Free Press, 1965), p. 710.

Furthermore, although some of these observable consequences might also confirm the statements of Jewish and Muslim theologians, there is at least one consequence specified by Hick that is distinctive in the sense that it would only serve to confirm Christian teachings: this is the rule of the Celestial City by the risen Christ.

Nielsen: the description of the celestial city is incoherent

Kai Nielsen raises a number of problems with this scheme:

1. He has questions about Hick's notion that there are statements that can be verified in principle, but that cannot, in principle, be falsified, but he does not press this. It is however, worth noting that, on the basis of Hick's analysis, it might be falsified. Hick has made his eschatological verification specifically Christian because it is Jesus Christ who rules the Celestial City. Christian Faith would, therefore, be falsified, if there were an afterlife in the Celestial City, but Mohammed or the Buddha rather than Jesus Christ were ruling over it.[2]

2. He regards Hick's talk of "resurrection bodies" and "celestial space" as conceptually confused. He thinks that Hick's use of these categories violates the rules of language so that we could not, even in the afterlife, observe resurrection bodies or be located in celestial space.

3. Nielsen emphasizes the charge that the theological conception of the transcendent God is incoherent. If this is the case, then even such utterly extraordinary experiences as those of Hick's Celestial City would not serve to confirm the truth of theological statements. This charge will be considered at length in the context of Nielsen's interchange with Crombie (see pp. 338 f.).[3]

Mavrodes: verification does not challenge theology

George Mavrodes's essay is directed with equal force against Hick, the believer, and Nielsen, the sceptic. They accept verification as a criterion of factual meaningfulness, but he claims that the use of this test involves circular reasoning in the most vicious sense of the term. He accuses

[2] Edward A. Langerak made this point in correspondence with the author.
[3] For a clear and brief restatement of these points, see Kai Nielsen, *Reason and Practice*, pp. 229ff.

philosophers who use it of actually understanding the factual meaning-fulness of statements, before they have tested them. Consider the state-ment, "It's high tide." According to philosophers who accept one version or another of verifiability, this statement, as it stands, is grammatically proper, but we do not know whether it is cognitively meaningful. First we decide that it is intended to tell us about a state of affairs in the world (which, of course, already presupposes that we know what it means) then we try to think of observations that would verify, or at least, confirm it. If we are successful, we declare the statement to be synthetic, that is, factually meaningful.

Mavrodes insists that unless philosophers understand the factual meaning of the statement, "It's high tide," they could not determine the observations that would verify it; for example: "The sand is almost com-pletely covered with water." Their ability to conceive of these tests is not a function of their having determined that the statement is factually meaningful. It is a function of their having grasped its factual meaning independently of the tests.

Mavrodes' argument drives a wedge between two activities that the positivists linked: (1) The analysis of meaning, and (2) Testing for the truth of factual statements. His point is typical of the post-positivist scene where philosophers have spent a considerable amount of time sundering what the positivists had joined together. Indeed, in dropping the use of verification as a theory of factual meaning, the positivists themselves did some of this sundering (see pp. 121 f.). Other contributions to this volume which deal with the distinction between meaning and testing are Flew's retrospective survey of falsification (see pp. 269 ff.), and Tooley's discussion of a recent effort to reformulate the use of verifica-tion as a criterion of factual meaningfulness (see pp. 481 ff.).

Mavrodes would, of course, be willing to concede the point that verification is needed in testing scientific hypotheses. What he is con-cerned to deny is that verification, in any of its forms, can be used to demonstrate the pseudo-synthetic character of theological statements, and to dismiss them as factually meaningless.

Mavrodes' contribution is typical of the thinking of a group of traditionally oriented religious thinkers who are competent in contempo-rary logic and epistemology and who scornfully reject the challenge of verification.[4] They are convinced that the view that it constitutes a threat to theology should have been abandoned years ago, at about the

---

[4] George I. Mavrodes, *Belief in God* (New York: Random House, 1970); Alvin Plantinga, *God and Other Minds*, pp. 156–168; James F. Ross, *Introduction to the Philosophy of Religion* (London: Macmillan, 1969), pp. 150ff.

time that positivism passed from the scene (if not sooner). They maintain that the problems involved in theology are similar to those involved
in such perennial philosophical issues as our knowledge of other minds,
and that they are not fundamentally more resistant to solution than
these other tough issues.

Mavrodes therefore advises theologians to ignore the subject of
verification and to get on with their proper concerns, by which he presumably means the study of the attributes of God, the Incarnation, and
the like.

This is a case of a good philosopher dispensing bad advice. Theologians who take it will be tempted to indulge in the obscure and sloppy
thinking that has characterized so much of the work in this discipline.
Mavrodes' example is must better than his advice. He is a first rate
logician and philosopher. He is not retreating from the issue of verification out of an inability to handle it. He has mastered the relevant disciplines and he dismisses the challenge of verification on technical
grounds. In reply, Nelsen tries to suggest that Mavrodes dimisses it too
quickly.

Nielsen's reply to Mavrodes

In answering Mavrodes' blistering criticism of the concept of verification,
Nielsen appeals to a "lesson we should have learned from G. E. Moore
years ago" (see p. 234). It is the lesson that there are things whose truth
we know with certainty, but which baffle us when we try to offer a
theoretical account of how it is that we know them. The truths which
Moore claimed to know in his way are, as we have seen (pp. 49 ff.), the
truths of common sense, such as "I have a body," and "There are such
things as chairs and tables."[5]

In applying Moore's lesson, Nielsen makes a distinction that is
important to his many criticisms of contemporary religious thinkers.[6] It
is the distinction between the operative level of discourse (first order)
and the theoretical one (second order). In our ordinary use of language
(at the operative or first order level) we understand commonsense statements of fact and we know how to verify them. When he is sitting behind a sand dune and cannot see the water, Nielsen insists that he knows

[5] In *Belief in God*, pp. 73–80, Mavrodes, without mentioning Moore, shows
how Moore's lesson can be applied to support theological truth claims.
[6] Kai Nielsen, "The Intelligibility of God-Talk," *Religious Studies*, 6, 1 (1970),
pp. 14–21.

what someone means in saying "It's high tide," and he knows how to
go about verifying it. The difficulties with verification emerge only at
the second order level of theoretical reflection when philosophers try to
achieve an adequate statement of verifiability.

Nielsen contrasts statements about God with statements about
verification on the grounds that theological statements are problematic
at both the operative and the reflective levels. It is not merely the case
that theologians have difficulties in formulating an adequate theoretical
concept of God, but rather that even nonreflective believers are confused. They do not really know what they mean by God. Therefore, it
is hard to know what it is that Hick's account of the Celestial City is
supposed to verify.

Theologians could reply that at the operative level believers are
not confused. In the context of prayer, Bible readings, and other forms
of religious ritual, they know what they mean by God. Furthermore,
theologians could also claim that the problems of ordinary believers
at the operative level are no worse than those of physicists and other
scientists. Statements like "Hydrogen atoms have one electron" are
much more problematic than commonsense statements of fact like "It's
high tide." Yet Nielsen and other sceptical empiricists take scientific
statements as one of their models of factual meaningfulness while denying this status to religious statements. Theologians charge that this
discrimination is the result of the anti-religious bias of these sceptics,
rather than of sound philosophical analysis.

I have driven the Mavrodes-Nielsen exchange a few steps further
by way of illustrating that the issue of theology and verification constantly drives beyond itself to the larger questions of religion and
science. Nielsen applies Moore's lesson in drawing a contrast, at the
operative level, between statements about God and statements about
verification. I don't think this contrast amounts to much apart from the
assertion that at the operative level scientists make good on their claims
to knowledge and believers do not. If sceptics like Nielsen can make
this assertion stand up, it follows that a concept like verification, which
is integral to the scientific method, has far more cognitive clout than a
concept like God, which is integral to religion.

In Reason and Practice, Nielsen reviews his controversy with
Mavrodes and he accepts the point that in order to know how to go
about verifying a statement we must already know what it means.
Nielsen then tries to salvage the test of verification by insisting that it
is not a general criterion of meaning, but only a standard of factual
meaningfulness:

As a criterion of factual significance, it serves as a principle of demarcation, distinguishing within the corpus of meaningful sentences those declarative ones used to make genuine factual statements from those employments of language that purport to make factual claims but are in reality pseudo-factual, that is, statements that purport to be factual—true or false assertions about what there is—but actually fail to have factual significance because they have no truth conditions and thus we have no idea of what counts or could count toward establishing or disestablishing their truth.[7]

This is an astonishing reply, because under the guise of presenting a defense of verification that takes account of an important criticism, Nielsen merely restates the classical positivist position. If we restore the more traditional positivist term 'synthetic,' where Nielsen uses 'factual,' we find that he is presenting the positivist definitions of genuinely synthetic and pseudo-synthetic statements. He subsequently tries to deal with other criticisms that have been directed against this positivist position, but he fails to take account of the fresh departures initiated by Wesley Salmon that are discussed in Section Ten (see pp. 456–480).

[7] Kai Nielsen, *Reason and Practice*, p. 423; for an elaboration of his views on Moore, see pp. 465ff.

John Hick/**Theology and verification**

To ask "Is the existence of God verifiable?" is to pose a question which is too imprecise to be capable of being answered.[1] There are many different concepts of God, and it may be that statements employing some of them are open to verification or falsification

From "Theology and Verification," *Theology Today,* 17 (April 1960), 12–31, by John H. Hick. Reprinted by permission of *Theology Today* and the author.

[1] In this paper I assume that an indicative sentence expresses a factual assertion if and only if the state in which the universe would be if the putative assertion could correctly be said to be true differs in some experienceable way from the state in which the universe would be if the putative assertion could correctly be said to be false, all aspects of the universe other than that referred to in the putative assertion being the same in either case. This criterion acknowledges the important core of truth in the logical positivist verification principle. "Experienceable" in the above formulation means, in the case of alleged subjective or private facts (*e.g.,* pains, dreams, after-images, etc.), "experienceable by the subject in question" and, in the case of alleged objective or public facts, "capable in principle of being experienced by anyone." My contention is going to be that "God exists" asserts a matter of objective fact.

while statements employing others of them are not. Again, the
notion of verifying is itself by no means perfectly clear and fixed;
and it may be that on some views of the nature of verification the
existence of God is verifiable, whereas on other views it is not.

Instead of seeking to compile a list of the various different
concepts of God and the various possible senses of "verify," I wish
to argue with regard to one particular concept of deity, namely the
Christian concept, that divine existence is in principle verifiable;
and as the first stage of this argument I must indicate what I mean
by "verifiable."

I

The central core of the concept of verification, I suggest, is the
removal of ignorance or uncertainty concerning the truth of some
proposition. That p is verified (whether p embodies a theory,
hypothesis, prediction, or straightforward assertion) means that
something happens which makes it clear that p is true. A question
is settled so that there is no longer room for rational doubt concerning it. The way in which grounds for rational doubt are excluded varies, of course, with the subject matter. But the general
feature common to all cases of verification is the ascertaining of
truth by the removal of grounds for rational doubt. Where such
grounds are removed, we rightly speak of verification having taken
place.

To characterize verification in this way is to raise the question whether the notion of verification is purely logical or is both
logical and psychological. Is the statement that p is verified simply
the statement that a certain state of affairs exists (or has existed),
or is it the statement also that someone is aware that this state of
affairs exists (or has existed) and notes that its existence estab-
lishes the truth of p? A geologist predicts that the earth's surface
will be covered with ice in 15 million years time. Suppose that in
15 million years time the earth's surface *is* covered with ice, but
that in the meantime the human race has perished, so that no one
is left to observe the event or to draw any conclusion concerning
the accuracy of the geologist's prediction. Do we now wish to say
that his prediction has been verified, or shall we deny that it has
been verified, on the ground that there is no one left to do the
verifying?

The range of "verify" and its cognates is sufficiently wide to permit us to speak in either way. But the only sort of verification of theological propositions which is likely to interest us is one in which human beings participate. We may therefore, for our present purpose, treat verification as a logico-psychological rather than as a purely logical concept. I suggest, then, that "verify" be construed as a verb which has its primary uses in the active voice: I verify, you verify, we verify, they verify, or have verified. The impersonal passive, it is verified, now becomes logically secondary. To say that p has been verified is to say that (at least) someone has verified it, often with the implication that his or their report to this effect is generally accepted. But it is impossible, on this usage, for p to have been verified without someone having verified it. "Verification" is thus primarily the name for an event which takes place in human consciousness.[2] It refers to an experience, the experience of ascertaining that a given proposition or set of propositions is true. To this extent verification is a psychological notion. But of course it is also a logical notion. For needless to say, not any experience is rightly called an experience of verifying p. Both logical and psychological conditions must be fulfilled in order for verification to have taken place. In this respect, "verify" is like "know." Knowing is an experience which someone has or undergoes, or perhaps a dispositional state in which someone is, and it cannot take place without someone having or undergoing it or being in it; but not by any means every experience which people have, or every dispositional state in which they are, is rightly called knowing.

With regard to this logico-psychological concept of verification, such questions as the following arise. When A, but nobody else, has ascertained that p is true, can p be said to have been verified; or is it required that others also have undergone the same ascertainment? How public, in other words, must verification be? Is it necessary that p could in principle be verified by anyone, without restriction, even though perhaps only A has in fact verified it? If so, what is meant here by "in principle"; does it signify, for example, that p must be verifiable by anyone who performs a

[2] This suggestion is closely related to Carnap's insistence that, in contrast to "true," "confirmed" is time-dependent. To say that a statement is confirmed, or verified, is to say that it has been confirmed at a particular time—and, I would add, by a particular person. See Rudolf Carnap, "Truth and Confirmation," Feigl and Sellars, Readings in Philosophical Analysis, 1949, pp. 119f.

certain operation, and does it imply that to do this is within every-one's power?

These questions cannot, I believe, be given any general an-swer applicable to all instances of the exclusion of rational doubt. The answers must be derived in each case from an investigation of the particular subject matter. It will be the object of subsequent sections of this article to undertake such an investigation concern-ing the Christian concept of God.

Verification is often construed as the verification of a pre-diction. However, verification, as the exclusion of grounds for rational doubt, does not necessarily consist in the proving correct of a prediction; a verifying experience does not always need to have been predicted in order to have the effect of excluding ratio-nal doubt. But when we are interested in the verifiability of propo-sitions as the criterion for their having factual meaning, the notion of prediction becomes central. If a proposition contains or entails predictions which can be verified or falsified, its character as an assertion (though not of course its character as a true assertion) is thereby guaranteed.

Such predictions may be and often are conditional. For ex-ample, statements about the features of the dark side of the moon are rendered meaningful by the conditional predictions which they entail to the effect that if an observer comes to be in such a posi-tion in space, he will make such-and-such observations. It would in fact be more accurate to say that the prediction is always con-ditional, but that sometimes the conditions are so obvious and so likely to be fulfilled in any case that they require no special men-tion, while sometimes they require for their fulfillment some un-usual expedition or operation. A prediction, for example, that the sun will rise within twenty-four hours is intended unconditionally, at least as concerns conditions to be fulfilled by the observer; he is not required by the terms of the prediction to perform any special operation. Even in this case, however, there is an implied negative condition that he shall not put himself in a situation (such as im-muring himself in the depths of a coal mine) from which a sunrise would not be perceptible. Other predictions, however, are ex-plicitly conditional. In these cases it is true for any particular indi-vidual that in order to verify the statement in question he must go through some specified course of action. The prediction is to the effect that if you conduct such an experiment you will obtain such a result; for example, if you go into the next room you will have such-and-such visual experiences, and if you then touch the table which you see you will have such-and-such tactual experiences, and so on. The content of the "if" clause is of course always determined by the particular subject matter. The logic of "table" determines what you must do to verify statements about tables; the logic of "molecule" determines what you must do to verify statements about molecules; and the logic of "God" determines what you must do [to] verify statements about God.

In those cases in which the individual who is to verify a proposition must himself first perform some operation, it clearly cannot follow from the circumstances that the proposition is true that everybody has in fact verified it, or that everybody will at some future time verify it. For whether or not any particular person performs the requisite operation is a contingent matter.

II

What is the relation between verification and falsification? We are all familiar today with the phrase, "theology and falsification." A. G. N. Flew and others,[3] taking their cue from John Wisdom,[4] have raised instead of the question, "What possible experiences would verify 'God exists'?" the matching question, "What possible experiences would falsify 'God exists'? What conceivable state of affairs would be incompatible with the existence of God?" In posing the question in this way it was apparently assumed that verification and falsification are symmetrically related, and that the latter is apt to be the more accessible of the two.

In the most common cases, certainly, verification and falsification are symmetrically related. The logically simplest case of verification is provided by the crucial instance. Here it is integral to a given hypothesis that if, in specified circumstances, A occurs, the hypothesis is thereby shown to be true, whereas if B occurs the hypothesis is thereby shown to be false. Verification and falsification are also symmetrically related in the testing of such a

---

[3] A. G. N. Flew, editor, *New Essays in Philosophical Theology*, 1955, Chapter VI.

[4] "Gods," *Proceedings of the Aristotelian Society*, 1944–45. Reprinted in A. G. N. Flew, editor, *Logic and Language*, First Series, 1951, and in John Wisdom, *Philosophy and Psycho-Analysis*, 1953. [Reprinted in this volume beginning on pp. 158ff.—Editors]

proposition as "There is a table in the next room." The verifying experiences in this case are experiences of seeing and touching, predictions of which are entailed by the proposition in question, under the proviso that one goes into the next room; and the absence of such experiences in those circumstances serves to falsify the proposition.

But it would be rash to assume, on this basis, that verification and falsification must always be related in this symmetrical fashion. They do not necessarily stand to one another as do the two sides of a coin, so that once the coin is spun it must fall on one side or the other. There are cases in which verification and falsification each correspond to a side on a different coin, so that one can fail to verify without this failure constituting falsification.

Consider, for example, the proposition that "there are three successive sevens in the decimal determination of π." So far as the value of π has been worked out, it does not contain a series of three sevens, but it will always be true that such a series may occur at a point not yet reached in anyone's calculations. Accordingly, the proposition may one day be verified, if it is true, but can never be falsified, if it is false.

The hypothesis of continued conscious existence after bodily death provides an instance of a different kind of such asymmetry, and one which has a direct bearing upon the theistic problem. This hypothesis has built into it a prediction that one will after the date of one's bodily death have conscious experiences, including the experience of remembering that death. This is a prediction which will be verified in one's own experience if it is true, but which cannot be falsified if it is false. That is to say, it can be false, but *that* it is false can never be a fact which anyone has experientially verified. But this circumstance does not undermine the meaningfulness of the hypothesis, since it is also such that if it be true, it will be known to be true.

It is important to remember that we do not speak of verifying logically necessary truths, but only propositions concerning matters of fact. Accordingly verification is not to be identified with the concept of logical certification or proof. The exclusion of rational doubt concerning some matter of fact is not equivalent to the exclusion of the logical possibility of error or illusion. For truths concerning fact are not logically necessary. Their contrary is never self-contradictory. But at the same time the bare logical possibility of error does not constitute ground for rational doubt as to the veracity of our experience. If it did, no empirical proposition could ever be verified, and indeed the notion of empirical verification would be without use and therefore without sense. What we rightly seek, when we desire the verification of a factual proposition, is not a demonstration of the logical impossibility of the proposition being false (for this would be a self-contradictory demand), but such weight of evidence as suffices, in the type of case in question, to exclude rational doubt.

III

These features of the concept of verification—that verification consists in the exclusion of grounds for rational doubt concerning the truth of some proposition; that this means its exclusion from particular minds; that the nature of the experience which serves to exclude grounds for rational doubt depends upon the particular subject matter; that verification is often related to predictions and that such predictions are often conditional; that verification and falsification may be asymmetrically related; and finally, that the verification of a factual proposition is not equivalent to logical certification—are all relevant to the verification of the central religious claim, "God exists." I wish now to apply these discriminations to the notion of eschatological verification, which has been briefly employed by Ian Crombie in his contribution to *New Essays in Philosophical Theology*,[5] and by myself in *Faith and Knowledge*.[6] This suggestion has on each occasion been greeted with disapproval by both philosophers and theologians. I am, however, still of the opinion that the notion of eschatological verification is sound; and further, that no viable alternative to it has been offered to establish the factual character of theism.

The strength of the notion of eschatological verification is that it is not an *ad hoc* invention but is based upon an actually operative religious concept of God. In the language of Christian faith, the word "God" stands at the center of a system of terms, such as Spirit, grace, Logos, incarnation, Kingdom of God, and many more; and the distinctly Christian conception of God can

[5] *Op. cit.*, p. 126.
[6] Cornell University Press, 1957, pp. 150–162.

only be fully grasped in its connection with these related terms.[7] It belongs to a complex of notions which together constitute a picture of the universe in which we live, of man's place therein, of a comprehensive divine purpose interacting with human purposes, and of the general nature of the eventual fulfillment of that divine purpose. This Christian picture of the universe, entailing as it does certain distinctive expectations concerning the future, is a very different picture from any that can be accepted by one who does not believe that the God of the New Testament exists. Further, these differences are such as to show themselves in human experience. The possibility of experiential confirmation is thus built into the Christian concept of God; and the notion of eschatological verification seeks to relate this fact to the logical problem of meaning.

Let me first give a general indication of this suggestion, by repeating a parable which I have related elsewhere,[8] and then try to make it more precise and eligible for discussion. Here, first is the parable.

Two men are travelling together along a road. One of them believes that it leads to a Celestial City, the other that it leads nowhere; but since this is the only road there is, both must travel it. Neither has been this way before, and therefore neither is able to say what they will find around each next corner. During their journey they meet both with moments of refreshment and delight, and with moments of hardship and danger. All the time one of them thinks of his journey as a pilgrimage to the Celestial City and interprets the pleasant parts as encouragements and the obstacles as trials of his purpose and lessons in endurance, prepared by the king of that city and designed to make of him a worthy citizen of the place when at last he arrives there. The other, however, believes none of this and sees their journey as an unavoidable and aimless ramble. Since he has no choice in the matter, he enjoys the good and endures the bad. But for him there is no Celestial City to be reached, no all-encompassing purpose ordaining their jour-

[7] Its clear recognition of this fact, with regard not only to Christianity but to any religion, is one of the valuable features of Ninian Smart's *Reasons and Faiths* (1958). He remarks, for example, that "the claim that God exists can only be understood by reference to many, if not all, other propositions in the doctrinal scheme from which it is extrapolated" (p. 12).

[8] *Faith and Knowledge*, pp. 150f.

ney; only the road itself and the luck of the road in good weather and in bad.

During the course of the journey the issue between them is not an experimental one. They do not entertain different expectations about the coming details of the road, but only about its ultimate destination. And yet when they do turn the last corner it will be apparent that one of them has been right all the time and the other wrong. Thus although the issue between them has not been experimental, it has nevertheless from the start been a real issue. They have not merely felt differently about the road; for one was feeling appropriately and the other inappropriately in relation to the actual state of affairs. Their opposed interpretations of the road constituted genuinely rival assertions, though assertions whose assertion-status has the peculiar characteristic of being guaranteed retrospectively by a future crux.

This parable has of course (like all parables) strict limitations. It is designed to make only one point: that Christian doctrine postulates an ultimate unambiguous state of existence *in patria* as well as our present ambiguous existence *in via*. There is a state of having arrived as well as a state of journeying, an eternal heavenly life as well as an earthly pilgrimage. The alleged future experience of this state cannot, of course, be appealed to as evidence for theism as a present interpretation of our experience; but it does suffice to render the choice between theism and atheism a real and not a merely empty or verbal choice. And although this does not affect the logic of the situation, it should be added that the alternative interpretations are more than theoretical, for they render different practical plans and policies appropriate now.

The universe as envisaged by the theist, then, differs as a totality from the universe as envisaged by the atheist. This difference does not, however, from our present standpoint within the universe, involve a difference in the objective content of each or even any of its passing moments. The theist and the atheist do not (or need not) expect different events to occur in the successive details of the temporal process. They do not (or need not) entertain divergent expectations of the course of history viewed from within. But the theist does and the atheist does not expect that when history is completed it will be seen to have led to a particular end-state and to have fulfilled a specific purpose, namely that of creating "children of God."

The idea of an eschatological verification of theism can

make sense, however, only if the logically prior idea of continued personal existence after death is intelligible. A desultory debate on this topic has been going on for several years in some of the philosophical periodicals. C. I. Lewis has contended that the hypothesis of immortality "is an hypothesis about our own future experience. And our understanding of what would verify it has no lack of clarity."[9] And Morris Schlick agreed, adding, "We must conclude that immortality, in the sense defined [i.e. 'survival after death,' rather than 'never-ending life'], should not be regarded as a 'metaphysical problem,' but is an empirical hypothesis, because it possesses logical verifiability. It could be verified by following the prescription: 'Wait until you die!' "[10] However, others have challenged this conclusion, either on the ground that the phrase "surviving death" is self-contradictory in ordinary language or, more substantially, on the ground that the traditional distinction between soul and body cannot be sustained.[11] I should like to address myself to this latter view. The only self of which we know, it is said, is the empirical self, the walking, talking, acting, sleeping individual who lives, it may be, for some sixty to eighty years and then dies. Mental events and mental characteristics are analyzed into the modes of behavior and behavioral dispositions of this empirical self. The human being is described as an organism capable of acting in the "high-level" ways which we characterize as intelligent, thoughtful, humorous, calculating, and the like. The concept of mind or soul is thus not the concept of a "ghost in the machine" (to use Gilbert Ryle's loaded phrase[12]), but of the more flexible and sophisticated ways in which human beings behave and have it in them to behave. On this view there is no room for the notion of soul in distinction from body; and if there is no soul in distinction from body, there can be no question of the soul surviving the death of the body. Against this philosophical background the specifically Christian (and also Jewish) belief in the resurrection of the flesh, or body, in contrast to the Hellenic notion of the survival of a disembodied soul, might be expected to have at-

[9] "Experience and Meaning," *Philosophical Review*, 1934, reprinted in Feigl and Sellars, *Readings in Philosophical Analysis*, 1949, p. 142.
[10] "Meaning and Verification," *Philosophical Review*, 1936, reprinted in Feigl and Sellars, *op. cit.*, p. 160.
[11] E.g. A. G. N. Flew, "Death," *New Essays in Philosophical Theology*; "Can a Man Witness his own Funeral?" *Hibbert Journal*, 1956.
[12] *The Concept of Mind*, 1949, which contains an important exposition of the interpretation of "mental" qualities as characteristics of behavior.

tracted more attention than it has. For it is consonant with the conception of man as an indissoluble psycho-physical unity, and yet it also offers the possibility of an empirical meaning for the idea of "life after death."

Paul is the chief Biblical expositor of the idea of the resurrection of the body.[13] His view, as I understand it, is this. When someone has died he is, apart from any special divine action, extinct. A human being is by nature mortal and subject to annihilation by death. But in fact God, by an act of sovereign power, either sometimes or always resurrects or (better) reconstitutes or recreates him—not, however, as the identical physical organism that he was before death, but as a *soma pneumatikon*, ("spiritual body") embodying the dispositional characteristics and memory traces of the deceased physical organism, and inhabiting an environment with which the *soma pneumatikon* is continuous as the *ante-mortem* body was continuous with our present world. In discussing this notion we may well abandon the word "spiritual," as lacking today any precise established usage, and speak of "resurrection bodies" and of "the resurrection world." The principal questions to be asked concern the relation between the physical world and the resurrection world, and the criteria of personal identity which are operating when it is alleged that a certain inhabitant of the resurrection world is the same person as an individual who once inhabited this world. The first of these questions turns out on investigation to be the more difficult of the two, and I shall take the easier one first.

Let me sketch a very odd possibility (concerning which, however, I wish to emphasize not so much its oddness as its possibility!), and then see how far it can be stretched in the direction of the notion of the resurrection body. In the process of stretching it will become even more odd than it was before; but my aim will be to show that, however odd, it remains within the bounds of the logically possible. This progression will be presented in three pictures, arranged in a self-explanatory order.

First picture: Suppose that at some learned gathering in this country one of the company were suddenly and inexplicably to disappear, and that at the same moment an exact replica of him were suddenly and inexplicably to appear at some comparable meeting in Australia. The person who appears in Australia is ex-

13 I Cor. 15.

actly similar, as to both bodily and mental characteristics, with the person who disappears in America. There is continuity of memory, complete similarity of bodily features, including even fingerprints, hair and eye coloration and stomach contents, and also of beliefs, habits, and mental propensities. In fact there is everything that would lead us to identify the one who appeared with the one who disappeared, except continuity of occupancy of space. We may suppose, for example, that a deputation of the colleagues of the man who disappeared fly to Australia to interview the replica of him which is reported there, and find that he is in all respects but one exactly as though he had travelled from say, Princeton to Melbourne, by conventional means. The only difference is that he describes how, as he was sitting listening to Dr. Z reading a paper, on blinking his eyes he suddenly found himself sitting in a different room listening to a different paper by an Australian scholar. He asks his colleagues how the meeting had gone after he ceased to be there, and what they had made of his disappearance, and so on. He clearly thinks of himself as the one who was present with them at their meeting in the United States. I suggest that faced with all these circumstances his colleagues would soon, if not immediately, find themselves thinking of him and treating him as the individual who had so inexplicably disappeared from their midst. We should be extending our normal use of "same person" in a way which the postulated facts would both demand and justify if we said that the one who appears in Australia is the same person as the one who disappears in America. The factors inclining us to identify them would far outweigh the factors disinclining us to do this. We should have no reasonable alternative but to extend our usage of "the same person" to cover the strange new case.

Second picture: Now let us suppose that the event in America is not a sudden and inexplicable disappearance, and indeed not a disappearance at all, but a sudden death. Only, at the moment when the individual dies, a replica of him as he was at the moment before his death, complete with memory up to that instant, appears in Australia. Even with the corpse on our hands, it would still, I suggest, be an extension of "same person" required and warranted by the postulated facts, to say that the same person who died has been miraculously recreated in Australia. The case would be considerably odder than in the previous picture, because of the existence of the corpse in America contemporaneously with the existence of the living person in Australia. But I submit that, although the oddness of this circumstance may be stated as strongly as you please, and can indeed hardly be overstated, yet it does not exceed the bounds of the logically possible. Once again we must imagine some of the deceased's colleagues going to Australia to interview the person who has suddenly appeared there. He would perfectly remember them and their meeting, be interested in what had happened, and be as amazed and dumbfounded about it as anyone else; and he would perhaps be worried about the possible legal complications if he should return to America to claim his property; and so on. Once again, I believe, they would soon find themselves thinking of him and treating him as the same person as the dead Princetonian. Once again the factors inclining us to say that the one who died and the one who appeared are the same person would outweigh the factors inclining us to say that they are different people. Once again we should have to extend our usage of "the same person" to cover this new case.

Third picture: My third supposal is that the replica, complete with memory, etc. appears, not in Australia, but as a resurrection replica in a different world altogether, a resurrection world inhabited by resurrected persons. This world occupies its own space, distinct from the space with which we are now familiar. That is to say, an object in the resurrection world is not situated at any distance or in any direction from an object in our present world, although each object in either world is spatially related to each other object in the same world.

Mr. X, then, dies. A Mr. X replica, complete with the set of memory traces which Mr. X had at the last moment before his death, comes into existence. It is composed of other material than physical matter, and is located in a resurrection world which does not stand in any spatial relationship with the physical world. Let us leave out of consideration St. Paul's hint that the resurrection body may be as unlike the physical body as is a full grain of wheat from the wheat seed, and consider the simpler picture in which the resurrection body has the same shape as the physical body.[14]

In these circumstances, how does Mr. X know that he has been resurrected or recreated? He remembers dying; or rather he remembers being on what he took to be his death-bed, and becoming progressively weaker until, presumably, he lost consciousness.

[14] As would seem to be assumed, for example, by Irenaeus (*Adversus Haereses*, Bk. II, Ch. 34, Sec. 1).

But how does he know that (to put it Irishly) his "dying" proved fatal; and that he did not, after losing consciousness, begin to recover strength, and has now simply waked up?

The picture is readily enough elaborated to answer this question. Mr. X meets and recognizes a number of relatives and friends and historical personages whom he knows to have died; and from the fact of their presence, and also from their testimony that he has only just now appeared in their world, he is convinced that he has died. Evidences of this kind could mount up to the point at which they are quite as strong as the evidence which, in pictures one and two, convince the individual in question that he has been miraculously translated to Australia. Resurrected persons would be individually no more in doubt about their own identity than we are now, and would be able to identify one another in the same kinds of ways, and with a like degree of assurance, as we do now.

If it be granted that resurrected persons might be able to arrive at a rationally founded conviction that their existence is *post-mortem*, how could they know that the world in which they find themselves is in a different space from that in which their physical bodies were? How could such a one know that he is not in a like situation with the person in picture number two, who dies in America and appears as a full-blooded replica in Australia, leaving his corpse in the U. S. A.—except that now the replica is situated, not in Australia, but on a planet of some other star?

It is of course conceivable that the space of the resurrection world should have properties which are manifestly incompatible with its being a region of physical space. But on the other hand, it is not of the essence of the notion of a resurrection world that its space should have properties different from those of physical space. And supposing it not to have different properties, it is not evident that a resurrected individual could learn from any direct observations that he was not on a planet of some sun which is at so great a distance from our own sun that the stellar scenery visible from it is quite unlike that which we can now see. The grounds that a resurrected person would have for believing that he is in a different space from physical space (supposing there to be no discernible difference in spatial properties) would be the same as the grounds that any of us may have now for believing this concerning resurrected individuals. These grounds are indirect and consist in all those considerations (e.g., Luke 16: 26) which lead most of those who consider the question to reject as absurd the possibility of, for example, radio communication or rocket travel between earth and heaven.

V

In the present context my only concern is to claim that this doctrine of the divine creation of bodies, composed of a material other than that of physical matter, which bodies are endowed with sufficient correspondence of characteristics with our present bodies, and sufficient continuity of memory with our present consciousness, for us to speak of the same person being raised up again to life in a new environment, is not self-contradictory. If, then, it cannot be ruled out *ab initio* as meaningless, we may go on to consider whether and how it is related to the possible verification of Christian theism.

So far I have argued that a survival prediction such as is contained in the *corpus* of Christian belief is in principle subject to future verification. But this does not take the argument by any means as far as it must go if it is to succeed. For survival, simply as such, would not serve to verify theism. It would not necessarily be a state of affairs which is manifestly incompatible with the non-existence of God. It might be taken just as a surprising natural fact. The atheist, in his resurrection body, and able to remember his life on earth, might say that the universe has turned out to be more complex, and perhaps more to be approved of, than he had realized. But the mere fact of survival, with a new body in a new environment, would not demonstrate to him that there is a God. It is fully compatible with the notion of survival that the life to come be, so far as the theistic problem is concerned, essentially a continuation of the present life, and religiously no less ambiguous. And in this event, survival after bodily death would not in the least constitute a final verification of theistic faith.

I shall not spend time in trying to draw a picture of a resurrection existence which would merely prolong the religious ambiguity of our present life. The important question, for our purpose, is not whether one can conceive of after-life experiences which would *not* verify theism (and in point of fact one can fairly easily conceive them), but whether one can conceive of after-life experiences which *would* serve to verify theism.

I think that we can. In trying to do so I shall not appeal to the traditional doctrine, which figures especially in Catholic and mystical theology, of the Beatific Vision of God. The difficulty presented by this doctrine is not so much that of deciding whether there are grounds for believing it, as of deciding what it means. I shall not, however, elaborate this difficulty, but pass directly to the investigation of a different and, as it seems to me, more intelligible possibility. This is the possibility not of a direct vision of God, whatever that might mean, but of a *situation* which points unambiguously to the existence of a loving God. This would be a situation which, so far as its religious significance is concerned, contrasts in a certain important respect with our present situation. Our present situation is one which in some ways seems to confirm and in other ways to contradict the truth of theism. Some events around us suggest the presence of an unseen benevolent intelligence and others suggest that no such intelligence is at work. Our situation is religiously ambiguous. But in order for us to be aware of this fact we must already have some idea, however vague, of what it would be for our situation to be not ambiguous, but on the contrary wholly evidential of God. I therefore want to try to make clearer this presupposed concept of a religiously unambiguous situation.

There are, I suggest, two possible developments of our experience such that, if they occurred in conjunction with one another (whether in this life or in another life to come), they would assure us beyond rational doubt of the reality of God, as conceived in the Christian faith. These are, *first*, an experience of the fulfillment of God's purpose for ourselves, as this has been disclosed in the Christian revelation; in conjunction, *second*, with an experience of communion with God as he has revealed himself in the person of Christ.

The divine purpose for human life, as this is depicted in the New Testament documents, is the bringing of the human person, in society with his fellows, to enjoy a certain valuable quality of personal life, the content of which is given in the character of Christ—which quality of life (i.e. life in relationship with God, described in the Fourth Gospel as eternal life) is said to be the proper destiny of human nature and the source of man's final self-

fulfillment and happiness. The verification situation with regard
to such a fulfillment is asymmetrical. On the one hand, so long as
the divine purpose remains unfulfilled, we cannot know that it
never will be fulfilled in the future; hence no final falsification is
possible of the claim that this fulfillment will occur—unless, of
course, the prediction contains a specific time clause which, in
Christian teaching, it does not. But on the other hand, if and when
the divine purpose *is* fulfilled in our own experience, we must be
able to recognize and rejoice in that fulfillment. For the fulfillment
would not be for us the promised fulfillment without our own
conscious participation in it.

It is important to note that one can say this much without
being cognizant in advance of the concrete form which such fulfillment will take. The before-and-after situation is analogous to that
of a small child looking forward to adult life and then, having
grown to adulthood, looking back upon childhood. The child possesses and can use correctly in various contexts the concept of
"being grown-up," although he does not know, concretely, what it
is like to be grown-up. But when he reaches adulthood he is nevertheless able to know that he has reached it; he is able to recognize
the experience of living a grown-up life even though he did not
know in advance just what to expect. For his understanding of
adult maturity grows as he himself matures. Something similar
may be supposed to happen in the case of the fulfillment of the
divine purpose for human life. That fulfillment may be as far removed from our present condition as is mature adulthood from
the mind of a little child; nevertheless, we possess already a comparatively vague notion of this final fulfillment, and as we move
towards it our concept will itself become more adequate; and if
and when we finally reach that fulfillment, the problem of recognizing it will have disappeared in the process.

The other feature that must, I suggest, be present in a state
of affairs that would verify theism, is that the fulfillment of God's
purpose be apprehended *as* the fulfillment of God's purpose and
not simply as a natural state of affairs. To this end it must be ac-
companied by an experience of communion with God as he has
made himself known to men in Christ.

The specifically Christian clause, "as he has made himself
known to men in Christ," is essential, for it provides a solution to
the problem of recognition in the awareness of God. Several writ-

ers have pointed out the logical difficulty involved in any claim to have encountered God.[15] How could one know that it was *God* whom one had encountered? God is described in Christian theology in terms of various absolute qualities, such as omnipotence, omnipresence, perfect goodness, infinite love, etc., which cannot as such be observed by us, as can their finite analogues, limited power, local presence, finite goodness, and human love. One can recognize that a being whom one "encounters" has a given finite degree of power, but how does one recognize that he has unlimited power? How does one observe that an encountered being is *omni-present*? How does one perceive that his goodness and love, which one can perhaps see to exceed any human goodness and love, are actually infinite? Such qualities cannot be given in human experience. One might claim, then, to have encountered a Being whom one presumes, or trusts, or hopes to be God; but one cannot claim to have encountered a Being whom one recognized to be the infinite, almighty, eternal Creator.

This difficulty is met in Christianity by the doctrine of the Incarnation—although this was not among the considerations which led to the formulation of that doctrine. The idea of incarnation provides answers to the two related questions: "How do we know that God has certain absolute qualities which, by their very nature, transcend human experience?" and "How can there be an eschatological verification of theism which is based upon a recognition of the presence of God in his Kingdom?"

In Christianity God is known as "the God and Father of our Lord Jesus Christ."[16] God is the Being about whom Jesus taught; the Being in relation to whom Jesus lived, and into a relationship with whom he brought his disciples; the Being whose *agape* toward men was seen on earth in the life of Jesus. In short, God is the transcendent Creator who has revealed himself in Christ. Now Jesus teaching about the Father is a part of that self-disclosure, and it is from this teaching (together with that of the prophets who preceded him) that the Christian knowledge of God's transcendent being is derived. Only God himself knows his own infinite nature; and our human belief about that nature is based upon his self-revelation to men in Christ. As Karl Barth expresses it, "Jesus

---

[15] For example, H. W. Hepburn, *Christianity and Paradox*, 1958, pp. 56f.
[16] II Cor. 11:31.

Christ is the knowability of God."[17] Our beliefs about God's infinite being are not capable of observational verification, being beyond the scope of human experience, but they are susceptible of indirect verification by the removal of rational doubt concerning the authority of Christ. An experience of the reign of the Son in the Kingdom of the Father would confirm that authority, and therewith, indirectly, the validity of Jesus' teaching concerning the character of God in his infinite transcendent nature.

The further question as to how an eschatological experience of the Kingdom of God could be known to be such has already been answered by implication. It is God's union with man in Christ that makes possible man's recognition of the fulfillment of God's purpose for man as being indeed the fulfillment of *God's* purpose for him. The presence of Christ in his Kingdom marks this as being beyond doubt the Kingdom of the God and Father of the Lord Jesus Christ.

It is true that even the experience of the realization of the promised Kingdom of God, with Christ reigning as Lord of the New Aeon, would not constitute a logical certification of his claims nor, accordingly, of the reality of God. But this will not seem remarkable to any philosopher in the empiricist tradition, who knows that it is only a confusion to demand that a factual proposition be an analytic truth. A set of expectations based upon faith in the historic Jesus as the incarnation of God, and in his teaching as being divinely authoritative, could be so fully confirmed in *post-mortem* experience as to leave no grounds for rational doubt as to the validity of that faith.

VI

There remains of course the problem (which falls to the New Testament scholar rather than to the philosopher) whether Christian tradition, and in particular the New Testament, provides a sufficiently authentic "picture" of the mind and ·character of Christ to make such recognition possible. I cannot here attempt to enter into the vast field of Biblical criticism, and shall confine myself to the logical point, which only emphasizes the importance of the historical question, that a verification of theism made possible by the Incarnation is dependent upon the Christian's having a genuine

---

[17] *Church Dogmatics*, Vol. II, Pt. I, p. 150.

contact with the person of Christ, even though this is mediated through the life and tradition of the Church.

One further point remains to be considered. When we ask the question, *"To whom* is theism verified?" one is initially inclined to assume that the answer must be, "To everyone." We are inclined to assume that, as in my parable of the journey, the believer must be confirmed in his belief, and the unbeliever converted from his unbelief. But this assumption is neither demanded by the nature of verification nor by any means unequivocally supported by our Christian sources.

We have already noted that a verifiable prediction may be conditional. "There is a table in the next room" entails conditional predictions of the form: if someone goes into the next room he will see, etc. But no one is compelled to go into the next room. Now it may be that the predictions concerning human experience which are entailed by the proposition that God exists are conditional predictions and that no one is compelled to fulfill those conditions. Indeed we stress in much of our theology that the manner of the divine self-disclosure to men is such that our human status as free and responsible beings is respected, and an awareness of God never is forced upon us. It may then be a condition of *post-mortem* verification that we be already in some degree conscious of God by an uncompelled response to his modes of revelation in this world. It may be that such a voluntary consciousness of God is an essential element in the fulfillment of the divine purpose for human nature, so that the verification of theism which consists in an experience of the final fulfillment of that purpose can only be experienced by those who have already entered upon an awareness of God by the religious mode of apperception which we call faith.

If this be so, it has the consequence that only the theistic believer can find the vindication of his belief. This circumstance would not of course set any restriction upon who can become a believer, but it would involve that while theistic faith can be verified—found by one who holds it to be beyond rational doubt— yet it cannot be proved to the nonbeliever. Such an asymmetry would connect with that strain of New Testament teaching which speaks of a division of mankind even in the world to come.

Having noted this possibility I will only express my personal opinion that the logic of the New Testament as a whole, though admittedly not always its explicit content, leads to a belief in ultimate universal salvation. However, my concern here is not to seek to establish the religious facts, but rather to establish that there are such things as religious facts, and in particular that the existence or non-existence of the God of the New Testament is a matter of fact, and claims as such eventual experiential verification.

Kai Nielsen/Eschatological verification

Professor John Hick, in carrying on a discussion initiated by Professors Wisdom and Flew, argues that (1) divine experience, as it is understood in the New Testament, is taken to be a matter of objective fact, and (2) statements which assert that existence are empirically verifiable.[1] Hick does not try to show that "God exists" is true and that Christian claims have been established; rather, in "Theology and Verification" he is concerned with the *logically* prior question of whether it is *intelligible* to claim that divine existence is a fact.

I shall argue that Hick has not at all succeeded in establishing what he has set out to establish and that we have no good reasons for believing that such crucial theistic utterances are used

---

From "Eschatological Verification," *Canadian Journal of Theology*, 9 (1963), 271–281, by Kai Nielsen. Reprinted with the permission of the *Canadian Journal of Theology* and the author.
[1] John Hick, "Theology and Verification," *Theology Today*, 17 (1960), 12–31. [This article is reprinted in this volume beginning on p. 188.—Editors]

to make statements of fact that are either verifiable or confirmable in principle. (Although I cannot accept Hick's central claims, I should like to record that it is a pleasure to read and evaluate critically Hick's writings, for he writes with a clarity and forthrightness of statement that allows his arguments to be appraised readily. The turgid obscurity typical of Tillich, Bultmann, Niebuhr, Buber, and Maritain may give some the illusory sense that they have grasped the esoteric "essence" of religion, but such a manner of writing does not actually contribute to an understanding of religion or to an appraisal of the claims of religion. There is enduring intellectual value in writing so that one's claims can be understood and appraised.)

I

Recognizing that the central intellectual perplexity for enlightened contemporary theists is not the difficulty of proving theistic claims but the difficulty of establishing their intelligibility, Hick's primary concern is to refute claims that religious sentences have uses which are *merely* mythical, quasi-moral, ceremonial, emotive, or ideological, and to establish that they characteristically are used to make factual statements—that is, that such sentences as "God exists" or "The world was created by an act of God" typically function to make assertions of "supernatural fact."

It is Hick's contention that "divine existence is in principle verifiable" (p. 189). For a statement to have *factual meaning* it must, Hick argues, contain or entail "predictions which can be verified or falsified" (p. 191). Hick does not contend that God's existence can be *falsified* but, contending that verification and falsification are in this context asymmetrically related, Hick argues that God's existence can in principle be verified. He does not claim that the verification can come in this life. The verification is eschatological; it will come, if at all, in the next life. It need not necessarily come as a "vision" but may be an experience of the fulfilment of God's purpose for ourselves, as it has been given to us in Christian revelation, in conjunction with "an experience of communion with God as he has revealed himself in the person of Christ" (p. 203).

Hick claims in "Theology and Verification," as he did in

Faith and Knowledge,[2] that the notion of "eschatological verification is sound; and further, that no viable alternative to it has been offered to establish the factual character of theism" (p. 194). He also claims that it is not "an *ad hoc* invention but is based upon an actually operative religious concept of God" (p. 194).

It is important to note how Hick's insistence that the verification must be eschatological allows him to come to terms with Wisdom's argument that the existence of God is not *now* an experimental issue. Hick contends, in opposition to Wisdom, that the sophisticated Christian does not merely have different feelings or attitudes about the world and man's place in it. He does not view life in just a different way; that is, his difference with the atheist is not the same as that which exists where two people see the same ambiguous figure in two different ways (e.g. the duck-rabbit, seen as either a duck or a rabbit). The Christian's and the atheist's "opposed interpretations" of man's life and the nature of reality are "genuinely rival assertions, though assertions whose assertion-status has the peculiar characteristic of being guaranteed retrospectively by a future crux" (p. 196). There is then a real factual issue between the atheist and theist; it is not just a matter of rival ways of "seeing," "viewing," or "looking" at man's nature and destiny. But Hick does agree with Wisdom that in *this life* we are like men looking at an ambiguous figure. We cannot now settle by any appeal to experience the issue between the theist and atheist. There are no signs that can unambiguously count as pointing to God; there is no *present* evidence adequate to make it meaningful to assert "There is a God" where this sentence is used to make a statement of objective fact; but "Christian doctrine postulates an ultimate unambiguous state of existence in *patria* as well as our present ambiguous existence in *via*" (p. 196). But Hick makes it perfectly clear that this postulated state of an "eternal heavenly life as well as an earthly pilgrimage" cannot "be appealed to as evidence for theism as a present interpretation of our experience . . ." (p. 196). If we simply regard our experiences in this life they are too ambiguous to allow us correctly to claim that theism is a verifiable position. If we so limit our appeal, a claim such as Wisdom's is quite compelling. But, Hick argues, we do not need so to limit it. We can *conceive* what it would be like to have an

---

[2] Ithaca: Cornell University Press, 1957.

after-life and we can *conceive* what it would be like to verify that there is a God in the "resurrection world" of the next life. Thus, while we cannot possibly have any present evidence for or against theism, and must now live by faith if we are to believe, we can *conceive* what it would be like to have evidence in the next life; and so the existence of God is, after all, a factual issue and "the choice between theism and atheism is a real and not a merely empty or verbal choice" (p. 196).

It seems to me that Hick is correct in affirming that any reasonably orthodox Christian—I do not speak of Tillichians— would surely wish to regard the question of divine existence as a factual, substantive issue. If an orthodox Christian discovered that he and the atheists were *only* differing in picture preferences, he would then assert that the very foundations of Christianity had been destroyed. Religious talk is certainly embedded in myth and overlaid with ceremonial expressions; and it most certainly guides our behaviour and calls for a basic alteration of our attitudes; but, as Hick recognizes, certain key religious statements are also thought by believers to be factual assertions. If utterances such as "There exists a creator of the heavens and the earth" are not taken by believers to be factual assertions—myth-embedded as they are—theistic religious talk and hence Christianity itself would lose the character it has. If our task is to understand Christianity and not simply to redefine it to fit some antecedently held intellectual or moral ideal, we must come to grips with this assertional element in Christianity. Hick has courageously and honestly attempted to do just that. Like Barth and Crombie, and unlike Tillich and Braithwaite, Hick attempts to elucidate the Christian religion that we actually meet, and in one way or another contend with, in daily life; we sense here that Hick is actually trying to analyse the claims the Christian ordinarily makes. And this, to my way of thinking, is just what we must do if we ever are to get anywhere in an understanding of religion. I am not saying that this is all that either a theologian or a philosopher needs to do, but he at least must do this. Perhaps in that way he will make Christianity or Judaism sound very absurd; but perhaps they are absurd. (We must not forget Kierkegaard here.)

While I am in complete agreement with Hick on this methodological issue, Hick fails, in my judgment, to make the basic claims of Christianity intelligible on the very grounds on which he rightly recognizes that the believer demands they should be intelligible. Hick's arguments are clear and straightforward until he gets to the very crux of his argument and then they become incoherent. Hick recognizes the difficulty of trying to speak to God and he argues that language is never quite adequate to state the facts of which religious people are aware. He speaks as if thought could speed ahead of language and, independently of the forms of language, grasp what is the case. It is natural to want to say this, but can we really "escape language" in this way? Is it really an intelligible claim?[3] Given such complications, it seems to me apparent that we are in real darkness as to whether "there are such things as religious facts" (p. 208). It seems to me that the more plausible conclusion, given such a situation, would be that religious discourse itself is in conceptual confusion (and not just the theological and philosophical accounts of it).[4] This, of course, would be welcome news to the secularist and most unwelcome news to all but the most rabidly Kierkegaardian defenders of the faith. Thus it is understandable that theologians such as Hick, Farrer, and Crombie should try to make an intelligible elucidation of religious concepts. I shall not attempt here to show that religious discourse itself is in a state of conceptual confusion, but merely try to show that Hick's account of such discourse is not successful. But if my analysis is correct, the following problem, relevant to the wider issue mentioned above, is suggested. If Hick utterly fails to establish how "There is a God" is in any way verifiable and if Hick is right (as I think he is) in his claim that statements asserting divine existence typically are intended to be factual, verifiable claims, then, given the care and the skill with which he has stated the arguments pro and con, would it not be reasonable to assume there is something wrong with our first-order God-talk itself? If it can be shown, as I think it can, that the analyses of Crombie, Farrer, and Mascall result in similar failures, does not the assumption of the incoherent quality of the discourse itself grow stronger? It seems to me that this issue needs

[3] I shall not pursue this question here, but a study of the work of Peirce or Wittgenstein raises serious questions about the very possibility of thoughts that have no linguistic expression. For brief and more readily accessible analyses that bring out some of the crucial difficulties, see Alice Ambrose, "The Problem of Linguistic Inadequacy," in Max Black (ed.), *Philosophical Analysis* (Ithaca: Cornell University Press, 1950), pp. 15–37, and William Kennick, "Art and the Ineffable," *Journal of Philosophy*, 58 (1951), 309–20.

[4] I have tried to show how this is so in an article, "Speaking of God," *Theoria*, 28 (1962), 110–37.

to be faced by theologians in a way in which it has not yet been faced.[5]

The above assumes that Hick's arguments will not do. I have yet to establish this. But it should make apparent the importance for the Christian of making out a case somewhere along the lines that Hick attempts.

II

In making out his case for eschatological verification, Hick argues that it is intelligible to say that there is a continued existence after death. Hick is perfectly aware that we cannot take such a claim as simply a noble myth, but that it must be regarded as an empirical assertion if his case for eschatological verification is to be made out. As Hick himself recognizes, the truth of such a claim is not sufficient for his case, but without it eschatological verification is unintelligible (pp. 196 ff.).

Hick does not argue for what he takes to be the "Hellenic notion of the survival of a disembodied soul" (p. 197) but for "the specifically Christian (and also Jewish) belief in the resurrection of the flesh or body." God "by an act of sovereign power . . . resurrects or (better) reconstitutes or recreates" at least some human beings, giving them a "resurrection body" in "the resurrection world." The relation of the "resurrection body" to the "resurrection world" is obscure and puzzling, to put it conservatively. Hick readily acknowledges that such conceptions are very odd, but, however odd, they are (he avers) intelligible empirical claims. (Even *assuming* their *intelligibility*, I should think their very oddness and extreme implausibility would be a very good reason for those who tie their belief in God to such notions to give up their belief and place a belief in God in the same class with a belief in Santa Claus or in the Easter Bunny.) I doubt very much that either conception is intelligible. After all, what is this "resurrection world"? What counts as a space that is "a different space" from physical space? Has any meaning or use been given to the words "non-physical space"? What are we supposed to be contrasting with physical space, that either has or fails to have "properties

[5] This issue is obviously evaded in J. N. Hartt's obscure survey of the state and prospects of contemporary theology, "The Theological Situation after Fifty Years," *Yale Review*, 51 (1961), 84f.

which are manifestly incompatible with its being a region of physical space"? What is it to have a property manifestly incompatible with being a region in physical space? There is the assumption that these words have a use or a sense, but they do not and Hick does not provide us with one. But I wish to bypass all these questions here. For the sake of the discussion, I shall not only grant Hick that all these notions are meaningful as empirical statements but I shall also grant that they are true.

The survival of a "resurrection body" in a "resurrection world" is only a necessary but not a sufficient condition for the verifiability of theism. Hick puts it this way:... "survival, simply as such, would not serve to verify theism. It would not necessarily be a state of affairs which is manifestly incompatible with the non-existence of God. It might be taken just as a surprising natural fact" (p. 202). Hick must now show how it can be the case that when our "resurrection body" gets to "the resurrection world" we shall then come to know God.

In trying to complete his case for eschatological verification, Hick attempts to show that one can "conceive of after-life experiences which *would* serve to verify theism" (p. 203). He is looking for a conceivable *situation* "which points unambiguously to the existence of a loving God" (p. 203). Hick suggests that there are "two possible developments of our experience such that, if they occurred in conjunction with one another, . . . they would assure us beyond rational doubt of the reality of God, as conceived in the Christian faith" (p. 203). As we have seen, they are (1) an experience of God's purpose for ourselves as it has been disclosed in Christian revelation, and (2) "an experience of communion with God as he has revealed himself in the person of Christ" (p. 203).

The initial difficulty we feel about (1) and (2) is that they seem to presuppose some understanding of that very thing we are trying to understand. But let us see what Hick tries to do with these claims. He starts by telling us (a) that the content of (1) is "depicted in the New Testament documents" and (b) that these documents indicate (at least to the believer) that to experience the "divine purpose for human life" is "to enjoy a certain valuable quality of personal life, the content of which is given in the character of Christ . . ." (p. 203). This experienced "quality" is "said to be the proper destiny of human nature and the source of man's final self-fulfillment and happiness" (pp. 203 f.). That there is such a divine purpose cannot be falsified but it can be verified.

(I am troubled about the claim that something can be verified but not falsified, but for the sake of the argument I shall let Hick's claim here pass unexamined.) But how is Hick's claim here even verifiable in principle, without the *assumption* of God—a divine Creator? We are trying to come to understand how "There is a God" or "God created man" could have a factual meaning, but Hick's analysis requires us to presuppose the very thing we are trying to understand, for to speak of "the proper *destiny* of human nature" or of "man's *final* self-fulfilment" *assumes* that man is a creature of God, a divine artefact created by God with a purpose— an "essential human nature" that can be realized. Without such an *assumption*, talk of man's proper destiny or final self-fulfilment is without sense. Hick is asking us to pull ourselves up by our own bootstraps, for unless we understand what it is for there to be a God who created man with a purpose we can make nothing at all of (1).

I add "nothing at all" deliberately, for the believer's understanding of "God exists" or "God loves us" is not—as Hick claims —sufficiently analogous to a child's understanding of what it is to be an adult. Hick's analogy is faulty because the child, as soon as he can recognize anything at all, sees adults around him and is constantly in their presence, but Hick has not shown us how we can have a like idea of what "the divine purpose for us is" or what we mean by "God." We indeed know that these words have great emotional appeal for us, and we know that they would not have that appeal if religious discourse were treated simply as (*a*) a species of ceremonial discourse, (*b*) moral discourse touched with emotion, or (*c*) expressions of human commitment embedded in a mythical framework. Beyond this, we know that there are certain analytic statements we can make about "God" (e.g. "God is eternal" and the like). But what we do not know is what it would be like to verify "There is divine existence." We have no idea at all of what it would be like for that statement to be either true or false. Here the believer is in a much worse position than the child. And, as we have seen, to appeal to the divine purpose for man assumes we already know what it would be like to verify that our lives have such a purpose. We do not know what must be the case for it to be true or false that our lives have a purpose, a *telos*, a destiny or final fulfilment. Our actions may be purposive and we may so live that there is some purpose in our lives without its even being intelligible that human life has a purpose or some final end.[6] We do not understand how to break into this closed circle with either God or man's destiny or a Christian revelation of our "essential human nature." It is indeed true that we, who have been brought up as Christians or in close proximity to Christians, know how to use this discourse. In *that sense* it is sheer nonsense to say Christian chatter is meaningless, but Hick has not shown us how we understand this use of language as a factual or statement-making type of discourse. We do not know what must happen for us to assert correctly that so and so is "apprehended *as* the fulfillment of God's purpose and not simply as a natural state of affairs" (p. 204).

Can (2) help? I think we are no better off here. (2) is the "experience of communion with God as he has revealed himself in the person of Christ" (p. 203). Hick acknowledges that we do not know what it would be like to encounter directly an infinite, almighty, eternal Creator. But Jesus, or Christ, comes in as the mediator. "Only God himself knows his own infinite nature; and our human belief about that nature is based upon his self-revelation to men in Christ" (p. 205). Hick quotes with approval Barth's contention that "Jesus Christ is the knowability of God" (pp. 205 ff.).

There is—as R. W. Hepburn has stressed in his *Christianity and Paradox*[7]—an ambiguity in this sort of claim. "Jesus was born in Bethlehem" or "Jesus died on the cross" are straightforward empirical statements. There is no puzzle at all about their logical status. Where "Jesus" and "Christ" are equivalent we can of course make substitutions and the resulting statements will also be uncontroversial. But "Jesus" and "Christ" are not equivalent, for "Jesus is the Christ" is supposed to be informative. "Christ" or "The Christ" is not intended simply to refer to a man—no matter how extraordinary. "Jesus," by contrast, simply refers to an extraordinary man. We well enough understand the referent of "Jesus," but where "Christ" is not equivalent to "Jesus," what does "Christ" refer to? Unless we already understand what is meant by "God," how can we possibly understand words such as

[6] Kurt Baier, *The Meaning of Life* (Canberra: University College, 1957), pp. 20f., has remarked appropriately that religionists often "mistakenly conclude that there can be no purpose *in* life because there is no purpose *of* life; that men cannot themselves adopt and achieve purposes because man, unlike a robot or a watchdog, is not a creature with a purpose."
[7] London: Watts, 1958.

"Christ," "The Christ," "The Son of God," or "Our Lord Jesus Christ"? How can utterances incorporating them be used to make verifiable statements? What would count as verifying them? What *conceivable* experiences, post-mortem or otherwise, would tell us what it would be like to encounter not just Jesus, but the Christ, the Son of God, and the Son of Man, or our Lord, where "Our Lord" does not just mean a wise teacher or a monarch whom we meet either now or hereafter? If we do not know what it would be like to verify "God exists" directly, we have no better idea of what it would be like to verify "The Son of God exists," where "The Son of God" is not identical in meaning with "Jesus." (*If* they are identical in meaning, "The Son of God exists" can provide no logical bridge to "God exists.") The same sort of thing can be said for "The Christ"; and if it is said that "Jesus" and "The Christ" are not identical but we have verified that Jesus is the Christ, then I will reply that Hick has not shown us how we can verify this statement. He has not shown us how we can logically move from "Jesus exists" to "The Christ exists" where they are not identical.

Hick apart, how could we verify "Jesus is the Christ"? What would count as evidence for it? If we say we verify it indirectly by verifying "Jesus lived and acted in a certain way," then again it can be asked what grounds warrant our saying that the verifiable statement, "Jesus lived and in his thirty-third year died on the cross," or any statement or statements of that logically unambiguous type, counts as evidence for "Jesus is the Christ." I do not see that we have any warrant for saying that it is evidence for such a claim. We might decide that Jesus was a powerful man; we might verify that he did many quite amazing things; our moral insight might lead us to say he was a superlatively good and wise man; but how would this at all point, ambiguously or unambiguously, to Jesus' being the Christ, unless we independently understood what was meant by "The Christ" or "X's being the Christ"?

No empirical sense has been given to Hick's "an experience of the reign of the Son in the Kingdom of the Father"; and we are in no position to say, as Hick does, that this confirms Jesus's authority to reveal God's nature and purpose and thus we can verify that there is a God. No method of verification has been given; we do not know what conceivable experiences would count for or against "God exists" and thus Hick has failed to give us any grounds for saying that "There is a God" or "God exists" "asserts a matter of objective fact" (Note 1, p. 188).

Hick might reply that I am, in effect, arguing like a ration-

alist. I want a purely logical argument to prove that such experiences are experiences which point to God; but, as Hick correctly
remarks, "the exclusion of rational doubt concerning some matter
of fact is not equivalent to the exclusion of the logical possibility
of error or illusion" (p. 193). To ask for the latter is to ask for what
is self-contradictory; it is (in effect) to ask that a factual proposition be analytic. If we take this rationalist stand, then to have
a post-mortem experience of "the Kingdom of God, with Christ
reigning as Lord of the New Aeon, would not constitute a logical
certification of his claims nor, accordingly, of the reality of God"
(p. 206). If in our "resurrection bodies" in "the resurrection world"
we assert "Jesus is ruling over us all with love and justice" the truth
of this statement would not entail the truth of the statement "There
is a God" or "There is a divine purpose which is revealed through
Jesus," but, Hick argues, such a postmortem experience of Jesus's
reign would leave no grounds for rational doubt of these theistic
claims.

I of course agree with Hick that a statement of evidence for
a statement p need not be equivalent to the statement p. My evidence for "My glasses are on the desk" may be "I looked around
a moment ago and I saw them there," but the first statement is not
equivalent to, and is not entailed by, the second statement; but
if this is granted should we not say the same thing here about
Jesus as the mediator for God? Our evidence is a certain post-
mortem experience of Jesus. It is true that I know what it would
be like to see my glasses, while, apart from claims about a "direct
vision of God"—claims which Hick does not espouse—I cannot,
even in the next life, directly observe God (p. 203). But, after all,
there are certainly very many statements that are only indirectly
verifiable. We speak of a magnetic field or a superego and we
cannot see either, but there are recognized procedures for verifying statements embodying such conceptions. They are a part of a
whole network of conceptions, but within the appropriate scientific context there are recognized procedures of verification for
statements using such concepts. Why can we not properly say the
same thing about Jesus and Christianity?

One important difference is that in science we are more and
more willing to take a conventionalist attitude towards such
theoretical conceptions. Such conceptions can be seen as useful
devices for systematically predicting and retrodicting certain observable events. But once having learned the lesson that not all
substantives have a substance, we no longer feel incumbent to ask

if there are any such things as magnetic fields or superegos. Such concepts are pragmatically useful constructs since they enable us to make predictions and assessments of behaviour with greater ease than if we did not have such concepts, but we can be quite agnostic about whether there are such things.[8] But the believer cannot be agnostic in this way about God, and he cannot regard the concept of God *simply* as an important construct or as a useful heuristic device in his confessional group, and still remain a believer. (Note that this last statement is analytic.) As Hick argues, to claim "There is a God" is to make what purports to be an objective factual claim. But where we are willing to say that so-and-so is an objective factual claim we must know what could count as a confirmation of it. Sometimes our evidence is only indirect, but to know what the evidence unambiguously points to we must know what would count as observing or experiencing what the indirect evidence is indirect evidence of. As I sit upstairs I say to my wife, "The children are playing downstairs." I could give as indirect evidence: "They are laughing down there and someone is running around in the living room." But I only do this because I know what it would be like to see the children laughing and running around in the living room. But if we have no idea of what it would be like to experience that which we *supposedly* have indirect evidence for, then we in fact do not actually understand what it would be like to have evidence (direct or indirect) for it. We do not even understand what it could *mean* to say there is a so-and-so such that we have no idea at all of what it would be like to experience it, but something else can be experienced which is evidence for it. The "it" here cannot refer to anything, for in such a case how could we *possibly understand* what it is that our putative "evidence" is supposed to be evidence for? This is just the difficulty we have in using Jesus as the evidence for God. Hick's correct remarks about statements of evidence not being equivalent to statements of what they are evidence for is thus not to the point. We still do not know what is *meant* by saying that a post-mortem encounter with Jesus counts as the indirect (but sole) evidence for the existence of God. Thus we do not have a right to say, as Hick does, that we know what it would be like for our faith to be "so fully confirmed in *post-mortem* experience as to leave no grounds . . . as to the validity of that faith" (p. 206).

[8] Cf. J. J. C. Smart, "The Reality of Theoretical Entities," *Australasian Journal of Philosophy*, 34 (1956), 1–12.

III

Such conclusions as I have arrived at here might, if correct, lead Hick to a conclusion he merely suggests at the end of his essay. There he suggests certain considerations that would lead one to the conclusion "that only the theistic believer can find . . . vindication of his belief" (p. 207). If one becomes a believer one's theistic faith can be verified; but the non-believer cannot verify it. Hick's reasoning is as follows. It may be that predictions concerning human experience which give us good grounds for asserting that God exists are conditional predictions; since they are conditional, one is compelled to fulfil the relevant conditions.

> It may then [Hick argues] be a condition of *post-mortem* verification that we be already in some degree conscious of God by an uncompelled response to his modes of revelation in this world. It may be that such a voluntary consciousness of God is an essential element in the fulfillment of the divine purpose for human nature, so that the verification of theism which consists in an experience of the final fulfillment of that purpose can only be experienced by those who have already entered upon an awareness of God by the religious mode of apperception which we call faith (p. 207).[9]

Once more Hick in effect asks us to assume just what is in question. Granted, we can only verify "There is a table in the next room" if we can carry out certain conditional predictions which the statement entails. But these conditional predictions, these operations, are themselves very well understood. No one needs to approach them by faith, for any normal observer (where "normal observer" can itself be objectively and empirically specified) can verify them. But we have seen above how "God exists" does not have any comparable conditional statements which can be so verified or are so verifiable and hence so understood by a normal observer. We must, instead, appeal to that "apperception" we call faith.

This necessity makes "God exists" a very different sort of chowder. There is a further logical difficulty. If we understand

[9] Hick presents a similar argument in his "Meaning and Truth in Theology," in Sidney Hook (ed.), *Religious Experience and Truth* (New York: New York University Press, 1960), pp. 208–10. Cf. Paul Edwards' response, *ibid.*, pp. 245–7.

what a statement (conditional or otherwise) *means*, then it is proper to speak of having faith in its truth, or having faith that the evidence for it outweighs the evidence against it, or that certain experiences will verify it. *Given* these conditions, we could be fideists and approach God simply on trust. But what we cannot do is have faith in a proposition we do not understand, for in such a situation we literally cannot know *what* it is we are supposed to have faith in. If we cannot conceive of there being a state of affairs that would make "God exists" true or false, we cannot understand what conceivable state of affairs we are being asked to accept on faith. We can, by an act of faith, accept as true an antecedently understood proposition. In *that sense,* faith can precede understanding; but it does not make sense to say that we can certify the *meaning* of a proposition by faith; in that sense, understanding must precede faith. We can only have faith in something whose meaning we already understand; otherwise we cannot possibly have any idea what we are being asked to accept on faith. Hick assumes that, as knights of faith, we can somehow be conscious of God even though there is no understanding of what it would be like for there to be a God. But in such a situation we literally cannot have faith in God, for the statement "He has faith in God" cannot be used by him or by anyone else to make a factual claim and thus it cannot, in the requisite sense, have a meaning or a use.

There may indeed be a place for fideism but not on the level at which Hick sets the discussion. Questions of what is *meant* by x cannot possibly be settled by faith or trust. At the most, faith might lead us to try to fulfil certain conditions, but we would still have to understand independently of our faith *what* to fulfil. If my argument is in the main correct, we do not understand what it would be like to fulfil conditions which, once fulfilled, would result in anything that would count as a verification of God's existence. This being so, Hick's forthright argument has not established "that the existence or non-existence of the God of the New Testament is a matter of fact, and claims as such eventual experiential verification."

George I. Mavrodes/God and verification

In a recent paper in this journal Professor Kai Nielsen has criticized John Hick's attempt to show that Christian theological statements, e.g., about the existence of God, are meaningful as straightforward assertions of fact.[1] Hick accepts the doctrine that such an assertion of fact must be verifiable in principle, and he argues that these statements about God could conceivably be verified, at least posthumously by experiences in the resurrection life. Hick gives as examples of such possible verifying experiences the discovery that God's purpose for ourselves is being fulfilled, and an experience of communion with God through Christ. Nielsen's criticism, in effect, is based on the claim that Hick's descrip-

From "God and Verification," *Canadian Journal of Theology*, 10 (1964), 187–191, by George I. Mavrodes. Reprinted with the permission of the *Canadian Journal of Theology* and the author.

[1] *Canadian Journal of Theology*, 9 (1963), no. 4, 271–81. [The Nielsen article immediately precedes and begins on p. 209.—Editors]

tions of these alleged possible verifying experiences are not themselves meaningful. For, he says, we cannot understand expressions such as "the divine purpose for man," "Christ," "the Son of God," etc., unless we already understand what it is for there to be a God who created man with a purpose, a God to whom Jesus might bear a special relation, etc. But it is just the claim that there is such a God whose meaningfulness is in doubt. And that meaningfulness cannot be validated by reference to descriptions whose own intelligibility depends upon the assumption that talk about God's existence is meaningful. Nielsen therefore concludes that Hick's attempt to show the meaningfulness of talk about God has failed.

From this alleged failure, and his belief that all other such attempts have also failed, Nielsen goes on to conclude that probably all first-order talk about God is incoherent and conceptually confused. And he suggests that this is perhaps the most serious intellectual issue which faces contemporary theism.

I am afraid that Nielsen is unduly optimistic about theism. If this were indeed its most serious intellectual challenge, then theism would be in a powerful position. For the challenge itself is so muddled that theologians, as well as religious laymen, might reasonably be excused from responding to it until philosophers have formulated it in some more coherent terms. It is the confusion in the challenge itself which I wish to discuss here.

I

The first, and perhaps the most fundamental, failure of clarity concerns the term "verification" (and its complement, "falsification"). Nielsen writes as if we all understand perfectly well what it is for any assertion to be verified or verifiable, and that now all we need to do is to determine whether Hick or someone else has described something which would verify some statement about God. But Nielsen gives us no account at all of what he means by verification, or any account of the logical (or other) relations which must obtain between the statement to be verified and the statement, description, or state of affairs which is supposed to verify it. But without clarity at this point it is impossible to carry on a discussion about verification profitably.

In this respect contemporary discussions of meaningfulness based upon verifiability compare very unfavourably with those of the logical positivists. The positivists were generally enemies of God-talk and made no bones about it. They thought it was meaningless because it was not verifiable. But at least they tried to say precisely what they meant by "verifiability." They laid a criterion on the line where it could be examined. And therefore a reasonably clear discussion could ensue about whether verifiability had the significance attributed to it, and whether God-statements, and other types of statements, did or did not meet the criterion.

The results of these discussions were largely disappointing to the positivists. Early formulations of the verifiability criterion did seem to exclude God-statements. But they also excluded such commonplace scientific and ordinary life statements as "All of John's children have measles" or "Some marsupials are carnivorous." These too turned out to be "unverifiable" and therefore "meaningless." So if religious statements were also "meaningless" they were at least in good company.

Most positivists thought that the exclusion of statements actually used in scientific discourse was an intolerable consequence for any criterion of meaning. It was not hard to amend the first attempts in such a way as to include statements of the types given above. But some of these amendments still could not handle such a simple scientific hypothesis as "Some poisons have no antidote." And so finally more sophisticated versions of the verifiability criterion appeared, such as those in the first and second editions of A. J. Ayers' *Language, Truth and Logic.*

These criteria did, indeed, include every scientific statement within their scope. But it was soon shown that these criteria included *all other statements* within their scope just as well as they did scientific statements. Theological statements satisfied them perfectly well, and were validated as "verifiable" and hence "meaningful." In fact, it was shown that these criteria would be satisfied by any indicative sentence whatever, and that they would validate as "verifiable" and "meaningful" such non-theological nonsense as "The absolute is lazy" and "The square root of three is tired." They were completely useless as touchstones for distinguishing the meaningful from the meaningless. *And no more satisfactory criteria have been proposed.* They all either include everything, or else they exclude many perfectly ordinary state-

ments. And in either case there is nothing for the theologian to
fear from them.[2]

There are two surprising things about this. One is the fact
of the very failure itself, the failure of such an extraordinary
amount of philosophical thought to draw a viable distinction between religious talk and scientific talk on the basis of verifiability.
This failure makes it seem probable to me that verifiability does
not actually play the role which these philosophers wanted to
assign to it (in common life, in science, or in religion), and that
it cannot provide a base for a distinction between the cognitively
meaningful and the cognitively meaningless. I shall try to argue
further for this conclusion in the second part of this paper.

The second surprise is that philosophers of religion continue to talk about "verifiability" as if it were a perfectly clear
notion with no problems, a notion which we could use to identify
"unintelligibility" and "conceptual confusion" in religious discourse. But if there is ever to be a philosophical application of
Jesus' statement about the beam in one's own eye that application
must surely be here. I therefore agree that philosophers should be
welcomed to the theological arena. But a theologian (or a layman)
will be well advised to respond to challenges pertaining to the
verifiability of his talk as follows:

> I welcome your interest, and I respect your concern for clarity
> and intelligibility. Therefore please tell me just what you mean
> by "verifiability." Exactly what is it, and how are we to determine
> whether any given statement or sentence is or is not verifiable?
> If you present me with a clear account of verifiability then we
> can investigate the question of whether my talk satisfies it. But I
> warn you that I shall also apply your account to some other
> kinds of talk, perhaps even your own, and shall see if you are

---

[2] Since these failings have been discussed at length elsewhere, I do not repeat the arguments here. There is a discussion of some early formulations of
the verifiability criterion in A. J. Ayer, *Language, Truth and Logic* (2nd ed.,
New York: Dover Publications, 1946), pp. 35–9. It also includes the criticism
of Ayer's own first formulation of the criterion (pp. 11–13). The fundamental
criticism of Ayer's second criterion (p. 13) is made by Alonzo Church in a
review of Ayer's second edition in *The Journal of Symbolic Logic*, 14 (1949),
52–3. A concise account of the history and tribulations of this criterion is
given in Carl Hempel "Problems and Changes in the Empiricist Criterion of
Meaning," in Leonard Linsky, *Semantics and the Philosophy of Language*
(Urbana: The University of Illinois Press, 1952), pp. 163–85. Hempel's own
attempt to reformulate the criterion allows meaning to any indicative sentence, just as did Ayer's formulations.

satisfied with the results of it there. On the other hand, if you cannot provide me with a clear account of verifiability, then I do not see how we can pursue a profitable discussion along these lines. If I should try to respond to your challenge one confusion would compound another.

II

Nielsen complains that Hick's description of possible verifying experiences for, for example, "There is a God" cannot be understood unless we already understand the statement (or sentence) which is to be verified. But if its cognitive meaningfulness is in doubt, then so also must we doubt the meaningfulness of the descriptions of the allegedly conceivable verifying experiences. Hick's procedure is circular. It is an attempt to pull ourselves up by our theological bootstraps, and so must fail.

I am not concerned here to defend Hick. Since he, too, proceeds without a clear account of verifiability, it will not be surprising if his response is confused. What I do want to argue is that the attempt to use verifiability as a criterion or condition of cognitive meaningfulness itself involves the very type of circularity of which Nielsen accuses Hick. The demand that we should show that our talk is meaningful by showing that it is verifiable is itself a challenge to pull ourselves up by our bootstraps. The confusion in the response is the mirror image of the confusion in the challenge.

In arguing this point I shall assume that any account of verification which is to be provided by these philosophers will have something to do with the truth (or a justified belief in the truth) of the statement to be verified. That is, whatever statement, experience, or state of affairs verifies the statement p will have to be somehow relevant to the truth of p or to the justification of our belief that p is true. Let us call such a statement, experience, or state of affairs E.

Now, I am apparently asked to determine (or to show) that some statement p is meaningful by determining (or showing) that there is a conceivable E which would verify it. Suppose someone proposes an E for this purpose. How can I determine whether E would, in fact, verify p? I suppose that what I must do is to try the thought experiment of assuming that E is true and then asking myself whether, given that assumption, the following statement is true:

(1) E verifies that p.

Clearly, however, the truth of a statement having the form of (1) is in part a function of what is filled in for p. An experiment which would verify the special theory of relativity probably would not verify the Mendelian theory of inheritance. For it is unlikely that a single experiment will have the required type and degree of relevance to the truth of both of these diverse theories. And it certainly seems that if I do not understand what the Mendelian theory is (i.e., if I do not understand what assertions are made by the sentences used to express the theory), then I am in no position to decide whether a given E verifies it.

When I attempt a response to a challenge such as that of Nielsen I am, however, in an even worse position. For in this case I am presumed to be in doubt not only as to just *what* assertion is made by p but also as to whether *any* assertion is made by it. I am not supposed to know that p is cognitively meaningful at all *until after I have determined (or shown) that (1) is true*. And so far as I can see that is an impossible task.

This impossibility is not merely contingent. The verifiability approach to the determination of meaningfulness requires us to do something which is *necessarily* impossible. And this impossibility has nothing *special* to do with theology or religion. No matter what is the content of p I cannot determine the truth of (1) before I have determined what is the meaning of p and, *a fortiori*, that p is meaningful.

This point can be put in a way which parallels Nielsen's critique of Hick and shows the isomorphism of their confusion. Statement (1), since it includes p, will be unintelligible to someone who does not understand p. Consequently, if anyone is inclined to think that p is cognitively meaningless, he will also be equally inclined to think that (1) is meaningless.[3] The verifiability approach, then, requires us to determine the meaningfulness of a disputed statement by determining the truth of another statement which cannot be understood until the meaning of the disputed statement is understood. But we are supposed to determine the truth of the second

[3] Cf. "The Michelson-Morley experiment verified that the square root of three is tired." Is that conceivably true (and only contingently false)? Does not the failure of "The square root of three is tired" infect the entire statement?

statement *before* we are entitled to understand the first one at all. This is, of course, a necessarily impossible task. It is not the subject matter, theological or otherwise, which renders it impossible. Rather, the impossibility is due to the stipulated structure of the task itself. The challenge is itself circular, and it is not surprising that a circular challenge should provoke a circular and fallacious response.

We cannot, then, discover that a given statement or sentence is verifiable in principle *before* we understand what assertion is being expressed in it. And therefore we cannot make verifiability a criterion for determining, in disputed cases, whether the given statement or sentence is cognitively meaningful. That puts the cart before the horse.

I conclude, therefore, that theologians have no logical reason to be troubled by the current state of the philosophical challenge to the meaningfulness of God-talk. Perhaps at a later time some philosopher will formulate such a challenge in some coherent way. But until then theologians will probably be justified in devoting the major part of their attention to the more substantive problems of their discipline.

Kai Nielsen/God and verification again

Professor Mavrodes's criticisms of my "Eschatological Verification" are searching and incisive, but (perhaps failing to note the beam in my own eye) I remain unconvinced.[1] There are three points I wish to make by way of counter-argument.

    1. Mavrodes maintains that the most fundamental failure of clarity in my (and for that matter in Hick's) account concerns a failure to be clear about what is meant by "verification." "Nielsen," Mavrodes tells us, "writes as if we all understood perfectly well what it is for an assertion to be verified or verifiable, and

From "God and Verification Again," *Canadian Journal of Theology*, 11 (1965), 135–141, by Kai Nielsen. Reprinted with the permission of the *Canadian Journal of Theology* and the author.

[1] George I. Mavrodes, "God and Verification," *Canadian Journal of Theology*, 10 (1964), 187–91. This article was a response to my "Eschatological Verification," *Canadian Journal of Theology*, 9 (1963), 271–81, which in turn was a critique of John Hick's "Theology and Verification," *Theology Today*, 17 (1960), 12–31. Hick's essay has recently been reprinted in John Hick (ed.), *The Existence of God* (New York: Macmillan, 1964). [All three articles are reprinted in this section.—Editors]

that now all we need to do is to determine whether Hick or someone else has described something which would verify some statement about God."[2]

I did not give an analysis of "verification" or "verifiability,"
but I protest that I did not need to in order to make the points I
made in my essay. Any given philosophical analysis must start
somewhere—must assume that we understand the meaning of
some terms in order to analyse the meaning of others. I assumed
that we have a reasonably decent understanding of "verification"
and of what it is for an assertion to be verified or verifiable; and
I proceeded to show, in a way that Mavrodes does not assail, that
Hick has not shown how a purportedly factual statement like
"There is a God" is verifiable in principle. Now Mavrodes calls a
plague on both our houses by arguing that it is impossible to carry
on such a discussion profitably until we have a more satisfactory
account of verification than the one we have at present. I would
agree with Mavrodes if it were true that we do not understand
perfectly well what it is for a factual assertion to be verified or
verifiable. For ordinary purposes and for the problems raised by
the "Theology and Falsification Issue," we perfectly well understand what it is for a factual assertion to be verified or verifiable.
We have clear paradigms of different sorts of verification. We
know how to operate with these words though we may not know
their correct analysis; when in an ordinary case someone asks us
to verify a factual statement we have at least some idea of what
is required of us. I am sitting behind a sand dune screened from
the sea and my brother-in-law calls out to me, "Let's go swimming!
It's high tide." I know perfectly well how to verify "It's high tide."
Exactly the same thing is true of the following statements: "Many
union men will switch their vote this year and vote for Gold-
water"; "There is vegetation on Mars," or "People in the great
cities generally feel more alienated than do people in Saskatch-
ewan." We understand perfectly well what it is for an assertion
that is unequivocally factual to be verified; that is, we know what
it would be like to have evidence that counted for or against its
truth. Mavrodes has done nothing to show that this is not so.
Mavrodes writes as if the concept of verification were entirely un-
clear, but he presents no evidence of this. He only shows that
people who try to use verifiability as a base for a distinction be-

[2] Mavrodes, "God and Verification," pp. 187f. [See our pp. 223f.—Editors]

tween the cognitively meaningful and the cognitively meaningless get into irresolvable difficulties.

Mavrodes would no doubt protest that I have not given an analysis of what it is to verify a statement, but my point is that I do not need to. As Moore taught us, it is perfectly possible to know the meaning of a word without knowing the proper analysis of it.[3] I may understand perfectly well what is meant by "chair." I can identify chairs; I may know a lot about how they are made and know the uses to which they are put. I may never use "chair" incorrectly, but I still might not be able to give some formula to the effect that x is a chair if and only if y and z. But I know how to use "chair" properly enough, though I cannot *say* very well what "chair" means and I cannot state the necessary and sufficent conditions that must obtain if some artifact is properly to be called "a chair." But a failure to do this would not constitute grounds for denying that I know what chairs are or for denying that I understand the meaning of "chair." Similarly, given our paradigms, we can with good conscience assert that we know how to verify factual statements and that we understand what "to verify factual statements" means.

Mavrodes might reply that knowledge of such paradigms is not enough. The paradigms are themselves different, and in a different situation, perhaps in how we verify that there is a God, we still would not know, given only these paradigms, whether it was logically possible to verify such a statement. Before we can argue, as Hick did, that "There is a God" is verifiable or deny that it is, as I did, we must be much clearer about what counts as verification here.

Why? Let us call the statement to be verified "p" and the statement or state of affairs that verifies p "E." Where E is a statement it must either describe some observable state of affairs or entail some further statement "E" that describes such an observable state of affairs. Why, for the purposes at hand, does this not give us a sufficient account of what it is to verify a statement?

To this it might be replied that if we accept that account of verifiability it is plainly the case that "There is a God" is verifiable. We might try to say that "There is a God" (p) has factual significance if the statement "There are human beings" (E) has empirical significance; and E has empirical significance, so p must have fac-

---

[3] G. E. Moore, *Philosophical Papers* (New York: Macmillan, 1959), pp. 32–59.

tual significance. Since E is true, we have some evidence, though of course not conclusive evidence, for p.

Does p really have factual significance? Suppose the sceptic remarks: "As far as I can make out, the only thing you are asserting when you assert p is E. What more are you asserting?" If the theist replies that "the more" is that there are not only human beings but many kinds of contingent beings (F) and that these beings might not have existed (G), the sceptic can ask: "But I still do not see what E, F, and G have to do with God, with the truth of p. What more are you asserting when you assert p than E, F, and G?" If the theist says, "nothing more," then his position is indistinguishable from atheism; if he says, "something more," then he must specify some further statement or state of affairs that would be incompatible with something a non-believer could properly say, but it is just this that he has not done.

Hick, unlike Mavrodes, sees this problem clearly enough and tries to meet it, but, as I argued in "Eschatological Verification," Hick fails, for his possible verifying experiences (a discovery that God's purpose for ourselves is being fulfilled and a communion with God through Christ) already make reference to the very conceptions whose factual intelligibility is in question.[4] Hick is in effect trying to lift himself up by his own bootstraps. But Mavrodes does nothing to take us around the bog. He neither shows us how we could in principle verify p, nor does he show us that we have no clear conception of what it is to verify a factual assertion. He only recounts a by now familiar story concerning the verifiability criterion of meaning, namely, that within natural languages (and that is all that is relevant here) no one has been able to elucidate adequately the exact logical relations between the statement to be verified and the verifying statement or statements. But this, as I have shown, does not at all show that we do not understand what it is to verify a statement, any more than the fact that we do not know how to give an adequate definition or analysis of "chair" shows that we do not perfectly well know what a chair

[4] I make my intent perfectly plain in "Eschatological Verification," when I remark: "It is indeed true that we, who have been brought up as Christians or in close proximity to Christians, know how to use this discourse. In that sense it is sheer nonsense to say Christian chatter is meaningless, but Hick has not shown us how we understand the use of language as a factual or statement-making type of discourse" (p. 217). I would only explicitly state here, what I thought the context would make evident enough, that I am only talking about factual statements.

is. That lesson we should have learned from G. E. Moore years ago.

2. Mavrodes misses my intent and misses, I believe, Hick's intent as well. I certainly was not (and I do not believe Hick was either) trying to provide a general criterion of meaning or even a general criterion of cognitive meaning—some touchstone for distinguishing the meaningful or cognitively meaningful from the meaningless or cognitively meaningless. Certainly I have never implied, as Mavrodes says I do,[5] that verifiability is "a criterion or condition of cognitive meaningfulness." Certainly, "How far is the train station?" "Close the window," "I declare him *persona non grata*," have cognitive meaning, and yet they are plainly not verifiable: they do not even purport to be verifiable.[6] Furthermore, it seems to me very questionable that all ethical statements are verifiable; yet non-verifiability does not divest them of cognitive meaning. I would argue and did argue that non-verifiability (logical impossibility of confirmation or disconfirmation) divests a statement of *factual* intelligibility, but that is a different matter.[7] Hick argues that believers intend "There is a God" and many key religious and theological statements to be factual statements; and he also argues, and I argue, that in order for them to be genuinely factual statements it must be logically possible, directly or indirectly, to verify (confirm or disconfirm) them. Hick claims that they are so verifiable; I argue that neither he nor anyone else has shown this to be so. I further suggested, not that they were meaningless, but that they were without *factual significance.* I have further agreed with Hick (and many others) that reasonably orthodox believers *believe* that they are factual; but I have argued, as they did

---

[5] Mavrodes, "God and Verification," p. 190. [See this volume, pp. 227f.—Editors]

[6] Many of the points I would make about verification are clearly made by G. J. Warnock in his masterful essay "Verification and the Use of Language," *Revue Internationale de Philosophie,* 17–18 (1951), 307–22.

[7] It might be replied that questions, imperatives, and performatives are in a technical sense cognitively meaningless, for unlike declarative statements they do not make knowledge claims. By contrast, sentences used to make declarative statements can be used to state items of knowledge. Because of this, "cognitive" should be identified with "factual." But why identify "cognitive" with "factual"? Cannot one know that one ought to help one's parents and that one has a duty to provide for one's children? Certainly the onus is on the critic to show that "factual" and "cognitive" have the same meaning or that *only* factual considerations are cognitive considerations. (Again he could stipulate this, but very similar considerations would become relevant when we ask ourselves whether we should accept his stipulation.)

not, that believers do not actually use such religious sentences to make factual statements, but—though unwittingly—they use them to make ideological statements, i.e., statements that appear to have factual significance, statements that are believed by their users to be grand factual claims, but statements which actually function (though in an essentially surreptitious manner) to recommend that we act in a certain way or take a certain attitude towards life. They literally are value judgments, but someone who thinks they are something more, who makes such ideological statements, believes (though mistakenly) that the norm involved in any such religious statement has a massive backing by a mysterious kind of fact asserted by that statement. In other words the ideologist gains what in reality is simply psychological reinforcement, but what he takes to be additional objective support for certain of his value judgments by making it appear—though, of course, not deliberately—that they are a conceptually odd and essentially mysterious kind of factual statement.[8] But these religious utterances are most surely not devoid of meaning and they are not even devoid of "cognitive meaning," for value judgments are not without cognitive meaning. There is nothing in Mavrodes' arguments to gainsay that.

3. Given that I am not using verifiability as an over-all criterion of meaning or of cognitive meaning, Mavrodes' case against me in section II of his essay collapses.

I shall show why Mavrodes' argument does not apply to me or for that matter to Hick. Mavrodes points out, quite correctly, the logical untenability of verificationist attempts to show that some statement p is meaningful by determining that there is some conceivable E, some statement, experience, or state of affairs, which would verify p—would count as evidence for the truth or justified belief of p.[9] Verificationists must claim that I am not supposed to

---

[8] This point is rather cryptically expressed here, but I have argued for it in detail in my "Speaking of God," Theoria, 28 (1962), 110–137. A "Moorean approach" might be taken against me here. Someone might argue that, since it is commonly believed by their users that such God-sentences are used to make factual statements, my theory, which denies that they are actually used by present-day believers to make factual statements, must be wrong. Why must my theory be wrong because of this? Native speakers' linguistic behaviour indeed determines what meaning such sentences have, but their beliefs about their linguistic behaviour are certainly not in such an authoritative position. Native speakers need not be, and normally are not, either linguists or philosophers.

[9] Mavrodes, "God and Verification," p. 190. [See this volume, p. 227.—Editors]

know, on the verifiability criterion, whether p is cognitively meaningful or not until I have verified p, but I cannot, logically cannot,
verify p until I know what p asserts. The verifiability criterion puts
the cart before the horse and, in effect, unwittingly asks me to do
what is logically impossible, for only if p's meaning is already
known can we intelligibly ask what would verify p. The verifiability criterion of meaning is logically untenable, for it would
require us to do something that is logically impossible. Consider
(1) "E verifies that p." As Mavrodes points out, "No matter what
. . . the content of p I cannot determine the truth of (1) before I
have determined what is the meaning of p and, *a fortiori,* that p is
meaningful."[10] But on the verifiability theory of meaning I am not
supposed to know or even be able to know whether p is meaningful until after I have determined that (1) is true.

    Neither my account nor Hick's is caught up in such a mud-
dle, for we are *not* setting out a general criterion of meaning, but
trying to determine whether "There is a God" is used to make a
factual statement, and we have assumed what could, of course, be
questioned, namely that a statement is a factual statement only if
it is logically possible to confirm or disconfirm it. We use verifiability to demarcate *within the class of meaningful sentences* those
sentences that are used to make factual statements. Thus where we
assume that p has *some meaning* and then say that p is a factual
claim only if some E would count as verifying p, we are not pulling
ourselves up by our own bootstraps, not doing anything that is
logically inappropriate, but only developing a test to determine
whether a purportedly factual statement is indeed factual.

    I have not tried to do the impossible, e.g., to discover
whether a given statement is verifiable before I have at all understood its meaning; but where p stands for a statement utilizing a
linguistic unit that is part of the corpus of some natural language
and thus, in one plain sense, meaningful, I have tried to show, by
setting out a test, how we can determine whether p actually makes
a factual claim by determining whether p is verifiable. "The square
root of three is tired" is not part of the corpus of English; we do
not understand it. It is not part of some scientific discourse attached to English, and native speakers cannot think of discourses
(philosophical or linguistic ones apart) in which it would naturally

----

[10] *Ibid.,* p. 191. [See this volume, p. 238.—Editors]

occur. But "There is a God" plainly is part of the corpus of English, native speakers can paraphrase it, and they can readily think of discourses in which it would naturally occur. But nothing that I said denies the intelligibility of religious utterances. In fact my theory that they are or are very like ideological statements requires that they be meaningful. Yet religious people claim that it is a fact that there is a God, but if it is a fact, then "There is a God" must have factual intelligibility, but if it has factual intelligibility it should be verifiable in principle, but "There is a God" does not appear to be verifiable in principle, and Hick's attempts to show that it is verifiable fail on the very grounds I marked out in "Eschatological Verification." Nothing that Mavrodes has said touches that argument.

I have tried to show how Mavrodes' arguments do not establish that the general conditions for argument concerning the theology and falsification issue are muddled. Religious people, as Hicks avers, believe that it is a fact that there is a God.[11] If it is not a fact their faith is in vain; but if it is a fact, then to assert that there is a God is to make a factual statement, but then the statement must be verifiable in principle, i.e., there must be some empirical evidence that would count for or against its truth. But given the way in which "There is a God" is actually used by believers, or at least by many contemporary believers, its truth or falsity seems to be equally compatible with anything and everything that could conceivably occur. But, if this is so, it can hardly be a genuine factual claim. This is the challenge raised by the theology-and-falsification issue and this is the challenge that Hick quite properly tried to meet. Hick failed and Mavrodes has not shown that the challenge itself involves a conceptual muddle. Perhaps someone can show that such religious statements can be verified and thus show

---

[11] In this exchange with Binkley this side of Hick's approach becomes even more evident. See Luther Binkley, "What Characterizes Religious Language?" and John Hick, "Comment," in *Journal for the Scientific Study of Religion*, 2 (1962–63), 18–24, and Binkley again in "Reply to Professor Hick's Comment on 'What Characterizes Religious Language?' " and Hick, "Comment on Professor Binkley's Reply," *ibid.*, 228–32. In his final comment Hick even remarks that while "the factual" is wider than "the empirical" (p. 230) he would "define fact in terms of 'making an actual or possible experienceable difference' and wish experience to show what various kinds of facts there are" (p. 230). It was such a position that I was criticizing and I see no reason to retract my criticisms of it.

that they actually have factual intelligibility, or perhaps someone can show that Hick and I are both mistaken in thinking that a statement, to be factual, needs to be verifiable (confirmable or disconfirmable) in principle. Mavrodes has shown neither of these two things, but until either such claim can be made out, I persist in my challenge and persist in my contention that even first-order God-talk is incoherent and conceptually confused.[12]

[12] I do not wish to suggest that this is the only reason why I find such talk incoherent and conceptually confused; and I must reiterate that to be incoherent is one thing, to be meaningless or linguistically unintelligible is another. "The square root of three is tired" belongs in the latter class, but certainly not "God made the heavens and the earth." (I am indebted to Professor Kenneth Stern for his comments on an earlier draft of this essay.)

John *Hick*/**Faith and knowledge**

It is not . . . being suggested that the existence of God has the status in the believer's mind of a tentatively adopted hypothesis which awaits verification after death.[1] The believer can already have, on the basis of his religious experience, a warrant as to the reality of God. He may already know God in a way which requires no further verification.

Now to the extent to which the believer actually has a present consciousness of God, he does indeed need no future verification of God's reality, and the life of heaven will not fundamentally

From *Faith and Knowledge* by John Hick, 2d ed. rev., (Ithaca: Cornell University Press, 1966), pp. 194–199. First ed. © 1957, 2d ed. © 1966 by Cornell University. Reprinted by permission of Cornell University Press and the author.

[1] It is misinterpreted in this way by D. R. Duff-Forbes in his discussion of I. M. Crombie's use of the idea of eschatological verification in *New Essays in Philosophical Theology*, p. 126. See Duff-Forbes' "Theology and Falsification Again," *Australasian Journal of Philosophy*, 39 (1961), p. 153. See also a reply to this article by Antony Flew, "Falsification and Hypothesis in Theology," *Australasian Journal of Philosophy*, 40 (1962), and further reply by Duff-Forbes.

change his cognitive relation to his Maker. But this does not render the notion of eschatological verification any less apposite to the function for which it has been advanced—namely, establishing the factual character of theistic belief in response to questions raised by contemporary philosophy. It is not that the believer needs further confirmation of his faith, but that the philosopher— whether believer or not—wants to know what aspects of Christian belief bring that system of belief within the accepted criteria of factual meaningfulness. The religious man has always assumed— usually without formulating this as a philosophical position—that the propositions expressing his faith-awareness of God have the character of factual statements: that they are factually true or false, and of course, according to him, true. That is to say, the ordinary religious believer has always taken it for granted that the dispute between himself and an atheist concerns a momentous question of fact: the existence or nonexistence of a transcendent divine Being. But in our own time, as a result of investigations of the concepts of meaning and verification, this assumption has been questioned. Do the core religious statements (such as "God loves mankind") really have the logical character of factual assertions? Or are they incapable in principle of either verification or falsification, and thus factually vacuous? These questions challenge the religious apologist to point to any features of theological discourse which establish its factual character. The task is not to show that religious statements are true, but to show that they make factual assertions, and are accordingly true-or-false. And it is this task that the notion of eschatological verification is invoked to perform. It draws out of the system of Christian belief—which can be regarded as a complex expansion of the Christian concept of God— that element which makes an experientially verifiable claim, in virtue of which the belief-system as a whole is established as being factually true-or-false. Thus the purpose of the reference to eschatological verification is simply to show the inquirer who is concerned about the questions raised by logical positivism and its philosophical descendants that the theistic assertion is indeed— whether true or false—a genuinely factual assertion.

It must be added, however, that a state of faith which is so complete that it leaves no room for doubt, and therefore no room for the exclusion of doubt by further verifying experiences, represents an ideal that is seldom attained in this life. Faith is in practice a variable state, with both its moments of indubitable consciousness of God and its times of precarious living upon the memory of those moments. Even the perfect God-consciousness of Jesus seems to have faltered in the experience which evoked his cry of dereliction on the cross, "My God, my God, why hast thou forsaken me?" Thus whilst in its strongest possible form faith needs no further verification, in its common forms it does not exclude the possibility of such future confirmation.

An important philosophical objection has been presented by Kai Nielsen in an article on "Eschatological Verification."[2] He offers several secondary criticisms, but his main criticism is that the argument begs the question by presupposing that which is to be shown. Nielsen focuses attention upon the two suggested conditions fulfillment of which, it is claimed, would remove grounds for rational doubt as to the existence of the God of Christian faith: namely, the completion of God's purpose for us as this has been disclosed in the New Testament, and an eschatological confirmation of the authority of Jesus and hence of his revelation of God. Nielsen claims that these conditions presuppose that we already know what it is for God to exist, to have a purpose for us, and to be encountered in Christ, and that they cannot be used to establish the meaning, nor therefore the factual meaning, of these religious ideas. Speaking of the first of the two allegedly verifying conditions, Nielsen says:

> But what we do not know is what it would be like to verify "There is divine existence." We have no idea at all of what it would be like for that statement to be either true or false. . . . And . . . to appeal to the divine purpose for man assumes we already know what it would be like to verify that our lives have such a purpose. We do not know what must be the case for it to be true or false that our lives have a purpose, a *telos*, a destiny or final fulfillment. . . . We do not know what must happen for us to assert correctly that so and so is "apprehended as the fulfillment of God's purpose and not simply as a natural state of affairs."[3]

And referring to the second condition, he says:

> Unless we already understand what is meant by "God," how can we possibly understand words such as "Christ," The Christ," "The Son of God," or "Our Lord Jesus Christ"? How

[2] In *Canadian Journal of Theology*, IX, no. 4 (1962). See also a reply by George Mavrodes, "God and Verification," in X, no. 3 (1964), and a reply to this by Nielsen, "God and Verification Again" in XI, no. 2 (1965). [All three articles are reprinted in this section.—Editors]

[3] Nielsen, "Eschatological Verification," pp. 276–277. [See this volume, pp. 216f.—Editors]

can utterances incorporating them be used to make verifiable statements? What would count as verifying them? What *conceivable* experiences, post-mortem or otherwise, would tell us what it would be like to encounter not just Jesus, but the Christ, the Son of God, and the Son of Man, or our Lord, where "Our Lord" does not just mean a wise teacher or a monarch whom we meet either now or hereafter? If we do not know what it would be like to verify "God exists" directly, we have no better idea of what it would be like to verify "The Son of God exists," where "The Son of God" is not identical in meaning with "Jesus."[4]

Certainly the philosophical elucidation of the Christian concept of God raises the most profound, elusive, and perhaps insoluble problems. And it is therefore correspondingly difficult, or even impossible, to state in full what it is for God to be real. For to set forth the complete truth-conditions of "God exists" would require an exhaustive definition of the divine nature. And Nielsen is right in saying that the notion of eschatological verification does not enable us to do this. But it was not invoked to do this. It was invoked to establish that the statement "God exists" is factually true-or-false. It does this by showing that the concept of deity, in its Christian context, involves eschatological expectations which will be either fulfilled or not fulfilled. But it is not suggested that the fulfillment of these expectations, by participation in the ultimate Kingdom of God, defines the *meaning* of "God exists." In trying to describe a situation in which it would be irrational for a human being to doubt the reality of God, as allegedly revealed in Christ, one is not undertaking to define exhaustively the nature of God or, therefore, the truth-conditions of "God exists."

If it is asked how we can be in a position to tell the difference between God existing and God not existing without fully knowing what "God" means, the general answer is that such combined knowledge and ignorance is a very common epistemological situation. As Nielsen himself emphasizes on another occasion, we can often use a word correctly, applying it to the right objects or situations, and yet be unable to give a satisfactory philosophical analysis of its meaning.[5] We all know what "This is a material

---

4 *Ibid.*, p. 277. [See this volume, pp. 217f.—Editors]

5 "God and Verification Again," *Canadian Journal of Theology*, XI, no. 2 (1965) pp. 136–137. [See this volume, pp. 233f.—Editors] Cf. G. E. Moore, *Some Main Problems of Philosophy* (London, 1953), pp. 205–206 and *Philosophical Papers* (London, 1959), pp. 36ff.

object" or "He is alive" means, and we may have an assured knowledge of many things that they *are* material objects and of many people that they *are* alive, and yet be unable to define fully what it is to be a material object or to be alive. And so in the theological case we must not rule out a priori that one might be able to be aware of the presence of God, to identify an act of God, and to recognize God's rule, without being able fully to define or comprehend the divine nature.

Within Christianity it is possible to talk about the infinite God, incomprehensible though he still remains, because he has become finitely incarnate in Jesus of Nazareth. That is to say, God is identified as the Being about whom Jesus taught and whose attitude to mankind was expressed in Jesus' deeds. Building upon Jesus' teaching, together with that of the Hebrew prophets before him, Christian theologians have developed the philosophical conception of this Being as infinite, uncreated, eternal, and so on. But the starting point and basis of the Christian use of the word "God" remains the historical figure of Jesus, as known through the New Testament records. Under his impact we come (in some degree and at some times) to experience life in a distinctively new way, as living in the presence of the God whose love was revealed in the words and actions of Jesus. Is the appropriateness of this response to the haunting figure of Jesus—this response of personal discipleship, of acceptance of his teaching, and of coming to experience life in its relation of "the God and Father of our Lord Jesus Christ"—in any way verifiable by future events? Surely our participation in an eschatological situation in which the reality of God's loving purpose for us is confirmed by its fulfillment in a heavenly world, and in which the authority of Jesus, and thus of his teaching, is confirmed by his exalted place in that world, would properly count as confirmatory. It would not (to repeat) amount to logical demonstration, but it would constitute a situation in which the grounds for rational doubt which obtain in the present life would have been decisively removed. Such eschatological expectations —without the detailed imagery in which earlier ages have clothed them—are an integral part of the total Christian conception of God and his activity. And they suffice, I suggest, to ensure the factual, true-or-false character of the claim that God, as so conceived, exists.

Seven/Theology and falsification

Introduction/Do theologians take facts seriously?

I N the early fifties the debate on the factual meaningfulness of theological statements shifted to the issue of theology and falsification.
Antony Flew's retrospective survey (see pp. 269 ff.), shows how
provocative the challenge of falsification has proved to be. All participants in the discussion of "Theology and Falsification," Flew, R. M. Hare,
and Basil Mitchell, follow Wisdom's example insofar as they deal with
the issue in terms of parables or far-out illustrations. These are subject
to different interpretations. I believe that those which follow are both
faithful to the texts and helpful in getting at the issues.

Flew: the challenge of falsification

The passion with which Antony Flew introduced falsification as a
challenge to the factual meaningfulness of theological statements goes
a long way toward accounting for the continuing interest in this issue.
Previous positivistic criticisms of religious language had generally been
bloodless: they made relatively little impact on believers. By focusing

on the statement "God loves us as a father loves his children" which I will shorten to "God loves us," Flew linked his challenge to one of the perennial problems of Christian thought, namely, to the problem of evil. Furthermore, this statement has deep biblical roots. In the Book of Hosea (11:1) we read, "When Israel was a boy I loved him, I called my son out of Egypt." The New Testament is full of talk about the loving concern of the heavenly Father, culminating in the statement of this theme in the First Letter of John (4:9): "God is love."

As Flew understands it, the statement "God loves us" is not only intended to be informative (synthetic), but the information conveyed is clearly regarded by believers as being one of the most important truths that we can know in orienting ourselves to reality. Flew's searing assault on the meaningfulness of the statement, "God loves us," contrasts the love of earthly fathers for their children with the love that is attributed to God, the heavenly Father. If a child is suffering from cancer of the throat, his earthly father frantically tries to help by comforting the child, seeking the best doctors, and so on. The Heavenly Father does not do anything that can be taken as an equally clear effort to help. Flew thinks that the obvious conclusion to be drawn is that the statement, "God loves us," is not true. Yet he notes that theologians shrink from the obvious. In an effort to make them face up to it, Flew invokes the test of falsification. He challenges theologians to specify an observable set of circumstances that would falsify the statement "God loves us." In effect, Flew confronts theologians with the following unpalatable options (unpalatable to them, not to Flew):

Analytic

One clearly meaningful option would be to declare that "God loves us" is analytic. In that case it would be necessarily true, but it would no longer be doing the job that believers want it to do. Believers want a guarantee that a limitless power will console us, somehow, for human suffering. If the statement "God loves us" is analytic, it can offer no such guarantee. It can only express the theologians' definition of God, that is, their intention of inextricably associating the word love with the word God. This verbal formula would be logically impeccable, but religiously vacuous.

Synthetic

Theologians might insist that "God loves us" is a genuine synthetic statement. In that case they would claim that "God loves us" means that we are loved by a center of consciousness that is aware of all states *of affairs and that is infinitely powerful. This is a strong claim. It is, in Flew's view, factually meaningful, because he thinks it is falsifiable in principle. Indeed, although this is not his main point, he thinks that it has actually been falsified. Human suffering through the ages has falsified, many times over, the claim that we are loved by an all-knowing and all-powerful God.*

Pseudo-synthetic

In this context we must again appreciate the importance of the rise of science to religious thought. Religious thinkers are not generally prepared to stake belief on the outcome of observable tests. They would not be prepared to have the parents of the child pray to God for help, and to say that if the child is cured "God loves us" is true, and that if the child suffers and dies, the statement is false. Instead, theologians emphasize the mystery of divine transcendence and they qualify the meaning of "God loves us." They fall back on such traditional moves as saying that God's love is mysterious and we cannot understand it. A similar qualification is to note that we human beings are finite; we cannot see the whole picture. If we could see reality as a whole, we would be able to realize that God does love every human being, even the child dying of inoperable cancer.

Flew insists that qualifications of this kind erode the straightforward meaning of the biblical assurances of God's love. That is the point of his accusation that at the hand of theologians biblical statements suffer "death by a thousand qualifications."

At the end of this process, the statement still appears to be synthetic, but as actually used by the theologians, it is compatible with any state of affairs whatever, including the suffering of a child dying of inoperable cancer. Therefore, the statement, "God loves us," as used by theologians who reject fundamentalism, is not genuinely synthetic. Flew's third option, the one he is clearly most concerned to emphasize, is that this statement is pseudo-synthetic and, therefore, factually meaningless.

Hare: "bliks" are not falsifiable, but we use them to assess the facts

R. M. Hare's reply to Flew stresses a point that has gained wide acceptance. Language, even when we restrict our consideration to its empirical functions, has many levels or strata. One important kind of statement is what Hare calls a blik. A blik is not verified or falsified by evidence; it is rather, a statement about the world which is used to assess the evidence. Hare's main illustration is sensational. A deluded student is convinced that all members of the faculty want to kill him. Since he uses this blik to weigh the evidence, he cannot be persuaded that he is mistaken. If members of the faculty try to show him that he is wrong by being especially friendly, he interprets this as a diabolical effort on their part to throw him off guard. Hare concludes that the student's statement (or one he might make) that "All members of the faculty are trying to kill me" is not, therefore, falsifiable. It may, nevertheless, (to recall a point of Wisdom's), tell us something about "what is so."

Hare's passing reference to Hume shows that he thinks something important is at stake. Bliks need not express delusions like that of the student. They may play an important role in science. When we deal with assumptions that underlie scientific work, like causality and induction, we come across statements that may be understood as bliks. They cannot be falsified, but they are crucial to our forming a notion of what is so. This point, which is only suggested by Hare, is treated at length in J. F. Miller's contribution to this volume. In Flew's retrospective essay on falsification, he clarifies the meaning of bliks by considering the question of whether they can properly be characterized as sane or insane (see pp. 279 ff.).

Mitchell: theological statements can be confirmed and disconfirmed

Basil Mitchell's contribution is a religiously relevant response to Flew's religiously relevant challenge. Mitchell's parable of The Partisan and the Stranger says a great deal about the way that faith actually operates in the lives of believers. It is in the nature of faith to persist in spite of the doubts engendered by disappointed hopes and by observations that run contrary to its expectations.

In the parable, a Partisan, that is, a member of the Resistance, meets a mysterious Stranger. In a conversation of great intensity he is convinced that the Stranger is the secret head of the Movement. They never have another direct meeting, but the Partisan continues to see the Stranger in a way that confronts him with a swirl of conflicting evidence. Sometimes the Stranger seems to help the Resistance; at other times, he appears in the uniform of the police and arrests members of the Movement. Other members of the Resistance decide that the Stranger is really an enemy, but the Partisan who had the intimate conversation with him persists in his trust.

Mitchell uses this parable to meet Flew's challenge head on:

1. He refuses to qualify the meaning of "love" in the statement "God loves us." This is the point of his admitting that the Stranger's work in arresting members of the Resistance does count against the truth of the statement, "The Stranger is one of us."

2. Mitchell insists that theological statements (he calls them assertions) are factually meaningful. To make good on this claim, he shifts the issue from Flew's challenge, which is expressed in terms of conclusive falsification, to the test of confirmation and disconfirmation. This point needs elaborating.

In the biblical story of Elijah and the Priests of Baal, we have a conclusive test (see pp. 153, 159). As it is told, Elijah's claim that the Lord God of Israel is the true God is conclusively verified, and the priests' claim that Baal is the true God is conclusively falsified. By contrast, in Mitchell's parable the test is not conclusive. When members of the Resistance are unaccountably released the events confirm, or count for the truth of, the statement "The Stranger is on our side." On the other hand, when members of the Resistance are unexpectedly captured the statement is disconfirmed because these events count against its truth.

One reason for the lack of conclusiveness in Mitchell's parable is that it is not possible to quantify the test. Even when quite a few members of the Resistance have been captured, it is open to the Partisan to argue that "The Stranger is on our side." He can, for example, claim that the Stranger must permit these tragic episodes to occur because, if he interfered too openly on the side of the Resistance, the Nazis would discover his true identity and his utility to the Resistance (as well as his life) would come to an end. Furthermore, it is obvious that the Partisan who had the special conversation with the Stranger is in a different situation from the rest of his comrades. His conversation was a source of privileged access (what Martin Buber would call an I-Thou relation) to the Stranger. As a result, he sets the evidence in the context of that special relation. Therefore, evidence that would conclusively falsify the statement "The Stranger is on our side" for other members of the Resistance, might well not do so for the Partisan who talked directly to him.

Mitchell's important contribution is to show that the logic of confirmation is permissive enough to render theological statements factually meaningful. Theologians can claim that their statements are factually meaningful even though, like the statement "The Stranger is on our side," their statements cannot be conclusively verified or conclusively falsified. However, Flew tells us that Mitchell never intended to say that theological statements cannot be conclusively falsified (see p. 279). In that case, The Parable of the Partisan and the Stranger only communicated a limited part of Mitchell's intention, because a number of commentators thought that the parable was intended to exclude the possibility of conclusive falsification.[1]

Flew's retrospective survey of "theology and falsification"

In his retrospective essay on "Theology and Falsification," Flew makes a number of important points. The main one involves his recognition that the effort to eliminate theology by preliminary examination has failed. Falsification proved no more effective for this purpose than verification. He is, therefore, calling for interchanges that are more like the traditional arguments between theists and atheists, but he seeks interchanges which will have benefited from the work of contemporary empiricists.

A number of Flew's important points should be noted:

a. Thinkers like Litzenburg stress the need to be specific about the theologians that are to be criticized (see pp. 285 f.). Yet one of the points that Flew made in his original contribution to "Theology and Falsification" is still valid: it is hard to pin theologians down because they shift their positions under fire. As Crombie puts it, theologians oscillate "backwards and forwards between a literal interpretation of what we say when we say it, and a scornful rejection of such anthropomorphism when anybody challenges us" (see p. 312).

b. There is an important distinction between observations that "count against" the truth of a statement and those that are logically incompatible with it. "The sun is shining" counts against the truth of the statement "It is raining," but it is not logically incompatible with it. We have all experienced the suprising phenomenon of sunshowers. On the other hand, the statement that "There is no moisture whatever in the air," is logically incompatible with the statement, "It is raining."

c. Flew's report of the origin of the debate on theology and falsi-

---

[1] In addition to the essays cited by Flew, see Howard R. Burkle, "Counting Against and Counting Decisively Against," The Journal of Religion XLIV, 3, pp. 223–229.

fication explains its peculiar character: it is long on poetry and short on prose. By this I mean that the illustrations are vivid, but there is little philosophical elaboration. This is one reason why the debate has evoked so many comments in philosophical journals; the illustrations and parables that appear in the original debate are open to many interpretations. Flew reviews some of the high points of twenty years of philosophical commentary and uses them to clarify the points of the original contributors to show their similarities and differences.

d. Michael Tooley discusses a number of ways in which Flew's original challenge may be understood (see pp. 484 ff.). In reply, Flew admits that his challenge is open-ended. He is not committed to conclusive falsifiability as a criterion of factual meaningfulness. The original challenge was designed only to make theologians "come clean" on the way that empirical evidence affects their beliefs. He renews that challenge in this essay.

e. Flew's discussion of the burden of proof and Litzenburg's response to it will be considered in the following section.

Litzenburg: the burden of proof

Litzenburg's challenge to Flew's survey must be understood against the background of the post-postivist situation with its looser approach to questions of cognitive meaning.

Flew's criticisms of theology take account of this new situation. They are moderate in tone, and he avoids dogmatism. He neither insists that the believer demonstrate the falsifiability of theological statements, nor does he insist that theological statements conform to any particular pattern. He merely asks that the theologian specify some initial grounds for the truth, or possible truth, of his statements. In this way Flew tries to shift the "onus" or "burden" of proof to the theologian.

In response, Litzenburg claims that despite his moderate tone Flew is still up to the positivist's game of subjecting theology to a preliminary examination. Before theology can be taken seriously as cognitively meaningful, it must demonstrate some degree of evidential confirmation of its claims. Yet in proposing this preliminary examination Flew refuses to commit himself to any specific criterion of cognitive meaning nor will he specify the particular theology that he thinks is sadly deficient in evidential confirmation. Litzenburg insists that at this level of vagueness, the argument can scarcely proceed. Many theologies, Thomism for one, Calvinism for another, have long histories of consistent usage. If Flew wants to claim that these theologies lack cognitive meaning, the burden of proof is on him. In fairness to Flew, it should be noted that he thinks he has successfully borne this burden in his book, God and Philosophy.[2] He could not hope to reproduce that kind of argument here. Yet, there is no denying that his remarks here are characterised by a rather high level of generality.

Ogden: a metaphysical response by a neoclassical theologian

Schubert Ogden's contribution is directed to Flew's retrospective survey of the "Theology and Falsification" issue and to his God and Philosophy. As a metaphysically-oriented theologian, Ogden provides an important counterweight to a major theme stressed here in the introductory essays, namely the relation of theology and falsification to the larger issue of religion and science and the importance of technology as an influence on the cultural scene. By contrast, Ogden deals directly with the role of metaphysics in coping with "limiting questions," that is, with questions about the world as a whole.

Ogden concedes the point that factually meaningful statements must, as Flew insists, be falsifiable by observations. He then makes what seems to be a further concession, namely, that statements about God cannot be falsified by observations. Actually, this second point is not a concession at all for Ogden, since he regards it as part of the meaning of "God," and he thinks that anyone who supposed that theological statements could be falsified by observations would show that he did not understand the word. Ogden insists that not only theological statements, but all statements which deal with reality as a whole will not be factual. He then claims that "the universe," a term that Flew regards as both cognitively meaningful and conceptually indispensable, displays the same features as "God."

Ogden charges that no conceivable observation could falsify the statement "The universe exists," because if there were no universe, then no human (or other) beings would be around to observe it; what is more, there would be no facts to observe. Ogden concludes that Flew must agree that there are statements which are not factual, but which nevertheless make meaningful existential claims. In other words, the

[2] Antony Flew, God and Philosophy (London: Hutchinson, 1966).

claims that "God exists" and that "The universe exists" are both cognitively meaningful. It is, however, clear that neither of them can be factually meaningful because neither of them is falsifiable by observations. Yet, because they make claims that involve existence, they cannot be analytically meaningful. Ogden therefore insists that Flew is too restrictive in his view of meaningful statements. To the analytic and the synthetic, Ogden adds theological and metaphysical statements as cognitively meaningful. It is in this context that Ogden's talk about classes of assertions (statements) must be understood. He insists that "the class of factual assertions is smaller than the class of meaningful assertions [which includes the analytic as well as the synthetic] but . . . also it is . . . smaller than the class of meaningful existential assertions [which includes the theological and metaphysical as well as the factual]" (see p. 293).

The more specific theological point being made by Ogden is that classical theism is more vulnerable to the challenge of contemporary empiricism than neoclassical theism. This point cannot be made fully accessible to readers who are not familiar with both Thomism (classical theism) and Charles Hartshorne's adaptation of Alfred North Whitehead's process philosophy to theological purposes (neoclassical theism). The general point concerns God's relation to the world. Thomists claim that God is perfect, eternal, omnipotent, omniscient, and that he has a number of other distinctive attributes or characteristics. For our purposes, the most important of these characteristics is the immutability (unchangeability) of God. Thomists claim that purely rational considerations force us to conceive of God as being unaffected by changes that take place in the world, even though we cannot imagine him in this way. In that case, there is an unbridgeable gulf between the transcendent God of classical theism and the world.

Hartshorne (and Ogden, of course) regards this classical view as incoherent. One way of understanding his criticisms is to focus on God's knowledge in relation to the problem of change. The Thomists claim that God is omniscient (all-knowing), yet they simultaneously claim that although change in our world is real, God's knowledge does not change. Hartshorne insists that this is contradictory, because if change is real, then even an omniscient being could not know actual states of affairs as actual in advance of their occurrence. In other words, if God is all-knowing, he could know in advance of my doing so, that I will paint my house brown. Yet he could not possibly know my present house as actually brown until I had done the painting. When I paint it,

God's knowledge will change from knowledge that my house is poten-tially brown to knowledge that it is actually brown. Therefore, God changes with changes of states of affairs (facts) in the world.[3]

Hartshorne also insists that the utterly changeless God of the classical theistic tradition is a religiously inadequate God. In everyday life we find that the superior being is the being that changes in response to others, not the being that is unaffected. If a man sees a tree, the tree is not conscious of the man and is presumably unaffected by the rela-tion. The man however acquires a new item of consciousness and his knowledge of the world changes. This is one of the things that makes the man superior to the tree. Hartshorne insists that God is utterly su-perior to any other reality by virtue of the fact that he is maximally changeable and not because he is changeless.

In his contribution to this volume Ogden spells out one impli-cation of this view for the question of God's relation to the factual order. Although no specific observations will falsify statements about God, which means that no theological statements are factual in character, there is, unlike the situation in classical theism, no gulf between God and the facts of this world. God is maximally responsive to factual changes, in part, because he knows everything that happens. As Ogden puts it:

> Although for this kind of theism [neoclassical] the truth that God exists is strictly metaphysical, and therefore factually nonfalsi-fiable, his essential nature as God, as modally coincident with all actuality and all possibility, implies that he is also the ever-growing integrity of all factual truth, and therefore precisely "supremely relevant" (see p. 295).

Ogden thinks that classical theism is far more vulnerable to the challenge of falsifiability than his own neoclassical variety. Father Copleston (see Section Three) and many of the theists mentioned in note 35, pp. 46 f., would strenuously disagree. This is in keeping with theological tradition. The theologians argue among themselves and agree only in rejecting reductionistic secularism.

---

[3] Charles Hartshorne, *Man's Vision of God* (Chicago: Willett, Clark 1941), pp. 97–105; *Philosophers Speak of God*, ed. Charles Hartshorne and William L. Reese (Chicago: University of Chicago Press, 1953), pp. 11ff, 18ff.

Theology and falsification
Antony Flew

Let us begin with a parable. It is a parable developed from a tale
told by John Wisdom in his haunting and revelatory article 'Gods'.[1]
Once upon a time two explorers came upon a clearing in the jungle.
In the clearing were growing many flowers and many weeds. One
explorer says, 'Some gardener must tend this plot.' The other dis-
agrees, 'There is no gardener'. So they pitch their tents and set a
watch. No gardener is ever seen. 'But perhaps he is an invisible
gardener.' So they set up a barbed-wire fence. They electrify it.
They patrol with bloodhounds. (For they remember how H. G.
Wells's *The Invisible Man* could be both smelt and touched though
he could not be seen.) But no shrieks ever suggest that some in-
truder has received a shock. No movements of the wire ever betray
an invisible climber. The bloodhounds never give cry. Yet still the
Believer is not convinced. 'But there is a gardener, invisible, intangible, insensible to electric shocks, a gardener who has no scent
and makes no sound, a gardener who comes secretly to look after
the garden which he loves.' At last the Sceptic despairs, 'But what
remains of your original assertion? Just how does what you call
an invisible, intangible, eternally elusive gardener differ from an
imaginary gardener or even from no gardener at all?'

In this parable we can see how what starts as an assertion,
that something exists or that there is some analogy between certain complexes of phenomena, may be reduced step by step to an
altogether different status, to an expression perhaps of a 'picture

From "Theology and Falsification" by Antony Flew, Richard M. Hare, and
Basil Mitchell in *New Essays in Philosophical Theology,* ed. Antony Flew and
Alasdair MacIntyre (London: SCM Press; New York: Macmillan, 1955), pp. 96–
108. Reprinted by permission of SCM Press, Ltd., The Macmillan Company,
and the authors.

[1] Proceedings of the Aristotelian Society, 1944–45, reprinted as Ch. X of *Logic
and Language,* Vol. 1 (Blackwell, 1951), and in his *Philosophy and Psychoanalysis* (Blackwell, 1953). ["Gods" is reprinted in Section Five of this volume, beginning on pp. 158ff.—Editors]

preference'.[2] The Sceptic says there is no gardener. The Believer says there is a gardener (but invisible, etc.). One man talks about sexual behaviour. Another man prefers to talk of Aphrodite (but knows that there is not really a superhuman person additional to, and somehow responsible for, all sexual phenomena).[3] The process of qualification may be checked at any point before the original assertion is completely withdrawn and something of that first assertion will remain (Tautology). Mr. Wells's invisible man could not, admittedly, be seen, but in all other respects he was a man like the rest of us. But though the process of qualification may be, and of course usually is, checked in time, it is not always judiciously so halted. Someone may dissipate his assertion completely without noticing that he has done so. A fine brash hypothesis may thus be killed by inches, the death by a thousand qualifications.

And in this, it seems to me, lies the peculiar danger, the endemic evil, of theological utterance. Take such utterances as 'God has a plan', 'God created the world', 'God loves us as a father loves his children'. They look at first sight very much like assertions, vast cosmological assertions. Of course, this is no sure sign that they either are, or are intended to be, assertions. But let us confine ourselves to the cases where those who utter such sentences intend them to express assertions. (Merely remarking parenthetically that those who intend or interpret such utterances as crypto-commands, expressions of wishes, disguised ejaculations, concealed ethics, or as anything else but assertions, are unlikely to succeed in making them either properly orthodox or practically effective).

Now to assert that such and such is the case is necessarily equivalent to denying that such and such is not the case.[4] Suppose then that we are in doubt as to what someone who gives vent to an utterance is asserting, or suppose that, more radically, we are sceptical as to whether he is really asserting anything at all, one way of trying to understand (or perhaps it will be to expose) his

[2] Cf. J. Wisdom, 'Other Minds,' *Mind*, 1940; reprinted in his *Other Minds* (Blackwell, 1952).

[3] Cf. Lucretius, *De Rerum Natura*, II, 655–60,

Hic siquis mare Neptunum Cereremque vocare/Constituet fruges et Bacchi nomine abuti/Mavolat quam laticis proprium proferre vocamen/Concedamus ut hic terrarum dictitet orbem/Esse deum matrem dum vera re tamen ipse/ Religione animum turpi contingere parcat.

[4] For those who prefer symbolism: $p \equiv \sim \sim p$.

utterance is to attempt to find what he would regard as counting against, or as being incompatible with, its truth. For if the utterance is indeed an assertion, it will necessarily be equivalent to a denial of the negation of that assertion. And anything which would count against the assertion, or which would induce the speaker to withdraw it and to admit that it had been mistaken, must be part of (or the whole of) the meaning of the negation of that assertion. And to know the meaning of the negation of an assertion, is as near as makes no matter, to know the meaning of that assertion.[5] And if there is nothing which a putative assertion denies then there is nothing which it asserts either: and so it is not really an assertion. When the Sceptic in the parable asked the Believer, 'Just how does what you call an invisible, intangible, eternally elusive gardener differ from an imaginary gardener or even from no gardener at all?' he was suggesting that the Believer's earlier statement had been so eroded by qualification that it was no longer an assertion at all.

Now it often seems to people who are not religious as if there was no conceivable event or series of events the occurrence of which would be admitted by sophisticated religious people to be a sufficient reason for conceding 'There wasn't a God after all' or 'God does not really love us then'. Someone tells us that God loves us as a father loves his children. We are reassured. But then we see a child dying of inoperable cancer of the throat. His earthly father is driven frantic in his efforts to help, but his Heavenly Father reveals no obvious sign of concern. Some qualification is made—God's love is 'not a merely human love' or it is 'an inscrutable love', perhaps—and we realize that such sufferings are quite compatible with the truth of the assertion that 'God loves us as a father (but, of course, . . .)'. We are reassured again. But then perhaps we ask: what is this assurance of God's (appropriately qualified) love worth, what is this apparent guarantee really a guarantee against? Just what would have to happen not merely (morally and wrongly) to tempt but also (logically and rightly) to entitle us to say 'God does not love us' or even 'God does not exist'? I therefore put to the succeeding symposiasts the simple central questions, 'What would have to occur or to have occurred to constitute for you a disproof of the love of, or of the existence of, God?'

University College of North Staffordshire, England

[5] For by simply negating $\sim p$ we get $p:\sim\sim p \equiv p$.

R. M. Hare

I wish to make it clear that I shall not try to defend Christianity in particular, but religion in general—not because I do not believe in Christianity, but because you cannot understand what Christianity is, until you have understood what religion is.

I must begin by confessing that, on the ground marked out by Flew, he seems to me to be completely victorious. I therefore shift my ground by relating another parable. A certain lunatic is convinced that all dons want to murder him. His friends introduce him to all the mildest and most respectable dons that they can find, and after each of them has retired, they say, 'You see, he doesn't really want to murder you; he spoke to you in a most cordial manner; surely you are convinced now?' But the lunatic replies 'Yes, but that was only his diabolical cunning; he's really plotting against me the whole time, like the rest of them; I know it I tell you'. However many kindly dons are produced, the reaction is still the same.

Now we say that such a person is deluded. But what is he deluded about? About the truth or falsity of an assertion? Let us apply Flew's test to him. There is no behaviour of dons that can be enacted which he will accept as counting against his theory; and therefore his theory, on this test, asserts nothing. But it does not follow that there is no difference between what he thinks about dons and what most of us think about them—otherwise we should not call him a lunatic and ourselves sane, and dons would have no reason to feel uneasy about his presence in Oxford.

Let us call that in which we differ from this lunatic, our respective *bliks*. He has an insane *blik* about dons; we have a sane one. It is important to realize that we have a sane one, not no *blik* at all; for there must be two sides to any argument—if he has a wrong *blik,* then those who are right about dons must have a right one. Flew has shown that a *blik* does not consist in an assertion or system of them; but nevertheless it is very important to have the right *blik*.

Some references to intervening discussion have been excised—Editors. [This note written by editors of original material, not of this volume.]

Let us try to imagine what it would be like to have different *bliks* about other things than dons. When I am driving my car, it sometimes occurs to me to wonder whether my movements of the steering-wheel will always continue to be followed by corresponding alterations in the direction of the car. I have never had a steering failure, though I have had skids, which must be similar. Moreover, I know enough about how the steering of my car is made, to know the sort of thing that would have to go wrong for the steering to fail—steel joints would have to part, or steel rods break, or something—but how do I know that this won't happen? The truth is, I don't know; I just have a *blik* about steel and its properties, so that normally I trust the steering of my car; but I find it not at all difficult to imagine what it would be like to lose this *blik* and acquire the opposite one. People would say I was silly about steel; but there would be no mistaking the reality of the difference between our respective *bliks*—for example, I should never go in a motor-car. Yet I should hesitate to say that the difference between us was the difference between contradictory assertions. No amount of safe arrivals or bench-tests will remove my *blik* and restore the normal one; for my *blik* is compatible with any finite number of such tests.

It was Hume who taught us that our whole commerce with the world depends upon our *blik* about the world; and that differences between *bliks* about the world cannot be settled by observation of what happens in the world. That was why, having performed the interesting experiment of doubting the ordinary man's *blik* about the world, and showing that no proof could be given to make us adopt one *blik* rather than another, he turned to backgammon to take his mind off the problem. It seems, indeed, to be impossible even to formulate as an assertion the normal *blik* about the world which makes me put my confidence in the future reliability of steel joints, in the continued ability of the road to support my car, and not gape beneath it revealing nothing below; in the general non-homicidal tendencies of dons; in my own continued well-being (in some sense of that word that I may not now fully understand) if I continue to do what is right according to my lights; in the general likelihood of people like Hitler coming to a bad end. But perhaps a formulation less inadequate than most is to be found in the Psalms: 'The earth is weak and all the inhabiters thereof: I bear up the pillars of it'.

The mistake of the position which Flew selects for attack is to regard this kind of talk as some sort of *explanation,* as scientists are accustomed to use the word. As such, it would obviously be ludicrous. We no longer believe in God as an Atlas—*nous n'avons pas besoin de cette hypothèse.* But it is nevertheless true to say that, as Hume saw, without a *blik* there can be no explanation; for it is by our *bliks* that we decide what is and what is not an explanation. Suppose we believed that everything that happened, happened by pure chance. This would not of course be an assertion; for it is compatible with anything happening or not happening, and so, incidentally, is its contradictory. But if we had this belief, we should not be able to explain or predict or plan anything. Thus, although we should not be *asserting* anything different from those of a more normal belief, there would be a great difference between us; and this is the sort of difference that there is between those who really believe in God and those who really disbelieve in him.

The word 'really' is important, and may excite suspicion. I put it in, because when people have had a good Christian upbringing, as have most of those who now profess not to believe in any sort of religion, it is very hard to discover what they really believe. The reason why they find it so easy to think that they are not religious, is that they have never got into the frame of mind of one who suffers from the doubts to which religion is the answer. Not for them the terrors of the primitive jungle. Having abandoned some of the more picturesque fringes of religion, they think that they have abandoned the whole thing—whereas in fact they still have got, and could not live without, a religion of a comfortably substantial, albeit highly sophisticated, kind, which differs from that of many 'religious people' in little more than this, that 'religious people' like to sing Psalms about theirs—a very natural and proper thing to do. But nevertheless there may be a big difference lying behind—the difference between two people who, though side by side, are walking in different directions. I do not know in what direction Flew is walking; perhaps he does not know either. But we have had some examples recently of various ways in which one can walk away from Christianity, and there are any number of possibilities. After all, man has not changed biologically since primitive times; it is his religion that has changed, and it can easily change again. And if you do not think that such changes make a difference, get acquainted with some Sikhs and some Mussulmans of the same Punjabi stock; you will find them quite different sorts of people.

There is an important difference between Flew's parable and my own which we have not yet noticed. The explorers do not mind about their garden; they discuss it with interest, but not with concern. But my lunatic, poor fellow, minds about dons; and I mind about the steering of my car; it often has people in it that I care for. It is because I mind very much about what goes on in the garden in which I find myself, that I am unable to share the explorers' detachment.

Balliol College, Oxford

Basil Mitchell

Flew's article is searching and perceptive, but there is, I think, something odd about his conduct of the theologian's case. The theologian surely would not deny that the fact of pain counts against the assertion that God loves men. This very incompatibility generates the most intractable of theological problems—the problem of evil. So the theologian *does* recognize the fact of pain as counting against Christian doctrine. But it is true that he will not allow it—or anything—to count decisively against it; for he is committed by his faith to trust in God. His attitude is not that of the detached observer, but of the believer.

Perhaps this can be brought out by yet another parable. In time of war in an occupied country, a member of the resistance meets one night a stranger who deeply impresses him. They spend that night together in conversation. The Stranger tells the partisan that he himself is on the side of the resistance—indeed that he is in command of it, and urges the partisan to have faith in him no matter what happens. The partisan is utterly convinced at that meeting of the Stranger's sincerity and constancy and undertakes to trust him.

They never meet in conditions of intimacy again. But sometimes the Stranger is seen helping members of the resistance, and the partisan is grateful and says to his friends, 'He is on our side'.

Sometimes he is seen in the uniform of the police handing over patriots to the occupying power. On these occasions his friends murmur against him: but the partisan still says, 'He is on our side'. He still believes that, in spite of appearances, the Stranger did not deceive him. Sometimes he asks the Stranger for help and receives it. He is then thankful. Sometimes he asks and does not receive it. Then he says, 'The Stranger knows best'. Sometimes his friends, in exasperation, say 'Well, what *would* he have to do for you to admit that you were wrong and that he is not on our side? But the partisan refuses to answer. He will not consent to put the Stranger to the test. And sometimes his friends complain, 'Well, if *that's* what you mean by his being on our side, the sooner he goes over to the other side the better'.

The partisan of the parable does not allow anything to count decisively against the proposition 'The Stranger is on our side'. This is because he has committed himself to trust the Stranger. But he of course recognizes that the Stranger's ambiguous behaviour *does* count against what he believes about him. It is precisely this situation which constitutes the trial of his faith.

When the partisan asks for help and doesn't get it, what can he do? He can (a) conclude that the stranger is not on our side or; (b) maintain that he is on our side, but that he has reasons for withholding help.

The first he will refuse to do. How long can he uphold the second position without its becoming just silly?

I don't think one can say in advance. It will depend on the nature of the impression created by the Stranger in the first place. It will depend, too, on the manner in which he takes the Stranger's behaviour. If he blandly dismisses it as of no consequence, as having no bearing upon his belief, it will be assumed that he is thoughtless or insane. And it quite obviously won't do for him to say easily, 'Oh, when used of the Stranger the phrase "is on our side" *means* ambiguous behaviour of this sort'. In that case he would be like the religious man who says blandly of a terrible disaster 'It is God's will'. No, he will only be regarded as sane and reasonable in his belief, if he experiences in himself the full force of the conflict.

It is here that my parable differs from Hare's. The partisan admits that many things may and do count against his belief: whereas Hare's lunatic who has a *blik* about dons doesn't admit that anything counts against his *blik*. Nothing *can* count against *bliks*. Also the partisan has a reason for having in the first instance committed himself, viz. the character of the Stranger; whereas the lunatic has no reason for his *blik* about dons—because, of course, you can't have reasons for *bliks*.

This means that I agree with Flew that theological utterances must be assertions. The partisan is making an assertion when he says, 'The Stranger is on our side'.

Do I want to say that the partisan's belief about the Stranger is, in any sense, an explanation? I think I do. It explains and makes sense of the Stranger's behaviour: it helps to explain also the resistance movement in the context of which he appears. In each case it differs from the interpretation which the others put upon the same facts.

'God loves men' resembles 'the Stranger is on our side' (and many other significant statements, e.g. historical ones) in not being conclusively falsifiable. They can both be treated in at least three different ways: (1) As provisional hypotheses to be discarded if experience tells against them; (2) As significant articles of faith; (3) As vacuous formulae (expressing, perhaps, a desire for reassurance) to which experience makes no difference and which make no difference to life.

The Christian, once he has committed himself, is precluded by his faith from taking up the first attitude: 'Thou shalt not tempt the Lord thy God'. He is in constant danger, as Flew has observed, of slipping into the third. But he need not; and, if he does, it is a failure in faith as well as in logic.

Keble College, Oxford

Antony Flew

It has been a good discussion: and I am glad to have helped to provoke it. But now—at least in *University*—it must come to an end: and the Editors of *University* have asked me to make some concluding remarks. Since it is impossible to deal with all the issues raised or to comment separately upon each contribution, I will concentrate on Mitchell and Hare, as representative of two very different kinds of response to the challenge made in 'Theology and Falsification'.

The challenge, it will be remembered, ran like this. Some theological utterances seem to, and are intended to, provide explanations or express assertions. Now an assertion, to be an assertion at all, must claim that things stand thus and thus; *and not otherwise*. Similarly an explanation, to be an explanation at all, must explain why this particular thing occurs; *and not something else*. Those last clauses are crucial. And yet sophisticated religious people—or so it seemed to me—are apt to overlook this, and tend to refuse to allow, not merely that anything actually does occur, but that anything conceivably could occur, which would count against their theological assertions and explanations. But in so far as they do this their supposed explanations are actually bogus, and their seeming assertions are really vacuous.

Mitchell's response to this challenge is admirably direct, straightforward, and understanding. He agrees 'that theological utterances must be assertions'. He agrees that if they are to be assertions, there must be something that would count against their truth. He agrees, too, that believers are in constant danger of transforming their would-be assertions into 'vacuous formulae'. But he takes me to task for an oddity in my 'conduct of the theologian's case. The theologian surely would not deny that the fact of pain counts against the assertion that God loves men. This very incompatibility generates the most intractable of theological problems, the problem of evil'. I think he is right. I should have made a distinction between two very different ways of dealing with what looks like evidence against the love of God: the way I stressed was the expedient of qualifying the original assertion; the way the theologian usually takes, at first, is to admit that it looks bad but to insist that there is—there must be—some explanation which will show that, in spite of appearances, there really is a God who loves us. His difficulty, it seems to me, is that he has given God attributes which rule out all possible saving explanations. In Mitchell's parable of the Stranger it is easy for the believer to find plausible excuses for ambiguous behavior: for the Stranger is a man. But suppose the Stranger is God. We cannot say that he would like to help but cannot: God is omnipotent. We cannot say that he would help if he only knew: God is omniscient. We cannot say that he is not responsible for the wickedness of others: God creates those others. Indeed an omnipotent, omniscient God must be an accessory before (and during) the fact to every human misdeed; as well as being responsible for every non-moral defect in

the universe. So, though I entirely concede that Mitchell was absolutely right to insist against me that the theologian's first move is
to look for an *explanation*, I still think that in the end, if relentlessly pursued, he will have to resort to the avoiding action of
qualification. And there lies the danger of that death by a thousand
qualifications, which would, I agree, constitute 'a failure in faith
as well as in logic'.

Hare's approach is fresh and bold. He confesses that 'on
the ground marked out by Flew, he seems to me to be completely
victorious'. He therefore introduces the concept of *blik*. But while
I think that there is room for some such concept in philosophy,
and that philosophers should be grateful to Hare for his invention, I nevertheless want to insist that any attempt to analyse
Christian religious utterances as expressions or affirmations of a
blik rather than as (at least would-be) assertions about the cosmos
is fundamentally misguided. *First*, because thus interpreted they
would be entirely unorthodox. If Hare's religion really is a *blik*,
involving no cosmological assertions about the nature and activities of a supposed personal creator, then surely he is not a
Christian at all? *Second*, because thus interpreted, they could
scarcely do the job they do. If they were not even intended as
assertions then many religious activities would become fraudulent, or merely silly. If 'You ought *because* it is God's will' asserts
no more than 'You ought', then the person who prefers the former
phraseology is not really giving a reason, but a fraudulent substitute for one, a dialectical dud cheque. If 'My soul must be immortal *because* God loves his children, etc.' asserts no more than
'My soul must be immortal', then the man who reassures himself
with theological arguments for immortality is being as silly as
the man who tries to clear his overdraft by writing his bank a
cheque on the same account. (Of course neither of these utterances
would be distinctively Christian: but this discussion never pretended to be so confined.) Religious utterances may indeed express false or even bogus assertions: but I simply do not believe
that they are not both intended and interpreted to be or at any
rate to presuppose assertions, at least in the context of religious
practice; whatever shifts may be demanded, in another context,
by the exigencies of theological apologetic.

One final suggestion. The philosophers of religion might
well draw upon George Orwell's last appalling nightmare *1984*
for the concept of *doublethink*. '*Doublethink* means the power of

holding two contradictory beliefs simultaneously, and accepting both of them. The party intellectual knows that he is playing tricks with reality, but by the exercise of *doublethink* he also satisfies himself that reality is not violated' (*1984*, p. 220). Perhaps religious intellectuals too are sometimes driven to doublethink in order to retain their faith in a loving God in face of the reality of a heartless and indifferent world. But of this more another time, perhaps.

University College of North Staffordshire, England

Antony Flew/"Theology and falsification" in retrospect

I

By the time when the present volume appears more than twenty-one years will have passed since the original publication of my first piece on "Theology and Falsification." So it is not surprising that the idea emerged, during correspondence with the editors about reprinting the material which appears in the previous article, that I might compose a sort of coming-of-age review of the ensuing controversy. Such a review may, and perhaps should, be more historical, and even biographical, than an ordinary purely philosophical paper. Certainly in this particular case some appreciation of the background can help a little to advance the discussion. I shall not, however, attempt a comprehensive survey of the literature. This is partly because I am sure that there must be more which has escaped me, partly because the exercise would be intolerably self-important, and partly for other reasons also.

The general background is very satisfactorily described in

Professor Diamond's Introduction. But we need to remember also what was more particular to Oxford: For that many-times-reprinted paper "Theology and Falsification" was originally commissioned as the opening contribution for the first number of a new journal, University, founded by Oxford undergraduates and now long since dead.[1] All contributors to this initial symposium were, quite properly, restricted to a maximum of one thousand words. So it was only with an apology that Professor MacIntyre and I gave some of them their first encore in New Essays in Philosophical Theology. "We have included contributions to the 'Theology and Falsification' controversy, by Flew, Hare, and Mitchell and pieces on 'Death' by MacKinnon and Flew, in spite of the fact that all of these are much shorter and slighter than the rest of the contents; and because they are often referred to, though they originally appeared in a journal now unfortunately defunct and consequently unobtainable."[2]

This occasional background explains not only the remarkable brevity of all the initial contributions but also the fact that I began with a challenge. Visitors have often commented upon the gladiatorial aspects of philosophy as it is pursued in Oxford. The favourite arena for the contests in the philosophy of religion had for many years been the meetings of the Socratic Club. This was founded either just before or during World War II on the initiative of Professor C. S. Lewis, a distinguished teacher of English literature, who originally—like most Oxford philosophers of his generation—was a product of the School of Literae Humaniores ("Greats"). Lewis later became a convert to Christianity and perhaps the most influential Anglican apologist of his time. The Socratic Club flourished, especially in the war and immediate post-war years. It provided the forum for all those, both faculty and undergraduates, who wanted no-holds-barred discussion of every sort of intellectual issue bearing on the truth or falsity of systems of religion which, for obvious local reasons, involved primarily the Christian religion.

This club was, therefore, not a group of professional philosophers. Nor were its interests by any means confined to the philosophy of religion, nor even indeed to philosophy. Again, although it held to its Socratic motto that "We must follow the argument wherever it leads," the club gave no encouragement to

[1] Oxford: Basil Blackwell, 1950 onwards. [Flew's paper first appeared in 1951. For details, see the Bibliography.—Editors]

[2] London: SCM Press, 1955, p. xi.

any comfortable donnish pretences that it really does not matter what the conclusions turn out to be. Within the framework of free yet personally concerned inquiry all comers were welcome; and many of us were, in a way which in some academic contexts would be felt to be indecent, openly committed and to that extent partisan. So when the Socratic Club went in for philosophy this was usually—to borrow a fine phrase from the *Autobiography* of Gilbert Ryle's predecessor, R. C. Collingwood—"gloves-off philosophy."[3]

These discussions referred frequently to Logical Positivism. But by the late forties that system had lost its clan. It was a sign of the times that the second edition of *Language, Truth and Logic*, appearing in 1946, just ten years after it first appeared, began with an Introduction of the author's afterthoughts.[4] This made the whole production a model object for Professor J. L. Austin's cynical epitome of one kind of philosophical essay: "First you say it. And then you take it all back." The all-destroying Logical Positivist of the twenties and thirties had come to seem an arbitrary and dogmatic manipulator. Not only was he apparently unable to provide compelling reasons why others should accept his principle of verifiability: he was himself forever fiddling with the formulation of that principal in order that it should include and exclude precisely all and only those utterances which he had by his own decision antecedently resolved to include or to exclude, as the case might be. The result was that the religious apologists, all by now equipped with their ready replies to Logical Positivism, were having it pretty easy—at least on the philosophical front.

II

The time was thus ripe for a fresh secular initiative. The final version of "Theology and Falsification" was printed after preliminary oral trials at the Socratic Club. The aim was to set the discussion off on a new and more fruitful tack, which, hopefully, it did. The method was to reverse the previous strategy. The Logical Positivist started from a general account of what he called "literal meaning;" itself a technicality equivalent to the "cognitive meaning" of some contributors to the present volume. This was summed up in his principle of verifiability, to which he appealed

3 Oxford: Oxford University Press, 1940.
4 London: Victor Gollancz, 1946.

as the instrument for the exclusion of ill-favoured utterances from the honoured society of the literally meaningful. But the new strategy eschewed any commitment to a general account of any sort of meaning—save in so far as such may be implicit in the ordinary notion of assertion. This totally familiar and untechnical notion provides the starting point. The crucial development consists in spelling out that "to assert that such and such is the case is necessarily equivalent to denying that such and such is not the case."[5] With this absolutely minimal commitment of theory—a commitment surely to a tautology only—the challenge is put to the believer himself to expound how much or how little the assertion of his belief amounts to: "what is this assurance of God's . . . love worth, what is this apparent guarantee really a guarantee against? Just what would have to happen not merely . . . to tempt but also . . . to entitle us to say 'God does not love us' or even 'God does not exist'?"

Where the Logical Positivist would boldly, not to say recklessly, launch his immediate offensive against whatever he could characterize as metaphysical, the new strategy begins by adopting what is fundamentally a defensive posture. This defensive and calculatedly non-committal posture is apt for response in all directions. The direction and the nature of the appropriate response necessarily depends upon the sense of the answers given to such questions; and no member of the Socratic Club could fail to be aware of the possibility of receiving radically different answers from different answerers, who all perhaps think of themselves as professing the same religion. Yet until we do have definite answers to work on it must be too early to offer a categorical report on the kind or kinds of meaning possessed or lacked by the supposed assertions thus construed. Just as I tried not to assume any general account of meaning, in order not to give grounds for charges of prejudice and dogmatism, so I studied not to make any premature statement on the present particular case or collection of cases of ostensible assertions about God.

Also, and I think appropriately to the original polemical context, my challenge is deliberately open and indeterminate as between the four possibilities which Professor Tooley distinguishes as (A) through (D) (p. 487). It is only and precisely when a

[5] Antony Flew, "Theology and Falsification" in *New Essays in Philosophical Theology*, ed. A. Flew and A. MacIntyre (London: SCM Press; New York: Macmillan, 1955), p. 98 [Essay appears in this section, p. 257.—Editors]

particular spokesman is confronted by the falsification challenge that it becomes possible to determine whether, for him, the ostensible disconfirmation is: either (A), not a disconfirmation at all of what he was wanting to say; or (B), something the decisive relevance of which he has somehow overlooked; or (C), something the decisive relevance of which he has fully grasped, but is irrationally refusing to allow to affect his beliefs; or (D), something the decisive relevance of which he has fully grasped, but which for Pascalian "reasons of the heart" he refuses to allow to disturb his faith.

III

We can now look at a few of the very many published comments on "Theology and Falsification," in the light of what I have already said in part one about the Oxford background and in part two about my own aim and method. I shall, for obvious reasons of economy, try not to repeat anything which I have put previously in print elsewhere.

1. In the first section of an article reprinted in part in Section Eight Professor Kai Nielsen writes: "Now, there is surely one way . . . to answer Flew's challenge, that is so very obvious that one wonders, perhaps fearing one's own naiveté, whether Flew would possibly have overlooked it. Asked to specify what would count against the assertion 'God loves mankind,' we could say 'God hates mankind' or 'God is really jealous of human beings' counts against such a religious claim."[6]

As so often in philosophy, to state the obvious is to make a useful move. In suggesting my likely counter-move Nielsen is characteristically sympathetic: ". . . what is needed, Flew would no doubt argue, are straightforward non-religious non-theological empirical statements to serve as evidence for the religious statement."[7] Nielsen then proceeds to draw on and to support the moral: "Religious statements purporting to make factual assertions must be confirmable or disconfirmable in principle by non-religious, straightforwardly empirical, factual statements."[8]

[6] Kai Nielsen, "On Fixing the Reference Range of 'God'," *Religious Studies* 2 (1966), 15.
[7] *Ibid.*
[8] *Ibid.*

In this, I think, after choosing so to speak the right sally-port, Nielsen presses his counter-offensive imprudently far. It is neither necessary nor, surely, correct to insist that in order to rate as factual assertions religious utterances must in principle be confirmable or disconfirmable by another and a particular sort of factual statement; namely, "non-religious, straightforwardly empirical, factual statements." Any such insistence must present that same appearance of arbitrariness which it was a main aim of the new strategy to avoid. It is quite sufficient, as well as more cautious and less provocative, to indicate that, if some candidate assertion cannot even in principle be confirmed or disconfirmed by anything which happens or which conceivably might happen in the ordinary world, then by the same token it can neither itself be an assertion about that ordinary world nor can any factual implications be deducible from it, whether general about the whole thing or particular and about us.

That religious statements are not about the everyday world need perhaps worry no one immediately; since in that sense of the word *Universe* in which the Universe is everything there is (with the exception only of its Creator, if such there be) a candidate assertion about God has to be not about the Universe but about God. But this concession is valueless. For the further implication that from such statements nothing can then be deduced about that everyday world must be unacceptable to anyone for whom the putative fact of God is supposed to be—in a modish catch-phrase—"supremely relevant." Immunity against even the theoretical possibility of falsification in this our world would have been achieved only and precisely at the cost of a complete and necessary irrelevance to it. If anyone were to choose to accept this consequence, and to construe his supposed religious assertions as making statements about another and a wholly isolated world, then the safely defensive response would be to say—with apologies to Thurber—that that is his world, and welcome to it. We ought, however, to add some warning of the semantic and still more the epistemological difficulties which must beset a religion so peculiarly exclusive and withdrawn.

2. An appropriate motto for the strategy proposed is, as I have suggested elsewhere, the Spanish proverb: " 'Take what you like,' said God, 'take it; and pay for it'." For this strategy just consists of insisting that assertion has its price, and that this price

corresponds exactly to the scope of the assertion proposed. You cannot make an assertion without incurring its charge, and that charge is always the theoretical possibility of falsification by whatever the actual realities may be. If you want to limit the charges, then you have to restrict the scope of your assertions accordingly. But then again, the more you restrict the scope of your assertions the less you succeed in saying. The truth is that there is no escape. Yet it is all too humanly understandable to want to have something without paying the price.

A second illustration of the application of the same principle in the present context can be got from Father Thomas Corbishley's first reply in University. He wrote: "So . . . to the question 'What would have to occur, or to have occurred to constitute for you a disproof of the love of, or of the existence of, God?' the only thing to be said is, quite literally, 'Nothing.' . . . for me the existence of nothing at all, i.e. the non-existence of anything at all, would constitute for me a disproof of the existence of God."[9]

This is a clear, straight answer. It is probably representative of at least one school of Thomist thought. Nevertheless, as it stands, without prefix or suffix, it carries an implication which Corbishley would have to regard as catastrophic. For if in asserting the existence of God he really is denying nothing else but the nonexistence of a Universe, then for him this assertion is formally equivalent to an assertion that there is a Universe; and, when you bring into the reckoning the further consideration that he must allow worthiness to be worshipped to be one of the essential characteristics of God, it seems that Corbishley would thereby become committed to the heretical and, hence to him, unacceptable doctrine of pantheism.

3. A third and comparatively massive response to "Theology and Falsification" is to be found in Professor R. S. Heimbeck's book Theology and Meaning.[10] Heimbeck faults my essays on three main counts: (1) "the assumption that the meaning of a sentence is equivalent to the empirical expectations of the statement it makes"; (2) "the identification of the 'counts against' and the 'is incompatible with' relations"; and (3) "the suggestion that G-statements expressing the love of God and the existence of

[9] Thomas Corbishley, "Theology and Falsification," University, 1 (1950), 10.
[10] London: C. Allen and Unwin, 1969.

God are unfalsifiable."[11] (The expression 'G-statement' has earlier been defined as "any statement about God, any statement entailing a statement about God, or any statement presupposing a commitment to the existence of God."[12])

In pressing the first and the third of his three charges I think that Heimbeck greatly underrates my calculated reluctance to make bold initial assumptions in the manner of the old Logical Positivists. For, with regard to his first objection, my point was not (in his words) "that the meaning of a sentence is equivalent to the empirical expectations of the statement it makes,"[13] but that (quoting myself) "to assert that such and such is the case is necessarily equivalent to denying that such and such is not the case." The latter is only an analytic truth about statements, whereas the former is a general claim about all meaning. And the latter specifies no particular kind of verification or falsification, whereas the former requires empirical expectations.

On Heimbeck's third charge my innocence is perhaps less easy to establish. Certainly I did suggest that "the death by a thousand qualifications" constitutes "the peculiar danger, the endemic evil, of theological utterance," and that "it often seems to people who are not religious as if there were no conceivable event or series of events the occurrence of which would be admitted by sophisticated religious people to be a sufficient reason for conceding 'There wasn't a God after all' or 'God does not really love us then'."[14] Had I when I wrote that I enjoyed my present advantage of having read Nielsen's paper partly reprinted in Section Eight above, I would not have resisted quoting again his very striking illustration: " 'Good fortune without reveals the hand of God; bad fortune, if it is not a matter of just punishment, teaches that God's ways are unintelligible, not that there are no ways of God'."[15] But I should still have wanted to insist that to maintain that something is the besetting danger to which particularly the sophisticated often seem in fact to succumb, is certainly not to

[11] *Ibid.*, p. 123.
[12] *Ibid.*, p. 29n.
[13] *Ibid.*
[14] Flew, "Theology and Falsification," in *New Essays in Philosophical Theology,* pp. 97–98. [Essay appears in this Section, p. 257.—Editors]
[15] Nielsen, "On Fixing the Reference Range of 'God'," p. 15. [Nielsen is quoting from Emil L. Fackenheim, "On the Eclipse of God," *Commentary* 37 (1964), 55.—Editors]

say, nor surely is it even to suggest, that this always does happen
with every spokesman or even with every sophisticated spokesman. (A danger which is inescapable is not a danger but a fate!)

What has perhaps put me at cross-purposes with both
Heimbeck and many others is a widespread failure, which the
present paper may help to restore, to appreciate differences between the two approaches. Tooley, for instance, explains at the
very beginning of his article in Section Ten: "Because of the ever
widening range of interpretations that are assigned to the term
'God,' it is important to specify the interpretation that one intends
to place upon it, before embarking upon a discussion of philosophical issues concerned with theological statements" (p. 482).
Tooley thus commits himself to taking this specified object
position as static. There is to be no question of a defender ma-
noeuvring himself, perhaps all unwittingly, into some other and
maybe radically different stance. But in "Theology and Falsification" I was attempting something else. What I proposed, I proposed with a calculated mixture of provocation and restraint, as a
first move in a discussion. And in a discussion, especially an hard-
driving polemical discussion, participants may be pressed into
new positions.

One passage in my second contribution to the original *University* symposium is most likely to have confused someone who
did not realize the relevance of the differences between these two
different, and on different occasions, equally legitimate approaches. I allowed that although Professor Basil Mitchell was
"right to insist against me that the theologian's first move is to
look for an *explanation* . . . in the end, if relentlessly pursued, he
will have to resort to the avoiding action of *qualification*. And
there lies the danger of that death by a thousand qualifications,
which would, I agree, constitute 'a failure in faith as well as in
logic' "[16] [italics in original]. To Tooley and Heimbeck this passage
may have appeared, despite that last sentence, to carry the implication "that G-statements," in the last analysis, "are unfalsifiable." What it actually does imply is that the ostensibly assertive
statements usually are falsifiable; but that, under pressure showing that if falsifiable they must be false, such genuine statements

[16] Flew, "Theology and Falsification," *New Essays,* p. 107. [See p. 267 in this
volume.—Editors]

may be but certainly are not always abandoned in favour of what is really something else.

Yet even this does too little justice to the dynamics of belief. For under such strong conflicting pressures as can be involved in these basic issues of ideology a man may oscillate between two incompatible interpretations of the same form of words, or else insist on having it both ways at once. In the Parthian shot from my second contribution I transfixed the latter possibility with a cruel definition from George Orwell's 1984: " 'Doublethink means the power of holding two contradictory beliefs simultaneously, and accepting both of them.' . . . Perhaps religious intellectuals too are sometimes driven to doublethink in order to retain their faith in a loving God in the face of the reality of a heartless and indifferent world."[17] This passage is of course further evidence against Heimbeck's third charge. But it is still static, and thus fails to embrace the former possibility.[18]

4. Heimbeck's second charge deserves a subsection to itself. To this one I plead guilty. It was a serious offence. To say that some occurrence counts against the truth of a given utterance is not at all the same as saying that that occurrence is incompatible with its truth. It was wrong to conflate the two cases, or try to deal with both at the same time. My main argument bore directly only on the latter: "to know the meaning of the negation of an assertion is . . . . to know the meaning of that assertion. And if there is nothing which a putative assertion denies then there is nothing which it asserts either: and so it is not really an assertion" (p. 259).

To deal satisfactorily with the former, the case of counting against, is another and much trickier matter. It was to this that Mitchell, among my earlier critics, in fact addressed himself. He made the compelling point that any believer who accepts that the traditional theist Problem of Evil is indeed a problem for him thereby allows that the occurrence of the evil in question does count against what he wants to assert about his God; and that he thus becomes committed to maintaining that there is some saving

---

[17] Flew, "Theology and Falsification," New Essays, p. 108. [See p. 268 of this volume.—Editors]

[18] One may in this connection recall a similar suggestion made by Professor P. F. Strawson in his Introduction to Logical Theory about certain equivocal utterances in another and a much less emotionally engaged context: "under pressure they may tend to tautology; and, when the pressure is removed, assume an expansively synthetic air" (London: Methuen, 1952), p. 252.

explanation, even if he does not himself know what it is. This point I accepted immediately, though with the warning that the difficulties of finding excuses for omnipotence are necessarily so intractable that the apologist "in the end, if relentlessly pursued . . . will have to resort to the avoiding action of *qualification*".

Mr. D. R. Duff-Forbes, in a paper published in the *Australasian Journal of Philosophy* in 1961, took Mitchell to be saying that while many things do count against the truth of assertions of faith, no single occurrence, and no accumulation of occurrences, conceivably could count decisively.[19] I then suggested that this was a misreading, arising from a common but interesting confusion.[20] Mitchell has since assured me privately that my interpretation, rather than that of Duff-Forbes, was correct. Nevertheless, Duff-Forbes certainly was right to insist that, if anyone did take the line which he attributed to Mitchell, then that would be to deprive the expression "count against" of most if not all of its present meaning. It would also erode the difference by which Hare's position is supposed to be distinguished from that of Mitchell. For in discussing what we might label the ur-*blik*-paranoia about dons—Hare says of his lunatic: "There is no behaviour of dons . . . which he will accept as counting against his theory. . . ." He then comments: "But it does not follow that there is no difference between what he thinks about dons and what most of us think about them—otherwise we should not call him a lunatic and ourselves sane, and dons would have no reason to feel uneasy about his presence in Oxford."[21]

What makes this difficult to sort out is, first, that neither of the examples of bliks which Hare himself provides actually succeeds in satisfying Hare's own stipulation of what a blik is supposed to be; and second, that Hare, after insisting that his lunatic will accept nothing "as counting against his theory," then forthwith proceeds to describe him as doing precisely this. Hare's two examples fail to meet his own requirement that bliks are not to be distinguished from one another by reference to any characteristic assertions. For those who have the abnormal blik about steel

---

[19] 39 (August 1961), pp. 143–154.

[20] "Falsification and Hypothesis in Theology," *Australasian Journal of Philosophy* 40 (December 1962): 318–323.

[21] R. M. Hare, "Theology and Falsification," *New Essays in Philosophical Theology*, p. 100. [Both quotations appear on p. 260 of this volume.—Editors]

would differ from the rest of us with the normal one precisely and only in respect of their different, perverse, stubbornly maintained, and in fact, false, beliefs about the structural properties of steel; while the exemplar of the ur-*blik* is, as we have just this minute reminded ourselves, distinguished from the normal man of sense by the "difference between what he thinks about dons and what most of us think about them" (p. 260).

Again and similarly, Hare's statement that there is nothing which his lunatic "will accept as counting against his theory" is not consistent with Hare's own specification, that, after being introduced to one of "the mildest and most respectable dons," his "lunatic replies, 'Yes, but that was only his diabolical cunning. . . '." For what, Mitchell might have asked, is the point of postulating such diabolical cunning if it is not to provide a saving explanation for what is accepted as being ostensibly contrary evidence? Mitchell might indeed have asked this. In fact he contrasted Hare's lunatic with the hero of his own Parable of the Stranger: "The partisan admits that many things may and do count against his belief: whereas Hare's lunatic who has a *blik* about dons doesn't admit that anything counts against his *blik*.[22] Duff-Forbes, on the other hand, saw the similarity between the two cases: "*both* the lunatic *and* the partisan allow that certain states of affairs count against their respective theories. . . ." But he interprets this in the opposite sense, by adding immediately: "but only in the sense that they *appear* to count against, but in fact don't."[23]

It looks to me now as if both Hare and Duff-Forbes went wrong because they followed in my false footsteps. For, surely, the reason why Hare, and more obviously, Duff-Forbes refuse to accept these as genuine cases of counting against is that for them nothing really counts against if it is only ostensibly and immediately, and not really and ultimately, irreconcilable with the hypothesis. But then such ultimate irreconcilability is logical incompatibility, which ought, as Heimbeck insists, to be distinguished from merely counting against.

Can I now offer any kind of summing up? First, then, considered as what it was originally intended to be, an attempt to set

---

[22] Basil Mitchell, "Theology and Falsification," *New Essays in Philosophical Theology,* p. 105. [Essay appears in this Section, p. 263.—Editors]

[23] *Ibid.,* p. 151. Italics his.

discussion on a fresh and more fruitful course, "Theology and Falsification" must be rated as vastly successful. I have long since lost count of the number of times it has been reprinted in philosophical anthologies. Certainly the total is now well into double figures. And, whatever its deficiencies and the misdirections of the discussions which it has helped to focus or to provoke, I know no one who would wish in this particular to return to the conditions of the thirties and the forties.

But, second, the paper had two gross and admitted faults: the first was pointed out by Mitchell in the second issue of *University*, and the second has just been considered in the fourth subsection of Part Three above. In a paper of little more than a thousand words that is perhaps a formidably bad score. The question arises whether if these were removed anything fit for salvage would remain.

To this I reply, third, that the heart of the matter does still remain. This heart of the matter as I see it is the challenging insistence that assertion has its price: " 'Take what you like', said God, 'take it; and pay for it'." Within the present coming-of-age review, the importance of this is surely adequately vindicated by the arguments of the first two subsections of Part Three. Certainly I failed—at the time of my philosophical birth, so to speak—to take due account of the enormous difficulties of applying this principle in detail to claims which have to be appraised indirectly by the examination of evidences for and against, rather than directly, by searching for the presence or absence of the criteria supplied by the sum of their entailments. I do nevertheless still want to maintain that the principle does apply to both.

Notoriously, any hypothesis, given sufficient ingenuity and a willingness to make whatever arbitrary postulates may be required, can be squared with any recalcitrant fact. Often such saving explanations are actually correct. Yet, equally notoriously, the process of saving the hypothesis is one which can go on too long. It can, as Mitchell says, become "just silly", and in Hare's lunatic it is what makes that lunatic a lunatic. Because counting against is not the same as being incompatible with, it is impossible to draw precise and proven lines to show when too long begins. Yet that does not make it any the less true that the man—be he the lunatic, the lover, the man of theory, or the man of faith—who goes on too long is by such perseveration trying to get his assertion on the cheap.[24] To demand at this stage of the game that he himself specify his own sticking point can be a salutary shock treatment for the epicyclic degeneration of an hypothesis.[25]

Fourth, and finally, suppose that I were to undertake to produce today another short piece again presenting methodology with a polemical secular edge, would it be a revised version of "Theology and Falsification" corrected in the ways indicated above? No, not now. In part the reason is one of the possibilities of expression rather than of philosophical content: even if I am right on the point just made in the previous paragraph it would surely be excessively difficult both to distinguish and to deal faithfully with the two cases, of incompatibility and of counting against, within the same one thousand words. But the main reason is that I should now prefer to begin from the presumption of atheism—a thesis about the onus of proof—leaving a falsification challenge until a rather later stage in the discussion. The nub of this thesis, which can certainly be developed very forcefully within the original length limit, is that it is up to the spokesman for any sort of theism: first, to introduce and explain his proposed concept of God; and, second, to provide some good reason for believing that this concept does in fact have an object.

To accept this always defeasible presumption is again to adopt a powerful defensive posture, combining the minimum of possibly disputatious assumption with the maximum of aptness for response in all directions. And yet it contrives to cover a wider front than that occupied in "Theology and Falsification". For by starting from this presumption of atheism we put all the problems of meaning and coherence together at the beginning where they belong, whereas the approach of "Theology and Falsification" concentrated on the single notion of falsifiability. And this suggested new approach makes the demand that it is really up to the believer or the potential believer himself to take the initiative of offering

[24] [On the cheap is a British colloquialism meaning, roughly, "easily" or "cheaply."—Editors]

[25] Consider some very relevant remarks made by John Stuart Mill in his essay on "Nature": "If a tenth part of the pains which have been expended in finding benevolent adaptations in all nature, had been employed in collecting evidence to blacken the character of the Creator, what scope for comment would not have been found in the entire existence of the lower animals, divided, with scarcely an exception, into devourers and devoured, and a prey to a thousand ills from which they are denied the faculties for protecting themselves!" (Three Essays on Religion. London: Longmans Green, 1874, p. 58).

some reason for thinking that his proposition is true; whereas that old challenge asked only that his assertions should be falsifiable, not that they should be shown to be true, or at least in some degree plausible.[26] To go on from here, however, would be to begin another story.[27]

[26] This requirement constitutes another dimension to the problem about falsifiability. For falsifiability may be secured only at the cost of enormous implausibility. Consider here the fair comment made in Section Six, p. 214 above: "Even *assuming* their *intelligibility,* I should think their very oddness and extreme implausibility would be a very good reason for those who tie their belief in God to such notions to give up their belief and place a belief in God in the same class as a belief in Santa Claus or in the Easter Bunny."

Incidentally, is it not unnecessarily provocative for Professor Hick to locate his "resurrection world" in "a different space"? This gives purchase for Nielsen's rhetorical questions: "What counts as a space that is 'a different space' from physical space? Has any meaning been given to the words 'non-physical space'", (p. 214), and so on. Surely if faith were still strong our universe would be sufficiently large for a very remote location "in physical space" to provide an acceptable combination of falsifiability in principle with security against falsification in, and by, fact.

[27] One which I have indeed myself begun elsewhere: in *God and Philosophy* (London: Hutchinson, 1966; New York: Harcourt Brace and World, 1966; and New York: Delta Paperbacks, 1967); and in a Howard Hintz Memorial Foundation lecture delivered at the University of Arizona in January 1971, and ultimately to be published with other lectures in the same series by the University of Arizona Press, Tucson.

Although the editors of the present volume were kind enough to offer me the opportunity to add a comment on Professor Litzenburg's final contribution (pp. 284f.), it seemed to me that that contribution was opening the door wider on a new discussion, and one to which any further contribution from me had best be made later and elsewhere.

I make this occasion to mention the critical notice of my *God and Philosophy* by Professor Schubert Ogden: The editors of *The Journal of Religion* published, so to speak, reciprocal reviews of his *The Reality of God* (New York: Harper and Row, 1963) and of this book of mine in 48(April 1968), pp. 150–181.

Thomas V. Litzenburg, Jr./"Any sort of theism" and the "onus of proof"

Flew's provocative review of the "Theology and Falsification" debate is a conscious effort to benefit from past mistakes and to initiate fresh and fruitful moves. This is a worthy goal, but I do not think Flew succeeds, because I am not convinced by Flew's protestation—if such it be—that he "eschewed any commitment to a general account of any sort of meaning" in setting forth his original challenge. I am suggesting, in a word, that his challenge of falsifiability looks very much like a claim about the sorts of meaning statements can have.

Surely, the view of meaning that is operative in Flew's original challenge is more than "a totally familiar and untechnical notion" (p. 272), more than an "absolutely minimal commitment of theory" (p. 272), and more than "a commitment . . . to a tautology only." It is also more than the mere contention that "to assert that such and such is the case is necessarily equivalent to denying that

284

such and such is not the case" (p. 258). That it is more is evidenced, in large part, by Flew's supplementary contention that "to know the meaning of the negation of an assertion, is as near as makes no matter, to know the meaning of that assertion"[1] (p. 259).

I am not at all clear as to just how close this "near as makes no matter" shuffle in logic brings us to the "meaning" of an "assertion." But I dare say that if it does bring us anywhere within the general vicinity then surely we are having to do with the problem of meaning. This, of course, should come as no surprise if we recall that the principle of falsifiability as a criterion—if not a theory—of meaning has been seriously entertained as a more satisfactory philosophical proposal than the principle of verifiability. This being—as it most surely is—a matter of record, it behooves Flew to say considerably more than he has in order to disassociate himself from those philosophers who have employed falsifiability as the cutting edge of meaning.

My point, I think, has been made—namely, to indicate that I approach Flew with a certain bias concerning what counts as a "commitment to a general account of any sort of meaning." The relevance of my particular bias will become evident as I turn to Flew's most recent discussion of his challenge of falsifiability.

It would appear that in reformulating his challenge Flew has cast his net too far in his effort "to cover a wider front than that occupied in 'Theology and Falsification.'" For it could be argued that in his zeal to widen the horizon of the discussion he has come very close to "throwing out the baby with the bath water." I say this because nowhere in the formulation of his "new challenge"— if I may be allowed to dub it that—do I find reference to any of the rather stock-in-trade philosophical ploys that confine the

---

[1] Thomas McPherson has chided a critic of Flew for failing to distinguish between saying (1) "The negation of the denial of an assertion *means the same thing as* the assertion" and (2) *"The meaning of an assertion* is the negation of its denial" ("The Falsification Challenge: a Comment," *Religious Studies,* 5 [1969], 83.). While his point is well taken it also is applicable to Flew. McPherson, it seems, simply assumes that Flew's supplementary contention ("to know the meaning of the negation of an assertion, is as near as makes no matter, to know the meaning of that assertion") cannot be read as anything other than a restatement of his contention that "to assert such and such is the case is necessarily equivalent to denying that such and such is not the case." But that is *precisely* what is at issue—namely, whether Flew is *only* dealing with a *tautology* ("the negation of the denial of an assertion means the same thing as the assertion") or with a *criterion* (principle of falsifiability) *of meaning* ("the meaning of an assertion is the negation of its denial") as well.

original debate to what Flew insisted was the normative or orthodox version of theism. Because I have never understood how one
manages to determine just what that version might be, I am more
interested in Flew's new and, by comparison, somewhat unrestricted "thesis about the onus of proof"—namely, "that it is up to
the spokesman of any sort of theism first, to introduce and explain
his proposed concept of God; and, second, to provide some good
reason for believing that this concept does in fact have an object."

I want to examine this "thesis" not because I care to speak
to it by way of a theological apology—although I might find that
to be an inviting task if I could be certain that Flew would stand
foursquare behind this position. In point of fact, however, I do not
see how he can do so and it is for this reason that I prefer, instead,
to confine myself to a discussion of the thesis.

Flew is quite right in arguing that his new challenge "puts
all the problems of meaning and coherence together at the beginning." He clearly is affording the believer an opportunity to say
straight away what it is that *he* means by his concept of God.
While I commend him for his newly found magnanimity toward
the theist, I am inclined to suspect that therein lies both the weakness as well as the charm of his new challenge.

No longer confronted at the outset by implied stipulative
definitions of theism, the believer is being asked to state how it is
that he uses his concept of God. In other words, I am taking Flew
seriously when he challenges the "spokesman for *any sort* [italics
mine] of theism" to "introduce and explain his proposed concept
of God" and that is why I assume that he is not asking for a
definition in the strictest—if, indeed, in any—sense of the word.
This being the case, I find nothing in Flew's *first* condition that
prohibits the believer from responding to his challenge with an
introduction and explanation that meet "the problems of meaning
and coherence" by way of a series of more or less detailed descriptions of how he uses his concept of God.

Perhaps Flew would reply that he was not asking for descriptions of use. If so, I would be inclined to note that—inten-
tionally or otherwise—he has failed in the first instance to specify
what sort of introduction and explanation of a proposed concept of
God he would find acceptable. In the absence of any such specification it is wholly proper for the believer to make the first move
and step into the breech by adopting the not unfamiliar position
that "for a *large* class of cases—though not for all—in which we

employ the word 'meaning' it can be defined thus: the meaning of a word is its use in the language."[2]

I am, of course, aware of the fact that Wittgenstein continues this passage by adding that "the *meaning* of a name is sometimes explained by pointing to its bearer."[3] Critics of theology may insist that this "rider" ought to be applied to "God" if the concept is to have factual meaning. Yet surely, we cannot determine, in advance of a consideration of specific theological arguments, whether the factually meaningful use of *God* depends on the ability of theologians to point to the bearer of this name.[4] Yet, as I will shortly show, Flew seems to make this demand.

On the basis of the first condition stipulated in Flew's thesis it would seem logically possible that a "spokesman" for some sort of theism could give an adequate account of what he meant by *God* provided, of course, that the account was both consistent and coherent. That the account rendered was not to Flew's liking would be quite beside the point. This is so precisely because within the limits of the *first* condition of his thesis he has neither stated what he means by *theism* nor proposed a criterion of meaning but, instead, has left it to the "spokesman for any sort of theism" to do both.

Lest I prematurely proclaim the death of Flew's thesis, it is advisable to take up his *second* condition—namely, that the believer "provide some good reason for believing that this concept does in fact have an object." At first blush it looks as though the believer's effort to meet Flew's new challenge may have been in vain, that I have misunderstood Flew, and that the "presumption of atheism" wins the day. For unlike the *first* condition of his thesis, Flew's *second* condition does entail a criterion or theory of meaning—one that is often characterized as the "word-object" theory. In effect, Flew has said that the believer must "provide some good reason for believing" that there exists an *object* which is *denoted* by the believer's concept of God. If this condition stands, then clearly it must be met.

[2] Ludwig Wittgenstein, *Philosophical Investigations,* 3rd ed. (New York: The Macmillan Company, 1969), p. 20e, para. 43. I am not suggesting that the adoption of this particular criterion of meaning is free of difficulties. Rather, I am contending that, at this point, it is quite in order for the believer to specify whatever criterion he thinks is sound.

[3] Ibid., p. 21e, para. 43.

[4] This caveat would become the cutting edge of a reply to the critics of theology if one were proposing a non-cognitive use for the concept of *God.*

There are several ways in which one might try to deal with the dilemma posed by this *second* condition. I might argue that while there are reasons and there are reasons, it is a wholly open question, at this point, as to what will count as a "good reason." Then, again, I might choose the more difficult task of showing that it is one thing to explain why I believe something to be the case and quite another to demonstrate that something in fact *is* the case. Thirdly, I could, I suppose, contend that with respect to the concept of God it is none too clear as to what is meant by saying that "this concept does *in fact* [italics mine] have an object"— thereby, of course, raising the murky question of what it means to speak of the *existence* of God. Lastly, I might wax philosophical on the subject of how theologically wrong-headed it is to conceive of God as a *being* or an *entity*. For myself, however, I find none of these alternatives too attractive. They each point toward roads once smoothly paved with good theological intentions that are now closed for repairs occasioned by the presence of an excessive number of philosophical potholes.

I prefer, instead, to take a detour which may well turn out to be a shorter way around the problem. I think it can be argued that in accepting the *first* condition it is logically possible that a believer could "introduce and explain his proposed concept" without having to meet Flew's *second* condition. It is conceivable, in other words, that precisely by meeting the *first* condition the believer can show, by the particular and specific use to which he puts his concept of God, that the *second* condition is not applicable. Nothing in Flew's *first* condition excludes this possibility. Moreover, this move would still remain a logical possibility for the believer even if he accepted the "rider" that "sometimes" the "*meaning* of a name" is "explained by pointing to its bearer." All he would have to show is that, in this instance, the "rider" is not applicable, which, in effect, is what Crombie tries to do in his contribution to this volume.

Granted, Flew can reply that the believer has rejected rather than met the *second* condition. However, if he takes this tack then surely the "onus of proof" has now fallen to Flew and he must (1) explain what he means by "any sort of theism" and (2) justify his employment of a restrictive criterion (theory) of meaning. It is not at all clear to me that having to take on either of these tasks is part of what Flew envisioned as a new and more "powerful defensive posture" which leaves it up to the "believer himself to take the initiative of offering some reason for thinking that his proposition is true."

Flew has pointed to a new direction. He cannot, however, be said to have successfully set the discussion going in that direction until he is more specific about his criterion of meaning and about the kind of theology he is challenging.

Schubert M. Ogden/'"Theology and falsification' in retrospect": a reply

I hope it will be understood if I do not attempt to give a balanced account of my reaction to Professor Flew's essay by considering the many points where I tend to share his position. I will concentrate, instead, on the main points where I have difficulty with it. Because my response to his essay will be thus one-sided, I would like to state right at the outset that I nevertheless remain grateful for, and personally indebted to, his contribution to contemporary theistic discussion. More than that, I would like to repeat the judgment I have made elsewhere that, if the theistic issue were the kind of issue he assumes, and if the theism he chooses to consider were the only theism there is, then he might well be considered to have made his case against the theistic conclusion.

But this judgment evidently leaves room for further discussion, and I must now try to indicate the direction that I, for one, hope it might take.

Obviously, the assumption shared by all the participants in the original "theology and falsification" debate is Flew's own assumption that if theological assertions are meaningful assertions at all, they must be factual assertions—by which I mean simply assertions that at least in principle are falsifiable because there are at least conceivable facts that could count against them. Except for this shared assumption, there would have been nothing about theological assertions for the "falsification challenge" to challenge, and neither of the typical responses to it—whether "right-wing" or "left-wing"—would have been intelligible responses.[1] And yet, significantly, I think, each of the main participants in the original discussion in his own way admitted that theological assertions—especially those of a so-called "sophisticated theism"—do not in fact perform as factual assertions. The pertinent question, therefore, is why, despite this admitted fact, they nevertheless all agreed in Flew's initial assumption.

I submit that the likely answer is that they also all agreed more or less in his tacit presupposition which appears fundamental to the position of his present paper: that factual assertions are the only meaningful assertions there are. Yet, so far from being, as he avers, a "tautology," or even an "absolutely minimal commitment of theory" (p. 272), this presupposition as it stands seems to me clearly controversial—and that on at least two counts.

In the first place, it does not follow that the premise stated in the paper that "to assert that such and such is the case is necessarily equivalent to denying that such and such is not the case" (p. 272), that to assert that such and such is the case is necessarily equivalent to denying that such and such is not *factually* the case. Why? Because there is a whole class of assertions commonly recognized as meaningful, any one of which would illustrate the truth of the premise while also illustrating the falsity of the conclusion. I refer, of course, to the class of mathematical and logical assertions. Of all such assertions it is indeed true that they are equivalent to the denials of their contradictories; and yet, because the assertions themselves are not factual, neither are their contradictories and neither, therefore, are the denials to which they are logically equivalent.

Having made so elementary a point, however, I hasten to

---

[1] "Right wing" responses are those that claim cognitive meaning for theological statements, such as Crombie's contribution to this volume; "left wing" responses are those which deny that theological statements are cognitively meaningful, for example, Braithwaite's contribution to this volume.—Editors.

say that I do not make it because I imagine Flew, or anyone else, would wish seriously to dispute it. From what he has often written in other contexts, it is no doubt reasonable to infer that the premise stated and employed in his paper is subject to an unspoken restriction that in effect concedes the point I have bothered to make. Even so, if the assumption of the "falsification challenge" is that theological assertions must be of a certain kind, and if that assumption, in turn, rests on some presupposition as to the kinds of assertion that are logically possible, it strikes me as terribly important that presupposition not be left unexpressed but, rather, explicitly formulated, together with whatever refinements may be essential to it.

To this end, therefore, I propose to restate Flow's premise so as to make explicit the restriction he no doubt understands in employing it in his paper. Seeing that mathematical and logical assertions, though commonly recognized to be meaningful, are also commonly recognized to be nonexistential, I suggest the following restatement: "to assert that such and such is *existentially* the case is necessarily equivalent to denying that such and such is not *existentially* the case."

But then, in the second place, it does not follow even from this restated premise that to assert that such and such is existentially the case is necessarily equivalent to denying that such and such is not *factually* the case. Why? Because there is a whole class of assertions recognized by some of us to be meaningful—at least some of which must perhaps be recognized by all of us to be meaningful—which show this conclusion to be false, even though they also show the premise to be true. My reference here is to the class of what I should call metaphysical assertions. Although it is true of all such assertions that they are indeed equivalent to the denials of their contradictories, neither the assertions nor their contradictories, nor, perforce, the implied denials of their contradictories, are factual—even though they are, or, at any rate, purport to be— existential.

The pertinent question at this point, of course, is what reason I have for recognizing such metaphysical assertions as included in the class of meaningful assertions. Flew, at least, evidently agrees with me in recognizing one such assertion:—the assertion, namely, that "The universe exists." He tells us in his paper that he uses the term *universe* in the sense in which "the Universe is everything there is (with the exception only of its

Creator, if such there be)" (p. 274). Elsewhere he further explains: "The universe is, as an immediate consequence of the definition, unique: for inasmuch as it includes everything there is there can be no possibility of another; if there were a second there would not be a second but only two parts of the one."[2] Noting the modal form of this explanation, I think we may say not only that Flew recognizes the assertion, "The universe exists," to be meaningful, because obviously true, but also that he would have to grant that it is in my sense a metaphysical, as distinct from a merely factual assertion. For, clearly, it could not be even "theoretically falsifiable," if that means that there are at least conceivable facts that could count against it. If there cannot be even the possibility of a fact that would not be included in the universe as "everything there is," then any even conceivable fact could only verify the assertion, and no fact, not even a conceivable fact, could ever falsify it.

If this line of argument is sound, however, it seems to me there is reason to believe not only that the class of factual assertions is smaller than the class of *meaningful* assertions, but also that it is smaller than the class of meaningful *existential* assertions. But, then, so far as I can see, Flew's initial assumption that theological assertions, if they are meaningful at all, can only be factual assertions is not likely to seem very plausible, since the presupposition that factual assertions are only meaningful assertions, or even the only meaningful existential assertions, is itself so far from being "only an analytic truth about statements" (p. 276) as to be quite evidently open to dispute. And his assumption seems to me all the more implausible, I repeat, because, as he himself admits, " 'the religious hypothesis' of a really sophisticated theism entails no straightforwardly falsifiable consequences."[3] The inference he inclines to draw from this admitted fact, of course, is that such a theism provides "a textbook example of degenerate assertion"[4]; hence the allusion in his paper to "the epicyclic degeneration of an hypothesis" (p. 282). But I submit that a nonarbitrary account of the possible kinds of meaningful assertions permits another, rather more plausible inference from the same admission: that, whatever must be said of its grammar, the *logic* of "the religious hypothe-

2 Antony Flew, *God and Philosophy* (New York: Harcourt, Brace and World, Inc., 1966), par. 3.24.
3 *Ibid.*, par. 8.25, 1.24–1.25.
4 *Ibid.*, par. 8.28.

sis" (as well, naturally, as the *anti*-religious hypothesis) is the logic of existential assertions—the most fundamental of which neither are nor could be merely factual.

Which brings me to the other main point where I have difficulty with Flew's position: if the question of theism, in my view, is logically different from what he—along with many others —assumes it to be, I also see no good reason to suppose that the theism he selects for criticism is the only theistic alternative to his own "presumption of atheism" (p. 282). As a matter of fact, I would suggest that the rather different kind of theism I myself should want to defend is by no means without a reply to his criticisms, including what I suspect might well be his major objection to the first part of my argument.

You will recall his insistence in the paper that "immunity against even the theoretical possibility of falsification in this our world" can be achieved "only and precisely at the cost of a complete and necessary irrelevance to it." This is so, he reasons, because, if any "candidate assertion about God has to be not about the Universe but about God," it follows that "from such statements nothing can then be deduced about that everyday world," and that, therefore, "the putative fact of God" must be anything but "supremely relevant" (p. 274). Now, as against the kind of classical theism that Flew alone takes into account, I readily grant that this is a forcible objection. For, given the axioms of such theism, especially the arch-axiom of the divine "simplicity," it necessarily follows that no assertion about God can be nonfalsifiable unless all assertions about God are so. In other words, the classical theist can consistently construe the theistic issue as a properly metaphysical issue only by accepting the implication that it is nothing but a metaphysical issue—with the further implication, then, that God is insofar forth irrelevant to our life in the world.

Yet how different the case of the neoclassical theist, by which I mean the kind of theist who frankly rejects the axiom of "simplicity," maintaining instead that God is not a monopolar but a dipolar God, who—though he exists necessarily—essentially exists only as the God of *some* world of contingent individuals other than himself, to all of which he is related not only externally but also internally. Given these axioms, the fundamental assertions that God exists and that he exists as God, as the eminent individual who is the integral ground and end of all other individuals, are all strictly metaphysical assertions and as such immune to factual falsification. But, if these assertions are true, they necessarily imply that any number of other, merely factual assertions must also be true, even though they do not imply, of course, just which such assertions actually are true. Furthermore, necessarily included among such assertions are certain factual assertions about God himself, all of which have the general form of asserting that he is somehow appropriately related internally to just this or that world of contingent individuals that in fact happens to exist. Being factual, these assertions about God are so far from being immune to falsification as to be factually falsifiable in a perfectly straightforward sense. For had some other world existed than actually exists, God would be somehow appropriately related to it instead, and any assertion that he is somehow related to the actual world would of necessity be false. This need not imply, naturally, that such factual assertions as may be made about God are also *empirically* falsifiable in some particularly strict sense of the word *empirical*. For, as Professor Flew himself rightly points out in replying to Heimbeck, the "falsification challenge" as such "specifies no particular kind of verification or falsification," such as might be specified, say, in holding the meaning of an assertion to be equivalent to its "empirical expectations" (p. 276).

In sum, not the least virtue of a neoclassical theism is to provide a way out of the very dilemma from which Flew assures us "there is no escape" (p. 275). Although for this kind of theism the truth that God exists is strictly metaphysical and therefore factually nonfalsifiable, his essential nature as God, as modally coincident with all actuality and all possibility, implies that he is also the ever-growing integrity of all factual truth, and therefore precisely "supremely relevant." One may also observe that while the sheer existence of God as metaphysically necessary can indeed make no factual difference, this is not at all so of my belief in his existence or of my willingness to trust here and now in his real, factual relation to myself and my world. To both belief in God and trust in Him there are very real factual alternatives; and, so far as the witness of faith is concerned, they make just the factual differences that for each of us are by far the most important.

I would add one further comment on Flew's thesis toward the end of his paper about "the onus of proof" (p. 282). If one simply must somehow make a presumption in this matter, I should myself suppose that he is hardly any better advised to make the "presumption of atheism" than to presume the truth of the theism to which such atheism is logically the extreme contrary. I should suppose this, of course, because of the existence long since and in an elaborately developed form of just that neoclassical theism to which I have here appealed, which—being logically something like their common contradictory—is about equally far removed from *both* of the classical alternatives. It is the very genius of this kind of "sophisticated theism" that it is not the least less critical than Flew of the inadequacies of classical theism, even while it gives all kinds of reasons—backed up by strictly philosophical arguments—for thinking that his own "presumption of atheism" may also be, however unintentionally, presumptuous. But you will have observed, I trust, that I make this point only on the hypothesis that it is necessary that some particular position be saddled with the burden of proof. My own advice, quite frankly, is that we do well to abjure any such hypothesis, acknowledging instead that each position must take full responsibility for its particular claims in face of the counterclaims of *all* the others. There are various reasons for this, but what they all come to, I think, is that experience has shown that there is very little of importance in matters philosophical and theological that is not in some way or other controversial. At this absolutely radical level of human reflection, there can be no unique starting point simply because all starting points are in a way also conclusions, the movement of such reflection being in the very nature of the case circular rather than linear.

But, if this advice can be accepted, then I, for one, could not only view the "theology and falsification" debate in retrospect as on the whole fruitful, in having helped to clarify more sharply what the question of theism is all about, but could also join with Flew in speaking of it as having at last "come of age."

Eight/The complexities of theological contexts

Introduction/**Verification inside the theological language game**

T HE exchange between Ian Crombie and Kai Nielsen in this section is reminiscent of a type that Wisdom describes. (See pp. 168 ff.) A man is in love and a friend tries to convince him, on rational grounds, that he is mistaken in his view of the woman. They agree as to the facts pertaining to the woman's behavior. The friend attacks her by calling attention to patterns in her behavior that the lover cannot stand when he encounters them in other people. If the lover had not been aware of these connections he might be shaken in his judgment and his attitude would change. On the other hand, if the lover claims that he was aware of these connections, but that he has found other patterns in her behavior that more than compensate for them, then it is the critic who may be shaken.

The Crombie-Nielsen exchange recalls Wisdom's example because Nielsen's criticisms of the problematic aspects of the concept of God are not only familiar to Crombie, they constitute his point of departure.

299

Crombie: theological statements are confirmable, but not in a straightforward way

Crombie's essay is a subtle yet compact statement of the difficulty of applying any version of the empiricist criterion of meaning to theological statements. Crombie's treatment of the issue is reminiscent of Wisdom's. There are, however, two important differences:

1. Wisdom brings out the complexity of theological arguments by showing their similarity to a variety of nontheological modes of argument. Crombie plunges right into the theological context.

2. Wisdom avoids direct statements on the issue of verification. At the end of his essay Crombie deals with it directly, although he is more concerned with falsification and confirmation than with the older forms of verifiability.

Like the positivists, Crombie is impressed by the fact that theologians strain language to say strange things.[1] The sort of thing he has in mind is that at times theologians talk of God as a particular individual, as in "God freed the Israelites from slavery in Egypt." Yet at other times they talk as though God could be identified with universals, that is, with general terms like "love" that are used to describe individuals or relations between individuals. An example of this has already been given: "God is love". (See p. 248.)

Crombie knows that there are many theologians who fully appreciate the differences between a particular and a universal, or between a person and the characteristics of a person. They do not speak about God in ways that run athwart these distinctions because (as the positivists assumed) they are confused. They deliberately talk in very strange ways.

The positivists' response to theology is to dismiss it as cognitively meaningless because it does not conform to the patterns of analyic statements (math and logic), on the one hand, and of synthetic statements (common sense and science), on the other. By contrast, Crombie follows the lead of Wittgenstein and Wisdom. He probes religious experience and religious language in an effort to discover why theologians choose to talk this way and what validity their talk may have.

[1] I. M. Crombie, "The Possibility of Theological Statements," in *Faith and Logic*, ed. B. Mitchell (London: Allen and Unwin, 1957), pp. 31–48. This essay is considerably longer than the one in this volume (it runs from pp. 31–83 of *Faith and Logic*). Nevertheless, it does not deal as directly with the issue of verification, and it does not cover the important issue of parables which is discussed in the essay that is reprinted in this volume. It should, however, be read as an important elaboration of the essay reprinted here.

The logical parents of religious belief

Crombie focuses on the statement, "God loves us," and deals with it in terms of what he calls the "logical parents" of religious belief. The phrase is an odd one, but it is well chosen. When we look at a child we know that both parents influenced him, and at the same time, not one after the other. Furthermore, although for purposes of reflection and discussion we can isolate the influence of each parent, we know that in the child they are inextricably involved. Crombie wants to say the same thing about the sources that enter into the kind of belief that lead a person to say, "God loves us." He calls the considerations that lead the believers to use the term God the "logical mother" of religious belief. The considerations that lead them to use "love us" and other predicates are called the "logical father" of religious belief. They come to the believer together, but they can be discussed separately, and it is important to do so because different kinds of difficulties relate to each "parent". In the case of God, we have to find out what people mean by this strange term; there seems to be no clearcut parallel to it in our language. In the case of "loves us" and other qualities that are attributed to God, the problem is to find out why these particular terms are used and what they mean when used in this strange context.

Crombie realizes that we cannot, in principle, have direct access to God. Therefore, we cannot deal with the statement, "God loves us," in the way we can deal with the statement, "My father loves me," namely, by directly observing the subject of the statement. All we can do is to examine those elements in human experience that elicit the response, "God loves us," from believers.

Experience: the logical mother

When theologians talk of God they deliberately "strain and distort our media of communication" (see p. 317). Why? Crombie maintains that they do so in response to certain distinctive experiences. What kind? His own list is brief: contingency, morality, beauty, order, and mysticism, but a fuller statement is provided by Donald Evans's account of "depth experiences" (see pp. 387 ff.). Crombie and Evans agree on an important point: these experiences can also be interpreted in nontheological terms.

In this essay, Crombie elaborates only one of these experiences, the sense of contingency. It is important to note that contingency has figured prominently in the history of Christian thought. A leading Protestant theologian, Friedrich Schleiermacher (1768–1834), called it the sense of "absolute dependence," and claimed that it was the heart of the religious experience.[2] As Crombie puts it, the sense of contingency or dependence is the conviction "that we, and the whole world in which we live, derive our being from something outside us" (see p. 315). It is the sense that "all that is" need not be, and that it is sustained by a reality of a totally different order whose existence is necessary and is not derived. The argument from contingent to necessary being is the third of St. Thomas Aquinas's (1224–1274) five ways of demonstrating the existence of God.[3] Crombie does not think that the argument is effective as a proof; he thinks it is, however, a fitting way of communicating the experience that leads brilliant thinkers to distort our language in order to express their beliefs.

There are two difficulties with the talk of contingent and necessary being, and Crombie acknowledges both of them.

Contingent and necessary are logical terms.   In their normal, and (at least relatively) nonproblematical uses, contingent and necessary function in the field of logic. We have seen that analytic statements are necessarily true or necessarily false. It is possible for synthetic statements to be either true or false (see p. 14). Contingent, as used in logic is a substitute for possible. Positivists insisted that talking about "necessary being" was as bad a mistake as talking about a "hyperthyroid mountain." In doing so, one committed a category mistake, one took a category, "necessity," which is only applicable in logic, and transferred it to talk of things.[4]

Statements of contingency are pseudo-synthetic.   In its religious use, the term contingent is clearly intended to inform us about a very important property of things, therefore, it is putatively synthetic. Yet contingency is a property which theologians ascribe to all observable beings at all times. No particular state of affairs can verify the statement, "This being is contingent." Its truth is compatible with every state of affairs. Positivists would therefore brand it as pseudo-synthetic.

[2] Friedrich Schleiermacher, The Christian Faith (Edinburgh: T. & T. Clark, 1928), pp. 12ff.

[3] Summa Theologica, Ques. 2, Art. 3.

[4] J. N. Findlay, "Can God's Existence Be Disproved?" in New Essays in Philosophical Theology, ed. A. Flew and A. MacIntyre (New York: Macmillan, 1955), pp. 47–56. This is still the best statement of this point, even though Findlay has subsequently repudiated it. The discussion of the issue between Findlay and G. E. Hughes and A. C. A. Rainer which is reproduced on pp. 56–75 of that volume is also well worth reading.

Crombie acknowledges the pressure of these criticisms. Neverthe-less, he is persuaded that this odd use of contingency and of necessary being ought not to be dismissed as the product of mere confusions. Theo-logians are deliberately distorting language in an effort to say what they mean by God. In doing so, they refer us out of our experience, but in a determinate direction. In this case, we are referred to necessary being as to a being that, in the words of Anthony Kenny, "is, always will be and always was; and cannot nor could not, nor will not be able not to be."[5] What this means remains mysterious, because we cannot directly encounter God, yet theologians have achieved a considerable measure of agreement in using the term necessary being as a means of indicating certain features of normal experience that would definitely not hold true of God.

The logical mother of religious belief is then a bearer of mystery as well as of confusions. Clearly, a thinker of Crombie's astuteness might dismiss them out of hand, if it were not for the echoes this language finds in his own experience. The cumulative effect of the experience of con-tingency, moral obligation, the beauty and order in nature, and in some cases, mystical experiences, drives men to talk of God and to try to say what they mean by this term.

Parables: the logical father

"God" is the mysterious subject of the statement "God loves us." Many predicates, like "loves us," provide the vital religious content of the term God. Crombie calls the considerations that lead theologians to use these predicates, "the logical father" of religious belief. Basically he describes them as certain events or records of events which are regarded by be-lievers as special manifestations of God. In Christianity, the Bible is the chief record of these events. It is the record of Israel and of Jesus Christ. Jesus tells parables or stories that communicate something of what the love of God is like. In the parable of The Prodigal Son, for example, he tells the story of a father who forgives a son who has defied him and left home. He not only permits him to return, he receives him joyfully. In the Book of Hosea the prophet comes to see his problems with his faith-less wife as a mirror of God's suffering because of his faithless people Israel. God forgives them beyond the power of any earthly father to forgive. Stories like these tell the believer which elements of our experi-ence are most properly referred to God. They provide an authorized in-terpretation of our experience. They drive us beyond our experience in

[5] Anthony Kenny, "Necessary Being," in Sophia, I, 1, (1962), p. 8.

the direction of limitless compassion and forgiveness. This is why theologians say "God loves us," rather than, for example, "God hates us."

Yet the mystery remains. In human love we observe the person who loves us. We cannot observe God. We cannot see how his limitless love is operative in God himself. Yet we are driven to trust the biblical accounts, because it accords with our experiences. The communication involved in "God loves us" is limited, but it is adequate to enable believers to communicate with one another and to sustain a religious life.

Verification, confirmation, and falsification

Once he has set the statement, "God loves us," in its theological context, Crombie turns to the explicit consideration of the controversy over theology and falsification. He claims that the statement "God loves us" can be understood and that it is neither analytic nor contradictory. Therefore, there is no rule of theological language that precludes our testing it; it is supposedly synthetic. When it comes to conceiving the circumstances that would verify or falsify it, we are on difficult ground.

Any statement dealing with love is difficult to check. It is, for example, notoriously difficult to verify the statement, "My father loves me." Fathers may behave harshly out of love for their children. Verifying "God loves us" is incomparably more problematic because we cannot observe God and the very concept of God is shrouded in mystery. Nevertheless, Crombie claims that the statement is factually significant because there are conceivable circumstances which are relevant to testing it.

Eschatological verification.   One test of the statement, "God loves us," is mentioned but not developed by Crombie. It is the Christian hope for the afterlife. This issue is the subject of Section Six.

Confirmation.   Crombie follows Mitchell's lead (see pp. 263 ff.) in refusing to qualify the meaning of "God loves us" to the point where it is open to Flew's charge of suffering "death by a thousand qualifications." Crombie concedes that suffering counts against (disconfirms) the statement, "God loves us."

Conclusive falsification.   Crombie proposes a state of affairs that would conclusively falsify the statement, "God loves us." It would involve the observation of "suffering that was utterly, eternally, and irredeemably pointless" (see p. 325). At this point Crombie is forced to resort to qualifications that seem to weaken his proposal to the point of death. He claims that conclusive falsification is not possible in this life because we cannot, in principle, see the whole picture. Yet his appeal to the afterlife does not help with this problem. Even if there were no difficulties involved with the notion of eschatalogical verification, we could not, in principle, see the whole picture, even in the afterlife. Only God, who is eternal, can see the whole picture. Therefore, Crombie's effort to show that "God loves us" can be conclusively falsified boils down to the claim that it could be conclusively falsified only by God himself. As far as human beings in this life are concerned, Crombie's position is, in effect, that statements like "God loves us" can be confirmed and disconfirmed, but they cannot be conclusively falsified or conclusively verified.

Christ.   The Christian cannot see God directly. Yet in the life and teachings of Jesus Christ he finds convincing verification of God's love and a specification of the character of that love. It should be obvious that this "verification" would not be observable by the non-Christian. To understand why Crombie, nevertheless, appeals to it, we must recall the fact that he regards the test of verification in terms of "communication value." A person fully understands a statement when he can conceive of circumstances that would verify it. For the Christian, the account of Jesus Christ in the New Testament specifies the circumstances that verify the statement "God loves us."

Life context.   Crombie claims that the life of faith is an aspect of verification that falls outside the scope of the "logical parents" of religious belief. It is the place where the individual "puts it all together." In responding to experience and the parables he comes to learn the meaning of God's love for his personal existence. It is confirmed, not by the absence of suffering, but in the way that it enables him to cope with it.

Crombie's final sentence is worth quoting: "Seen as a whole religion makes rough sense, though it does not make limpidity" (p. 329).

Nielsen: theological statements are factually meaningless

Crombie writes from inside the theological camp, yet no critic could put the case against the cognitive meaningfulness of theological statements more forcefully than he does: ". . . is it not true that they only appear to be statements to those of us who use them, because we deceive ourselves by a sort of conjuring trick, oscillating backwards and forwards between a literal interpretation of what we say when we say it, and a scornful rejection of such anthropomorphism when anybody challenges us?" and again, "Theology is not a science; it is a sort of art of enlightened ignorance" (see pp. 312, 328). Nevertheless, Crombie claims that theological statements are factually meaningful.

Crombie's candor is disarming, but Nielsen refuses to be disarmed. He claims that Crombie's thorough exploration of the nature of theological statements points to the conclusion that theological statements are factually and cognitively meaningless.

Theological statements cannot be verified or confirmed

Nielsen presents a definition of God that he claims is used by Crombie and other sophisticated theologians: ". . . a proper name standing for an infinite, non-spatio-temporal, non-indicable individual, utterly transcendent to the cosmos" (see p. 339). This is accurate, as is Nielsen's further point that "Anything that we could apprehend or could be acquainted with would eo ipso not be such a reality" (see p. 339). In other words, since God is defined as being a nonobservable reality that is utterly beyond the world, anything that could be directly observed could not possibly be God. Nielsen, therefore, agrees with sophisticated theologians when he claims that the case for the factual meaningfulness of statements about God hinges on the possibility that they can be indirectly confirmed. (See pp. 30 f.)

Nielsen recognizes the legitimacy of only two kinds of indirect confirmation, and he denies that either of them can be applied to God.

Scientific.   Scientists talk of magnetic fields, superegos, and other nonobservables whose operations are indirectly confirmed. Nielsen is an operationalist (see pp. 219 f.). He claims that the nonobservable theoretical entities of the scientists do not exist in the sense that tables, chairs, and persons exist, but rather that "Such concepts [as magnetic fields] are pragmatically useful constructs since they enable us to make predictions and assessments of behavior with greater ease than if we did not have such concepts, but we can be quite agnostic about whether there are such things" (see p. 220). This model is inapplicable to Crombie's use of "God" where the reference is to an all-powerful and all knowing agent who "loves us."

Common sense. Nielsen considers the indirect confirmation of the ordinary statement "The children are playing downstairs." Hearing laughter and running feet constitutes indirect confirmation, because one has often heard these same sounds while directly observing them at play. Nielsen insists that this mode of indirect confirmation is also inapplicable to the statement "God loves us." He notes that, "Hick acknowledges [and Crombie would surely agree] that we do not know what it would be like to encounter directly an infinite, almighty, eternal Creator" (see p. 217). Nielsen then claims that "If we have no idea of what it would be like to experience that which we supposedly have indirect evidence for, then we in fact do not actually understand what it would be like to have evidence (direct or indirect) for it." Nielsen immediately generalizes this point and claims that if we cannot state what it would be like to experience a certain reality by direct observation then "we do not even understand what it would mean to say there is a so-and-so. . . ." (see p. 220).

To summarize Nielsen's case:

1. He assumes that theologians do not intend their statements to be analytic; they are supposed to be synthetic.

2. God cannot, in principle, be observed directly; therefore, theological statements cannot be conclusively verified by inspection.

3. Statements about God are not indirectly confirmable because God is comparable neither to a theoretical entity in science nor to a physical object.

4. Therefore, theological statements are neither directly verifiable nor indirectly confirmable. They are pseudo-synthetic and both factually and cognitively meaningless.

Challenges to Nielsen's case

Nielsen has clearly moved beyond positivism in one respect. He does not issue blanket pronouncements condemning theological statements as a class. He treats individual efforts at religious thought and plays the role of a counter-puncher. In this sense, he has, along with Flew, carried out the program that Flew proposes in his retrospective survey of the controversy on theology and falsification (see pp. 269 ff.).

Yet, when one examines the cumulative impact of his arguments against both Hick and Crombie, Nielsen appears closer to a straight line positivist position than one might, at first reading, suppose.

Nielsen demands that theological statements conform to those of science or common sense. Nielsen claims that theological statements

are pseudo-synthetic because they can neither be verified by direct observation nor indirectly confirmed. His charge that they are not indirectly confirmable depends on his appeal to two standard types of
statements. One type involves the theoretical entities of science, such as
electrons. The other involves physical objects that are, in principle, observable. His illustrations are the ocean at high tide, and children playing
in the living room.

Nielsen is, therefore, confronting theologians with the positivist
either/or; theological statements must either conform to the patterns of
nontheological statements, or they must be rejected as factually meaningless. Yet, as we have seen, Wittgenstein's reaction against this kind
of positivist restrictiveness was one of the major factors in the emer-
gence of a post-positivist mode of philosophical analysis which is looser
in its approach to questions of cognitive meaningfulness (see pp. 39 ff.).

Confining "experience" to sense experience may be too restrictive.   Nielsen states that "if we have no idea of what it would be like to
experience that which we supposedly have indirect evidence for, then
we in fact do not actually understand what it would be like to have evidence (direct or indirect) for it." He clearly means sense experience such
as seeing or hearing. Yet Crombie went to great lengths to develop a
meaning of experience that is broader than this; so too, did Evans in his
discussion of "depth experiences," and Robison, in his contribution to
this volume (see pp. 409 ff.). Nielsen does not argue against these wider
uses of experience. He assumes that if a wider use of experience is factually meaningful, it must, in principle, be expressible in terms of statements about direct observation by means of the senses.

Concluding remarks

These critical observations may have been unfair to Nielsen. He is, after
all, charging Crombie with covertly borrowing the legitimate uses of
indirect confirmation and illegitimately applying them to theological
statements like "God loves us." Having done so, Crombie then claims
that he is confirming this statement by a distinctive method which is appropriate to the unique reality of God. Furthermore, Nielsen can claim
that Crombie's involved mode of confirming theological statements
would lack all persuasiveness unless it traded on these standard models
of confirmation. After all, Crombie himself called attention to the theologians' trick of oscillating between standard and utterly strange uses of
their terms.

In response, theologians can accuse Nielsen of treating controversial philosophical positions as though they were well established: (1) the operationalist view of theoretical entities, which Nielsen invokes almost casually, is certainly subject to challenge; and (2) the use of verification as a criterion of factual meaningfulness has been subjected to crippling criticisms, as Nielsen admitted in his reply to Mavrodes (see pp. 234 ff.). Yet Nielsen continues to appeal to it on the grounds that, at the level of practice, we know how to go about verifying the statements of science and common sense. As we have seen (pp. 185 f.), this appeal to the practical utility of verification cannot provide conclusive justification for its theoretical use as a standard of factual meaningfulness.

In light of the many theoretical difficulties involved in his effort to discredit the cognitive meaningfulness of theology, Nielsen's case rests heavily on his appeal to the distinction between the operative and the theoretical levels of intellectual activity. He must continually stress the point that at the operative level scientists make good on their claims to knowledge; religious believers do not.

Phillips and Jones: the Wittgensteinian influence

D. Z. Phillips is one of the leading exponents of the Wittgensteinian point of view in contemporary religious thought.[6] *In his discussion with J. R. Jones on "Belief and Loss of Belief," he focuses, in very clear language, on many of the points that have already been covered:*
1. The distrust of technical jargon that is used as a prefabricated mold to determine what can and cannot be cognitively meaningful.
2. The rejection of the positivist either/or with regard to theological statements, that is, either factually meaningful like scientific and common sense statements, or factually meaningless and merely emotively significant.
3. The importance of personal and cultural contexts to the question of meaningfulness. I will deal with this point more extensively.
Phillips claims that the model of disputes about "the facts" is

[6] D. Z. Phillips, *Faith and Philosophical Enquiry* (London: Routledge and Kegan Paul, 1970) is the collection of his essays from which this discussion was taken. Two important full length studies of the importance of Wittgenstein for religious thought are Dallas High, *Language, Persons and Belief* (New York: Oxford, 1967) and W. Donald Hudson, *Ludwig Wittgenstein: The Bearing of his Philosophy on Religious Belief* (Richmond, Virginia: John Knox Press, 1968).

singularly inapplicable to disputes between believers and sceptics. If a theist says, "I believe in the Last Judgment," and the nonbeliever replies, "I do not believe in it," their difference is not about a future event, like a horse race, which will be settled in a factual way. In this dispute the sceptic is not even denying what the believer affirms, because, in an important sense, he does not know what the believer is talking about. The sceptic is not part of the personal and cultural situation to which this belief is relevant. He cannot contradict the believer any more than someone who is not on a football field can tackle a runner.

Disputes about the Last Judgment can be carried on meaningfully only within the framework of Christian Faith where certain assumptions are shared. As a result of these arguments, faith may be lost. This is not like changing one's mind about the facts, for example, by conceding that a house which one thought was white turned out to be gray. To lose faith involves opting out of a community of the faithful who have a way of life as well as a framework of belief. It is to find that certain options are no longer live. As we have seen, this is what happened when sophisticated theologians stopped arguing with fundamentalists (see pp. 53 f.). Loss of belief is, in part, attributable to matters of fact. An individual may discover certain facts about Christian history that shake his faith. Yet the patterns of the facts and the way in which they are connected and disconnected are more important.

Ian M. Crombie/**Theology and falsification**

There are some who hold that religious statements cannot be fully meaningful, on the ground that those who use them allow nothing to count decisively against them, treat them, that is, as incapable of falsification. This paper is an attempted answer to this view; and in composing it I have had particularly in mind an article by Antony Flew [p. 257 ff. above], and an unpublished paper read by A. M. Quinton to the Aquinas Society of Oxford. I shall offer only a very short, and doubtless tendentious, summary of my opponents' views.[1]

From "Theology and Falsification" by Ian M. Crombie in *New Essays in Philosophical Theology,* ed. Antony Flew and Alasdair MacIntyre (London: SCM Press, New York: Macmillan, 1955). pp. 109–130. Reprinted by permission of SCM Press, Ltd., The Macmillan Company, and the author.

[1] This paper was composed to be read to a non-philosophical audience. In composing it I have also filched shamelessly (and shamefully no doubt distorted) some unpublished utterances of Dr. A. M. Farrer's.

Briefly, then, it is contended that there are utterances made from time to time by Christians and others, which are said by those who make them to be statements, but which are thought by our opponents to lack some of the properties which anything must have before it deserves to be called a statement. 'There is a God', 'God loves us as a father loves his children', 'He shall come again with glory . . .' are examples of such utterances. *Prima facie* such utterances are neither exhortations, nor questions, nor expressions of wishes; *prima facie* they appear to assert the actuality of some state of affairs; and yet (and this is the objection) they are allowed to be compatible with any and every state of affairs. If they are compatible with any and every state of affairs, they cannot mark out some one state of affairs (or group of states of affairs); and if they do not mark out some one state of affairs, how can they be statements? In the case of any ordinary statement, such as 'It is raining', there is at least one situation (the absence of falling water) which is held to be incompatible with the statement, and it is the incompatibility of the situation with the statement which gives the statement its meaning. If, then, religious 'statements' are compatible with anything and everything, how can they be statements? How can the honest inquirer find out what they mean, if nobody will tell him what they are incompatible with? Are they not much more like such exhortations as 'Keep smiling', whose confessed purpose is to go on being in point whatever occurs? Furthermore, is it not true that they only appear to be statements to those of us who use them, because we deceive ourselves by a sort of conjuring trick, oscillating backwards and forwards between a literal interpretation of what we say when we say it, and a scornful rejection of such anthropomorphism when anybody challenges us? When we *say:* 'He shall come again with glory . . .', do we not picture real angels sitting on real clouds; when asked whether we really mean the clouds, we hedge; offer perhaps another picture, which again we refuse to take literally; and so on indefinitely. Whatever symbolism we offer, we always insist that only a crude man would take it literally, and yet we never offer him anything but symbolism; deceived by our imagery into supposing that we have something in mind, in fact there is nothing on which we are prepared to take our stand.

This is the position I am to try to criticize. It is, I think, less novel than its clothes; but none the less it is important. I turn to criticism.

Let us begin by dismissing from our inquiry the trouble-some statement 'There is a God' or 'God exists'. As every student of logic knows, all statements asserting the existence of something offer difficulties of their own, with which we need not complicate our embarrassment.

That being dismissed, I shall want to say of statements about God that they consist of two parts. Call them, if you like, subject and predicate. Whatever you call them, there is that which is said, and that which it is said about—namely God. It is important to make this distinction, for different problems arise about the different parts. As a first approximation towards isolating the difference, we may notice that the predicate is normally composed of ordinary words, put to un-ordinary uses, whereas the subject-word is 'God', which has no other use. In the expression 'God loves us', the word 'God' is playing, so to speak, on its Home Ground, the phrase 'loves us' is playing Away. Now there is one set of questions which deal with the problem of why we say, and what we mean by saying, that God loves us, rather than hates us, and there is another set of questions concerned with the problem of what it is that this statement is being made about.

To approach the matter from an angle which seems to me to afford a good view of it, I shall make a few observations about the epistemological nature of religious belief. Let me caution the reader that, in doing so, I am not attempting to describe how religious belief in fact arises.

Theoretically, then, not in how it arises, but in its logical structure, religious belief has two parents; and it also has a nurse. Its logical mother is what one might call *undifferentiated theism*, its logical father is particular events or occasions interpreted as theophanic, and the extra-parental nurture is provided by religious activity.

A word, first, about the logical mother. It is in fact the case that there are elements in our experience which lead people to a certain sort of belief, which we call a belief in God. (We could, if we wished, call it rather an attitude than a belief, so long as we were careful not to call it an attitude to life; for it is of the essence of the attitude to hold that nothing whatever in life may be identified with that towards which it is taken up.) Among the elements in experience which provoke this belief or attitude, perhaps the most powerful is what I shall call a sense of contingency. Others are moral experience, and the beauty and order of nature.

Others may be actual abnormal experience of the type called religious or mystical. There are those to whom conscience appears in the form of an unconditional demand; to whom the obligation to one's neighbour seems to be something imposed on him and on me by a third party who is set over us both. There are those to whom the beauty and order of nature appears as the intrusion into nature of a realm of beauty and order beyond it. There are those who believe themselves or others to be enriched by moments of direct access to the divine. Now there are two things that must be said about these various theistic interpretations of our experience. The first is that those who so interpret need not be so inexpert in logic as to suppose that there is anything of the nature of a deductive or inductive argument which leads from a premiss asserting the existence of the area of experience in question to a conclusion expressing belief in God. Nobody who takes seriously the so-called moral argument need suppose that the *prima facie* authority of conscience cannot be naturalistically explained. He can quite well acknowledge that the imperativeness which so impresses him could be a mere reflection of his jealousy of his father, or a vestigial survival of tribal taboo. The mystic can quite well acknowledge that there is nothing which logically forbids the interpretation of the experience which he enjoys in terms of the condition of his liver or the rate of his respirations. If, being acquainted with the alternative explanations, he persists in rejecting them, it need not be, though of course it sometimes is, because he is seized with a fallacious refutation of their validity. All that is necessary is that he should be honestly convinced that, in interpreting them, as he does, theistically, he is in some sense facing them more honestly, bringing out more of what they contain or involve than could be done by interpreting them in any other way. The one interpretation is preferred to the other, not because the latter is thought to be refutable on paper, but because it is judged to be unconvincing in the light of familiarity with the facts. There is a partial parallel to this in historical judgment. Where you and I differ in our interpretation of a series of events, there is nothing outside the events in question which can over-rule either of us, so that each man must accept the interpretation which seems, on fair and critical scrutiny, the most convincing to him. The parallel is only partial, however, for in historical (and literary) interpretation there is something which to some extent controls one's interpretation, and that is one's general knowledge of human nature;

and in metaphysical interpretation there is nothing analogous to this. That, then, is my first comment on theistic interpretations; for all that these journeys of the mind are often recorded in quasi-argumentative form, they are not in any ordinary sense arguments, and their validity cannot be assessed by asking whether they conform to the laws either of logic or of scientific method. My second comment upon them is, that, in stating them, we find ourselves saying things which we cannot literally mean. Thus the man of conscience uses some such concept as the juridical concept of authority, and locates his authority outside nature; the man of beauty and order speaks of an intrusion from another realm; the mystic speaks of experiencing God. In every case such language lays the user open to devastating criticism, to which he can only retort by pleading that such language, while it is not to be taken strictly, seems to him to be the natural language to use.

To bring these points into a somewhat stronger light, let me say something about the sense of contingency, the conviction which people have, it may be in blinding moments, or it may be in a permanent disposition of a man's mind, that we, and the whole world in which we live, derive our being from something outside us. The first thing I want to say about this is that such a conviction is to no extent like the conclusion of an argument; the sense of dependence feels not at all like being persuaded by arguments, but like seeing, seeing, as it were, through a gap in the rolling mists of argument, which alone, one feels, could conceal the obvious truth. One is not *persuaded* to believe that one is contingent; rather one feels that it is only by persuasion that one could ever believe anything else. The second thing I want to say about this conviction of contingency is that in expressing it, as Quinton has admirably shewn, we turn the word 'contingent' to work which is not its normal employment, and which it cannot properly do.

For the distinction between necessity and contingency is not a distinction between different sorts of entities, but between different sorts of statement. A necessary statement is one whose denial involves a breach of the laws of logic, and a contingent statement is one in which this is not the case. (I do not, of course, assert that this is the only way in which these terms have been used in the history of philosophy; but I do assert that this is the only use of them which does not give rise to impossible difficulties. I have no space to demonstrate this here; and indeed I do not think that it is any longer in need of demonstration.) But in this, the only coherent, sense of 'contingent', the existence of the world may be contingent fact, but so unfortunately is that of God. For *all* existential statements are contingent; that is to say, it is never true that we can involve ourselves in a breach of the laws of logic by merely denying of something that it exists. We cannot therefore in this sense contrast the contingent existence of the world with the necessary existence of God.

It follows that if a man persists in speaking of the contingency of the world, he must be using the term in a new or transferred sense. It must be that he is borrowing[2] a word from the logician and putting it to work which it cannot properly do. Why does he do this, and how can he make clear what precisely this new use is? For it is no good saying that when we are talking about God we do not use words in their ordinary senses unless we are prepared to say in what senses it is that we do use them. And yet how can we explain to the honest inquirer what is the new sense in which the word 'contingent' is being used when we use it of the world? For if it is proper to use it, in this sense, of everything with which we are acquainted, and improper to use it only of God, with whom we are not acquainted, how can the new use be learnt? For we normally learn the correct use of a word by noticing the differences between the situations in which it may be applied and those in which it may not; but the word 'contingent' is applicable in all the situations in which we ever find ourselves. If I said that everything but God was flexible, not of course in the ordinary sense, but in some other, how could you discover what the new sense was?

The answer must be that when we speak of the world as contingent, dependent, an effect or product, and so contrast it with a necessary, self-existent being, a first cause or a creator, we say something which on analysis will not do at all (for devastating criticisms can be brought against all these formulations), but which seems to us to be the fittest sort of language for our purpose. Why we find such language appropriate, and how, therefore, it is to be interpreted, is not at all an easy question; that it does in some way, it may be in some logically anomalous way, convey the meaning of those who use it, seems however to be an evident fact.

[2] It might be argued that, historically, the borrowing was the other way round. To decide that we should have to decide where the frontier between logic and metaphysics really comes in the work of those whose doctrine on the relationship between these disciplines is unsatisfactory.

How it is that the trick is worked, how it is that this sort of distortion of language enables believers to give expression to their beliefs, this it is the true business of the natural theologian to discuss. Farrer, for example, in *Finite and Infinite,* has done much to elucidate what it is that one is striving to express when one speaks of the contingency of the world, and so to enlighten the honest inquirer who wishes to know how the word 'contingent' is here being used.

What I have said about contingency and necessity applies also to obligation and its transcendent ground (or goodness and its transcendent goal), to design and its transcendent designer, to religious experience and its transcendent object. In all these cases we use language which on analysis will not do, but which seems to us to be appropriate for the expression of our beliefs; and in all these cases the question can be, and is, discussed, why such language is chosen, and how it is to be understood.

That then is the logical mother of religious belief; call her natural theism, or what you will, she is a response, not precisely logical, and yet in no sense emotional or evaluative, to certain elements in our experience, whose characteristic is that they induce us, not to make straightforward statements about the world, but to strain and distort our media of communication in order to express what we make of them. In herself she is an honest woman; and if she is sometimes bedizened in logical trappings, and put out on the streets as an inductive argument, the fault is hardly hers. Her function is, not to prove to us that God exists, but to provide us with a 'meaning' for the word 'God'. Without her we should not know whither statements concerning the word were to be referred; the subject in theological utterances would be unattached. All that we should know of them is that they were not to be referred to anything with which we are or could hope to be acquainted; that, and also that they were to be understood in terms of whatever it is that people suppose themselves to be doing when they build churches and kneel down in them. And that is not entirely satisfactory; for while there is much to be said in practice for advising the honest inquirer into the reference of the word 'God' to pursue his inquiry by familiarizing himself with the concrete activity of religion, it remains true that the range and variety of possible delusions which could induce such behaviour is theoretically boundless, and, as visitors to the Pacific coast of the United States can testify, in practice very large.

The logical father of religious belief, that which might bring us on from the condition of merely possessing the category of the divine, into the condition of active belief in God, this consists, in Christianity (and if there is nothing analogous in other religions, so much the worse for them), in the interpretation of certain objects or events as a manifestation of the divine. It is, in other words, because we find, that, in thinking of certain events in terms of the category of the divine, we can give what seems to us the most convincing account of them, that we can assure ourselves that the notion of God is not just an empty aspiration. Without the notion of God we could interpret nothing as divine, and without concrete events which we felt impelled to interpret as divine we could not know that the notion of divinity had any application to reality. Why it is that as Christians we find ourselves impelled to interpret the history of Israel, the life and death of Christ, and the experience of his Church as relevatory of God, I shall not here attempt to say; it is an oft-told tale, and I shall content myself with saying that we can hardly expect to feel such an impulsion so long as our knowledge of these matters is superficial and altogether from without. Whyever we feel such an impulsion, it is not, of course, a logical impulsion; that is, we may resist it (or fail to feel it) without thereby contravening the laws of logic, or the rules of any pragmatically accredited inductive procedure. On the anthropological level the history of Israel, Old and New, is certainly the history of a religious development from its tribal origins. We may decide, or we may not, that it is something more, something beyond the wit of man to invent, something which seems to us to be a real and coherent communication from a real and coherent, though superhuman, mind. We may decide, or we may not; neither decision breaks the rules, for in such a unique matter there are no rules to conform to or to break. The judgment is our own; and in the language of the New Testament it judges us; that is, it reveals what, up to the moment of our decision, the Spirit of God has done in us—but that, of course, is to argue in a circle.

Belief, thus begotten, is nurtured by the practice of the Christian life—by the conviction so aroused (or, of course, not aroused; but then it is starvation and not nurture) that the Christian warfare is a real warfare. Something will have to be said about this later on, but for the moment I propose to dismiss it, and to return to the consideration of the significance of religious utterances in the light of the dual parentage of religious belief.

I have argued that unless certain things seem to us to be
signs of divine activity, then we may hope that there is a God,
but we cannot properly believe that there is. It follows from this
that religious belief must properly involve treating something as
revelatory of God; and that is to say that it must involve an element of authority (for to treat something as divine revelation is to
invest it with authority). That what we say about God is said on
authority (and, in particular, on the authority of Christ) is of the
first importance in considering the significance of these statements.
In what way this is so, I shall hope to make clear as we go along.

If we remember that our statements about God rest on the
authority of Christ, whom we call his Word, we can see what
seems to me the essential clue to the interpretation of the logical
nature of such utterances, and that is, in a word, the notion of
parable. To elucidate what I mean by 'parable' (for I am using the
word in an extended sense) let us consider Christ's action on Palm
Sunday, when he rode into Jerusalem on an ass. This action was
an act of teaching. For it had been said to Jerusalem that her king
would come to her riding upon an ass. Whoever, therefore, deliberately chose this method of entry, was saying in effect: 'What
you are about to witness (namely my Passion, Death and Resurrection) is the coming of the Messianic King to claim his kingdom'.
The prophecy of Messiah's kingdom was to be interpreted, not in
the ordinary sense, but in the sense of the royal kingship of the
Crucified. To interpret in this way is to teach by violent paradox,
indeed, but none the less it is to teach. Part of the lesson is that it
is only the kings of the Gentiles that lord it over their subjects; if
any man will be a king in Israel (God's chosen people), he must
humble himself as a servant; part of it is that the Crucifixion is to
be seen as Messianic, that is as God's salvation of his chosen people. Now the logical structure which is involved here is something
like this:—You are told a story (Behold, thy king cometh, meek
and lowly, and riding upon an ass). You will not know just what
the reality to which the story refers will be like until it happens.
If you take the story at its face value (an ordinary, though humble,
king, bringing an ordinary political salvation), you will get it all
wrong. If you bring to bear upon its interpretation all that the Law
and the Prophets have taught you about God's purposes for his
people, though you will still not know just what it will be like
until it happens, none the less you will not go wrong by believing
it; for then you will know that Christ ought to have suffered these

things, and to enter into his glory, and so you will learn what
the story has to tell you of God's purposes for man, and something
therefore, indirectly, of God. If you remember what Isaiah says
about humility and sacrifice, you will see that what is being fore-
cast is that God's purposes will be accomplished by a man who
fulfils the Law and the Prophets in humble obedience.

This story is that one that can be fairly fully interpreted.
There are others that cannot. There is, for example, Hosea's parable in which he likens himself to God, and Israel to his unfaithful
wife, and expresses his grief at his wife's unfaithfulness. If, now,
you ask for this to be fully interpreted, if you ask Hosea to tell
you what he supposes it is like for the Holy One of Israel, of whom
no similitude may be made, to be grieved, demanding to know, not
what would happen in such a case to the unfaithful sinner who had
provoked the divine wrath, but what was the condition of the divine mind in itself, then no doubt he would have regarded the very
question as blasphemous. As an inspired prophet, he felt himself
entitled to say that God was grieved, without presuming to imagine
what such a situation was like, other than in its effects. What he
said was said on authority; it was not his own invention, and
therefore he could rely on its truth, without supposing himself to
understand its full meaning. In so far as Hosea's parable is 'interpreted', the interpretation is confined to identifying the *dramatis
personae* (Hosea=God, his wife=Israel). It is noteworthy that the
interpretation which is sometimes given to the parables of the
New Testament is usually of the same sketchy kind (The reapers
are the angels). In Plato's famous parable of prisoners in a cave, it
is quite possible to describe the situation which the parable seeks
to illuminate. One can describe how a man can begin by being
content to establish rough laws concerning what follows what in
nature, how he may proceed from such a condition to desire explanations of the regularities which are forced on his attention,
rising thus to more abstract and mathematical generalizations, and
then, through the study of mathematics, to completely abstract
speculation. One cannot similarly describe the situation which the
parable of the Prodigal Son is intended to illustrate (or rather one
can only describe the human end of it); and no attempt is ever
made to do so.

I make no apology for these paragraphs about the Bible;
after all the Bible is the source of Christian belief, and it cannot
but illuminate the logical nature of the latter to consider the com-

municational methods of the former. But we must turn back to more general considerations. It is, then, characteristic of a parable that the words which are used in it are used in their ordinary senses. Elsewhere this is not always so. If you speak of the virtues of a certain sort of car, the word 'virtue', being applied to a car, comes to mean something different from what it means in application to human beings. If you speak of hot temper, the word 'hot' does not mean what it means in the ordinary way. Now many people suppose that something of the latter sort is happening in religious utterances. When God is said to be jealous, or active in history, it is felt that the word 'jealous' or 'active' must be being used here in a transferred sense. But if it is being used in a transferred sense, some means or other must be supplied whereby the new sense can be taken. The activity of God is presumably not like the activity of men (it does not make him hot or tired); to say then that God is active must involve modifying the meaning of the word. But, if the word is undergoing modification, it is essential that we should know in what direction. In the case of ordinary transfers, how do we know what sort of modification is involved? This is a large question, but roughly, I think, the answer is, in two ways. Firstly there is normally a certain appropriateness, like the appropriateness of 'hot' in 'hot temper'; and secondly we can notice the circumstances in which the word gets used and withheld in its transferred sense. If I hear the phrase 'Baroque music', the meaning of the word 'Baroque' in its normal architectural employment may set me looking in a certain direction; and I can clinch the matter by asking for examples, 'Bach? Buxtehude? Beethoven?' But for either of these ways to be of any use to me, I must know something about *both* ends of the transfer. I must know something about Baroque architecture, *and* I must be able to run through musical styles in my head, to look for the musical analogue of Baroque features. If I cannot stumble on your meaning without assistance, I can still do so by eliciting from you that Bach and Buxtehude are, Handel and Mozart are not, examples of the sort of music you have in mind. This is informative to me if and only if I know something of Buxtehude and Bach, Handel and Mozart.

Now we all know what it is like for a man to be active. We can quote examples, decide correctly, and so forth. But what about divine activity? Surely we cannot have it both ways. Either God can be moderately like a man, so that the word 'active', used of him, can set us looking in the right direction; or he can be quite unlike a man, in which case it cannot. Nor can we be helped by the giving of examples, unless it is legitimate to point to examples of divine activity—to say, 'Now here God is being active, but not there.' This constitutes the force of Flew's demand that we should tell him how statements about God can be falsified. In essence Flew is saying: 'When you speak about God, the words which occur in the predicate part of your statement are not being used in the ordinary sense; you make so great a difference between God and man, that I cannot even find that the words you use set me looking in anything that might perhaps be the right direction. You speak of God as being outside time; and when I think what I mean by "activity", I find that that word, as used about a timeless being, suggests to me nothing whatsoever. There is only one resort left; give me examples of when one of your statements is, and is not, applicable. If, as no doubt you will say, that is an unfair demand, since they are always applicable (e.g. God is always active, so that there are no cases of his inactivity to be pointed to), I will not insist on actual examples; make them up if you like. But do not point to *everything* and say, "*That* is what I mean"; for *everything* is not *that,* but this and this and this and many other mutual incompatibles; and black and white and red and green and kind and cruel and coal and ink and everything else together cannot possibly elucidate to me the meaning of a word.'

As I have said, the answer must be that when we speak about God, the words we use are intended in their ordinary sense (for we cannot make a transfer, failing familiarity with both ends of it), although we do not suppose that in their ordinary interpretation they can be strictly true of him. We do not even know how much of them applies. To some extent it may be possible to take a word like 'activity' and whittle away that in it which most obviously does not apply. It is, however, an exaggeration, at the least, to suppose that this process of whittling away leaves us in the end with a kernel about which we can say that we know that it does apply. A traditional procedure is to compose a scale on which inanimate matter is at the bottom, the characteristically human activities, such as thinking and personal relationship, at the top, and to suppose that the scale is pointing towards God; and so on this assumption the first thing to do is to pare away from the notion of human activity whatever in it is common to what stands below it on the scale—for example actual physical moving about. Taking the human residue, we try to decide what in it is positive, and what is negative, mere limitation. The tenuous ghost of a concept remaining we suppose to be the essential structure of activity (that structure which is common to running and thinking) and so to be realized also in divine activity. Perhaps this is how we imagine our language to be related to the divine realities about which we use it; but such ghostly and evacuated concepts are clearly too tenuous and elusive to be called the meanings of the words we use. To think of God thus is to think of him not in our own image, but in the rarefied ghost of our own image; and so we think of him in our own image, but do not suppose that in so thinking of him we begin to do him justice. What we do, then, is in essence to think of God in parables. The things we say about God are said on the authority of the words and acts of Christ, who spoke in human language, using parable; and so we too speak of God in parable—authoritative parable, authorized parable; knowing that the truth is not literally that which our parables represent, knowing therefore that now we see in a glass darkly, but trusting, because we trust the source of the parables, that in believing them and interpreting them in the light of each other, we shall not be misled, that we shall have such knowledge as we need to possess for the foundation of the religious life.

So far so good. But it is only the predicates of theological utterances which are parabolic; it is only in what is *said about* God that words are put to other than customary employment. When we say 'God is merciful', it is 'merciful' that is in strange company—deprived of its usual escort of human sentiments. But the word 'God' only occurs in statements about God. Our grasp of this word, therefore, cannot be derived from our grasp of it in ordinary human contexts, for it is not used in such contexts. How then is our grasp of it to be accounted for? In other words, if I have given some account of how, and in what sense, we understand the meaning of the things we say about God, I have still to give some account of how, and in what sense, we know what it is that we are saying them about.

In thus turning back from the predicate to the subject of religious utterances, we are turning from revealed theology to natural theology, from the logical father to the logical mother of religious belief. And the answer to the question: 'What grasp have we of the meaning of the word "God"?' must be dealt with along the following lines. Revelation is important to the believer not for what it is in itself (the biography of a Jew, and the history of his forerunners and followers), nor because it is revelation of nothing in particular, but because it is revelation of God. In treating it as something important, something commanding our allegiance, we are bringing to bear upon it the category of the transcendent, of the divine. Of the nature of that category I have already spoken. In other words, there must exist within a man's mind the contrast between the contingent and the necessary, the derivative and the underivative, the finite and the infinite, the perfect and the imperfect, if anything is to be for him a revelation of God. Given that contrast, we are given also that to which the parables or stories are referred. What is thus given is certainly not knowledge of the object to which they apply; it is something much more like a direction. We do not, that is, know to what to refer our parables; we know merely that we are to refer them out of experience, and out of it *in which direction.* The expression 'God' is to refer to that object, whatever it is, and if there be one, which is such that the knowledge of it would be to us knowledge of the unfamiliar term in the contrast between finite and infinite.

Statements about God, then, are in effect parables, which are referred, by means of the proper name 'God', out of our experience in a certain direction. We may, if we like, by the process of whittling away, which I have mentioned, try to tell ourselves what part of the meaning of our statements applies reasonably well, what part outrageously badly; but the fact remains that, in one important sense, when we speak about God, we do not know what we mean (that is, we do not know what that which we are talking about is like), and do not need to know, because we accept the images, which we employ, on authority. Because our concern with God is religious and not speculative (it is contemplative in part, but that is another matter), because our need is, not to know what God is like, but to enter into relation with him, the authorized images serve our purpose. They belong to a type of discourse —parable—with which we are familiar, and therefore they have communication value, although in a sense they lack descriptive value.

If this is so, how do we stand with regard to verification and falsification? Must we, to preserve our claim to be making assertions, be prepared to say what would count against them?

Let us see how far we can do so. Does anything count against the assertion that God is merciful? Yes, suffering. Does anything count decisively against it? No, we reply, because it is true. Could anything count decisively against it? Yes, suffering which was utterly, eternally and irredeemably pointless. Can we then design a crucial experiment? No, because we can never see all of the picture. Two things at least are hidden from us; what goes on in the recesses of the personality of the sufferer, and what shall happen hereafter.

Well, then, the statement that God is merciful is not testable; it is compatible with any and every tract of experience which we are in fact capable of witnessing. It cannot be verified; does this matter?

To answer this, we must make up our minds why the demand for verification or falsification is legitimate. On this large matter I shall be summary and dogmatic, as follows. (1) The demand that a statement of fact should be verifiable is a conflation of two demands. (2) The *first* point is that all statements of fact must be verifiable in the sense that there must not exist a *rule of language* which precludes testing the statement. That is to say, the way the statement is to be taken must not be such that to try to test it is to show that you do not understand it. If I say that it is wrong to kill, and you challenge my statement and adduce as evidence against it that thugs and headhunters do so out of religious duty, then you have not understood my statement. My statement was not a statement of fact, but a moral judgment, and your statement that it should be tested by anthropological investigations shows that you did not understand it. But so long as there exists no *logical* (or we might say *interpretational*) ban on looking around for verification, the existence of a *factual* ban on verification does not matter. 'Caesar had mutton before he crossed the Rubicon' cannot in fact be tested, but by trying to devise ways of testing it you do not show that you have not understood it; you are merely wasting your time. (3) The *second* point is that, *for me, fully* to understand a statement, *I* must know what a test of it would be like. If I have no idea how to test whether somebody had mutton, then I do not know what 'having mutton' means. This stipulation is concerned, not with the logical nature of the expression, but with its communication value for me. (4) There are then two stipulations, and they are different. The first is a logical stipulation, and it is to the effect that nothing can be a statement of fact if it is untestable in the sense that the notion of testing it is precluded by correctly interpreting it. The second is a communicational stipulation, and it is to the effect that nobody can fully understand a statement, unless he has a fair idea how a situation about which it was true would differ from a situation about which it was false.

Now with regard to these two stipulations, how do religious utterances fare? With regard to the first, there is no language rule implicit in a correct understanding of them which precludes putting them to the test (there may be a rule of faith, but that is another matter). If a man says, 'How can God be loving, and allow pain?' he does *not* show that he has misunderstood the statement that God is loving. There *is* a *prima facie* incompatibility between the love of God, and pain and suffering. The Christian maintains that it is *prima facie* only; others maintain that it is not. They may argue about it, and the issue cannot be decided; but it cannot be decided, not because (as in the case of e.g. moral or mathematical judgments) the appeal to facts is *logically* the wrong way of trying to decide the issue, and shows that you have not understood the judgment; *but* because, since our experience is limited in the way it is, we cannot get into position to decide it, any more than we can get into position to decide what Julius Caesar had for breakfast before he crossed the Rubicon. For the Christian the operation of getting into position to decide it is called dying; and, though we can all do that, we cannot return to report what we find. By this test, then, religious utterances can be called statements of fact; that is their *logical* classification.

With regard to the second stipulation, the case is a little complicated, for here we are concerned with communication value, and there are the two levels, the one on which we remain within the parable, and the other on which we try to step outside it. Now, on the first level we know well enough how to test a statement like 'God loves us'; it is, for example, like testing 'My father loves me'. In fact, of course, since with parents and school-masters severity is notoriously a way of displaying affection, the decisive testing of such a statement is not easy; but there is a point beyond which it is foolish to continue to have doubts. Now, within the parable, we are supposing 'God loves us' to be a statement like 'My father loves me', 'God' to be a subject similar to 'My father', 'God loves us' being thus related to 'My father loves me' as the latter is related to 'Aristotle's father loved him'. We do

not suppose that we can actually test 'God loves us', for reasons
already given (any more than we can test the one about Aristotle);
but the communication value of the statement whose subject is
'God' is derived from the communication value of the same statement with a different proper name as subject. If we try to step
outside the parable, then we must admit that we do not know
what the situation about which our parable is being told is like;
we should only know if we could know God, and know even
as also we have been known; see, that is, the unfolding of the
divine purposes in their entirety. Such ignorance is what we ought
to expect. We do not know how what we call the divine wrath differs from the divine mercy (because we do not know how they respectively resemble human wrath and mercy); but we do know how
what *we mean* when we talk about the wrath of God differs from
what *we mean* when we talk about his mercy, because then we are
within the parable, talking within the framework of admitted
ignorance, in language which we accept because we trust its
source. We know what is meant *in* the parable, when the father of
the Prodigal sees him coming a great way off and runs to meet
him, and we can therefore think in terms of this image. We know
that we are here promised that whenever we come to ourselves
and return to God, he will come to meet us. This is enough to
encourage us to return, and to make us alert to catch the signs
of the divine response; but it does not lead us to presume to an
understanding of the mind and heart of God. In talking we remain
within the parable, and so our statements communicate; we do
not know how the parable applies, but we believe that it does
apply, and that we shall one day see how. (Some even believe,
perhaps rightly, that in our earthly condition we may by direct
illumination of our minds be enabled to know progressively more
about the realities to which our parables apply, and in consequence about the manner of their application.)

    Much of what I have said agrees very closely with what the
atheist says about religious belief, except that I have tried to
make it sound better. The atheist alleges that the religious man
supposes himself to know what he means by his statements only
because, until challenged, he interprets them anthropomorphically;
when challenged, however, he retreats rapidly backwards towards
complete agnosticism. I agree with this, with two provisos. The
first is that the religious man does not suppose himself to know
what he means by his statements (for what religious man sup-

poses himself to be the Holy Ghost?); he knows what his statements mean within the parable, and believes that they are the
right statements to use. (Theology is not a science; it is a sort of
art of enlightened ignorance.) The second proviso is that the
agnosticism is not complete; for the Christian, under attack, falls
back not in any direction, but in one direction; he falls back upon
the person of Christ, and the concrete realities of the Christian
life.

Let us consider this for a moment with regard to the divine
love. I could be attacked in this sort of way:—'You have contended', my opponent might argue, 'that when we say that God
loves us the communication value of the statement is determined
by the communication value of a similar statement about a human
subject; and that we know the statement to be the right statement,
but cannot know *how* it is the right statement, that is, what the
divine love is like. But this will not do. Loving is an activity with
two poles, the lover and the loved. We may not know the lover,
in the case of God, but we *are,* and therefore *must know,* the
loved. Now, to say that the image or parable of human love is
the right image to use about God must imply that there is some
similarity or analogy between human and divine love. Father's
love may be superficially very unlike mother's, but, unless there
is some similarity of structure between them, we cannot use the
same word of both. But we cannot believe that there is any
similarity between the love of God and human love, unless we
can detect some similarity between being loved by God and being
loved by man. But if being loved by God is what we experience
all the time, then it is not like being loved by man; it is like being
let down right and left. And in the face of so great a discrepancy,
we cannot believe that God loves us, if that is supposed to be in
any sense a statement of sober fact.'

I cannot attempt to answer this objection; it involves the
whole problem of religion. But there is something I want to say
about it, which is that the Christian does not attempt to evade
it either by helter-skelter flight, or by impudent bluff. He has his
prepared positions on to which he retreats; and he knows that if
these positions are taken, then he must surrender. He does not
believe that they can be taken, but that is another matter. There
are three main fortresses behind which he goes. For, *first,* he looks
for the resurrection of the dead, and the life of the world to come;
he believes, that is, that we do not see all of the picture, and that
the parts which we do not see are precisely the parts which

determine the design of the whole. He admits that if this hope be vain then we are of all men the most miserable. *Second,* he claims that he sees in Christ the verification, and to some extent also the specification, of the divine love. That is to say, he finds in Christ not only convincing evidence of God's concern for us, but also what sort of love the divine love is, what sort of benefits God is concerned to give us. He sees that, on the New Testament scale of values, it is better for a man to lose the whole world if he can thereby save his soul (which means his relationship to God); and that for that hope it is reasonable to sacrifice all that he has, and to undergo the death of the body and the mortification of the spirit. *Third,* he claims that in the religious life, of others, if not as yet in his own, the divine love may be encountered, that the promise 'I will not fail thee nor forsake thee' is, if rightly understood, confirmed there. If, of course, this promise is interpreted as involving immunity from bodily suffering, it will be refuted; but no reader of the New Testament has any right so to interpret it. It is less glaringly, but as decisively, wrong to interpret it as involving immunity from spiritual suffering; for in the New Testament only the undergoing of death (which means the abdication of control over one's destiny) can be the beginning of life. What then does it promise? It promises that to the man who begins on the way of the Christian life, on the way that is of seeking life through death, of seeking relationship with God through the abdication of the self-sovereignty claimed by Adam, that to him the fight will be hard but not impossible, progress often indiscernible, but real, progress which is towards the paring away of self-hood, and which is therefore often given through defeat and humiliation, but a defeat and humiliation which are not final, which leave it possible to continue. This is the extra-parental nurture of religious belief of which I spoke earlier, and it is the third of the prepared positions on to which the Christian retreats, claiming that the image and reflection of the love of God may be seen not only hereafter, not only in Christ; but also, if dimly, in the concrete process of living the Christian life.

One final word. Religion has indeed its problems; but it is useless to consider them outside their religious context. Seen as a whole religion makes rough sense, though it does not make limpidity.

Wadham College, Oxford

Kai Nielsen/On fixing the reference range of 'God'

Crombie has some important things to say about the role of parables in religion. The Bible abounds in parables and they are essential for our understanding of the claims of religion. 'Parable', Crombie admits, is used by him in an extended sense. The description of Christ's action of riding into Jerusalem on an ass on Palm Sunday would in Crombie's terms count as a parable, for it helps us to understand something about the extraordinary nature of the Messianic King and the non-political nature of the Messiah's kingdom.[1]

Our knowledge of what God is like is only given in parables. Our understanding of many sentences like 'God is wrathful toward sinners' or 'God is our merciful Father' can only be understood within the parables of our religion. But we also come to under-

From "On Fixing the Reference Range of 'God'," *Religious Studies*, 2(1966), 29–36, by Kai Nielsen. Reprinted by permission of Cambridge University Press and the author.

[1] I. M. Crombie, "Theology and Falsification" in *New Essays in Philosophical Theology*, ed. A. MacIntyre and A. Flew (London, 1955), p. 118. [This article is reprinted in this volume beginning on p. 311.—Editors]

stand that our parables do not tell us, in any literal fashion, what God is really like, e.g. how he is merciful, wrathful, etc. But we *trust* the *source* of our parables. We trust, taken on faith, that our images given in the parables are faithful: that the parables are faithful, that they refer us, and refer us in *a certain direction* 'out of experience. . . .'[2] They point to an incomprehensible reality, totally out of our own or anyone else's experience, which is the underlying reality that we get at through a faithful parable.[3]

Why do we accept these parables as *faith*ful parables—as parables which truly 'point out of our experiences'? If we are Christians, we do this because we trust Jesus and he authorises the parables. Jews and Moslems would accept other religious authorities as authorising certain parables as faithful, reliable parables. We, as knights of faith, simply trust the source of our parables. We trust (have faith) that our parabolic language refers beyond the parable to a God whom we cannot positively comprehend. But, if we are Christians, our trust in Jesus leads us to believe that we will not be misled by the parables as to the nature of the underlying reality referred to in the parables.

This talk, tempting as it may seem to some, won't do. I can only detail some of the reasons here. Unless we understand what is meant by saying, outside of the parable and quite literally, that there is a God and he is merciful, how could we possibly trust that Jesus or any other religious authority is not misleading us in the parable, for we could not, if we did not understand the utterance literally in its non-parabolic context, know what could count as being misled or as failing to be misled by Jesus or by anyone else.[4] Without some independent way of indicating what we are

---

[2] *Ibid.* p. 124. [See p. 324 of this volume.—Editors]

[3] I. M. Crombie, "The Possibility of Theological Statements," *Faith and Logic*, ed. B. Mitchell (London, 1957), p. 71.

[4] Wittgenstein has well remarked '. . . in ethical and religious language we seem constantly to be using similes. But a simile must be the simile for something. And if I can describe a fact by means of a simile I must also be able to drop the simile and to describe the facts without it'. Ludwig Wittgenstein, 'A Lecture on Ethics', *The Philosophical Review*, vol. LXXIV (January, 1965), p. 10. In spite of Wittgenstein's emotional disquietude about this, his conclusion seems unassailable. If we have a putative non-literal or figurative mode of speech (as a simile or metaphor) and cannot possibly say *what* it is a simile or metaphor *of*, then what at first appears as a non-literal expression 'now seems mere nonsense'. If we cannot in some literal fashion assert what facts stand behind what appeared to be a metaphor or a simile then we are, in using such expressions, talking nonsense. That it is 'deep nonsense' expressive of a powerful human drive does not make it any the less nonsense.

talking about when we are talking about God, we cannot understand what is meant by saying that the image or the parable *is or
is not* faithful. And we cannot take on trust what we cannot
understand, for we cannot know *what* it is we are supposed to
take on trust. If, as Crombie avers, we can *only* talk about God
in images, then we cannot intelligibly speak of faithful or unfaithful images any more than we can speak of married or widowed
stones. And to add insult to injury, we must note that the phrase
'parables referred out of our experience' like 'unconscious toothache' has no use. Wittgenstein *gave* 'unconscious toothache' a
use; Crombie has *not* given 'referred out of our experience' a use.

It might be replied that in general we know what it is like
to be misled. We know it to be a distressing, unpleasant and dis-
heartening experience. We, in trusting Jesus, at least trust that we
won't have this experience. We can know something about Jesus
and we can trust that he will not mislead us about God. But this
misses my last point. It is just this that we can't do, no matter
how much we may *want* to, for only if we can understand what is
meant by 'God' could we take anything about him on trust. In
this way faith cannot precede understanding.[5]

Crombie, like Hick, makes a further argument that is important in trying to establish the factual status of theism. (I have
dealt with this argument in more detail elsewhere with specific
reference to Hick, so here I shall be brief.[6]) The argument I have
in mind is Crombie's appeal to eschatological verification. To first
put the matter metaphorically: we see now through a glass darkly
but after our bodily death we shall see face to face. It is a mistake
to argue, as some have, that Crombie here uses a theological concept to explicate a theological concept.[7] An atheist can, and some
did, believe in immortality. Let us grant—which is most surely
to grant a whale of a lot—that immortality is an intelligible notion,
and furthermore let us even grant that it is true that man is
immortal. But even granting that, we still have not got to the

[5] Bernard Williams, 'Tertullian's Paradox', *New Essays in Philosophical The-
ology,* ed. A. MacIntyre and A. Flew (London, 1955), pp. 187–211. Kai Nielsen,
'Can Faith Validate God Talk?' *New Theology,* no. 1, ed. Martin E. Marty and
Dean G. Peerman (New York, 1964), pp. 131–149.

[6] Kai Nielsen, 'Eschatological Verification', *Canadian Journal of Theology,* vol.
IX (1963), no. 4, pp. 271–281. [Reprinted in this volume beginning on p. 209.—
Editors] See also William Bean 'Eschatological Verification: Fortress or Fairy-
land', *Methodos,* vol. XVI, no. 62 (1964), pp. 91–107.

[7] William Blackstone, *op. cit.* p. 123.

promised land, the concept of eschatological verification still will not do the job it was designed to do by Crombie. Consider the putative statement 'God is merciful'. Crombie asks:

> Does anything count against the assertion that God is merciful? Yes, suffering. Does anything count decisively against it? No, we reply, because it is true. Could anything count decisively against it? Yes, suffering which was utterly, eternally and irredeemably pointless. Can we then design a crucial experiment? No, because we can never see all of the picture. Two things at least are hidden from us; what goes on in the recesses of the personality of the sufferer, and what shall happen hereafter.[8]

But presumably in the hereafter, we would be in a position to know, or have some grounds for believing, that the suffering was, or was not, utterly, irremediably and eternally pointless, for then we would be in a position to see all of the picture.[9] But how could we even then be in such a position? No matter how long we lived in the hereafter, after any point of time, we would *not* have good grounds for asserting or denying the suffering was *eternally* pointless. We could never—and this is a conceptual and not an empirical point—be in a position to see things *sub specie aeternitatis* and grasp what the whole picture is like. At any point in time, the believer or the non-believer could justly claim that we could not make such a judgment because the whole picture wasn't in. In fact we couldn't know or even have reasonable grounds for believing that a fair sample had been taken. But even if we drop the requirement that the suffering be seen to be *eternally* pointless, Crombie's account has still not been saved.

Suppose we were somehow to discover after our bodily death that there is no suffering which is utterly and irredeemably pointless, then according to Crombie, we would have good evidence for believing in God. How so? Someone might well agree that there is no utterly and irredeemably pointless suffering and

---

[8] I. M. Crombie, 'Theology and Falsification', *New Essays in Philosophical Theology,* ed. A. MacIntyre and A. Flew (London, 1955), pp. 124–125. [Reprinted here beginning on p. 311.—Editors]

[9] I. M. Crombie, 'The Possibility of Theological Statements', *Faith and Logic,* p. 72. There is a clash here between the two essays. In his later essay Crombie sets conditions that are open to disconfirmation while in 'Theology and Falsification' they are not. In 'Theology and Falsification' Crombie speaks of 'suffering which was utterly, *eternally* and irredeemably pointless' (p. 124 italics mine) while in 'The Possibility of Theological Statements' he only speaks of 'utterly and irremediably pointless suffering. . . .' (p. 72).

still assert that he doesn't understand what is meant by 'God' and so he doesn't understand what it means to say that God is merciful. After all the sentence 'In spite of the fact that there is no God there is no utterly and irredeemably pointless suffering' is not a self-contradiction. What, after all, is meant by the subject term 'God'? How could suffering or the lack thereof do anything to show how there might exist an object of discourse which is particular but not indicable? If we could understand what 'God' meant, Crombie's remarks might help us to give sense to 'God is merciful', but since we do not understand what 'God' means, we cannot understand 'God is merciful'.

To this Crombie might well reply: 'Indeed I haven't shown how "There is no utterly pointless and irredeemable suffering" allows us to conclude that God is merciful or to understand the word "God", but I did not try to. Furthermore, I grant that I have not shown how, on purely intellectual grounds, one could conclude that naturalistic interpretations of such experiences are inadequate. That cannot be done. But I have done what I set out to do, namely to meet Flew's challenge. I have shown under what conditions I would be prepared to give up my claim that God is merciful. I have shown how such a claim is falsifiable "in principle".'

But I do not see how Crombie has met Flew's challenge. If the statement and denial that God is merciful are both equally compatible, as they have been shown to be, with the statement 'There is no utterly pointless, irredeemable suffering' and with any possible empirical statement, which reports experiences we have or might conceivably have in our bodily life and in our non-bodily life (whatever that may mean), then we have not shown, as Crombie must, how the assertion or denial of the mercifulness of God have different factual content, and thus we have not shown how such religious statements can be used to make factual statements, for it is the believer's claim that 'God is merciful' asserts something different from 'There is no merciful God'. It is not enough that different strings of marks are used, but different factual assertions are supposed to have been made—statements with different experiential consequences. But Crombie has not been able to show how this is so; and as a result he has not been able to show that his God-statements have the kind of intelligibility that he claims for them.

Crombie, like Hick, is perfectly prepared to admit that both naturalistic and non-naturalistic interpretations of our religious experience are perfectly possible and quite plausible. He *trusts,* he says, that the non-naturalistic theistic interpretations more adequately depict the facts. But this, he claims, is for him, and should be for all believers, a matter of *faith* and not a matter of knowledge. But if my above arguments are correct it could not possibly be a matter of *faith* for him, for he has not succeeded in establishing that his theistic beliefs are indeed beliefs of the sort he takes them to be, for he has not shown how they are expressible in factual statements, and thus he has not shown how they form an intelligible alternative to naturalism. He is in the same boat as the Edwardian who steadfastly denied that lovely young ladies sweat—they only glow. The Edwardian shows by his speech that he no doubt has a different attitude toward young ladies than the plainest of plain men, but he doesn't show that he has different factual beliefs about them.

There is one further line of argumentation that Crombie avails himself of that might be taken as establishing the factual status of theism. The claim that a sentence is used to make a factual statement if and only if it is verifiable (confirmable or disconfirmable) is, Crombie argues, a confused conflation of two distinct claims. Once they are separated, we should come to see that we have no good grounds for *denying* that our key religious or theological claims assert facts, have the logical status of factual statements.

What are these quite two different claims? The first one is the claim that a statement of fact 'must be verifiable in the sense that there *must NOT be a rule of language* which precludes testing the statement'. Whether we can *in fact* test it does not matter, but it must be *testable* in principle; that is, there must be no logical ban on verifying it, as there is (or so let us assume) on verifying moral statements like 'You ought *NOT* to kill puppies just for the fun of it' and on analytic statements like 'Puppies are young dogs'. To try to verify these statements, Crombie argues, is to show that you do not *understand* what they *mean.* That is to say, there is a logical or conceptual ban against verifying them. But if something is a factual statement there *can* be no logical ban on verifying it, but whether or not it is *in fact* verifiable is quite another matter.

Crombie claims that we only require, as a necessary condition for factuality, that there be no logical ban on verifying a statement if it is to count as a genuine factual statement.

The second claim—a claim that must not, if clarity is prized, be confused with the first—is that *for any individual* fully to understand a statement, he must know what a test of it would be like. If he has no idea how to test whether a person had mutton for lunch, then he does not know what 'having mutton' means. This Crombie argues, has nothing to do with the logical status of the expression in question, but merely with its 'communication value' for the person in question. To count as a factual statement, a statement need *not* be verifiable *in this sense* or have such communication value. We would say, however, that if utterances did not have 'communication value' we could have no fair idea as to what would make them true and what would make them false.

Crombie argues that our key religious statements are only unverifiable in this *second,* quite harmless, sense. *But since they are about a mystery this is just as it should be.* But they are verifiable in the *first sense* and this is enough to ensure that they have *factual* meaning. Recall that there is no *linguistic rule* to the effect that there can be no test for 'God is loving' or 'God made man in his image and likeness'. The Christian argues that we cannot confirm or disconfirm that 'God is loving' or 'God created man in his image and likeness' because, since our experience is limited in the way it is, we as a matter of fact cannot get into the position of verifying such claims. But there is no *logical ban* on verifying them. They are perfectly verifiable in principle. This being so, they have factual meaning and after the death of the body we shall then in fact be in a position to verify such claims. This is enough to preserve their factual status.

Within the parable, 'God is merciful' and 'God loves us' even have communication value. The communication value is derived from similar utterances with a different proper name. Within the parable we understand such talk, but we do not know the 'communication value of such utterances *outside* of the parable'. But, Crombie argues, given the hiddenness, the wholly otherness, the mysteriousness of God, this is just what we should expect. As Kierkegaard has well argued, any being who didn't have these features couldn't be God. Talking within the framework of the parable—the biblical stories for example—we work in a context of 'admitted ignorance', but we accept this language because we *trust* its source. We do not know how our parable applies, but we believe—have faith—that it applies 'and that we shall one day see how'.[10] The religious man—if he knows what he is about, that is if he understands his religion—does 'not suppose himself to know what he means by his statements'. He does not suppose himself to be the Holy Ghost. But it is also incorrect to claim that he falls back, when pressed, on complete agnosticism, for he can turn for a check—for a test—to the person of Jesus, the mediator, and to the concrete process of living the Christian life. There, in the anguishing struggle to pare away 'self-hood', he will encounter divine love directly. Thus these key religious and theological statements are verifiable in principle; there is no *logical ban* on verifying them. They meet the minimum requirements for being factual statements, so it is a mistake to say that they are cognitively or factually meaningless on the very grounds that Flew and the logical positivists mark out as relevant for determining factual intelligibility. In fact we should say that within the proper religious contexts they even have communication value. 'Seen as a whole', Crombie can conclude, 'religion makes rough sense though it does not make limpidity'.[11]

We have already discussed the specific difficulties in trying to move from what we understand *in the* parable to understanding how the parable could refer to that which is 'out of experience'; and we have discussed the difficulty in trying to appeal to authority, Jesus' or otherwise, to settle questions of meaning. We can, as Hepburn has shown, know a lot about Jesus and about Christian living, but this does not, and cannot, take us to God unless we *already understand* what 'God' *means*. No matter how much we love and trust Jesus, his saying 'There is a God. Love Him with your whole heart and your whole mind' cannot *mean* anything to us unless we already understand the meaning of 'God'.[12] It would be like Jesus' telling us to put our trust in Irglig when we had no idea of what was meant by 'Irglig'. But what is new in Crombie's arguments above, and what must be examined is Crombie's claim that there is no *logical ban* on verifying (con-

[10] I. M. Crombie, 'Theology and Falsification', *New Essays in Philosophical Theology* ed. A. MacIntyre and A. Flew (London, 1955), p. 127 [See p. 327 in this volume.—Editors]
[11] *Ibid.* p. 130. [See p. 329.—Editors]
[12] Ronald Hepburn, *Christianity and Paradox* (London, 1958), pp. 50–90.

firming/disconfirming) 'There is a God', 'God loves us', 'God is merciful' and the like. *Perhaps* there is no such ban, but they still have not been shown to be verifiable (confirmable/disconfirmable) in principle, for we do not have any idea of what it would be like to confirm or disconfirm such claims. We do not understand at all what it would be like for such claims to be either true or false or probably true or probably false. It isn't that these utterances just lack 'communication value' for some (say non-believers), but since believers and non-believers alike have no idea of what would or could count as confirming them or disconfirming them, neither a believer nor a non-believer can know what it *means* to say that they are used to assert facts.

Now, Crombie could reply that to argue in this way is to miss his point. When Schlick and Carnap put forth the verifiability criterion as a criterion for what is to count as a factual statement, they were talking about verifiability *in principle*. To speak of 'verifiability in principle' is to speak, as they stressed, of the *logical* possibility of verification. When you say, Crombie could continue, that we cannot specify what would or could count as a verification/falsification or confirmation/disconfirmation of these theistic claims, your 'cannot' is a *factual* 'cannot'. You just mean that, as a matter of fact, we can think of none, but you don't rule out, by definition, that there might be some such verification. Thus you can't consistently say that it is *logically impossible* to verify them, as it is in the case of moral statements, imperatives, analytic statements, and the like. Since it makes *sense* to look for evidence for these claims, they remain verifiable (confirmable or disconfirmable *in principle*) and thus they do have a *factual meaning and content,* even under a criterion of meaning like that of Carnap or Schlick.

I think there is such a ban or at least an implicit ban on verifying non-anthropomorphic God-talk. The crucial, yet inessential, difference between analytic statements and theological statements in this respect is that in the case of these non-anthropomorphic theological statements the ban is not so obvious. We know that it is a conceptual blunder to try to verify whether 'Bachelors are really unmarried' or 'Wives are really women'. Given an understanding of the constituent terms, we know there can be no question of confirming or disconfirming such statements. But this is not true for 'There are matzos in the centre of the sun' or 'There are beings as folksy as Johnson on Mars'. There is no way of detecting whether these statements can, as a matter of fact, be verified from examining the meanings of the constituent terms in such sentential contexts. Thus, unlike with our analytic statements, we have not ruled out the logical possibility of their verification. But consider now such sentences as 'There is an infinite being' or 'A being transcendent to the universe and not spatio-temporally related to the universe directs the universe in an incomprehensible way' or 'There is a reality in all ways greater than nature'. Such sentences, sentences which are (according to Crombie) an integral part of a non-anthropomorphic theism, are sentences which, given the meanings of their constituent terms, cannot be used to form statements which admit of the logical possibility of verification/falsification or confirmation/disconfirmation. Where 'infinite being' is being used non-anthropomorphically, there can, *logically* can, be no observing an infinite being. To understand this term, in the only way we can understand it, is to understand that there can, logically can, be no way of indicating or identifying what it purportedly refers to. The same is true of 'being transcendent to the universe', 'not spatio-temporally related to the universe', 'directs the universe in an incomprehensible way' and 'greater than nature'. Yet, if Crombie is correct, such talk is not just a part of the theologian's febrile chatter about 'God', but is embedded, as well, in a sophisticated religious man's talk of God. But Crombie's own remarks about such phrases *in effect* show that to understand the conventions governing such talk is to understand that such sentences cannot be used to make statements capable of confirmation or disconfirmation. (Of course, as we have seen at other places in his argument, he speaks as if such statements were verifiable; but we have shown that none of his arguments show that there are traces or indicia in the world pointing to an infinite individual transcendent to the cosmos.)

The fundamental thing to be noted here is this: God is *not* for a believer some kind of theoretical construct. God is *not* consciously conceptualised by the believer as a mystifying term we insert in our discourse to allay anxieties. Rather 'God' is supposed to be a proper name standing for an infinite, non-spatio-temporal, non-indicable individual, utterly transcendent to the cosmos. When we reflect on the meanings of these terms, we recognise that it would be logically impossible to verify that such an alleged individual exists. Anything that we could apprehend or could be acquainted with would *eo ipso* not be such a reality. (To speak of 'indirect verification' here will not do, for if it is *logically* impossible to directly verify x, it makes no sense to speak of indirectly verifying x, for 'indirectly' cannot here qualify 'verifying x'.)

The above line of argument indicates that there is a logical ban on the verification of such God-statements; it is only not so obvious and not so explicit. Furthermore, we are easily tricked into thinking there is no such ban, for there are different uses of 'God', including anthropomorphic uses of 'God', where 'God created the heavens and the earth' or 'God governs the world' are factual (confirmable or disconfirmable) and known to be false. But given the non-anthropomorphic uses of 'God' that Crombie so patiently details, such sentences are not used to form statements which are logically possible to verify. Crombie has not shown how his key theistic claims, when construed non-anthropomorphically, have factual intelligibility and yet, as he rightly claims, their having such intelligibility is crucial to the soundness of the fundamental claims of Christianity, Judaism and Islam.

D. Z. Phillips and J. R. Jones/Belief and loss of belief

D.Z.P.: Jargon is the enemy of philosophy. It creates a screen between the enquirer and the possibility of understanding. Furthermore, if a certain jargon has become a prevalent fashion in philosophical circles, using it, and hearing it used, may lead a person to think he has understood, when, in fact, he has not. There is a great need to cut through some prevalent jargon in contemporary philosophy of religion. We need to be forced to see that many religious beliefs cannot be understood in terms of the neat categories which, we are tempted to think, are the only categories which intelligible notions have. For example, in his lectures on religious belief,[1] Wittgenstein considers religious beliefs like belief

From "Belief and Loss of Belief" by D. Z. Phillips and J. R. Jones in *Faith and Philosophical Enquiry,* ed. D. Z. Phillips (London: Routledge and Kegan Paul, New York: Schocken, 1970), pp. 111–121. Reprinted by permission of Routledge and Kegan Paul, Ltd., Schocken Books, Inc. and D. Z. Phillips. Copyright © 1970 by D. Z. Phillips. This discussion first took place on B.B.C. radio.
[1] Wittgenstein, Ludwig, *Lectures and Conversations on Aesthetics, Psychology and Religious Belief,* ed. Barrett, Cyril, Blackwell, 1966. The lectures on religious belief belong to a course of lectures on belief given by Wittgenstein sometime during the summer of 1938.

in the Last Judgment, or that one's life is being lived under the eye
of God. We cannot grasp the nature of these beliefs by forcing them
into the alternatives: empirical propositions or human attitudes.
And yet, again and again, philosophers of religion force our hands
by saying, 'But come now, which is it? Is the Last Judgment a
future event? Is it something which is going to happen at a certain
time? Or is belief in the Last Judgment simply your own attitude,
a value, a way of looking at things, which you confer on the world
about you?' What Wittgenstein does is to free us from this jargon.
It is as if he said to us, 'Don't say it *must* be one or the other. Look
and see what kind of things these beliefs are. Don't let the jargon
determine your thinking.' Or, as Wittgenstein used to say, 'Don't
think, look.' Don't say that religious beliefs *must* be of this kind or
that, but look to see what kind of beliefs they are. And when we
do this, Wittgenstein suggests, we stop asking many questions of
religious belief which, before, we thought it quite reasonable to
ask. For example, we stop thinking of religious beliefs as conjectures, hypotheses, for which the evidence is not particularly good.
In the light of our reflections on religious beliefs, we may be led
to revise our opinions about the distinction between the rational
and the irrational, and to think again about what might be meant
by saying that one does not have any religious beliefs. What does
it mean to believe in the Last Judgment? What does it mean to say
that one does not believe in it? Must we say one or the other, or is
this a mistake we are led into because of the hold of a certain jargon on us? These are some of the questions Professor Jones and I
are going to try to discuss. We do no more than touch lightly on
them. At this stage, all we are attempting to do is to indicate a
direction in which these questions can be pursued with profit.

J.R.J.: I should like to draw you out first, Mr. Phillips, on the
point that religious belief is nothing like the acceptance of a hypothesis or the holding of an opinion, however well- or ill-founded.
I wonder whether this can be seen to be so by just looking at the
role beliefs have in the believers' lives. We have been told, in this
kind of context, not to think and allow ourselves to get into the
grip of a jargon, but to just look. Well, what is it that shows that,
to take Wittgenstein's example, belief in the Last Judgment has obviously nothing in common with a hypothesis?

D.Z.P.: I think that if we do look at the role this belief plays in at
least many believers' lives, we find that it is not a hypothesis, a
conjecture, that some dreadful event is going to happen so many

thousand years hence. We see this by recognizing that a certain range of reactions is ruled out for the believer. What I mean is this: if it were a conjecture about a future event, he might say, 'I believe it is going to happen' or 'Possibly it might happen' or 'I'm not sure; it may happen', and so on. But that range of reactions plays no part in the believer's belief in the Last Judgment. It is not a conjecture about the future, but, as it were, the framework, the religious framework, within which he meets fortune, misfortune, and the evil that he finds in his own life and in life about him.

J.R.J.: It would seem, then, that you could say that a genuine religious belief has a certain firmness which is quite peculiar to itself. That indeed, in a sense, the expression of a genuine religious belief could be described as the firmest of all judgments. Well, I wonder what is the character of this firmness, because it doesn't seem to mean the same thing as, for example, firmly grounded; because, of course, the whole notion of grounding, of obtaining good evidence, of weighing evidence, is right out of place here. What, then, is the character of the firmness?

D.Z.P.: Well, certainly the firmness does not mean, as you say, what it means in 'firmly grounded prediction'. Wittgenstein considers the example of a man who said, 'I had a dream last night in which I dreamt of the Last Judgment, and now I know what it is.' Well, Wittgenstein says, if you compare that with a prediction of what weather we are going to get next week, it isn't any kind of prediction. 'I had a dream—therefore—Last Judgment.' We don't know what to make of that, if it is taken as an inference. So, in that sense, one might say the belief in the Last Judgment isn't firm at all, isn't well-established at all. So what could be meant, then, by firm belief here? Wittgenstein suggested that belief in religion has much more this role: I have this picture of the Last Judgment before my mind whenever, perhaps, I am tempted to perform a despicable deed. It regulates my thinking. It is firm in that it is to this picture that I appeal in such situations as these.

J.R.J.: If this, then, is the sort of firmness that a religious belief has, that is to say, not at all the firmness of a well-founded hypothesis or conjecture, what, then, is the non-believer doing when he rejects belief? You see, in not having a use for what you have called 'the picture', and in rejecting it because it has no force or significance in his life at all, is he then, or could he then be said to be, contradicting the believer?

D.Z.P.: In his lectures, Wittgenstein suggests that in certain cases, anyway, the non-believer would not be contradicting the believer. He takes the example of a man who, when he is ill, says, 'This is a punishment from God.' Wittgenstein asks, 'What am I saying if I say that this plays no part in my life? Am I contradicting the man who does believe this?'[2] Wittgenstein wants to deny this. What he would say is: 'It plays no part in my life at all; this collection of words means nothing to me, in the sense that it does not regulate my life; I do not adhere to it; I do not aspire to what it stands for. Therefore, I am not involved in the same form of life as the man who does regulate his life by this picture and aspires to it.' On the other hand, if I said, 'There is a German aeroplane overhead'[3] and you doubted this, we would both be participating in the same activity, namely, locating the German aeroplane; we would be appealing to the same criteria: I would be certain, you would be doubtful. But if I say that the idea of a Last Judgment plays no part in my life, then I am saying that in this respect you are on an entirely different plane from me; we are not participating in the same language-game, to use Wittgenstein's phrase, at all.

J.R.J.: It looks, then, that no evidence could count against or for; in that no evidence can count for, then, of course, it follows that no evidence can count against, what might naïvely be called the truth of these pictures. And yet, we know well, from experience and from the history of religions, that belief, religious belief, is something which can be undermined by scepticism; and scepticism would be in this case scepticism concerning what is thus naïvely called the truth of the picture. But, when this happens—and this is what interests me—when belief is thus undermined, or weakened, it then looks as though the picture itself begins to lose its hold on the life of the believer. And I wonder what this really signifies? Doesn't it suggest that there is some sort of internal relation between the weight or force of the picture—and I mean by that, it's having weight for me—and the state of my mind that is capable of being undermined by doubt? This seems to reintroduce the notion of a literal truth, as against a literal falsity, you see. It is in this kind of connection that doubt and scepticism work upon people's minds, and it looks as though it does do its job here. When there is this corrosion by doubt, the pictures are somehow corroded; they lose their hold.

[2] These are not quotations.
[3] Wittgenstein's example.

D.Z.P.: I think this is an extremely important and difficult region to be reflecting about, and the best I can do, I think, is to make the following initial distinction. Let us distinguish between, on the one hand, someone, that is, a given believer, for whom the force of the Last Judgment no longer means anything. In his life, this picture of the Last Judgment means nothing at all, whereas it used to once. Now, what has happened here, I suggest, is that the *attention* of the individual has been won over either by a rival secular picture, or, of course, by worldliness, etc. Because his energies are now focused in another direction, this picture which was once powerful in his life, has lost its grip. Interestingly enough, when you say that the notion of literal truth is reintroduced, I suggest that it is reintroduced in this way: that when the old force of the picture is lost, the new force it has is that of a literal picture, which, as far as I can see, is simply a matter of superstition. But we might want to distinguish between the case of the picture losing its hold for a given individual, with religious pictures losing their hold anyway, not through the fault of any particular individual, but because of changes in the culture. Certain religious pictures decline, and yet you can't ask, 'But whose fault is it that they are declining?' You can't trace the decline to the biographical details of the life of any single individual.

J.R.J.: This cannot be done because it is a decay of belief which is affecting a whole culture or a whole epoch. Couldn't we be said to be living in such a period today—a period of what you might call prevalent disbelief? And I would be interested to know what you would say to this: why doesn't it make sense, then, in a period such as this, of the decay of belief, to suppose a group of people—of well-minded people—trying to bring about a renewal of faith, possibly from within a religious context or even from entirely without it; people with a secular background, noting the effect of the decay of belief on the morals of the culture generally, trying to bring about a renewal of faith by devising new and more acceptable pictures, and then trying to induce belief in them? Why is this somehow nonsensical? Why couldn't such a thing work?

D.Z.P.: I think this is linked to a point that we have neglected. So far, we have been concerned to emphasize that these religious beliefs are not conjectures, or hypotheses, with insufficient evidence for them. The beliefs are not empirical propositions. Once this is said, many philosophers assume that the beliefs must be human attitudes, values conferred, as it were, by individuals on to the world about them. But this does not follow and is in fact untrue. It is important to recognize that these pictures have a life of their own, a possibility of sustaining those who adhere to them. Part of the answer, though I think not the complete answer, to the question why it would be nonsensical to imagine theologians, let us say, creating pictures—new pictures—to meet the crisis of the age, the declining faith that they perceive about them, is that whatever they created would precisely be their creation, and you would have a curious reversal of the emphasis needed in religion, where the believer does not want to say that he measures these pictures and finds that they are all right or finds that they are wanting. On the contrary, the believers wish to claim that it isn't they who measure the pictures, since in a sense, the pictures measure them; they are the measure in terms of which they judge themselves. They do not judge the picture. Or again, to link with the earlier points we made, when people do judge the picture that is the time when they are beginning either to rebel against it, or when the picture is beginning to lose its hold on their lives as individuals.

J.R.J.: Yes, I agree with this, but there seems to me to be another thing that could be added to that. Isn't it, or wouldn't it be, precisely the element of believing as part of a tradition of belief that would be wanting or lacking in this attempt on the part of a group of people to bring about a renewal of faith by devising new pictures? You see, this group of would-be reformers wouldn't be dealing with a faith nourished by time and handed down from the past within which certain pictures are to be found. They would, rather, be presenting their new-fangled pictures first, and then trying to get people to believe them. Well, now, in such a situation, it seems to me, pictures degenerate into mere pictures; but— and this is interesting—not because they would be in the nature of hypotheses or conjectures for which the evidence is found wanting. Not that at all, but because they would be, as it were, trying to become, or trying to be made to become, operative as beliefs outside the sphere of, or you might say, in the absence of the surroundings of, belief—all that goes with believing in a tradition of belief, I mean, in an historical faith. I can't see that anything could be a substitute for that.

D.Z.P.: I agree entirely. This makes it necessary to say something about our use of the term 'picture'. Sometimes, at a casual glance, it might look as if by 'pictures' we meant what you have now referred to as 'mere pictures'. Indeed, many philosophers of religion today have spoken of devising new pictures, finding new symbols, to communicate the essence of the divine to people. It's as if there were a deliberate use of the picture to communicate the essence of the divine. 'We now find that that picture isn't working, so let us revise what is called, naïvely, our image of God.' 'Our image of God must go', we are told. As if, independently of the picture, we have a notion of divinity. You then compare the picture with this notion and you say, 'Oh, well, it's not doing its job properly', and we have another picture. Wittgenstein stressed in his lectures that the whole weight may be in the picture. The picture is not a picturesque way of saying something else. It says what it says, and when the picture dies, something dies with it, and there can be no substitute for that which dies with the picture.

J.R.J.: Well, could this, then, have the implications that when the picture, which is a picture of the divine, as it were, which is God, having a role through faith in the whole life of a believer, is corroded by doubts and scepticism, the picture can be said to have died; but that when the picture dies or decays or is phased out in a whole culture, that in a sense, on your own presuppositions, God could be said to have died?

D.Z.P.: Yes, this is a difficulty that some people have felt about this way of talking. For instance, if you said that certain modes of moral conduct were to pass away, some people might say that there would be no goodness in the world any more. So why do we not want to say that if these pictures were to die, God dies, as it were, with the pictures? I think the answer to that, though I don't see this very clearly, is that the desire to say that God dies is literal-mindedness attempting to reassert itself. The point is that from within the picture something can be said now about such a time, that is, a time when people might turn their backs on it altogether. What can be said is that in such a time, people will have turned their backs on God. In other words, if people believe, there is nothing within belief which allows them to say that God can die. What they say is that there may come a time when people will turn their backs on God.

J.R.J.: It is as though you were saying that although the picture has, in one sense, died, not only in the lives of particular individuals, but even prevalently through the whole of a culture, it is still possible to speak from within the picture.

D.Z.P.: I am saying that it is possible for believers to say something now about such a time. You may find, of course—perhaps we do find—that only a handful of people do derive sustenance from this picture. But a picture may die in a culture because believing in it is not an isolated activity. To call the belief a language-game can be misleading if it does suggest an isolated activity. Other cultural changes can affect people's worship. For example, in *Brave New World* there is a decline in the notion of moral responsibility. In such a society one can see, without too much difficulty, how the notion of God as a Judge might also be in decline.

J.R.J.: So that, in that kind of society, the picture 'Last Judgment' would have no power over people's lives. But the interesting thing is that it wouldn't be this because it was a hypothesis for which people found that there wasn't sufficient evidence. It is not as a weak hypothesis that it declines, but because everything else surrounding it has declined out of that particular society.

D.Z.P.: As I said at the outset, we aimed to do no more in this discussion than to point out a direction in which the hold of a certain jargon could be avoided, a jargon which forces us to think of religious beliefs either as hypotheses about some future events or as human attitudes in which values are conferred on the world by the believers. In trying to elucidate what such a direction involves we have discussed what kind of beliefs religious beliefs are; the kind of firmness they have; in what sense they are unshakeable for the believer; on the other hand, what can happen to a believer when an unshakeable belief begins to lose its hold on him, and he becomes an unbeliever—what happens to him then; and also what is happening despite all his efforts to believe; what is happening in the culture in which he does believe, where, as it were, the surroundings from which the religious picture is nourished are changing, so bringing about changes in the nature of that religious picture itself.

Nine/**Religion and science**

Introduction/Verification in its wider cultural context

WE have seen the importance of the question of the burden of proof to the issue of theology and verification. When we explore this issue, it inevitably drives us back to the more traditional problem of religion and science.

The issue of theology and verification revolves around a contrast that the positivists drew between scientific and theological statements. Observations are relevant to checking the truth of scientific statements. The positivists claimed that this was not the case with theological statements made by nonfundamentalists. A number of contributions to this volume deal with this issue. They make it clear that, if there is a contrast, it is not a simple one.

Similarities between religion and science

Most of the similarities between religion and science that are emphasized in the contributions to this volume stress the fact that the role of observation in science is not straightforward.

Scientific laws are not straightforwardly falsifiable

J. F. Miller, III, tries to show that the more important a statement is to a given science, the more reluctant the scientists are to permit it to be falsified. In this connection, he deals with the principle of conservation of energy (see pp. 361 ff.). D. D. Evans invokes Thomas Kuhn's well known discussion of "scientific paradigms" to make the same point.[1] There are laws that are so important to a given science that, confronted with data that does not conform, scientists will modify the law, rather than abandon it (see p. 362). This is similar to the accusation that Flew levels at theologians for qualifying the meaning of "God loves us." Indeed, this similarity was the inspiration for Miller's essay. Miller strengthens his point by dealing with the presuppositions of science. These are assumptions which are supposed to underlie scientific work as such, rather than research in some particular field. They are far more resistant to falsification than the most well established laws of any particular science.

Thus close attention to the actual practice of theoreticians of science erodes the alleged sharp contrast between religion and science in the matter of falsification.

Confirmation in scientific work is not simple

The role of experimentation and observation in science seems straightforward. By contrast, we have already considered Crombie's somewhat tortuous efforts to show the complexities of the role of verification and confirmation in checking on the truth of theological statements. Yet, Evans's discussion of the actual role of observation in scientific work shows that it too is extremely complicated (see pp. 396 ff.). It is not nearly as simple as checking on the truth of "This book has white pages and black print." There are many levels of meaning, and many degrees of theoretical generality involved in scientific work. It takes an expert to understand how a blur on a photographic plate is related, through a series of ascending layers of theoretical complexity, to statements about electrons or other sub-atomic particles.

Scientific hypotheses and religious beliefs

We argued earlier that a crucial result of the abandonment of fundamentalism was that it deprived theologians of an appeal that made reli-

[1] Thomas S. Kuhn, The Structure of Scientific Revolutions, 2d ed. enlarged (Chicago: University of Chicago Press, 1970).

gion comparable to science, namely, the appeal to miracle. As we have seen (p. 159), Wisdom referred to the contest between Elijah and the priests of Baal as a crucial experiment. And the supernatural behavior of the waters of the Red Sea could be taken as confirmation of the activity of the supernatural God. Theologians, like the representatives of the new orthodoxy, are far removed from this quasi-scientific way of confirming theological statements. They vehemently reject the idea of confirming the truth of theological statements by empirical observations. They claim that the notion of empirical confirmation belongs to the domain of science and of magic; it has no place in authentic faith. The man of faith believes the truth of theological statements like "God loves us," in spite of evidence that runs against it. This is brought out by the way that Mitchell's Partisan persists in believing in the Stranger despite the contrary evidence (see pp. 263 ff.).

Andrew Robison argues that the position of the new orthodoxy is misguided. Properly understood, religious beliefs are to a significant degree, comparable to scientific hypotheses. He considers a number of confusions that have obscured this point for many contemporary theologians (see pp. 413 ff.). One of them is the distinction between logic and faith. A mother who has faith in her son's integrity may trust him despite the fact that she is shown strong evidence of his having robbed a bank. The evidence counts against her statement that "My son is honest," even though her faith leads her to preserve her trust. Robison claims that the strong faith orientation of many theologians, especially among the representatives of the new orthodoxy, prevents them from seeing the relevance of this point for theology. From a logical standpoint, the suffering of a child from inoperable cancer counts against the truth of "God loves us," even though a Christian may continue to persevere in his faith and to trust God. This point is clearly relevant to Mitchell's parable of the Partisan and the Stranger (p. 263), and Flew's discussion in his retrospective essay (pp. 281 f.) bears on this issue.

Robison claims that appropriate religious attitudes like faith cannot affect the logic of disconfirmation. Therefore, theological statements, and the religious beliefs they express, are comparable to scientific hypotheses.

In general, thinkers who stress the similarities between religion and science do so by undercutting the supposedly simple and straightforward character of scientific inquiry. Robison makes this sort of point, but he also picks things up at the other end. He tries to show that theological statements are theoretical in character and that they can be confirmed by an appeal to religious experiences. They are, therefore, factually meaningful.

A major purpose of Tooley's ambitious program, which is treated in Section Ten, is to show that Ayer and Carnap fail in their effort to drive a sharp wedge between science and religion by means of what he calls the "translatability challenge." Tooley may, therefore, also be numbered among philosophers who stress the structural similarity between scientific and religious thought.

The differences between science and religion

The essay by Donald Evans that is reprinted in this volume is a succinct and effective statement of the differences between science and religion. It would be pointless to summarize his statement of the differences (see pp. 404 ff.); his presentation is itself a summary. Instead I will supplement his observations by emphasizing issues that bear directly on the question of the burden of proof.

Science is successful at the operative level

A point that has already been dealt with in connection with Kai Nielsen's criticisms of religious thought is worth repeating in this context. It is the distinction between the theoretical and the operative levels. The issue of theology and verification is debated between theoreticians, between theologians, who are the theoreticians of religion, and philosophers of science. One of the major lessons of the issue of theology and verification is that verification has not been effective as a concept that will demonstrate a contrast between science and religion, at the theoretical level.

At the operative level there seems to be a contrast between science and religion which damages the case of thinkers who stress their similarity. Scientists know what they mean by the terms they use and they know how to resolve their differences. They successfully confirm and falsify their hypotheses and they manage to work quite well with nonobservables like genes and electrons. They gladly leave theoretical reflections about the difficulties of verification and the status of nonobservables to the philosophers of science.

It might seem that ordinary religious believers are in the same relation to theologians. They have no difficulties at the operative level where they worship and engage in other rituals, and they gladly leave theoretical problems, like the meaning of God, to the theologians. This is not the case. Believers who represent different religious traditions, and even members of the same one, do not agree on the meaning of God.

Furthermore, they cannot agree on procedures for resolving their disputes (see pp. 406 f.).

The role of technology

Most people do not understand the first thing about science. They do not understand the concepts of any particular science and they do not know anything about the scientific method. Yet they respect science because of its technological applications. Although the uninitiated layman cannot understand the connection between television and scientific theory, he is apt to be impressed with the idea that there is a connection, because the technological application of science can be produced on demand. Religions, in the past, promised practical benefits. Many of them still do. Technology has proved far more reliable at delivering the goods in the here and now.

When the preceding observations are tied to the differences between religion and science that Evans enumerates, the list is impressive. It would seem that the burden of proof is on the theologians. As Flew insisted, they need to provide some evidence of the cognitive effectiveness of religion.

As we have seen, the issue isn't that simple. Theologians can reply by noting that religion is a far more difficult subject than science. It involves ultimate mysteries. It is unreasonable to expect religion to be as effective as science at the operative level. Considering the difficulty of the subject, its cognitive performance is about what one would expect. Therefore, the appeal to the contrast between religion and science at the operative level does not work. When the failure of verification to do the job of discrediting theology at the theoretical level is added to the picture, theologians can claim that the burden of proof is on the sceptic.

John F. Miller, III/Science[1] and religion: their logical similarity

I

In his "Theology and Falsification" Professor Antony Flew challenges the sophisticated religious believer to state under what conceivable occurrences he would concede that there really is no God Who loves mankind:

> 'Just what would have to happen not merely (morally and wrongly) to tempt but also (logically and rightly) to entitle us to say "God does not love us" or even "God does not exist"? I

From "Science and Religion: Their Logical Similarity," *Religious Studies*, 5(1969), 49–68, by John F. Miller, III. Reprinted by permission of Cambridge University Press and the author.

[1] Throughout this paper I intend by 'science' that systematic body of knowledge which at any given time has been achieved by physics, chemistry, biology etc., rather than the methodology employed in the acquisition of this knowledge.

therefore put . . . the simple central questions, "What would have to occur or to have occurred to constitute for you a disproof of the love of, or of the existence of, God"?'

Flew's claim is that religious statements are 'killed by inches, the death by a thousand qualifications': religious believers so qualify their statements about what constitutes evidence for and against God that the statements become no longer assertions. 'They look at first sight very much like assertions' and 'those who utter such sentences intend them to express assertions'. But 'to assert that such and such is the case is necessarily equivalent to denying that such and such is not the case. . . . For if the utterance is indeed an assertion it will necessarily be equivalent to a denial of the negation of that assertion.' And if there are no specifiable conditions denied by a statement, then the statement is really not a statement at all. Thus, Professor Flew concludes, religious statements have 'been so eroded by qualification' that they cease to be assertions.

This statement of the problem is straightforward. For example, if someone claims that this paper is white, then he must know under what conditions this statement (that the paper is white) would be false, specifically: any case in which the paper is brown, purple, orange, green, blue, etc., or any case in which there is no paper at all. For in order for a statement, whether true or false, to have a discernible meaning (unless, of course, it is a tautology), the user of the statement must be able to specify at least under what conditions the statement would be false. In short, Flew's challenge assumes the falsifiability criterion of meaning.

This is not the place to discuss the falsifiability criterion of meaning. Rather, what I will argue is that it is a misapplication to apply this criterion to such statements as 'God exists' or 'God loves mankind'. For these statements are *religious first-order principles* of the Judeo-Christian *Weltanschauung* and *as such* are not amenable to falsification. These first-order religious principles bear resemblance to first-order scientific principles which, I will argue, are *unfalsifiable* since they are the fundamental tenets of the contemporary scientific *Weltanschauung*.

Two concepts must be explicated before the aforementioned claim can be argued: 'Weltanschauung' and 'first order principles'. The German word 'Weltanschauung' literally means a way of *looking* at the world or a way of *seeing* the world *as* something. Translated concisely as 'world-view', it refers to one's conception of events, things, and life in general, including the purpose of life, the constitution of the world, and a general cosmological and philosophical outlook. Whatever would be considered essential in understanding the world would be an integral part of one's *Weltanschauung*, for it would definitely have an influence on the way in which one saw the world. At this point in the explication of a world-view it becomes necessary to introduce a Wittgensteinian distinction between 'seeing' and 'seeing as'. In *Philosophical Investigations*, Wittgenstein says that if he looks at something twice and sees each time something different, it is not a matter of interpreting it differently but rather of seeing something different each time. What could be meant, since the physical object does not change? In one sense, he would see the same thing in the sense that the image passing through the pupil to the retina would be 'the same'. 'To see' here means to take a picture as with a camera or to reflect as a mirror. But 'seeing-as' is quite different, and, Wittgenstein seems to argue, we can see something only as something, that is, we must always *interpret* our experience for it to be experience. It must be carefully pointed out that seeing something is not a double experience: first seeing it and then seeing it as something, which is tantamount to interpreting it. Rather it is *one* experience.

Since 'seeing-as' means *seeing* something *as* something, it is our conceptual framework or the categories and concepts within our *Weltanschauung* which force this situation upon us. A concept, Wittgenstein tells us, forces itself upon us because we hold a certain view of the world. In a famous passage, Wittgenstein writes that we think that we are 'tracing the outline of a thing's nature over and over again' but really we are only tracing around the 'frame through which we look at it'. It is, by analogy, as though everyone were wearing green-tinted glasses: everything would be *seen as* green. We all wear conceptual glasses, glasses which consist of our world view. For example, when the primitive man looked at lightning, he *saw* it *as* the thunderbolt thrown by an angry god, as, for instance, when the Greeks saw it as the personified wrath of Zeus. Similarly our present-day scientists *see* lightning *as* electricity. Likewise when primitive men looked at nature, they *saw* it *as* god-infested. When Plato looked at the same phenomena, he saw them as resembling the divine forms, yet inferior to them and striving to attain their *telos*. Nature for Democritus was both a mechanistic and naturalistic atomism; for Newton it was like a mechanical clock. Darwin saw nature as striving to live, in a world where only the fittest were privileged to survive. And today our scientists see the world in still a somewhat different way. For what we see depends upon what pair of conceptual glasses we are using, that is, with what *Weltanschauung*-lenses we view the world. A man who is committed to a particular world view is necessitated to seeing the world in the way which the concepts of his *Weltanschauung* suggest. No one, for instance, who accepts our world-view would ascribe feeling to trees or stones. But this was not so for the primitive man, who treated many objects, for us inanimate, as possessing feeling and spirits which had to be dealt with as one deals with persons. Indubitably, the world-view of the Greeks in the time of Plato, the world-view of the wandering Jew in his Exile, the Egyptian world-view during the reign of King Tut, the view of life of St Francis or St Thomas in the Middle Ages, and our own diverse world-view all differ greatly concerning the meaning, structure, origin, constituents, etc., of life and the world. To adopt one view is tantamount to seeing the world in a particular way. To take but an insignificant example: whereas we see snow, more or less, as either dry or wet, the Eskimo has many different words for snow. In short, *he sees* more than we do; he differentiates and verbalises what he sees. Wittgenstein's point—a most important one—is that although we think that we are tracing the true reality of an object, actually we are tracing with *words* and *symbols* which do not allow us to get beyond them, in the sense that these concepts determine what it is that we *see* the world *as*. And a system of integrated concepts is what constitutes a *Weltanschauung*.

We have next to consider the notion of 'first-order principle'. The only way to determine what constitutes a first-order principle in either science or religion is to examine how the statements so characterised function in these differing *Weltanschauungen*. That is, we must examine the logical relation between statements, notice which ones are statements from which others are derived and which are statements in accordance with which other statements are derived. This last-mentioned distinction is well known to philosophers of science. There are some statements in science as we know it today (viz., 'the principle of causality, according to which an event is causally determined only if it can be accurately foretold';[2] the law of conservation of energy according to which

[2] Max Planck, *The Philosophy of Physics*, p. 53.

the total amount of energy in the universe remains constant[3]) which are used logically as principles in accordance with which evidence is interpreted, and as such logically could not ever *be falsified* if continued to be used *in this manner.* In religion, such statements as 'There is a God' and 'God loves mankind' are used in the *same way logically,* since they are statements *in accordance with which* all evidence is interpreted and are hence unfalsifiable. These statements, both in science and religion, hereafter termed 'first-order principles', function specifically to harmonise and to incorporate into a consistent whole the widest possible range of phenomena. Coherence and consistency are the test for truth, implicitly. Thus it will be argued that basically religion and science present alternative *Weltanschauungen,* neither of whose first-order principles are amenable to empirical testing in that they actually function as principles in accordance with which all reasoning within the *Weltanschauung* takes place.[4]

Two brief comments must be made before continuing. First, it does not matter whether 'first-order principles' in the sense in which it is used in this paper refers to something such as what Professor Strawson in *Individuals* calls 'categories and concepts which, in their most fundamental character, change not at all' or whether it refers to something less Kantian and thus more mutable in human religious and scientific reasoning. Whether more or less permanent, 'first-order principle' refers to what at this stage in our conceptualising is fixed and being used logically in such a way that nothing could falsify it. Perhaps this will change; but if it does, it will not affect our analysis of either religion or science at the *present time.* Second, it might be argued that science does not require causation. As will be pointed out in due course, science *is*

---

[3] For specific problems, this principle is assumed before deductions can be made and insures that the total increase of energy of a system is equal to the net work done on the system, which is tantamount to asserting that total energy is constant.

[4] One may ask, if this is so, whether these first-order statements can then be considered 'factual'. Strictly speaking, one might be inclined to deny this. This would mean, as the positivists and a host of philosophers criticising religion have urged, that these important religious statements are not factual. But similarly we would also have to deny that the law of causation and the law of conservation of energy are factual. We may not want to do this. But in any case, if the religious ones are non-factual, so too are the scientific ones; and if the scientific ones are factual, so too are the religious ones. It seems to me that 'factual' is merely an honorific term: 'facts' are what is based upon evidence, but evidence is determined by the *Weltanschauung* with its concepts, categories, and first-order principles.

now using the principle of causality to introduce states and properties, to determine what constitutes an 'event', and to decide which rules of correspondence may be used. Whether science *needs* to employ the principle of causality or not, the point is that it is so employing it now. Whether religion *needs* to define God as a non-spatial, non-temporal, eternal and infinite being which is transcendent and immanent etc. is not the issue at stake: indications from Buber, Tillich, and the death-of-God theologians illustrate that possibly this is not so. But the point in question is merely that this is the way in which the majority of believers define God and thus the way in which 'God' functions in most religious discourse. It is this fact about the logical use of terms which is relevant for our discussion.

II

Professor Ernest Nagel in his *The Structure of Science,* in explaining why, in spite of evidence against or at least 'apparent exception to' certain laws, scientists are reluctant to abandon them, states that this is due to two factors, the second of which is most relevant to our discussion. First, the direct and indirect confirmatory evidence combined to support a law may outweigh the apparent exceptions. Second, the relationship of the law in question to other laws and indeed to the entire structure of science may be such that the rejection of the law in question would force a serious structural reorganisation and revision of scientific knowledge which might be unfeasible because an adequate alternative may be available. Writing about what has been labelled a 'scientific first-order principle', namely the law of conservation of energy, Professor Nagel writes:

> 'In that event, both L and the system to which it belongs can be "saved", despite the ostensible negative evidence for the law. This point is illustrated when an apparent failure of a law is construed as the result of careless observation or of inexpertness in conducting an experiment. But it can be illustrated by more impressive examples. Thus the law (or principle) of the conservation of energy was seriously challenged by experiments on beta-ray decay whose outcome could not be denied. Nevertheless, the law was not abandoned, and the existence of a new kind of entity (called a "neutrino") was assumed in order to bring the law

into concordance with experimental data. The rationale for this assumption is that the rejection of the conservation law would deprive a large part of our physical knowledge of its systematic coherence.'[5]

It is obvious from this example that the logical relationship of the law of the conservation of energy to other laws is such that its abandonment would necessitate a conceptual revision of the sort which physicists would not enjoy. When a principle such as this one harmonises many elements, it often is used as a principle *in accordance with which* evidence is drawn. In this case, the law of the conservation of energy was used logically in this way; thus the 'discovery'—perhaps 'invention' would be a more accurate term here—was made in order to 'save' this most important principle. *Used in this way,* the law of the conservation of energy *could never be falsified.* This situation in science definitely counts against Flew's analysis: it is true, as he claims, that some religious statements are used in such a way that nothing *could* count against them and it *looks* as though something could count against the law of the conservation of energy, since it was stated above that the principle was 'seriously challenged', but this is *not* the case. The serious challenge was only an apparent one, for the subsequent developments indicated the decision to *use* the law of the conservation of energy as a *first-order principle in accordance with which* facts were to be drawn: the fact drawn here was the 'discovery' of the 'neutrino'. Thus, as Professor Nagel points out, such apparent exceptions are not 'genuine' at all.

That the same situation occurs in religion with respect to its first-order principles is indubitable. There are many apparent exceptions to the claim that God loves mankind. Theodicy, or the problem of reconciling the existence of an all-good, powerful, and knowing God with the evidence of an evil world, provides concrete evidence that there are apparent possible exceptions to God's love. But the religious believer will no more allow anything to count *conclusively* against his assertion that God loves mankind than the scientist will allow anything to count *decisively* or *conclusively* against the law of the conservation of energy, at least for the present.

Before we examine another example of a scientific first-

[5] Ernest Nagel, *The Structure of Science,* Harcourt, Brace, and World, Inc., New York, 1961, pp. 65–6.

order principle, it is important to consider a crucial aspect of Flew's Challenge, namely the claim that important religious statements are unverifiable *in principle*. Now it is important to distinguish between what it is *in fact* not possible to verify and what is *in principle* not possible to verify. We cannot in fact verify whether there is life elsewhere in the universe or whether in 75,000 B.C. people in a certain part of the world were arguing over property rights. But—and this is Professor Flew's point—we do know *how* one would go about verifying these propositions. Nevertheless, argues Flew and a host of other philosophers, there are some propositions such that we do not know *what* we would have to do to verify them: these are *in principle* unverifiable, in that one is *in principle* unable to specify under what conditions they would be true or false. What, for instance, would constitute possible evidence against the existence of a non-spatial, non-temporal, eternal, infinite Being which is transcendent, immanent, omnipotent, omniscient, and wholly good? Just how could one possibly get into a situation to verify that? Eschatological verification is illegitimate as possible verification, for it assumes the intelligibility of the very discourse in question. The question then is how one could verify or falsify theological utterances.

The first point that must be made is that the distinction between verification/falsification *in fact* and verification/falsification *in principle* is an *empirical distinction*. By this is meant that it is because of the nature of the world and our experience that certain things are *in principle* impossible for us. To claim that certain things are logically impossible for us to do, strictly speaking, would entail a contradiction in the proposition requested. No one, for example, could legitimately demand that one draw a round square or find a married bachelor. But it is not a logical impossibility—it is only an empirical impossibility, if that—to experience a non-spatial etc. God. Perhaps 'impossible' is a poor choice of words here. For if 'to experience' means 'to have sense experience of one of the five senses', then it becomes a logical impossibility to experience a non-sensible God. On the other hand, if 'to experience' means something similar to 'to feel' or 'to love' or even 'to see as through a glass darkly', then a failure to experience God would be a personal empirical limitation, an empirical impossibility based upon our possible experience in this sort of world as we stipulate it to be. Only if one could substantiate the claim that this is the only possible world would it be logically impossible for human beings ever to experience God, verify his love etc. The cognizance of this point is imperative: what must be meant by the phrase 'unverifiable in principle' is 'unverifiable in principle in the world as we now stipulate it'. This is a less strong claim. And if what has been argued is cogent, then *it is possible* to answer Flew's challenge of specifying 'just what would have to happen not merely (morally and wrongly) to tempt but also (logically and rightly) to entitle us to say "God does not love us" or even "God does not exist"?' Of course, in specifying an answer, we must conceive of the world and human experience as perhaps drastically different and stipulate possibly different or at least somewhat new rules for verification. And only if one's metaphysical position would require that human experience can be of one, and only one, kind should there be objections to this procedure.[6]

One can even specify a situation in which the question of a God's existence would not even be raised. If, for instance, the world were not very orderly, if material spontaneously appeared where there had been no material before, if nothing were discernibly responsible for the occurrence of anything, if nothing showed the slightest indication of purpose or conscious design, if there were no morality, if no event were mysterious, and if human beings indicated no signs of insecurity—under such circumstances the question of the existence of a Judeo-Christian God may not even arise. And if it did not arise, it would be absurd to ask what could falsify the existence of it. To make this clear: suppose someone were to ask you to falsify the existence of a nonsensible gwackypoo. You would reply that this would be unintelligible, for you do not even know what it is that you are to prove false. Exactly this situation would occur with God, in the above example. It is, in short, illegitimate to ask for the falsification of the existence of an entity of the sort described.

The eschatological argument attempts to show that if human experience can be of such and such a kind, then it is possible to verify and/or falsify the existence and the love of God. Those who criticise the argument do so by stating that this argument assumes the intelligibility of the very discourse in question, namely theological discourse, in order to prove the intelligibility of theological discourse—a question-begging procedure. But, as has been pointed

---

[6] The inclusion of this point is to demonstrate that Flew's challenge rests upon the verification principle of meaning, specifically in that it considers empirical evidence alone as admissible—a clearly moot assumption.

out, those who make this objection do so on the assumption that human experience can be of only one kind. And this metaphysical assumption, which is wholly unwarranted, need not be granted. It is a peculiar feature of the religious *Weltanschauung* that certain non-empirical experience is said to be possible to human beings. To rule out this possibility is to set the limits of possible verification and falsification within only an empirically scientific domain: this is tantamount to committing oneself to a *Weltanschauung* preference.

What must be pointed out here is that people do give up the proposition 'God exists' either because they take certain evidence as counting against this proposition or because they see nothing as counting in favour of it: in either case they abandon the religious *Weltanschauung*. A believer, on the other hand, is one who under no circumstances rejects this fundamental proposition. Now what has just been stated is trivially true, but nevertheless fundamentally important. The way to 'disprove' the claim that God exists is a pragmatic, rather than a logical one: it involves persuading people to give up their *Weltanschauung* in which 'God exists' is a first-order unfalsifiable principle in accordance with which they interpret experience and determine evidence. Similar situations occur *in science,* and it is to this that we shall now turn.

III

Let us then consider an example of a scientific first-order principle which is so important for the harmonisation of data and for the coherence of science that nothing is allowed to count conclusively against it, for it is undoubtedly the most important principle in accordance with which evidence is drawn: this is the principle of causation. It is indubitable that this principle is of a somewhat different status from the principle of the conservation of energy, for without the former, science as we know it would not exist. That is, if we gave up the law of the conservation of energy, we would have to give up a great part of physics and chemistry, specifically those domains for which a constant energy system is a necessary condition for determining values for those systems. Likewise, if we gave up the Principle of the Rectilinear Propagation of Light, we would have to abandon the principle of what is now geometrical optics. But were we to abandon the principle of causation, we would have to completely give up physical science as we now have it. Exactly the same sort of situation would occur if we were, in religion, to give up the proposition, 'God exists'. We could perhaps think of situations in which we would give up both propositions, but the world would have to be constituted so differently that it is a moot question just what drastic changes would have to occur for us to do this. Flew's challenge is incorrect in claiming that religious statements are *in principle* unverifiable. Rather, they are unverifiable *in principle* in the world as we find (or specify) it. That this is so seems so obvious that it is hardly worth arguing. Flew's challenge depends for its plausibility upon the assumption that only empirical evidence is legitimate. This of course loads the question in such a way that it allows only one type of answer; by limiting the possibility of other answers, it begs the question manifestly. If physical and spiritual phenomena were as commonplace as our everyday daily empirical experience, there would be no incentive to so load the question. Thus it seems that the insistence upon empirical evidence as the only evidence is dependent upon the world being characterised as it is. To conclude: religious statements are unverifiable and unfalsifiable in principle —if they are—*only given* our world as it is characterised, not in principle qua every possible world. Therefore, the claim made above is true: were the world different, we would not have science as we have it; for our science depends upon the use of the principle of causation as an ordering principle for experience and for evidence. Similarly, were the world different, men might very well not assert 'God exists'; but the world would have to be very different indeed, for religion uses 'God exists' as a non-falsifiable principle in accordance with which evidence is construed as evidence and is interpreted. To summarise: if we can conceive of a world in which we would not ask what caused this or that phenomenon, we could think of a world in which we would not ask what was responsible for this or that being as it was. The principle of causation in science and the religious claim that God exists are logically of the same type.

IV

Let us now consider the status of the principle of causation and of determinism in science. It is clear that physics, the epitome of the physical sciences, is deterministic. In fact, as the famous physicist Planck writes in *The Philosophy of Physics*:

'Physics has hitherto developed on the . . . assumption [of determinism]. . . . In other words, in order to be preserved intact, the principle of causality, according to which an event is causally determined only if it can be accurately foretold, has been slightly modified. What has been done is to change the sense in which the term "event" is employed. Theoretical physics does not consider an individual measurement as an event, because such a measurement always contains accidental and unessential elements. By an event, physics means a certain merely intellectual process. It substitutes a new world in place of that given to us by the senses or by the measuring instruments which are used in order to aid the senses. This other world is the so-called physical world image; it is merely an intellectual structure. To a certain extent it is arbitrary. It is a kind of model or idealization created to avoid the inaccuracy inherent in every measurement and to facilitate exact definition.'[7]

What is being stated here, however philosophically inadequately, is that every measurement of distance, time, length, mass, space, and electrical charge has two meanings: the immediate result of actual measurement in which case it is always inaccurate; the application of the 'physical world image' to the model, the intellectual exact picture of the world in which mathematics makes possible exactly specified and perfectly defined measurements. But—and this is the important point—these two are different.

'The world image contains no observable magnitudes at all; all that it contains is symbols. More than this: it invariably contains certain components having no immediate meaning as applied to the world of the senses nor indeed any meaning at all, e.g., ether waves, partial oscillations, reference coordinates, etc. Such component parts may seem to be an unnecessary burden; yet they are adopted because the introduction of the world image brings with it one decisive advantage. This advantage consists in the fact that it permits strict determinism to be carried through.'[8]

This physical world image or conceptual framework in which one's scientific concepts apply exactly is what this writer would call the scientific *Weltanschauung*. That and how science is such a world-view will be explicated in the next section; what must be clarified here is what sort of claim is being made. The following examples may suffice to clarify the meaning of this claim. No scientist would claim that he has observed atoms, yet physics in

[7] Planck, *op. cit.*, p. 53.
[8] Planck, *op. cit.*, p. 55.

the twentieth century is atomic or particle physics. The predication of a conceptual framework in which reality is interpreted in terms of atomic particles would be an example of the claim that science is a world-view. Numerous other examples could be given. Theories are examples of conceptual frameworks for which the evidence is not direct. Evolution with its concept of genes to explain phenomena in its domain would constitute an example in science where a picture or image of the world functions to organise and explain biological phenomena. Einstein's conception of space as curved—that is, the application of Riemannian geometry instead of Euclidean geometry to space—is an example of what is meant by the claim that science has its picture preferences or world images. Determinism and causality also are part of the over-all scientific *Weltanschauung*. Other examples will be given in the next section.

Then let us continue to examine the claim that causation and determinism are non-falsifiable first-order principles of science.[9] Professor Nagel has suggested that a deterministic theory is one in which from one instant someone who analyses the system can logically determine the state of any other instant in the system. But 'determinism' may be extended to refer to systems in which one can statistically (with high probability) determine any state of a system from a given instant description.[10] Using the example of the molecular theory of gases, Nagel makes this point explicit:

> 'Although statistical mechanics does not predict the individual mechanical states of the molecules of a gas, it would be a mistake to conclude that statistical mechanics is not a determin-

[9] Perhaps it would be better to view causation and determinism as the necessary conditions for the possibility of science as we now have it. For it may be that these principles stipulate what can and cannot be science, rather than being principles which science uses in accordance with which to adduce evidence. However, this may be merely a linguistic distinction without any methodological value: perhaps methodologically the two amount to the same thing.

[10] Ernest Nagel, *op. cit.*, p. 292. 'According to this definition, a theory is deterministic if, and only if, given the values of its state variables for some initial period, the theory logically determines a unique set of values for those variables for any other period. If this definition is adopted, it is incorrect to deny that a theory is deterministic on either of the following two grounds: on the ground that a theory does not establish such unique one-to-one correspondences between the values at different times of *every* set of magnitudes mentioned by the theory; or on the ground that experimentally measured values of theoretical state variables are not in precise agreement with their theoretically calculated ones.'

istic theory. For in the first place, statistical mechanics includes the assumptions of classical particle mechanics, so that at least in theory the initial mechanical state of the individual molecules uniquely determines the mechanical state for any other time. But what is more to the point is that the statistical-mechanical state-description is defined in terms of *statistical* state variables, not in terms of the state variables of particle mechanics. With respect to its *own* mode of specifying the state of a system, statistical mechanics is a strictly deterministic theory.'[11]

A similar situation obtains with the pressure-density-temperature law. As Max Planck tells us, 'the simple law of pressure is valid only for relatively extensive surfaces on which a very great number of molecules exert an impact; for here the irregularities cancel each other'.[12] Further, the emissions of radioactive phenomena provide another example: considered in brief times, the action of emission is irregular; it is regular only statistically considered over a long period of time.

Still another illuminating example where causality and determinism are clearly operating as first-order non-falsifiable principles of science occurs in quantum mechanics. Let us examine what takes place conceptually when in particle physics it is theoretically impossible to determine the exact 'position' and 'velocity' of an individual 'particle' simultaneously, because this would entail illuminating the particle with light which itself is composed of particles which then would alter the position of the particle to be illuminated. If we keep in mind Flew's objection that religious claims die the death of a thousand qualifications, perhaps we could claim that the same sort of qualifying is going on in science as regards the causation-determinism in quantum mechanics. Perhaps it would be well to list these qualifications.

(Qualification One): Planck states that the conclusion that it is impossible to apply strict causality to particle physics 'rests upon a confusion between the world image and the world of sense'.[13] Rather he suggests that we use a method

> which consists in assuming that it is meaningless, with respect to physics, to ask for the simultaneous values of the coordinates and of the velocities of a material point or for the path of a photon of a given colour. Evidently the law of causality cannot be blamed

[11] Ernest Nagel, *op. cit.*, p. 291.
[12] Planck, *op. cit.*, pp. 51–2.
[13] Planck, *op. cit.*, p. 63.

because it is impossible to answer a meaningless question; the blame rests with the assumptions which lead to the asking of the question, i.e., in the present case with the assumed structure of the physical world image.[14]

(Qualification Two): Professor Frank, in his *Modern Science and its Philosophy,* makes a somewhat different point. One often reads, he says, that 'it is impossible to measure the position and the velocity of a moving particle simultaneously', and that particles 'in general do not possess definite positions and velocities simultaneously'. But these statements postulate physical objects (particles) with certain states (position and velocity) which cannot be known, a sort of Kantian *ding-an-sich,* which is neither necessary nor helpful to empirical science. In Professor Frank's words:

> 'Quantum mechanics speaks neither of particles the positions and velocities of which exist but cannot be accurately observed, nor of particles with indefinite positions and velocities. Rather it speaks of experimental arrangements in the description of which the expressions "position of a particle" and "velocity of a particle" can never be employed simultaneously.'[15]

Construed in this way, particle physics or quantum mechanics would not violate determinism or causation. The statement that the position and velocity of a particle cannot be measured simultaneously becomes a grammatical or syntactical comment, not a material-mode statement. This is the point of Professor Nagel too: it follows that if the variables 'p' and 'q' which must satisfy the

> 'uncertainty relations, are interpreted as the measures, respectively, of the "momentum" and "position" of an electron, then despite the names used for these measurable traits of electrons, these traits cannot be identified with characteristics of particles denoted by the words "momentum" and "position" as they are used in classical physics. For it is evident that though "p" and "q" in quantum mechanics are *called* coordinates of "momentum" and "position", the words are now being employed in an unusual sense. In classical mechanics these words are so used that a particle always must have a determinate position and simultaneously a determinate momentum, and in theory both the position and momentum can be ascertained with unlimited precision. In this usage it is nonsense to say that a particle has a determinate posi-

[14] Planck, *op. cit.,* pp. 63–4.
[15] Frank, *Modern Science and its Philosophy,* Harvard University Press, Cambridge, 1949, p. 163.

tion but not a determinate momentum, or that it is logically impossible to discover the precise value of one but not the other. But in quantum mechanics the uses legislated for these words are patently different. Accordingly, if in conformity with the assumptions of quantum theory an electron is said to be a "particle", possessing magnitudes represented by the symbols "p" and "q" whose simultaneous values cannot be ascertained with unlimited precision even in principle, then either the word "particle" is being used in some Pickwickian sense or these symbols cannot represent momenta and positions in the familiar classical meanings of the words.'[16]

Concerning 'position' and 'momentum' of 'an electron', Nagel points out that 'since no experimental arrangements can be instituted within which both phases can be simultaneously interpreted, it follows trivially that no measurement can ever assign precise values to both conjugate coordinates simultaneously.'[17] Because these concepts are necessarily construed differently from similar concepts in classical physics, one would erroneously conclude that quantum mechanics is not deterministic.

(Qualification Three):[18] If we understand the law of causation as stating that if a state of the universe X is followed by state Y, then whenever X occurs Y will occur (assuming that this is a causal relation and not coincidence), the following objections obtain: (1) we can never know the state of the whole universe; (2) it is not certain whether state X could ever exactly return. Actually in science the law of causality is put somewhat as follows: 'if, in a finite region of space, the state A is at one time followed by the state B and at another time by the state C, we can make the region sufficiently large by adding to its environment that the state C becomes as close to the state B as we please.'[19] This means that we determine, by including various aspects of environment, that B and C are in 'the same state' and thus uphold the law of causality. An example would be the investing of objects with 'qualities' or 'properties' which are not perceivable: chemical affinity,

[16] Nagel, op. cit., p. 301.

[17] Nagel, op. cit., p. 303.

[18] The qualifications following do not apply to causality in quantum mechanics only, but in general.

[19] Cf. Henri Poincaré's Science and Hypothesis and The Value of Science Poincaré makes the point that the law of inertia, the law of conservation of energy, the law of casuality are conventional, not open to verification or falsification.

electrical charges, magnetism. To take the last example: if two iron bars look alike but in the presence of iron filings one behaves differently, we impute to the one magnetism and not to the other. It is not that magnetism is 'indirectly observable' here. What is the case is that the results are different, so *in accordance with* the principle of causality we assign the 'cause' a different *state,* in terms of imperceptible variables if perceptible ones are not forthcoming. As Professor Frank says, 'this in turn means that if the law of causality is not valid according to one definition of the state, we redefine the state in such a way that the law is valid'. Thus the law of causality functions as the principle *in accordance with which* we determine what is taken to constitute a state and with which we define the word 'state'.[20]

Cassirer takes a similar position: as logical empiricism argues that the form of a physical law is dependent upon what variables are used to describe the state of the system, so Cassirer argued that by introducing an appropriate conception of an 'object' one can always insure the validity of the causal principle. Indeed, this may be the very task of science, according to Frank. 'The task of theoretical science is to provide bodies with fictitious properties the chief purpose of which is to insure the validity of the law of causality.[21] This 'sort of remodelling of nature' not only indicates that the law of causality as it is used in science could never be falsified in principle but also attests to the fact that science is a *Weltanschauung.*

(Qualification *Four*): A very similar observation was made by Planck, but he construes causality as defining what is an 'event' rather than what constitutes a 'state'. Writing about the laws concerning radioactive emission and the pressure-density-temperature law, Planck states that individual measurements are not considered 'events', for then the law of causality would not hold. Such measurements must be regarded statistically, rather than individually:

> 'In other words, in order to be preserved intact, the principle of causality . . . has been slightly modified. What has been done is to change the sense in which the term "event" is employed. Theoretical physics does not consider an individual measurement as an event, because such a measurement always contains accidental and unessential elements.'[22]

20 Cf. Nagel, *op. cit.,* pp. 292–3.
21 Frank, *op. cit.*
22 Planck, *op. cit.,* p. 53.

Here once again then is an example of the use of the principle of causality as a non-falsifiable first-order principle.

(Qualification *Five*): Often in science a new concept is introduced to insure that the law of causality can be applied. For example, although the law cannot be applied in its classical form to quantum mechanics, by introducing the concept of wave,

> 'we see then that there is fully as rigid a determinism in the world image of quantum physics as in that of classical physics. The only difference is that different symbols are employed and that different rules of operating obtain.'[23]

Thus, Heisenberg's principle of uncertainty notwithstanding,

> 'the uncertainty in forecasting events in the world of the senses disappears and in its place we have an uncertainty with regard to the connection between the world image and the world of the senses. In other words, we have the inaccuracy arising from a transfer of the symbols of the world image to the sense-world and vice versa. The fact that physicists have been willing to put up with this double inaccuracy is an impressive demonstration of the importance of maintaining the rule of determinism within the world image.'[24]

(Qualification *Six*): These considerations have led many philosophers of science to regard the principle of causality as 'an imperative, a precept to seek regularity, to describe events by laws'[25] in which case it is clearly neither true nor false nor verifiable nor falsifiable, or as a 'heuristic principle',[26] 'a maxim for inquiry',[27] or a maxim expressing 'the general objective of theoretical science to achieve *deterministic* explanations'.[28] Professor Nagel suggests that we view it in this way:

> 'The principle of causality so construed is thus a generalised recommendation. It bids us construct theories and find appropriate systems to which those theories can be successfully applied, with no restrictions upon the detailed form of the theories, except for the requirement that, when the state of a system is given for some initial time . . ., the theory for it must determine a unique state of the system for any other time.'[29]

[23] Planck, *op. cit.*, p. 65.
[24] Planck, *op. cit.*, p. 66.
[25] Moritz Schlick, 'Causality in Contemporary Physics', *The British Journal for the Philosophy of Science*, Vol. XII (February 1962).
[26] Nagel, *op. cit.*, pp. 82–3.
[27] Nagel, *op. cit.*, p. 320.
[28] Nagel, *op. cit.*, p. 323.
[29] Nagel, *op. cit.*, p. 320.

(Qualification *Seven*): As we have seen already, another way to uphold the causal relation and determinism is to 'substitute a new world in place of that given to us by the senses', a new world image designed especially 'to avoid the inaccuracy inherent in every measurement and to facilitate exact definition',[30] containing no observable magnitudes but only symbols, the events of which we view as happening in accordance with what we can formulate as causally determined laws.[31] By adopting this qualification, we can be assured that the law of causality and determinism will be universally applicable, but only within our *Weltanschauung* or world image. As Planck writes, this is done by symbolising the system of material bodies of our sense experience in terms of measured states, which is tantamount to transferring them to the world image. The result is a physical structure with an initial state. External influences acting upon the initial state and the object are subsequently symbolised in terms appropriate to the world image.

> 'As a result of this second step we obtained the external forces acting upon the structure; in other words, the liminal conditions. These data causally determine the behaviour of the system for all time, and it can be calculated with absolute accuracy from the differential equations furnished by theory. In this way the coordinates and the velocities of all material points of the system are found to be perfectly definite functions of time. If now at any later point we translate the symbols used for the world image back into the world of the senses, the result we obtain is that a later event of the sense-world has now been connected with an earlier event of the sense-world, so that the latter can be used in order to allow us to make an approximate forecast of the former.'[32]

(Qualification *Eight*): Still another way of insuring that causation and determination will hold is to introduce a new concept where an old one failed. In discussing quantum mechanics Planck tells us that the classical Newtonian image failed and in its place was put the new world image of quantum mechanics, which ultimately was due to the desire to keep the rigid determinism in which a place could be found for the Planck quantum. Material waves, he tells us, 'are the elements of the new world image'.[33]

30 Planck, *op. cit.*, p. 53.
31 Planck, *op. cit.*, pp. 55–7.
32 Planck, *op. cit.*, p. 56.
33 Planck, *op. cit.*, p. 64.

Conclusion: The above qualifications from selected philosophers and scientists are but a few of the many ways in which
the principle of causality has been used to qualify evidence to
insure its validity and application. This procedure, however, is
tantamount to making it a non-falsifiable (*in principle,* at least as
it is used) principle. As in religion with its first-order non-
falsifiable statements, *nothing is allowed to count against* these
important first-order scientific principles which have been discussed (causality, determinism, the principle of the rectilinear
propagation of light, the law of the conservation of energy). Therefore, religion and science are logically similar in this respect: both
have within their conceptual frameworks or world-views non-
verifiable principles of a first-order status which are principles *in
accordance with which* inferences are drawn and evidence is
adduced.

V

Let us now consider another crucial claim, namely that science,
like religion, is fundamentally a *Weltanschauung.* Even a superficial reading of the preceding portions of this paper will indicate
that science is most certainly a *Weltanschauung,* as defined above.
References to 'world images', and imputing properties to objects
in order to assure the validity of first-order principles indubitably
indicate what has been described as 'seeing the world' in a particular way, thus constituting a picture preference. For example,
light travelling in straight lines, material waves, atomic particles,
and many other scientific concepts are *theoretical* and not part of
the observable world. It is not that light does travel in straight
lines; it is that we *represent* it as doing so. It is not that particles
and light do travel in waves, but rather that this is how we choose
to view it. It is not that there 'really are' atoms so much as that
atomic theoretical physics is productive. To talk of a system of
material bodies, symbolise them and submit them to laws is to
transfer them to a world image. In providing 'bodies with fictitious properties the chief purpose of which is to insure the
validity of the law of causation' one is obviously creating features
of a world-view or *Weltanschauung.* There are, however, alternatives to a particular world-view, and we find them even in science:

> 'For example, I can introduce only the motion of masses;
> but then, in order to obtain the necessary diversity, I must take

refuge in unconfirmable hidden motions. This leads to the purely mechanical picture of the world, which Democritus dimly conceived as an ideal, and which occurs mostly in the form of atomism. . . . In a quite different way, H. A. Lorentz and his pupils have created a qualitative world picture by breaking away from the mechanistic tradition and introducing as state variables electric charge and electric and magnetic field intensities. Thus arose the electro-magnetic picture of the world. Among all these, it is not possible to choose uniquely on the basis of experience.[34]

It is thus clear that, whatever science is, it is at least at crucial points a non-verifiable world-view, a particular view of the world which excludes alternatives which would be equally compatible with the 'facts' and 'evidence'. What is considered fact and evidence could be interpreted in such a way as to make alternatives equally plausible.

A well-known philosopher of science, Stephen Toulmin, clearly states that 'physics presents new ways of regarding phenomena'.[35] For example,

'in geometrical optics it is not the data which are fresh, for we have known about shadows for a very long time. The novelty of the conclusion comes, not from the data, but from the inference: by it we are led to look at familiar phenomena in a new way, not at new phenomena in a familiar way.'[36]

What Toulmin is pointing out is that the 'optical discovery' that light 'travels' in a straight line (the Principle of the Rectilinear Propagation of Light) was rather the discovery that talk about light travelling in straight lines was profitable, suggestive, useful in the sense of being predictive. Regarding light in this new way gave intelligibility to questions such as 'How fast?' and 'From where to where?' to which one could then begin to look for answers, which one could not have done when one regarded light in the old way. What has happened is that we have changed our way of looking at the phenomena. Now must we accept this new way of looking at the world? No, but if we do not we cannot explain certain phenomena which, perhaps, we might like to explain. With this first-order principle of optics, we can explain why a shadow is exactly 15½ feet instead of 50 or 35 feet. The shadow must be exactly so many feet if the sun is at such and such an angle

[34] Frank, op. cit., p. 59.
[35] Stephen Toulmin, The Philosophy of Science, Harper Torchbooks, Harper & Brothers, New York, 1960, p. 17.
[36] Ibid., p. 20.

and if the tree or wall, etc., is at such an angle and if the tree or wall, etc., is at such and such a height. 'It just follows from the Principle of the Rectilinear Propagation of Light that the depth of the shadow must be what it is.' But to say that it must be such and such, one must add 'given our model (picture of the world)'. 'The depth of the shadow is therefore not a necessary fact, but a necessary consequence of applying the principle as it is meant to be applied.'[37] For it is from this *picture* of the world that the necessity in the inference comes. That is, the Principle of the Rectilinear Propagation of Light is the legislating principle *in accordance with which* we decide to view phenomena.

> 'The discovery that light travels in straight lines . . . was a double one: it comprised the development of a technique for representing optical phenomena which was found to fit a wide range of facts, and the adoption along with this technique of a new model, a new way of regarding these phenomena, and of understanding why they are as they are.'[38]

'We do not *find* light atomised into individual rays: we represent it as consisting of such rays'[39] in our newly developed scientific *Weltanschauung*.

Toulmin writes that 'the heart of all major discoveries in the physical sciences is the discovery of novel methods of representation'.[40] This is but another way of saying that the developments in science are brought about by novel ways of viewing the phenomena. There is no doubt that the 'Copernican Revolution' was primarily a conceptual upheaval, the replacing of the Aristotelian world-view with the atomic world-view. New categories are imposed upon phenomena and as a result new concepts emerge. With these imposed upon experience, experience becomes something different from what it was: it becomes viewed in a new way. This new viewing of phenomena leads to new conceptions and consequently new questions. When these questions are answered in terms of the categories and concepts, a new world-view forms. And it is the first-order principles of this newly emerging *Weltanschauung* which are unfalsifiable, for they are those principles *in accordance with which* inferences in the world-view are drawn. We see many examples of this in our models: the

---

37 *Ibid.*, p. 93.
38 *Ibid.*, p. 29.
39 Stephen Toulmin, *The Philosophy of Science*, p. 93.
40 *Ibid.*, p. 34.

atomic model of energy, the kinetic model for thermal phenomena, the spherical model of space. The world viewed as composed of atomic particles, heat viewed as a form of motion of these particles, light viewed as travelling in rays, space viewed as curved— all these conceptions are dependent upon a particular scientific picture of reality, a picture which in its more fundamental aspects is not falsifiable. To take light once again as an example:

> 'To justify the conclusion that the light travels in straight lines, we do not have to make observations which *entail* this conclusion: what we have to do is to show how the data we have can be accounted for *in terms of* this principle [of the Rectilinear Propagation of Light]'.[41]

It is interesting to note not only that the principles determine what data are accounted for but also what is *meaningful* and *not meaningful*. Toulmin, discussing principles in optics, writes that

> 'questions about refractive index will have a *meaning* only in so far as Snell's Law holds . . .—the law is an essential part of the theoretical background against which alone the notion of refractive index can be discussed. This is something we find generally in physical theory. Theoretical physics is *stratified*: statements at one level have a meaning only within the scope of those in the level below.'[42]

This is a fundamentally significant point for our argument, namely that the meaning of statements within science and religion is dependent ultimately upon the *Weltanschauung* and its concepts and categories.

If, for another example, we were to take Newton's Laws of Motion, we would find that

> 'they do not set out by themselves to tell us anything about the actual motions of particular bodies, but rather provide a form of description to use in accounting for these motions. The heart of the matter is put forcibly, and almost to the point of paradox, in a celebrated passage of Wittgenstein's: "The fact that it can be described by Newtonian mechanics tells us nothing about the world; but this tells us something, namely, that it can be described in that particular way in which as a matter of fact it is described." But we must notice that it is no denigration of a system of mechanics to say that, by itself, it tells us nothing about the world.

[41] *Ibid.*, pp. 42–3.
[42] *Ibid.*, p. 80.

. . . The laws themselves do not do anything: it is we who do things with them.[43] . . . .

There are many other examples which could be used to illustrate this important point. The existence of an Absolute Zero is not a fact of the world but rather a conceptual way of giving meaning to the concept of temperature and of ordering numerically degrees of warmth and cold. An Absolute Zero is not experimentally discoverable, but is 'ensured by our way of introducing the ideal gas scale'.[44] 'It is a conceptual matter, a fact about our *notion* of temperature, not as one might at first suppose, a fact about thermal phenomena at very low temperatures.'[45] The crucial point to realise here is that the very meaning of 'temperature' depends upon our introducing a concept which cannot be empirically proven. Obviously harmonisation of the science is of prime consideration in the introduction of this concept, for the coherence and consistency of the discipline are dependent upon it. And it is trivially obvious that if this is how the concept operates, it cannot be proven false.[46]

VI

It is the commonly well-known ideal of science to contain only what experience forces upon it. There are two reasons why this aspiration towards realism will probably never be realised and most certainly is not now. First, 'their historical origins are against them'.[47] Secondly, 'the structure of a scientific theory may be built up entirely from bricks of observation, but the exact positions the bricks occupy depend on the layout of the scientist's conceptual scaffolding'.[48] Cassirer seemed to have this in mind when he wrote:

> 'We no longer deal with a being, self-contained and absolutely determined, from which we directly read off the laws, and to which we can attach them as its attributes. What really forms the content of our empirical knowledge is rather the aggregate of

[43] Stephen Toulmin, *The Philosophy of Science*, pp. 88–9.
[44] *Ibid.*, p. 132.
[45] *Ibid.*
[46] Cf. Nagel, *op. cit.*, p. 67.
[47] Stephen Toulmin, 'Scientific Theories and Scientific Myths', in *Science and Language*, Alfred M. Bock, ed., Heath & Company, Boston, 1966, p. 18.
[48] *Ibid.*, p. 18.

observations which we group together in a certain order, and which we represent through theoretical concepts of laws according to this order.

As far as the dominion of these concepts extends, so far extends our objective knowledge. There is "objectivity" or "objective reality" because, and in so far as, there are laws—not conversely.'[49]

VII

Many philosophers use Flew's challenge to attack theological discourse on the grounds that religious and theological propositions such as 'God loves mankind' or 'There is a God' are immune from falsification and are hence non-factual: such propositions 'die the death of a thousand qualifications', since any challenge will be countered by a new qualification. But these philosophers fail to comprehend the logical extension of their criticism. For the very feature to which they object is not a feature peculiar to religious discourse or systematic theology but rather is a feature which is characteristic of every intellectual discipline employing elaborate systematic conceptual structures. Exactly the criticism directed toward religion could be directed toward science either in general or in specific systematic accounts such as classical physics or thermodynamics. Their first-order principles are hardly more open to falsification by 'contrary instances' than are those general religious propositions which take the brunt of criticism by these philosophers. The very point of this paper is to argue that if one understands properly the structure and operation of scientific conceptual systems with their first-order principles, then if one admits the legitimacy of Flew's falsification argument against religion, one would find it exceptionally difficult to defend *scientific discourse* against the same charge. There is no doubt that religion and science differ, but it is certainly not at the point where Flew and others think.

Science like religion is most certainly a *Weltanschauung*, employing first-order principles which it constantly defends against seemingly contrary evidence by qualifications and exceptions. But to employ Flew's challenge is to exact too high a price for rejecting theological utterances; for it would entail rejecting science for the same reason.

[49] Cassirer, *Determinismus und Indeterminismus in der Moderner Physik*, quoted in Frank, *op. cit.*, p. 178.

Donald D. Evans/Differences between scientific and religious assertions

Two conflicting views concerning comparisons between religion and science are current today. On the one hand, both existentialist theologians and positivist critics of religion maintain that religious assertions and scientific assertions are radically *different*. On the other hand, some scientific thinkers who are keen to humanize science or to legitimize religion maintain that religion and science are essentially *similar*, and that they differ mainly in subject matter rather than in method. It seems to me that although there are a few genuine similarities between religious theory (theology) and scientific theory, there are fundamental differences between religion and science which the second view fails to acknowledge. The first view, properly qualified in response to cogent criticisms from the second, seems closer to the truth.

From "Differences Between Scientific and Religious Assertions" by Donald D. Evans in *Science and Religion,* ed. I. G. Barbour (London: SCM Press, New York: Harper and Row, 1968), pp. 101–133. Copyright © 1968 by Ian G. Barbour. Reprinted by permission of SCM Press, Ltd., Harper and Row Publishers, Inc., and the author.

This paper has four parts. I shall discuss religion, then science, and then their similarities and differences. Finally, I shall summarize my conclusions.

I. Religious faith and depth-experiences

There are many varieties of religion. Some, such as classical Buddhism, are not theistic. Others, such as the modern so-called "religionless Christianity," attempt a theism without religion. The kind of religion which we shall consider is one in the Judeo-Christian tradition which equates *religious* faith with faith in *God*. Faith in God is best understood, it seems to me, by reference to "depth-experiences." This term will become clear as we look at five different kinds of depth-experience.

Depth-experiences

Personal encounter. I encounter John Brown. He has an I-Thou attitude toward me, as Martin Buber would say.[1] That is, he is outgoing, open, available, and responsive. He focuses his whole self exclusively on me in my uniqueness, involving himself in my world and committing himself to me. If I respond in kind, even though less profoundly, something mysterious flashes between us, changing both of us so that we become more truly human, more real as persons. I emerge from the encounter aware of a new meaning in life, a meaning which is expressed more in a new mode of life than in any words.

This personal encounter is a depth-experience. If an agnostic or an atheist has had a similar experience and agrees with me that it is real and important, he does not thereby agree that there is a God. He only agrees that there are mysterious depths in human relations. But he does enter a context in which I can begin to explain part of what I mean by "God." God is, in part, a hidden being whose unlimited and perfect I-Thou attitude toward me is revealed in the limited and imperfect I-Thou

[1] My debt to Martin Buber will be evident in this section. Similarly my account of numinous experience is partly derived from Rudolph Otto, moral responsibility from John Baillie, radical despair from Paul Tillich, and indignant compassion from D. M. Mackinnon and Dietrich Bonhoeffer. In each case, however, my own account differs somewhat from theirs.

attitude which John Brown and others have toward me. That is, I interpret the I-Thou encounter with John Brown as a revelation of God. I look on John Brown's "presence with a meaning" as a revelation of a divine presence, an eternal meaning. I see in his I-Thou attitude toward me a revelation of God, the Eternal Thou whose I-Thou attitude toward me is complete and constant and utterly trustworthy. A believer looks on a depth-experience of personal encounter as a revelation of God and tries to live accordingly; that is, he is open to the "address" of the Eternal Thou, which comes through the words and deeds of men whom he meets in personal encounter. An agnostic or atheist interprets the depth-experience in purely human terms: "Yes, human beings are mysterious; there are depths in man which can only be known in personal encounters; but why bring in God?"

In general, depth-experiences are interpreted in one of two ways: as revelations concerning *man* or as revelations concerning both *man* and *God*. Faith involves the latter interpretation. Faith is an ongoing practical commitment to an interpretation of some depth-experiences as revelations not only of man but also of God. Sometimes a depth-experience "hits" the believer as a divine revelation, so that he is aware of no alternative interpretation at the time; but honest reflection afterwards should lead him to acknowledge the possibility of interpreting his depth-experience in purely human terms. His faith presupposes a belief that there is a hidden personal being called "God" who sometimes reveals Himself in depth-experiences. Note that his faith thus involves both commitment and belief.

Let us consider another kind of depth-experience.

Numinous experience. I look at a sunset or a waterfall. I have an overwhelming feeling of awe, a sense of my own littleness coupled with a joy in being so much alive and a dumbfounded wonder at the mystery of beauty. Or I meet a man whom religious people call a "saint," and I have similar feelings of reverence, self-abasement, exhilaration, and bewilderment.

Such "numinous" feelings need not be interpreted in a religious way. An agnostic or atheist who is profoundly impressed by sunset or saint is not being illogical if he refrains from bringing in God. On the other hand, it is not unreasonable for a man of faith to look on the impressive features of sunset or saint as

expressions of a hidden numinous being.[2] An unbeliever can
understand part of what is meant by "God" in this context. God
is the numinous, worshipful being who expresses Himself, reveals Himself, in such a way as to evoke numinous feelings. The
man of faith interprets the depth-experience as a revelation concerning both man and God. Like many unbelievers he sometimes
finds in men a mysterious depth, a capacity for awe, self-abase-
ment, exaltation, and wonder; and in a few men he finds a mysterious impressiveness which evokes such responses in their fellows.
For the man of faith, however, the depth-experience is also a revelation of God, the hidden personal being who reveals His inner
nature through the numinous sunset or saint. Each element in the
numinous depth-experience is correlated in meaning with an attribute of God: awe with "holiness," self-abasement with "majesty," exaltation with "spirit," and wonder with "glory." In each
case the transcendence of a divine attribute is correlated with the
unlimited character of the appropriate numinous response.

Moral responsibility.   Some men have a strong sense of
moral responsibility. Moral obligations come, as it were, from outside oneself, imperiously subordinating one's own inclinations and
interests, urgently demanding acknowledgment and action.

Such moral seriousness is common to both unbelief and
belief at their best. A believer differs in that he looks on his own
sense of moral responsibility as a revelation of a hidden moral
Sovereign who has a rightful and righteous authority over his life.
He looks on the unconditional and awesome demands of the moral
imperative as divine imperatives. Such faith does not equate conscience with the voice of God, for no infallibilty is assumed or
assured. The question, "What ought I to do?" is the same question
for a believer as the question, "What does God require me to do?"
—but he has no infallible method for answering his question, and
his certainty and uncertainty concerning particular moral obligations may be the same as that of an unbeliever. Rather, he differs
in having a sobering sense of being responsible and answerable
not merely to himself or to society or to an impersonal moral law,
but to a hidden personal being who is a moral Sovereign, whose
wisdom is perfect, and whose demand for obedience is unqualified.

An unbeliever, however, may interpret his own moral seri-

[2] For a detailed analysis of "impressive" and "expressive," see Donald Evans,
The Logic of Self-Involvement (London: SCM Press, 1963), chaps. 2, 4.

ousness and that of others as an indication of something profound
and mysterious in human nature, without going on to interpret it
as a revelation of God as well. For the believer, it reveals both man
and God. Note that the morally serious unbeliever is in a position
to understand part of what the believer means by "God" because
they share a common sense of moral responsibility. Here again the
depth-experience provides a context for meaningful language
concerning God. On the other hand, to the extent to which a man
lacks depth-experience he will be unable to understand such language.

   We have considered three depth-experiences: personal encounter, numinous experience, moral responsibility. We now turn
to a fourth.

   Radical despair.   A man is in a state of radical despair. Life
seems meaningless and pointless—not only life around him, but
his own life. Nevertheless he protests passionately against this
meaninglessness. His despair is not a state of apathy or indiffer-
ence, although he finds no basis for deciding between life and
death, between right and wrong; his despair is vital and vehement;
meaninglessness is for him a matter of ultimate concern.

   Such radical despair is sometimes paradoxical. In such
cases, the more the man protests against the meaninglessness of
life, the more meaning he gives to life by his very protest. The
more ultimate his concern about meaninglessness, the more meaning he gives to life by his very concern. The more vehement his
rejection of this supposed meaning and that supposed meaning,
the more transcendent his own sense of what a meaningful existence would be. The more profound and vital his anxiety in the
face of meaninglessness, the more profound and vital his own
courage in facing this anxiety.

   Radical despair, like other depth-experiences, is open to
alternative interpretations. The man of faith interprets his own
concern for meaning as a revelation of a being who is the source
of meaning in life. He interprets his own existential courage as a
revelation of a being who is its source, and his own passionate
yearning for an ultimate as itself a revelation of the ultimate. The
man of faith believes that Pascal was right when he put those
famous words into the mouth of God: "You would not be seeking
me unless you had already found me." The unbeliever, however,
interprets his radical despair in terms of man alone. His concern

for meaning, his existential courage, and his passionate yearning for an ultimate may reveal mysterious depths in human personality. But the unbeliever does not share the believer's conviction that there is also a revelation of God, that both God and man are active in the depth-experience.

Indignant compassion. Some believers and unbelievers have this in common: they identify themselves compassionately with other human beings in their suffering, sharing in it, but also grieving and rebelling against it. Like Dostoievsky's atheist Ivan Karamazov, or Camus' atheist Dr. Rieux, their compassion is compounded with a sense of outrage and revulsion that nature and men should inflict mental and physical torture on human beings. Karamazov and Rieux focus their revolt on the alleged God who made a world in which children can be torn to pieces by hunting dogs as a sport, or in which children writhe helplessly in the pains of the plague.

This atheistic protest is, for some believers, supreme blasphemy; but for other believers it is an admirable attitude which can be a profound revelation of God. For example, D. M. Mackinnon of Cambridge says, "The man who revolts, determined somehow to affirm in this most desperate situation that God did not so make the world, is met by the mystery of God's own revolt against the world He made."[3] On such a view, a man interprets his own indignant compassion as a revelation of the infinite indignant compassion of a hidden personal being, as well as an indication of myterious depths in human nature. For the unbeliever, however, it is only the latter.

Belief in a God of indignant compassion involves a belief in a God who suffers, God as depicted by Bonhoeffer when he wrote "Christians stand by God in his hour of grieving." Bonhoeffer's image is vivid and daring. In a Nazi prison, he interprets his own grieving for humanity as a participation in God's grieving. It is as if he were standing by a friend who grieves over the sufferings of the friend's child. His own grieving is as nothing compared to his friend's. His own compassion for the child is a sharing in his friend's compassion. Similarly a man's finite concern for others is a way of sharing in the infinite divine concern.

We have considered five kinds of depth-experience. There

[3] D. M. Mackinnon, *Christian Faith and Communist Faith* (London: Macmillan & Co., 1953), pp. 247–48.

are others which might have been included, but I shall not discuss them in this paper. Let us now examine depth-experiences more closely in relation to religious faith.

Religious faith

Religious faith is a practical commitment to an interpretation of depth-experiences as divine revelations. Such faith presupposes a belief that there exists a hidden personal being who reveals himself in these ways. This being, who has the proper name "God," reveals Himself as the Eternal Thou, the awesome numinous, the moral Sovereign, the source of meaning, and the grieving friend. The believer holds that in each case the depth-experience has limitations and imperfections, but that the God who is thereby revealed does not. For example, the I-Thou attitude of the Eternal Thou is *perfect* in its constancy and openness. Although I am far from being clear as to what I mean when I describe God in these ways, and although I assume that any attempted description will be inadequate, and although the meaning of the descriptions cannot be understood in abstraction from elusive and mysterious depth-experiences, my faith does involve a *"belief-that."* I stress this, because I want to make clear my disagreement with those religious philosophers who rightly stress the element of commitment in faith, but who wrongly deny that the commitment presupposes a *belief-that.*

　　I also wish to distinguish my account of religious faith from some which resemble it in taking a depth-experience seriously and in finding common ground between believers and some unbelievers, but which differ in *equating* a depth-experience with faith or with God. Paul Tillich, for example, says that faith *is* the state of being ultimately concerned.[4] He also says, in a passage made famous by being quoted in *Honest to God*, "If you know that God means depth, you know much about him. . . . You cannot think or say: Life has no depth! Life is shallow. Being itself is surface only. If you could say this in complete seriousness, you would be an atheist; but otherwise you are not. He who knows about depth knows about God."[5] Elsewhere Tillich seems to equate faith (his "absolute faith") with the radical despair which protests against

[4] Paul Tillich, *Dynamics of Faith* (New York: Harper & Row, 1958), p. 1.
[5] J. A. T. Robinson, *Honest to God* (London: SCM Press, 1963), p. 22.

meaninglessness.[6] I reject Tillich's equation.[7] God is not the same as the depths in man, and faith is not the same as an experience of these depths. If Tillich wants to use the words "God" and "faith" in a peculiar way which abolishes any radical distinction between belief and unbelief he is free to do so, but both believers and unbelievers have a right to protest, indeed to protest with Tillichian passion! Similarly it is a mistake to equate faith with numinous experience or personal encounter or moral responsibility or indignant compassion. Faith involves an interpretation of a depth-experience as a revelation of God.

The various descriptions of God are indirect. God is a being such that various unlimited depth-experiences are appropriate responses to Him. This does not mean that God *is* a depth-experience. Such an account would be an unwarranted reductionism, similar to a reduction of material objects to sense-data or a reduction of other minds to observable public behavior. The meaning of a statement is linked with its method of verification, but the two need not be equivalent. Nor is an indirect description of God a matter of *acting-as-if*. Religious faith is not an *acting-as-if* there were a God to whom various responses would be appropriate if He really did exist. No, there really does exist such a God, though what is meant by talk about Him cannot be understood in abstraction from human depth-experiences.

Christian faith

Thus far in this paper I have talked about a religious faith which is not specifically Christian. A Christian faith differs in that depth-experiences are interpreted in relation to Jesus, the man of Nazareth whom Christians believe to be now alive and present in the depth-experience. For example, in the case of personal encounters, the Christian looks on another man's "presence with a meaning" as a revelation of Jesus Christ. In the words of Hopkins:

[The just man]
Acts in God's eye what in God's eye he is—

[6] Paul Tillich, *The Courage to Be* (London: Nisbet & Co., 1952), esp. p. 167.
[7] Sometimes Tillich does not equate God with a depth-experience or a depth in man; God is the "ground" or even the "source" of these. This strand in Tillich's thought is not in conflict with my approach.

Christ—for Christ plays in ten thousand places,
Lovely in limbs, and lovely in eyes not his
To the Father through the features of men's faces.[8]

Also, the Cross of Christ transforms our ordinary notions of what is supremely *numinous*. A Christian looks on the Cross as the normative expression of divine glory: transcendence revealed in humility, majesty revealed in sacrifice, life and spirit revealed in death, mystery revealed in agony. Others, both believers and un-believers, may look on the Cross as the unfortunate death of a good man; but the Christian looks on the Cross in such a way that, more than sunsets and saints, it arouses his awe, his self-abase-ment, his exultation, and his wonder. In other words, the Christian worships Christ crucified.

The Christian also interprets his moral experience in rela-tion to Jesus Christ. His sense of moral responsibility to the divine sovereign is modified in various ways because of this. For example, insofar as a man is a Christian, he looks on his status before God as something which he cannot earn, something which he receives as a gift from God through Christ. He is justified by grace, and so his moral seriousness has an underlying joy and an absence of anxious strain.

I shall not try to indicate the specifically Christian interpre-tation of radical despair and indignant compassion. Perhaps I have said enough to show that the Christian reinterpretation of a depth-experience may involve a more or less radical revision of a man's religious interpretation. We should also note two additional points. On the one hand, my conviction concerning Jesus of Nazareth may reinforce an original decision of faith. Indeed, some elements in a step from agnosticism to faith may seem implausible unless the Christian claims for Jesus are true; for example, the interpretation of one's own grieving as a revelation of God's grieving may seem implausible unless one believes that Jesus was divine, so that the Cross reveals God's grieving. On the other hand, my conviction concerning Jesus is in some respects not a basis for faith but rather something which itself requires a basis. It is only rational to in-terpret depth-experiences today in terms of Jesus if there is an adequate basis for believing two things about him: that as an historical figure he was a normative medium for God's self-reve-lation, and that he conquered death in such a way as to become

[8] *Poems of Gerard Manley Hopkins*, ed. W. H. Gardner (New York: Oxford University Press, 1948), p. 95. Reprinted by permission.

a living presence in the depth-experiences of multitudes of men. These beliefs concerning the character and the resurrection of Jesus depend, in turn, partly on historical evidence. But this cannot be explored further here.

II. Scientific language and objectivity

Some writers have claimed not only that some science is non-objective but that objectivity is not even a tenable ideal for science. Such a claim may contain many valid objections against popular notions of scientific objectivity, but it is far too extreme. There are three important ways in which scientists actively, and often successfully, seek for objectivity. In each of these ways, as we shall see, science differs radically from religion. A scientific assertion should be *logically neutral, comprehensible impersonally,* and *testable by observations.* The first requirement has to do with the logic of scientific assertions, the second with conditions for understanding them, and the third with their method of verification.

Before we consider each requirement in turn, I should indicate how I am using two terms: "assertion" and "objective." "Assertion" will be used in a very loose and general way so that it covers scientific observation-reports, laws, hypotheses, or theories; the differences between these will be noted only when necessary. An "objective" assertion is one whose truth or falsity can in principle be established on the basis of maximal intersubjective agreement.

Scientific assertions are logically neutral

The term "neutral" can mean a great many different things. The meaning which I shall select and refine is one which makes "neutral" the opposite of *"self-involving."* A self-involving assertion is one which commits the person who asserts it or accepts it to further action, or which implies that he has an attitude for or against whatever the assertion is about, or which expresses such an attitude. For example, in saying "I promise to return this book tomorrow," I commit myself, logically, to a specific future action. In saying, "I commend Jones for his restraint," I imply that I approve of Jones' restraint. In saying, "I look on you as a father," I express an attitude toward you. In each case I *cannot* deny the self-involvement. I cannot deny that "I promise . . ." commits me, or that "I commend . . ." implies a favorable attitude, or that "I look on you as a father" expresses an attitude. The "cannot" is a *logical* one. It is based on part of the *meaning* of the utterance, namely its performative force: what one is doing in saying such-and-such.[9] This meaning or force depends on public linguistic and institutional conventions, though it sometimes also depends on special contexts of meaning or on the special intentions of the speaker (what *he* means in saying such-and-such).

Of course a man may be deceitful when he promises or commends or expresses an attitude. Although he implies that he intends to return the book or that he has a favorable attitude toward Jones, he may have no such intention or attitude. Similarly an utterance which expresses an attitude may be quite insincere. But deceit or insincerity does not affect the meaning of the utterance. Although the speaker does not "mean what he says," what he says *has* a meaning; his deceit or insincerity depends on this linguistic fact. As I propose to use the terms "self-involvement" and its opposite "neutrality," they have to do with matters of logic and meaning rather than introspective psychology.

Let us now consider scientific assertions. It is a requirement of science that scientific language should be *neutral*. In asserting or accepting a scientific theory, law, or observation-report, I give assent to it without committing myself to future conduct (other than verbal consistency), and without implying or expressing any personal attitude for or against what is asserted. If the scientific assertion were not neutral, agreement between scientists would depend partly on each one's personal commitments and attitudes, especially his moral commitments and attitudes. For example, if the Kinsey report says, "Such-and-such sexual behavior is normal," and the word "normal" here does not mean "average" or "usual" but "normative," a scientist's assent to the assertion would depend partly on whether or not he approves of the behavior. Scientists rightly seek a language which is as neutral as possible in order to minimize any dependence on such considerations. The objectivity which can be achieved through intersubjective testing in

---

[9] See *The Logic of Self-Involvement*, pp. 27–46, which depends on J. L. Austin's account of "illocutionary force" in *How to Do Things with Words* (Oxford: Clarendon Press, 1962).

science depends partly on the logical neutrality of scientific assertions. Science can discover what *is* the case, what *is* being done, only if scientists do not have to agree concerning what *ought* to be the case, what *ought* to be done.

Logical neutrality must not be confused with *psychological neutrality*. A particular scientist may be a bitter opponent or an enthusiastic practitioner of the sexual conduct which he is reporting; or he may be very detached and disinterested. In each case, however, his report can and ought to be logically neutral if it is to be a scientific report. Which attitude tends to promote scientific progress, scientific "detachment" or scientific "passion"? Whatever the answer to this question (my own answer is "both, but in different ways and different contexts"), the issue has nothing to do with the requirement that scientific language be neutral in its public meaning. Nor does the logical neutrality of scientific language mean that science is doomed to be existentially trivial. A scientific report (for example, the results of a test for cancer) may be both logically neutral and profoundly important.

Logical neutrality must also not be confused with *absence of belief*. In making a scientific assertion, a speaker usually implies that he believes it. The strength of the belief implied varies according to the type of assertion. Where a scientific hypothesis is presented, no belief need be implied at all. But where a belief is implied, this belief is not itself an attitude for or against something, nor is it a commitment to a future pattern of conduct. The belief may provide a basis for such an attitude or commitment, but it is not itself an attitude or commitment. Furthermore, whether or not a speaker actually *has* the belief which he implies is an empirical or psychological matter. He may be sweating with conviction or inwardly sneering with scepticism, but the kind of belief which he *implies* depends on conventions of language concerning the meaning (performative force) of what he says. If a scientist is testing a new hypothesis, will his work be better if he passionately believes in it or if he cautiously entertains it as a mere possibility? Whatever the answer to this question—and there are conflicting answers given—the issue has nothing to do with the requirement that scientific language be logically neutral.

One final clarification concerning logical neutrality. Critics of objectivity-claims for science often point out that all investigations involve a *selection* of subject matter and that these involve implicit *judgments concerning importance*. This seems to me to be a legitimate point. No investigation, whether scientific or non-scientific, deals with everything or with every aspect of an event, and what is included is presumably regarded as being more important for the investigation than what is omitted. But this point does not show that logical neutrality is impossible. When I say, "The litmus paper has turned red," my assertion may involve some implicit judgments concerning the importance of such color changes, but I do not imply that I have a pro-attitude or a con-attitude. The term "implicit" may mislead us here, for I do not *imply* a judgment (or attitude) concerning importance in the way that I *imply* a pro-attitude when I say, "I commend you for your restraint." The so-called "implicit judgment" is one which a speaker might make in giving a *reason* for having selected changes in *color* rather than, say, changes in *shape*. Furthermore, any implicit judgment concerning importance—assuming there are such judgments—could itself be logically neutral. In saying, "X is important" I imply no pro-attitude or con-attitude toward X. We should also notice that the scientific importance of X lies in its relation to other matters in science. X may *also* be of profound personal relevance to the investigator, but this is not necessary.

Scientific assertions are comprehensible impersonally

Obviously *all* comprehension or understanding, including scientific understanding, is "personal" rather than "impersonal" in the sense that it is *persons* who understand. But we also say, "He's an unusual person, he deals with every problem so impersonally." In a somewhat similar way we can say, "Scientific assertions are understood by persons, but they are understood impersonally." That is, if a man has sufficient intelligence and scientific training, he should be able to understand a particular scientific assertion regardless of his personal attitudes concerning what the assertion is about, and regardless of his moral, aesthetic, or spiritual appreciation of what the assertion is about. The conditions for understanding are scientific, not intimately personal. For example, let us suppose that John Brown does not understand what is meant by "Light travels in straight lines." If he has enough brain power and if he studies enough physics he should be able to understand the assertion. This understanding should be possible whether or not light is something that matters tremendously to him, whether or not he is a self-centered or an altruistic person, whether or not he has ever contemplated a beam of light with the eye of an artist. The conditions for understanding a particular scientific assertion are independent of these variable personal factors. It is a matter of intelligence and scientific training.

Scientific training, however, involves a good deal of *attitudinal* training, especially for people who have not grown up in a scientific culture. There are various scientific virtues to be inculcated if a student is to become a scientist: industry, patience, curiosity, open-mindedness, detachment, self-discipline, rigorous and orderly thinking, scrupulous honesty in reporting results, etc. These virtues are conditions for understanding science. If too many are lacking, a student will not make any progress in understanding. Thus he may fail to understand "Light travels in straight lines," not because of his attitudes toward light or his failure to appreciate light aesthetically, but because he is lazy—or more generally, because he has not been sufficiently interested in science to continue his studies. When I say that scientific assertions are "comprehensible impersonally" I am not denying that the understanding of a particular scientific assertion depends *indirectly* on the fulfillment of prior personal conditions.

Science does differ from many other disciplines in that its indirect dependence on personal conditions is, on the whole, less; and the conditions themselves are less profoundly and intimately personal than those in some other disciplines; obviously they differ from basic conditions in aesthetics, morality, or religion. But the main point is that the understanding of a particular scientific assertion does not depend *directly* on personal conditions. There is no direct relation between the meaning of a particular scientific term and a particular scientific virtue or attitude. The meaning of "electron" is not correlated with an attitude of detachment, or with any other attitude. The meaning of "holy," however, *is* correlated with an attitude of reverence; that is, "X is holy" means (in part) "X is such that an attitude of reverence is an appropriate response." More generally, the meaning of "God" is correlated with various attitudinal depth-experiences.

The requirement of impersonal comprehensibility (like that of logical neutrality) is rightly designed to minimize the relevance of personal factors in science. It is an attempt at maximal mutual understanding in spite of the profound and numerous personal differences which exist among men, especially differences in aesthetic, moral, and spiritual attitudes. There are limits, of course, not only because of variations in degree of intelligence and kind of scientific training, but also because of variations in *kind* of intelligence. Also, the more theoretical and frontier-exploratory the nature of the scientific work, the fewer the scientists who can, at the time, understand one another fully.

We should also notice that there are a great many different levels of understanding; a man only gradually gets to "know his way around" in a field, grasping more and more of the significance of various terms or theories. Nor is all scientific language easily intelligible because precisely defined; the fertility of some theoretical concepts depends partly on their open texture. In short, the requirement that scientific assertions be comprehensible impersonally does not mean that all science should be like a ten-year-old's scientific textbook! It does nevertheless mean three things. First, the indirect dependence on personal conditions is less than in many other disciplines. Second, these conditions are less profoundly personal than those in many other disciplines. Third (most important), the comprehensibility of a particular scientific assertion is not directly dependent on profoundly personal conditions.

We have considered two requirements of scientific assertions, each of which in a different way is designed to promote the objectivity of science: logical neutrality and impersonal comprehensibility. The first is a matter of logic, and can be stated with precision. The second is a matter of conditions for understanding, and is much less clearly statable. The third requirement, which also is designed to promote objectivity, has to do with methodology; it is fairly clear, but complex.

Scientific assertions are testable by observations

A scientific assertion should be, in principle, testable by observations. That is, a scientist should be able to specify the observable states of affairs which would verify his assertion—or at least help to support it. And he should also be able to specify the observable states of affairs which would falsify his assertion—or at least help to undermine it. He may not be able to test his assertion at the moment; he may have to wait until further evidence comes in, or until technicians build an apparatus. But he must be able to say what observable states of affairs *would* verify or support his assertion, and what *would* falsify or undermine his assertion; his assertion must be testable in principle. It must not be compatible with any and every possible state of affairs.

In the early days of positivism, the requirement that scientific assertions be testable by observations was mistakenly regarded as the key to the whole of science. Today, however, philosophers of science set forth many qualifications and objections concerning it, so much so that there is considerable danger of its being ignored in comparisons between science and religion. Let us consider some of the qualifications and objections which have been propounded, looking successively at four different kinds of scientific assertion: observation-reports, theories, paradigms, and presuppositions.

Observation-reports. The claim that scientific assertions are testable by observations needs to be qualified, since all observation involves interpretation. There are no "pure" observations, "given" perceptions, or "raw" experiences. Human minds impose various conceptual frameworks on all observations, perceptions, or experiences. What we "observe" depends on the conceptual framework which we bring to the observations; we can never disentangle observations completely from interpretations so as to "test" interpretations by reference to "pure" observations. Scientific observations, moreover, involve a special kind of interpretation. They are "theory-laden"; that is, what one observes as a scientist is already interpreted in terms of concepts drawn from scientific theory. Where common sense observes a swinging stick, the scientist observes a pendulum. Where common sense observes a flash, the scientist observes an electrical discharge.

Does this mean that scientific assertions are not testable by observations? Surely not. It means that there are differing levels of interpretation of experience, and that "higher" levels cannot be reduced to lower ones. That is, if we consider a common-sense observation-report ("The stick is swinging") this involves terms such as "stick" which are not reducible to lower-level talk about sense-impressions. Above the common-sense level, a scientific observation-report ("The pendulum is swinging") involves terms such as "pendulum" which are not reducible to lower-level common-sense talk about sticks. At a still higher level, a scientific theory will use terms like "gravity," which are not reducible to terms used in scientific observations.

At each level, including the "bottom" level of sense-impression reports, there is an element of interpretation. Yet the different levels are linked. Although a higher-level assertion is not reducible to a lower-level one since it is *not equivalent in meaning,* the *truth* of the higher-level one depends partly on the *truth* of the lower-level one. This hierarchical picture of language is an oversimplification; however, it does seem to me to provide a way to avoid a possible misunderstanding of the testability requirement. The requirement need involve neither reductionism nor a belief in an uninterpreted basis for all knowledge. It does not depend on a crudely empiricist epistemology.

More important, the testability requirement is part of scientific practice as this is described even by such antipositivists as Harold Schilling.[10] There is an accumulation of established scientific knowledge which has been tested by observation and which is permanent (or virtually so) *because* of this testing. Such knowledge includes experimental (that is, observational) laws which are not undermined by changes in scientific theory.[11] It is true that the laws may be reinterpreted by being explained in relation to new theories, so that the newly interpreted law is not equivalent in meaning to the old one; nevertheless the law also has a relatively uninterpreted meaning, and its truth in this form has been established by reference to observations. Probably the observations would not have been made were it not for the existence of a scientific theory, but this does not show that the testability requirement is unnecessary. It is also true that the observations are usually reported in a language which includes scientific terms that are relatively theoretical or interpretive as compared with the everyday language of common sense. But the scientific terms are linked to commonsense terms, though they are not reducible to commonsense terms. If a nonscientist in the laboratory sees no spark or feels no tingling pain on touching a wire, the scientist's report concerning an electrical discharge may be undermined or even falsified.

[10] Harold Schilling, *Science and Religion* (New York: Charles Scribner's Sons, 1962), esp. chaps. 5–8.
[11] Cf. Schilling, *op. cit.,* and Ernest Nagel, *The Structure of Science* (New York: Harcourt, Brace & Co., 1961), chap. 5.

Theories. Someone might concede that perhaps experimental laws are testable by observations, but insist that theories are not. It is clear that the evaluation of a theory involves various criteria which are not observational.[12] There are *formal* criteria: internal consistency, coherent conceptual relations, and simplicity or relative independence from *ad hoc* assumptions. There is an *aesthetic* criterion of "elegance"; although minimized by some scientists, it is stressed by others. Then there is the *explanatory power* of the theory in displaying a pattern in many previously unrelated states of affairs. Some would stress the role of scientific models in this respect. Then there is the *"fertility"* of the theory in stimulating the invention or discovery of new theories, concepts, and experimental laws, and its consistency and coherence with other highly rated theories. Since there are many different criteria, there is no such thing as a "knockdown" falsification or a "conclusive" verification of a theory by reference to observations.

This objection is extremely important in destroying crude positivist conceptions of scientific "verification." But with reference to the testability requirement, all it shows is that the requirement is only one among many. A theory may pass observational tests as well as its rival does, and yet be rejected because it is inferior when appraised by reference to its fertility, say, or its internal coherence. If, as some experts claim, it is true that *no* theory ever fits *all* the relevant observations, then obviously the testability requirement is not as strict as one might imagine. Also, if it is true that no theory is ever "falsified" by observations, this is an important point in understanding the requirement properly. But none of this shows that no theory is ever *undermined* by observations. A theory is not compatible with any and every conceivable state of affairs that might be observed. Finally, however much philosophers of science may insist that scientific theories are not evaluated *solely* in terms of whether or not they enable scientists to make precise and specific *predictions* of observable states of affairs, or to *produce* these at will, surely these features of science are important; and surely they mark important differences between scientific theories and theories in metaphysics or in theistic religion.

[12] Most of these are outlined in Ian Barbour, *Issues in Science and Religion* (Englewood Cliffs, N.J.: Prentice-Hall, 1966), pp. 144–50. I am greatly indebted to Dr. Barbour for his balanced and lucid discussions of various issues throughout his book.

A different, but related, objection to the testability requirement is that scientific theories are not representations of the real
world at all, but are merely useful fictions or regulative maxims.
A theory can be neither true nor false, it is said, so it can be neither
verified nor falsified; indeed, observations can neither support nor
undermine the alleged truth of a theory, for a theory cannot be
"true." This objection is relevant only if we accept a nonrealist
view of scientific theories. Yet even if we do, we need not reject
the testability requirement. Rather, we understand the "test" of a
theory to be a test of usefulness rather than of truth.

Paradigms. The term "paradigm," as used by Thomas
Kuhn,[13] refers to a type of scientific theory which has a special role
in science. The paradigm theory, together with certain laws which
it explains and perhaps an exemplary application and instrumenta-
tion, dominates a whole area of scientific investigation. It not only
provides solutions to scientific problems; it largely determines
what *counts* as a scientific problem and what *counts* as a scientific
solution. It provides a framework of presumptions within which
detailed scientific investigation can flourish. When a paradigm is
replaced by another paradigm, this is no minor change; it is a scientific revolution. An established paradigm is scarcely affected at
all by some of the observations which do not fit in with it. In
the overthrow of a paradigm, nonobservational criteria play a
major role, and these criteria themselves may be modified or
reinterpreted.

It is clear that in the paradigm we find science in a form
most remote from observational testing, from "knockdown" falsification or "conclusive" verification by means of specific observations. Paradigms are very different from restricted generalizations
such as "All the boys in this room right now have blue eyes." Nevertheless, even Kuhn says that "observation and experience can
and must drastically restrict the range of admissible scientific belief, else there would be no science."[14] More specifically, in his
account of the "anomalies" which force scientific revolutions he
notes that a paradigm makes possible a precision of observational
expectations which renders it specially sensitive to possible under-

---

[13] Thomas Kuhn, *The Structure of Scientific Revolutions* (Chicago: University
of Chicago Press, 1962).
[14] Thomas Kuhn, *op. cit.,* p. 4.

mining by anomalous observational findings.[15] Without the paradigm, one would not notice that such-and-such an observed state of affairs is anomalous, yet the paradigm is put in question by this observed state of affairs. When Kuhn says that paradigms "provide all phenomena except anomalies with a theory-determined place in the scientist's field of vision,"[16] he is indicating both a way in which paradigms are relatively *immune* from being undermined by observations and a way in which they are peculiarly *sensitive* to such undermining. Indeed, his account of paradigm sensitivity helps to explain a fact noted by Nagel:

> Prescientific beliefs are frequently incapable of being put to definite experiential tests, simply because those beliefs may be vaguely compatible with an indeterminate class of unanalyzed facts. Scientific statements, because they are required to be in agreement with more closely specified materials of observation, face greater risks of being refuted by such data.[17]

Presuppositions.   Antipositivist writings on science, especially those which stress alleged similarities between science and religion, often maintain that science involves unfalsifiable presuppositions which constitute the "faith" of a scientist. The argument goes as follows: a scientist believes that the world has an order, that it has regularity, that it is dependable. No observable state of affairs could falsify this claim. His faith is not testable by observations. So if a religious faith is not testable by observations, this is not a feature of religion which distinguishes it from science.

Later I shall indicate the one strength and the many weaknesses of this argument. Here I shall distinguish between two different kinds of scientific presupposition. First, there is the paradigm, which we have already considered. A paradigm involves belief in a specific kind of order, regularity, and dependability within a specific area to be investigated by a subcommunity of scientists. Investigations which are carried out within the framework of a paradigm involve a great many implicit or explicit presuppositions. We have seen that paradigms are remote from "knockdown" falsifiability by observations, but nevertheless have not only a resistance but also a *sensitivity* to possible undermining by obser-

---

15 *Ibid.*, p. 65.
16 *Ibid.*, p. 96.
17 Ernest Nagel, *op. cit.*, p. 9.

vations. It would be misleading to say that paradigms are in principle unfalsifiable, for old paradigms *are* replaced by new ones, and this happens partly because of anomalous observations.

Although I suspect that most of what practicing scientists might mean by "scientific faith" arises from paradigms, there is a second type of presupposition which also has a role to play. It has the general form, *"Every X has a Y,"* where it is possible to verify "This X has a Y," but not to falsify it. Consider, for example, *"Every event has a sufficient condition."* Whenever scientists discover an experimental law and apply it to a particular event which is covered by the law, the proposition "This event has a sufficient condition" is verified. But what if scientists cannot find a sufficient condition for an event, for example, the particular movement of a particular electron? They may go on looking, but they may abandon the search. The proposition "Every event has a sufficient condition" is not falsifiable, yet it may be so undermined by failure to verify that it is abandoned—at least in a specific area of science. In so far as scientists believe in a world "order" or a "regularity," where these terms have a definite sense, the belief is not immune from being undermined by observations, though observations alone do not suffice to overthrow it.

In this section we have examined the requirement that scientific assertions be testable by observations, and we have noted various ways in which it needs to be qualified. Observation involves interpretation. Theories are not tested solely by reference to observations. Paradigms and presuppositions are not falsifiable by observations. In previous sections we considered two other requirements of scientific assertions: logical neutrality and impersonal comprehensibility. Before we move on to see whether religious assertions fulfill any of the three requirements, I should note one important omission in my account: I have not considered the requirements in relation to *social* science. My own view is that special difficulties arise only in relation to the second requirement. Some assertions in social studies, though logically neutral and testable by observation, are not comprehensible impersonally. In that respect, they are not "scientific," though they are nevertheless respectable and important. I am referring to assertions concerning how an agent views his situation, where the agent's view may be very difficult for an investigator to understand unless there is some affinity or rapport between the two men. But I cannot discuss this matter further here.

III. Religious language and objectivity

Religious assertions are not logically neutral

Religious faith, as it was described in Part I, is expressed in such assertions as the following:

> "I look on this man's I-Thou attitude toward me as a revelation of a hidden being whose I-Thou attitude is complete and constant."
>
> "I look on the impressive beauty of this sunset as an artistic expression of a hidden numinous being."
>
> "I look on this unconditional moral demand as a command from a hidden being who has rightful authority over my life."
>
> "I look on my concern for meaning in life as a revelation of a being who is the source of the concern and of ultimate meaning."
>
> "I look on my indignant compassion as a revelation of a hidden being whose compassion is infinite."

These assertions are not neutral, but *self-involving*. Each is an expression of attitude, a commitment to interpret a depth-experience as a revelation. In religious assertions where the word "God" occurs, the meaning of the word "God" is roughly "the hidden being who is such that various attitudinal depth-experiences are appropriate responses." God is the hidden being who is worthy of worship. In using the word "God," a member of a religious community is using self-involving langauge. He may, of course, be insincere. He may be, as a matter of fact, psychologically neutral. But his language is not logically neutral. It is a requirement of the religious community that his language be self-involving in its meaning.

There are two important exceptions to this. First, many *theological* assertions are second-order statements *about* religious assertions, and are not themselves self-involving. Talk about self-involving assertions need not itself be self-involving. In saying, "I promise . . . ," I do promise; my utterance is self-involving. But in saying, "I promised . . . ," or "He is promising . . . ," or "Promises are self-involving," I do not promise; nor are my utterances in any other way self-involving. Similarly if a theologian says

"What Christians mean by 'God' is 'the being worthy of worship,' "
the assertion is not self-involving. And even when he says "God
is the being worthy of worship," although his assertion is not
explicitly a second-order statement about religious assertions, it
may be second-order implicitly, especially if the context is descriptive.

This leads us to the second exception. The context in which
self-involving language is used may be artificially made a "descriptive" one. That is, there may be an implicit agreement among
speakers or writers that self-involving elements are to be set aside.
A man can use the word "God" to mean, say, "the [alleged] being
whom [some] people believe to be worthy of worship," without
implying or expressing any religious attitudes himself. In this way
it is possible for unbelievers or wavering members of the religious
community (or theologians!) to talk about God without insincerity.[18]

Neither of these exceptions detracts from the self-involving
character of primary religious assertions. The secondary theological or descriptive uses of religious language are parasitic on the
primary use; that is, they depend on the primary use for their
meaning. Similarly second-order talk about promises depends on
the existence of first-order promise-making, and descriptive uses
of the word "good" depend on self-involving uses of the word
"good."

Religious assertions are not comprehensible impersonally

The main point can be dealt with briefly. The account of religious
faith in Part I and of this requirement in Part II have already indicated my conclusion. Religious assertions require special personal conditions for understanding. Each depth-experience is an
elusive and mysterious experience which a man will not have had
unless he has fulfilled various personal conditions. In order to
understand what an I-Thou attitude is, one must be responsive to
it in others, and this depends on one's own basic life-experience
and attitudes to people. Similar conditions apply in the case of
other depth-experiences. There are intelligent men, well-trained

[18] For a further discussion of "descriptive" contexts see *The Logic of Self-Involvement*, pp. 50–51, 160–62, 183–85.

men, for whom some or all of the descriptions of depth-experiences have little meaning. Yet one can understand the meaning of talk about "God" only to the extent that one understands talk about the depth-experiences. Religious language is directly correlated to depth-experiences in its meaning. So religious assertions are not comprehensible impersonally.

This conclusion, however, needs some clarification and qualification. What constitutes an "understanding" of an assertion? A man may be able to use the words of the assertion without making any gross mistakes concerning its relations with other words. A psychopath, for example, might pick up much of what Wittgenstein calls the "logical grammar" of the word "conscience" by listening to other people talk. Yet in terms of his own experiences he does not understand what a conscience is. Similarly a deprived but intelligent child might learn how to use the word "love," without having had any deep experience of what it is to love and to be loved. Similarly a man of no depth-experiences might learn how to use religious language, for example, that "God" is connected with "worship"; he need not have had a personal experience of worship in order to do this. We seem to need a distinction between *"verbal"* and *"experiential"* understanding or comprehension of language. I cannot explore this further here, but some such distinction is required if the comprehensible-impersonally requirement is to be properly clarified. A man needs depth-experiences for *experiential* understanding of religious language.

Religious assertions are not
testable by observations

In Part II we saw that scientific assertions should be testable by observations. We also noted that science has a presupposition, "Every event has a sufficient condition," which is unfalsifiable. Are religious assertions testable by observations? Are there any unfalsifiable religious presuppositions of the form "Every X has a Y"?

My answer to the second question is, "Maybe." Some believers do hold, for example, that every event has a divine purpose. But religious faith is fundamentally a conviction that *some* depth-experiences are divine revelations. The word "faith" is appropriate for two different reasons. First, "This depth-experience is a revelation" is *unfalsifiable*, like "This event has a sufficient condition." Second, "This depth-experience is a revelation" is *"verified"* only by presupposing the existence of God. The second reason is what distinguishes religious faith from so-called scientific faith.

Do religious assertions resemble scientific assertions in being testable by observations? In four important ways they do not. We shall consider these ways in turn, considering scientific assertions first in each case.

First, although scientific presuppositions, paradigms, and theories are evaluated in terms of various nonobservational criteria, they are also open to support or undermining by *observational tests*. And although scientific observation-reports are not reducible to commonsense observation-reports, they can be supported or undermined by commonsense observation-reports, which thus provide a base on which the whole hierarchical superstructure of science is built. The superstructure of religious and theological assertions, however, is based on reports of elusive and mysterious depth-experiences rather than on commonsense observations. Although talk about God is not reducible to talk about depth-experiences, the former cannot be understood in abstraction from the latter; and if there had never been any depth-experiences, there would be no empirical basis for religion.

Second, scientific observation-reports are in principle open to *intersubjective testing* by anyone with the requisite intelligence and scientific training. If I think I observe an electrical discharge, but no other scientist does, my observation-report is radically undermined. The intersubjective element in religion, however, is very different. Suppose that other people report fewer depth-experiences or very different ones, or that other people stop having depth-experiences which seem to them to be divine revelations. As a believer I am committed to go on believing in spite of this. I may, as a matter of fact, falter, especially if my own spiritual life has gone dry. But I ought not to falter, for this runs contrary to my religious commitment. Depth-experiences depend on elusive personal conditions, and those which are divine revelations also depend on the free action of God. Men ought not to try to test God; it is God who "tests" men by sometimes withdrawing His presence. There is, to be sure, an intersubjective element in religious faith. The believer holds that God has revealed Himself to other members of the religious community in the *past*. Moreover, the believer's convictions concerning what counts as revelation are derived mainly from the religious community. Faith is a trust in

God which is based partly on a trust in intersubjective testimony. But it is not a matter of intersubjective testing or experimenting similar to that in science, for there are two open "variables" in the venture of faith: God and human sin. If God seems to be absent (or dead!) this is either because He has chosen to withhold His presence or because men are not responsive to it.

Third, the interpretive move from commonsense descriptions of events to scientific descriptions is so designed as to enable men to make *precise predictions of observables.* Covering laws are discovered: whenever conditions $C1$ to $C5$ hold, an event of type $T1$ occurs. And if men can produce conditions $C1$ to $C5$, they can thereby produce events of type $T1$. (They can explode an H-bomb.) Scientific theories work not only in that they make the world more intelligible, but also in that they make possible such prediction and control. In religion, however, the interpretive move from depth-experiences to divine revelations does not enable men to make predictions on the basis of covering laws, and still less to produce divine revelations at will.

Fourth, the move from common sense to scientific observation-reports begins with an ontological assumption that there is a real external world which we can observe. A *realist* view of scientific theories may involve some further ontological conviction concerning the nature of the world. No further ontology, however, is entailed. In religion a further ontology is entailed. The move from reports of depth-experiences to religious assertions involves an assumption that there exists a hidden divine being, distinct from the world but revealing Himself through the world, a being such that various human attitudes are appropriate responses. This assumption differs even from the scientific realist's assumption concerning the world, a world such that various scientific theories "work." Religious theory, for those who make the crucial assumption that God exists, works in two ways. On the one hand it meets *intellectual needs* by making more intelligible the various depth-experiences-interpreted-as-divine-revelations; for example, it might link the numinous aspect of God with the moral aspect. On the other hand, it meets *spiritual needs* by helping to promote those depth-experiences and interpretations which are believed to bring men into right relation with God; that is, it promotes faith.

In four important ways the testable-by-observations requirement in science thus differentiates science from religion. We should note, however, that religious theory (theology) *may* resemble scientific theory in so far as various nonobservational

criteria are used to evaluate it. I say may, because theologians disagree moderately concerning the extent to which theology should
be appraised in terms of consistency, internal coherence, and simplicity, and they disagree greatly concerning the attempt to fit
theology into a consistent and coherent relation with other disciplines. Even more generally, the spiritual-need emphasis in theology may become more and more dominant in contrast with an
intellectual interest in producing a system. The more this happens,
the more remote becomes the analogy between theology and scientific theory.

Before I close this section of the paper, I should expose a
major weakness. I have failed to grapple with one way in which
religious faith *is* in principle testable by observations.[19] Since revelation is a divine *action,* it should make a difference to what happens. A depth-experience must be partially *caused* by God if it is
to be a *revelation* of God. Of course some convictions concerning
God might be true even though God did not produce them. A critic
of religion is committing the "genetic fallacy" if he attacks the
truth of some religious convictions by exposing their nondivine
causal origin. It is possible that a Freudian explanation of my belief that God is like a father could be correct, yet my belief might
nevertheless be true, by a happy coincidence. Or perhaps it is not
a coincidence; perhaps God the Creator made the world in such
a way that natural causation would lead to my having this true
religious belief. But if my religious conviction is that *God sometimes actively reveals Himself* in depth-experiences, this specific
conviction involves a causal claim concerning God. If *all* religious
convictions of this specific kind could be accounted for by reference to nondivine sufficient conditions, then faith in an actively
self-revealing God would be falsified. Such falsification is not possible in practice, only in principle. But a substantial and rightful
undermining of religious faith is a possibility. If this were not so,
the religious believer would not be making any claim concerning
a God who *acts* in the world. Nothing ventured, nothing claimed.

What kind of *causal claim* is involved? The nearest analogy,
I think, is something like "Without your encouragement, John, I
could not have done it" (or "would not have done it" or "would
not have felt it"). Such a claim can be undermined by behavioral
evidence, yet the basis for the claim is not simply a Humean con-

[19] *Christian* faith, as we saw at the end of Part I, is also testable by observation (i.e., historical investigation) in so far as it depends on beliefs concerning
the man Jesus.

stant conjunction. The recipient of the action is in a privileged position to back his claim by referring to his own private experience. Yet his claim may become untenable in the face of overwhelming contrary evidence. Similar issues arise when a man claims that God actively revealed Himself in a depth-experience, so that a human action or a human feeling was partially caused by God. The recipient of the divine action is in a privileged position to back his claim, yet it may become untenable in the face of overwhelming contrary evidence.

For some philosophers no problems arise concerning the need to test claims concerning divine action by reference to observations. These men hold that there are two complementary and nonconflicting ways to talk about some events: as the action of a personal agent (human or divine) and as an effect of a set of nonpersonal sufficient conditions. I do not think that this account will stand up to scrutiny. I do not think that we can have our cake of agent causality if we eat it up with a determinism of natural causality. Perhaps I am mistaken concerning this, but if I am not, then my faith in a God who sometimes acts by revealing Himself in depth-experiences is a faith which is open to undermining by reference to observations.

IV. Conclusions

Three conclusions can be drawn concerning differences between religious and scientific assertions. *First*, religious assertions are self-involving, though second-order theological assertions may be logically neutral, and there may be special descriptive contexts in which self-involving elements are set aside. Scientific assertions are logically neutral. *Second*, religious assertions are understood experientially only to the extent that men have had various depth-experiences. Scientific assertions are not directly or indirectly dependent on such conditions for their comprehensibility, and they are indirectly dependent on different and less personal conditions. *Third*, religious assertions are not testable by observations, except where they involve causal claims concerning divine actions (or where they depend on historical claims concerning the man Jesus). Scientific assertions are testable by observations, although many are evaluated by reference to nonobservational criteria as well, and many are not falsifiable solely by observations.

Andrew C. Robison/Religious experience

With the exception of permutations on the history of philosophy or the history of religions, it seems to me that the most important questions in the philosophy of religion have to do with justification, i.e., with the general question of whether and how religious beliefs may or may not be justified.

In this century it has been popular with some philosophical analysts and with some liberal Protestant Christians to try to avoid such questions by means of noncognitivist interpretations of what were supposed to be theological assertions. However, I think there are decisive objections of two different kinds to such a move. Such interpretations cannot make sense of the cognitivist way in which at least some religious language (e.g., the creedal statements) has been used through the history of Christianity before this century, as well as the way it still seems to be used by the majority of Christians. Such noncognitivist interpretations also cannot make sense of the cognitivist use of religious language by atheists and metaphysical rebels, of whom the Christian Devil would be the most notable supernatural example.[1]

[1] For argument supporting both of these points, see the extensive and clear presentation by Michael Tooley in his dissertation *A Defense of the Cognitive Significance of Experientially Transcendent Theological Statements* (Princeton University, 1968).

If one rejects noncognitivism, there are a number of approaches to, or arguments for, the justification of theological assertions. Unfortunately for believers, however, most of the approaches or arguments do not go very far towards succeeding in such a justification.[2] Arguments based on past miracles do not get very far, nor do those based on fulfilled prophecy, nor those based simply on various types of religious authorities, whether of sacred scriptures, contemporary prophecies, charismatic religious leaders, or men whose eminence is notable in aspects or fields other than their religious beliefs. As for the old warhorse rational arguments for and against the existence and character of a deity, another ride on them might give us a few new and interesting sights around the philosophical ranch, but I do not really believe it would get us any nearer or farther away from the supernatural pastures which are the point.

All of this, however, still leaves untouched one of the major approaches to justification. It is major not only in terms of the extent to which it is actually used by believers in various traditions, but also major in terms of being, in my opinion, the most promising approach for any positive conclusion about the possibility of justifying belief in theological assertions. This is the attempt to justify such beliefs on the basis of one or another kind of religious experience.

Arguments concerning the cognitive value of religious experiences may be organized in terms of a movement through several stages of debate. A fruitful beginning for an epistemological treatment is a distinction between particularist experiences or claims and universalist experiences or claims. By a particularist claim I mean the claim that an experience supports one particular religion or theological system in contradistinction to others. A universalist claim might be either of the two following things: first, based on the view that all religions are in essence theoretically

[2] While I shall not be strict or technical about it, "justification of theological assertions" will be my normal language for the statement of the problem in this essay. In reference to the terminology elsewhere in this volume, I would have no objections to stating the issue as the "confirmation of theological statements" if those words were understood in terms of recent broadenings of the scope and method and presuppositions of confirmation. However, I am cautious about the latter terminology because it still smacks strongly of a rather simple positivism which sees the issue as merely one of applying the right criteria and determining the yes-or-no verification or confirmation of single statements. Hempel and Quine, among others, have made it clear for some time that this view will not do.

consistent or combinable, it might be the claim that any confirming religious experience supports such a universal doctrinal distillation; and a second kind of universalist claim might be that in all religions there is one main type of religious experience, or perhaps the claimant would say one type of religious experience at the basis of all religions, but that the experience is interpreted in different fashions depending on the experiencers' background theological beliefs.

The first of my several stages of argument concerning religious experience deals with the question of whether particularist claims by an individual based on his own experiences may in some cases be of such a nature, and in such a relation to the experiences neutrally described, that the individual has sufficient reason to hold to the claims. Of course, *sufficiency* here would be judged in relation to the way other types of claims are supported by experiences, i.e., sufficient in relation to the picture in one's epistemology of what counts as warranted belief. A full treatment of this question would begin with an outline and defense of one's general approach to epistemology. For me, this would be a type of reconstructionist empiricism, similar to the epistemological aspects of traditional phenomenalists, though not necessarily including their doctrines in semantics and ontology. While I acknowledge that it makes a truncated presentation to omit further specification and defense, there is hardly room in an essay to do everything; and I hope that after indicating my presuppositions I may proceed to spend the time here in investigating further aspects of what I called the first stage question.

Before continuing with the work thus delimited, perhaps I should briefly indicate how the further stages in a debate concerning religious experience would arise. Even if a positive conclusion might be reached in the first stage of argument, that would still leave open the question of what regard a non-experiencer should have for particularist religious experiences. This immediately raises two issues. First, there is the general philosophical question whether and how we may have good reason to believe other people's assertions on the basis of their experiences. Second, since the obvious problem for any positive regard toward particularist claims is that there are many conflicting particularist claims made by different religious experiencers, we have the question of whether there is any reasonable way for the non-experiencer to decide between particular theologies. The universalist positions I sketched above are two different attempts to solve the apparent particularist conflict by denying, in various ways, that the conflict is conclusive. Thus, a full epistemological treatment of religious experience would need to consider in turn whether either of the two moves to universalism work: first, whether one can extract a meaningful common theology which all confirming religious experiences may be said to support; or, second, whether there is any plausible candidate for a basic type of experience common to all religions, and whether that experience under a neutral description —independent of its particularist contexts—would support theological assertions. Even presuming the following essay successful in dealing with the first stage question, it would still remain to solve the above issues of further stages in the argument concerning religious experience. Hopefully, I may try my hand at them in a later publication.

Two final cautions on what follows: I make no pretense of giving either an account which is immediately applicable to all religious assertions, or an account of the way in which every religious assertion might be properly justified by either an experiencer or a non-experiencer. First, I make no pretense to the former because I am concerned primarily with basic theological assertions of the kind which would occur in minimal creedal statements. But just as in other epistemological contexts, one may also have assertions in theology which are rhetorical, symbolic, metaphorical, etc., and which would need to be explained or translated into more straightforward or precise statements before one could investigate the manner or degree of their confirmation. However, just as in other contexts—with the exception of fictive literature—given a rich language or a rich command of language, one would hope to be able to give an account of such rhetorical/symbolic/metaphorical statements in order to show what their cognitive content is, and why experience is relevant for confirmation or disconfirmation, so also one would expect to be able to do so in religion.[3] Second, I make no pretense to a comprehensive account of justification in religion because just as in other epistemological contexts, some

[3] For example, "Like the hart, he panteth after the Lord, his water-brook" is surely brought into question by the proof that he never prays; and that may be clarified even by a minimal translation of the former such as "He loves and seeks contact with God." Of course, it remains clear that just as in other epistemological contexts, so also in religion some statements may be subject to debate—even among those who accept them—as to the proper clarification of their cognitive content; e.g., "He ascended into heaven from which he shall come again to judge the quick and the dead."

theoretical assertions may be justified to one who accepts the broad theory, not by supporting them on the basis of experience but by showing their connection with those previous theoretical statements he already accepts. So also in religion, if the interlocutor accepts some statements in the theology, then one might justify the new statement in question by reference to those theological statements already accepted and to the decision procedure provided by the theological context. However, just as in natural science, coherence is not the only aspect of a well-constructed or well-justified theory, so also in theology one attempts to support the theoretical structure at various crucial points by statements referring to experience, both past experiences which are supposed to be confirming and future experiences which are predicted.

II

Suppose an empiricist of reconstructionist bent agreed not to restrict his conception of experience to sense-experience, but to investigate his approach to epistemology for what relevance it might have to understanding the logic of justifying claims based on experiences which we might label *moral, aesthetic,* or *religious.* Suppose we set out to investigate religious experiences to see to what extent they might function as the evidential base from which one might or might not be justified in adopting a theology, though remembering that most religions have highly elaborated systems which depend only in small part on any evidence from experience which might be available now. That is, religious systems have been elaborated on the basis not only of evidence from the experiences of believers, but also from more or less stable sources of codified revelation in the form of sacred scriptures, theological tradition developing in relation to changing philosophical movements, and pastoral problems, etc. Thus, what we should be concerned with is not how every aspect of a religious system might be elaborated from experience, but rather the first level problem of whether the most basic sorts of theological affirmation might be justifiable by the believer as theoretical statements which explain and which he adheres to on the basis of his religious experiences.

The first major problem is that it can by no means be taken for granted that tolerance towards investigating theological assertions as theoretical assertions justifiable from experience is going to be met with equal tolerance on the part of religious theorists. To take an example from classical mysticism, one might be inclined to analyse the justification of a religious claim based on a mystic experience by setting up an inference hierarchy moving from a supposedly highly inferred and corrigible description of the experience as one of God being born in the soul, down to a supposedly more basic description of the experience as one of overwhelming joy, fulfillment, peace, etc. But this might well be met at the very beginning by a claim that the so-called higher order description neither always must be nor always could be justified by reference to reasons or grounds, inference from some evidence, e.g., more basic beliefs or descriptions of experience.[4] The claim would be that the experience *just is* an experience of communion with God or of God being born in the soul—that statement about it may be just as incorrigible as any so-called lower order description of the experience. This latter claim in particular might be correlated with perennial theological talk about religious experiences being self-confirming or self-justifying, i.e., not open in their reports to any further correction or further justification. Thus, it might be argued that my epistemological approach is irrelevant to religious experience from the beginning, as one might see by considering the way religious persons talk about their experiences, especially those persons who are clearly concentrating on the task of giving an honest and straightforward report of their experiences and not trying to connect them with some preconceived philosophical position.

There are a number of replies which should be made to such an argument. First of all, just as with the questions of epistemology more generally, it is not simply a matter of how people actually make their assertions, and whether they always state or think that their assertions concerning their experiences stand in need of justification. It is rather a matter of whether those assertions are corrigible, if so whether they may be defended as warranted by certain evidence, and how such a defense might best proceed.

Secondly, it is not by any means only the non-believer or the secular psychoanalyst who thinks that religious experiences do not come with their proper interpretation written on their faces.[5]

[4] This would be a theological correlate to Austin's objection concerning sense-experience. Cf. J. L. Austin, *Sense and Sensibilia* (New York: Oxford University Press, 1962), Lecture X.
[5] Cf. A. E. Taylor, in *The Existence of God,* ed. John Hick (New York: Macmillan, 1964), p. 156.

Common to many religious traditions is the assumption that what I would call highly inferred theological descriptions of religious experiences, or assertions based on religious experiences, are in fact corrigible. This can be seen especially in the widespread religious stories of believers being deceived in their experiences, especially being deceived by other forces or powers than what they took their experiences to manifest. As another example, the Catholic Church has elaborate and careful procedures for investigating whether a claimed vision or other kind of striking religious experience should, in fact, be taken as the believer has reported it. These procedures include not only an investigation of the veracity and responsibleness of the experiencer, but also tests of consistency with widely accepted theological theory, pragmatic tests of the beneficial results in the behavior of the experiencer, etc. In terms of common Western parlance more generally, it is widely agreed by religious persons that the Devil knows Scripture thoroughly and quotes it to suit his own purposes, so he surely would not be above taking the form of light in order to mislead the Lord's true disciples.

Finally, it is not even true that this theory of the given interpretation and justification of religious experiences has the support of all those persons who are "clearly concentrating on the task of an honest and straightforward report of their experiences." A good example of such a straightforward and unsystematized report might be taken from William James's collection, this piece by Stephen H. Bradley.[6] One night Bradley had what he interpreted to be an experience of the power of the Holy Spirit. Earlier that evening he had been to a church service, something he had surely done often before. This time he was temporarily stirred by the fiery preaching, though not seriously moved. He returned home, and claims to have had no expectation whatsoever of anything unusual, of any important religious experience. To continue with his own words,

> I retired to rest soon after I got home, and felt indifferent to the things of religion until I began to be exercised by the Holy Spirit, which began in about five minutes after, in the following manner: At first, I began to feel my heart beat very quick all on a sudden, which made me at first think that perhaps something is going to ail me, though I was not alarmed, for I felt no pain. My heart increased in its beating, which soon convinced me that it was the

[6] William James, *The Varieties of Religious Experience* (New York: Modern Library, n.d.), p. 188.

Holy Spirit from the effect it had on me. I began to feel exceedingly happy and humble, and such a sense of unworthiness as I never felt before.

Bradley continues, but for our purposes this early phase of his report is the important one. He portrays the experience straightforwardly, and at this crucial descriptive point in his long account, in nontheological language. First he attends to the palpitations of heart, and thinks he might be on the verge of illness. (Note the explicit possibility of a nonreligious interpretation—even recognized by the experiencer during the experience!) But then he takes the other effects into account and decides it must be the Holy Spirit. And surely it is his background theory, or shall I say "attendant beliefs," the doctrines of Christianity, which provide the identification of God or the Holy Spirit as the being which would be of the appropriate nature to cause such exceeding happiness and humility. Thus Bradley manifests a picture of justifying theological assertions based on inference from religious experiences which is similar in type, if not so elaborate or careful in the specification of stages, to the general picture of justification which a reconstructionist proposes.

Two notes here: first, the present issue is not the adequacy of Bradley's account and explanation of his experience, but rather the character of his method of approaching an account or explanation; and second, my claim is not that all religious experiencers justify their theological assertions in the way I am proposing. Obviously, even among those experiencers attending to the problem of justification—and certainly among the theologians so attending—one will find a variety of ways in which they actually do propose to justify their assertions, just as one will find that variety with experiencers—and theoreticians—in any other realm of experience. The point is rather to show that there is no reason to rule my approach to religious experience out of order from the beginning. In fact, though by no means universal, I believe the features Bradley shows are common enough in reports of religious experiences to need no more than an explicit example in order to ring true.[7]

I do not wish to take much more time cataloguing objections to the possibility of theologies as theories, which might to some

[7] For similar features in a couple of paradigm cases of religious experiences, cf.: Teresa of Avila: *Interior Castle*, Fifth Mansions, Chapter 1; and Augustine: *Confessions*, Book VIII, Chapter 12.

extent be justifiable by a believer on the basis of inferences from his experiences. However, there are two further common objections which it might be well to mention. The first is the objection that theologies cannot be at all like (scientific) theories because the latter are hypotheses which we believe in a tentative and detached fashion, whereas religious faith is a matter of total commitment to the truth of the religious system and complete personal involvement with the truth of those beliefs.[8] There are two things wrong with this objection. The minor problem is that it misrepresents the actual attitudes of believers in both scientific and religious theories. That even the specialists in the former field are not so tentative and detached would seem evident from scientific debates, either at contemporary symposia or as reported in historical writings such as Thomas Kuhn's *The Structure of Scientific Revolutions*. Nor are religious believers the simply and totally committed. It is a common feature of serious discussions of faith and of conversion to consider the extent to which doubts remain after definite commitment; and it is surely evident that, with the exception of the most basic tenets of the faith, beliefs are debated and changed even by adherents within a religious tradition.

In reaction to this point, I presume the objector might reply that his substantive argument can be reformulated: namely, that the most appropriate way for an epistemologist to view scientific theories is as hypothetical explanations, for which one might specify a greater or lesser degree of confirmation on available evidence. Further, since the evidence is never conclusive in favor of one theory as opposed to all others possible, scientific theories should be believed with a certain tentativeness appropriate to their degree of confirmation, whatever the degree of tenacity with which some less than fully self-conscious scientists might in fact hold to particular theories. This helpful reformulation clarifies not only the intended argument of the objector but also the major problem with this argument, namely, that in its approach to theology it depends upon a confusion between the psychology of belief and the logic of confirmation.[9] If, on a particular view of epistemology and of science, it can be claimed that sci-

---

[8] E.g., Antony Flew, *God and Philosophy* (New York: Harcourt, Brace and World, 1966), p. 151 (7.20, a subordinate but present part of Flew's argument in the paragraph).

[9] For a fuller discussion of this distinction, see Michael Tooley, *op. cit.,* pp. 98ff.

entific laws are to be treated as hypotheses and systematic views as theories, with a greater or lesser degree of confirmation, and that it does not matter to the adequacy of that account that some scientists may in fact hold to their views much more strongly than their status as theories warrants, then by the same token the same may be claimed of religious views. That is, the extent to which some religious believers may feel their theological views are certain, or may hold to them tenaciously in the face of criticism, is no reason why the theological views may not best be construed in an epistemological account as explanatory theories with a greater or lesser degree of confirmation.

A second common objection is the following: the religious person, more especially the theist, should not accept for his god the role of being the explanation for certain events, because that will somehow degrade or stigmatize the god, "reducing" him to some lower level of worth inhabited by "explanation" and "science".[10] In its full-blown form this argument usually depends on several polarities, with their terms left helpfully vague to aid their supposed coalescence: scientific/unscientific, natural/supernatural, and non-divine (or worldly)/divine. The claim is that a scientific account and a supernatural account are mutually exclusive, the supernatural is surely opposed to the natural, and the natural is opposed to the divine as common or unworthy of religious responses. Thus we finish with the opposition between the scientific and the divine. Often the argument is embellished with various rhetorical devices to saddle the opponents with a particularly denigrating view of the god: a liberal sprinkling of "simply" and "merely" (if He were treated as the explanation for certain events, God would become "simply one cause amongst others"), with the examples of other explanatory principles chosen from a rather lowly bag (God would be a causal explanation like a strong wind is a causal explanation).[11] The lack of force in the rhetorical side of the argument can be seen by substituting different examples into the sentence forms: one would hardly think it a difficulty with viewing the god as a creator/person/savior that he might be "simply another" creator/person/savior. The worth or dignity of the

10 E.g., John Wilson, *Philosophy and Religion* (New York: Oxford University Press, 1961), pp. 38f; Antony Flew, *op. cit.*, pp. 149ff. (7.15, 16, 21); Patrick Nowell-Smith, "Miracles", in *New Essays in Philosophical Theology*, ed. Antony Flew and Alasdair MacIntyre (London: SCM Press, 1955).

11 Wilson's words and example; see John Wilson, *op. cit.*, p. 38.

god presumably depends not on whether he fills any of these roles, but rather on how he might fill them. Again, there is no more reason at the beginning to compare the explanatory deity to a strong wind than to the sun, the source of warmth and light and life, which in many traditions has been thought an appropriately honorific analogy. As for the substantive argument based on polarities, it seems to have no more force than the rhetoric. If the supernatural is the same as the divine, then there is no reason—given the existence of a god—why there should not to some extent be laws of the supernatural (e.g., whom the Lord loveth, He chastiseth), and a science of the supernatural (a good ideal for theology). On the other hand, if the natural is no more specific than "whatever in fact occurs",[12] then any believer who sees his deity as acting in the world should have no difficulty in admitting divinely caused events to be "natural" in that sense of the word.

III

Having answered three of the most common objections to my program, this is a good point at which to give some rough account of just what sorts of things I intend "religious experiences" to range over, in order not to be mistaken for taking the data too narrowly. What counts as a religious experience is not determined by some constant feature characteristic of the basic descriptions of such experiences (e.g., a "numinous" quality), but rather is determined by whether the experiencer connects his experience in some definite and direct way with his religious theory. A more specific criterion, which I believe will work for now, is that an experience is a religious experience if the actor's normal explanation or account of the experience contains characteristically religious terminology. I do not know of an adequate typology of religious experiences in the literature; so I offer the following as a working organization of the kinds of experiences which at different times have been claimed as bases for religious knowledge:[13]

---

[12] Antony Flew, *op. cit.*, p. 149.

[13] From my remarks on epistemology it is undoubtedly clear that I use the word *experience* in terms of discrete experiences (e.g., I had an exhilarating intellectual experience last night when I finally understood why space and time are but forms of the sensibility), and not what one might call holistic experience (e.g., my experience tells me he is up to no good). To the extent that the latter usage is relevant to epistemology, it does not seem to be be-

1. *Miracles.* For example, the nature and healing miracles of the Bible.

2. *Visions and Voices.* That is, the supposed direct perception of the deity or a representative of the deity, either through sense-experience or through dreams.[14] Examples: the rather simple vision of the Virgin at Lourdes by Bernadette Soubirous; the much more complex vision by Arjuna in the eleventh chapter of the Bhagavad-Gita; the voice heard by Saul on the road to Damascus—note that the textual claim is that the sound was public, also heard by his companions (Acts 9); Solomon's dream dialogue with God (I Kings 3).

3. *Experiences of General Exaltation or Communion with Everything (including what has come to be called extrovertive mysticism).* Examples would stretch from the nature mysticism of hilltop feelings on a starry night to sensory drug experiences under the influence of marijuana, mescaline, etc.

4. *Sense of a Particular Presence.* Either of some impersonal power,[15] or of a personal being.[16] Rudolf Otto's analysis of numinous experience in terms of a *mysterium tremendum et fascinans* primarily concerns types of experience under this heading.[17]

5. *Sense of Being Addressed.* Either commands and challenges (such as Augustine's experience in the garden),[18] or

---

cause considering one's experience holistically adds some further confirmation to one's claim, but rather because it is a way of summarizing and balancing all of one's relevant particular experiences (e.g., I know he is a good boy and often goes around the house quietly like that; but every time he looks sideways when you call him, then you know he is doing something wrong).

[14] Cf. the first two of three traditional Catholic distinctions of kinds of visions: corporeal (an apparition—the eyes perceive some object); imaginative (caused in the imagination without use of the sense of sight, e.g., dreams); and intellectual (simple intuition of some truth).

[15] Such as is discussed in the first chapters of G. van der Leeuw, *Religion in Essence and Manifestation,* tr. J. E. Turner (New York: Harper and Row, 1963).

[16] Such as is discussed in Lecture III of William James's *The Varieties of Religious Experience.*

[17] See his *The Idea of the Holy,* tr. J. W. Harvey (Oxford: Oxford University Press, 1923).

[18] *Confessions,* VIII, 12.

comforts (such as Wesley's heartwarmings).[19] These types of experiences often occur indirectly in conjunction with the reading of religious texts, the hearing of religious exhortations, etc.

6. *Mystic Experiences.* That is, the classical mystic experiences, which have come to be called introvertive mysticism (contrast (3) above). For example, the Indian Yogins, Teresa of Avila, Plotinus.

7. *Metaphysical Experiences.* That is, strong feelings or senses of the contingency of the natural world, of the beauty and harmony of the natural order, of radical dependence for one's very being on some superior Cause.

8. *Moral Experiences.* For example, overwhelming remorse at some evil committed, or an unreasonably high valuation of persons or of charity in personal relationships.

While I may occasionally refer to problems connected with the first and the last two types of experiences, the middle four in this list are the experiences of most general and potent interest. With regard to miracles, contemporary ones seem rather infrequent, with the possible exception of faith healings; and I have little to add to Hume's classic discussion of the difficulties of confirming the mere occurrence, much less any theological explanation, of past miracles.[20] Much the same thing as that could also be said of visions and voices. To the extent that so-called metaphysical experiences are elaborated into more definite patterns of justification for theological assertions, they appear to result in just the classical rational arguments, which do not seem to me to require yet another treatment to show their great difficulties. (For example, the explanation sought is not really for the experience of contingency but for the posited contingency as a feature of the world, which would lead us to a type of cosmological argument.)

Having indicated the range of data that may be considered,

[19] See his Journal for May 24, 1738, extensively quoted in *John Wesley,* ed. A. Outler (New York: Oxford University Press, 1964), the crucial experience on p. 66).

[20] David Hume, *An Enquiry Concerning Human Understanding* (Oxford: Clarendon, 1902), Section X.

what are the main issues in approaching the epistemology of religious experience from a reconstructionist point of view? One of the most important questions is: if one is to set up inference hierarchies to show the pattern of justifying, and thus of evaluating theological assertions based on religious experiences, what are they going to look like in their lowest reaches? What is the basic language of report for religious experiences?

It seems to me that there are two approaches to answering this question. The first is to make use of some criterion such as that a more basic report or description of an experience is one which is "less particularizing."[21] This could be applied to both the objective and the subjective aspects of reports. For example, in objective terms, the criterion might lead from a report of an experience as one of being close to Shiva, to a report of the experience as one manifesting a fascinating personal power with tremendous aspects of both beneficence and destructiveness. In subjective terms, the criterion might lead from descriptions like "the touch of

[21] The specification of just what a basic descriptive or reporting language should contain is, of course, a major difficulty for any form of phenomenalism; and I have no suggestion with which I am finally happy. I do think one grasps intuitively rather easily what sort of thing is required, especially when one considers illustrations of the idea. For example, one thinks of "there is before me something relatively small, white, curved, solid" as a more basic observational or descriptional statement than "before me on my desk is the hand-carved meerschaum pipe which I bought in Istanbul." One would like if possible to avoid specifying the basic observational language by means of some static enumeration of its terms, and instead to give some rule for what it may include so that new observational terms may be admitted by passing the test. However, it is not at all easy to find the right rule. The "simplicity" of the basic observational statements is certainly not adequate, because they may not be at all simple in terms of the number and syntax of descriptional words or locutions used. Nor do I think that "ostensively definable" would be an adequate criterion, because of problems with how one might ostensively define various kinds of feelings or emotions, which seem to me to have a strong claim to be considered as observation terms. At present I am happiest, though only minimally happy, with saying that the basic descriptional statements are up to a point "less particularizing" or "less individualizing." "Up to a point", because the limit of less particularizing or less individualizing would be "there is something"; and one clearly wants to stop before that limiting lack of particularity is reached, after having eliminated specific object terms like "hand-carved meerschaum pipe", but before eliminating descriptional terms for elementary perceptual qualities like colors, shapes, etc. The general idea of course is to eliminate more and more possibilities of counterevidence to one's basic description, counterevidence in the form of evidence one has made false inferences and thus misdescribed, and by that elimination to make the assertion increasingly more nearly incorrigible.

God's love" to descriptions like "overwhelming peace, joy, and fulfillment."

The second approach to determining at least a working picture of the basic language for reports of religious experience would be the exegetical one. That would be to study many reports of religious experiences and see whether there is indeed a general distinction between the normal theological terminology used to refer to an experience, and the terminology used in critical contexts to report some inferential bases for the usual description of the experience. Naturally, this approach would require an outline of strong exegetical principles to be used, so as not merely to go through texts culling bits and pieces to support one's thesis. In the case of Stephen Bradley, quoted in part in Section II, I believe that this method would find such expressions as "my experience of the power of the Holy Spirit" to be Bradley's normal way of referring to his experience; but it would also find that when he came to describe the experience as closely as possible, his more basic descriptions were formed from such terminology as "exceedingly happy and humble" and "a sense of unworthiness."

IV

Whichever way of determining a basic reporting language were chosen, one will soon find major difficulties if one proposes to justify highly interpreted theological assertions by showing how they may be inferred from such careful and precise and even incorrigible basic descriptions of religious experiences. Whether we are religious experiencers or not, if we attend only to the nature of the experiences under these careful descriptions, then there will quickly appear two of Hume's monumental barriers looming in the way of positing any religiously satisfying theology on the basis of such religious experiences. *Barrier One:* no matter what quantity-determinants are hooked to the basic descriptions (*immense joy, overwhelming* love, etc.), the descriptions at this level could only support the existence of a being whose powers are *just great enough* to cause that degree of immense joy, etc.[22] Now, one might

22 Compare Hume's criticism of the teleological argument that a deity argued as the cause of certain effects in the world can, on that basis, only be claimed to be just *sufficient* to account for those effects (*Dialogues Concerning Natural Religion*, ed. N. Kemp Smith [Oxford: Oxford University Press, 1935], Part V).

regard theoreticians' talk about the "infinity" of the deity's attributes as, strictly speaking, unacceptable,[23] or as acceptable solely as a kind of religious rhetoric provoked by worshipful attitudes. However, even such a one will admit that the powers which are "just great enough" are hardly going to be great enough as a portrayal of the religious object for most devotees. *Barrier Two:* the experiences under these descriptions by themselves would not unambiguously indicate a being which should necessarily be connected with any specific theological picture, e.g., the Old Testament Yahweh, or the Zen buddha-nature.[24] These two barriers would mean for most people that such attention to these epistemological bases, or the lower order descriptions of religious experiences, would not be able to justify a theology at all honorific enough or at all specific and elaborate enough to be religiously satisfying.

The problem that the Humean Barriers pose, however, is not peculiar to religious contexts, but is present in analogous forms in other epistemological contexts, even in the strictest of them. In physical science, for example, one does not go straight from the data of an isolated chemical experiment, nor even from the data of a number of similar experiments, to a full-blown theory of valence. Nor does Sherlock Holmes go from the mere presence of a size 12 footprint to the condemnation of the butler. Rather, as Quine, Hempel, and others have stressed, the investigator works in a much richer context, the context of data from other sources, and especially the context of vast presumed and hypothesized theory, the more flexibly held as the investigator is more critically self-conscious. And it is in that rich context that one interprets data from experiments or experiences, which, if they occur at the

---

[23] Cf. F. R. Tennant, *Philosophical Theology* (Cambridge: Cambridge University Press, 1930), Vol. II, pp. 140–143.

[24] Compare Hume's further criticism of the teleological argument that a cause of the effects in question is not necessarily any specific kind of deity (in particular, not necessarily the deity of the theists) because of all the alternative hypotheses possible to account for the data, with their many different kinds of causal principles or deities (Hume, *op. cit.*, Parts V–VII). Antony Flew gives an altered version of this argument, namely, to the effect that we would not know enough about a posited God to make him function as an explanatory principle in any theory (see Antony Flew, *op. cit.*, p. 151). The same answers given below to the Humean Barrier are relevant to Flew, i.e., that at this stage in the argument the theoretical option for adoption as an explanation is not Flew's minimally defined God, but a deity or principle in a particular elaborated theology.

proper point according to a theory, and if they result in data correlating with the theory, are then regarded as confirming evidence for that theory. On this greatly oversimplified account, in viewing an event as confirming a particular theory, two broad aspects may be distinguished: that the event occurs in a context indicated by or appropriate to the theory, and that the character of the event correlates with the character indicated by the theoretical hypothesis.

What I vaguely called occurring "in a context indicated by or appropriate to the theory" is in the natural sciences generally thought to be a matter of definite predictions of events. By means of the theory one may predict that, given certain physical conditions, then at such and such a place and time an event of certain characteristics will occur. There might be both theological and philosophical objections to treating religious experiences as parallel to such confirming events for scientific theories. From the theologians one might hear that it is wrong to focus on such *particular* experiences as manifestations of the divine, because the theists' god is working *always* and *everywhere,* just as the advaitins and pantheists claim to be *always* unified with Brahman, Nature, or whatever their metaphysical principle may be termed. However, there is no real problem here, since there is no conflict between the theoretical claim that events or conditions of such and such a nature always occur or obtain, and the claim that particular events are especially appropriate for manifesting or justifying the assertion of this continuing order. It is true that on most religious theories one cannot exclude the possibility of revelation occurring at any point. However, for the theists there certainly are particularly appropriate times and places; e.g., for Christians in the reading of the Scriptures, or at the elevation of the Host, and for Hindu theists in the performance of temple ritual, or in the culmination of religious festivals. And there are similarly appropriate particular times and places for the pantheist; e.g., being confronted by a sublime spectacle of nature, or after a long course of meditation for purposes of discovering one's true inner self.

From the philosophical side one might hear the objection that the occurrence of religious experiences at times and places which accord with a religious theory is not really analogous to the occurrence of confirming events in contexts which accord with a scientific theory. With science it is a matter of simple and definite predictions of events, which do or do not occur, straightforwardly confirming or disconfirming the theory. However, the theologians can never make definite predictions from their religious theory but only offer post facto explanations of events, with more or fewer epicycles, depending on how closely the events correlate with the theory. Such a criticism would seem to me to misrepresent both science and theology. On the one hand, when a natural scientist predicts an event, he generally relies on many presumptions besides the particular hypothesis under consideration, e.g., presumptions about the adequacy of his method of observation, about the theoretical principles underlying the functioning of his instruments according to his conceptions, etc.[25] And whether the predicted event occurs or not, it confirms or disconfirms this much broader theoretical scheme, with the possibility of many epicycles to take account of uncongenial data.

On the other hand, most theologies can make definite predictions, of a lesser or greater degree of abstractness, and thus of a greater or lesser ease in checking. Religions without a personal deity may be able to make very definite predictions, e.g., that for any person willing to undergo the proper training, his performance of certain types of meditation will eventually lead to ecstatic experiences of unity with his object of meditation. However, with the religions positing a personal deity, because the occurrence of revelation depends on the deity's personal will, and because his will is usually claimed to be known only for the most general or long range events, such theologies are able to predict particular cases only with some degree of probability, and to make definite predictions only about the very general or long range or limit cases. Thus, one would not be able definitely to predict the answering of a particular prayer or the occurrence of some revelation at a particular time and place, because, while such events might well be in accord with the character of the deity, the god may have other or stronger purposes or beliefs, unknown to the predictor, which make the god's action on that particular occasion and in that fashion less desirable. On the other hand, the divine will certainly is claimed to be known to some extent; and thus such theologies can make definite general predictions, e.g., that God will not wholly abandon His Chosen People, or that at some unspecified time Christ will come again to judge the quick and the dead.

[25] For his clear summary of the point, see C. G. Hempel, *Philosophy of Natural Science* (Englewood Cliffs, N.J.: Prentice-Hall, 1966), pp. 22–28.

There certainly is a difference between the normal examples of scientific prediction and the predictions of theologies with a personal deity. However, I believe the difference has mainly to do with the fact that such examples for science are almost invariably drawn from the physical sciences; and it is obvious that, without the availability of a reductionistic psychology, predictions concerning a personal deity cannot be expected to be like predictions concerning an impersonal principle. In fact, if the examples for the natural sciences were only chosen over a wider range, instead of the inevitable kinetic theory of gases, etc., then it would be clear that even in those prestigious fields statistical laws and probabilistic predictions are not at all uncommon.[26] Man is the natural being claimed by theologies of personal deities to be closest in resemblance to their gods—no matter how many qualifications they may issue to restrict the resemblance. Thus, the sciences of man would seem to be the natural field for comparisons with such theologies. And by comparison with the social sciences, I do not believe theologies will look nearly so dissimilar on such subjects as definiteness of predictability concerning individual actions.

V

After dealing with the above objections, let me return to the main thread of the argument. Considering what I termed attention to theoretical context in relation to the value of some event for confirming a theory, I can now show why I set out at the beginning to investigate particularist religious claims at this first stage of the general argument concerning religious experience. The reason is that particularist claims might involve just that element of extra epistemological strength which would come from correlation of the experiences with a specific theory and context, which they are taken to support. Thus particularist claims could be shown stronger if there is shown to be not only a correlation between the presumed particularist theology and the character of the religious experiences under their lower order descriptions, but also a correlation between the points and methods of occurrence of the experiences and a context specifically indicated by or appropriate to the particularist theology.

[26] Again, for a beautiful summary, see Hempel, *op. cit.*, pp. 58ff.

Since this is terribly abstract, let me give two examples to show a *discorrelation* in the two fashions intended. (1) Suppose a rabbi has ecstatic experiences which he reports in characteristics appropriate to an effect of the Jewish God. However, he has these experiences only when he performs worship and yoga in a Vaishnavite temple. With only this data under consideration, suppose the experiences were consistent and overwhelming enough to seem to the rabbi to require a continuing supernatural cause. Although he might be drawn by the character of the experiences to talk of the Jewish God, the context and method of the experiences seem most inappropriate for that particular theology, and should weaken that interpretation considerably. (2) A converse discorrelation might be, say, having an experience of the sense of the presence of an overwhelmingly powerful and fascinating being which the experiencer would be inclined to take as the Christian God. His interpretation might be supported by the context of the experiences if they occurred always and only during the saying of the Mass. But though the context is right, the character of the experiences might still be wrong, e.g., if his lower order descriptions indicated a being combining creativity and grace with destructiveness and capricious violence, something more appropriate to Shiva than to the Christian God.

With those two examples I suppose it is clear what a positive correlation of the character and the context of the experiences would look like. Just such a dual correlation would, if it occurred, tend to overcome the Humean Barriers. It would tend to confirm not merely a theological hypothesis which is just adequate to explain the experiences. Rather, it would tend to confirm a particular, fully elaborated theology, which would provide not only an articulated picture of the divine but also a moral and social context sufficiently developed to be religiously satisfying.

The importance of the theoretical context for the experiencer's interpretation of his experiences is reinforced by the individualist bent of epistemological phenomenalism. For the system of science which one takes to be the right one, one's own experiences play the final, decisive role. One person's interpretation of his experience will of course be relevant to another's as in general other persons' experiences give us some prima facie reason to accept their assertions based on those experiences. However, given the presence of a very different kind of experience, then an experiencer's interpretation may be justifiable even though it is not congruent with a non-experiencer's justifiable interpretation.

This type of contextualism and individualism also necessitates a reevaluation of some features of religious experiences with regard to their role in confirmation. The primary example is what I might call the quantitative aspect of such experiences. It is a regular part of the reports of religious experiences that their characteristic features occur in unusual or excessive quantity; e.g., "overwhelming joy," "infinite peace," "a reality more real than any mere earthly objects or persons". As we saw, an attempt to construct a religious explanation for such features without regard to any theoretical context runs foul of one of the Humean Barriers. However, the experiencer is never in fact without such a context of background theory and conception of the possibilities of various explanatory options. And in that context the quantitative features of religious experiences might prove justifiably crucial. For example, imagine the option for an experiencer were between a divine or a subjective cause for his supposedly religious experience. His knowledge of the possible strength of self-induced psychological experiences, of hallucinations, Freudian mechanisms of the mind, etc., will appropriately be his basis for judging the adequacy of the latter explanation. And his understanding of the particular theology in question, not only in theory but also in reports of devotee's experiences, will give his basis for judging the particular religious interpretation. Given that choice, suppose he found features of his experiences correlating in both character and context with a certain theology, and that he found those features overwhelmingly different from or stronger than features of normal experience, or even of abnormal but hallucinatory experience. Then, given no particular reason to consider further types of explanations (e.g., nonhuman beings of a less than divine rank), the strength of his experiences would seem properly to be an important positive factor in confirming his theological interpretation.

Of course, if there were insoluble problems with every particular religious theory, then one could definitely argue against any particularist theological interpretation of religious experiences. However, while there are serious moral and theoretical difficulties with most of the traditional theologies, I have not seen any convincing specification which would prevent the problems from being mollified to the point of being acceptable, given strong experiential reasons for adopting the theology.[27] That seems even clearer given a strong component of holism in one's view of theoretical confirmation. This means, among other things, that it is quite possible that one might have experiences of such a nature as to be sufficient to revise even the innermost structure of one's theoretical explanation of the world, one's science in the broadest sense of that term.

In focusing on the role of crucial individual experiences, I have not yet taken adequate account of another holistic feature possible in the justification of a particularist theological interpretation. It may well be that in the experiencer's justification of a particularist religious interpretation, a crucial experience, perhaps a conversion experience, will play the dominant role. However, because of its concern with an elaborated theology, relevant to experience at many other points, such justification will generally also appeal to a broad range of other experiences and arguments. (And, by the same token, a particularist interpretation must deal with the problems raised for aspects of the theology by different kinds of experiences from the crucial or conversion experience.)

Perhaps the best way to bring all these last themes together is with an example. Imagine Raj, brought up in a Brahmin family, successful at school so that he is able to get a lucrative science scholarship to a university. Grouped with the smartest and most critical students, Raj considers himself a freethinker and a materialist, delights in quoting Bertrand Russell with his friends. While he still assists with any family rituals at home, he never goes to a temple except for fun at festivals. He has successfully made the transition to nonvegetarian food; and little remains of his Hinduism except that he does expect, of course, to marry a girl from his own caste.

Later in his university career Raj starts attending meetings at a Ramakrishna Mission house, first because he enjoys the dis-

[27] In "Can God's Existence be Disproved?" (reprinted in *The Ontological Argument*, Alvin Plantinga, ed., [Garden City: Doubleday, 1965]), J. N. Findlay claims to show how the characteristics of a deity necessitated by (Western) worship would make the deity be of such a nature that we could show the impossibility of his existence. However, beyond any problems with specific parts of his argument, the divine characteristics with which Findlay begins seem to me not at all derived from the language of worship and the reasons for worshipping given in such paradigm sources as psalms and prayers, but rather derived from a generally neo-Platonic type of theological speculation. Thus, Findlay's argument hardly seems to affect all options of a worshipful Christianity or Judaism, much less of all worshipful religions.

cussions about ethics, and only afterwards because of any interest in religious themes. However, the latter strike him as increasingly more interesting, especially the often abstruse but often delightful speculation of the Vedanta; and Raj decides to seek conversation with a guru. One thing leads to another; he embarks upon a stringent course of training and meditation; and months later, after periodic stretches of intense effort, Raj has an ecstatic experience.

When pressed, Raj describes this new experience as the lapse of ordinary consciousness, followed by the persistence of his own self grown limitless, and by feelings of certainty and of fulfilling bliss which are more intense than any he thought possible. Otherwise, he describes his experience only in words from the Upanishads, and reasonably considers it to be empirical confirmation, made stronger as he has more similar experiences, for an adherence to the philosophy which guided him to its achievement and with which its character exactly correlates. In arguments with his friends he insists that no activity of the ordinary conscious self can even approach the characteristics of the ecstatic experience, that the psychologists' account of the unconscious contains no mechanism powerful enough to account for them either, and that they can only be due to the uncovering of the unity between one's true inner self and the Self which underlies all things, Brahman, which is known as being, consciousness, and bliss.

Of course, Raj's theology does not stop there, but in affirming the Vedanta he affirms the other basic Hindu themes included in that philosophy, for example, reincarnation and the doctrine of karma. By reference to other kinds of experiences or patterns of experience than the ecstatic ones, he is beset with difficulties in some aspects of his broader theory of Vedanta; and he considers himself aided in justifying others. For example, his friends trouble him with the question why he should so obviously expend so much effort to seek again and again to be united with Brahman when he claims that he already is united with Brahman and that he already realizes that unity. On the other hand, Raj brings common psychological experiences of a feeling of *deja vu* in support of reincarnation, and he claims the "fact" that evil breeds evil and good is rewarded is a manifestation of the rule of karma even in this life.

Raj seems to me a typical example of the way in which religious experiencers, when conscious of the problem of justification or when made conscious of it by challenge, might approach an account of their reasons for holding to their theological assertions.

The elaborateness and care of such justifications by religious experiencers will certainly vary from case to case. And one's regard for the success of such attempted justifications will also vary, depending on a much closer examination of each particular case at issue. However, given the various considerations I have sketched above, it seems to me not only possible, but quite plausible that we should regard a religious experiencer, under certain circumstances, as justified in asserting his theology on the basis of his experiences. What I have done in my accounts of theoretical context, of the qualitative factor in religious experiences, etc., is to indicate what seem to me the most important aspects of those circumstances which would tend to make us conclude in approving a particularist theological interpretation by an experiencer.

Ten/A fresh approach to verification and theology

Introduction/Verificationism: difficulties and proposals

THIS section, the most technical in expression, begins with Alvin Plantinga's effort to follow what he calls "verificationism" to the end of the line. When he arrives he finds that there is nothing in it, and that its threat to theology was grossly exaggerated. In the next essay, Wesley Salmon, a leading logician, begins by acknowledging the lowly estate into which verification has fallen. Yet, convinced that the positivists were on the right track, he institutes some major modifications to get it moving again. Michael Tooley's contribution is a bold and controversial effort to revive verification and other "discredited" doctrines of positivism, and to apply them to the question of the cognitive meaningfulness of theological statements. In formulating his version of verification, he relies heavily, indeed almost exclusively, on Salmon's essay, but he goes beyond it. Tooley formulates his own highly controversial view of what the positivists called "protocol sentences," but which he calls "basic observation statements."[1] What is more, he sets them in the context of his

[1] Otto Neurath, "Protocol Sentences," in *Logical Positivism*, ed. A. J. Ayer, pp. 199–208.

version of the phenomenalistic epistemology that was characteristic of the early positivists but which, along with so many of their doctrines, was later widely repudiated.[2]

Plantinga: verification is futile and does not challenge theology

Alvin Plantinga's survey of what he calls "verificationism," by which he means all versions of the test, is a valuable launching pad for this concluding Section. In addition to his discussion of falsification, he picks up the story of confirmation where we left it at the end of Section Two. He deals with Ayer's second version of confirmation, and with Peter Nidditch's effort to salvage it in the face of Alonzo Church's criticism. Plantinga concludes that verificationism is a futile affair and he wonders why theologians have taken it so seriously.

The essays by Salmon and Tooley are an effort to show that an adequate version of the test of confirmation can be achieved. To that extent, they may be taken as highly sophisticated efforts to reply to Plantinga. Tooley's essay also contains a lengthy statement of his reasons for regarding verification as a serious challenge to the cognitive meaningfulness of theological statements, even though Tooley thinks the challenge can be met.

It should be added that, throughout the introductory materials (see especially Section One, parts I and IV), I have answered Plantinga's question regarding the importance of the issue by stressing the cultural framework. The test, in all its forms, represents a sophisticated version of the challenge of science to religion. Theologians have taken it seriously because many of them were concerned to relate to thinkers outside the circle of "true believers." They wanted to meet the challenges of a scientifically oriented culture head on. They felt threatened by verification because it seemed as though it could be used to show that theology was not a cognitive endeavor. Plantinga's surprise at the seriousness with which some theologians responded to the challenge of verification is, perhaps, understandable, because, by the time his survey appeared (1967), pessimism about verification was widespread among the empiricists who were most concerned to achieve an adequate statement of it.

In any case, theologians still need to take the lessons of verification-

2 A lucid introduction to phenomenalistic epistemology is provided in the Introduction to Part IV of A Modern Introduction to Philosophy, ed. P. Edwards and A. Pap, pp. 504–512.

ism to heart. They ought to become self-conscious about the circumstances would count for and against the truth of their statements.

Paul Tillich recognized the validity of this point and tried to respond to it.[3] He claimed that the positivists' standard of verification was too scientifically oriented (he called it "experimental verification") to be used in theology. Yet he accepted the demand for verification as a valid one, and he presented his existential mode of verification which he called "experiential." Many analytic critics thought that his application of this test was woefully inadequate.[4] That is another matter. The fact is that he tried, whereas subsequent generations of theologians will be discouraged from even making the effort if emphases like those of Plantinga take hold.

Salmon: the reports of verificationism's demise were premature

Tooley's claim that it is possible to achieve an adequate statement of verification (or confirmation) as the test for factual meaningfulness is based on Salmon's essay. I shall confine my treatment of Salmon to the major points that Tooley discusses and indicate one difficulty that applies to all of them.

Factual meaning and confirmation

Confirmation plays a crucial role in the notion of factual meaningfulness and it should do so. In this respect the positivists were on the right track. They bogged down on the problem of developing an adequate theory of confirmation. It is hard to say exactly what kinds of observations confirm statements of fact and how they actually do the job of confirming them. Yet the difficulties involved in the concept of confirmation should not lead us to deny the validity of the position that "A sentence (or statement) has factual meaning if, and only if, it is empirically verifiable (or confirmable)" (see p. 497).

[3] Paul Tillich, Systematic Theology, vol. I (Chicago: University of Chicago Press, 1951), pp. 100ff.

[4] Sydney Hook, ed., Religious Experience and Truth (New York: New York University Press, 1961), Part I; see also, Paul Edwards, "Professor Tillich's Confusions" in Cahn, ed., Philosophy of Religion (New York: Harper and Row, 1970), pp. 209–235. For a defense of Tillich from many of these charges, see William Rowe, Religious Symbols and God (Chicago: University of Chicago Press, 1968).

Verification and induction

The difficulties with verification that were elaborated in Section One of this volume involve deductive moves in logic (see pp. 446 ff., especially note 19 on p. 453). Readers who are familiar with this discipline will realize that a number of them hinge on modus pones and modus tollens. Salmon tries to show that many of these difficulties can be avoided by gearing verification (and confirmation) to inductive rather than deductive logic.

Factual synonymity

Verification or confirmation has been used as a test of whether a statement has factual meaning. Within the class of supposedly synthetic statements, it has been used to discriminate the genuine from the pseudo-synthetic. In order to avoid some of the difficulties that have plagued the test, Salmon stresses the point that confirmation can also be used to specify exactly what the factual content of a statement is. If all possible observations confirm different statements to the same extent, then the statements have the same factual content. Consider the following four statements:

1. "How splendid it was that John F. Kennedy carried Illinois in 1960!"

2. "That John F. Kennedy carried Illinois in 1960 was simply deplorable!"

3. "John F. Kennedy carried Illinois in 1960 and the Absolute is lazy."

4. "John F. Kennedy carried Illinois in 1960."

The first two statements express strong and contrasting attitudes. The third statement combines a nonsense clause with the statement about the results of the election. Yet, to the extent that they are factual, the first three statements would be confirmed in the same way as the fourth. We could look them up in the World Almanac or some other compendium of facts. Furthermore, the first three statements would not only be confirmed in the same way as the fourth one, they would be confirmed to the same degree. Therefore, according to Salmon and Tooley, they are factually synonymous, that is, they have the same factual content.

The major difficulty that haunts this fresh approach to verifiability is that it invokes three of the most problematic areas in contemporary philosophy: the logic of confirmation, inductive logic, and questions of synonymity. Salmon acknowledges this, at least with regard to in-

duction. This means that as matters stand, Salmon has made some important distinctions that revitalize the issue of verification. Yet, because of the problematic areas of philosophy that he is forced to invoke, he is, in effect, issuing a promissory note. If these problems can be overcome, then we shall, at last, have an adequate version of the test of whether a statement has factual meaning. Furthermore, we shall be able to specify the factual meaning that it has.

We do not yet know whether the promissory note issued by Salmon and Tooley can be made good. One ominous note is that it is several years since Salmon's essay appeared and, apart from Tooley's contributions to this volume, it has not elicited comment or controversy. Tooley's discussion may provide the needed stimulus.

Tooley: verification is fruitful, but it does not challenge an appropriately conceptualized theology

It is especially interesting to compare Tooley's work with that of George Mavrodes, Alvin Plantinga, and James F. Ross (see pp. 446 ff.). Tooley resembles them in style and approach; all of them work with the logical emphases of contemporary analytic thought, rather than with an emphasis on ordinary language. They all rely heavily on formal notation. Yet, where the others scornfully dismiss the use of verification as a criterion of factual meaningfulness, Tooley endorses Salmon's version of it. Tooley's acceptance of an adequate criterion of verification, and his effort to revive other positivist doctrines, suggests that he is out to demonstrate the factual meaninglessness of theology. He demonstrates a refreshing independence of purpose and judgment by arguing, contrary to our expectations, that his positivist system allows for the factual meaningfulness of theological statements.

Tooley claims that the verification challenge of Ayer and Carnap (translatability) when properly understood, is the most potent of all. He tries to show that the force of this challenge depends, in part, on confused views of transcendence that are used by many theologians. Two aspects of Tooley's case will be helpful in showing how the translatability challenge bears on the question of the similarities and differences between religion and science.

The challenge of translatability to transcendence

Evans stresses the complex character of scientific testing, but he notes that the most abstract statements of scientific theory are, ultimately, related to observations. The relation involves a progression of theoretical levels of discourse. Ayer and Carnap capitalize on this point. Statements about electrons, genes, or other nonobservable entities can be related to observations. The relation may not be simple but it is there. Statements about electrons are tied to observations of specific types of patterns on photographic plates. Therefore, the statements about nonobservable electrons can be translated into statements about observable data. One reason for this is that electrons are inside the fabric of the physical world.

By contrast, the transcendent God of Judaism and Christianity is utterly beyond the world; this is a standard meaning of transcendence. In that case, statements about God cannot, in any way, be translated into statements about observations or other experiences that take place within the world. There is simply no possibility, no logical possibility, of tying any events that take place within the world to a God who is utterly beyond it. It cannot be done even by working with a series of logical or linguistic levels that are more complex than those used in a science like physics. Therefore, religion is utterly unlike science, and theological statements are factually meaningless.

The response

Tooley's response to the translatability challenge has two major elements: (1) The rejection of the common theological notion of "conceptual transcendence" and its replacement by "experiential transcendence;" and (2) The appeal to a special type of observation statements that can confirm theological statements, but only when these theological statements are understood in terms of experiential transcendence. He calls his basic observation statements "existentially quantified phenomenalistic statements."

Experiential transcendence.   Tooley thinks that the translatability challenge is tough, but he claims that it can be answered if theologians abandon a mistaken view of transcendence. Many sophisticated theologians talk of God in terms of "conceptual transcendence." As Tooley puts it, . . . "to say that God is conceptually transcendent is to say (roughly) that there is no truth about God that can be adequately expressed in any human language" (see p. 483). He claims that by using this notion of transcendence theologians are going out of their way to make their statements vulnerable to the translatability challenge. Given this view of transcendence, no statement about our experiences can be linked to statements about God, not even by the most complicated chain *of reasoning. This is exactly what the translatability challenge was de-signed to demonstrate. In Tooley's view, theologians who use the con-ceptual notion of transcendence are giving up without a fight. They define God in a way that makes it impossible for statements about Him to be factually meaningful.*

In an effort to correct the confusions involved in the notion of conceptual transcendence, Tooley proposes his view of experiential transcendence. This amounts to the following claims:

1. God is a reality that transcends or is distinct from the world. He is not a person or physical object in the world. He cannot be reduced to the status of a symbol for the experiences that men call religious, for example, the depth experiences discussed by Evans (see pp. 382 ff.). He is a distinct and independent reality.

2. We can make true statements about God, and one of them is that God is "a person who is incorporeal and who transcends the realm of human existence, and . . . is . . . able to act in the world so as to communicate with man and to realize his purposes" (see p. 483). This straightforward description of God as "a person" conflicts with the thought of Paul Tillich who insists that God cannot be a being alongside other beings.[5] To be individuated in this way is, for Tillich, the mark of limited beings, but the notion of limitation is incompatible with the meaning of God. On the other hand, neoorthodox theologians would re-ject Tooley's view because they insist that we limited and sinful beings cannot formulate such straightforward statements about the infinite and mysterious reality of God. This is why Tillich and the neoorthodox theologians write in terms that Tooley characterizes as conceptual tran-scendence. Tooley claims that they are confused and that his own ap-proach allows for the uniqueness of God, but formulates it in a way that makes theological statements factually meaningful.

Existentially quantified phenomenalistic statements. Tooley pro-poses a daring and distinctive view of the observation statements that should be used to confirm statements of fact. Although his presentation of these statements, which he calls, "existentially quantified phenomenalis-tic statements," presupposes familiarity with both contemporary logic and epistemology, his goals can be stated in nontechnical form. It is, however, important to realize that his specific formulations cannot be criticized except by mastering the technical details of his discussion.

Tooley's observation statements are set up in a way that com-

[5] Paul Tillich, *Systematic Theology*, vol. I, pp. 235f.

pliments his view of the experiential transcendence of God. God is experientially transcendent, because he is a center of consciousness and power who does not have a body. What makes Tooley's observation statements distinctive is that they are not necessarily tied to experiencers with bodies. This eliminates the "bodily component" from both sides of the equation.

Tooley's thesis is radical but very restricted. He provides the following examples of statements of sense experience for which he claims it is not necessary to assume that the experiencers have bodies: "Someone is experiencing a rectangular brown appearance," "There is a sharp painful sensation," and "Some person is enjoying a tingling sensation" (see p. 518). Tooley does not claim that these reports cannot or ought not to be tied to bodies; he claims only that a proper analysis of quantification and phenomenalism shows that they are not necessarily linked to experiencers with bodies. Furthermore, it should be obvious that he thinks that they are legitimate examples of observation statements and that the burden of proof is on the philosophers who would deny this.

The use of these observation statements, according to Tooley, cuts the ground out from under the translatability challenge. This challenge depends on the view that factually meaningful statements must, ultimately, be expressible in terms of statements "about the natural world or about the experiences of human or other embodied beings" (see p. 519). His existentially quantified phenomenalistic statements are designed to show that this requirement is too restrictive. Meaningful observation statements can be made independently of bodies. They must, of course, be properly quantified and set in the framework of a phenomenalistic epistemology. Statements about God, conceived of as a person without a body, could then be expressed in terms of such statements.

Tooley's basic observation statements are not examples of mystical experiences or of any other distinctive form of religious experience. He appeals to ordinary experiences, such as seeing a brown rectangle or feeling sharp pain. This suggests that Tooley is tying the logic of religion as closely as possible to the logic by which we deal with normal experiences in everyday life. Yet his proposal to dissociate reports of sensory experiences from persons with bodies seems to bring us to the brink of science fiction or to the sort of Cartesian body-mind dualism that many contemporary philosophers disdain and ridicule.

Tooley's program is somewhat reminiscent of John Hick's. This is not surprising. Both of them try to meet the challenge of positivism on its own terms. Hick did so by appealing to observation statements that could be made with resurrection bodies in the afterlife. He insisted that he was not trying to demonstrate the truth of any specific theological statements, nor did he claim that his view of the afterlife was plausible. He merely claimed that his observation statements were logically possible, because no contradiction is involved in his description of the Celestial City. Therefore, theological statements, which are confirmed by these observation statements, are factually meaningful. Tooley's claims have the same limited character. He, too, does not try to demonstrate the truth of any specific theological statements. He claims only to show that statements about God—understood in terms of experiential transcendence—are factually meaningful. He also follows Hick's pattern in another respect. Tooley does not argue for the plausibility of his view that observation statements can be attributed to disembodied experiencers. He claims that after many centuries of work in the field of epistemology, philosophers have failed to come up with a plausible account of perception that precludes his view of observation statements. There is a vast body of contemporary literature devoted to the body-mind problem.[6] Despite this, Tooley thinks that the burden of proof is on philosophers who deny the possibility of existentially quantified phenomenalistic statements.

Many readers will respond by dismissing Tooley's thesis as outrageous and will insist that the burden of proof is on him. An example of the outraged dismissal of a philosophical thesis was provided by Dr. Johnson. Confronted with Bishop Berkeley's thesis that material objects do not exist, he kicked a stone and said, "That for Bishop Berkeley!" This "refutation" could only impress people who had no understanding of Locke's thesis about material objects and of Berkeley's reply to it. If Tooley's view is to be discredited it will have to be done by philosophical analysis of his essay and not by outraged appeals to its implausibility.

In any case, Tooley's contribution calls our attention to still another difficulty that plagued the positivists' program. This book focuses on many problems involved with verification, but the problems were

---

[6] The single most important discussion of the body-mind problem is still Gilbert Ryle's The Concept of Mind (New York: Barnes and Noble, 1949). For comprehensive introductions to the high points of recent discussions see Jerome A. Shaffer, Philosophy of Mind (Englewood Cliffs, N.J.: Prentice-Hall, 1968), Alan R. White, The Philosophy of Mind (New York: Random House, 1967), and Norman Malcolm, The Problems of Mind (New York: Harper and Row, 1971).

treated as though there were no difficulties connected with observation statements. This is not the case, and Tooley's presentation of the various options shows how problematic an issue it is. At the level of ordinary speech we may not have trouble with observation statements like, "This page is white." Yet as soon as we move to the second order level of the theory of perception or of knowledge, we run into problems.

Tooley's updated version of positivism is imaginative and it is executed with considerable technical skill. His thesis is that theological statements are factually meaningful because: (1) they can be understood in terms of experiential transcendence, and (2) they stand in confirmation relationships to, and hence are expressible in terms of, "existentially quantified phenomenalistic statements."

Tooley seems to provide theologians with considerable conceptual support, but they may prove reluctant to accept it. The reluctance might reflect disagreement with his controversial appeal to sensory experiences that are not necessarily linked to embodied experiencers. Yet other theologians may be far more upset by the fact that Tooley's view of meaning reverts to the positivists' set of options: (1) analytic, (2) synthetic, and (3) cognitively meaningless. To be sure, Tooley's difference from the positivists is striking. As far as they were concerned theological statements fall under the third option, whereas he regards them as factually meaningful and therefore as falling under option two. Yet many theologians will bristle at Tooley's return to the kind of positivistic restrictiveness that Wittgenstein's theory of meaning as use was designed to counteract. We have seen that a major form of theological protest was to insist that theological statements ought not to be forced into molds designed for other enterprises (pp. 96, 99, 118, 125 f.).

To this Tooley could doubtless reply, "But just what do these distinctive theological meanings amount to?" This is the question that Ayer directed to Copleston (see pp. 104 f.). It is one of the major themes of this book. One of the gains of the "revolution" in philosophy inaugurated by the positivists was to make theologians aware of the need to answer this question; as we have seen, many of them have tried (p. 46, note 35).

A final observation on Tooley's essay. He tries to revive a number of discredited positivist positions. If he were to succeed, he would add still another irony to the story of positivism. This movement tried to get philosophy to progress like science by burying major metaphysical options—like idealism and Thomism—once and for all. It did not succeed. Instead, many of the positivist doctrines were buried. This irony has already been noted (see pp. 96 f.). If Tooley, in following Salmon's lead, succeeds in resurrecting verification and other positivist doctrines, he will provide another illustration of the point that "Philosophical positions never die, they just fade out of focus." This would be extremely ironical because, in their effort to achieve philosophical progress, the positivists thought they had demonstrated that philosophical positions don't merely fade, they are killed by philosophical analysis.

Alvin Plantinga/**Verificationism**

In this chapter I shall examine a miscellany of atheological arguments, beginning with the claim that the *unverifiability* of religious assertions renders them in some way suspect.

I

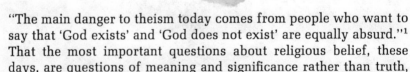

"The main danger to theism today comes from people who want to say that 'God exists' and 'God does not exist' are equally absurd."[1] That the most important questions about religious belief, these days, are questions of meaning and significance rather than truth,

From *God and Other Minds: A Study of the Rational Justification of Belief in God* by Alvin Plantinga (Ithaca: Cornell University Press, 1967), pp. 156–168.
Copyright © 1967 by Cornell University. Reprinted by permission of Cornell University Press and the author.
[1] J. J. C. Smart, "The Existence of God," in *New Essays in Philosophical Theology*, ed. A. Flew and A. MacIntyre (London, 1955).

is repeated often enough.[2] It seems to be widely believed that certain developments in twentieth-century philosophy (particularly twentieth-century "linguistic" philosophy) have shown that there is something semantically improper about typical religious utterances. Certainly this suspicion is not altogether misplaced; the writings of many theologians are of a granitic opacity designed, it may seem, more to conceal than to reveal their author's thought. And (as the Christian tradition has insisted from the beginning) some of the central concepts and doctrines of Christian theism as found in the Bible and the creeds are difficult to grasp. This much is undeniable. But just how is contemporary philosophy relevant here? How, exactly, have contemporary "linguistic" philosophers raised this ancient problem in a new and acute form?

Most of the discussion has concerned alleged difficulties in *verifying* or *falsifying* typical religious and theological utterances. And here a focal point of discussion has been Antony Flew's "Theology and Falsification."[3] Let us look carefully at what Flew says.

Flew begins the central part of his argument by stating the law of double negation:

> Now to assert that such and such is the case is necessarily equivalent to denying that such and such is not the case.[4] Suppose then we are in doubt as to what someone who gives vent to an utterance is asserting, or suppose that, more radically, we are skeptical as to whether he is really asserting anything at all, one way of trying to understand (or perhaps it will be to expose) his utterance is to attempt to find what he would regard as counting against, or as being incompatible with, its truth.[5]

So far, quite unexceptionable. It is doubtless true (if less than exciting) that one way to understand an assertion is to see what is incompatible with it. But Flew goes on to give for this

---

[2] See for example, Ronald Hepburn, *Christianity and Paradox* (London, 1958), pp. 6, 15; R. B. Braithwaite, *An Empiricist's View of the Nature of Religious Belief* (Cambridge, 1955); John Wilson, *Language and Christian Belief* (London, 1958), Chapter I; W. Blackstone, *The Problem of Religious Knowledge* (Englewood Cliffs, 1953), Introduction. Most of the authors in *New Essays in Philosophical Theology* seem to share this opinion.

[3] *New Essays in Philosophical Theology*, p. 96. [This essay is reprinted in this volume, p. 257.]

[4] Here Flew helpfully adds (in a footnote): "For those who prefer symbolism: $p \equiv \sim \sim p$." [p. 258.]

[5] *Loc. cit.*

truism an *argument* the first premise of which is again the law of double negation:

> For if the utterance is indeed an assertion, it will necessarily be equivalent to a denial of the negation of that assertion. And anything which would count against the assertion, or which would induce the speaker to withdraw it and to admit that it had been mistaken, must be part of (or the whole of) the meaning of the negation of that assertion.[6]

If the first premise of the argument is unexceptionable, the second is not nearly so innocent. Although Flew does not explain "count against," what he says suggests that anything *incompatible with* an assertion counts against it. Again, Flew does not explain what it is for something to be *part of the meaning of* an assertion. But presumably anything that is part of the meaning of an assertion is contained in or *entailed* by that assertion. If so, however, certain curious consequences ensue. Consider, for example, the assertion

(A) Feike Vander Horst is in Zeeland.

Now many things are incompatible with (and hence count against) A—for example,

(B) Feike Vander Horst is in Australia

and

(C) Feike Vander Horst is in Paterson, New Jersey.

(B) and (C), then, must be part of the meaning of the denial of (A); hence on this showing, *Feike Vander Horst is not in Zeeland* entails that Feike is both in Australia and in Paterson, New Jersey. But then the denial of (A) is logically inconsistent in that it entails the (inconsistent) conjunction of (B) with (C)[7] (A), therefore, is necessarily true; it is logically impossible that Feike be anywhere but in Zeeland. But of course by the very same sort of reasoning it will follow that (A) is logically inconsistent; both

(D) Feike Vander Horst is in the northern quarter of Zeeland

and

(E) Feike Vander Horst is in the southern quarter of Zeeland

[6] *Ibid.* [p. 259.]

[7] The purist who objects that (B) *and* (C) is not, in fact, logically inconsistent may be mollified if we conjoin the denials of (C) and (B) to (B) and (C) respectively.

are incompatible with (hence count against) the denial of (A);
therefore they are part of the meaning of (and hence entailed by)
the denial of (A)'s denial—that is, by (A); hence (A) is inconsistent
as well as necessary. Flew's second premise, therefore, seems to
entail a contradiction.

This is indeed a beguiling spectacle; Flew evidently means
to prove a truistic conclusion by deducing it from a self-contradictory premise. The argument is certainly valid (if a contradiction
entails just any proposition) but things do not auger well for its
soundness. Perhaps Flew is not being entirely serious. Or perhaps
I have misunderstood his argument. In any event, the theist will
be happy to accept its conclusion, as well as the consequence that

> ... if there is nothing which a putative assertion denies then there
> is nothing which it asserts either: and so it is not really an asser-
> tion.[8]

A theist who claimed that some of his assertions denied nothing
at all—not even their own negations—would be backward and
benighted indeed. Even Heidegger, the verificationist's favorite
whipping-boy, would no doubt concede that "the not negates itself" is inconsistent with its contradictory.

Having exegeted his text, Flew proceeds to the application:

> Now it often seems to people who are not religious as if there
> was no conceivable event or series of events the occurrence of
> which would be admitted by sophisticated religious people to be
> a sufficient reason for conceding 'There wasn't a God after all'
> or 'God does not really love us then'. . . . Just what would have to
> happen not merely (morally and wrongly) to tempt us but also
> (logically and rightly) to entitle us to say 'God does not love us'
> or even 'God does not exist'? I therefore put to the succeeding
> symposiasts the simple central questions, 'What would have to
> occur or to have occurred to constitute for you a disproof of the
> love of, or of the existence of, God?'[9]

Numberless hosts of writers (including some theologians)
have repeated this challenge and found in it a real difficulty for the
theist.[10] And several writers, both believers and unbelievers, have
suggested that religious beliefs be *reinterpreted* in such a way that

[8] Flew, *op. cit.*, p. 98. [p. 259.]

[9] *Ibid.* [p. 259.]

[10] E.g., R. Hepburn, *op. cit.*, p. 11; W. Blackstone, *op. cit.*, p. 53; R. B. Braithwaite, *op. cit.*, p. 6; John Wilson, *op. cit.*, pp. 7–8; and Duff-Forbes, in "Theology and Falsification Again," *Australasian Journal of Philosophy*, XXXIX
(1961), 143.

they turn out to be verifiable. A. C. MacIntyre in *Metaphysical Beliefs* suggests a way of understanding religious beliefs which, he thinks, shows that one can accept the beliefs and still hold to the view that all significant statements are verifiable.[11] In *An Empiricist's View of the Nature of Religious Belief* R. B. Braithwaite offers a reinterpretation of Christian beliefs according to which they are consistent with the verificationist thesis. Sometimes these reinterpretations assume truly heroic proportions, as, for example, when David Cox helpfully suggests that Christians resolve henceforth to use the statement "God exists" to mean "some men and women have had, and all may have, experiences called 'meeting God.' "[12] He also suggests that when we say "God created the world from nothing" what we should mean is "everything we call 'material' can be used in such a way that it contributes to the well-being of men." (I might remark here that certain Christian theologians—Bultmann and some of his followers in particular—seem to me to be doing something quite as outrageous.)

But the first thing to note is that the legitimacy of this challenge does not follow from what was previously established. No doubt the assertion that there is a God, if it is meaningful, must deny many other assertions and exclude many states of affairs; but it does not follow that it must exclude some conceivable *happening* or *event* or series of events—unless, indeed, we allow such Pickwickian events as God's going out of existence or his revealing to us that he no longer loves us. (Of course if "event" is to include these, then the challenge is easily answered.) Nonetheless the theist can perhaps meet the challenge head on. My discovering a contradiction in the proposition *God exists* would constitute a disproof of it; and if after death I were to meet Father Abraham, St. Paul, and St. John (I think I could recognize them), who united in declaring they had been duped, perhaps I should have sufficient reason for conceding that God does not love us after all.

But clearly enough this is not at all the sort of event or happening Flew has in mind. What he means is that meaningful assertions must be falsifiable by some *empirical* state of affairs, or some proposition with *empirical content*. What is empirical content and under what conditions does a proposition have it? Duff-Forbes takes Flew to be chiding the religious for trying to make assertions

---

[11] London, 1957.
[12] "The Significance of Christianity," *Mind*, LIX (1950), 47.

that no *observation statements* count against.[13] It appears, then, that according to Flew a meaningful (contingent) proposition must be falsifiable by observation statements; there must be some finite and consistent set of observation statements that entails its denial. If so, Flew is embracing a version of the famous *verifiability criterion of meaning*.

Oddly enough, a number of theologians have apparently joined forces with Flew. Paul van Buren, for example, declares that

> The empiricist in us finds the heart of the difficulty not in what is said about God but in the very talking about God at all. We do not know "what" (*sic*) God is and we cannot understand how the word "God" is being used.
>
> The problem of the Gospel in a secular age is a problem of its apparently meaningless language, and linguistic analysts will give us help in clarifying it.[14]

What sort of help will they give us?

> The heart of the method of linguistic analysis lies in the use of the verification principle—that the meaning of a word is its use in its context. The meaning of a statement is to be found in, and is identical with, the function of that statement. If a statement has a function, so that it may in principle be verified or falsified, the statement is meaningful, and unless or until a theological statement can be submitted in some way to verification, it cannot be said to have a meaning in our language game.[15]

One might expect a theologian to have about as much sympathy for verificationism as a civil rights worker for the Ku Klux Klan; yet van Buren is by no means the only theologian who believes that "linguistic analysis" has shown that we must accept the verifiability criterion. But in fact the lot of the verificationist has been far from enviable. The many attempts to state the verifiability criterion have met a common fate; each has been so restrictive as to exclude statements the verificationists themselves took to be meaningful, or so liberal as to exclude no statements at all.

[13] *Op. cit.*, p. 143. An observation statement is "any sentence which—correctly or incorrectly—asserts of one or more specifically named objects that they have, or that they lack, some specified observable characteristic" (cf. Carl Hempel, "Problems and Changes in the Empiricist Criterion of Meaning" in Leonard Linsky, ed., *Semantics and the Philosophy of Language* [Urbana, 1952], p. 165).

[14] *The Secular Meaning of the Gospel* (New York, 1963), p. 84.

[15] *Ibid.*, pp. 104–105.

Here I cannot trace the detailed history of these attempts,[16] but Flew, his numerous epigoni, and their theological allies, seem to have neglected this study altogether. The version Flew apparently accepts was recognized very early to be unsatisfactory. As Hempel remarks in a slightly different connection, one must suppose that if a given statement is meaningful, so is its denial. Flew's criterion does not meet this condition: for (as Hempel remarks) although a universal statement like *All crows are black* passes the test, its existential denial does not. *There is at least one pink unicorn* is consistent with any finite and consistent set of observation statements. (Apparently it is Flew rather than the theologian who is holding that some propositions have no denials.) So we must add —as the second clause of a recursive definition—that if a statement is meaningful, so is its denial. But the result is still far too restrictive; for now, as Hempel points out, statements of mixed quantification (*For every substance there is a solvent, every tree is about the same size as some other tree*) turn out to be meaningless.

We could repair this difficulty, perhaps, by adding further that the logical consequences of a meaningful statement are meaningful; but then our criterion no longer rules anything out. For consider such a "statement" as *The not regularly nothings itself* and call it *N*. Its conjunction with any falsifiable statement *S* will be meaningful (in that any set of observation statements inconsistent with *S* will be inconsistent with *S and N*); since it will entail *N*, the latter too is meaningful.

Upon perceiving the futility of some earlier versions (including the one Flew appears to adopt) A. J. Ayer restated the verifiability criterion as follows:

> A statement *p* is meaningful if and only if there is a statement *q* such that the conjunction of *p* with *q* entails an observation statement not entailed by *q* alone.[17]

It was quickly pointed out, however, that this confers meaning upon every statement: where *N* is *The not nothings itself* and *S* is any observation statement, *N* and *if N then S* entails *S*; since *if N then S* alone does not, *N* is meaningful.

In the introduction to the second edition of *Language, Truth and Logic* Ayer hoped to repair this difficulty as follows:

---

[16] See the Hempel article mentioned above, n. 13.

[17] *Language, Truth and Logic*, 2nd ed. (New York, 1946), p. 39.

I propose to say that a statement is directly verifiable if it is either itself an observation-statement, or is such that in conjunction with one or more observation-statements it entails at least one observation-statement which is not deducible from these other premises alone; and I propose to say that a statement is indirectly verifiable if it satisfies the following conditions: first, that in conjunction with certain other premises it entails one or more directly verifiable statements which are not deducible from these other premises alone; and secondly, that these other premises do not include any statement that is not either analytic, or directly verifiable, or capable of being independently established as indirectly verifiable.[18]

But in a review of the revised edition of *Language, Truth and Logic* Alonzo Church pointed out that this revision is no improvement:

> Let O_1, and O_2, and O_3 be three 'observation-statements' . . . such that no one of the three alone entails any of the others. Then using these we may show of any statement S whatever that either it or its negation is verifiable, as follows: Let $\sim O_1$ and $\sim S$ be the negations of O_1 and of S respectively. Then (under Ayer's definition) $(\sim O_1 \cdot O_2) \vee (O_3 \cdot \sim S)$ is directly verifiable, because with O_1 it entails O_3. Moreover S and $(\sim O_1 \cdot O_2) \vee (O_3 \cdot \sim S)$ together entail O_3. Therefore (under Ayer's definition) S is indirectly verifiable—unless it happens that $(\sim O_1 \cdot O_2) \vee (O_3 \cdot \sim S)$ alone entails O_2, in which case $\sim S$ and O_3 together entail O_2, so that $\sim S$ is directly verifiable.[19]

Here the matter rested until 1961, when Professor Peter Nidditch issued a rebuttal of Church's objection:

> Let p, q, and r, be any three specific observation-statements such that no one of them alone entails any of the others, and let s be *any statement whatever.* Church's thesis is that, on Ayer's definition, s, or its negation $\sim s$, is always verifiable. If this is correct, then it obviously completely destroys the point and utility of the Verifiability Principle.
>
> (a) To begin with, Church points out that
>
> p and $(\sim p \cdot q) \vee (r \cdot \sim s)$ jointly entail r.   (A)
>
> Since r is not entailed by p alone, it results from the second clause of Ayer's definition of directly verifiable statements that
>
> $(\sim p \cdot q) \vee (r \cdot \sim s)$ is directly verifiable   (B)

I certainly grant the correctness of (A) and (B).

(b) The next stage of the argument has two parts.

(bi) According to Church, if $(\sim p \cdot q) \vee (r \cdot \sim s)$ does not alone entail q, then

$$s \text{ and } (\sim p \cdot q) \vee (r \cdot \sim s) \text{ jointly entail } q, \qquad (C)$$

and from this, together with Ayer's definition, he concludes that

s is indirectly verifiable. (D)

This allegation is easily disposed of. Looking at Ayer's two conditions for indirectly verifiability, we can see that, in view of (B) and (C), s satisfies the first condition, while, *unless s is analytic or verifiable,* it cannot satisfy the second condition. (I assume that Ayer's "include" means "include *intra se*" and not "include *inter se*". If it does mean the latter, Church's criticism is very easily sidestepped by amending the original to mean "include *intra se*".)[20]

Now presumably a group of premises contains a proposition *p inter se* if p is one of the group; it contains *p intra se* if p is one of the group or a component of one of the group as s is a component of $(\sim p \cdot q) \vee (r \cdot \sim s)$. But this suggestion fares no better than its forebears. Where N is *the not nothings itself* and O_1 and O_2 are any observation statements logically independent of each other and of N, N and O_1 is directly verifiable, since in conjunction with O_2 it entails O_1. But then N is indirectly verifiable, for together with O_1 it entails the directly verifiable N *and* O_1. Here the "other premises" mentioned in Ayer's definition obviously include, *inter se,* or *intra se,* or in any other way, only O_1.

It was suggested to me[21] that the definition of direct verifiability be revised as follows:

p is directly verifiable if p is an observation statement or there is an observation statement q such that (1) p *and* q entails an observation statement r that neither p nor q alone entails, and (2) the argument from p *and* q to r is minimal in the sense that if any conjunct of p or q is deleted, the resulting argument is invalid.

This avoids the preceding difficulty (as well as some difficulties that arise if the second clause is not added) but is still vulnerable: $N \cdot (\sim O_1 \vee \sim N \vee O_2)$ will be directly verifiable, for conjoined with O_1 it entails O_2 in such a way that conditions (1) and (2) of the definition are met. And again N will be indirectly verifiable, for conjoined with O_2 it entails $N \cdot (\sim O_1 \vee \sim N \vee O_2)$.

[20] *Mind* (1961), pp. 88–89.
[21] By Messrs. Michael Slote, Michael Stocker, and Robert Shope.

The fact is that no one has succeeded in stating a version of the verifiability criterion that is even remotely plausible; and by now the project is beginning to look unhopeful.[22]

But suppose the criterion could be stated in a way which satisfied the verificationist. (We could, after all, say simply that the statements of science and "common sense" are meaningful and those of transcendental metaphysics and theology meaningless.) Why should anyone accept it? Why should the theist not retort as follows: "Your criterion is obviously mistaken; for many theological statements are not empirically verifiable; but theological statements are meaningful; hence it is false that all and only verifiable statements are meaningful"? What could the verificationist reply? What sort of argument could he bring forward to show the theologian that he ought to accept the verifiability criterion and stop proclaiming these meaningless theological pseudo-statements? About all he could say here would be that his criterion does fit scientific and commonsense statements and does not fit theological statements. And to this the theologian could agree with equanimity; there are, no doubt, many properties which distinguish scientific and commonsense statements from theological statements. But of course that does not suffice to show that theological statements are meaningless or logically out of order or anything of the sort.

In the light of this and of the fact that it seems impossible to state the verifiability criterion the question becomes acute: how *are* we to understand Flew's challenge? What exactly is he requiring of theological statements? Is he chiding the theist for ignoring some version of the verifiability criterion? If so, which version? Until these questions are answered it is impossible to determine whether his challenge is legitimate or even what the challenge *is*. If the notion of verifiability cannot so much as be explained, if we cannot so much as say what it is for a statement to be empirically verifiable, then we scarcely need worry about whether religious statements are or are not verifiable. How could we possibly tell? As a piece of natural atheology, verificationism is entirely unsuccessful.[23]

---

[22] See James Cornman, "Indirectly Verifiable: Everything or Nothing," *Philosophical Studies*, 18(1967), 49–56.

[23] And this makes the dizzy gyrations of those theologians who accept it more puzzling than ever; perhaps they would do well to study it before rushing to embrace it.

Wesley C. Salmon/**Verifiability and Logic**

Herbert Feigl has long been one of the ablest and most devoted champions of logical empiricism. On this occasion I should like to re-examine a complex of issues which lie at the heart of this doctrine. They center around the verifiability criterion of cognitive meaning.

Until 1949 it could have been said that the verifiability criterion was one of the cornerstones of logical empiricism. The criterion had been hotly debated and had undergone numerous reformulations. By that time it was quite generally recognized that the criterion had to be formulated in terms of verifiability in principle rather than actual verification and that verifiability itself had to be understood as the possibility of partial verification instead of

From "Verifiability and Logic" by Wesley C. Salmon in *Mind, Matter and Method*, ed. P. K. Feyerabend and G. Maxwell (Minneapolis: University of Minnesota Press, 1966), pp. 354–376. Copyright © 1966 University of Minnesota. Reprinted by permission of University of Minnesota Press and the author.

the possibility of complete and conclusive verification. Nevertheless, the notion that cognitive meaningfulness was to be explicated in terms of empirical verifiability remained a fundamental principle. The history of the criterion up to that time has been well recounted by Hempel.[1]

In 1949 an apparent disaster struck in the form of Church's critique[2] of Ayer's second formulation.[3] Shortly thereafter Hempel expressed grave doubts about the possibility of giving any satisfactory formulation of the verifiability criterion.[4] The view that the verifiability criterion faces insuperable difficulties has subsequently spread. In the past fifteen years the number of its defenders and the amount of attention it has received have dwindled considerably. Feigl has remained an exception to this general trend.[5] Writing in 1956[6] he referred to the "serious doubts" of Hempel and others "as to the adequacy of all [formulations] thus far suggested, or even as to any conceivable formulations of the meaning criterion." He goes on to say, "I admit that an all-around satisfactory and fully precise explication is difficult, but I am confident that confirmability-in-principle (for statements) or logical connectibility with the terms of a suitably chosen observation basis (for concepts) is the explicandum of at least a *necessary*

[1] Carl G. Hempel, "Problems and Changes in the Empiricist Criterion of Meaning," in *Semantics and the Philosophy of Language,* ed. Leonard Linsky (Urbana, Ill.: University of Illinois Press, 1952), pp. 163–185. Originally published in *Revue Internationale de Philosophie* 11 (1950).

[2] Alonzo Church, "Review of Ayer's *Language, Truth and Logic,*" *Journal of Symbolic Logic* 14 (1949): 52–53.

[3] Alfred Jules Ayer, *Language, Truth and Logic,* 2d ed. (New York: Dover, 1946).

[4] Carl G. Hempel, "The Concept of Cognitive Significance: A Reconsideration," *Contributions to the Analysis and Synthesis of Knowledge,* Proceedings of the American Academy of Arts and Sciences 80 (July 1951): 61–77.

[5] Herbert Feigl, "De Principiis Non Disputandum . . . ?" in *Philosophical Analysis,* ed. Max Black (Ithaca, N. Y.: Cornell University Press, 1950; Englewood Cliffs, N. J.: Prentice-Hall, 1963), pp. 113–147; "Logical Empiricism," in *Readings in Philosophical Analysis,* ed. Herbert Feigl and Wilfrid Sellars (New York: Appleton-Century-Crofts, 1949), pp. 3–26; "Philosophical Tangents of Science," in *Current Issues in the Philosophy of Science,* ed. Herbert Feigl and Grover Maxwell (New York: Holt, Rinehart and Winston, 1961), pp. 1–17; "Some Major Issues and Developments in the Philosophy of Science of Logical Empiricism," in *Minnesota Studies in the Philosophy of Science,* vol. 1, ed. Herbert Feigl and Michael Scriven (Minneapolis: University of Minnesota Press, 1956), pp. 3–37.

[6] Feigl, "Some Major Issues and Developments in the Philosophy of Science of Logical Empiricism."

condition for factual meaningfulness. Understood in this way, the meaning criterion still provides a sharp delimitation between sense and nonsense."[7]

The present essay will not offer any direct defense of the verifiability criterion. Instead it will attempt to diagnose and assess some of the major difficulties which have stood in the way of an adequate formulation. It is my view that certain difficulties, though familiar, are not sufficiently understood, and that other difficulties, though not much discussed, are of fundamental importance. My own attitude toward the verifiability criterion is, like Feigl's, optimistic. I hope that the present essay will clarify certain basic issues, thereby facilitating judgment as to whether such optimism is well grounded.

I

In order to achieve some degree of terminological clarity I shall construe the verifiability criterion to consist of the following series of explications:

1. A sentence (or statement) has factual meaning if and only if it is empirically verifiable (or confirmable).

2. A sentence (or statement) has formal meaning if and only if it is either analytic or self-contradictory.

3. A sentence (or statement) has cognitive (or literal) meaning if and only if it has either formal meaning or factual meaning.

4. A sentence (or statement) is either true or false if and only if it has cognitive (or literal) meaning.

These explications identify cognitive meaningfulness with the possibility of being either true or false, and they reduce these properties to empirical verifiability and analyticity (or self-contradiction). There remain, however, the tasks of explicating empirical verifiability and analyticity. Ayer undertook to provide an explication of empirical verifiability. A statement is empirically verifiable if and only if it is either directly or indirectly verifiable, where these latter concepts are explained as follows:

> I propose to say that a statement is directly verifiable if it is either itself an observation-statement, or is such that in conjunction with one or more observation-statements it entails at least one observation-statement which is not deducible from these other prem-

[7] Ibid., p. 15.

ises alone; and I propose to say that a statement is indirectly
verifiable if it satisfies the following conditions: first, that in conjunction with certain other premises it entails one or more directly verifiable statements which are not deducible from these
other premises alone; and secondly, that these other premises do
not include any statement that is not either analytic, or directly
verifiable, or capable of being independently established as indirectly verifiable.[8]

This explication is intended as an account of what Ayer calls
"weak" verifiability, that is, confirmability or verifiability to some
degree. It is meant to explain what is involved in the possibility
of having empirical or scientific evidence for or against a statement, recognizing that such evidence is often partial and inconclusive.

The inadequacy of this explication of empirical verifiability
was shown by Church as follows:

Let O_1, and O_2, and O_3 be three 'observation-statements' . . .
such that no one of the three alone entails any of the others.
Then using these we may show of any statement S whatever that
either it or its negation is verifiable, as follows: Let $\sim O_1$ and $\sim S$
be the negations of O_1 and of S respectively. Then (under Ayer's
definition) $(\sim O_1 \cdot O_2) \vee (O_3 \cdot \sim S)$ is directly verifiable, because
with O_1 it entails O_3. Moreover S and $(O_1 \cdot O_2) \vee (O_3 \cdot \sim S)$ together entail O_3. Therefore (under Ayer's definition) S is indirectly
verifiable—unless it happens that $(\sim O_1 \cdot O_2) \vee (O_3 \cdot \sim S)$ alone
entails O_2, in which case $\sim S$ and O_3 together entail O_2, so that $\sim S$
is directly verifiable.[9]

It is evident that Church's criticism has no bearing upon the verifiability criterion (see explications 1–4 above); it shows only that
Ayer's explication of empirical verifiability is faulty. Church did
not claim to have proved more.

Church's criticism also raises problems for the explication
of empirical verification. With respect to Ayer's explication of
empirical verifiability there seems only one plausible way of construing empirical verification. A statement is empirically verifiable
according to Ayer's definition if, in conjunction with certain verifiable premises, it has a verifiable consequence. Presumably, then,
that statement is verified to some degree if the verifiable premises
and conclusion have been verified to some degree. With this understanding of empirical verification, Church's criticism translates

[8] Ayer, p. 13.
[9] Church, pp. 52–53.

immediately into a recipe for verifying any hypothesis whatever by a trivial and obviously irrelevant procedure. For example, to verify the hypothesis

H: $E = mc^2$

formulate the auxiliary hypothesis

H': Either there is no ink bottle on my desk or I am sitting in a chair, or my copy of Language, Truth and Logic has a red cover and it is not the case that $E = mc^2$.

This hypothesis H' in conjunction with

O_1: There is an ink bottle on my desk,

which I find by observation to be true, entails

O_3: My copy of Language, Truth and Logic has a red cover.

I observe that my copy of Language, Truth and Logic does have a red cover, so H' is verified. From H' and H we can deduce

O_2: I am sitting in a chair.

I observe that I am sitting in a chair; hence, H is verified. Anyone who objects to my use of physical-object statements as observation statements may substitute three logically independent protocol statements for them.

Ayer's account of empirical verifiability and the related account of empirical verification are in many ways fairly typical of what is often said about scientific verification (or confirmation) and scientific verifiability (or confirmability). These matters fall within what may broadly be called inductive logic. Church's criticism raises fundamental difficulties concerning these basic concepts. In this respect it is analogous to Hempel's paradox of confirmation and Goodman's grue-bleen paradox. Any satisfactory theory of scientific verification (or confirmation) must avoid such paradoxical consequences.

It is of greatest importance to distinguish between the problem of explicating cognitive meaningfulness and the problem of explicating empirical verifiability. The problem of the meaning criterion is the problem of the propriety or desirability of explicating cognitive meaningfulness in terms of empirical verifiability. Leaving this problem entirely aside, there remains the problem of explicating empirical verifiability. This latter problem is surely an extremely important and fundamental one whether or not a verifiability criterion of meaning is to be adopted. This is the problem Church's criticism bears upon. It did not show Ayer's explication of cognitive meaningfulness to be inadequate; it showed that Ayer did not have an adequate conception of empirical confirmation. Considering the extreme difficulty of confirmation theory and the fact that there is no theory of confirmation which is generally accepted as satisfactory, this result is not too surprising.

The only way in which Church's criticism can be taken as a critique of the verifiability criterion is by construing it as an indication that the concept of empirical verifiability is inexplicable in principle. This seems like a harsh conclusion to draw from Ayer's failure to provide a satisfactory explication of empirical verifiability. It is my personal suspicion that many philosophers who have had little hesitation in dismissing the possibility of formulating an unobjectionable explication of cognitive meaningfulness in terms of empirical verifiability would be far more hesitant to conclude that the concepts of scientific confirmation and confirmability are inexplicable in principle.

It might be said that the problem of the verifiability criterion cannot be dealt with until the concept of empirical verifiability has been satisfactorily explicated. This, I think, would be a mistake. Even if we have no precise explicatum of the concept of empirical verifiability, it seems to me that we have a sufficiently clear notion of the explicandum to be able sensibly to consider the merits of explicating cognitive meaningfulness in terms of empirical verifiability. Feigl,[10] Reichenbach,[11] and many others have made amply clear the import of a *vindication*[12] of the verifiability criterion, whatever explication of empirical verifiability is ultimately accepted. It is not my purpose to add further arguments for the verifiability criterion. Instead I propose to examine certain consequences of accepting the verifiability criterion, and in the course of so doing I shall try to show how some alleged difficulties can be avoided.

II

If we ask what went wrong with Ayer's account of empirical verifiability, there is an obvious and in some respects easy answer. Ayer did not sufficiently restrict the kinds of statements which

[10] Feigl, "De Principiis Non Disputandum . . . ?", "Logical Empiricism", "Some Major Issues and Developments in the Philosophy of Science of Logical Empiricism."

[11] Hans Reichenbach, *Experience and Prediction* (Chicago: University of Chicago Press, 1938). See Chapter 1.

[12] Feigl, "De Principiis Non Disputandum . . . ?".

are directly and indirectly verifiable. In particular, he neglected to stipulate that to be verifiable a non-observation-statement must be a lawlike statement. If we look at the alleged verification of $E = mc^2$ in the relativity-made-easy example of the preceding section, it is apparent that one source of trouble lies in the use of the unlawlike auxiliary hypothesis H'. Leaving aside the difficulties in explicating the concept of a lawlike statement, we could perhaps patch up Ayer's explication of empirical verifiability by inserting the condition of lawlikeness at the appropriate places:

> . . . a statement is directly verifiable if it is either an observation-statement, or is *a lawlike statement* such that . . .

> . . . a statement is indirectly verifiable if it satisfies the following conditions: first, *that it is lawlike and* that in conjunction with certain other premises . . .

This emendation will block the exact form of the refutation presented by Church, but there is no assurance that a similar type of objection could not be formulated. In any case, it seems to me that the root of the problem goes much deeper.

Ayer's account of cognitive meaningfulness is ultimately question-begging. Very briefly, the situation is this. Cognitive statements are taken to be just those statements which are either true or false. Statements which are either true or false are the admissible substituends for the variables of truth-functional logic. But, for those statements which are neither analytic nor self-contradictory, a statement is cognitive if and only if it is empirically verifiable. The test for empirical verifiability involves using a statement as a substituend for a truth-functional variable (or larger expression involving variables) in the premise of a deductive argument. This procedure is logically permissible only if the statement in question is either true or false, which is precisely the question at issue. Although making no explicit reference to Ayer, Quine has expressed the point very cogently in a passing remark:

> As an empiricist I consider that the cognitive synonymy of statements should consist in sameness of the empirical conditions of their confirmation. A statement is analytic when its operational condition of verification is, so to speak, the null condition. But I am using terms here which we cannot pretend to understand until we have made substantial progress in the theory of confirmation. Considering what good hands the problem of confirmation is in,

it may seem that optimism is in order. However, if synonymy and
analyticity and the rest are to be made sense of only in terms of
an eventual account of confirmation, I think philosophers are
tending to be insufficiently chary of the circularity involved in
resting their eventual account of confirmation upon such concepts as synonymy and analyticity.[13]

One striking feature which Ayer's explication of factual
meaningfulness has in common with many others is that the meaningfulness of a statement is determined by its consequences and
not by what it is a consequence of. There is something extremely
misleading in supposing that any kind of argument from conclusions to premises is at issue. To say that a statement is verified is
to say that it is supported by evidence. To say that a statement is
verifiable is to say that it could be supported by evidence. The
evidence (actual or possible) plays the role of a premise—more
exactly, the statement of the evidence is a premise—and the verified or verifiable statement is the conclusion. Of course, in many
important instances the conclusion is not a deductive consequence
of the premise but is inductively supported by it. Strangely
enough, Ayer's explication of empirical verifiability makes no
reference to inductive relations. Empirical verifiability is explained entirely in terms of the deductibility of observation-
consequences.

Ayer apparently held that inductive inference is simply the
converse of deductive inference. According to this view (which is,
unfortunately, widely held) a valid deductive argument becomes
a correct inductive argument merely by interchanging the conclusion with one of the premises. Any number of considerations
show that this characterization of induction is untenable; in fact,
this is precisely what Church's criticism shows. The alleged
verification of H' in the preceding section is obviously a counterexample to the view that induction is the converse of deduction.
Furthermore, even assuming that H' has somehow been satisfactorily verified, the alleged verification of H is another
counterexample. Again it might be tempting to have recourse to
restrictions involving lawlikeness. This would amount to a view
that certain kinds of valid deductive arguments have correct inductive arguments as converses while other kinds of valid deduc-

[13] Willard Van Orman Quine, "Semantics and Abstract Objects," *Contributions to the Analysis and Synthesis of Knowledge,* Proceedings of the American Academy of Arts and Sciences 80 (July 1951): 90–96. See p. 92.

tions do not. Under this view serious questions would arise concerning the grounds for deciding which kinds of deductions have correct inductive arguments as converses. In any case it is an abandonment of the thesis that inductive correctness is simply a converse of deductive validity.

A more straightforward approach, it seems to me, is to admit inductive relations explictly into the explication of empirical verifiability. On this approach we might say, roughly, that a statement which is neither analytic nor self-contradictory is empirically verifiable if and only if it is either an observation-statement or the conclusion of a correct inductive or deductive argument from verifiable premises. Such a formulation leaves many problems unsolved, but it is a step in the right direction. In the first place, it places appropriate emphasis upon the role of inductive relations in the explication of empirical verifiability. It calls attention to the need to specify (and possibly justify) the rules of inductive inference. In the second place, it escapes the question-begging procedure of using a statement whose cognitive status is at issue as a premise in any argument, inductive or deductive.

Let us re-evaluate the situation now that the statement whose cognitive status is at issue has been shifted from the position of premise to the position of conclusion. Consider deduction first. A fundamental requirement of a satisfactory deductive logic is that it shall be truth-preserving. Such a logic will also be "verifiability-preserving"; that is, if a conclusion C is derivable from premises $P_1, \ldots, P_n$ and the conjunction of these premises is verifiable, then the conclusion C is *ipso facto* verifiable. One way to put this is to say that whatever is evidence for a statement is evidence for anything entailed by that statement. Another way to put it is to cite the theorem of the probability calculus to the effect that the degree of confirmation of C on any evidence e is at least as great as the degree of confirmation of P on e if C is derivable from P. This condition is so basic to the notion of evidence that it might well be listed as a condition of adequacy for an explication of degree of confirmation. Unfortunately for Ayer's attempted explication of empirical verifiability, the converse relation does not hold. Given that P entails C, it is not generally true that whatever is evidence for C is evidence for P. Just as one cannot argue legitimately from the truth of the conclusion to the truth of the premises, so one cannot argue from the verifiability of the conclusion to the verifiability of the premises.

The situation with respect to induction cannot be spelled out fully in the absence of a completed inductive logic and it goes almost without saying that no inductive logic is at present widely accepted as reasonably complete and satisfactory. Nevertheless, there are certain general considerations which would seem to hold regardless of the precise character of inductive logic. Two cases, which correspond closely to Ayer's direct and indirect verifiability, need to be distinguished.

First, a statement may be the conclusion of an inductive argument which has no premises which are not observation-statements. Let us say that such conclusions are directly inductively verifiable. This case presents no particular difficulty, for the conclusion is directly supported by empirical evidence. Admitting that the inductive rule which governs the argument is correct is tantamount to admitting that the observation-premises constitute inductive evidence for the conclusion.

Second, a statement may be the conclusion of an inductive argument which has among its premises at least one non-observation-statement which is the conclusion of another inductive argument. Let us say that such conclusions are indirectly inductively verifiable. In this case, the situation is more complex because the relation of inductive support, unlike the relation of deductive entailment, is not transitive. Even if P inductively supports Q and Q inductively supports R, P may not inductively support R. A simple example will illustrate this point. Consider a population known to consist of ninety white stones, nine white gumdrops, and one black gumdrop. All of the gumdrops are soft and all of the stones are hard. Let P be the statement that some particular randomly selected member of the population is a gumdrop, Q the statement that it is white, and R the statement that it is hard. P strongly supports Q and Q strongly supports R (each to about the degree 9/10), but P and R are incompatible by hypothesis.

Suppose H is indirectly inductively verifiable. It is the conclusion of an inductive argument which has at least one non-observation-premise D. For the sake of simplicity, let D be the only non-observation-premise and let D be directly inductively verifiable. This means that D is the conclusion of an inductive argument which has only observation-premises O. These premises provide inductive support for D. H is the conclusion of an inductive argument which has D as a premise and which might have other observation-premises O'. Do O and O' inductively support H? Not necessarily.

We must be careful not to be misled into attempting to answer the wrong question. Our problem is not whether H is inductively supported by the observation-statements given; rather, the question is whether the characteristic of empirical verifiability is transferred from O to D and thence from D and O' to H. The question is this. Given that H is the conclusion of an inductive argument of the kind specified, does it follow that there exist observation statements which would support H? No decisive answer can be given in the absence of a precisely specified inductive logic. Nevertheless, an affirmative answer is to be expected; indeed, this affirmative answer might be considered a condition of adequacy for an inductive logic. The reason is as follows. With what is given it is impossible to assess the support of H by O and O', but added information would make the assessment possible. We need to know the degree to which H would be supported by the conjunction of D and O and the degree to which H would be supported by the conjunction of not-D and O. For statements of the kind we are considering, it is not unreasonable to suppose that this added information is obtainable in principle. If so, the support of H by O can be established. It would follow that indirectly inductively verifiable statements are empirically verifiable and that inductive arguments have the property of "verifiability preservation." These considerations show, I believe, that the prospects of satisfactorily explicating verifiability improve when we regard a statement as empirically verifiable if and only if it is either an observation-statement or the *conclusion* of an argument of a specified type.

III

It might seem that the only remaining task is to construct an inductive logic and choose an appropriate observation basis. Then, with deductive logic, inductive logic, and the observation basis we could, in principle, determine unambiguously which statements are verifiable and which ones are not. We could then decide, if we had not already done so, whether we want to identify factual meaningfulness with empirical verifiability. Unfortunately, there are further complications, as a simple example will show. Consider the following two deductive arguments:

(i) Jack is lazy.
——————————————————
Jack is lazy or the Absolute is lazy.

(ii) Jack is lazy or the Absolute is lazy
Jack is not lazy.
——————————————————
The Absolute is lazy.

Let us agree that "Jack is lazy" is a verifiable statement. If we allow that (i) is a valid argument, then its conclusion is verifiable, for whatever evidence supports its premise also supports its conclusion. We would also maintain that the negation of any verifiable statement is verifiable. Thus (ii) has two verifiable premises, so its conclusion must be verifiable. But let us agree that "The Absolute is lazy" is not verifiable. Therefore, something has gone wrong. If we allow such proofs of verifiability, then it is trivial to show that every statement is verifiable.

However, we might question the validity of (i). The form of (i) seems to be

(iii) P.
——————
P ∨ Q.

which is certainly valid, but the statement "Jack is lazy or the Absolute is lazy" may be ruled an improper disjunction because of its noncognitive component. The trouble seems to stem from the fact that (iii) is an argument form which permits the addition of an arbitrary disjunct in the conclusion. Everything is all right if the addition is a cognitive statement, but we get into trouble if the addition is a noncognitive statement. Unfortunately, it seems that we have to know whether a conclusion is cognitive before we can tell whether it actually follows validly from verifiable premises. Under these circumstances we can hardly use the fact that a statement is a conclusion of verifiable premises as a criterion of verifiability. We are back in a circle again.

There is a very easy way of handling (iii) and the problem of arbitrary additions to conclusions. It is a well-known fact that truth-functional logic can be formalized using a finite set of axioms, a rule of substitution, and the rule of detachment. Rules like (iii) are then derived rules. For purposes of our criterion we could eliminate all derived rules. Substitution and detachment will

not permit arbitrary additions to conclusions. Form (iii) would
then become

(iv) P

P ⊃ P ∨ Q.

P ∨ Q.

where the second premise is taken as a logical truth. The problem
of the noncognitive part is now referred to the premises; it is the
question of whether "If Jack is lazy then Jack is lazy or the Absolute is lazy" is admissible as a premise in (iv). If not, of course,
we cannot get the unwanted conclusion "Jack is lazy or the
Absolute is lazy."

Arguments like (i) and the general problem of compound
statements having noncognitive components played a conspicuous
part in the considerations which led to Hempel's abandonment of
hope for a satisfactory formulation of the verifiability criterion.
Hempel laid down a condition of adequacy for meaning criteria
which merits careful consideration:

> . . . any general criterion of cognitive significance will have to
> meet certain requirements if it is to be at all acceptable. Of these,
> we note one, which we shall consider here as expressing a neces-
> sary, though by no means sufficient, *"condition of adequacy"* for
> criteria of cognitive significance.
>
> (A) If under a given criterion of cognitive significance, a
> sentence N is non-significant, then so must be all truth-functional
> compound sentences in which N occurs non-vacuously as a com-
> ponent. For if N cannot be significantly assigned a truth value,
> then it is impossible to assign truth values to the compound sen-
> tences containing N; hence, they should be qualified as non-sig-
> nificant as well.[14]

While Hempel's criterion seems rather straightforward, it is essential to distinguish between its application to sentences constructed
within formal logic and its application to sentences of a natural
language. A sentence of formal logic cannot have a nonsignificant
component, whether occurring vacuously or nonvacuously, for
the sentences of formal logic are all either true or false, and this
includes component sentences as well as complete sentences. It
is inadmissible to interpret any formula of truth-functional logic
as a sentence which is neither true nor false.

The conjunctions of natural language are not, however,

[14] Hempel, "The Concept of Cognitive Significance: A Reconsideration," p. 62.

truth-functional in the same way. There are restrictions upon logical operations which do not apply to ordinary conjunctions. In particular, while it is meaningless to join sentences which are neither true nor false with truth-functional connectives, it is patently admissible from the point of view of English grammar to join them with the conjunctions of English. For example, "Shut up *and* eat your dinner," "Alas *and* alack," and "Be sure to lock the door *if* you leave," are all perfectly grammatical. Nevertheless, "Shut up," "Eat your dinner," "Alas," "Alack," and "Be sure to lock the door," are all sentences which are neither true nor false. Furthermore, it is not clear that the following two sentences must be devoid of cognitive meaning:

(v) If Jack is lazy then the Absolute is lazy.
(vi) Jack is lazy and the Absolute is lazy.

Since "The Absolute is lazy" is (by hypothesis) noncognitive, it follows that sentences (v) and (vi) cannot be schematized in truth-functional logic as $S \supset N$ and $S \cdot N$ respectively. We need not conclude, however, that there is no correct way of schematizing them truth-functionally. If Hempel's criterion were applied directly to sentences like (v) and (vi), the result would be that the presence of any noncognitive part takes the cognitive content away from the cognitive parts of a compound sentence. It seems more reasonable to say that the cognitive parts render the compounds cognitive to some extent and that the noncognitive parts do not add to the cognitive content but do not detract from it either. One might adopt something like the following rules of thumb:

Let S be a cognitive sentence and N a noncognitive sentence; then:
   a. *Not-N* is noncognitive.
   b. *S and N* has the same cognitive meaning as *S*.
   c. *S or N* has the same cognitive meaning as *S*.
   d. *If S then N* has the same cognitive meaning as *not-S*.

It is essential, of course, that these rules be stated in terms of conjunctions of English rather than truth-functional connectives.

The foregoing rules are not to be regarded as hard and fast; they may, however, be somewhat indicative of the manner in which compound sentences with noncognitive parts may be treated. The intuitive rationale is simple. We treat the conjunction as false if and only if some component is false and the disjunction as true if and only if some component is true. Since the non-cognitive part has no truth value, the conjunctive and disjunctive compounds have the same truth value as their cognitive parts. It is as if to say that by adding conjunctively or disjunctively the noncognitive sentence, "The Absolute is lazy," to the cognitive sentence, "Jack is lazy," no cognitive content is added or taken away. To preserve some analogy with truth functions, the hypo-thetical is translated into a disjunction and treated by the appro-priate rule. Another way to look at it is this. Sentence (v) says that it is true that the Absolute is lazy if it is true that Jack is lazy. Since "The Absolute is lazy" cannot be true, Jack cannot be lazy. Sentence (v) says that Jack is not lazy much as "If Jack is lazy the moon is made of green cheese" does, except that "The moon is made of green cheese" is not true because it is false while "The Absolute is lazy" is not true because it is noncognitive. How-ever, all of this is only intuitive. Because English is informal and imprecise it is impossible to have formal rules to deal with all cases of compound sentences with noncognitive parts.

As Reichenbach long maintained,[15] the verifiability criterion of cognitive meaningfulness needs to be supplemented with a veri-fiability criterion of sameness of cognitive meaning. Sentences with noncognitive parts can be handled by means of this addi-tional criterion. The problem is to find other sentences which have the same cognitive meaning but which have no noncognitive parts. After this has been done we are in a position to schematize compound sentences in truth-functional notation. Sentences (v) and (vi) would be schematized as $\sim S$ and S respectively. Argu-ments (i) and (ii) would come out as follows:

(vii) Jack is lazy.   P.
      ――――――――――――――――――――――――――――――――――
      Jack is lazy or the Absolute is lazy.   Q.

(viii) Jack is lazy or the Absolute is lazy.   Q.
       Jack is not lazy. $\sim$P.
       ―――――――――――――――――――――――――――――――――
       The Absolute is lazy.

Because of the equivalence in meaning between "Jack is lazy" and "Jack is lazy or the Absolute is lazy" (vii) must be considered valid, but the nearest we could come to (viii) would be to conclude

[15] Reichenbach, *Experience and Prediction;* "The Verifiability Theory of Meaning," *Contributions to the Analysis and Synthesis of Knowledge,* Pro-ceedings of the American Academy of Arts and Science 80 (July 1951): 46–60.

"It is not the case that Jack is lazy or the Absolute is lazy," which is equivalent to "Jack is not lazy." We have blocked the proof of the cognitive meaningfulness of "The Absolute is lazy" without denying the validity of (i).

A similar approach will dispose of certain problems concerning the meaningfulness of theoretical systems. Hempel, after characterizing an *isolated sentence* as one which is neither logically true nor logically false and whose "omission from the theoretical system would have no effect on its explanatory and predictive power in regard to potentially observable phenomena," asks, "Should we not, therefore, require that a cognitively significant system contain no isolated sentences?"[16] Hempel answers his own question in the negative and so would I, but for very different reasons. Applying the verifiability criterion of sameness of cognitive meaning, I should say that a theoretical system containing an isolated sentence has precisely the same cognitive meaning as the system which would result from the deletion of the isolated sentence. Suppose that G is a physical (interpreted) geometry and that G′ is the system which results when "The Absolute is lazy" is added to that system as another postulate. G′ clearly is not lacking in cognitive significance; it has the same cognitive content as G. It is worth noting that a nonindependent postulate is, under Hempel's definition, an isolated sentence. Let T be a theorem of the system G and let G* be the system which results by making T a postulate. We would certainly, under these circumstances, want to say that the systems G and G* have the same cognitive meaning even though G* has an isolated sentence, especially in view of the logical truth:

$$(ix) \ (P \supset Q) \equiv (P \equiv P \cdot Q).$$

In large measure, the approach via a criterion of sameness of cognitive meaning circumvents Hempel's objections to a verifiability criterion.

A verifiability criterion of sameness of cognitive meaning would be the sort of thing suggested by Quine:

> ... the cognitive synonymy of statements should consist in sameness of the empirical conditions of their confirmation.[17]

This amounts, I take it, to saying that two statements have the same cognitive meaning if and only if every observation-statement

[16] Hempel, "The Concept of Cognitive Significance: A Reconsideration," p. 70.
[17] Quine, "Semantics and Objects," p. 92.

has equal inductive relevance to both. Reichenbach has formulated this criterion as follows:

> Two sentences have the same [cognitive] meaning if they obtain the same weight, or degree of probability, by every possible observation.[18]

The criterion of cognitive equisignificance is, I believe, an essential part of the verifiability criterion. Indeed, it may be regarded as basic, for we may define "noncognitive" in terms of it:

A statement is noncognitive if and only if it has the same cognitive meaning as its denial.

This formulation expresses the general idea that there is no empirical difference between the assertion and denial of a noncognitive sentence.

IV

We have not yet faced squarely enough the problem of the relation between truth-functional logic and the verifiability criterion of cognitive meaning. It is a familiar fact that logical systems can be treated in two distinct ways. On the one hand, a system can be regarded as an uninterpreted formal calculus consisting of meaningless marks which are manipulated by formal rules. From this standpoint, only the syntactical properties of the system are considered. On the other hand, a system may be regarded as an interpreted calculus which is endowed with semantical properties by virtue of semantical rules. From this standpoint, the system is one whose marks are meaningful symbols with some kind of reference.

Standard two-valued truth-functional logic (as found, for instance, in *Principia Mathematica*) is a system of this sort. There are many alternative formalizations of this logic; in fact, it can be handled either axiomatically or by truth-tables. All of these treatments are formally equivalent. Although some approaches may have certain formal advantages, the philosophical problems of interpretation will be the same for all of them. We shall consider the truth-table treatment as the most perspicuous for our purposes.

Truth-tables themselves can be regarded either syntactically

[18] Reichenbach, *Experience and Prediction*, p. 54.

or semantically. From the purely syntactical point of view, either the "T" and "F" are dissociated from the semantical concepts of truth and falsity, or else marks such as "1" and "0" which are already dissociated are used. One of the important interpretations of this system (the only one which shall interest us) is designed to provide a logic of deduction. For this interpretation it is required that the theorems be necessarily true and that the derivations be truth-preserving. Accordingly, the "T" and "F" of the truth-table are to be associated with truth and falsity.

The formulas of the system are constructed from two types of symbols, proper and improper. The proper symbols can be taken as variables or constants; for the sake of definiteness, let us regard them as variables, for the philosophical problems we are dealing with will be the same in any case. The improper symbols will include one or more truth-functional operation symbols. The first problem of interpretation is to choose a domain of interpretation, that is, a range for the variables of our system. The elements of the domain of interpretation must be entities which can be associated with truth and falsity. Again, there are various alternatives available, but for the sake of definiteness let us agree to let the variables range over whatever it is that sentences which are either true or false denote—propositions, truth values, or whatever you like. With this choice made, the substituends for truth-functional variables are sentences which are either true or false. Those who dislike "entities" like propositions or truth values can let the variables range over sentences which are either true or false and make names of such sentences the substituends for truth-functional variables. In any case, we cannot avoid the problem of deciding which sentences are true or false and how they are to be distinguished from those which are neither true nor false. The verifiability criterion has been proposed to fulfill this function.

There is a further complication. In order to provide an admissible interpretation for the propositional calculus, we must satisfy a *closure condition*.

> The result of applying an n-ary operation of the system to an n-tuple of elements of the domain of interpretation is an element of the domain of interpretation.

In other words, the negation of a sentence which is either true or false must be a sentence which is either true or false, the conjunction of two sentences which are either true or false must be a sentence which is either true or false, etc. Now this condition can be satisfied by fiat; we can define the class of sentences which are either true or false so that it includes the negation, conjunction, etc., of sentences which are either true or false. However, there might be good reasons to reject such a definition. Consider, for example, the following trivial argument form which is valid in ordinary logic:

$$(x) \quad \frac{\begin{array}{l} P. \\ Q. \end{array}}{P \cdot Q.}$$

Is it reasonable to say that the conjunction $P \cdot Q$ is verifiable if the conjuncts P and Q are separately verifiable? If P and Q are statements about conjugate parameters of a quantum-mechanical system, we might want to deny it. It is well known that quantum mechanics imposes severe limitations upon the possibility of verification. Even though we might define possibility of verification in such a way as to automatically satisfy the condition of closure with respect to ordinary two-valued truth-functional logic, the fact would remain that it is physically impossible to verify certain statements (though we shall see that the difficulties attach more directly to negations and disjunctions than to conjunctions).

Before going into a more concrete discussion of the situation in quantum mechanics, it is important to note that the difficulties being considered arise out of an ambiguity in the term "verifiability." Possibility of verification may mean logical possibility or it may mean physical possibility. The impossibilities of verification imposed by quantum mechanics are physical impossibilities. There is, as far as anyone knows, no logical impossibility in a universe something like the Newtonian in which there are no incompatible parameters and hence no restriction on the verifiability of compound statements involving different parameters. If we accept physical possibility of verification as a criterion of factual meaningfulness, then we are committed to the consequence that empirical matters of fact to some extent determine our deductive logic. This would result in a rather subtle relationship between the a priori and the a posteriori. Whether two-valued truth-functional logic is acceptable becomes, in some sense, an empirical question.

There are some philosophers, I am sure, who would regard the foregoing reasoning (if correct) as a conclusive argument against interpreting verifiability in terms of physical as opposed to logical possibility. However, there are strong reasons for adopting the physical sense of possibility. In the first place, physical impossibility is impossibility of an insurmountable kind; to speak of *mere* physical impossibility would surely be a solecism.[19] In the second place, the logical analysis of modern physics seems to require the interpretation of verifiability in terms of physical possibility. Reichenbach, who has given this problem considerable attention,[20] has put the point as follows:

> Schlick, and with him most members of the Vienna circle, have used logical possibility. But a definition of meaning in terms of logical possibility of verification makes the definition of meaning too wide, at least, when the interpretation of physics is concerned. For instance, Einstein's principle of equivalence, according to which being in accelerated motion means the same as being in a gravitational field, presupposes a definition of verifiability based on physical possibility. For these reasons I have advocated a definition of meaning in terms of the physical possibility of verification.[21]

Without further argument as to which sense of possibility should be selected, let us consider the situation which results in quantum mechanics from adopting physical possibility of verification as a criterion of factual meaningfulness.

A classic discussion of the adoption of an alternative propositional logic for quantum mechanics is that of Birkhoff and von Neumann.[22] The present brief discussion is based upon their treatment. In classical and quantum mechanics a phase-space Σ can be associated with a given physical system S in such a way that the state of the system at any instant is represented by a point of Σ.

[19] Physical impossibility is, of course, to be sharply distinguished from technical impossibility; this latter sort of impossibility can be overcome by increased knowledge and improved technology. Until recently it was technically impossible to obtain photographs of the opposite side of the moon, but now it is technically possible. It was never physically impossible to do so. See Reichenbach, *Experience and Prediction;* "The Verifiability Theory of Meaning."

[20] Reichenbach, *Experience and Prediction;* "The Verifiability Theory of Meaning."

[21] Reichenbach, "The Verifiability Theory of Meaning," p. 53.

[22] Garrett Birkhoff and John von Neumann, "The Logic of Quantum Mechanics," *Annals of Mathematics* 37 (October 1936): 823–843.

Given that S is at t_0 in a state represented by the point x_0, the physical laws governing the system determine what point x_1 will represent the state of S at a later time t_1. The laws of physics constitute, so to speak, the laws of motion of the points in phase-space. In classical mechanics the phase-space is a region of $2n$-dimensional Euclidean space (i.e., n position coordinates and n momentum coordinates); in quantum mechanics the phase-space is taken to be Hilbert space. In order to provide physical significance for the phase-space, its subsets must be made to correspond with "experimental propositions." (This, I take it, amounts to the verifiability criterion with possibility interpreted in the physical sense.) Even in classical mechanics it is unrealistic to identify each subset of phase-space with an experimental proposition, but it does seem reasonable "to assume that it is the *Lebesgue-measurable* subsets of a phase-space which correspond to experimental propositions, two subsets being identified, if their difference has *Lebesgue-measure* 0."[23] In any case it turns out that set-sums, set-products, and set-complements of subsets corresponding to experimental propositions are themselves subsets corresponding to experimental propositions. Because of its Boolean character, ordinary two-valued truth-functional logic is adequate for the experimental propositions of classical mechanics. The closure condition will not be violated because the subsets corresponding to experimental propositions constitute a field of subsets.

Owing to the existence of incompatible parameters in quantum mechanics, not every measurable subset of phase-space corresponds to an experimental proposition. The experimental propositions are associated instead with the closed linear subspaces of Σ. These do not constitute a field of subsets; although the set-product of two closed linear subspaces is a closed linear subspace, the set-sum of two closed linear subspaces and the set-complement of one closed linear subspace do not in general constitute closed linear subspaces. The closed linear subspaces form a lattice with respect to which the analogues of negation, conjunction, and disjunction are definable. The negation of an experimental proposition is represented by the *orthogonal complement* of the closed linear subspace which represents that proposition. Conjunction coincides with set-product. Disjunction is defined in terms of negation and conjunction by means of the De Morgan

23 *Ibid.*, p. 825.

relation; thus defined it differs from set-sum. With these definitions the closure condition is satisfied because negations, conjunctions, and disjunctions of experimental propositions are experimental propositions. The resulting logic is not a Boolean logic. The basic difference is that it fails to satisfy the distributive laws:

(xi) $P \cdot (Q \vee R) \equiv P \cdot Q \vee P \cdot R.$
       $P \vee Q \cdot R \equiv (P \vee Q) \cdot (P \vee R).$

In their place the "modular identity" is proposed which, though not satisfied by every lattice, seems plausible for quantum mechanics:

(xii) If P implies Q, then
       $P \vee R \cdot Q \equiv (P \vee R) \cdot Q.$

It is interesting to note that the paper concludes with the following two suggested questions:

(xiii) What experimental meaning can one attach to the meet [conjunction] and join [disjunction] of two given experimental propositions?

(xiv) What simple and plausible physical motivation is there for condition L5 [(xii) above]?

Question (xiii) is a question about the *physical* significance of *logical* connectives; question (xiv) is a question of *physical* grounds for adopting an axiom of *logic*. These authors are certainly not guilty of a naive failure to grasp the distinction between logical necessity and empirical fact; they are to be credited, in my opinion, with a deep insight into the fact that the adoption of a criterion of significance in terms of physical possibility of verification makes the selection of a propositional logic contingent upon physical theory. As they say near the close of their discussion, "The above heuristic considerations suggest in particular that the *physically significant* statements in quantum mechanics actually constitute a sort of projective geometry, while the *physically significant* statements concerning a given system in classical dynamics constitute a Boolean algebra".[24]

There is, I think, a germ of truth in the view, often attributed to Mill, that the laws of logic are extremely highly confirmed em-

[24] *Ibid.*, p. 836. Italics added.

pirical generalizations. Empirical fact does not determine the formal validity of any logic. The empirical question is this: If we choose a certain domain of interpretation and assign meanings to the improper symbols in a certain way, is the interpretation an admissible one? There seems to be ample empirical evidence that the physically verifiable statements about the macrocosm constitute a Boolean algebra and hence an admissible interpretation of ordinary two-valued truth-functional logic. The situation seems different for the microcosm. The importance of this point depends in no way upon the truth of quantum-mechanical theory. In the first place, even if the theory undergoes drastic modification, as it probably will, the same logical considerations will apply as long as the new theory involves incompatible parameters. More importantly, in the second place, as long as quantum-mechanical theory cannot be shown to be false a priori, there is no reason to rule out a priori the possibility that a logic different from the ordinary two-valued truth-functional variety may be required to satisfy the closure condition in the presence of the meaning criterion.

If this account of the situation is correct, then the syntactical features of a logical system are strictly a priori matters, but any application of the system involves empirical considerations. This means that any use of a logical system to determine whether a given English sentence is analytic, contingent, or self-contradictory, and any use of a system to determine whether one English sentence is a logical consequence of other English sentences, involve empirical considerations. Such applications of logic depend upon the admissibility of a given interpretaton.

The point I have been arguing is, perhaps, similar to one expressed figuratively but forcefully by Quine as follows:

> The totality of our so-called knowledge or beliefs, from the most casual matters of geography and history to the profoundest laws of atomic physics or even of pure mathematics and logic, is a man-made fabric which impinges on experience only along the edges. Or, to change the figure, total science is like a field of force whose boundary conditions are experience. A conflict with experience at the periphery occasions readjustments in the interior of the field. Truth values have to be redistributed over some of our statements. Reëvaluation of some statements entails reëvaluation of others, because of their logical interconnections—the logical laws being in turn simply certain further statements of the system, certain further elements of the field. Having reëvaluated one state-

ment we must reëvaluate some others, which may be statements logically connected with the first or may be the statements of logical connections themselves.[25]

Perhaps it amounts to the same thing to say that the interpretation of a formal logical system is always an empirical matter, the statement that an interpretation is admissible being an empirical generalization.

V

The main points I have been arguing may be summarized as follows. First, it is essential to distinguish the problem of explicating cognitive meaningfulness from the problem of explicating empirical verifiability. Second, empirical verifiability must be explicated in terms of inductive relations and not exclusively in terms of deductive relations. Induction is not simply the converse of deduction. If the explication of empirical verifiability is merged with the explication of cognitive meaningfulness, the joint explication must not be given solely in terms of the existence of observational consequences. Third, any criterion of cognitive meaningfulness needs to be supplemented with a criterion of cognitive equisignificance. Equisignificance must be explicated in terms of equal inductive support, not in terms of equal observational consequences. Fourth, if verifiability is to be understood as physical possibility of verification (as I think it should), then applications of deductive logic depend for their admissibility upon empirical considerations.

Where does all of this leave us? First, it reaffirms the fundamental importance of two old philosophical problems, the problem of specifying an observation-basis and the problem of constructing (and possibly justifying) an inductive logic. These two problems are intimately related, as is shown, for example, by Goodman's grue-bleen paradox. Second, it leads, I believe, to what might be called a formalistic theory of logic. Logical calculi are on a par with other uninterpreted formal systems; they admit physical interpretations but the question of admissibility is an empirical question. If such a view is correct it raises difficult problems concerning the status of logical truth. There is surely a question as to

[25] Willard Van Orman Quine, "Two Dogmas of Empiricism," in *From a Logical Point of View* (Cambridge: Harvard University Press, 1953), p. 42. Originally published in *Philosophical Review* 60 (January 1951).

whether it is possible in a nonarbitrary manner to distinguish logical calculi from other fully formalized calculi or, given what would be regarded as a nonlogical calculus, to distinguish its logical from its nonlogical parts. Furthermore, the serviceability of the distinction between analytic and synthetic statements is again called into question.

I think it would be overly hasty to conclude, however, that the distinction between analytic and synthetic statements breaks down entirely or becomes perniciously relativized. Given a fully formalized system and a metalanguage adequate to discuss it, it still makes good sense to describe its syntax. If the system is interpreted, it still makes good sense to discuss its semantics. I do not think that the concepts of definition, linguistic convention, and semantic rule dissolve. There may remain a sufficient basis for a distinction between logical (or linguistic) truth and factual truth. These are problems which deserve further careful consideration.

Michael Tooley/Theological statements and the question of an empiricist criterion of cognitive significance

Introduction

This paper is divided into four sections. The first section contains an informal characterization of what may, for the purposes of this discussion, be referred to as the standard interpretation of theological statements. Then, in the second section, I mention two challenges to the commonsense view that theological statements have cognitive content: the "falsifiability challenge" and the "translatability challenge."[1] Both of these challenges involve appeal to an empiricist criterion of cognitive content, but I contend that they are nevertheless very different arguments, and that clarity about the fundamental issues involved in the question of theology and verifi-

[1] Where I employ expressions such as "cognitive content" and "cognitively significant," one could, in most cases, instead use the more specific expressions "factual content" and "factually significant," since there is no need to give special consideration to analytic statements. My use of the more general expressions is simply a matter of terminological conformity with the articles that I happen to be referring to most frequently.

cationism cannot be achieved unless these two lines of argument are carefully distinguished. The third section is concerned with the question of the possibility of an empiricist criterion of cognitive significance. The underlying purpose of the discussion will be to arrive at an evaluation of the commonly advanced claim that verificationist objections to the meaningfulness of theological language can be refuted by simply arguing that it is not possible to formulate an adequate confirmability criterion of cognitive significance. I then conclude by suggesting some responses that seem more promising.

I. The standard interpretation of theological statements

Because of the ever widening range of interpretations that are assigned to the term "God," it is important to specify the interpretation that one intends to place upon it, before embarking upon a discussion of philosophical issues concerned with theological statements. The interpretation that will be assigned to the term *God* in the ensuing discussion is intended to meet the following two conditions:

1. It is an interpretation that represents one of the central strands of thought both in the theory and practice of monotheistic religion;

2. It is the interpretation that has given rise to the philosophical controversy that we are considering.

In this paper, theological statements are to be taken as being *cognitive*.[2] That is, they have truth-values (they are either true or false), and their primary function is to state facts, to describe states of affairs. The facts that they state are basically facts about

---

[2] A number of writers have defended the view that theological statements are to be interpreted as *noncognitive* in nature. See, for example, R. B. Braithwaite's essay, *An Empiricist's View of the Nature of Religious Belief* (Cambridge: Cambridge University Press, 1955), Paul Schmidt's book, *Religious Knowledge* (Glencoe: The Free Press, 1961), and Kai Nielsen's article, "On Speaking of God," in *Theoria* 28 (1962), 110–137. This contention that theological language is noncognitive is highly implausible on the face of it, and it is hard to believe that anyone would accept such a position except out of despair over the possibility of finding a cognitive account that avoids all the philosophical objections that have been directed against the view that theological statements have cognitive meaning. Moreover, I think that the noncognitive position, besides being highly counterintuitive, is open to decisive philosophical objections. This question falls outside the scope of the present discussion, however.

the individual referred to by the term "God." This term will not be taken as a logically proper name, but simply as an abbreviation for some definite description, such as the following: "the one person who, though he can act within the world and can communicate with man, is neither dependent upon the world nor simply a part of it, but rather transcends the realm of human existence, and who, in addition, is morally perfect, omnipotent, omniscient, eternal, and incorporeal."

The precise terms used in this suggested definition will not be of critical importance. Some might wish to eliminate some of the predicates that I have included, on the grounds either that the properties associated with them are not religiously significant, or that the predicates are obscure ones that cannot be adequately explicated (e.g., "omnipotent," "eternal"). Others might wish to add other predicates that they would take to be religiously important or philosophically illuminating: "the maker of heaven and earth," "immutable," "necessarily existent," "timeless," "infinite," and the like.

All that is critical here is that the term *God* be taken as referring to *a person who is incorporeal and who transcends the realm of human existence, and yet who is immanent in the sense of being able to act in the world so as to communicate with man and to realize his purposes.* Other properties will not enter into the argument.

Most critical of all is the notion of *transcendence:* when we turn to consider the translatability argument we will see that it pivots about this very notion. We shall consider this concept more closely before going any further. At least two basic notions can be distinguished in traditional discussions of the transcendence of God: (a) *conceptual transcendence,* and (b) *experiential transcendence.* To say that God is conceptually transcendent is to say (roughly) that there is no truth about God that can be adequately expressed in any human language. To say that God is experientially transcendent is to say that statements about God cannot be reduced to, or analyzed in terms of, statements about the physical world or about the experiences (actual or conditional[3]) of humans or other embodied perceivers.

To get an intuitive grasp of the concept of experiential tran-

---

[3] By a statement about conditional experiences I simply mean any statement about the experiences that someone *would* have if certain conditions *were* to be realized.

scendence, consider for the moment the following difference between chairs and headaches. In the case of a chair, there are two
things: our experiences of the chair and the chair itself. This isn't
so with a headache. In the case of a headache, there are only one's
experiences of it. To say that God is experientially transcendent is
to say that he is an object separate and distinct both from our experiences of him (both actual and conditional), and from the physical world in which he manifests himself.

In the present discussion, *transcendence* will be construed
as experiential transcendence, for the following three reasons:

1. I doubt that coherent sense can be assigned to the notion
of conceptual transcendence;

2. It would seem that what matters to the ordinary religious
believer is the experiential transcendence of God: when he utters
theological statements, such as "God is the Lord of all creation,"
"God will not forsake those who have faith in him," he believes
that he is referring to some real object beyond the physical world
that is separate and distinct from human experience;

3. It is the notion of experiential transcendence that is critical to the translatability challenge arguments advanced by logical
positivists such as Ayer and Carnap.

II. Verificationist challenges to the meaningfulness of theological statements

A number of philosophers have argued that if theological statements are interpreted in the manner indicated above, then they are
either conceptually incoherent or else completely devoid of cognitive significance (i.e., they are not such as are either true or false,
they cannot function to state facts or to describe states of affairs).
Of the various objections that have been raised,[4] two are of inter-

---

[4] Other important challenges to the meaningfulness of theological language
are these: First, many philosophers have contended that the notion of a nonembodied person, or at least the notion of a nonembodied agent, is incoherent. Secondly, doubts have been raised about the intelligibility of key
theological terms, such as "infinite," "totally other," "ground of being,"
"omnipotent," and so on. And thirdly, it has been argued that if theological
language is, as some have contended, irreducibly analogical, or metaphorical,
or symbolic, then there is an insoluble problem as to how anyone could ever
learn such language.

est to us here: (1) the falsifiability challenge (associated with Antony Flew), and (2) the translatability challenge (advanced by logical empiricists such as Ayer and Carnap). Since appeal to an empiricist criterion of cognitive significance plays a central role in both of these challenges, it is natural to view them as simply variations on a single verificationist theme. We shall see that this position is *radically* incorrect. It is true that the tenability of an empiricist criterion of cognitive significance is a necessary condition for the acceptability of either argument. But it is not sufficient. Both arguments require auxiliary assumptions, which are very different in the two cases. I shall attempt to show that, as a consequence, one of the arguments is much more formidable than the other.

Let us now examine these two challenges very carefully by looking at their critical premises and their logical structure. First, the falsifiability challenge,[5] which, as was noted above, is associated with Flew. The basic argument can be stated as follows:

1. Sophisticated religious believers do not seem to be willing to admit that there are any conceivable experiences or events whose occurrence would result in their abandoning some of their central theological affirmations.

2. Hence it is reasonable to conclude that there are no experiences or events whose occurrence would count against the truth of a typical theological statement.

3. A statement is cognitively significant if and only if there are experiential statements that would decisively count against the truth of that statement.

4. Hence theological statements cannot be cognitively significant.

This argument can be attacked in at least two very different ways. First, one might argue that it is not possible to formulate

---

[5] The label "falsifiability challenge" is not an entirely happy one, since it suggests that Flew requires that a statement must be *conclusively* falsifiable if it is to be cognitively significant. Some writers, such as Alvin Plantinga in his book, *God and Other Minds* (Ithaca, N.Y.: Cornell University Press, 1967), have mistakenly attributed this position to Flew: "It appears, then, that according to Flew a meaningful (contingent) proposition must be falsifiable by observation statements; there must be some finite and consistent set of observation statements that entails its denial" (*Ibid.*, p. 162) [Reprinted in this volume, pp. 446–455.—Editors' Note]. However, it is clear that all that Flew requires is that it be possible to specify observational evidence that would be sufficient to make it *unreasonable* to believe the statement in question.

an acceptable criterion of cognitive significance, or that, at the very least, the version of such a criterion that is set out at (3) above is inadequate. Secondly, one might challenge the claim advanced at (2), viz., that there are no experiential statements that would decisively disconfirm a typical theological statement. [Since in the above argument premise (1) is offered in support of (2), to challenge (2) involves questioning either (1) or the inference from (1) and (2).]

Let me comment briefly upon each of these possible responses. First, let's set aside the claim that it is not possible to formulate an acceptable criterion of cognitive significance. This question will be given detailed consideration in the next section. Here we can confine our attention to the weaker claim that the version of the criterion invoked at (3) is inadequate.

The claim that the version of the criterion of cognitive significance employed by Flew is unacceptable has often rested upon the mistaken assumption that Flew's criterion is that of *complete* or *conclusive* falsifiability. However as was emphasized above, all that Flew demands is that it be possible to specify evidence that would make it unreasonable to accept the statement in question. Once this is realized, it is far from clear that Flew's criterion is unacceptable. For if one believes that it is possible to formulate an adequate empiricist criterion of cognitive significance, it seems reasonable to agree with Flew that any cognitively significant statement that is nonanalytic must be such that there are experiential statements that would serve to decisively disconfirm it. This is not to say that Flew's criterion is entirely satisfactory. It is not. But its shortcoming is not that it is false, but that it is incomplete.

The second line of criticism seems much more forceful. In the first place, a number of writers have argued, convincingly in my opinion, that premise (1) is unacceptable.[6] But secondly, even if premise (1) were true, it would not adequately support the claim that theological statements cannot be decisively disconfirmed. For

[6] See, for example, the discussion of this point by A. C. Ewing in his article on "Religious Assertions in the Light of Contemporary Philosophy," *Philosophy* 32 (1957), 206–218. It is important to keep in mind here the interpretation that has been assigned to theological statements in this discussion. It may very well be the case that there are interpretations that some sophisticated religious believers assign to theological statements that effectively remove those statements from the realm of what can be rendered unreasonable by experiential evidence. (An interpretation of the term *God* according to which it meant simply being-itself might be a case in point.) Such offbeat interpretations of theological statements are not under consideration here.

even if it were true that there are no experiences that would convince a sophisticated religious believer to abandon his central theological beliefs, it would not automatically follow that theological
statements cannot be decisively disconfirmed. There are many
alternative ways that this behavior might be explained. To see this,
let us consider a nonreligious example. Suppose that John believes
that the earth is flat, even though he knows that the earth *appears*
spherical when photographed from rockets high above the surface
of the earth. The fact that John resists such negative evidence does
not show that the belief in question cannot be decisively disconfirmed. For there are a number of reasons why John might not
abandon some statement T (e.g., "The earth is flat") when he
comes to accept some other statement E (e.g., "The earth appears
spherical in pictures taken from rockets high above the surface of
the earth"):

    a. E may not decisively disconfirm T;

    b. John may not notice that E decisively disconfirms T;

    c. E may decisively disconfirm T and John may know this,
but simply behave irrationally and continue to believe T in spite
of the decisive negative evidence provided by E;

    d. E may decisively disconfirm T, and John may know this,
with the consequence that if he knows that E is true, it will be
epistemically unreasonable for him to continue to believe T; however there may be *other considerations*—of a moral or "pragmatic"
sort, rather than of a purely evidential or epistemic sort—that
make it *reasonable, all things considered,* for him to believe T even
though he knows that it is, in view of the truth of E, epistemically
unreasonable to believe T.

    The inference from (1) to (2) in the falsifiability challenge argu-
ment depends upon the assumption that (a), rather than (b), (c), or
(d), provides the correct explanation of the (purported) fact that
sophisticated religious believers would hold onto their theological
beliefs no matter to what experiences or events they were exposed. This assumption deserves to be argued as well as to be
made explicit. Once this is done, it is far from clear that it sur-
vives. The third explanation, for example, will surely find considerable support among those who are hostile to religion: the
suggestion that religious believers are irrational in that they hold
onto their religious beliefs even in the face of evidence that renders such beliefs unreasonable is hardly a novel theme. And, on
the other hand, many religious believers have argued that, in view

of the centrality of attitudes of loyalty, faith, and trust to the religious outlook, it is clear that no adequate ethic of belief in the religious sphere can restrict itself merely to evidential considerations. Perhaps it will turn out that the explanation that Flew and other defenders of the falsifiability challenge argument have implicitly opted for is the most plausible one. But this claim must be argued.

The conclusion seems to be this. Even if one sets aside entirely the question of the acceptability of an empiricist criterion of cognitive significance, there still appear to be at least two grave weaknesses in the argument as it stands:

a. The claim advanced at step (1) is false. It is extremely doubtful that sophisticated religious believers would hold on to their theological beliefs no matter what conceivable experiences or events were to occur;

b. Even if the claim advanced at (1) is granted, it is far from clear that the correct explanation of this behavior is that the theological statements in question are not open to decisive disconfirmation. There are alternative explanations that, *prima facie,* appear just as reasonable.

Let us now turn to the translatability challenge argument. This argument involves quite different assumptions, with the result that it is not open to the objections that appear to tell against the falsifiability challenge argument.

For clarity of exposition, the translatability challenge argument will be set out in a simplified form.[7] In this exposition of the argument the following two expressions will be used in semi-technical senses: (1) "empirical sentence"; (2) "basic observation sentence". These two expressions are to be interpreted as follows:

1. A sentence will be said to be an *empirical sentence* if and only if it is a sentence whose sole cognitive function is to describe some state of affairs of the natural world, i.e., it describes some physical state of affairs, or the experiences or other mental states

---

[7] The logical structure of the argument as set out here is quite similar to the logical structure of Ayer's formulation of the argument [Reprinted in this volume, pp. 64–92.—Editors' Note]. The argument will treat the cognitive content of a statement as if it depended only upon the *deductive* relations holding between the statement and the basic observation statements. In the next section we will see that this view is an oversimplification, in that one must also take into account the statement's *inductive* relations to observation statements. Taking this point into consideration here would only make the statement of the argument unnecessarily complex, without providing any additional insight into the basic structure.

of humans and other embodied beings inhabiting the spatio-temporal world.[8] (Given this definition of "empirical sentence," the sentence "There are no abominable snowmen" is empirical, whereas the sentences "God loves us" and "Ghosts rarely haunt new houses" are not empirical, though they may contain *components* that are.)

2. If one adopts a verificationist criterion of cognitive significance, one is in effect committing oneself to the view that there is *some special set of sentences* such that any sentence that is cognitively significant stands in certain confirmation relation to some sentences belonging to the set in question. Sentences that belong to the special set will be referred to as *basic observation sentences*.[9]

Let us now consider the basic translatability challenge argument:

1. A sentence S has cognitive significance if and only if there is at least one basic observation sentence O that is analytically entailed by S.[10]

2. If two sentences S and T analytically entail exactly the

[8] Empiricists who believe that all *synthetic* statements are *empirical* statements often employ the terms *synthetic* and *empirical* interchangeably. It is important to notice that I am *not* using the term *empirical* as synonymous with *synthetic*. If the position suggested in the final section of this paper is correct, then there are some statements that are synthetic but not empirical.

[9] A number of different labels have been employed to refer to this class of sentences, one of the most common being "protocol sentences."

I shall leave open, in the statement of the translatability challenge argument, the question of what type of sentences should be chosen as the basic observation sentences. This was a controversial question within logical positivism: some positivists, such as Carnap and Neurath, defended the choice of sentences about physical objects and their properties ("physicalistic sentences") as the protocol sentences, whereas other positivists, such as Ayer and Schlick, held that it was sentences about one's own present immediately given experiences that should be chosen as the basic observation sentences. Another, less frequently discussed, possibility for the basic observation sentences is the class of sentences about human experiences.

While the *statement* of the translatability challenge argument will be neutral with respect to these various possibilities, I shall suggest later that the question of the choice of basic observation sentences may very well be *critical* to the whole argument.

[10] Sentence Q of language L is *analytically entailed* by sentence P of language L just in case Q is deducible from P together with the meaning postulates for language L. (Some philosophers, most notably Quine, have rejected the whole notion of analytic entailment. A critical evaluation of this position will not be undertaken here, since the issues involved are very complex and would require a great deal of detailed argumentation.)

same basic observation sentences, then S and T have the same cognitive content.

3. Basic observation sentences are empirical sentences.

4. Any truth-functional combination of empirical sentences is an empirical sentence.

5. It follows from (3) and (4) that any truth-functional combination of basic observation sentences will be an empirical sentence.

6. Let S be any cognitively significant sentence. Then in virtue of (1) there must be some non-empty set of basic observation sentences $\{O_1, O_2, \ldots\}$ that is the set of *all* and *only* basic observation sentences that are analytically entailed by S.

7. Now consider the (possibly infinite) conjunction "O_1 and O_2 and . . ." (the conjuncts of which are all and only members of the set $\{O_1, O_2, \ldots \}$), and let E be any finite expression employed as synonymous with this (possibly infinite) conjunction. There are two important facts about E: (a) E is an *empirical* sentence, in virtue of (5); (b) E will analytically entail precisely the same basic observation sentences as S.

8. It follows from (6) and (7) that if S is any cognitively significant sentence, it is possible to define a sentence E that is an empirical sentence that has the same basic observation sentences as consequences as S does. And it follows from this, in virtue of (2), that for any cognitively significant sentence S there is an *empirical* sentence E that is *synonymous* with S with respect to cognitive content.

9. Let T be any theological statement. If the term *God* is interpreted as suggested above in section I, then T purports to refer to a being that transcends the physical world and the realm of human experience, both actual and conditional. Thus talk about God is *intended* (under the standard interpretation) to refer to *nonempirical* states of affairs.

10. It follows from (8) that reference to something transcending the empirical world (the physical world and the world of human experience) cannot be part of the cognitive content of any sentence. And this fact, together with (9), entails the conclusion: *either theological statements are not cognitively significant, or they do not have the sort of cognitive reference that they are, under the standard interpretation, intended to have.*

Three brief comments on this argument:

1. The conclusion of the argument is *not* that theological

statements are *devoid* of cognitive content. This would be the conclusion only if a theological statement did not analytically entail any basic observation sentence.[11] The conclusion is simply that if theological statements are cognitively significant, they cannot refer to an *experientially transcendent being*.

2. Both the translatability challenge argument and the falsifiability challenge argument employ a verificationist criterion of cognitive significance, although the versions invoked are different in important respects. However the translatability challenge argument also involves a *verificationist criterion of synonymy with respect to cognitive content*. This principle, introduced at (2), plays a critical role in the argument. The significance of this principle will become clearer in the next section of this paper.

3. The translatability challenge argument, unlike the falsifiability challenge argument, does not rest upon the assumption that theological statements are unfalsifiable. It is perfectly compatible with the translatability challenge argument that a given theological statement should analytically entail some empirical statement, with the consequence that if the empirical statement is falsifiable, the theological statement will also be falsifiable.

This is a critical point, since we have seen that one of the most dubious aspects of the falsifiability challenge argument is just this assumption that theological statements are not open to decisive falsification. The translatability challenge argument is thus free of one of the main weaknesses of the falsifiability challenge argument.

III. The prospects for a confirmability criterion of cognitive content

Both the falsifiability challenge argument and the translatability challenge argument appeal to some version of a confirmability criterion of cognitive content. They both assume that if a sentence is to be cognitively significant (i.e., if it is to function to assert facts, if it is to be such as is either true or false), then it must stand in certain confirmation relations to certain specified

---

[11] Actually all that is required is that there be some basic observation sentence that would either raise or lower the degree of confirmation (evidential probability) of a theological sentence. The condition here is a stronger one—in keeping with the simplified statement of the argument.

sentences called "basic observation sentences". That is, for any cognitively significant sentence there will be basic observation sentences that provide *evidence* either for or against the statement.

Thus one could dispose of both arguments at once by simply rejecting the whole notion of a confirmability criterion of cognitive content. This response is simple and economical. Before accepting it, however, one must ask: Are there good reasons to reject the whole idea of a confirmability criterion of cognitive content? What grounds are there for holding that the notion of such a criterion is fundamentally misguided?

Some philosophers of a rather strong metaphysical orientation have rejected the idea of a confirmability criterion of cognitive content simply because they were unsympathetic to any form of empiricism. Such philosophers naturally opposed the rather vigorous form of empiricism of which the confirmability criterion of cognitive content is a central principle—logical positivism. Other philosophers, though sympathetic to empiricism in general, have rejected the idea of a confirmability criterion of cognitive content because of some rather elementary confusions.[12]

The purpose of the discussion in this section will neither be to convince others of the glories of empiricism, nor to deal with individual confusions associated with discussions of the confirmability criterion. My goal here is more modest: to set out in a systematic fashion, and then to examine, the difficulties that those who are basically sympathetic to the general idea of a confirmability criterion of cognitive content have thought to be involved in any attempt to formulate such a criterion in a precise fashion.[13]

[12] This seems to be true, for example, of some of Bertrand Russell's criticisms of the confirmability criterion of cognitive significance, as set out in *Human Knowledge* (London: Allen and Unwin, 1948), pp. 445ff. For details, see Hempel's comments in his article on "Empiricist Criteria of Cognitive Significance: Problems and Changes" in C. G. Hempel, *Aspects of Scientific Explanation* (New York: The Free Press, 1965), pp. 103–105.

[13] A clear statement of most of these difficulties can be found in the article by Hempel mentioned in the preceding footnote. There is, however, one point about Hempel's discussion that it is important to notice: Hempel is concerned *not* with the question: (1) Can one formulate a confirmability criterion that will state, for any sentence, *what* the cognitive content of that sentence is?, but rather with the question: (2) Can one formulate a confirmability criterion that will state, for any sentence, *whether* that sentence has any cognitive content?

This point is noted by Hempel himself on the first page of the above article, when he remarks in passing that the testability criterion of *meaning* might more accurately be referred to as the testability criterion of *meaningfulness* (p. 101).

Suppose now that one is confronted with a proposed criterion of cognitive significance. How is one to decide whether it
is an acceptable criterion? There are, I think, two main considerations. The most important one is this: Does the proposed
criterion yield acceptable results in those cases that are *noncontroversial*? There is, for example, general agreement that declarative English sentences that assign physical properties to everyday
physical objects do have cognitive content, do function to assert
something that is either true or false. An example of such a sentence would be: "Giraffes eat leaves." Any proposed criterion
that had the consequence that some sentences of this sort were
not cognitively significant would have to be rejected as unsound.
Similarly, there is general agreement that nondeclarative English
sentences (imperatives, interrogatives, optatives, etc.) do not have
any cognitive content, are not such as are either true or false.
Any acceptable criterion would have to have this consequence.

The second consideration is this. If the proposed criterion is
intended as a criterion not only of *whether* a sentence is cognitively significant but of *what* its cognitive significance is, then
there will be a second condition of adequacy: whenever it is
agreed that two sentences S and T have *the same* cognitive content, a criterion must assign the same cognitive content to S and T
if it is to be acceptable; and whenever it is agreed that S and T
do not have the same cognitive content, any acceptable criterion
must assign different content to S and T.

It is a rather puzzling feature of Hempel's otherwise admirable discussions
of the confirmability criterion that he considers only question (2), since traditionally these two questions have been viewed as aspects of a single problem. Positivists such as Carnap, Ayer, and Reichenbach all held not only that
(a) to be cognitively significant, a sentence has to be related in certain specified ways to the basic observation sentences, but moreover that (b) if two
sentences are related in precisely the same ways to all possible sets of basic
observation sentences, then the two sentences are identical with respect to
cognitive content. See, for example, R. Carnap, "The Elimination of Metaphysics Through the Logical Analysis of Language" in *Logical Positivism*,
ed. A. J. Ayer (New York: The Free Press, 1959), p. 63, A. J. Ayer, *Language,
Truth and Logic* (New York: Dover, 1952), pp. 13, 16, 115, and H. Reichenbach,
Experience and Prediction (Chicago: University of Chicago Press, 1938), p. 54.

One might think that narrowing the discussion in the manner that Hempel
does is nothing more than a useful simplification for purposes of discussion;
however we will see shortly that this is doubtful, and that, in fact, some of
the difficulties that trouble Hempel appear to arise from viewing the confirmability criterion as simply a criterion of meaningfulness, rather than as a
criterion of meaning, and hence as involving a criterion of synonymy with
respect to cognitive content.

Each of the four difficulties to be considered here is connected with the first of the above two conditions of adequacy:
the claim in each of the four cases is that a confirmability criterion
of cognitive significance must be rejected either because it is too
generous, and admits as cognitively significant sentences that it
would be generally agreed do not function to assert anything,
or because it is too stringent, and excludes from the class of cognitively significant utterances sentences that it is generally agreed
are cognitive in nature. But while all four difficulties are of the
same general sort, we will see that quite different philosophical
considerations have to be introduced in order to deal with each
of them.

The first difficulty is this: It can be shown that certain proposed confirmability criteria of cognitive significance have the
unfortunate consequence of admitting absolutely all sentences,
from "Tigers have stripes" to "Squares eat fish smoothly," to the
class of cognitively significant sentences. It was shown by Alonzo
Church,[14] for example, that if one is granted the completely trivial
assumption that there are three logically independent basic observation sentences, then it follows from Ayer's second version of
the confirmability criterion that, for any sentence S, either S or its
negation must be cognitively significant. But if negation is interpreted in the standard way, the negation of a sentence S cannot
have a truth-value unless S has a truth-value. Thus we may say
that Church's criticism of Ayer shows in effect that absolutely any
sentence qualifies as cognitively significant if we accept Ayer's
second version of the confirmability criterion.

A second difficulty arises in connection with sentences
about so-called *theoretical entities*—objects such as genes, electrons, photons, and so on whose size is such that they are not
capable of being directly observed.[15] The problem with sentences
about such theoretical entities is that it often seems to be the case
that such sentences do not have any analytical consequences that
are expressible in terms simply of basic observation sentences.
Any confirmability criterion of cognitive significance that is for-

[14] Alonzo Church, "Review of Ayer's *Language, Truth, and Logic*," *Journal of
Symbolic Logic* 14 (1949), 52–3.
[15] Recent discussions of the notion of a theoretical entity have suggested
rather strongly that the distinction between entities that are directly observable and entities that are theoretical is far from being unproblematical. The
distinction certainly does not seem to be a sharp one.

mulated simply in terms of *deductive* relations holding between a sentence and the basic observation sentences will thus have the unacceptable consequence that theoretical sentences such as "Electrons have mass" and "Heredity is controlled by genes" will have to be rejected as devoid of cognitive content, since they do not entail any basic observational sentences.

The first two difficulties are ones that apply to atomic sentences as well as to complex or molecular sentences. The next two difficulties apply only to compound sentences, or to systems of sentences.

The third difficulty arises in connection with the question of the status of compound sentences such as "Jack is lazy and the number five is innocent"—sentences that contain one part that is cognitively significant but another part that is devoid of all cognitive content. In his article, "Empiricist Criteria of Cognitive Significance: Problems and Changes," Hempel argues that one ought to require that *any sentence containing a noncognitive component be judged cognitively meaningless.* But many versions of the confirmability criterion take it for granted that if a sentence has observational consequences, it is cognitively significant. And then it would appear that even if the sentence "The number five is innocent" has no cognitive content, the compound sentence "Jack is lazy and the number five is innocent" has at least the same observational consequences as the sentence "Jack is lazy," and thus will have to be judged cognitively significant. So that if Hempel's contention here is correct, it appears that one will have to reject all versions of the confirmability criterion that hold that the having of observational consequences is a *sufficient* condition of cognitive significance.

The fourth difficulty is closely related to the third. It is concerned with the problem of the cognitive status of cognitively theoretical systems (e.g., quantum theory) to which isolated sentences devoid of cognitive content (e.g., "The number five is innocent") have been added. Is one to say that the resulting system of sentences is cognitively significant, in spite of the fact that it contains a sentence that is devoid of cognitive content? Or is one to say that the resulting system is not cognitively significant, in spite of the fact that it has precisely the same observational consequences as the unsupplemented, and cognitively significant, system of sentences? How is this dilemma to be resolved?

Difficulties such as the above have led Hempel and other

philosophers who are basically sympathetic with the general idea of a confirmability criterion of cognitive significance to conclude that perhaps it is impossible to set out a precisely formulated version of such a criterion that will satisfy even the first condition of adequacy mentioned above, i.e., that will enable us to pick out exactly (no more than and no less than) the set of cognitively significant sentences.

For some time the feeling among most empiricists who were interested in this program was one of despair: the difficulties appeared insurmountable, and it looked as if the program would simply have to be abandoned. More recently, however, considerations have been advanced that suggest that the above difficulties are not insurmountable. The turning point in the discussion of the confirmability criterion was brought about by the publication of a brilliant article by Wesley Salmon, entitled "Verifiability and Logic."[16] Salmon's article has enabled empiricists to approach the question of a confirmability criterion of cognitive significance with renewed optimism.

My own discussion will be based almost entirely upon Salmon's, since his discussion is very complete, and there is very little in his article with which I disagree.[17] My purpose will not be to enter into a detailed and technical consideration of Salmon's article. I wish merely to touch upon some of his more important

---

[16] Available in *Mind, Matter, and Method,* ed. P. K. Feyerabend and G. Maxwell (Minneapolis: University of Minnesota Press, 1966), pp. 354–76 [Reprinted in this volume, p. 456.—Editors].

[17] There is only one really substantive point made by Salmon with which I am not in agreement. This is his contention that cognitive significance should be explicated in terms of *physical* or *nomological* possibility of verification, rather than in terms of *logical* possibility of verification. Salmon claims that "there are strong reasons for adopting the physical sense of possibility" (p. 371). However I do not find the reasons offered by Salmon at all convincing. Moreover, there seem to me to be decisive arguments against the choice of nomological possibility, and in favor of the choice of logical possibility. For, first of all, if one chooses to relate cognitive significance to *nomological* possibility of verification, the question arises as to the cognitive significance of lawlike statements that are incompatible with the actual laws of nature. It is not nomologically possible to verify such statements, although it is logically possibly to verify them. If nomological possibility of verification is required, such statements will have to be regarded as devoid of cognitive significance. And secondly, if cognitive significance is related to nomological possibility of verification, it will not be possible to decide, for every sentence, whether or not it is cognitively significant, until one knows what all the laws of nature are. These and other peculiar consequences are avoided by opting for *logical* possibility of verification.

points, and to indicate how they enable one to dispose of the four difficulties outlined above.

The first point that Salmon stresses in his article is that it is critical to distinguish between (1) the question of whether the possibility of confirmation via basic observation sentences should be taken as a criterion of cognitive significance, and (2) the question of how the notion of empirical confirmation is itself to be analyzed. Most presentations of the confirmability criterion of cognitive significance do not clearly separate these issues: the confirmability criterion is set out in such a way that it *implicitly* involves at least a partial analysis of the notion of confirmation.

Salmon suggests that the confirmability criterion of cognitive meaning itself can be construed as involving the following series of explications:

1. A sentence (or statement) has factual meaning if and only if it is empirically verifiable (or confirmable).
2. A sentence (or statement) has formal meaning if and only if it is either analytic or self-contradictory.
3. A sentence (or statement) has cognitive (or literal) meaning if and only if it has either formal meaning or factual meaning.
4. A sentence (or statement) is either true or false if and only if it has cognitive (or literal) meaning.

These explications identify cognitive meaningfulness with the possibility of being either true or false, and they reduce these properties to empirical verifiability and analyticity (or self-contradiction). There remain, however, the tasks of explicating empirical verifiability and analyticity.[18]

Salmon's distinction between the question of whether confirmability in terms of basic observation sentences should be taken as a criterion of cognitive meaning, and the question of the correct analysis of the notion of confirmation, is directly relevant to the first of the four difficulties mentioned above. Salmon points out that Church's criticism of Ayer's second formulation of the confirmability criterion has no bearing upon the confirmability criterion as set out by explications 1–4 above: ". . . it shows only that Ayer's explication of empirical verifiability is faulty. Church did not claim to have proved more."[19] Church's criticism is thus "analogous to Hempel's paradox of confirmation and Goodman's

[18] *Ibid.*, p. 355 [See this volume, p. 458.—Editors]
[19] *Ibid.*, p. 356. [See this volume, p. 459.—Editors]

grue-bleen paradox. Any satisfactory theory of scientific verification (or confirmation) must avoid such paradoxical consequences."[20]

The upshot is that a number of objections directed against
various attempts to formulate a confirmability criterion of cognitive significance are in reality objections to the analyses of the
concept of *empirical verifiability* that such formulations of the
confirmability criterion implicitly contain. As a consequence such
objections can have *no relevance* to the question of the reasonableness of employing empirical verifiability, properly analyzed,
as a criterion of cognitive significance, *unless* one is prepared to
regard such difficulties as showing that "the concept of empirical
verifiability is inexplicable in principle."[21] As Salmon suggests,
one suspects that "many philosophers who have had little hesitation in dismissing the possibility of formulating an unobjectionable
explication of cognitive meaningfulness in terms of empirical verifiability would be far more hesitant to conclude that the concepts
of scientific confirmation and confirmability are inexplicable in
principle."[22]

A simple example may be useful here. Suppose that one
were to put forward a confirmability criterion of cognitive significance that involved the following assertions:

1. A sentence S is cognitively significant if and only if it is confirmable in terms of basic observation sentences.

2. If there is some basic observation sentence O that is deducible
from S, then S is confirmable relative to basic observation sentences, since O will confirm S.

3. If S is confirmable relative to basic observation sentences, and
T is deducible from S, then T is also confirmable relative to basic
observation sentences, since any basic observation sentence O
that confirms S will confirm any analytical consequence of S,
such as T.

This criterion of cognitive significance would lead to the
unhappy conclusion that *any* sentence whatever is cognitively
significant. Consider the sentence, "The number five sleeps virtuously". The complex sentence "The number five sleeps virtu-

---

[20] *Ibid.*, p. 357. [See this volume, p. 460.—Editors]
[21] *Ibid.*, p. 358. [See this volume, p. 461.—Editors]
[22] *Ibid.*, p. 358. [See this volume, p. 461.—Editors]

ously and this table is brown" entails the sentence "This table is brown", which may here be regarded as a basic observation sentence. Hence, in view of (2) the complex sentence is confirmable. But if the complex sentence is confirmable, then the sentence "The number five sleeps virtuously," which is entailed by it, must also be confirmable, in virtue of clause (3) above. And thus, in view of (1), the sentence "The number five sleeps virtuously" must be cognitively significant.

The important point is not, however, that the above criterion has this absurd result, but that it has this result *because* it involves an unsound account of confirmation: clauses (2) and (3) together have the consequence that *any sentence confirms any other sentence*. The argument that shows this parallels the argument that showed that the sentence "The number five sleeps virtuously" must be cognitively significant. Consider *any* two sentences 'S' and 'T.' Then since 'S' is entailed by the complex sentence 'S and T,' it follows in view of clause (2) that 'S' confirms 'S and T.' But clause (3) involves the assertion that if one sentence confirms another sentence, it also confirms any consequence of that sentence. And thus, since 'T' is a consequence of 'S and T,' it follows from the fact that 'S' confirms 'S and T' that 'S' confirms 'T.' That is, it follows that any sentence is confirmed by any other sentence.

Given this absurd result, it follows that every sentence is confirmed by some (indeed, by any) basic observation sentence. So that if confirmability by basic observation sentences is taken as the criterion of cognitive significance, we have the result that every sentence is cognitively significant.

The defectiveness of the criterion set out by clauses (1), (2), and (3) is thus seen to be a direct consequence of the inadequate account of empirical confirmation embodied in clauses (2) and (3). The inadequacy of the criterion should thus not be taken as calling into question the whole program of employing confirmability as a criterion of cognitive significance. The conclusion is simply that one needs a more satisfactory account of the notion of empirical confirmation.

In brief, then, the answer to the first difficulty is this. If a proposed confirmability criterion of cognitive significance has the absurd result that it grants cognitive significance to absolutely every sentence, the reason that it does so is quite likely that the proposed formulation of the criterion also has the absurd result that every sentence confirms every other sentence. The defect is thus no indication that the very idea of a confirmability criterion of cognitive significance is untenable. It shows only that the formulation in question involves an unsatisfactory analysis of the notion of confirmation.

This brings us to the second of the difficulties mentioned above. Salmon indicates how the second difficulty should be handled in the following passage:

"... empirical verifiability must be explicated in terms of inductive relations and not exclusively in terms of deductive relations. Induction is not simply the converse of deduction. If the explication of empirical verifiability is merged with the explication of cognitive meaningfulness, the joint explication must not be given solely in terms of the existence of observational consequences."[23]

The basic reason why one must take into account the inductive relations that hold among sentences is that it is possible to have two sentences S and T that, as far as observation sentences go, have precisely the same consequences, but such that there is some basic observation sentence O that is rendered more probable by S than it is by T. If S and T do not lend the same degree of evidential support to some observation sentence O, then S and T must differ in cognitive content, in spite of the fact that as far as *deductive* observational consequences are concerned they are in complete agreement. Thus it is clear that to have an adequate criterion of cognitive content one will have to take into account the *inductive* (evidential, or confirmational) relations that a given sentence has to basic observation sentences, and not merely its deductive relations.

The second difficulty—that of cognitively significant theoretical sentences that have no analytical consequences that are expressible in terms of basic observation sentences—is closely related to the more general difficulty just mentioned, and it can be handled in the same way. Just as taking inductive relations into account enables one to assign different cognitive content to two sentences S and T that have same observational consequences, so it also enables one to assert that a sentence R that has no (deductive) observational consequences, but which does lend in-

23 *Ibid.*, p. 375. [See this volume, p. 479.—Editors]

ductive support to some observation sentence O, has cognitive content.

Before turning to the third and fourth difficulties, we must consider· another point that Salmon stresses in his article: that "any criterion of cognitive meaningfulness needs to be supplemented with a criterion of cognitive equisignificance. Equisignificance must be explicated in terms of equal inductive support, not in terms of equal observational consequences."[24]

This is an extremely important point. For, in the first place, we noticed in the previous section that such a confirmability criterion of synonymy with respect to cognitive content is essential to the translatability challenge argument. And secondly, by supplementing[25] the confirmability criterion of meaningfulness with a confirmability criterion of synonymy with respect to cognitive content, one is able to dispose of the third and fourth difficulties.

Let's turn to the third difficulty—that of complex sentences, such as "Either Jack is lazy or the number five is innocent," that contain both a cognitive part and a noncognitive part. Hempel, in his article on "Empiricist Criteria of Cognitive Significance: Problems and Changes", suggests that it should be a condition of adequacy for a criterion of cognitive significance that *any sentence containing a noncognitive sentence as a component be judged cognitively meaningless.* This recommendation has some initial plausibility. But, as noted earlier, it leads directly to the third difficulty mentioned above. For there are complex sentences, such as "This table is brown and the number five sleeps virtuously", that do have observational consequences in spite of the fact that they contain cognitively meaningless components. So that if Hempel's condition of adequacy is sound, one is forced to accept the conclusion that there can be sentences that have observational consequences but which are cognitively meaningless.

[24] *Ibid.,* p. 375. [See this volume, p. 479.—Editors]

[25] The reason that this is a genuine supplementation is that a criterion of *meaningfulness* provides answers only to questions of the form, "Is the linguistic expression 'S' meaningful?", whereas when the criterion of meaningfulness is transformed into a criterion of *meaning* by adding a criterion of sameness of meaning, one is in a position to answer other sorts of questions, such as "Do the linguistic expressions 'S' and 'T' have the same meaning?", "What is the meaning of 'S'?", and so on. (Compare this difference with the difference between a criterion that would tell you *whether* an object was an animal, and a criterion that would tell you *what sort* of animal a given object was.)

Why does Hempel accept the above condition of adequacy? His reason for doing so is indicated in the following passage:

> "If under a given criterion of cognitive significance, a sentence N is nonsignificant, then so must be all truth-functional compound sentences in which N occurs nonvacuously as a component. For if N cannot be significantly assigned a truth value, then it is impossible to assign truth values to the compound sentences containing N; hence, they should be qualified as nonsignificant as well."[26]

I think there are at least two reasons for rejecting the suggested criterion of adequacy, together with the argument that Hempel offers in support of it. In the first place, Hempel's argument rests upon the assumption that connectives such as "and," "or," "if . . . then" are such that it is a *necessary condition* of applying them to sentence-arguments that *the sentence-arguments in question possess truth-values*. This is a natural enough assumption to make, given that, in logic courses, these connectives are generally expressed formally by means of the truth-functional connectives.

But let us widen our perspective a bit. Consider the sentence: "Close the door and open the window." Or the sentence: "What movie would you like to see, and at what time would you like to go?" Or the sentence: "Long live the king, and may his reign be a peaceful one." Is it plausible to believe that the word "and" occurring in the last three sentences is *not* the same word as the word "and" that occurs in the sentence "The door is open and the window is closed"? Surely it is reasonable to hold that such a conclusion is highly implausible.

If this is correct, it follows[27] that the so-called truth-functional connectives such as "and," "or," and the like are not, as employed in ordinary English, functions that need have as their arguments either truth-values or entities possessing truth-values. Hempel's argument for his condition of adequacy rests, however, upon the assumption that connectives such as "and" and "or" connect only linguistic expressions that have truth-values. It is thus clear that Hempel's argument is unsound.

Another consideration is this. There are a number of ex-

[26] Hempel, "Empiricist Criteria of Cognitive Significance: Problems and Changes," p. 102.
[27] Assuming, what seems very reasonable, that imperatives, interrogatives, and optatives do not all have truth-values.

pressions that are intimately tied up with the notion of cognitive content. If an expression is cognitively significant, it can be used to *assert facts,* and thus to *provide one with information.* Consider, in this light, the sentence: "The cat is on the mat and God is being-itself." This sentence surely provides one with information, and asserts at least one fact. For even if one can make no sense at all of the sentence "God is being-itself," the complex sentence does at least tell one that the cat is on the mat. And in view of this it seems peculiar to say, as Hempel's suggested condition of adequacy would have us do, that the sentence "The cat is on the mat and God is being-itself" is devoid of cognitive significance. One wants to say that the complex sentence is cognitively significant, and that it has *at least as much* cognitive content as the first part: "The cat is on the mat."

This is the view that Salmon takes of the matter: ". . . it seems more reasonable to say that the cognitive parts render the compounds cognitive to some extent and that the noncognitive parts do not add to the cognitive content but do not detract from it either."[28] To say this, of course, is to construe the confirmability criterion as being a criterion of cognitive *meaning,* and not merely a criterion of cognitive *meaningfulness.*

This brings us to the fourth difficulty—that of cognitively meaningful theoretical sentences to which isolated sentences[29] have been added. This difficulty is also easily disposed of if one interprets the confirmability criterion as involving a criterion of synonymy with respect to cognitive content. For suppose that one adds the sentence "The number five is innocent" to some scientific system. In such a case one will *not* say that the resulting system containing the isolated sentence "The number five is innocent" is devoid of cognitive significance. Rather, one will say that the resulting system has "precisely the same cognitive meaning as the system that would result from the deletion of the isolated sentence."[30] By employing a confirmability criterion of sameness of cognitive meaning one is able to avoid the dilemma: either (1) the

---

[28] Salmon, "Verifiability and Logic," p. 366. [See this volume, p. 469.—Editors]

[29] A sentence within a given scientific system of sentences is *isolated* if the explanatory and predictive power of the system of sentences is in no way altered by the omission of the sentence in question. Any sentence that is devoid of cognitive content will thus be an isolated member of any system of sentences.

[30] *Ibid.,* p. 367. [See this volume, 471.—Editors]

resulting system containing the isolated sentence is devoid of cognitive significance, in spite of the fact that it has precisely the same observational consequences as the original system, which was cognitively significant, or (2) the isolated sentence ("The number five is innocent") is cognitively significant, since it can form part of a cognitively significant theoretical system. For now there is a third alternative. One can say that the resulting system is cognitively significant, but that the isolated sentence "The number five is innocent" *adds nothing* to the cognitive content of the original theoretical system; the two systems are synonymous with respect to cognitive content.

The importance of viewing the confirmability criterion as a criterion of *what* the cognitive content of a sentence is, rather than simply as a criterion of *whether* a sentence has cognitive significance, should now be apparent. In order to have such a confirmability criterion of cognitive content the series of four explications mentioned above (p. 497) must be supplemented with a criterion of synonymy with respect to cognitive content. The one suggested by Salmon[31] may be formulated as follows:

Two sentences (or statements) S and T have the same cognitive meaning if and only if for any set O of basic observation (or protocol) sentences the degree of confirmation of S by evidence O is equal to the degree of confirmation of T by evidence O.

This criterion of synonymy with respect to cognitive content, together with the four explications stated earlier, constitutes only an outline sketch. There are a number of rather difficult problems that would have to be disposed of before one could offer anything like a fully and explicitly formulated confirmability criterion of cognitive content. This point is emphasized by Salmon towards the end of his paper, where he asks: "Where does all of this leave us?" Part of his reply is that ". . . it reaffirms the fundamental importance of two old philosophical problems, the problem of specifying an observation-basis and the problem of constructing (and possibly justifying) an inductive logic."[32]

Fortunately it will not be necessary here to become entangled in these problems, although I will suggest in the next section that one of these problems—that of choosing the basic observation sentences—lies at the very heart of the translatability challenge argument.

31 *Ibid.*, p. 368. [See this volume, p. 472.—Editors]
32 *Ibid.*, p. 375. [See this volume, p. 479.—Editors]

Let me summarize the discussion in this section by indicating the important facts that have emerged. First, we have seen that it is possible to dispose of four of the serious difficulties that attempts to formulate a confirmability criterion of cognitive significance have encountered. To the extent that the difficulties considered are representative ones, this fact gives one grounds for believing that a rigorous formulation of a confirmability criterion of cognitive significance is possible. And secondly, this means that to reject the translatability challenge argument by simply rejecting the whole notion of a confirmability criterion of cognitive significance may very well be incorrect, and at the very least is philosophically premature. Finally, we have seen that if one is to avoid the problems that arise in connection with the formulation of a confirmability criterion, it seems essential to view the criterion as incorporating a criterion of synonymy with respect to cognitive content—a principle that, as was noted earlier, is critical in the statement of the translatability challenge argument.

IV. Possible responses to the translatability challenge argument

In this final section I wish to set out, and comment briefly upon, the most important responses to the translatability challenge argument. It will be easiest to do this if we have a fairly rigorous statement of the argument in front of us. The following is a revision, in the light of intervening considerations, of the formulation offered earlier in section II.

1. A sentence S is cognitively significant if and only if it stands in confirmation relations to basic observation statements.

2. Two sentences S and T have precisely the same cognitive content if and only if for any set O of basic observation statements, the degree of confirmation of S by evidence O is equal to the degree of confirmation of T by evidence O.

3. Any sentence that can either be explicitly constructed from basic observation sentences (by means of truth-functional connectives, quantifiers, and possibly other logical apparatus[33]), or introduced in terms of basic observation sentences, is an *empir-*

---

[33] The possibility of logical apparatus beyond that provided by the quantifiers and the truth-functional connectives certainly has to be left open, since there is, for example, the notorious problem of the analysis of sentences containing subjunctive conditionals.

ical sentence, i.e., a sentence about the natural world or about the experiences of humans or other embodied beings.

4. If we have a function that specifies, for every possible set of basic observation sentences, some number (between zero and one), then it is possible to construct from, or introduce in terms of, the basic observation sentences, some sentence that will have, upon each set of basic observation sentences, just the degree of confirmation that the function in question associates with that particular set.

5. In view of (3), it follows that any sentence so constructed is an empirical sentence.

6. It follows from (4) that, given any cognitively significant sentence *S*, it must be possible to construct an empirical sentence *E* such that *E* has precisely the same degree of confirmation as *S* upon any possible set of basic observation sentences.

7. It follows from (6), in view of (2), that it is possible to construct, for any cognitively significant sentence *S*, an empirical sentence *E* such that *S* and *E* have precisely the same cognitive content.

8. Let *T* be any theological sentence. If the term "God" is interpreted as suggested in section I, then *T* purports to refer to a being that transcends the physical world and the realm of human experience, both actual and conditional. Thus talk about God is *intended*, under the standard interpretation, to refer to *nonempirical* states of affairs.

9. It follows from (7) that reference to something transcending the empirical world (the physical world and the world of human experience) cannot be part of the cognitive content of any sentence.

10. It then follows from (8) and (9) that *theological statements cannot have the sort of reference that they are intended to have.* If theological sentences are cognitively significant, they must be equivalent in cognitive meaning to *purely empirical* statements.

How, then, is one to respond to this argument? The main possibilities would seem to be these:

1. One might try to argue that some of the inferences made in the argument are logically unsound. This would involve questioning one of the inferences made at steps (5), (6), (7), (9), and (10).

2. One might challenge the constructability claim advanced at step (4).

3. One might completely reject the idea of a confirmability

criterion of cognitive significance, even in the partial form advanced at step (1).

4. One might accept the idea of a confirmability criterion of *cognitive meaningfulness* (as formulated at step (1)), but reject the further notion of a confirmability criterion of cognitive *meaning* (as advanced at step (2)).

5. One might completely accept the idea of a confirmability criterion of cognitive content (as formulated at steps (1) and (2)), but argue that a *proper* choice of the basic observation sentences invalidates the claim advanced at step (3) of the argument. That is, one might claim that the basic observation sentences are not such that any sentence constructed from them is an *empirical* sentence.

The first of these responses need not be considered at any length. I think that the argument is stated in sufficiently explicit form to make it clear that the inferences are sound ones.

The second response, on the other hand, merits serious consideration, especially since traditional formulations of the translatability challenge argument have not focused attention upon this step in the argument. The main reason this step has been generally overlooked is that the argument has usually been formulated in terms of the assumption that the cognitive content of a sentence is expressible simply in terms of the deductive relations of that sentence to the basic observation sentences: inductive relations have generally been ignored. And when one takes the cognitive content of a sentence to be expressible simply in terms of its deductive relations to basic observation sentences, one is able to replace the constructability assumption at step (4) by a much weaker assumption, to the effect that any conjunction of empirical sentences will be an empirical sentence.[34]

But we cannot pursue this issue here. For while the question of the acceptability of the constructability assumption is an important one, it is also quite a technical one. And in any case I think that the basic flaw in the translatability challenge argument lies elsewhere.

The third response is the most popular one: one simply rejects the very idea of a confirmability criterion of cognitive significance. This response has in effect been considered in section III, where I set out, and tried to defend, the reasons that Salmon has offered for thinking that the widespread rejection of the confirma-

[34] See step (4) in the simplified version of the translatability challenge argument stated earlier in section II.

bility criterion of cognitive significance has been, at the very least, tenuously based and philosophically premature.

Section III also provided us with grounds for rejecting the fourth response. For as was pointed out by Salmon, some of the difficulties confronting the formulation of a confirmability criterion of cognitive significance can be avoided by supplementing the confirmability criterion of cognitive meaningfulness with a confirmability criterion of synonymy with respect to cognitive content. To reject a confirmability criterion of cognitive *meaning* while accepting a confirmability criterion of cognitive *meaningfulness* appears to be a nonviable philosophical position.

This brings us to the fifth response. I will first set out a capsule statement of this response, and then attempt to clarify the basic concepts and considerations that underlie the particular form of this response that I consider the most promising.

This fifth response turns about a point mentioned in section III, namely, that even after one accepts the general idea of a confirmability criterion of cognitive content, there are a number of tasks that must be completed before one has a precisely formulated criterion. One of the most critical of these tasks is *the selection of the proper class of sentences as the basic observation sentences*. An arbitrary choice of the class of basic observation sentences is clearly unacceptable, since different choices will lead to quite different results both as to what sentences are to be viewed as cognitively significant, and as to what the cognitive content of certain sentences is. The fifth response claims that *the translatability challenge argument depends upon an epistemologically unsound choice of the class of sentences that are to be taken as the basic observation sentences*. It is contended that the argument will break down once a proper choice of the class of basic observation sentences is made. Specifically, it is contended that given the correct class of basic observation sentences, the claim advanced at step (3) of the argument will no longer be acceptable: not every sentence that can be constructed from basic observation sentences will be an empirical sentence.

We now must try to get clearer as to precisely what is involved in this fifth response. I think it will be good to proceed in the following stages:

1. An informal and intuitive clarification of the concept of a basic observation statement;

2. A discussion of the general guidelines to be used in selecting the *proper* class of basic observation statements;

3. A setting out of the main alternatives for the role of basic observation statements;

4. A discussion of the respective merits of the different alternatives;

5. An indication of the relationship between the different possible choices of basic observation statements and the tenability of the translatability challenge argument;

6. A discussion of the possibility of basic observation statements of a distinctively theological sort.

The concept of a basic observation statement

Basic observation statements are statements that are basic in two respects: (a) *epistemologically,* and (b) *semantically.*

To understand the concept of a class of epistemologically basic statements one must understand the distinction between *inferential* knowledge and *noninferential* knowledge. The basic idea here is this: suppose that one were asked to justify one's knowledge claims. One might very well reply by showing how a given knowledge claim could be justified *relative* to some other knowledge claim. However it is clear that showing that one is justified in believing one thing *if* one is justified in believing certain other things does not in itself show that one is justified in believing anything at all. One must trace one's knowledge claim back to things that one is justified in believing *simpliciter,* and not merely relative to other things. Such justified true beliefs that do not rest upon other justified true beliefs constitute *noninferential* knowledge. The things that one knows on the basis of one's noninferential knowledge constitute *inferential* knowledge.

Given this distinction, the belief that there are epistemologically basic statements just comes down to the belief that there is a special class of statements such that all and only statements belonging to that limited class can be noninferentially known.[35]

---

[35] Some contemporary philosophers have rejected the claim that there is a special class of statements that are epistemologically basic. In some cases they have rejected this claim on the grounds that the distinction between inferential and noninferential knowledge upon which it rests cannot be coherently explicated. In other cases this distinction has been accepted, but it has been contended that *any* sentence can, under appropriate circumstances, be known noninferentially, so that there is no privileged class of sentences that are epistemologically basic.

This brings us to the second characteristic of basic observation statements: they constitute a set of statements that are semantically basic. The concept of a set of semantically basic statements is best approached by considering how one would go about explaining the meaning of certain sentences to someone with whom one shared *no language at all*. If there were some terms that both of you understood, you might be able to explain the meanings of the sentences in question in terms of them. But if there are no words that are mutually understood, verbal definition is clearly useless. The only approach will be to define some terms *ostensively,* i.e., to actually *use* some terms in circumstances that will enable the other person to formulate, and to test, likely hypotheses as to what the terms in question mean.[36] And then, once the meanings of some terms have been learned in this ostensive fashion, it will be possible to convey the meaning of other terms by means of verbal definition.

A set of sentences constitutes a semantical basis for a language if the set satisfies the following conditions: (a) the set is semantically adequate, i.e., it is possible to explain the meanings of all other sentences in the language in terms of sentences that belong to the set; (b) the sentences in the set are such that their meanings can be learned ostensively; (c) the predicates in the sentences in the set have as their meanings simple rather than complex properties; (d) the set is minimal, i.e., there is no proper subset of it that has the first three properties. Any sentence that belongs to such a semantical basis can then be characterized as *semantically basic.*

Given these concepts, one can say that the confirmability criterion of cognitive content presupposes, *first,* that there are epistemologically basic sentences, and *secondly,* that the set of epistemologically basic sentences is also a set of semantically basic sentences. For the confirmability criterion asserts that if one knows the meaning of those sentences that can be noninferentially known, then one knows the meaning of any other sentence once one knows its confirmation relations to the sentences that are epistemologically basic. Thus if there is an adequate criterion of cognitive content, it must be possible to explain the cognitive content of all sentences by reference to the meanings of the epistemologically basic sentences.

[36] For example, one might point at red objects while saying, "This is red," in order to convey the meaning of the term "red" to the other person.

Selection of the class of basic observation statements

There are two main considerations that should guide the choice of basic observation statements. First, it must be possible to justify all knowledge by appealing to knowledge of statements belonging to the set in question. Secondly, it must be possible to explain the cognitive meaning of every statement in terms of the meanings of sentences belonging to the set in question. A set of sentences that satisfies the first condition can be referred to as an adequate epistemological basis, while a set of sentences that satisfies the second condition is an adequate semantical basis. The class of basic observation statements must be both.

For our purposes here, however, it is the second consideration that turns out to be most crucial in assessing the relative merits of different possible choices of the class of basic observation statements. In choosing a semantical basis, the *general* idea is quite clear: one simply considers different types of sentences— e.g., sentences about everyday physical objects, sentences about theoretical entities, sentences about past events, sentences about one's own experiences, feelings, thoughts, and other psychological states, sentences about the psychological states of others—and asks, of each type of sentence, whether the sort of meaning it has can be plausibly explained or analyzed in terms of the class of statements being considered for the role of basic observation statements. A negative answer at any point will rule out the class in question. The problem, however, is that it is often very difficult to decide whether or not the meaning of sentences of one type can plausibly be explained in terms of sentences of some other type. Many of the classical philosophical controversies have centered upon just such questions.[37] The upshot is that it will often be impossible to determine whether a given set of sentences constitutes

---

[37] Examples of such questions are these: (1) Can sentences about physical objects, such as "There is a brown chair in the next room," be analyzed in terms of phenomenalistic sentences about one's immediate experiences and sensations, such as "Someone is having a brownish sensation"? (2) Can sentences about the experiences of others, such as "John has a headache," be analyzed in terms of sentences about their behavior, such as "John is moaning, holding his head, and taking aspirins"? (3) Can sentences about one's own experiences be analyzed in terms of talk about one's physical condition or one's behavior?

an adequate semantical basis without first answering a number of very difficult questions in epistemology and philosophy of mind. For the present, however, let's ignore these larger questions and turn to consider the main alternatives that have been suggested for a semantical basis.

The main alternatives for the role of basic observation statements

Let us now consider four different proposals as to the class of sentences that is to serve as the class of basic observation sentences. A knowledge of these four alternatives should enable the reader to understand the different versions of the translatability challenge argument that he is likely to encounter in philosophical and theological discussions.

One possibility for the role of basic observation statements is that of statements about *physical* objects, events, states of affairs, and so on. These may be either (a) everyday statements about physical objects, e.g., "The cat often lies in front of the fireplace," or (b) statements formulated in the technical language of physics and the other sciences, e.g., "There is a gravitational field of strength K at space-time point (x, y, z, t)." Sentences of either type may, for brevity, be referred to as *physicalistic* sentences.[38]

Those who favor this alternative usually do so because they hold a certain view on the nature of verification: the view that verification should be a *public procedure, an intersubjectively checkable operation.* The selection of physicalistic statements as the basic observation statements insures that this condition will be met. For if all verification must ultimately be formulated in terms of statements about the physical world, it follows that all verification is ultimately of an intersubjective nature.

This view of the nature of verification is probably familiar, since one often encounters it in philosophical discussions of religious knowledge. One of the objections that philosophers often raise to claims of religious knowledge turns about a contrast between the *private* nature of religious experiences and the *public* nature of the experimental procedures that characterize scientific knowledge.

[38] Among the logical positivists who favored selection of physicalistic sentences as the basic observation sentences were Otto Neurath and Rudolf Carnap.

A second possibility for the role of basic observation statements is that of pure, *first-person, phenomenalistic statements.* These are statements about one's own sensations or so-called "raw feels", construed as *private inner mental events that one has logically privileged access to,* and that are described without any reference to anything external or public, such as one's behavior. Examples might be: "I feel feverish," "The images in my visual field are complex, brightly colored, and blurred," "My after-image is green."

There is a great difference between this second possibility and the first one. In this case verification is not intersubjective, and does not refer to the public spatiotemporal world. Rather, it is subjective and private: verification is *verification by me, and by reference to the properties of my own private inner experiences.*

What sorts of considerations have motivated philosophers to accept one of these first two views? In part, the choice of physicalistic statements as the basic observation statements has often resulted from (possibly superficial) reflection upon the nature of scientific knowledge. And on the other hand, the choice of first-person phenomenalistic statements as the basic observation statements has often been suggested by the thought that everything that I know must somehow rest upon my experience: the only thing that I have direct access to is my own experience, and it is only through it and by means of it that I come to know anything about the external world and the experiences of others.

The next two positions can be viewed as attempts to mediate, at least partially, between the first two alternatives. Both the third and the fourth alternative agree with the second in its stress upon immediate experience as the end-point in the verification process. However they disagree with the solipsistic[39] orientation that characterizes the choice of *first-person* statements as the basic observation statements.

The third alternative is this: sentences about *the experiences of humans and other organisms* can be taken as the basic observation sentences. Examples of such sentences would be: "It seems to Macbeth that he sees a dagger before him," and "Bowzer is now experiencing the taste of 1961 Mouton Rothschild for the first time."

This choice is a fairly natural one if one feels that (a) the

[39] Solipsism is here understood as the belief that there are persons other than oneself is either meaningless, or incoherent, or false, or unreasonable.

end-points in the process of verification must be experiences, and (b) the solipsistic limitation of experience to one's own experience cannot be correct. Given such an outlook, it is natural to conclude that what is wanted is sentences about the experiences of *humans*. Further reflection may, in turn, convince one that what one really wants is sentences about the experiences of physical organisms in general (or at least the "higher" ones), on the grounds that it does not seem reasonable to limit experience to humans.

However considerations (a) and (b) can lead one to a different choice of the class of sentences that are to be taken as the basic observation sentences. This should be clear once one notices that the movement from the second alternative to the third involves both a widening and a narrowing. The widening has already been noted: the basic observation statements under the third alternative refer to the experiences of humans in general (and other organisms), and not merely to one's own experiences, as was the case under the second alternative. But there is also a narrowing here, since under the third alternative the experiences *must* be the experiences of *physical organisms,* whereas with the second alternative—that of first-person phenomenalistic statements— there is *no necessity* that the experiences be the experiences of a physical organism. Once this is noted, it is clear that one need not insist that the basic observation statements involve reference to the experiences of humans and other physical organisms in order to avoid the solipsism that is implicit in the second alternative. One can instead simply *generalize* from first-person phenomenalistic statements to statements that are about experiences that may be either one's own or someone else's. The addition of the restriction to physical organisms is not necessary in order to avoid the solipsism of the second alternative.

The generalization can take two different forms. The first form is arrived at by replacing the term "I" that occurs in first-person phenomenalistic statements by the term "someone." If we do this in the case of the examples of first-person phenomenalistic statements used earlier we have: "Someone feels feverish," "The images in someone's visual field are complex, brightly colored, and blurred," "Someone's after-image is green." The second form is arrived at by simply dropping all reference to persons, and instead speaking only of experiences. Doing this with the previous examples gives us: "There is a feverish feeling," "There is a visual field image that is complex, brightly colored, and blurred," "There is a

green after-image." For our present purposes the distinction between these two types of sentences is not important, and I shall
refer to sentences of either type as existentially quantified phenomenalistic sentences.[40]

Respective merits of the different alternatives

As I indicated earlier, the selection of the class of basic observation statements cannot be separated from the resolution of some
fundamental philosophical issues. In this section I will merely
comment upon the four alternatives suggested in the previous section: there is no intention of offering capsule refutations.

The choice of physicalistic statements as the basic observation statements seems implausible for a number of reasons. In the
first place, it is hard to believe that sentences about the physical
world refer to the *end-points* in the process of verification. Surely
a sentence such as "The table is brown" does not express something that is noninferentially known. Rather, it expresses a fact
that is known on the basis of other facts: one knows that the table
is brown because one knows, for example, that it *looks* brown to
all the people in the room. But to talk about how things *look* is to
talk about the (visual) experiences of people. Thus it would seem
reasonable to hold that one's knowledge of the physical world,
rather than being noninferential, is based upon knowledge of the
experiences people have. As a consequence, physicalistic sentences would not appear to constitute an adequate epistemological
basis.

Secondly, physicalistic statements would not seem to provide an adequate semantical basis, mainly because it is very difficult to see how talk about experiences, about sensations, about
"raw feels," can be even roughly translated into physicalistic
language. For if it were possible to *translate* statements about experiences into physicalistic statements, this would mean that there
would be physical states of affairs such that it would be logically
or analytically necessary that any organism that was in such physical states be having a certain specific experience. But surely the

---

[40] Some philosophers would argue that there is no real difference in meaning
between these two classes of sentences, possibly on the grounds that it is an
analytic truth that every experience is someone's experience. Complex issues
are involved here, one of the more important of which is the question of
whether the concept of a person is analyzable into other, simpler, notions.

existence of any such correlation between one's physical state and one's experiences is at most an empirically discoverable correlation. It is always *conceivable* that any such correlation should not exist, and hence there can be no logical necessity in any such correlation. It follows from this that statements about experiences *cannot be translated* into physicalistic statements. This in turn implies that physicalistic statements cannot constitute the basic observation statements.

The second alternative, that of first-person phenomenalistic statements, has the defect of entailing analytical solipsism, where *analytical solipsism* is the view that it is analytically impossible for there to be persons (i.e., subjects that have experiences—people, cats, dogs, etc.) other than oneself. On this view, *all* experiences are necessarily one's own experiences. Sometimes an attempt is made to disguise this commitment to solipsism in the following way: Sentences are introduced that *appear* to be about the *experiences* of others. However it turns out that the meaning that is being assigned to experience-expressions in such sentences is radically different from the meaning experience-expressions have in sentences about one's own experiences. For while sentences about one's own experiences are interpreted phenomenalistically, i.e., as referring to certain private inner mental events that one has privileged access to, sentences about the experiences of *others* are interpreted *physicalistically or behavioristically*, i.e., as referring to physical events, processes, or dispositions which are in principle open to public observation.[41] By thus assigning some meaning to talk about the experiences of others, one avoids a position that is openly solipsistic; however the fact that the meaning assigned to talk about the experiences of others is of a different sort from that assigned to talk about one's own experiences means that the position is still implicitly solipsistic. In addition, such a "two-meanings" view of talk about experience encounters serious logical difficulties of its own. Thus there seem to be good reasons for rejecting first-person phenomenalistic statements as the basic observation statements.

The third alternative mentioned above was that of sentences that assign experiences to humans and other physical organisms. There are a number of considerations that make this class of sentences an implausible choice for the role of basic observation sen-

---

[41] Compare Ayer's position in *Language, Truth and Logic*, pp. 120–133.

tences. First, these sentences are "hybrids;" they contain both a phenomenalistic component (the reference to experience), and a physicalistic component (the reference to the physical organism that is having the experience). This is important for a number of reasons. First, since a sentence of this sort will always entail some physicalistic sentence, sentences of this sort cannot be noninferentially known unless physicalistic sentences can be noninferentially known. And as was mentioned during the earlier discussion of physicalistic sentences, it is far from clear that any physicalistic sentences can be noninferentially known. If this is correct, then the present class of sentences cannot constitute an adequate epistemological basis. Secondly, many philosophers have held that the basic observation sentences should be *structurally atomic,* rather than molecular. This in itself would rule out hybrid sentences such as those involved in this third alternative. Thirdly, it is hard to see how such hybrid sentences could ever constitute an adequate epistemological basis: in what sense is one really explaining the meaning of physicalistic sentences, for example, if the explanation that one offers is in terms of sentences that contain a physicalistic component? Such explanation certainly appears circular.

A second reason for rejecting this third alternative is that many people believe that it makes sense to speak of one's surviving the destruction of one's body.[42] But it can be shown that sentences describing such a state of affairs cannot be adequately rendered in terms only of sentences assigning experiences to humans and other physical organisms.

A final consideration arises if one asks what view of verification is associated with the choice of sentences ascribing experiences to physical organisms as the basic observation sentences. The answer is obvious: the view is that verification must always be by reference to the experiences of embodied persons. But what is the reason for this restriction to the experiences of *embodied* persons? Why not instead simply require that verifica-

[42] A number of philosophers have challenged this belief. See, for example, Antony Flew's article, "Can a Man Witness His Own Funeral?", *Hibbert Journal,* 54 (1956), 242–250, and C. B. Martin, *Religious Belief* (Ithaca: Cornell University Press, 1959), pp. 95–120. There was explicit disagreement among the positivists on this question. Ayer, in *Language, Truth and Logic,* contended that "it is self-contradictory to speak of a man as surviving the annihilation of his body" (p. 127), while Schlick, on the other hand, in his article on "Meaning and Verification," *Philosophical Review,* 45 (1936), 339–369, maintained that the notion of survival in disembodied form was perfectly intelligible.

tion be by reference to the experiences of persons—either embodied or nonembodied? The restriction to the experiences of embodied persons seems arbitrary and unwarranted;[43] moreover, it necessitates the incorporation of physicalistic reference into the basic observation statements, and thus leads to the difficulties noted above.

This brings us to the fourth and final possibility for the basic observation statements—existentially quantified phenomenalistic statements, such as "Someone is experiencing a rectangular brown appearance," "There is a sharp, painful sensation," "Some person is enjoying a tingling sensation," and the like. This alternative would be a natural one to adopt if one thought that the restriction of verification to the experiences of embodied persons was unjustified. For when one drops the reference to physical organisms that one finds in the sentences considered under the third alternative, one will be left with sentences about experiences in general: existentially quantified phenomenalistic sentences.

But is this fourth alternative acceptable? The choice of existentially quantified phenomenalistic sentences as the basic observation sentences encounters difficulties that confront the selection of *any* type of phenomenalistic sentences as the basic observation sentences. One central difficulty is this: Is it really possible to explain the meanings of sentences about physical objects in terms of phenomenalistic statements?

The critical point here, however, is that many of the objections that philosophers have advanced against the selection of phenomenalistic sentences for the role of basic observation sentences will not, even if they are sound, undermine the present argument. If one's purpose is merely to refute the translatability challenge argument, it is not necessary to show that the set of basic observation sentences is *identical* with an appropriately selected set of existentially quantified phenomenalistic sentences. One need only show that the set of basic observation statements

[43] Some philosophers might defend this restriction of verification to the experiences of embodied persons on the grounds that the notion of a nonembodied person is an incoherent notion. However even if this were correct, there would still be no reason to incorporate this fact into the formulation of one's basic criterion of meaning. While on the other hand, since it is far from clear that it's an analytic truth that all persons are embodied, there is an excellent reason *not* to incorporate this claim into one's criterion of cognitive meaning.

must *contain* existentially quantified phenomenalistic statements. This latter claim is *much* weaker, and yet it is sufficient to establish that no form of the translatability challenge argument can succeed.

The tenability of the translatability challenge argument

Let us now consider the connection between the selection of the class of basic observation statements and the structure of the translatability challenge argument. The relevant point is the claim advanced at step (3) of the argument, viz., the claim that *any sentence that can be constructed out of basic observation statements is an empirical statement,* i.e., a statement about the natural world or about the experiences of humans or other embodied beings. If one selects either physicalistic statements or statements about the experiences of humans or other physical organisms (alternatives [1] and [3]) as one's basic observation statements, then any statement that can be constructed by logical means out of the basic observation statements will be an empirical statement. If, on the other hand, first-person phenomenalistic statements are selected as the basic observation statements, it seems reasonable to hold that it will be possible to construct statements on the basis of the basic observation statements that are *not* empirical. For unless some form of physicalism or behaviorism is correct, phenomenalistic statements about my experience need not involve any reference to the physical world. One might object that in ascribing the experiences to a person one is implicitly referring to the body of the person in question. But this does not seem to be true: the fact that I am having some experience or other does not seem to analytically entail that I have a body.[44] And if this is right, then sentences about one's own experiences *need not* refer either to the physical world or to the experiences of humans or other embodied persons, and hence need not be empirical sentences. Conclusion: if one selects first-person phenomenalistic statements as the basic observation statements, the claim advanced at step (3) must be rejected.

[44] But it must be stressed that the concept of a nonembodied person cannot be accepted without serious scrutiny. As was pointed out in section II, a number of philosophers have contended that the idea of a nonembodied person is ultimately incoherent.

In *Language, Truth and Logic,* Ayer selected first-person phenomenalistic statements as the basic observation statements. As a consequence the translatability challenge argument that he offers there is not completely sound. It does not *in itself* show that absolutely all theological statements are either devoid of cognitive content or else equivalent to empirical statements. For there is at least one theological sentence, namely "I am God," that can be assigned cognitive content in a way that both (1) satisfies the version of the confirmability criterion employed by Ayer in *Language, Truth and Logic,* and (2) does not turn the sentence into an empirical sentence, i.e., into a sentence about the natural world or about experiences of humans or other embodied beings.[45]

This point is considerably more important than it may at first appear. For if Ayer's choice of *first-person* phenomenalistic statements as the basic observation statements robs his version of the translatability challenge argument of strict universality, in that cognitive content of a nonempirical sort must be granted at least to the *first-person* theological statement "I am God," one might suspect that if one were to select some class of phenomenalistic statements other than first-person ones as the basic observation statements, one might be able as a result to assign cognitive content of a nonempirical sort to other, more interesting theological statements. Such is in fact the case. In particular, if the class one selects is the class of existentially quantified phenomenalistic statements, it turns out that *all* theological sentences can, in a completely natural way, be assigned cognitive content of a nonempirical sort.

The critical feature of phenomenalistic statements that makes this possible is the feature noted above in connection with first-person phenomenalistic statements: they need not be empirical statements, i.e., statements about the physical world or about the experiences of humans or other physical organisms. It is precisely this feature that causes the translatability challenge argu-

---

[45] It is important to notice that Ayer does contend in *Language, Truth and Logic* that the correct criterion of personal identity is a physical one: people are to be identified in a way that involves reference to their bodies. If this contention is correct, then it is *not* possible to assign coherent cognitive sense to *any* theological sentence, including the sentence "I am God". My point, however, is not that one can assign cognitive significance to some theological sentences without coming into conflict with *any* of the basic philosophical claims made in *Language, Truth and Logic.* It is rather that the *verificationist* argument advanced in *Language, Truth and Logic* does not apply to absolutely all theological sentences.

ment to break down if phenomenalistic statements are selected as the basic observation statements: step (3) will be unsound, since there will be sentences that can be constructed from the basic observation sentences that will not be empirical sentences.

While the selection of existentially quantified phenomenalistic statements as the basic observation statements is a natural one, and does lead to a satisfactory answer to the translatability challenge, it is important to notice that this approach does involve a partial abandonment of a verificationist viewpoint, the acceptance of a confirmability criterion of meaning as defined above notwithstanding.[46] For at the heart of the verificationist position is the insistence that any factually significant statement must be in principle verifiable by any human who understands the statement. This demand may not be met if the view that I am advocating is espoused. It will be true that any factually significant statement must be verifiable by someone, but there is no guarantee that it need be verifiable by any embodied person. Consequently there may be factually significant statements that are in principle outside the scope of human knowledge. This is a possibility that a strict verificationist would like to exclude.

Distinctively religious observation sentences?

In view of the preceding discussion it is tempting to say that the translatability challenge argument raises a problem, not within philosophy of religion, but within philosophy of mind. But that would be a needlessly paradoxical way of putting things. What one can say is this: There are certain fundamental problems in philosophy of mind—among them the problem of the selection of an adequate semantical basis—such that a resolution of those problems will automatically, and without further reflection, lead to an answer to the translatability challenge argument.

[46] In his article "Problems and Changes in the Empiricist Criterion of Meaning," *Revue internationale de Philosophie* 11 (1950), 41–63, Hempel distinguished four general types of empiricist criteria of factual meaning: those appealing to verifiability; those appealing to falsifiability; those appealing to confirmability; and those appealing to translatability into an empiricist language. The criterion that results when existentially quantified phenomenalistic statements are chosen as the basic observation statements is something of a hybrid; however I think it is best described as a criterion of the translatability sort, even though the confirmability criterion of synonymy with respect to factual content is an essential part of it.

In sharp contrast to this view is the view that the solution of the problem of the cognitive content of theological language requires an appeal to observation statements that refer to experiences of a peculiarly religious sort, such as the experience of encountering God. On this latter view, theological language has cognitive meaning because the meaning of theological sentences can be explained in terms of the meaning of observation statements of a distinctively religious sort.

What are we to say of this position? It seems to me that it is completely untenable. For it is incompatible with the following two claims, both of which can, I suggest, be supported by convincing argumentation: (1) the existence of experiences of a distinctively religious sort is not a necessary condition of theological language having the meaning it is supposed to have; (2) even if there are experiences of a distinctively religious sort, the meaning of theological statements cannot be explained in terms of statements about such experiences.

Turning first to the contention that theological language would still be cognitively significant even if there were no experiences of a distinctively religious sort, the primary consideration that I would offer in support of this contention would be this. A man who has never experienced a kangaroo can certainly believe that there are kangaroos, whereas a man who has been blind from birth, and who thus has never experienced red things, cannot in the same way believe that there are red objects. For a man who has never seen a kangaroo can be given a verbal definition of the term *kangaroo,* and thus be enabled to understand what the word "kangaroo" means. However in the case of the man who has been blind from birth, there is no verbal definition of the term "red" that can be used to convey to him the meaning that the term "red" has for us. Now it has certainly often been held that it is possible to believe in God, and hence to know what the word "God" means, without having had any experiences of God: one can accept the existence of God "on faith." But the man blind from birth *cannot* accept the existence of red things on faith, since he does not understand what it is for red things to exist. It follows, then, that special experiences of God cannot be necessary for an understanding of the meaning of the term "God." If such experiences were necessary, a person who had not had such special religious experiences would be unable to believe in God.

Secondly, it is not even possible to give an adequate account of the meaning of theological language in terms of statements about religious experiences. The reason is that the introduction of statements about human religious experiences merely constitutes *a special case* of the third alternative mentioned earlier: the selection of statements about the experiences of humans and other physical organisms as the basic observation statements. All such sentences about human experiences—religious or otherwise—are by definition *empirical* sentences, and to attempt to explain the meaning of theological sentences in terms of such sentences is thus to attempt to reduce theological statements to empirical statements. But this conflicts with what most people mean by the term "God". Under the standard interpretation God is more than just a pattern in nature, history, and human experience: he is the *transcendent personal cause* of such patterns. And while talk about the patterns may be translated into empirical terms, talk about the transcendent personal cause of the patterns cannot.[47]

My position is thus that (1) the translatability challenge argument can be answered without appeal to distinctively religious observation statements, and (2) the appeal to distinctively religious observation statements does not even provide an alternative answer. The introduction of sentences about religious experiences gets one nowhere, as far as the problem of the meaning of theological language is concerned.

This is not, of course, to deny that there might be peculiar experiences—quite unlike one's everyday experiences—that were religiously significant. Nor is it to deny that such experiences might be critical in connection with the question of *knowledge* of God. What is being contended is simply that reference to such experiences does not help one to deal with the problem of the meaning of theological language.

---

[47] Some philosophers have contended that theological language functions *simply* to describe certain complex patterns in nature, in history, and in human experience. This seems to have been the view that John Wisdom, for example, advanced in his famous article "Gods," and also in his less well-known article "The Modes of Thought and the Logic of God." This construal of theological language clearly diverges from what has here been referred to as the standard interpretation, since the term "God" under the pattern-interpretation no longer refers to an entity that transcends the realm of human experience. It is no accident that the translatability challenge argument turns about God's transcendence, since it is precisely this feature to it is so difficult to assign cognitive sense. The pattern-interpretation (or: theoretical term interpretation) skirts this difficulty by reinterpreting the term "God" so that it involves no transcendent elements.

Concluding comment

I have tried to show that the translatability challenge argument must be taken seriously. It has too often been lightly dismissed— sometimes because it has been confused with other, much weaker arguments, such as the falsifiability challenge argument, and at other times, because the whole idea of a confirmability criterion of cognitive significance has been dismissed without due consideration. I have tried to set the argument out in such a way that it is clear exactly how difficult it is to refute it if one approaches it in a sympathetic manner. Nevertheless I do think that the argument is ultimately unsound, and I have tried to indicate precisely why this is so.

Although the translatability challenge argument is undoubtedly very important, there are a number of other very significant problems in theology and philosophy of religion. Some of these, as I indicated in the first section, are also connected with the claim that theological discourse (under the standard interpretation) is cognitively significant: there are the difficulties involved in the analysis of certain special predicates, such as *omnipotent;* there is the general question of whether predicates applied to God are employed with meanings that make it impossible to reduce them to predicates applied to creatures; there is the question of whether the notion of a nonembodied person is ultimately intelligible. But there are also many important problems that have little or no connection with the question of the exact analysis of theological language. The failure of philosophers to find a completely convincing answer to the translatability challenge argument has had the unfortunate consequence that these other very important problems have not received the careful attention they deserve.

Bibliography

Introduction

The bibliography covers a wide range of topics from logical positivism, contemporary empiricism, and philosophy of science to "ordinary language analysis," philosophy of religion and contemporary theology. An attempt has been made to provide sufficient references on these and other related topics to afford the interested reader ready access to most of the important literature bearing on the issues discussed in this volume. Wherever possible, references to reprints in anthologies and collections of essays have been given. In the case of collections of essays by a single author that contain essays of special relevance, I have listed both the original essay as well as the book in which it is reprinted.

The main bibliography is preceded by a shorter topical bibliography. The latter bibliography follows the section divisions of this volume: materials of special importance are listed by name of author and, where appropriate, are followed by a number indicating the specific entry in the main bibliography that is to be consulted for a full reference. Readers who are unfamiliar with the literature discussed in this volume should consult the topical bibliography first.

For specialized bibliographies the reader should consult the following:

Ayer, A. J., ed. *Logical Positivism.* New York: Free Press, 1959.

Edwards, Paul and Pap, A., eds. *A Modern Introduction to Philosophy,* 2d ed. rev. New York: Free Press, 1965.

Fann, K. T., ed. *Symposium on J. L. Austin.* London: Routledge and Kegan Paul, 1969.

————. "A Wittgenstein Bibliography." *International Philosophical Quarterly,* 7 (June 1967), 311–339.

Ferré, Frederick, *Language, Logic and God.* New York: Harper and Row, 1961.

Hall, R. "Analytic-Synthetic—A Bibliography." *Philosophical Quarterly,* 16 (April 1966), 178–181.

Heimbeck, R. S. *Theology and Meaning.* Stanford: Stanford University Press, 1969.

Rorty, Richard M., ed. *The Linguistic Turn.* Chicago: University of Chicago Press, 1967.

Topical bibliography

One/Introduction: The challenge of contemporary empiricism

Ayer [1], [5]; Bartley [1]; Ewing [4]; Feigl [1]; Heimbeck [1]; Hempel [1], [2], [3], [4]; Kraft [1]; Lewis [1]; Nielsen [15]; Plantinga [1]; Putnam [1]; Quine [1]; Reichenbach [1], [2]; Rorty [1]; Rynin [1], [2]; Salmon [1]; Scheffler [1], [2], [3], [4].

Two/The elimination of metaphysics and theology

See listings under One; Carnap [6]; Church [1]; Niddith [1]; Scriven [1].

Three/The thomistic response

Clarke [1]; Copleston [2], [5]; Preller [1]; Ross [1], [2]; Trethowan [2].

Four/The noncognitivist response

Blackstone [1]; Ferré [1], [3]; McPherson [2]; Miles [2]; Munz [1]; Randall [1]; Schmidt [1]; van Buren [1].

Five/The complexities of arguments between believers and atheists

Allen [1]; Bambrough [1]; Bell [1]; Bendall [1]; Crombie [1], [2]; Dilley [1]; Ewing [5]; Farrer [1]; Ferré [1], [3]; Hepburn [1]; High [1]; Holmer [1], [2]; Hudson [2], [3]; MacIntyre [2], [4]; McPherson [4]; Mavrodes (2); Mitchell [2], [3]; Phillips [2], [3], [4], [6]; Plantinga [1]; Ramsey [2], [3], [7], [8], [9]; Richmond [1]; Robinson [1], [2]; Smart [2], [4]; Trethowan [2]; van Buren [1], [2], [3], [5]; Wisdom [2], [9]; Wittgenstein [5], [7].

Six/Eschatological verification

Bean [1]; Crombie [1]; Flew [7]; Heimbeck [1]; Hick [1], [5], [6], [8]; MacKinnon [2]; Mavrodes [1]; Nielsen [3], [4]; Penelhum [3], [4]; Phillips [5]; Plantinga [1].

Seven/Theology and falsification

Allison [1]; Burkle [1]; Crombie [1], [2]; Duff-Forbes [1], [2]; Ferré [1]; Flew [1], [2], [6], [7], [8]; Hare [1]; Heimbeck [1]; Horsburgh [1]; Kellenberger [1], [3]; McPherson [5]; Miller [1], [3]; Mitchell [1]; Nielsen [6], [10], [11], [15].

Eight/The complexities of theological contexts

See listings under Five

Nine/Religion and science

Barbour [1]; Coulson [1], [2], [3], [4]; Dillenberger [1]; Evans [2]; Ferré [2], [4]; Heim [1]; Lakatos [1]; Mascall [1]; Miles [1]; Miller [1] [3]; Ramsey [5], [6]; Schilling [1]; Siefferman [1].

Ten/A fresh approach to verification and theology

Hempel [1], [2], [4]; Lakatos [1]; Nielsen [15]; Rynin [1], [2]; Salmon [1].

Thomas V. Litzenburg, Jr./
A selected bibliography
(1930–1974)

List of Abbreviations

Periodicals

A	Analysis	IPQ	International Philosophical Quarterly
AJ	Australasian Journal of Philosophy (formerly titled Australasian Journal of Psychology and Philosophy)	JP	Journal of Philosophy
		JR	Journal of Religion
		JSL	Journal of Symbolic Logic
APQ	American Philosophical Quarterly	JSSR	Journal for the Scientific Study of Religion
BJPS	British Journal for the Philosophy of Science	M	Mind
		ME	Methodos
CJP	Canadian Journal of Philosophy	MO	Monist
		NS	New Scholasticism
CJT	Canadian Journal of Theology	P	Philosophy
CQR	Church Quarterly Review	PER	Personalist
D	Dialogue	PF	Philosophy Forum (formerly titled Pacific Philosophy Forum)
HJ	Hibbert Journal		
I	Inquiry	PPR	Philosophy and Phenomenological Research
IJPR	International Journal of Philosophy of Religion	PQ	Philosophical Quarterly

Periodicals

PR   *Philosophical Review*
PS   *Philosophy of Science*
PSt   *Philosophical Studies*
PT   *Philosophy Today*
PAPA *Proceedings of the American Philosophical Association*
PAS   *Proceedings of the Aristotelian Society*
PAS, SV *Proceedings of the Aristotelian Society, Supplementary Volume*

RIP   *Revue Internationale de Philosophie*
RM   *Review of Metaphysics*
RS   *Religious Studies*
S   *Sophia*
SJP   *Southern Journal of Philosophy*
SR   *Studies in Religion*
TT   *Theology Today*
U   *University*

Anthologies and collections

APW   *American Philosophers at Work.* S. Hook, ed. New York: Criterion Books, 1956.

ASR   *Analyticity: Selected Readings.* F. Harris, Jr. and R. H. Severens, eds. Chicago: Quadrangle Books, 1970.

CAP   *Classics of Analytic Philosophy.* R. R. Ammerman, ed. New York: McGraw-Hill, 1965.

CIPS *Current Issues in the Philosophy of Science.* H. Feigl and G. Maxwell, eds. New York: Holt, Rinehart and Winston, 1961.

CNE   *Clarity Is Not Enough.* H. D. Lewis, ed. New York: Humanities Press, 1963.

ECA   *Essays in Conceptual Analysis.* A. Flew, ed. London: Macmillan, 1960.

FL   *Faith and Logic.* B. Mitchell, ed. London: Allen and Unwin, 1957.

FP   *Faith and the Philosophers.* J. Hick, ed. New York: St. Martin's Press, 1964.

GMR   *God, Man and Religion.* K. E. Yandell, ed. New York: McGraw-Hill, 1973.

LL(I) *Language and Logic.* First Series. A. Flew, ed. Oxford: Blackwell, 1951.

LL(II) *Language and Logic.* Second Series. A. Flew, ed. Oxford: Blackwell, 1953.

LP   *Logical Positivism.* A. J. Ayer, ed. New York: Free Press, 1959.

LT   *The Linguistic Turn.* R. Rorty, ed. Chicago: University of Chicago Press, 1967.

MIP   *A Modern Introduction to Philosophy.* Rev. ed. P. Edwards and A. Pap, eds. New York: Free Press, 1965.

MMM   *Mind, Matter and Method.* P. F. Feyerabend and G. Maxwell, eds. Minneapolis: University of Minnesota Press, 1966.

MSPS *Minnesota Studies in the Philosophy of Science.* 3 vols. H. Feigl, M. Scriven, and G. Maxwell, eds. Minneapolis: University of Minnesota Press, 1956, 1958, 1962.

NE   *New Essays in Philosophical Theology.* A. Flew and A. MacIntyre, eds. London: SCM Press, 1955.

NERL *New Essays on Religious Language.* D. M. High, ed. New York: Oxford University Press, 1969.

NM   *The Nature of Metaphysics.* D. F. Pears, ed. London: Macmillan, 1957.

OL   *Ordinary Language.* V. C. Chappell, ed. Englewood Cliffs, N.J.: Prentice-Hall, 1964.

PA   *Philosophical Analysis.* M. Black, ed. Ithaca: Cornell University Press, 1950.

PL   *Philosophy and Linguistics.* Colin Lyas, ed. New York: Macmillan, 1971.

PM   *Prospects for Metaphysics.* I. Ramsey, ed. London: Allen and Unwin, 1961.

POL   *Philosophy and Ordinary Language.* C. Caton, ed. Urbana: University of Illinois Press, 1963.

PR   *The Philosophy of Religion.* B. Mitchell, ed. Oxford: Oxford University Press, 1971.

Anthologies and collections

PRSR *Philosophy of Religion: Se-*
      lected Readings. W. L. Rowe
      and W. J. Wainwright, eds.
      New York: Harcourt, Brace,
      Jovanovich, 1973.

PSM   *Philosophy, Science and*
      Method. S. Morgenbesser, P.
      Suppes, and M. White, eds.
      New York: St. Martin's Press,
      1969.

PST   *Philosophy and Science To-*
      day. S. Morgenbesser, ed. New
      York: Basic Books, 1967.

RET   *Religious Experience and*
      Truth. S. Hook, ed. New York:
      New York University Press,
      1961.

REV   *The Revolution in Philosophy*
      by A. J. Ayer et al. London:
      Macmillan, 1956.

RL   *Religious Language and the*
      Problem of Religious Knowl-
      edge. R. E. Santoni, ed. Bloom-
      ington: Indiana University
      Press, 1968.

RPA   *Readings in Philosophical*
      Analysis. H. Feigl and W. Sel-
      lars, eds. New York: Apple-
      ton-Century-Crofts, 1949.

RPM   *Readings in the Philosophy of*
      Mathematics. P. Benacerraf
      and H. Putnam, eds. Engle-
      wood Cliffs, N.J.: Prentice-
      Hall, 1964.

RPS   *Readings in the Philosophy of*
      Science. H. Feigl and M. Brod-
      beck, eds. New York: Apple-
      ton-Century-Crofts, 1953.

RU   *Religion and Understanding.*
      D. Z. Phillips, ed. Oxford:
      Blackwell, 1967.

SPL   *Semantics and the Philosophy*
      of Language. L. Linsky, ed.
      Urbana: University of Illinois
      Press, 1952.

SR   *Science and Religion.* I. G.
      Barbour, ed. New York:
      Harper and Row, 1968.

TCP   *Twentieth Century Philoso-*
      phy. W. P. Alston and G.
      Nakhnikian, eds. New York:
      Free Press, 1963.

TG   *Talk of God,* "Royal Institute
      of Philosophy Lectures," 2,
      1967–1968. New York: St. Mar-
      tin's Press, 1969.

TM   *The Theory of Meaning.* G. H.
      R. Parkinson, ed. New York:
      Oxford University Press, 1968.

Abelson, R. [1] "Meaning, Use and Rules of Use." *PPR* 18 (1957):48–58.

———. [2] "A Reply to Evans." *PPR* 22(1961):262–263.

Achinstein, P., and Barker, S. F., eds. [1] *The Legacy of Logical Positivism.* Baltimore: Johns Hopkins Press, 1969.

Allen, D. [1] "Motives, Rationales, and Religious Beliefs." *APQ* 3(1966):111–
127. Included in *RL*, (1968), pp. 348–361.

Allison, H. E. [1] "Faith and Falsifiability." *RM* 22(1969):499–522.

Alston, W. P. [1] "Are Positivists Metaphysicians?" *PR* 63(1954):43–57.

———. [2] "Pragmatism and the Verifiability Theory of Meaning." *PSt* 6(1955):
65–71.

———. [3] "Ontological Commitments." *PSt* 9(1958):8–17. Included in *RPM*,
(1964), pp. 249–257.

———. [4] "Philosophical Analysis and Structural Linguistics." *JP* 59(1962):
709–720.

———. [5] "The Quest for Meaning." *M* 72(1963):79–87.

———. [6] "Meaning and Use." *PQ* 13(1963):107–124. Included in *TM*, (1968),
pp. 141–165.

———. [7] *Philosophy of Language.* Englewood Cliffs, N.J.: Prentice-Hall, 1964.

Ambrose (Lazerowitz), A. [1] "The Problem of Linguistic Inadequacy." In *PA*,
(1950), pp. 14–35.

————. [2] "Linguistic Approaches to Philosophical Problems." *JP* 49(1952): 289–301. Included in *LT,* (1967), pp. 147–155.

Anscombe, G. E. M., and Geach, P. T. [1] *Three Philosophers.* Oxford: Blackwell, 1961.

Ashby, R. W. [1] "Use and Verification." *PAS* 56(1955–56):149–166.

Austin, J. L. [1] *Sense and Sensibilia.* Edited by G. J. Warnock. Oxford: Clarendon Press, 1962.

————. [2] *How to Do Things With Words.* Edited by J. O. Urmson. New York: Oxford University Press, 1965.

————. [3] *Philosophical Papers.* Edited by J. O. Urmson and G. J. Warnock. 2d ed. rev. New York and London: Oxford University Press, 1970.

————. [4] "The Meaning of a Word." In Austin, *Philosophical Papers,* pp. 23–43. Included in *ASR,* (1970), pp. 122–130.

Austin, W. H. [1] "Waves, Particles and Paradoxes." *Rice University Studies* 53, No. 2. Houston: Rice University Press, 1967.

————. [2] "Models, Mystery and Paradox in Ian Ramsey." *JSSR* 7(1968):41–55.

————. [3] "Religious Commitment and the Logical Status of Doctrine." *RS* 9(1973)39–48.

Ayer, A. J. [1] *Language, Truth and Logic.* London: Victor Gollancz, 1936; 2d ed., London: Victor Gollancz, 1946, New York: Dover Publications, 1952.

————. [2] *The Problem of Knowledge.* London: Macmillan, 1956; New York: St. Martin's Press, 1956.

————. [3] *The Concept of a Person and Other Essays.* New York: St. Martin's Press, 1963.

————. [4] "Philosophy and Language." In Ayer, *The Concept of a Person and Other Essays,* (1963), pp. 1–35. Included in *CNE,* (1963), pp. 401–428.

————, ed. [5] *Logical Positivism.* Glencoe, Ill.: Free Press, 1959.

————, and Copleston, F. C. [6] "Logical Positivism—A Debate." Third Program, BBC (June 13, 1949). Reprinted in *MIP,* (1965), pp. 726–756.

Ayers, R. H. [1] *See* Blackstone, W. T.

Baier, K. [1] "The Ordinary Use of Words." *PAS* 52(1951–52):47–70.

Bambrough, R. [1] *Reason, Truth and God.* London: Methuen, 1969.

Barbour, I. G. [1] *Issues in Science and Religion.* Englewood Cliffs, N.J.: Prentice-Hall, 1966.

Barker, S. F. [1] *See* Achinstein, P.

Barrett, R. [1] "On the Conclusive Falsification of Scientific Hypotheses." *PS* 36(1969):363–374.

Bartley, W. W., III. [1] *The Retreat to Commitment.* New York: Alfred A. Knopf, 1962.

Bean, W. [1] "Eschatological Verification: Fortress or Fairyland?" *ME* 16 (1964):91–107.

Bell, R. H. [1] "Wittgenstein and Descriptive Theology." *RS* 5(1969):1–18.

Bendall, K., and Ferré, F. [1] *Exploring the Logic of Faith*. New York: Association Press, 1962.

Bennett, J. [1] "Analytic-Synthetic." *PAS* 59(1958–59):163–189. Included in *ASR*, (1970), pp. 152–178.

Berenda, C. W. [1] "A Five-Fold Scepticism in Logical Empiricism." *PS* 17 (1950):123–132.

Bergmann, G. [1] *The Metaphysics of Logical Positivism*. New York and London: Longmans, Green, 1954.

———. [2] *Meaning and Existence*. Madison: University of Wisconsin Press, 1960.

———. [3] *Logic and Reality*. Madison: University of Wisconsin Press, 1964.

Berlin, I. [1] "Verification." *PAS* 39 (1938–39):225–248. Included in *TM*, (1968), pp. 15–34.

Binkley, L. J. [1] "What Characterizes Religious Language?" *JSSR* 2(1962): 18–22.

———. [2] "Reply to Professor Hick's Comment on 'What Characterizes Religious Language?' " *JSSR* 2(1963):228–230.

Black, M. [1] "Language and Reality." *PAPA* 32(1959):5–17. Reprinted in Black, *Models and Metaphors*. Ithaca: Cornell University Press, 1962. Also included in *CNE*, (1963), pp. 170–184, and *LT*, (1967), pp. 331–339.

Blackstone, W. T. [1] *The Problem of Religious Knowledge*. Englewood Cliffs, N.J.: Prentice-Hall, 1963.

———, and Ayers, R. H., eds. [2] *Religious Language and Knowledge*. Athens: University of Georgia Press, 1972.

Blanshard, B. [1] *Reason and Analysis*. LaSalle, Ill.: Open Court, 1962.

Bochenski, J. M. [1] "Some Problems for a Philosophy of Religion." In *RET*, (1961), pp. 39–47.

———. [2] *Logic of Religion*. New York: New York University Press, 1965.

Boyd, B. P. [1] "A Defense of the Complete Verifiability and Complete Falsifiability Criteria of Empirical Meaningfulness." *D* 15(1972):74–81.

Braithwaite, R. B. [1] *Scientific Explanation*. Cambridge: Cambridge University Press, 1953.

———. [2] *An Empiricist's View of the Nature of Religious Belief*. Cambridge: Cambridge University Press, 1955. Included in *GMR* (1973), pp. 215–229.

Brown, R. [1] "Meaning and Rules of Use." *M* 71(1962):494–511.

———, and Watling, J. [2] "Amending the Verification Principle." *A* 2(1951): 87–89.

Brown, S. C. [1] *Do Religious Claims Make Sense?* New York: Macmillan, 1969.

Buchdahl, G. [1] "Science and Metaphysics." In *NM*, (1957), pp. 61–82.

Burkle, H. R. [1] "Counting Against and Counting Decisively Against." *JR* 44 (1964):223–229.

Butchvarov, P. [1] "Meaning—As—Use and Meaning—As—Correspondence." *P* 35(1960):314–325.

———. [2] "Knowledge of Meanings and Knowledge of the World." *P* 39 (1964):145–160.

Carnap, R. [1] *Philosophy and Logical Syntax.* London: Kegan Paul, French, Trukner and Co., 1935.

———. [2] *Meaning and Necessity.* Chicago: University of Chicago Press, 1947.

———. [3] "Empiricism, Semantics, and Ontology." *RIP* 4(1950):20–40. Included in *RPM* (1964), pp. 233–248; *SPL* (1952), pp. 208–228.

———. [4] "Meaning and Synonymy in Natural Languages." *PSt* 6(1955): 33–47. Included in *APW* (1956), pp. 58–74; *ASR* (1970), pp. 131–151.

———. [5] "The Methodological Character of Theoretical Concepts." In *MSPS* (I), (1956), pp. 38–76.

———. [6] "The Elimination of Metaphysics Through Logical Analysis of Language." In *LP*, translated by A. Pap, (1959), pp. 60–81.

Cavell, S. [1] "Must We Mean What We Say?" *I* 1(1958): 172–212. Included in *OL*, (1964), pp. 75–112; *PL* (1971), pp. 131–165.

———. [2] *Must We Mean What We Say?* New York: Charles Scribner's Sons, 1969.

Cell, E. [1] *Language, Existence and God.* New York: Abingdon Press, 1971.

Charlesworth, M. J. [1] *Philosophy and Linguistic Analysis.* Pittsburgh: Duquesne University Press, 1959.

Chisholm, R. [1] "Philosophers and Ordinary Language." *PR* 40(1951):317–328. Included in *LT*, (1967), pp. 175–182.

Christensen, W. N. [1] *See* King-Farlow, J.

Christian, W. A. [1] "Truth-Claims in Religion." *JR* 42(1962):52–62. Included in *RL*, (1968), pp. 67–82.

———. [2] *Meaning and Truth in Religion.* Princeton: Princeton University Press, 1964.

Church, A. [1] "Review of Ayer's *Language, Truth and Logic.*" *JSL* 14(1949): 52–53.

Churchill, L. R. L. [1] "Flew, Wisdom and Polanyi: the Falsification Challenge Revisited." *IJPR* 3(1972):185–194.

Clarke, B. L. [1] "The Contribution of Logical Positivism." *ME* 15(1963):73–88.

Clarke, W. N. [1] "Analytic Philosophy and Language About God." In *Christian Philosophy and Religious Renewal*, edited by G. McLean. Washington: Catholic University of America Press, 1966.

———. [2] "How the Philosopher Gives Meaning to Language About God." In *The Idea of God*, edited by E. H. Madden, R. Handy, and M. Farber, pp. 1–27. Buffalo: University of Buffalo Press, 1969.

Clifford, P. R. [1] "The Factual Reference of Theological Assertions." *RS* 3 (1967):337–346.

Coburn, R. C. [1] "A Neglected Use of Theological Language." *M* 72(1963):369–385. Included in *NERL*, (1969), pp. 215–235.

———. [2] "The Concept of God." *RS* 2(1966):61–74.

Cohen, C. B. [1] "The Logic of Religious Language." *RS* 9(1973):143–156.

Cole, R. [1] "On the Impossibility of Metaphysics." *PSt* 14(1963):43–48.

———. [2] "Falsifiability." *M* 77(1968):133–135.

Conway, D. E. [1] "Mavrodes, Martin and the Verification of Religious Experience." *IJPR* 2(1971):156–171.

Copleston, F. C. [1] "The Possibility of Metaphysics." *PAS* 50(1949–50):65–82.

———. [2] "Some Reflections on Logical Positivism." *The Dublin Review* 224 (1950):71–86. Included in Copleston, *Contemporary Philosophy*, pp. 26–44.

———. [3] *Contemporary Philosophy*. London: Burns and Oates, 1956.

———. [4] "The Philosophical Relevance of Religious Experience." *P* 31(1956): 229–243.

———. [5] *See* Ayer, A. J.

Corbishley, T. [1] "Theology and Falsification" (II). *U* 1(1950):8–11.

Cornforth, M. [1] *In Defense of Philosophy Against Positivism and Pragmatism*. London: Lawrence and Wishart, 1950.

Cornman, J. W. [1] "Uses of Language and Philosophical Problems." *PSt* 15 (1964):11–16. Included in *LT*, (1967), pp. 227–231.

———. [2] "Linguistic Frameworks and Metaphysical Questions." *I* 7(1964): 129–142.

———. [3] *Metaphysics, Reference and Language*. New Haven: Yale University Press, 1966.

———. [4] "Indirectly Verifiable: Everything or Nothing." *PSt* 18(1967):49–56.

Coulson, C. A. [1] *Science and Christian Belief*. Chapel Hill, N.C.: University of North Carolina Press, 1955.

———. [2] *Science and Religion*. Cambridge: Cambridge University Press, 1955.

———. [3] *Science and the Idea of God*. Cambridge: Cambridge University Press, 1958.

———. [4] *Science, Technology and the Christian*. New York: Abingdon Press, 1960.

Coval, S. [1] "Worship, Superlatives and Concept Confusion." *M* 68(1959):218–222.

Cox, D. [1] "The Significance of Christianity." *M* 59(1950):209–218.

———. [2] "A Note on 'Meeting'." *M* 60(1951):259–261.

Crombie, I. M. [1] "Theology and Falsification." In *NE*, (1955), pp. 109–130.

———. [2] "The Possibility of Theological Statements." In *FL*, (1957), pp. 31–83. Included in *PR*, (1971), pp. 23–52; *RL*, (1968), pp. 83–116.

Daher, A. [1] "God and Factual Necessity." *RS* 6(1970):23–39.

Daly, C. B. [1] "Logical Positivism, Metaphysics and Ethics." *The Irish Theological Quarterly* 23(1956):111–150.

———. [2] "Metaphysics and the Limits of Language." In *PM*, (1961), pp. 178–205.

Demos, R. [1] "The Meaningfulness of Religious Language." *PPR* 18(1957):96–106.

Diamond, M. L. [1] "Contemporary Analysis: The Metaphysical Target and the Theological Victim." *JR* 47(1967):210–232.

Dickie, J. S. [1] "What Are the Limits of Metaphysics?" In *PM*, (1961), pp. 50–63.

Dillenberger, J. [1] *Protestant Thought and Natural Science*. Garden City: N.Y.: Doubleday, 1960.

Dilley, F. B. [1] *Metaphysics and Religious Language*. New York: Columbia University Press, 1964.

Downing, F. G. [1] "Games, Families, the Public and Religion." *P* 47(1972):38–54.

Duff-Forbes, D. R. [1] "Theology and Falsification Again." *AJ* 39(1961):143–154.

———. [2] "Reply to Professor Flew." *AJ* 40(1962):324–327.

Durrant, M. [1] *The Logical Status of 'God'*. New York: Macmillan, 1973.

———. [2] *Theology and Intelligibility*. Boston: Routledge and Kegan Paul, 1973.

Edwards, R. B. [1] *Reason and Religion*. New York: Harcourt, Brace, Jovanovich, 1972.

Evans, D. D. [1] *Logic of Self-Involvement*. London: SCM Press, 1963.

———. [2] "Differences Between Scientific and Religious Assertions." In *SR*, (1968), pp. 101–133.

———. [3] "Ian Ramsey on Talk About God." *RS* 7(1971): 125–140.

Evans, J. L. [1] "On Meaning and Verification." *M* 62(1953):1–19.

———. [2] "Meaning and Use." *PPR* 22(1961):251–261.

———. [3] *The Foundations of Empiricism*. Cardiff: University of Wales Press, 1965.

Ewing, A. C. [1] "Is Metaphysics Impossible?" *A* 8(1948):33–38.

———. [2] "The Necessity of Metaphysics." In *Contemporary British Philosophy* (Third Series), edited by H. D. Lewis, pp. 143–164. London: George Allen and Unwin, 1956.

———. [3] "Pseudo-Solutions." *PAS* 57(1956–57):31–52.

———. [4] "Religious Assertions in the Light of Contemporary Philosophy." *P* 32(1957):206–218.

———. [5] "Awareness of God." *P* 40(1965):1–17.

Farrer, A. [1] "Revelation." In *FL*, (1957), pp. 84–107.

———. [2] "A Starting-Point for the Philosophical Examination of Theological Belief." In *FL*, (1957), pp. 9–30.

Feibleman, J. K. [1] "The Metaphysics of Logical Positivism." *RM* 5(1951): 55–82.

Feigl, H. [1] "Logical Empiricism." In *Twentieth Century Philosophy*, edited by D. D. Runes. New York: Philosophical Library, 1943. Included in *RPA*, (1949), pp. 3–26.

———. [2] "De Principiis Non Disputandum . . . ?" In *PA*, (1950), pp. 113–147.

———. [3] "Scientific Method Without Metaphysical Presuppositions." *PSt* 5 (1954):17–29.

———. [4] "Some Major Issues and Developments in the Philosophy of Science of Logical Empiricism." In *MSPS*, I, (1956), pp. 3–37.

———. [5] "Philosophical Tangents of Science." In *CIPS*, (1961), pp. 1–17.

———. [6] "The Power of Positivistic Thinking: An Essay on the Quandaries of Transcendence." *PAPA* 36(1963):21–42.

———, and Maxwell, G. [7] "Why Ordinary Language Needs Reforming." *JP* 58(1961):488–498. Included in *LT*, (1967), pp. 193–200.

Ferré, F. [1] *Language, Logic and God.* New York: Harper and Row, 1961.

———. [2] "Mapping the Logic of Models in Science and Theology." *Christian Scholar* 46(1963):9–39. Included in *NERL*, (1969), pp. 54–96.

———. [3] *Basic Modern Philosophy of Religion.* New York: Scribner, 1967.

———. [4] "Science and the Death of 'God'." In *SR*, (1968), pp. 134–156.

———. [5] "The Logic of Our Current Opportunity." *PF* 8(1970):61–87.

———. [6] *See* Bendall, K.

Feuer, L. S. [1] "The Paradox of Verifiability." *PPR* 12(1951):24–41.

Findlay, J. N. [1] "Can God's Existence Be Disproved?" *M* 57(1948):176–183. Included in *NE*, (1955), pp. 47–55.

———. [2] "God's Non-existence. A Reply to Mr. Rainer and Mr. Hughes." *M* 58(1949):352–354. Included in *NE*, (1955), pp. 71–75.

———. [3] "Religious Belief and Logical Analysis" (IV). *U* 1(1951):96–98. (Originally published as part of the *University* discussion of "Theology and Falsification.")

———. [4] "Use, Usage and Meaning." *PAS*, SV 35(1961):231–242. Included in *CNE*, (1963), pp. 429–441; *TM*, (1968), pp. 116–127.

Flew, A. [1] "Theology and Falsification" (I). *U* 1(1950):1–8. Included in *NE*, (1955), pp. 96–99; *PR* (1971), pp. 13–15; *PRSR*, (1973), pp. 419–421.

———. [2] "Religious Belief and Logical Analysis" (VI). *U* 1(1951):143–145. (Originally published as part of the *University* discussion of "Theology and Falsification.") Included under the title "Theology and Falsification" in *NE*, (1955), pp. 106–108.

———. [3] "Death" (II). *U* 2(1952):31–36. Included in *NE*, (1955), pp. 267–272.

———. [4] "Divine Omnipotence and Human Freedom." *HJ* 53(1954–55):135–144. Included in *NE*, (1955), pp. 144–169.

———. [5] "Philosophy and Language." *PQ* 5(1955):21–36. Revised and included in *ECA*, (1960), pp. 1–20.

———. [6] "Falsification and Hypothesis in Theology." *AJ* 40(1962):318–323.

———. [7] *God and Philosophy.* New York: Harcourt, Brace and World, 1966.

———. [8] "The Falsification Response." *RS* 5(1969):77–79.

———. [9] "The Presumption of Atheism." *CJP* 2(1972):29–46.

Foster, M. B. [1] "Religious Belief and Logical Analysis" (II). *U* 1(1951):91–93. (Originally published as part of the *University* discussion of "Theology and Falsification.")

———. [2] " 'We' in Modern Philosophy." In *FL*, (1957), pp. 194–220.

Gaskin, J. C. A. [1] "Disclosures." *RS* 9(1973):131–142.

Geach, P. T. [1] "Quine's Syntactical Insights." *Synthese* 19(1968):118–129.

———. [2] *God and the Soul*. New York: Schocken Books, 1969.

———. [3] "God's Relation to the World." *S* 8(1969):1–9.

———. [4] *See* Anscombe, G. E. M.

Gibson, A. B. [1] "Modern Philosophers Consider Religion." *AJ* 35(1957):170–185.

Gill, J. H. [1] *Theism and Empiricism*. New York: Schocken Books, 1970.

———. [2] *The Possibility of Religious Knowledge*. Grand Rapids: Eerdmans, 1971.

Glasgow, W. D. [1] "D. Cox: The Significance of Christianity: A Note." *M* 40 (1951):100–102.

Glickman, J. [1] "Hoffman on Ziff 'About 'God' '." *S* 4(1965):33–39.

Grice, H. P.; Pears, D. F.; and Strawson, P. F. [1] "Metaphysics." In *NM*, (1957), pp. 1–22.

Grice, H. P., and Strawson, P. F. [2] "In Defense of Dogma." *PR* 65(1956):141–158. Included in *ASR*, (1970), pp. 54–74; *CAP*, (1965), pp. 340–352.

Grunbaum, A. [1] *Falsifiability and Rationality*. Pittsburgh: University of Pittsburgh Press, 1973.

Hall, R. [1] "Analytic-Synthetic—A Bibliography." *PQ* 16(1966):178–181.

Hampshire, S. N. [1] "Are All Philosophical Questions Questions of Language?" *PAS, SV* 22(1948):31–48. Included in *LT*, (1967), pp. 284–293.

———. [2] "Metaphysical Systems." In *NM*, (1957), pp. 23–38.

Hanson, N. R. [1] *Patterns of Discovery*. Cambridge: Cambridge University Press, 1958.

———. [2] "On the Impossibility of Any Future Metaphysics." *PSt* 11(1960): 86–96.

———. [3] "Is There a Logic of Discovery?" In *CIPS*, (1961), pp. 20–35.

Hare, R. M. [1] "Theology and Falsification" (IV). *U* 1(1950): 16–20. Revised and included in *NE*, (1955), pp. 99–103; *PR* (1971), pp. 15–18; *PRSR*, pp. 421–424.

———. [2] "Religion and Morals." In *FL*, (1957), pp. 176–193.

———. [3] "Philosophical Discoveries." *M* 69(1960):145–162. Included in *LT* (1967), pp. 206–217; and, in part, under the title "Are Discoveries About Uses of Words Empirical?" *JP* 54(1957):741–750.

———. [4] "Religion and Analytic Naturalism." *PF* 5(1967):52–61.

Harrison, F. R. [1] "Metaphysics and Common Sense: An Appraisal." *PT* 14 (1970):33–37.

Harvey, V. A. [1] *The Historian and the Believer*. New York: Macmillan, 1966.

Hawkins, D. J. B. [1] "Toward the Restoration of Metaphysics." In *PM*, (1961), pp. 111–120.

Heath, P. L. [1] "The Appeal to Ordinary Language." *PQ* 2(1952):1–12. Included in *CNE*, (1963), pp. 185–200.

Heim, K. [1] *Christian Faith and Natural Science*. New York: Harper and Row, 1953.

Heimbeck, R. E. [1] *Theology and Meaning*. Stanford: Stanford University Press, 1969.

Hempel, C. G. [1] "Problems and Changes in the Empiricist Criterion of Meaning." *RIP* 11(1950):41–63. Included in *CAP*, (1965), pp. 214–230; *SPL*, (1952), pp. 163–185.

———. [2] "The Concept of Cognitive Significance: A Reconsideration." *Contributions to the Analysis and Synthesis of Knowledge*, Proceedings of the American Academy of Arts and Sciences 80(1951):61–77.

———. [3] *Aspects of Scientific Explanation*. New York: The Free Press, 1965.

———. [4] "Empiricist Criteria of Cognitive Significance: Problems and Changes." In Hempel, *Aspects of Scientific Explanation*, (1965), pp. 101–122.

Henle, P. [1] "Do We Discover Our Uses of Words?" *JP* 54(1957):750–758. Included in *LT* (1967), pp. 218–223.

———. [2] "Meaning and Verifiability." In *The Philosophy of Rudolf Carnap*, edited by P. A. Schilpp, pp. 165–181. LaSalle: Open Court, 1963.

Henze, D. F. [1] "Faith, Evidence and Coercion." *P* 42(1967):78–85.

Hepburn, R. W. [1] *Christianity and Paradox*. London: Watts, 1958.

———. [2] "From World to God." *M* 72(1963):40–50. Included in *PR*, (1971), pp. 168–178.

———; MacIntyre, A.; and Toulmin, S. [3] *Metaphysical Beliefs*. London: SCM Press, 1957.

Hick, J. [1] "Theology and Verification." *TT* 17(1960):12–31. Included in *PRSR*, (1973), pp. 437–451.

———. [2] "Meaning and Truth in Theology." In *RET*, (1961), pp. 203–210.

———. [3] "Comment." *JSSR* 2(1962):22–24.

———. [4] "A Comment on Professor Binkley's Reply." *JSSR* 2(1963):231–232.

———. [5] *Philosophy of Religion*. Englewood Cliffs, N.J.: Prentice–Hall, 1963.

———. [6] *Faith and Knowledge*. 2d ed., rev. Ithaca: Cornell University Press, 1966.

———. [7] "Religious Faith As Experiencing—As." In *TG*, (1967–68), pp. 20–35.

———, ed. [8] *The Existence of God*. New York: Macmillan, 1964.

High, D. M. [1] *Language, Persons and Belief*. New York: Oxford University Press, 1967.

———. [2] "Belief, Falsification and Wittgenstein." *IJPR* 3(1972), pp. 240–250.

Hodges, H. A. [1] "Religious Belief and Logical Analysis" (VII). *U* 1(1951):145–146. (Originally published as part of the *University* discussion of "Theology and Falsification.")

Hoffman, R. [1] "Professor Ziff's Resurrection of the Plain Man's Concept of God." *S* 2(1963):1–4.

———. [2] "On Being Mindful of 'God': Reply to Kai Nielsen." *RS* 6(1970): 289–290.

Holland, R. F. [1] "Religious Discourse and Theological Discourse." *AJ* 34 (1956):147–163.

Holmer, P. L. [1] "The Nature of Religious Propositions." *Review of Religion* 19(1955):136–149. Included in *RL,* (1968), pp. 233–247.

———. [2] "Wittgenstein and Theology." *Reflection* 65(1968):1–4. Included in *NERL,* (1969), pp. 25–35.

Hordern, W. [1] *Speaking of God.* New York: Macmillan, 1964.

Horsburgh, H. J. N. [1] "Mr. Hare on Theology and Falsification." *PQ* 6(1956): 256–259.

———. [2] "The Claims of Religious Experience." *AJ* 35(1957):186–200.

———. [3] "Professor Braithwaite and Billy Brown." *AJ* 36(1958):201–207.

Hudson, W. D. [1] *Ludwig Wittgenstein: the Bearing of his Philosophy upon Religious Belief.* Richmond: John Knox Press, 1968.

———. [2] "On Two Points Against Wittgensteinian Fideism." *P* 43(1968):269–273.

———. [3] "Some Remarks on Wittgenstein's Account of Religious Belief." In *TG,* (1969), pp. 36–51.

———. [4] *A Philosophical Approach to Religion.* New York: Barnes and Noble, 1974.

———. [5] *Wittgenstein's Influence on the Philosophy of Religion.* New York: Macmillan, forthcoming.

Hughes, G. E. [1] "Has God's Existence Been Disproved?" *M* 58(1949):67–74. Included in *NE,* (1955), pp. 56–67.

Hutchinson, J. A. [1] *Language and Faith.* Philadelphia: Westminster Press, 1963.

Joad, C. E. M. [1] *A Critique of Logical Positivism.* London: Victor Gollancz, 1950.

Joergensen, J. [1] *The Development of Logical Empiricism.* Chicago: University of Chicago Press, 1951.

Jones, J. R. *See* Phillips, D. Z.

Kellenberger, J. [1] "The Falsification Challenge." *RS* 5(1969):69–76.

———. [2] "We No Longer Have Need of that Hypothesis." *S* 8(1969):25–32.

———. [3] "More on the Verification Challenge." *RS* 5(1969):235–242.

———. [4] *Religious Discovery, Faith and Knowledge.* Englewood Cliffs, N.J.: Prentice-Hall, 1972.

———. [5] "The Language-Game View of Religion and Religious Certainty." *CJP* 2(1972):255–275.

Kennick, W. [1] "The Language of Religion." *PR* 65(1956):56–71.

Kenny, A. [1] "Necessary Being." *S* 1(1962):1–8.

———. [2] *The Five Ways.* New York: Schocken Books, 1969.

Khatchadourian, H. [1] "Criteria and Conditions: With Applications to Synonymity and the Verifiability 'Criterion' of Meaning" (Abstract). *JP* 67 (1970):829–830.

King, R. H. [1] "The Conceivability of God." RS 9(1973):1–10.

King-Farlow, J. [1] "Religion, Reality, and Ordinary Language." PF 5(1967): 4–95. Comments by Huber, C. E.; Bailiff, J. D.; and McClendon, J. W.

———. [2] "Cogency, Conviction and Coercion." IPQ 8(1968):464–473.

———, and Christensen, W. N. [3] "Faith—and Faith in Hypotheses." RS 7 (1971):113–124.

Klemke, E. D. [1] "Are Religious Statements Meaningful?" JR 40(1960):27–39.

Kneale, W. [1] "Verifiability." PAS, SV 19(1945):151–164.

Kordig, C. R. [1] "Falsifiability and the Cosmological Argument." NS 46(1972): 485–487.

Kraft, V. [1] The Vienna Circle. New York: Philosophical Library, 1953.

Kuhn, T. [1] The Structure of Scientific Revolutions. 2d ed., rev. Chicago: University of Chicago Press, 1970.

Lakatos, I., and Musgrave, A. [1] Criticism and the Growth of Knowledge. Cambridge: Cambridge University Press, 1970.

Lazerowitz, M. [1] The Structure of Metaphysics. London: Routledge and Kegan Paul, 1955.

Lehrer, K. [1] "A Note on the Impossibility of Any Future Metaphysics." PSt 13(1962):49–51.

Lewis, H. D. [1] "Contemporary Empiricism and the Philosophy of Religion." P 32(1957):193–205.

———. [2] Our Experience of God. London: Allen and Unwin, 1959.

———. [3] "God and Mystery." In PM, (1961), pp. 206–237.

———, and Whitely, C. H. [4] "The Cognitive Factor in Religious Experience." PAS, SV 29(1955):59–84. Included (in part) in RL, (1968), pp. 248–265.

Lloyd, A. C. [1] "Meaning Without Verifiability." PAS, SV 42(1968):1–6.

Lucas, J. R. [1] "The Soul." In FL, (1957), pp. 132–148.

McClendon, J. W. [1] "Religion and Language." PF 5(1967):77–82.

McGrath, P. J. [1] "Professor Flew and the Stratoniscian Presumption." Philosophical Studies (Ireland) 18(1969):150–159.

McKay, D. M. [1] "Language, Meaning and God." P 47(1972):1–17.

MacIntyre, A. [1] "Visions." In NE, (1955), pp. 254–260.

———. [2] Difficulties in Christian Belief. London: SCM Press, 1959.

———. [3] "Is Understanding Religion Compatible With Believing?" In FP, (1964), pp. 115–133.

———, and Ricoeur, P. [4] The Religious Significance of Atheism. New York: Columbia University Press, 1969.

———. [4] See Hepburn, R. W.

MacKinnon, D. M. [1] "Verifiability." PAS, SV 19(1945):101–118.

———. [2] "Death" (I). U 2(1952):25–30. Included in NE, (1955), pp. 261–266.

McPherson, T. [1] "The Existence of God." M 59(1950):545–550.

———. [2] "Positivism and Religion." *PPR* 14(1954):319–330. Revised and reprinted as "Religion as the Inexpressible" in *NE,* (1955), pp. 131–143.

———. [3] "Assertion and Analogy." *PAS* 60(1959–60):155–170. Included in McPherson, *The Philosophy of Religion,* (1965), pp. 182–196; *NERL,* (1969), pp. 198–214.

———. [4] *The Philosophy of Religion.* London and New York: Van Nostrand, 1965.

———. [5] "The Falsification Challenge: A Comment." *RS* 5(1969):81–84.

Makinson, D. [1] "Nidditch's Definition of Verifiability." *M* 74(1965):240–247.

Malcolm, N. [1] "The Verification Argument." In *PA,* (1950), pp. 229–279. Included in Malcolm, *Knowledge and Certainty.* Englewood Cliffs, N.J.: Prentice-Hall, 1963.

———. [2] "Is It a Religious Belief that 'God Exists'?" In *FP,* (1964), pp. 103–110.

Martin, C. B. [1] "A Religious Way of Knowing." *M* 61(1952):497–512. Included in *NE,* (1955), pp. 76–95.

———. [2] "The Perfect Good." *AJ* 33(1955):20–31. Included in *NE,* (1955), pp. 212–226.

———. [3] *Religious Belief.* Ithaca: Cornell University Press, 1959.

Mascall, E. L. [1] *Christian Theology and Natural Science.* New York: Ronald Press, 1956.

———. [2] *Words and Images.* London: Longmans, Green; New York: Ronald Press, 1957.

Mates, B. [1] "On the Verification of Statements About Ordinary Language." *I* 1(1958):161–171. Included in *OL,* (1964), pp. 64–74.

Matson, W. I. [1] "Bliks, Prayers, and Witches." PF 5(1966): 3–92. Comments by Mavrodes, G. I.; Mayer, John R.; Penelhum, T.

Matthews, G. B. [1] "Theology and Natural Theology." *JP* 61(1964):99–108. Included in *PRSR* (1973), pp. 428–437.

Mavrodes, G. I. [1] "God and Verification." *CJT* 10(1964):187–191.

———. [2] *Belief in God.* New York: Random House, 1970.

———. [3] "Some Recent Philosophical Theology." *RM* 24(1970):82–111.

Maxwell, G. [1] "Meaning Postulates in Scientific Theories." In *CIPS,* (1961), pp. 169–183.

———. [2] "The Ontological Status of Theoretical Entities." In *MSPS,* III, (1962), pp. 3–27.

———. [3] "Criteria of Meaning and Demarcation." In *MMM,* (1966), pp. 319–327.

———. [4] *See* Feigl, H.

Miles, T. R. [1] *Religion and the Scientific Outlook.* London: Allen and Unwin, 1959.

———. [2] "On Excluding the Supernatural." *RS* 1(1966):141–150.

———. [3] *Religious Experience.* New York: Macmillan, 1972.

Miller, J. F., III. [1] "Science and Religion: Their Logical Similarity." *RS* 5 (1969):49–68.

———. [2] "Theology, Falsification and the Concept of Weltanschauung." *CJT* 16(1970):54–60.

———. [3] "First Order Principles in Science and Religion." *The Iliff Review* 28(1971):47–58.

———. [4] "Why 'God Loves Mankind' is Unfalsifiable." *SJP* 4(1973):81–92.

Mitchell, B. [1] "Religious Belief and Logical Analysis" (III). *U* 1(1951):93–95. (Originally published as part of the *University* discussion of "Theology and Falsification.") Included under the title of "Theology and Falsification" in *NE*, (1955), pp. 103–105; *PR*, (1971), pp. 18–20; *PRSR*, (1973), pp. 424–426.

———. [2] "The Grace of God." In *FL*, (1957), pp. 149–175.

———. [3] "The Justification of Religious Belief." *PQ* 11(1961):213–226. Included in *NERL*, (1969), pp. 178–197.

———. [4] *The Justification of Religious Belief.* New York: Macmillan, 1973.

Monson, T. [1] "The Analysis of Religious Discourse." *PT* 12(1968):100–113.

Munz, P. [1] *Problems of Religious Knowledge.* SCM Press, 1959.

Musgrave, A. [1] *See* Lakatos, I.

Nagel, E. [1] *The Structure of Science.* New York: Harcourt, Brace and World, 1961.

Neurath, O. [1] "Protocol Sentences." Translated by G. Schick in *LP*, (1959), pp. 199–208. (Originally published as *Protokollsätze* in *Erkenntnis* 3 [1932–33].)

Niddith, P. [1] "A Defense of Ayer's Verifiability Principle Against Church's Criticism." *M* 70(1961):88–89.

Nielsen, K. [1] " 'Christian Positivism' and the Appeal to Religious Experience." *JR* 42(1962):248–261.

———. [2] "On Speaking of God." *Theoria* 28(1962):110–137.

———. [3] "Eschatological Verification." *CJT* 9(1963):271–281.

———. [4] "God and Verification Again." *CJT* 11(1965):135–141.

———. [5] "Religious Perplexity and Faith." *Crane Review* 7(1965):1–17.

———. [6] "On Fixing the Reference Range of 'God.' " *RS* 2(1966):13–36.

———. [7] "On Believing That God Exists." *The Southern Journal of Philosophy* 5(1967):161–172.

———. [8] "Language and the Concept of God." *Question Two* (1969):34–52.

———. [9] "The Significance of God-Talk." *Religious Humanism* 3(1969):16–20.

———. [10] "The Intelligibility of God-Talk." *RS* 6(1970):1–21.

———. [11] "In Defense of Atheism." In *Contemporary Philosophic Thought*, vol. 3, *Perspectives in Education, Religion, and the Arts*, pp. 127–156. Albany: State University of New York Press, 1970.

———. [12] "On the Logic of 'Revelation.' " *S* 9(1970):8–13.

———. [13] "On Waste and Wastelands: A Response." In *Contemporary Philosophic Thought*, vol. 3, *Perspectives in Education, Religion, and the Arts*, pp. 117–126. Albany: State University of New York Press, 1970.

———. [14] "The Primacy of Philosophical Theology." *TT* 27(1970):155–169.

———. [15] *Reason and Practice.* New York: Harper and Row, 1971.

———. [16] *Contemporary Critiques of Religion.* London: Macmillan, 1971.

———. [17] "The Coherence of Wittgensteinian Fideism." *S* 11(1972):4–12.

———. [18] "The Challenge of Wittgenstein: An Examination of his Picture of Religious Belief." *SR* 3(1973):29–46.

Norburn, G. [1] "The Philosophical Quest and the Logical Positivists." *CQR* 150(1950):141–154.

Nowell-Smith, P. [1] "Miracles—The Philosophical Approach." *HJ* 48(1949–50):354–360. Included in *NE*, (1955), pp. 243–253.

———. [2] "Theology and Falsification" (III). *U* 1(1950):12–15.

Oakes, R. A. [1] "Is Probability Inapplicable—In—Principle—to the God—Hypothesis?" *The New Scholasticism* 44(1970):426–430.

Pap, A. [1] *Elements of Analytic Philosophy.* New York: Macmillan, 1949.

———. [2] *An Introduction to the Philosophy of Science.* New York: The Free Press, 1962.

Passmore, J. [1] "Review Article: Christianity and Positivism." *AJ* 35(1957):125–136.

———. [2] *Philosophical Reasoning.* London: Gerald Duckworth; New York: Charles Scribner's Sons, 1961.

Paton, H. J. [1] *The Modern Predicament.* London: Allen and Unwin, 1955.

Pears, D. F. [1] *See* Grice, H. P.

Penelhum, T. [1] "Logic and Theology." *CJT* 5(1958):255–265.

———. [2] "Divine Necessity." *M* 49(1960):175–186. Included in *PR*, (1971), pp. 179–190.

———. [3] *Survival and Disembodied Existence.* London: Routledge and Kegan Paul, 1970.

———. [4] *Problems of Religious Knowledge.* London: Macmillan, 1971.

———. [5] *Religion and Rationality.* New York: Random House, 1971.

Phillips, D. Z. [1] *Concept of Prayer.* New York: Schocken Books, 1966.

———. [2] "Religion and Epistemology: Some Contemporary Confusions." *AJ* 44(1966):316–330. Included in Phillips, *Faith and Philosophical Enquiry*, (1971), pp. 123–145.

———. [3] "Wisdom's Gods." *PQ* 19(1969):15–32. Included in Phillips, *Faith and Philosophical Enquiry*, (1971), pp. 170–203.

———. [4] "Religious Beliefs and Language-Games." *Ratio* 12(1970):26–46. Included in Phillips, *Faith and Philosophical Enquiry*, (1971), pp. 77–110, and *PR*, (1971), pp. 121–142.

———. [5] *Death and Immortality.* New York: Macmillan, 1971.

————. [6] *Faith and Philosophical Enquiry.* New York: Schocken Books, 1971.

————, and Jones, J. R. [7] "Belief and Loss of Belief: A Discussion." *S* 9 (1970):1–7. Included in Phillips, *Faith and Philosophical Enquiry,* (1971), pp. 111–122.

Plantinga, A. [1] *God and Other Minds.* Ithaca: Cornell University Press, 1967.

————, ed. [2] *Faith and Philosophy.* Grand Rapids, Mich.: Eerdmans, 1964.

Popper, K. P. [1] *The Logic of Scientific Discovery.* 2d ed., rev. New York: Harper and Row, 1958.

————. [2] *Conjectures and Refutations.* New York: Basic Books, 1963.

Preller, V. [1] *Divine Science and the Science of God.* Princeton: Princeton University Press, 1968.

Presley, C. F. [1] "Arguments About Meaninglessness." *BJPS* 12(1961):225–234.

Price, H. H. [1] "Clarity Is Not Enough." *PAS, SV* 19(1945):1–31. Included in *CNE,* (1963), pp. 15–41.

————. [2] *Essays in the Philosophy of Religion.* Oxford: Oxford University Press, 1972.

Prior, A. N. [1] "Can Religion Be Discussed?" *AJ* 20(1942):141–151. Included in *NE,* (1955), pp. 1–11.

Putnam, H. [1] "The Analytic and the Synthetic." In *MSPS,* III, (1962), pp. 358–397.

Quine, W. V. [1] "Two Dogmas of Empiricism." *PR* 60(1951):20–43. Included in Quine, *From a Logical Point of View,* (1961), pp. 20–46; *ASR,* (1970), pp. 23–53; *CNE,* (1963), pp. 15–41; *RPM,* (1964), pp. 346–365.

————. [2] *Word and Object.* Cambridge: Technology Press of M.I.T., 1960.

————. [3] *From a Logical Point of View.* 2d ed., rev. New York: Harper and Row, 1961.

————. [4] *The Ways of Paradox and Other Essays.* New York: Random House, 1966.

————. [5] *Ontological Relativity and Other Essays.* New York: Columbia University Press, 1969.

Rainier, A. C. A. [1] "Necessity and God: A Reply to Professor Findlay." *M* 58(1949):75–77. Included in *NE,* (1955), pp. 67–71.

Ramsey, I. T. [1] *Miracles.* Oxford: Clarendon Press, 1952.

————. [2] *Religious Language.* London: SCM Press, 1957.

————. [3] "Paradox in Religion." *PAS, SV* 33(1959):195–218. Included in *NERL,* (1969), pp. 138–161.

————. [4] "On the Possibility and Purpose of a Metaphysical Theology." In *PM,* (1961), pp. 153–177.

————. [5] "Religion and Science: A Philosopher's Approach." *CQR* 162(1961): 77–91. Included in *NERL,* (1969), pp. 36–43.

————. [6] *Religion and Science.* London: S.P.C.K., 1964.

————. [7] *Models and Mystery.* London: Oxford University Press, 1964.

————. [8] "Contemporary Philosophy and the Christian Faith." *RS* 1(1965): 47–62.

————. [9] *Christian Discourse*. London: Oxford University Press, 1965.

————, ed. [10] *Christian Ethics and Contemporary Philosophy*. London: SCM Press, 1966.

Randall, J. H., Jr. [1] *The Role of Knowledge in Western Religion*. Boston: Starr King Press, 1958.

Reichenbach, H. [1] *The Rise of Scientific Philosophy*. Berkeley: University of California Press, 1951.

————. [2] "The Verifiability Theory of Meaning." *Contributions to the Analysis and Synthesis of Knowledge*, Proceedings of the American Academy of Arts and Sciences 80(1951):46–60. Included in *RPS*, (1953), pp. 93–119.

Richmond, J. [1] *Theology and Metaphysics*. London: SCM Press, 1970.

Ricoeur, P. [1] *See* MacIntyre, A.

Robinson, N. H. G. [1] "The Logic of Religious Language." In *TG*, (1969), pp. 1–19.

————. [2] "The Logical Placing of the Name 'God'." *Scottish Journal of Theology* 24(1971):129–148.

Root, H. [1] "Metaphysics and Religious Belief." In *PM*, (1961), pp. 64–79.

Rorty, R. [1] "Metaphilosophical Difficulties of Linguistic Philosophy." In *LT*, (1967), pp. 1–39.

Ross, J. F. [1] *Introduction to the Philosophy of Religion*. New York: Macmillan, 1969.

————. [2] *Philosophical Theology*. New York: Bobbs-Merrill, 1969.

Ruja, H. [1] "The Present Status of the Verifiability Criterion." *PPR* 22(1961): 216–222.

Russell, B. [1] "Logical Positivism." *Polemic* (1946):6–13.

————. [2] "Logical Positivism." *RIP* 4(1950):3–19.

Ryle, G. [1] "Systematically Misleading Expressions." *PAS* 32(1931–32):139–170. Included in *LL*(I), (1951), pp. 11–36; *LT*, (1967), pp. 85–100.

————. [2] "The Verification Principle." *RIP* 5(1951):243–250.

————. [3] "Ordinary Language." *PR* (1953):167–186. Included in *POL*, (1963), pp. 108–127; *OL*, (1964), pp. 24–40.

————. [4] *Dilemmas*. Cambridge: Cambridge University Press, 1954.

————. [5] "The Theory of Meaning." In *British Philosophy in the Mid-Century*, edited by A. C. Mace, pp. 239–264. London: Allen and Unwin; New York: Macmillan, 1957. Included in *POL*, (1963), pp. 128–153.

————. [6] "Philosophical Arguments." In *LP*, (1959), pp. 327–344.

————. [7] "Use, Usage and Meaning." *PAS, SV* 35(1961):223–230. Included in *TM*, (1968), pp. 109–127.

Rynin, D. [1] "Vindication of L*G*C*L*P*V*SM." *PAPA* 30(1957):45–67.

————. [2] "Cognitive Meaning and Cognitive Use." *I* 9(1966):109–131.

Salmon, W. C. [1] "Verifiability and Logic." In *MMM*, (1966), pp. 354–376.

Scheffler, I. [1] "Prospects of a Modest Empiricism, I." *RM* 10(1957):383–400.

——. [2] "Prospects of a Modest Empiricism, II." *RM* 10(1957):602–625.

——. [3] *Science and Subjectivity.* Indianapolis: Bobbs-Merrill, 1967.

——. [4] *The Anatomy of Inquiry.* New York: Alfred A. Knopf, 1967.

Schilling, H. [1] *Science and Religion.* New York: Charles Scribner's Sons, 1962.

Schillp, P. A., ed. [1] *The Philosophy of Rudolf Carnap.* LaSalle, Ill.: Open Court, 1963.

Schlick, M. [1] "The Future of Philosophy." *College of the Pacific Publications in Philosophy* I (1932):45–62. Included in *LT*, (1967), pp. 43–53.

——. [2] "Meaning and Verification." *PR* 45(1936):339–369. Included in *RPA*, (1949), pp. 146–170; *TCP*, (1963), pp. 468–492.

——. [3] "The Turning Point in Philosophy." Translated by D. Rynin, in *LP*, (1959), pp. 53–59.

Schmidt, P. F. [1] *Religious Knowledge.* Glencoe, Ill.: Free Press, 1961.

Schrag, C. O. [1] "Ontology and the Possibility of Religious Knowledge." *JR* 42(1962):87–95. Included in *RL*, (1968), pp. 201–212.

Scriven, M. [1] *Primary Philosophy.* New York: McGraw-Hill, 1966.

Searle, J. R. [1] "Meaning and Speech Acts." *PR* 71(1962):423–432.

——. [2] *Speech Acts.* Cambridge: Cambridge University Press, 1969.

Shapere, D. [1] "Philosophy and the Analysis of Language." *I* 3(1960):29–48. Included in *LT*, (1967), pp. 271–283.

Sherry, P. L. [1] "Is Religion a 'Form of Life'?" *APQ* 9(1972):139–167.

——. [2] "Truth and the Religious 'Language-Game'." *P* (1972), pp. 18–37.

Shorter, M. [1] "Meaning and Grammar." *AJ* 34(1956):73–91.

Siefferman, N. C. [1] "Science and Religion: A Reply to John F. Miller." *RS* 6 (1970):281–288.

Smart, J. J. C. [1] "The Existence of God." *CQR* 156(1955):178–194. Included in *NE*, (1955), pp. 28–46.

——. [2] "Metaphysics, Logic and Theology." In *NE*, (1955), pp. 12–27.

Smart, N. [1] "Paradox in Religion." *PAS, SV* 33(1959):219–232.

——. [2] *Reasons and Faiths.* New York: Humanities Press, 1959.

——. [3] "Myth and Transcendence." *MO* 50(1966):475–487.

——. [4] *Philosophy of Religion.* New York: Random, 1969.

——. [5] *Philosophers and Religious Truth.* New York: Macmillan, 1970.

Smith, J. E. [1] "Religious Insight and the Cognitive Problem." *RS* 7(1971):97–112.

Stead, G. C. [1] "How Theologians Reason." In *FL*, (1957), pp. 108–131.

Storer, T. [1] "An Analysis of Logical Positivism." *ME* 3(1951):245–272.

Strawson, P. F. [1] "On Referring." *M* 59(1950):320–344. Included in *ECA*, (1960), pp. 21–52; *POL*, (1963), pp. 162–193.

——. [2] "Construction and Analysis." In *REV*, (1956), pp. 97–110.

——. [3] "Analysis, Science, and Metaphysics." Translated by R. Rorty, in *LT*, (1967), pp. 312–320.

———. [4] *See* Grice, H. P.

Swinburne, R. G. [1] "Confirmability and Factual Meaningfulness." *A* 33 (1973):71–76.

Thompson, M. [1] "When Is Ordinary Language Reformed?" *JP* 58(1961):498–504. Included in *LT*, (1967), pp. 201–205.

Tomberlin, J. E. [1] "Is Belief in God Justified?" *JP* 67(1970):31–38.

Toulmin, S. [1] "Logical Positivism and After, or Back to Aristotle." *Universities Quarterly* 11(1957):335–347.

———. [2] *See* Hepburn, R. W.

Trethowan, D. I. [1] "Religious Belief and Logical Analysis" (V). *U* 1(1951): 141–143. (Originally published as part of the *University* discussion of "Theology and Falsification.")

———. [2] "In Defense of Theism—A Reply to Professor Kai Nielsen." *RS* 2(1966):37–48.

Tyson, R. [1] "Philosophical Analysis and Religious Language: A Selected Bibliography." *Christian Scholar* 43(1960):245–250.

van Buren, P. M. [1] *The Secular Meaning of the Gospel.* New York: Macmillan; London: Collier-Macmillan, 1963.

———. [2] *Theological Explorations.* New York, London: Collier-Macmillan, 1968.

———. [3] "On Doing Theology." In *TG*, (1969), pp. 52–71.

———. [4] "Theology and Philosophy of Religion From the Perspective of Religious Thought." *Union Seminary Quarterly Review* 25(1970):467–476.

———. [5] *The Edges of Language: An Essay in the Logic of a Religion.* New York: Macmillan, 1972.

Veatch, H. B. [1] "A Case for Transempirical and Supernaturalistic Knowledge Claims." In *MMM*, (1966), pp. 391–405.

Wainwright, W. J. [1] "Religious Statements and the World." *RS* 2(1966):49–60.

———. [2] "The Presence of Evil and the Falsification of Theistic Assertions." *RS* 4(1969):213–216.

Waismann, F. [1] "Verifiability." *PAS, SV* 19(1945):119–150. Included in *TM*, (1968), pp. 35–60.

———. [2] "Language Strata." In *LL*(II), (1953), pp. 11–31.

———. [3] "How I See Philosophy." In *Contemporary British Philosophy* (Third Series), edited by H. D. Lewis, pp. 447–490. London: Allen and Unwin, 1956. Included in *LP*, (1959), pp. 345–380.

———. [4] *The Principles of Linguistic Philosophy.* Edited by R. Harré. London: Macmillan; New York: St. Martin's Press, 1965.

Warnock, G. J. [1] "Verification and the Use of Language." *RIP* 5(1951):307–322. Included in *MIP*, (1965), pp. 715–725.

———. [2] "Analysis and Imagination." In *REV*, (1956), pp. 111–126.

———. [3] "Criticisms of Metaphysics." In *NM*, (1957), pp. 124–141.

Watling, J. *See* Brown, R.

Wertz, S. K. [1] "Logic, Theology and Falsification." *PER* 54(1973):75–79.

Wheeler, A. M. [1] "Are Theological Utterances Assertions?" *S* 8(1969):33–37.

White, A. R. [1] "A Note on Meaning and Verification." *M* 63(1954):66–69.

White, M. G. [1] "The Analytic and the Synthetic: An Untenable Dualism." In *John Dewey*, edited by S. Hook, pp. 316–330. New York: Dial, 1950. Included in *ASR*, (1970), pp. 75–91; *SPL*, (1952), pp. 272–286.

———. [2] *Toward Reunion in Philosophy.* New York: Atheneum, 1963.

Whitehouse, W. A. [1] *Christian Faith and the Scientific Attitude.* New York: Philosophical Library, 1952.

Whitely, C. H. *See* Lewis, H. D.

Williams, B. A. O. [1] "Tertullian's Paradox." In *NE*, (1955), pp. 187–211.

———. [2] "Metaphysical Arguments." In *NM*, (1957), pp. 39–60.

Wilson, J. [1] *Language and Christian Belief.* London: Macmillan, 1958.

———. [2] *Philosophy and Religion.* London: Oxford University Press, 1961.

Wisdom, John. [1] "Is Analysis a Useful Method in Philosophy?" *PAS, SV* 13(1934):65–89. Included in Wisdom, *Philosophy and Psycho-Analysis*, (1953), pp. 16–35.

———. [2] "Philosophical Perplexity." *PAS* 37(1936–37):71–88. Included in Wisdom, *Philosophy and Psycho-Analysis*, (1953), pp. 36–50; *LT*, (1967), pp. 101–110.

———. [3] "Metaphysics and Verification." *M* 47(1938):452–498. Included in Wisdom, *Philosophy and Psycho-Analysis*, (1953), pp. 248–282; *TCP*, (1963), pp. 513–552.

———. [4] "Philosophy, Anxiety and Novelty." *M* 53(1944):170–176. Included in Wisdom, *Philosophy and Psycho-Analysis*, (1953), pp. 112–119.

———. [5] "Gods." *PAS* 45(1944–45):185–206. Included in Wisdom, *Philosophy and Psycho-Analysis*, (1953), pp. 149–168.

———. [6] "Metaphysics." *PAS* 51(1950–51):i–xxiv. Included in Wisdom, *Other Minds*, (1952), pp. 236–259.

———. [7] *Other Minds.* Oxford: Basil Blackwell, 1952.

———. [8] *Philosophy and Psycho-Analysis.* Oxford: Basil Blackwell, 1953.

———. [9] "The Metamorphosis of Metaphysics." *Proceedings of the British Academy* 47(1961):37–59. Included in Wisdom, *Paradox and Discovery*, (1965), pp. 57–81.

———. [10] *Paradox and Discovery.* New York: Philosophical Library; Oxford: Basil Blackwell, 1965.

———. [11] "The Logic of God." In Wisdom, *Paradox and Discovery*, (1965), pp. 1–22.

Wisdom, J. O. [1] "Metamorphosis of the Verifiability Theory of Meaning." *M* 72(1963):335–347.

Wittgenstein, L. [1] *Remarks on the Foundations of Mathematics.* Edited by G. H. von Wright, R. Rhees, and G. E. M. Anscombe. Translated by G. E. M. Anscombe. Oxford: Basil Blackwell, 1956.

————. [2] *The Blue and Brown Books*. New York: Harper and Row; Oxford: Basil Blackwell, 1958.

————. [3] *Tractatus Logico-Philosophicus*. 2d. ed., rev. Translated by D. F. Pears and B. F. McGuiness. London: Routledge and Kegan Paul; New York: Humanities Press, 1961.

————. [4] *Zettel*. Edited by G. E. M. Anscombe and G. H. von Wright. Translated by G. E. M. Anscombe. Berkeley and Los Angeles: University of California Press, 1967.

————. [5] *Lectures and Conversations on Aesthetics, Psychology and Religious Belief*. Edited by C. Barrett. Berkeley and Los Angeles: University of California Press, 1967.

————. [6] *On Certainty*. Edited by G. E. M. Anscombe and G. H. von Wright. Translated by D. Paul and G. E. M. Anscombe. Oxford: Basil Blackwell, 1969.

————. [7] *Philosophical Investigations*. 3d ed. Translated by G. E. M. Anscombe. New York: Macmillan, 1969.

————. [8] *Philosophical Grammar*. Edited by R. Rhees. Translated by A. Kenny. Oxford: Basil Blackwell, 1974.

————. [9] *Philosophical Remarks*. Edited by R. Rhees. Translated by R. Hargreaves and R. White. Oxford: Basil Blackwell, 1974.

Wood, O. P. [1] "The Force of Linguistic Rules." *PAS* 51(1950–51):313–328.

Ziff, P. [1] *Semantical Analysis*. Ithaca: Cornell University Press, 1960.

————. [2] "About 'God'." In *RET*, (1961), pp. 195–202. Included in Ziff, *Philosophical Turnings,* (1966), pp. 93–102.

————. [3] *Philosophical Turnings*. Ithaca: Cornell University Press, 1966.

Zimmerman, M. [1] "The Status of the Verifiability Principle." *PPR* 22(1962): 334–343.

Zuurdeeg, W. F. [1] *An Analytical Philosophy of Religion*. New York: Abingdon Press, 1958.